Quality Measurement in Early Childhood Settings

D1413615

Quality Measurement in Early Childhood Settings

edited by

Martha Zaslow, Ph.D.
Society for Research in Child Development and Child Trends

Ivelisse Martinez-Beck, Ph.D.
U.S. Department of Health and Human Services

Kathryn Tout, Ph.D.
Child Trends

and

Tamara Halle, Ph.D.
Child Trends

Washington, D.C.

·P·A·U·L·H·
BROOKES
PUBLISHING CO.®

Baltimore • London • Sydney

Paul H. Brookes Publishing Co.
Post Office Box 10624
Baltimore, Maryland 21285-0624
USA

www.brookespublishing.com

Typeset by Aptara, Inc., Falls Church, Virginia.
Manufactured in the United States of America by
Sheridan Books, Inc., Chelsea, Michigan.

This work may be reproduced in whole or in part for the official use of the U.S. government or any authorized agency thereof. The following materials were written by U.S. government employees within the scope of their official duties and, as such, shall remain in the public domain: Introduction, Chapter 1, Chapter 8, and Chapter 9. The views expressed therein are those of the authors and do not necessarily reflect positions of the U.S. Department of Health and Human Services or its agencies.

Library of Congress Cataloging-in-Publication Data

Quality measurement in early childhood settings / edited by Martha Zaslow
... [et al.].
    p.   cm.
Includes bibliographical references and index.
ISBN-13: 978-1-59857-161-5 (pbk.)
ISBN-10: 1-59857-161-3 (pbk.)
1. Child care services—United States. 2. Early childhood
education—United States. 3. Children—Services for—United States.   I.
Zaslow, Martha J.   II. Title.

HQ778.7.U6Q36 2011
372.12'070973—dc22   2010042538

British Library of Congress Cataloguing in Publication data are available from the British Library.

2015   2014   2013   2012   2011

10   9   8   7   6   5   4   3   1

Contents

About the Editors

Martha Zaslow, Ph.D., Director, Society for Research in Child Development (SRCD) Office for Policy and Communications, 1313 L Street NW, Washington, D.C., 20005, and Senior Scholar, Child Trends, 4301 Connecticut Avenue NW, Suite 350, Washington, D.C. 20008

As Director of the Office for Policy and Communications of SRCD, Dr. Zaslow works to bring research on children's development to policy makers and the broader public and to bring information about policy developments to the SRCD membership. She also oversees the SRCD Policy Fellowship program. As Senior Scholar at Child Trends, Dr. Zaslow's research focuses on early childhood development and takes an ecological approach, considering the role of multiple contexts including the family, early care and education (ECE) settings, and programs and policies for families with young children.

Ivelisse Martinez-Beck, Ph.D., Senior Social Science Research Analyst and Child Care Research Coordinator; Division of Child and Family Development; Office of Planning, Research and Evaluation (OPRE); Administration for Children and Families (ACF) Department of Health and Human Services (DHHS); 370 L'Enfant Plaza Promenade SW, Washington, D.C. 20447

Dr. Martinez-Beck coordinates the work of the child care research team in OPRE, developing the child care policy research agenda, managing large research projects, and representing OPRE and the child care policy research perspective in diverse federal interagency research work groups. Prior to joining ACF, Dr. Martinez-Beck held a Society for Research in Child Development Executive Branch Policy Fellowship with the Child Care Bureau where she was involved in designing a research agenda to answer policy-relevant questions for Child Care and Development Fund State Administrators and other key stakeholders. A recent focus of her work has been on issues related to the quality of early care and education settings and links to young children's developmental outcomes.

Kathryn Tout, P.h.D, Codirector of Early Childhood Research, Child Trends, 4301 Connecticut Avenue NW, Suite 350, Washington, D.C. 20008

Dr. Tout oversees projects in Child Trends's Minnesota office. Her research focuses on policies and programs to improve the quality of early care and education and families' access to quality settings and programs to improve the quality and effectiveness of the early childhood workforce.

Tamara Halle, Ph.D., Codirector of Early Childhood Research, Child Trends, 4301 Connecticut Avenue NW, Suite 350, Washington, D.C. 20008

Dr. Halle oversees projects in Child Trends's Washington, D.C., office. She conducts research on children's early cognitive and social development, children's school readiness, family and community supports for school readiness, and school characteristics associated with ongoing achievement and positive development. Her recent work focuses on early literacy development among children who are English language learners and evaluations of early childhood curricula, programs, and professional development aimed at supporting children's school readiness.

Contributors

Susan S. Aronson, M.D., FAAP
Pediatrician and Consultant on Health and
  Safety in Early Education and Child Care
  Programs
Clinical Professor of Pediatrics and Pediatric
  Advisor for the PA Chapter of the
  American Academy of Pediatrics
University of Pennsylvania, The Children's
  Hospital of Philadelphia
605 Moreno Road
Penn Valley, PA 19072

Sally Atkins-Burnett, Ph.D.
Senior Researcher
Mathematica Policy Research
600 Maryland Avenue SW, Suite 550
Washington, D.C. 20024

Lauren R. Barton, Ph.D.
Early Childhood Development Researcher
SRI International
Center for Education and Human Services
333 Ravenswood Avenue, BS 185
Menlo Park, CA 94025

Elena Bodrova, Ph.D.
Principal Researcher
Mid-continent Research for Education and
  Learning
4601 DTC Boulevard, Suite 500
Denver, CO 80237

Kimberly Boller, Ph.D.
Senior Research Psychologist
Mathematica Policy Research
600 Alexander Road
Princeton, NJ 08543

Suzanne M. Bouffard, Ph.D.
Research Fellow
Harvard Graduate School of Education
Larsen Hall 606
14 Appian Way
Cambridge, MA 02138

Kimberly Brenneman, Ph.D.
Assistant Research Professor
National Institute for Early Education
  Research and Rutgers Center for Cognitive
  Science
120 Albany Street, Suite 500, Tower 1
New Brunswick, NJ 08901

Juliet Bromer, Ph.D.
Assistant Research Scientist
Herr Research Center for Children
  and Social Policy
Erikson Institute
451 North LaSalle Street
Chicago, IL 60654

Donna M. Bryant, Ph.D.
Senior Scientist
FPG Child Development Institute
Campus Box 8180
University of North Carolina at
  Chapel Hill
Chapel Hill, NC 27599

Margaret Burchinal, Ph.D.
Senior Scientist
FPG Child Development Institute
Campus Box 8185
University of North Carolina at
  Chapel Hill
Chapel Hill, NC 27599
Professor
University of California, Irvine
Department of Education
3200 Education
Irvine, CA 92697-5500

Yaping Cai, M.S.
Senior Biostatistician
PAREXEL International
2520 Meridian Parkway
Durham, NC 27713

Judith J. Carta, Ph.D.
Senior Scientist, Professor
Juniper Gardens Children's Project
University of Kansas
444 Minnesota Avenue Suite 300
Kansas City, KS 66101

Dina C. Castro, Ph.D.
Senior Scientist
Director, Center for Early Care and Education
  Research: Dual Language Learners
FPG Child Development Institute
University of North Carolina at Chapel Hill
105 Smith Level Road
Chapel Hill, NC 27599

Jason Downer, Ph.D.
Senior Research Scientist
Center for Advanced Study of Teaching and
    Learning,
University of Virginia
350 Old Ivy Way, Suite 100
Charlottesville, VA 22903

Barbrina B. Ertle Ed.D.
Assistant Professor
Adelphi University
Ruth S. Ammon School of Education
Harvey Hall, Room 130
1 South Avenue
Garden City, NY 11530

Linda M. Espinosa, Ph.D.
Professor of Early Childhood Education (Retired)
Townsend Hall
College of Education
University of Missouri–Columbia
Columbia, MO 65211

Nicole D. Forry, Ph.D.
Research Scientist
Child Trends
4301 Connecticut Avenue NW, Suite 350
Washington, D.C. 20008

Teresa Foulkes
Assistant Director
OPEN Initiative
Center for Family Policy and Research
University of Missouri
1400 Rock Quarry Road
Columbia, MO 65211

Ellen Frede, Ph.D.
Codirector
National Institute for Early Education
    Research
120 Albany Street, Suite 500, Tower 1
New Brunswick, NJ 08901

Lucia French, Ph.D.
Earl B. Taylor Professor of Education and
    Human Development
University of Rochester
Warner School
1-312 Dewey Hall
Rochester, NY 14627

Kathryn L. Fuger, Ph.D.
Director of Early Childhood and Youth
    Programs
University of Missouri–Kansas City
Institute for Human Development
215 West Pershing Road, Sixth Floor
Kansas City, MO 64108

Herbert P. Ginsburg, Ph.D.
Jacob H. Schiff Foundation Professor of
    Psychology and Education
Department of Human Development
Teachers College Columbia University
525 West 120 Street
New York, NY 10024

Bridget K. Hamre, Ph.D.
Associate Director/Senior Scientist
Center for Advanced Study of Teaching and
    Learning
University of Virginia
350 Old Ivy Way, Suite 100
Charlottesville, VA 22903

Jacqueline S. Hawks, Ph.D.
Senior Policy Research Analyst
Center for Family Policy & Research
University of Missouri
1400 Rock Quarry Road
Columbia, MO 65211

Kathleen M. Hebbeler, Ph.D.
Program Manager
SRI International
600 Mockingbird Place
Davis, CA 95616

Susan M. Hegland, Ph.D.
Associate Professor
Iowa State University
Department of Human Development &
    Family Studies
4380 Palmer
Ames, IA 50011

Julia R. Henly, Ph.D.
Associate Professor
University of Chicago
School of Social Service Administration
969 E. 60th Street
Chicago, IL 60637

Marilou Hyson, Ph.D.
Consultant, Early Childhood Development
    and Education
Affiliate Faculty, Applied Developmental
    Psychology
George Mason University
Fairfax, VA 22030

Patricia Isbell, Ph.D.
Social/Clinical Research Specialist
University of North Carolina at Chapel Hill
Department of Maternal and Child Health
Gillings School of Global Public Health
Rosenau Hall
421 Pittsboro Street, CD# 7445
Chapel Hill, NC 27599

Stephanie M. Jones, Ph.D.
Assistant Professor of Education
Harvard Graduate School of
    Education
14 Appian Way, Larsen 603
Cambridge, MA 02138

Kirsten Kainz, Ph.D.
Statistician
FPG Child Development Institute
University of North Carolina at
    Chapel Hill
521 South Greensboro Street
Carrboro, NC 27510

Marilyn J. Krajicek, Ed.D.
Professor, Director
National Resource Center for Health
    and Safety in Child Care and Early
    Education
University of Colorado
College of Nursing
ED 2 North, Mail Stop F541
13120 East 19th Avenue
Aurora, CO 80045

Deborah Leong, Ph.D.
Professor Emerita of Psychology
Metropolitan State College of Denver
Campus Box 54, Post Office Box 173362
Denver, CO 80217-3362

Denise Mauzy, LCSW
Director
OPEN Initiative
Center for Family Policy and Research
University of Missouri
1400 Rock Quarry Road
Columbia, MO 65211

Wayne A. Mayfield, Ph.D.
Senior Research Analyst
Center for Family Policy and Research
University of Missouri
1400 Rock Quarry Road
Columbia, MO 65211

Meagan McSwiggan, B.A.
Clinical Ph.D. Doctoral Student
University of Central Florida
4000 Central Florida Boulevard
Orlando, FL 32816

Shannon Moodie
Senior Research Assistant
Child Trends
4301 Connecticut Avenue NW
Washington, D.C. 20008

Judy A. Mumford, Ph.D.
Senior Policy Research Analyst
Center for Family and Policy
    Research
University of Missouri
1400 Rock Quarry Road
Columbia, MO 65211

Sara Benjamin Neelon, Ph.D.
Assistant Professor
Duke University
2200 W Main Street DUMC 104006
Durham, NC 27705

Susan B. Neuman, Ed.D.
Professor, Educational Studies
University of Michigan
School of Education
610 East University
Ann Arbor, MI 48109

Mariela M. Páez, Ph.D.
Associate Professor
The Carolyn A. and Peter S. Lynch School of
    Education
Boston College
126 Campion Hall
Chestnut Hill, MA 02467

Diane Paulsell, M.P.A.
Associate Director of Human Services
    Research
Mathematica Policy Research
Post Office Box 2393
Princeton, NJ 08543

Robert C. Pianta, Ph.D.
Dean, Curry School of Education
University of Virginia
405 Emmet Street South
Charlottesville, VA 22903

Toni Porter, M.A.
Director, Institute for a Child Care
    Continuum
Bank Street College of Education
610 West 112th Street
New York, NY 10025

Dawn Ramsburg, Ph.D.
Child Care Program Specialist
Office of Child Care
Administration for Children
    and Families
370 L'Enfant Promenade SW
Fifth Floor, East
Washington, D.C. 20447

Beth S. Rous, Ed.D.
Associate Professor
Education Leadership Studies
University of Kentucky
111A Dickey Hall
Lexington, KY 40506

Kay Sanders, Ph.D.
Assistant Professor, Child Development
Whittier College
Department of Education and Child
   Development
13406 Philadelphia Street
Post Office Box 634
Whittier, CA 90608

Heather Sandstrom, Ph.D.
Research Associate
Urban Institute
2100 M Street NW
Washington, D.C. 20037

Thomas Schultz, Ed.D.
Project Director, Early Childhood Initiatives
Council of Chief State School Officers
One Massachusetts Avenue NW, Suite 700
Washington, D.C. 20001

Eva Marie Shivers, Ph.D.
Director
Institute for Child Development Research and
   Social Change
Indigo Cultural Center, Inc.
2942 North 24th Street, Suite 114-321
Phoenix, AZ 85016

Sheila Smith, Ph.D.
Director, Early Childhood
National Center for Children in Poverty
Mailman School of Public Health
Columbia University
215 West 125th Street, 3rd Floor
New York, NY 10027

Amber Sparks, B.S.
Coordinator
OPEN Initiative
Center for Family Policy and Research
University of Missouri
1400 Rock Quarry Road
Columbia, MO 65211

Donna Spiker, Ph.D.
Program Manager
Early Childhood Program
SRI International
333 Ravenswood Avenue, BS 190
Menlo Park, CA 94025

Deborah Stipek, Ph.D.
Dean, School of Education
Stanford University
485 Lasuen Mall
Stanford, CA 94305

Deborah Swenson-Klatt, M.A.
Director, Child Development Services
Minnesota Department of Human Services
Post Office Box 64962
St. Paul, MN 55164

Kathy R. Thornburg, Ph.D.
Director
Center for Family Policy and Research
University of Missouri
1400 Rock Quarry Road
Columbia, MO 65211

Roberta B. Weber, Ph.D.
Faculty Research Associate
Family Policy Program
219 Bates Hall
Oregon State University
Corvallis, OR 97331

T'Pring R. Westbrook, Ph.D.
Research Fellow
Administration for Children and Families
370 L'Enfant Promenade SW
7th Floor West
Washington, D.C. 20447

Jessica E. Vick Whittaker, Ph.D.
Research Scientist
Center for Advanced Study of Teaching and
   Learning,
University of Virginia
Post Office Box 400877
Charlottesville, VA 22903

Foreword

As this book goes to press, federal policies and programs related to early care and education are the subject of increasing attention. Head Start, Early Head Start, and the Child Care and Development Fund (CCDF) have received infusions of funds through the American Recovery and Reinvestment Act of 2009. Health care reform legislation has made funding available to states to expand home visiting programs to pregnant women and families with young children through the Maternal, Infant, and Early Childhood Home Visiting Programs. Collaborative efforts are underway between the U.S. Department of Education and the U.S. Department of Health and Human Services, in which the largest federal early childhood programs (Head Start, the CCDF, and the new home visiting program) reside. Nonetheless, there continue to be large numbers of unserved children (e.g., Government Accountability Office, 2010), and large numbers of children who are served in settings in which quality of services is a concern. The economic recession of recent years has been marked by a drop in state preschool enrollment, decreased attention to quality standards, and concerns that parents will be forced to choose less expensive informal child care of uncertain quality (National Association of Child Care Resource and Referral Agencies, 2009; National Institute for Early Education Research, 2010). Especially in times of diminished funding, it is of critical importance that we understand how to maximize our investments to achieve the best possible results for our youngest children.

The array of early childhood programs is staggeringly diverse, mirroring the patchwork of frameworks for funding and regulating these programs and the range of motivations, resources, and expectations of parents who seek out these services and experiences for their children. Policy makers and providers are challenged with identifying and implementing early care and education programs that will respond to the unique needs and conditions of local communities while supporting the health, growth, and development of young children. Moreover, policy makers and the public have increasingly high expectations of early childhood programs for establishing trajectories that lead to success in school and even later in life. What are the elements of early care and education that promote positive developmental outcomes for children and families? How can we ensure the highest quality of services for our youngest children?

The fact that this book originated from a 2008 federally sponsored workshop ("Developing the Next Wave of Quality Measures for Early Childhood and School-Age Programs: A Working Meeting") on quality in early care and education that included researchers, policy makers, and practitioners speaks to the importance of the topic to multiple audiences and to the potential value of the information to these diverse stakeholders. Definitions and measures of quality are essential for building a common understanding of the key components across early childhood settings and to building the knowledge base about what programs and services are most beneficial. Moreover, careful measurement ultimately can be used to determine the areas in which programs need improvement, to direct training and professional development efforts, and to assess the effects of program improvement efforts. As systems embrace the use of quality measures, it is necessary to strengthen the available measures to ensure confidence in the information that results.

Systemwide use of quality measures is an increasing part of the early childhood landscape. At the end of 2010, more than 25 states had integrated quality ratings into efforts to improve their early care systems and, to varying degrees, have adopted measures of quality as part of their quality rating and improvement systems (Administration for Children and Families, 2010). In addition, federal legislative requirements have resulted in the systematic implementation of a research-based quality measure for reviewing Head Start programs (Improving Head Start for School Readiness Act, 2007). As these measures are assuming a more prominent role in program improvement, in providing guidance to parents, and in accountability efforts, it is necessary to take stock of the adequacy of currently available measures and to move toward a stronger and more comprehensive approach to quality measurement. A series of key questions must be addressed:

- What should be the focus of quality measures? What specific domains should be included, and how does the research literature support the inclusion of these domains?

- What should be the empirical basis of quality measures? How can we ensure that our measures meet strong technical standards?

- How can measures be more carefully linked to professional development and other quality improvement efforts?

- How can stakeholders in communities and states inform the development of quality measures?

- What are the research and evaluation strategies that can be used to track implementation of quality rating and improvement systems? How do those systems affect outcomes for children, families, providers, and markets?

These questions provided the focus for the 2008 meeting from which this book evolved. The chapters that follow provide a framework for strengthening the measurement strategies that increasingly are laying the foundation for early childhood quality improvement efforts.

Mary Bruce Webb
Director
Division of Child and Family Development
Office of Planning, Research and Evaluation
Administration for Children and Families

References

Barnett, W.S., Epstein, D.J., Friedman, A.H., Sansanelli, R., & Hustedt, J.T. (2010). *The state of preschool, 2009.* New Brunswick, NJ: National Institute for Early Education Research.

Government Accountability Office. (2010). *Multiple factors could have contributed to the recent decline in the number of children whose families receive subsidies* (GAO Publication No. GAO-10-344). Washington, DC: Government Printing Office.

Improving Head Start for School Readiness Act of 2007, 42 U.S.C. 9801 *et seq.*

National Association of Child Care Resource and Referral Agencies. (2009). *Child care centers and family child care homes across the nation are on the decline and vacancy rates on the rise.* Retrieved May 8, 2010, from http://www.naccrra.org/news/press-releases/52/

Tout, K., Starr, R., Soli, M., Moodie, S., Kirby, G. & Boller, K. (2010). *ACF-OPRE Report. Compendium of Quality Rating Systems and Evaluations.* Washington, DC: Office of Planning, Research and Evaluation, Administration for Children and Families, U.S. Department of Health and Human Services.

Acknowledgments

This book was made possible in part by funding from the Office of Planning, Research and Evaluation (OPRE) of the Administration for Children and Families, U.S. Department of Health and Human Services (DHHS), through Contract GS10F0030R, the Child Care and Early Education Policy and Research Analysis and Technical Expertise Project, to Child Trends.

- The "Working Meeting on Developing the Next Wave of Quality Measures for Early Childhood and School-Age Programs," held in Washington, D.C., in January 2008, was sponsored by OPRE. This meeting provided the starting point for in-depth discussions focusing on the current status of measurement of specific aspects of quality and the potential for strengthening the measurement of quality.

- The working groups that convened at the meeting, and additional working groups formed after the meeting, continued to work together to analyze available measurement tools and to identify next steps for strengthening quality measurement.

The editors thank OPRE for identifying the issue of the measurement of quality as a critical one, and for providing support for the meeting and specific follow-up steps. The editors are also extremely grateful to Naomi Goldstein and Mary Bruce Webb for their review and feedback on all of the chapters in this book. Their review helped to ensure that quality was a priority throughout the process of preparation of this book, as well as the book's focus.

The structure and agenda for the roundtable on quality measurement, which provided the framework for the present book, benefitted from the thoughtful input of a planning group, which convened multiple conference calls over the months prior to the meeting. In addition to the staff members from Child Trends and OPRE who collaborated in the editing of this book, the planning group included leading researchers from the Child Care Policy Research Consortium who have substantial expertise in different aspects of quality measurement. The editors are grateful to the following representatives from the planning group for helping to shape both the format and content of the meeting: Barbara Goodson from Abt Associates, Margaret Burchinal from the FPG Child Development Institute at the University of North Carolina at Chapel Hill and the University of California at Irvine, Dale Farran from Vanderbilt University, Lee Kreader from the National Center for Children in Poverty, Toni Porter from Bank Street College, Deborah Stipek from Stanford University, and Roberta B. Weber from Oregon State University.

The issue of the measurement of quality in early childhood settings is a high priority in multiple agencies within the federal government. The planning group for the roundtable on quality measurement included representatives from multiple federal agencies, with research focusing on quality in early childhood care and education settings. The editors greatly appreciated the input of Colleen Rathgeb and Amy Madigan from the Office of the Assistant Secretary for Planning and Evaluation, DHHS; James Griffin from the Eunice Kennedy Shriver National Institute of Child Health and Human Development; and Caroline Ebanks from the U.S. Department of

Education, Institute of Education Sciences. Their reactions after the meeting were also very helpful in making the decision to move forward with this book. We note that the views expressed in this book are those of the authors and do not necessarily reflect the positions of any federal agencies.

Whereas the discussions at the meeting occurred over a period of 2 days, the working groups formed at the meeting and afterward continued to meet for months. The work of analyzing the strengths and limitations of quality measurement in specific areas, and identifying fruitful next steps for quality measurement, was exciting but also challenging. Ensuring the input and review of working group members, and working toward chapters that reflected the views of sometimes quite large working groups, required not only scholarship but also diplomacy and perseverance. The book editors had the great pleasure of working with these groups as their ideas took shape, were put onto paper, and were refined. We want to convey our deep appreciation and respect for the authors of the chapters of this book for the care and thoughtfulness with which they looked at the field's current measurement tools and the exciting and original conceptualizations of ways that the field can move forward. Please see the complete listing of working group participants at the end of the acknowledgments of those whose involvement with this set of issues started at the roundtable, but was sustained to provide the chapters of this book. We anticipate that we will be joined by many others in acknowledging their contributions.

The editors express their deep appreciation for the staff from the Early Childhood Program Area at Child Trends, who provided critical support in preparing for the roundtable meeting and without whom it would have been impossible to summarize the discussions of the multiple working groups at the meeting. Tracking the book chapters through multiple rounds of revision and ensuring that key edits were entered and references located would not have been possible without the competence and dedication of this wonderful team. We thank, in particular, Nicole D. Forry, Laura Wandner, Meagan McSwiggan, Julia Wessel, Kathleen Sidorowicz, Shannon Moodie, and Margaret Soli.

Finally, we are very grateful for the close working relationship we have developed with Astrid Zuckerman and Julie Chávez of Paul H. Brookes Publishing Co. Astrid attended the roundtable meeting from beginning to end. She understood immediately both the importance and the complexity of developing a book based on the meeting. We are deeply grateful for the overall plan for the book that the editorial team at Brookes helped us to develop. We thank Astrid and Julie for their wonderful guidance and encouragement in the long process of bringing this book to completion. There is no doubt that, through this book and through multiple other Brookes publications, Astrid and Julie are now among the most knowledgeable individuals in the country on the issue of quality in early childhood settings. We are indebted to them for helping us share the thinking on this critical set of issues with researchers, policy makers, and practitioners.

LIST OF WORKING GROUPS AND WORKING GROUP PARTICIPANTS FROM 2008 QUALITY MEASURES ROUNDTABLE AND ROUNDTABLE FOLLOW-UP, NOTED IN ALPHABETICAL ORDER[1]

Children with Disabilities (Working Group Formed after Roundtable)
Donna Spiker (Lead)
Lauren R. Barton
Kathleen M. Hebbeler

Culturally Responsive Care
Eva Marie Shivers (Lead)
Behnosh Najafi
Kay Sanders
T'Pring R. Westbrook

Dual Language Learners (Working Group Formed After Roundtable)
Dina C. Castro (Lead)
Linda M. Espinosa
Mariela M. Páez

Family Sensitive Caregiving
Juliet Bromer (Lead)
Rena Hallam
Julia Henley
Susan Jekielek
Lee Kreader
Diane Paulsell
Toni Porter
Dawn Ramsburg
Roberta B. Weber

Health
Susan M. Hegland (Lead)
Susan S. Aronson
Sara Benjamin Neelon
Patricia Isbel
Marilyn J. Krajicek
Beth S. Rous

Language and Literacy
Susan B. Neuman (Lead)
Margaret Burchinal
Judith J. Carta
Dina C. Castro
David Dickinson
Linda M. Espinosa
Barbara Goodson
Kerry Hofer
Sharon Ramey
Adelaida Restrepo
Jerry West

Math
Kimberly Boller (Lead)
Sally Atkins-Burnett
Kimberly Brenneman
Barbrina B. Ertle
Nicole D. Forry
Ellen Frede
Lucia French
Herbert P. Ginsburg
Thomas Schultz
Deborah Stipek

Social and Emotional
Deborah Leong and Elena Bodrova (Co-Leads)
Donna M. Bryant
Lori Connors-Tadros
Kathleen Dwyer
Dale Farran
Grace Funk
Bridget K. Hamre
Marilou Hyson
Stephanie M. Jones
Carolyn Layzer
Kerry Kriener-Althen
Sheila Smith
Lauren Supplee
Kathy R. Thornburg
Jessica E. Vick Whittaker

PARTICIPANTS AT THE ROUNDTABLE WHO PROVIDED INPUT AT FULL-GROUP SESSIONS AND WHO ROTATED AMONG DIFFERENT WORKING GROUPS

Jennifer Brooks
Rachel Chazan Cohen
Caroline Ebanks
James Griffin
Tamara Halle
Amy Madigan
Ivelisse Martinez-Beck

Robert C. Pianta
Colleen Rathgeb
Louisa Tarullo
Kathryn Tout
Mary Bruce Webb
Martha Zaslow
Astrid Zuckerman

Endnote

[1]Participants who were present at the meeting or who joined working groups after the meeting are noted. Working groups are listed in alphabetical order, and participants within working groups are also listed in alphabetical order after noting the lead. We also note participants at the meeting who contributed primarily during the full group sessions and rotated among different working groups.

*To those in communities, states, and the federal government
who have accepted the challenge of working at the intersection
of research, policy, and practice in order to pursue the goal of
strengthening the quality of early childhood settings*

Introduction

Why Strengthening the Measurement of Quality in Early Childhood Settings Has Taken on New Importance

Ivelisse Martinez-Beck

The purpose of this book is to summarize what is known about how our existing measures of quality in early childhood settings are functioning and what the potential is for strengthening the measurement of quality in these settings. A focus throughout is the characteristics of measures that are needed when the measurement of quality in early childhood settings is brought to scale—that is, when quality is measured widely as part of a local, state, or federal policy initiative.

Growing Utilization of Measures of Quality in Policy Initiatives

Measures of quality in early childhood settings have taken on new importance as states and localities increasingly use them as a core component in policy initiatives to assess and improve quality. These initiatives grew out of evidence documenting the importance of quality for young children's development and concerns that quality is low to moderate in many settings. For example, at the end of 2010, more than 25 states and a number of local communities had quality rating and improvement systems that provide consumers with summary ratings of the quality of participating early care and education settings and provide support for programs to improve their quality. Many more states and localities are in the process of developing quality rating and improvement systems. Observational measures of quality are a key component in most of these systems.

Observational measures of quality are also central in evaluations of national early childhood programs. For example, the national evaluation of Head Start—the Head Start Impact Study—funded by the U.S. Department of Health and Human Services (DHHS), included observational measures of Head Start classrooms, along with other measures of quality such as teacher qualifications and the use of a curriculum. The Head Start Family and Child Experiences Survey, which includes a nationally representative sample of Head Start programs, incorporates multiple measures of classroom quality. The Early Childhood Educator Professional Development Program, a U.S. Department of Education program aimed at improving the knowledge and skills of early childhood teachers working in low-income communities across the country, included a reporting requirement for grantees to collect observational data on the quality of the language and literacy stimulation provided in early childhood settings.

Selection of quality measures with a focus on features of quality in early care and education programs that make the most difference for young children's learning and development is critical for implementation of federal programs as well. Programs targeting children's access to, and experiences in, early care and education (e.g., CCDF; Head Start) have refocused efforts to improve the quality of children's early learning experiences and are relying on the strength and effectiveness of measures of quality to assess the success of their efforts.[1]

With the widespread measurement of quality as part of these federal, state, and local policy initiatives, as well as evaluations of programs funded with public dollars, greater attention has been given to the measures of quality themselves. A key issue in assessing the effectiveness of existing measures of quality is to understand the extent to which they capture aspects of the environment that support development and improve children's school readiness. If the goal of policy initiatives is to strengthen the school readiness of children, and especially children from low-income families, quality measures that are predictive of child outcomes are critical to this effort.

The particular measures selected for use in a policy initiative could help to gauge whether children from low-income families are in early childhood settings that are supporting progress toward school readiness. The measures selected could also be used to set goals for quality improvement efforts. Use of a measure that misses key supports in the environment for development in specific areas (e.g., language development, task focus and motivation, development of positive relationships with teachers and peers) may result in characterization of overall quality that does not predict the outcomes of interest, or may fail to guide quality improvement to focus on those aspects of the environment.

Indeed, findings from recent research call into question how well existing measures of quality predict child outcomes at school entry. As is described in greater detail by Burchinal, Kainz, and Cai in Chapter 2, findings from both a meta-analysis of early childhood studies looking at the relationship of measures of quality and child outcomes and from a coordinated analysis of data from multiple large-scale studies of early childhood environments suggest that the strength of prediction of child outcomes from existing measures of quality is modest at best. These recent analyses raise the possibility that we may find stronger relationships if we focus on aligned measures of the environment and child outcomes (e.g., measures focusing specifically on language and literacy stimulation when the interest is children's language and literacy development). These analyses also raise the possibility that, rather than child outcomes improving steadily as quality improves, improvements in child outcomes may occur especially or only within a certain range of quality, suggesting that there may be thresholds of quality needed before children's development begins to show benefits. An important implication of these findings is that, in existing measures, specific facets of quality that are important to children's early academic adjustment and progress may not be captured, or captured in sufficient detail, to provide a strong basis for prediction to key child outcomes.

Opportunity to Update Measures of Quality in Light of New Basic and Evaluation Research on Young Children's Development

At the same time that questions are being raised about the strength of the relationship between existing measures of quality and child outcomes, new research is emerging that could guide efforts to strengthen the measurement of quality. Longitudinal descriptive research is strengthening our understanding of children's development in key areas. For example, we have a much greater understanding of the key facets of early language and literacy development and the types of stimulation that support development in these areas. (See Neuman & Carta, Chapter 4, for an overview of the research in this area.) We have an emerging body of research identifying how children's early mathematical understanding develops and can be supported in early childhood settings. (See Brenneman et al., Chapter 5, for a summary of the emerging evidence in this area that can inform measures of quality.) Our knowledge of health outcomes in young children is being substantially extended through a focus in recent research not only on accidents and illness, but also on aspects of early care and education environments that support positive health outcomes. (See Hegland et al., Chapter 7, for a summary of research in this area.)

There has also been a burgeoning of intervention research examining a range of approaches to strengthening quality and children's outcomes. Much of this work involves experimental evaluations of program approaches to strengthening children's development in particular domains, including language outcomes, social and emotional development, and health. Evidence suggests, for example, that specific approaches can strengthen ways in which early educators and caregivers guide young children's social and emotional development and can diminish the occurrence of problematic behaviors in early childhood settings. (See Hyson et al., Chapter 6.) By intentionally manipulating aspects of the early childhood environment, with the aim of improving child outcomes, these intervention studies are yielding critical information on aspects of early childhood settings that are malleable and that contribute to specific developmental outcomes. Intervention research is summarized across the chapters of this book. These findings can help to sharpen our identification of the aspects of early childhood environments that are important to specific child outcomes and that should be captured in measures of quality.

Young Children's Participation in Early Childhood Settings

National data indicate widespread participation of young children in a range of different types of nonparental early care and education settings. The range, and degree of accessibility, of different types of early childhood settings with varying levels of quality and cost affect the process of decision-making for parents. Until the late 1990s, there was no common rubric for comparing quality across such different settings as center-based child care, school-based and community-based prekindergarten programs, private preschool programs, and Head Start programs. Similarly, it has been extremely difficult to consider differences in quality across center-based and home-based early childhood settings. The emergence and growth of quality rating and improvement systems hold the potential of providing parents with readily interpretable tools that permit consideration of quality across different types of early childhood settings. (See Swenson-Klatt & Tout, Chapter 15, for a discussion of state perspectives on quality measurement and Thornburg et al., Chapter 16, for a description of ways in which data can be used in the development and implementation of state quality rating and improvement systems.) States and communities have been mindful that consumers may want information on particular facets of quality and have made available both overall quality ratings (such as a summary rating in which a different number of assigned stars indicates differing overall quality) and information on the individual indicators of quality that contribute to the overall rating.

New research is needed that is aimed at understanding the extent to which parents seek out and use summary ratings of quality in their decision making or seek out information on component ratings of quality. A brief review of the demographic data on young children's participation in early childhood settings underscores the substantial number of families who might *potentially* use this information. As noted in greater detail by Halle, Martinez-Beck, Forry, and McSwiggan in Chapter 1, more than half of the population of children from birth to age 5 are in nonparental care on a regular basis. More than 4 in 10 infants in the first year of life are regularly in a nonparental care arrangement, and the percentage increases to almost three quarters of children between the ages of 3 and 5.

With so many young children participating in early childhood settings on a regular basis, it will be important to provide information to parents built upon the strongest possible measures of quality and research establishing the validity of measurement rubrics used across different types of settings. (See Bryant, Burchinal, & Zaslow, Chapter 3, for a discussion of the empirical approaches that can be taken to strengthen the measurement of quality in early childhood settings.) The demographic data presented in Chapter 1 underscore how important it will be for states and communities to have access to strong measures of quality that are appropriate in both center-based and home-based settings, and that can measure quality in the settings in which infants and toddlers as well as preschool-age children are most likely to participate. These data also highlight the need to consider quality from the perspective of key demographic subgroups, such as families in which one or both parents are not English speakers, and families living in poverty. A demographic overview also underscores the need for measures of quality appropriate for settings serving children with disabilities.

A National Meeting on Strengthening the Measurement of Quality

This book grew out of a meeting convened to address this set of issues. In January 2008, the Office of Planning, Research and Evaluation (OPRE) of the DHHS's Administration for Children and Families, sponsored a meeting on strengthening the measurement of quality, called "Developing the Next Wave of Quality Measures for Early Childhood and School-Age Programs: A Working Meeting." The meeting grew out of 1) recognition of the growing utilization of measures of quality in early childhood policy initiatives aimed at improving quality and raising awareness about its importance for young children, 2) the growing body of research that can contribute to the strengthening of measures of quality for early childhood settings, and 3) the substantial utilization of nonparental care during the years from birth to school entry.

A planning group helped to develop the structure and agenda for the meeting. The planning group included, in addition to staff from Child Trends (Martha Zaslow, Kathryn Tout, and Tamara Halle) and OPRE (Ivelisse Martinez-Beck), Margaret Burchinal from the Frank Porter Graham Child Development Institute at the University of North Carolina at Chapel Hill, Barbara Goodson from Abt Associates, Dale Farran from Vanderbilt University, Lee Kreader from the National Center for Children in Poverty, Toni Porter from Bank Street College, Deborah Stipek from Stanford University, and Roberta B. Weber from Oregon State University. The planning group also included representatives from other federal agencies, including Colleen Rathgeb and Amy Madigan from the Office of the Assistant Secretary for Planning and Evaluation, DHHS; James Griffin from the Eunice Kennedy Shriver National Institute of Child Health and Human Development; and Caroline Ebanks from the Institute of Education Sciences, U.S. Department of Education.

The meeting started with a consideration of why this is an important time to take stock and strengthen measures of quality for early childhood as well as school-age settings. Working groups then met for in-depth discussions of the potential for strengthening the measurement of quality in specific domains, including language and literacy; early math, science and cognitive development; social and emotional development; and health. A working group focusing on supporting families decided at the meeting to give separate consideration to cultural sensitivity and to aspects of quality in early childhood settings that involve supports to the family. The meeting concluded with a consideration of cross-cutting issues, such as strengthening the empirical basis for measures of quality and issues in the implementation of quality measurement when applied widely as part of policy initiatives.

Follow-Up Steps to the Meeting

During the working meeting, it became clear that there were further perspectives on quality beyond the ones designated to be addressed by the working groups. Discussions at the meeting raised the possibility that children learning English in addition to a different home language may benefit from specific interactions and features of the environment in early childhood settings; therefore, a separate working group was formed to focus on children learning two or more languages. The discussions at the meeting also made clear that separate and in-depth consideration was needed on the issue of how overall quality could be enhanced through strengthening the facets of quality that are particularly important for children with disabilities. Following the meeting, additional small groups were formed to review the evidence on quality in early childhood settings from the perspectives of dual language learners and children with disabilities.

Although the meeting itself focused on strengthening the measurement of quality for school-age as well as early childhood settings, the follow-up steps to the meeting were narrowed to focus specifically on the early childhood period. Concern was expressed that even within the age range of birth to 5 there were significant gaps in the measurement of quality, with most measures focusing on formal settings for 3- to 5-year-olds. The decision was made to examine the potential for strengthening measures of quality throughout the birth-to-5 age range, with a separate focus on measures for infants and toddlers and measures in home-based early care and education settings (see Sandstrom, Moodie, & Halle, Chapter 14), rather than to attempt to cover a broader age range in follow-up work.

The working groups that had been formed at the meeting and by way of follow-up to the meeting continued to hold conference calls and to work together for a period of months (and, in some cases, even a year) after the meeting. Each working group developed a chapter that could lay the groundwork for strengthening the measurement of quality in early childhood settings, considering a different facet of quality or cross-cutting issue.

The working groups focusing on aspects of quality underlying particular domains of development worked in their chapters to address these questions: *Why is this aspect of the environment important to include in measures of quality? What is the current status of the measurement of quality for this aspect of the environment? What are the gaps and limitations in current measures that should be addressed in strengthening the measurement of this aspect of quality? What does recent and emerging research suggest should be the focus in measuring this aspect of quality? What are methodological issues that measures of quality should seek to address?* Other groups of coauthors focused on cross-cutting issues.

Much careful thought has gone into the original reviews and analyses completed for this book by the working groups. Each group of authors has not only taken into account the perspectives of the members of the working group or group of coauthors, but also responded to feedback from editors as well as to input from senior staff at the Office of Planning, Research and Evaluation of the Administration for Children and Families, DHHS. The book owes much to the members of the planning group and to the working groups and groups of coauthors who worked long after the meeting to identify and give voice to the multiple ways in which measures of quality may be strengthened.

Organization of the Book

The book follows closely the overall organization of the meeting on strengthening the measurement of quality, augmented with the addition of further working groups.

As at the meeting, the book starts in *Section I* with a focus on the issue of why there is a need to take stock of and to strengthen our measures of quality. The chapters in this part of the book provide a demographic context for the utilization of nonparental early childhood settings (Chapter 1), present new analyses on the prediction from existing measures of quality to child outcomes (Chapter 2), and underscore the need to strengthen the empirical basis for the measurement of quality (Chapter 3).

Section II provides an in-depth focus on the measurement of quality related to specific domains of children's development, emphasizing the potential for strengthening measurement in each separate aspect of quality. The chapters in this part of the book focus on aspects of quality that are important to the development of language and literacy (Chapter 4); math, science, and general cognition (Chapter 5); social and emotional development (Chapter 6); and health (Chapter 7). This section of the book also focuses on facets of quality important to supporting families (Chapter 8) and on cultural sensitivity as an aspect of quality (Chapter 9).

Section III provides a cross-cutting perspective, complementing the in-depth examination of specific domains of development in Section II. This part of the book includes chapters by the working groups focusing on children with disabilities (Chapter 10) and dual language learners (Chapter 11). Whereas earlier chapters look in detail at supporting specific domains of development, in this section there is a discussion of the need for measures of quality that take an integrative perspective, considering how features of quality can simultaneously support several aspects of development (Chapter 12). The chapters in

Section III also discuss the need for aligning the measurement of quality both with professional development efforts and with the intended child outcomes (Chapter 13), and the need for measures of quality that are appropriate for the youngest children in the birth-to-5 age range as well as those in home-based care settings (Chapter 14).

Finally, *Section IV* focuses on applications of quality measurement in policy and practice. Chapters in this part of the book consider how policy priorities combine with issues of measurement content, reliability, and validity to shape measurement selection within states and communities (Chapter 15), how data can be used in the development and implementation of state quality measurement and improvement initiatives (Chapter 16), and how measurement selection and use must take into account differing underlying purposes for measuring quality (Chapter 17).

A *concluding chapter* connects the themes that emerge across the chapters of the book, highlighting the highest priority and most feasible next steps for strengthening the measurement of quality for early childhood settings.

Endnote

[1]For more information on the Office of Head Start's plan, see *Improving School Readiness & Promoting Long-Term Success: The Head Start Roadmap to Excellence*; for more information on the Office of Child Care's Plan, see *Pathways to Quality.* Both are available on the web site of the Administration for Children and Families of the U.S. Department of Health and Human Services.

Reasons to Take Stock and Strengthen Our Measures of Quality

CHAPTER 1

Setting the Context for a Discussion of Quality Measures

The Demographic Landscape of Early Care and Education

Tamara Halle, Ivelisse Martinez-Beck, Nicole D. Forry, and Meagan McSwiggan

One of the most compelling justifications for strengthening measures of quality in early care and education (ECE) settings is that a significant proportion of young children in the United States participates regularly in nonparental ECE. The demand for ECE has grown substantially over the last 3 decades due to both demographic trends and changes in social policies that affect the work life of American families. For example, only two out of every five mothers with a child under age 6 (39%) worked outside of the home in 1975, whereas almost two out of three mothers with children under age 6 (64%) were in the labor force in 2008 (U.S. Department of Labor, Bureau of Labor Statistics, 2009). As a result of higher rates of maternal employment, as well as growing numbers of single-parent families, many children are spending a substantial amount of time every week in nonparental care (Hofferth, 1999; Iruka & Carver, 2006). The 1996 welfare reform legislation known as the Personal Responsibility and Work Opportunity Reconciliation Act (PL 104-193) also influenced the number of children in ECE through the creation of Temporary Assistance for Needy Families (TANF), a block-grant welfare program in which benefits are conditioned upon work requirements designated by the state (Cabrera, Hutchins, & Peters, 2006). Under TANF, the proportion of welfare recipients engaged in work-related activities increased, resulting in an increased demand for child care, including infant and toddler care (Cabrera, Hutchins, & Peters, 2006). In addition to welfare reform, the increased emphasis on ECE settings as places to support children's school readiness led to increased funding for Head Start (U.S. Department of Health and Human Services (DHHS), Administration for Children and Families, 2008a) and investments in the Child Care and Development Block Grant Program (CCDBG) and the Social Service Block Grant (Adams, Tout, & Zaslow, 2006; Zaslow, Acs, McPhee, & Vandivere, 2006). Moreover, the increased availability of state prekindergarten (pre-K) programs may affect ECE utilization rates (National Center for Education Statistics, 2008).

Demographic trends in the utilization of ECE for young children make clear that the widespread measurement of quality throughout a community or state has the potential to inform many families about the quality of ECE settings. Measures of quality that are summarized in readily interpretable formats—such as numbers of stars or ratings of gold, silver, or bronze—can serve as a resource for parents seeking to choose ECE for their young children, helping them to distinguish among the settings available to them. An increasing number of states and communities are making such summary ratings of quality available to the general public through Quality Rating and Improvement Systems (QRIS) (Tout, Zaslow, Halle, & Forry, 2009). At the end of 2010, more than 25 states had launched statewide Quality Rating and Improvement Systems. Many more states and communities are in the planning stages for implementing such systems. Most of these systems include, as a core indicator of quality, an observed measure of quality. They also tend to include a summary rating of quality, incorporating indicators pertaining to educator/caregiver professional development, the use of a learning curriculum, and the degree of parental engagement.

However, demographic data provide some important cautions about the measures of quality that are available for such efforts and the extent to which they are likely to be informative to families across the full range of demographic subgroups. As will be shown in this chapter, the pattern of ECE utilization varies by age of the child, household economic status, and primary home language. Many of the currently available measures of quality may not capture elements of quality that are most pertinent to certain subgroups or to settings that are frequented by these subgroups. Furthermore, more work may be needed in order to define the unique aspects of quality that are important in ECE settings for children with special needs and to create comparable measures of quality across types of settings so that parents who concurrently have children in multiple ECE settings can judge the overall level of quality of those settings.

In this chapter, we provide a descriptive portrayal of the ECE participation of young children overall in the United States and for key demographic subgroups. We focus first on overall participation in nonparental ECE settings and then on participation in different types of ECE, including center-based care, home-based care, and subtypes of these. Both for overall participation and for participation in particular types of ECE, we consider participation by age of the child, household economic status, and primary home language. We also provide brief discussions of data on children with multiple care arrangements and children with disabilities. We conclude with a summary of key findings and implications of these findings for measuring quality in ECE settings.

Data Source

Estimates of the utilization of nonparental ECE in this chapter are based primarily on data from the 2005 National Household Education Survey (NHES). This data set was selected because it is one of the most recent national studies providing estimates of utilization of ECE. Unless otherwise stated, estimates in the remainder of the chapter refer to at least once-a-week participation in some form of nonparental ECE arrangement.

The NHES uses a repeated cross-sectional design to provide snapshots and trend data that describe Americans' educational experiences (Hagedorn, Roth, Carver, Van de Kerckhove, & Smith, 2009). Eleven surveys were used to field the NHES between 1991 and 2007. Data for this chapter are taken from the most recent (2005) administrations of the Early Childhood Program Participation and After School Programs and Activities Surveys (Hagedorn et al., 2009).

Estimates of Participation in Nonparental ECE Overall and in Key Subgroups

According to the 2005 NHES, 60% of children from birth to 5 years (and not yet in kindergarten) were enrolled in at least one weekly nonparental care arrangement (Iruka & Carver, 2006). Patterns of nonparental ECE participation varied by the child's age, household economic status, and primary language spoken at home.

Child Age and Participation in ECE

Participation in nonparental ECE increased through early childhood (from birth to age 5), particularly during the preschool years (from ages 3 to 5). According to the 2005 NHES, approximately 4 in 10 (42%) infants under the age of 1 year were regularly cared for in a nonparental ECE arrangement (Iruka & Carver, 2006). In contrast, almost three-quarters (73%) of preschoolers between the ages of 3 and 5 were regularly in nonparental ECE (Iruka & Carver, 2006).

Household Economic Status and Participation in ECE

Household economic status was also associated with different patterns of nonparental ECE utilization. Across the early childhood years, fewer children living in households below the poverty threshold were in nonparental ECE than those in higher income households. According to the 2005 NHES, among children from birth to 5 years of age, 49% of those in households below the poverty threshold were in at least one weekly nonparental ECE setting, compared with 63% of those in households at or above the poverty line (Iruka & Carver, 2006).

Primary Home Language and Participation in ECE

Different patterns of participation in nonparental ECE were also seen in a comparison of children from English-speaking homes with children from homes where the primary language is not English. According to 2005 NHES data, more children ages birth to 5 were in weekly nonparental care if both of their parents or their single parent spoke English (63%) than if only one of their parents (37%) or neither parent (42%) spoke English (Iruka & Carver, 2006).

As may be expected, immigration status also is related to the use of nonparental ECE. Using 2000 U.S. Census data, Hernandez, Denton, and Macartney (2007) concluded that children of immigrants were less likely to be enrolled in preschool programs at ages 3 and 4 (32% and 55%, respectively) than were 3- and 4-year-old children of U.S. citizens (39% and 63%, respectively). This might put children of immigrants at a disadvantage with respect to cognitive aspects of school readiness that are supported by participation in formal ECE settings (Adams, Tout & Zaslow, 2006).

Participation in Different Types of ECE

Among families that rely regularly on nonparental ECE for their young children, multiple types of ECE are available. The NHES data set uses three categories for distinguishing among types of ECE: center-based care, relative care, and nonrelative care. Center-based care includes private child care centers and preschools, Head Start, and public pre-K. Relative care refers to any care provided by a relative, in either the child's or another person's home. Nonrelative care refers to any care provided by a nonrelative, either in the child's or another person's home. In this section we summarize differences in the use of various types of nonparental ECE by the child's age, household economic status, use of a child care subsidy, and home language.

Child Age and Participation in Different Types of ECE

Age plays a significant role in the utilization of different types of nonparental ECE. Among children in nonparental ECE, as reported by the 2005 NHES, the use of center-based care increases dramatically with age, with only 28% of infants (under 1 year of age), compared with 78% of preschoolers (ages 3 to 5), participating weekly in a center-based ECE setting (Iruka & Carver, 2006).

Conversely, the use of relative care decreases as children grow older. According to 2005 NHES data, among children in a nonparental ECE arrangement, approximately one-half (48%) of infants used relative care at least once a week, compared with approximately one quarter (29%) of preschoolers (Iruka & Carver, 2006).

Household Economic Status and Participation in Different Types of ECE

The use of nonrelative care is more prevalent among children in higher income households. According to the 2005 NHES, among children ages birth to 5 years in nonparental ECE, 24% were from households at or above the poverty threshold, whereas only 16% were from impoverished households.

Among children cared for in nonparental ECE arrangements, those living in impoverished households were more likely to be in relative care than their peers in higher income households. The 2005 NHES estimated an 11-percentage-point difference in the proportion of children using relative care, comparing those in impoverished households with those in higher income households (44% versus 33%, respectively).

Utilization of Child Care Subsidies and Participation in Different Types of ECE

Child care subsidies serve as a financial support to low-income parents in need of a nonparental ECE arrangement. In 2008, among children ages birth to 13 whose families received a child care subsidy from the CCDF, the U.S. federal child care subsidy program, 61% used a center-based program, 12% used relative care in their own home or the relative's home, and 21% were cared for by a nonrelative in their own home or the provider's home (DHHS, Administration for Children and Families, 2008b).[1] Although these national estimates reported that the greatest proportion of child care subsidy recipients used center-based ECE, this pattern did not hold for all states (Adams et al., 2006; DHHS, Administration for Children and Families, 2008b).

Primary Home Language and Participation in Different Types of ECE

NHES data for 2005 show similar utilization patterns of center-based, nonrelative, and relative care, regardless of whether a child was raised in a household in which both parents or the single parent spoke English, one of two spoke English, or neither parent spoke English. In each case, the majority of children (birth to age 5) were in center-based care and the fewest were in nonrelative home care (Iruka & Carver, 2006). Among children from birth to age 5 in nonparental care, between 56% and 66% are in center-based care, with 56% from families in which neither parent spoke English and 66% from families in which one of two parents spoke English. Among children in nonparental care, between 29% and 35% of children are in relative care, with 35% from families in which English was spoken by both parents or by the single parent, 32% from families in which neither parent spoke English, and 29% from families in which one of the two parents spoke English. Finally, among children in nonparental care, between 11% and 23% are in nonrelative care, with 23% from families in which both parents or the single parent spoke English, 21% from families in which no parent spoke English, and 11% from families in which one of the two parents spoke English.

Children with Disabilities and Participation in Different Types of ECE

The Individuals with Disabilities Education Improvement Act (IDEA) of 2004 mandates that community-based child care and preschool settings be inclusive of children (birth to age 6) with disabilities (Devore & Russell, 2007). Despite this provision, many ECE programs (both center- and home-based) do not accept children with disabilities, citing a lack of appropriate qualifications by employees and a lack of appropriate facilities to provide inclusive care (Wall, Kisker, Peterson, Carta, & Jeon, 2006). Estimating the utilization of ECE arrangements for children with disabilities is challenging for a number of reasons, including the difficulties in defining which health conditions are to be considered a "disability" and in obtaining a reliable estimate of children with disabilities (particularly in a preschool sample in which disabilities may not yet be diagnosed). (For additional information on estimations of ECE participation by children with disabilities, see Spiker, Hebbeler, and Barton, Chapter 10, this volume.)

Children Participating in Multiple Arrangements

Thus far, we have addressed the primary ECE arrangements of children in nonparental care. However, many children concurrently participate in multiple care arrangements during the early childhood period. According to 2002 data from the Survey of Income and Program Participation, 25% of children under age 5 with working mothers were in multiple child care arrangements (Overturf Johnson, 2005).

Similar estimates from 2005 NHES data were found: 16% of children from birth to age 5 were in a combination of multiple types of nonparental arrangements and 6% were cared for by a combination of providers within a single type of care (Iruka & Carver, 2006). The concurrent use of multiple types of nonparental arrangements increases with age throughout early childhood.[2]

Summary and Implications

Recent demographic data for the United States indicate that nonparental ECE partici-pation is common for infants and toddlers, but becomes even more widespread for chil-dren between the ages of 3 and 5. Specifically, about 4 in 10 infants are in regular non-parental care during their first year of life, whereas almost 8 in 10 preschoolers are in at least one nonparental care arrangement on a regular basis. Participation in nonparental care is more common among families with household incomes above the poverty line than among those living below the poverty threshold and more common among native English speakers compared with families in which one or both parents speak a lan-guage other than English at home. For those who participate in nonparental ECE, home-based care is more common than center-based care for infants and toddlers, as well as for children in impoverished households; for these two subgroups, relative care in the home is the most common type of ECE. Among 3- to 5-year-olds in nonparental care, center-based care is the most common type of ECE utilized. In addition, center-based care is the most common type of ECE used among children whose families re-ceived a child care subsidy in 2008. Among children who are in nonparental ECE, espe-cially during the first year of life, there are some distinct differences in the types of ECE utilized, based on the children's home language. Information on the number of children with a disability who are participating in ECE is difficult to determine.

In light of the varying ECE settings that children experience from birth through school entry, it is important to understand how quality is characterized for each ECE setting and for all types of children during the early childhood years. Many parents stand to benefit from readily interpretable information that permits them to look across multiple types and subtypes of ECE and compare them with regard to quality. Such in-formation would also allow policy makers to have a broad portrayal of quality, cutting across types and subtypes of ECE. This information can guide investments in quality im-provement so that limited funds can be used most effectively.

Whereas the demographic data suggest that both parents and policy makers could benefit from the collection and dissemination of information on the quality of ECE set-tings, the success of such efforts relies heavily on the availability of measures that are appropriate for the types and subtypes of ECE that major population subgroups are utilizing. Unfortunately, many of the existing measures of quality were not designed to examine the types of care most frequently used among children at certain ages and in particular subgroups, as identified by the population estimates noted in this chapter. For example, many infants and toddlers, and many children in low-income families across the full period from birth to school entry, are cared for primarily in home-based settings. Yet a compendium profiling the content, reliability, and validity of existing measures of quality finds that most existing measures of quality are designed for use in center-based programs serving children between the ages of 3 and 5 (Halle, Vick Whittaker, & Anderson, 2010).

Furthermore, our existing measures have limited content related to cultural sensi-tivity as a facet of quality, to practices that are important to the development of dual language learners, and to the features of ECE that foster positive development among children who have a disability (beyond the features of ECE that foster positive devel-opment among all children). There is a clear need for the measurement of quality to be extended so that measures can serve as sources of guidance on ECE that support the development of all children, including the population subgroups highlighted in this chapter and elsewhere in this volume.

Consideration of the demographic data also suggests that, in addition to developing robust measures of quality that are appropriate to the full range of settings in which children of varying ages and backgrounds participate, there is a need to develop effective strategies to disseminate information on quality in a way that is appropriate for diverse families.

Strengthening the measurement of quality will require the development of new measurement tools, or the extension of existing measurement tools, to focus on the features of ECE settings that define high-quality care for various subgroups of children and within different settings. This chapter has provided a demographic context for the discussions of strengthening quality measures articulated in the remaining chapters of the book. The estimates presented here highlight the importance of having strong quality measures that can be utilized in different care settings, including home-based care, and with children of various ages, including infants and toddlers. The demographic information provided in this chapter also underscores the importance of considering quality from the perspective of key demographic subgroups, such as families in which one or both parents are non–English speakers, families with children with disabilities, and families living in poverty.

References

Adams, G., Tout, K., & Zaslow, M. (2006). *Early care and education for children in low-income families: Patterns of use, quality, and potential policy implications.* Washington, DC: Paper presented at The Urban Institute and Child Trends Roundtable on Children in Low-Income Families. Retrieved May 27, 2009, from http://www.urbaninstitute.org

Cabrera, N., Hutchens, R., & Peters, H.E. (2006). *From welfare to childcare: What happens to young children when mothers exchange welfare for work?* Mahwah, NJ: Lawrence Erlbaum Associates.

DeVore, S., & Russell, K. (2007). Early childhood education and care for children with disabilities: Facilitating inclusive practice. *Early Childhood Education Journal, 35*(2), 189–198.

Hagedorn, M., Roth, S.B., Carver, P., Van de Kerckhove, W., & Smith, S. (2009). *National Household Education Surveys Program of 2007: Methodology report.* (NCES 2009–047). Washington, DC: National Center for Education Statistics, Institute of Education Sciences, U.S. Department of Education.

Halle, T., Vick Whittaker, J.E., & Anderson, R. (2010). *Quality in Early Childhood Care and Education Settings: A Compendium of Measures* (2nd ed.). Washington, DC: Prepared by Child Trends for the Office of Planning, Research and Evaluation, Administration for Children and Families, U.S. Department of Health and Human Services. Retrieved October 10, 2010, from http://www.research-connections.org/childcare/resources/18804/pdf

Hernandez, D.J., Denton, N.A., & Macartney, S.E. (2007). Children in immigrant families— the U.S. and 50 states: National origins, language, and early education [electronic version]. *Children in America's newcomer families.* Retrieved May 27, 2009, from http://www.childtrends.org/Files/Child_Trends-2007_04_01_RB_ChildrenImmigrant.pdf

Hofferth, S.L. (1999). Child care, maternal employment, and public policy. *Annals of the American Academy of Political and Social Science, 563,* 20–38.

Iruka, I.U., & Carver, P.R. (2006). *Initial results from the 2005 NHES Early Childhood Program Participation Survey* (NCES 2006–075). Washington, DC: National Center for Education Statistics, U.S. Department of Education.

National Center for Education Statistics. (2008). Enrollment in public elementary and secondary schools, by grade: Selected years, fall 1980 through fall 2006. Retrieved January 7, 2010, from http://nces.ed.gov/programs/digest/d08/tables/dt08_037.asp

Overturf Johnson, J. (2005). *Who's minding the kids? Child care arrangements: Winter 2002.*

Current Population Reports, P70-101. Washington, DC: U.S. Census Bureau.

Tout, K., Zaslow, M., Halle, T., & Forry, N. (2009). ACF-OPRE Issue Brief. *Issues for the Next Decade of Quality Rating and Improvement Systems.* Office of Planning, Research and Evaluation, Administration for Children and Families, U.S. Department of Health and Human Services. Washington, DC.

U.S. Department of Health and Human Services, Administration for Children & Families. (2008a). Head Start program fact sheet fiscal year 2008. Retrieved January 7, 2010, from http://eclkc.ohs.acf.hhs.gov/hslc/Head%20Start%20Program/Head%20Start%20Program%20Factsheets/dHeadStartProgr.htm

U.S. Department of Health and Human Services, Administration for Children and Families. (2008b). *Table 6. Average monthly percentages of children served in all types of care (FFY 2008).* Retrieved January 10, 2010, from http://www.acf.hhs.gov/programs/ccb/data/ccdf_data/08acf800_preliminary/table6.htm

U.S. Department of Labor, Bureau of Labor Statistics. (2009). *Table 7. Employment status of women by presence and age of youngest child, March 1975–2008.* Retrieved January 6, 2010, from http://www.bls.gov/cps/wlftable7.htm

Wall, S., Kisker, E.E., Peterson, C.A., Carta, J.J., & Jeon, H. (2006). Child-care for low income children with disabilities: Access, quality, and parental satisfaction. *Journal of Early Intervention, 28*(4), 283–298.

Zaslow, M., Acs, G., McPhee, C., & Vandivere, S. (2006). *Children in low-income families: Change and continuity in family context and measures of well-being.* Washington, DC: Paper prepared for The Urban Institute and Child Trends Roundtable on Children in Low-Income Families.

Endnotes

[1]The remaining 6% of children whose families received subsidies in 2007 are accounted for by 5% in licensed or regulated group homes and 1% from invalid or unreported data. (See U.S. Department of Health and Human Services, Administration for Children and Families, 2008b, Data Tables 3 and 6, FFY 2008: http://www.acf.hhs.gov/programs/ccb/data/ccdf_data/08acf800_preliminary/table6.htm)

[2]According to 2005 NHES data, among infants less than 1 year of age, 7% of children are in multiple ECE arrangements with a mix of provider types. The percentage increases to 11% among toddlers (1- to 2-year-olds) and to 22% among preschoolers (3- to 5-year-olds; Iruka & Carver, 2006).

CHAPTER 2

How Well Do Our Measures of Quality Predict Child Outcomes?

A Meta-Analysis and Coordinated Analysis of Data from Large-Scale Studies of Early Childhood Settings

Margaret Burchinal, Kirsten Kainz, and Yaping Cai

C hildren who attend higher quality early care and education (ECE) are more likely to start school with better cognitive, academic, and social skills, according to the extensive child care research literature (Lamb, 1998; NICHD [National Institute of Child Health and Human Development] Early Child Care Research Network, 2006; Peisner-Feinberg et al., 2001; Vandell, 2004). For this reason, parents and policy makers have focused on improving the quality of ECE to increase school readiness for all children and especially for children from low-income families (Barnett, Hustedt, Hawkinson, & Robin, 2006). Both the federal government and state governments have invested heavily in early childhood programs on the basis of research findings and have tended to focus on the results from the most successful programs when advocating for ECE. The purpose of this chapter is to provide a more comprehensive overview of the research relating ECE quality to child outcomes, especially for children from low-income families.

Both experimental and observational studies have examined the impact of ECE experiences on children's development. The clinical trials in which children are randomly assigned to child care programs or control groups test the extent to which these programs change children's development. Random assignment should reveal causal links but may not lead to generalization due to the limited diversity among families usually included in these studies. The observational studies examine the extent to which ECE experiences are related to child outcomes. They tend to have larger, more diverse samples, but cannot eliminate the possibility that other factors, such as family characteristics, could cause the observed associations.

A number of experimental studies have demonstrated that high-quality ECE experiences produce stronger cognitive and academic skills in children entering school; in turn, these skills translate into better adolescent and adult outcomes (Campbell, Ramey, Pungello, Sparling, & Miller-Johnson, 2002; Lazar, Darlington, Murray, Royce, & Snipper, 1982; Martin, Brooks-Gunn, Klebanov, Buka, & McCormick, 2008; Nores, Barnett, Belfield, & Schweinhart, 2005). The studies in question randomly assigned children to either the ECE program or to a comparison group, thereby testing the extent to which the ECE experiences changed the children's development. The effect sizes (reported in terms of the difference between the means for the treatment and control groups divided by the standard deviation) ranged from $d = 0.13$ to $d = 1.23$. The largest effect sizes were obtained in the most intensive interventions—in assessments of children after the age of 2 years. The Abecedarian Project, a single-site experimental intervention that delivered 5 years of full-time high-quality child care, had effect sizes of $d = 1.23$ at 36 months and long-term effects on employment and schooling outcomes at 21 years of age (Campbell, Pungello, Miller-Johnson, Burchinal, & Ramey, 2001). The Perry Preschool Project, a single-site program that delivered 2 years of child care between the ages of 3 and 5 years and included a home-visiting/parenting education component, yielded effect sizes of $d = 0.83$ on a cognitive test at 3 years of age (Nores et al., 2005). In contrast, the less intensive intervention programs resulted in much smaller effects. For example, effect sizes of $d = 0.13$ were found at 36 months for Early Head Start (Love et al., 2005), a large, multisite program for the first years of life that delivered 2–3 years of home visiting and, in some sites, high-quality child care.

Several meta-analyses have examined the magnitude of these programs on children's short- and long-term development. Nelson and colleagues (Nelson, Westhues, & MacLeod, 2003) estimated effect sizes for 34 preschool intervention programs, with at least one follow-up assessment. Moderately large effects for cognitive outcomes during preschool ($d = .52$) were still detectable at eighth grade ($d = .30$). Similarly, smaller effects for social–emotional outcomes during preschool ($d = .27$) were still detected at the end of high school ($d = .33$). Bigger cognitive effects were observed when programs had an intentional instruction component. Overall, programs that started with children at younger ages and provided more years of intervention had the largest effects. Similarly, in a Rand Corporation study, Karoly, Kilburn, and Cannon (2005) examined 20 programs implemented in the United States that provided services to children and/or families during early childhood. They reported that approximately two-thirds of the programs produced statistically significant benefits for children's outcomes, with larger effects for IQ or standardized achievement test scores for intensive full-time ECE interventions focused on improving school readiness, and smaller effects for parent ratings of social-emotional outcomes in typically less intensive programs focused on both mother and child.

Descriptive or quasi-experimental studies (i.e., studies that did not involve random assignment to ECE conditions) have provided further support for an association between higher quality ECE and positive child outcomes; such studies involved larger, more representative samples (Gormley, Gayer, Phillips, & Dawson, 2005; Howes et al., 2008; NICHD Early Child Care Research Network, 2005; Peisner-Feinberg et al., 2001; Reynolds, Temple, Robertson, & Mann, 2002). These studies varied widely in terms of the degree to which they accounted for possible selection biases. If parents who provided more cognitive stimulation and responsive care at home selected higher quality ECE programs, then some of the statistical association between ECE quality and child outcomes could be due to these parental characteristics serving as a confound. Whereas the experimental studies have examined the impact of specific center-based ECE programs, many of the observational studies have focused on the extent to which ECE that neither involves intervention nor demonstrates projects predicts child outcomes during the preschool years or at entry to kindergarten. Overall, studies have tended to report associations between child care quality and cognitive, language, and academic outcomes and, less consistently, links with social-emotional outcomes (Vandell, 2004). However, to date, this literature has not been summarized in a meta-analysis. Such a summary would be especially important because many child care advocates have used the results from the individual experimental studies or the meta-analyses of those studies to justify state and federal programs such as Head Start and pre-Ks and the use of funding to improve ECE quality through such initiatives as Quality Rating Systems. It is important to know how much the quality of ECE is related to child outcomes, especially for low-income children.

Methods

Two sets of secondary analyses were conducted. The first set involved a meta-analysis of studies of ECE that related the quality of the setting to child outcomes. This analysis of studies that usually included at least some child and family covariates to account for potential family selection bias addressed questions about how strong the association is between the quality of ECE and child outcomes. The second set of analyses involved the reanalysis of five large data sets that included a moderate-to-large number of low-income preschoolers to estimate the strength of the association between observed classroom quality and child outcomes in studies in which some child and family factors are included as covariates.

Meta-Analysis

The meta-analysis began with searching the published literature and the Internet for studies or evaluations that measured and related observed quality and child outcomes. We identified 20 different studies that met the following criteria: The studies 1) reported associations between widely used measures of child care quality and child outcomes, 2) included more than 10 classrooms, and 3) met some minimum criteria regarding peer review. That is, they had to be published either in a peer-reviewed journal or online in an evaluation report that, presumably, involved some sort of peer review. Table 2.1 lists the papers or reports that were included. Note that there were multiple reports or papers for some of the studies. In all, the studies generated 97 effect sizes that described the association between observed quality and child outcomes. Appendix B describes the details of the meta-analysis.

All associations between child care quality and child outcomes were converted to partial correlations for the meta-analysis. A partial correlation of 0.10 is considered modest, 0.30 is considered moderate, and 0.5 is considered large (Cohen, 1987).

The meta-analysis estimated the effect size, describing the association between child care quality and child outcome overall and by age and type of outcome. Child outcomes were categorized as language/cognitive, academic, and social-emotional outcomes. Children's age ranges were 2-3, 3-4, and 4-6 years. The results are shown in

Table 2.1. Studies included in the meta-analysis

Author/year	Study	Quality measures	Child outcomes	Covariates	Coefficients with controls
McCartney (1984)	Bermuda Intervention (n = 131)	ECERS, verbal interaction	PPVT, preschool language assessment	Family background & home environment, center care experience, age at entry & hours in current center care	ECERS—standardized coefficients: PPVT = 0.19,* preschool language assessment = 0.23,** ALI = 0.43,*** communication task = 0.46**
Peisner-Feinberg and Burchinal (1997)	CQO (n = 757)	ECERS, CIS, ECOF, AIS—a composite formed	PPVT, WJ prereading, WJ premath, CBI sociability, problem behavior, cognitive/attention	Maternal education, child ethnicity, child gender	Quality composite—unstandardized coefficient (standard error): PPVT = 2.05 (0.48),*** WJ prereading = 0.74 (0.34),* math = 0.68 (0.38), CBI sociability = 0.02 (0.02), problem behavior = 0.07 (0.03),* cognitive/attention = 0.02 (0.02)
NICHD ECCRN (2000)	NICHD SECCYD	ORCE positive caregiving and language stimulation	15 mos.: Bayley & CDI; 24 mos.: Bayley & CDI; 36 mos.: Bracken & Reynell	Site, child gender, ethnicity, maternal PPVT, HOME total, maternal stimulation	ORCE positive caregiving—standardized coefficients: Bayley (15/24mos.) = 0.08/0.16,* CDI vocab. prod. (15/24mos.) = 0.12*/0.07, comprehension = 0.15*/0.12,* Bracken (36mos.) = 0.12,* Reynell (36mos.) expressive = −0.10,* verbal comprehensive = 0.15*
Burchinal et al. (2000b)	CQO and two other NC projects	ECERS	PPVT, WJ Letter-Word ID and Applied Problems	Gender, ethnicity, poverty	ECERS—effect size (high versus low quality): language skills d = 1.01, prereading d = 0.52, premath d = 0.48
Peisner-Feinberg, et al. (2001)	CQO	ECERS, CIS, ECOF, AIS—a composite formed	PPVT-R, WJ reading, math, CBI cognitive/attention, problem behavior, sociability	State, age, maternal education, gender, ethnicity, age of entry, teacher–child closeness	ECERS—partial correlation (48mos., K, G2): PPVT: 0.18***/0.11**/0.04, WJ reading = 0.06/−0.05/0.02, WJ Math = 0.08*/0.07*/0.11,** CBI cognitive/attention = 0.03/−0.08/0.06, CBI problem behavior = 0.11**/0.02/0.04, CBI sociability = 0.04/−0.15/0.05
NICHD ECCRN & Duncan (2003)	NICHD SECCYD	ORCE positive caregiving rating	Bayley MDI 24 mos. cognitive composite of WJ-R memory and language scales, and PLS language scales; academic composite of WJ-R academic scales	Extensive demographic, parental characteristics and beliefs about child care, quality of home environment, amount and type of child care	ORCE quality 6–24mos. unstandardized coefficient (standard error): 24mos. MDI = 1.66 (0.48),*** 54mos. achievement = 0.90 (0.41),* 54mos. cognitive composite = 1.36 (0.49)** ORCE quality 36–54mos. B(se): 54mos. cognitive composite 1.17 (0.43),** 54mos. achievement = 1.12 (0.36)**

Author (year)	Study/data	Quality measure	Outcome measures	Covariates	Results
NICHD ECCRN (2003)	NICHD SECCYD	ORCE positive caregiving rating	term memory; Preschool Language Scale; Continuous Performance Task; M and CG ratings of SSRS and CBCL	Site, child gender, ethnicity, maternal education, partner status, maternal depression, quality of parenting, family income, hours of child care, type of care	ORCE unstandardized coefficient (standard error): WJ reading = 2.21 (1.07),* math = 2.49 (1.20),* phonemic skill = 2.52 (1.11),* memory = 3.37 (1.52),* language comprehension = 3.00 (1.44),* expressive = 4.47 (1.43)* Attention: omission errors = −1.10 (0.66), commission errors = −3.98 (1.75),* M SSRS competence = 1.70 (1.11), M behavior problems = −0.25 (0.79), CG social competence = 3.91 (1.29),** CG behavior problems = −1.04 (1.01)
Burchinal and Cryer (2003)	CQO and NICHD SECCYD	CQO—a composite formed from ECERS, CIS, ECOF, and AIS. For NICHD SECCYD, ORCE positive caregiving rating	CQO: PPVT, WJ-school readiness, CBI prosocial, CBI behavior problems. NICHD: 36 mos. Reynell Language Scale, 36 mos. Bracken School Readiness, mother and caregiver ratings of ASBI social skills and CBCL behavior problems	For CQO: maternal education, gender, ethnicity, child care quality index. For NICHD: site, gender, ethnicity, maternal education, type of care, amount of care	CQO quality composite unstandardized coefficient (standard error): PPVT = 1.89 (0.46),*** WJ-R school readiness = 0.57 (0.28)* NICHD SECCYD quality rating B(se): Reynell receptive language = 0.63 (0.17),*** Bracken school readiness = 1.51 (0.20)***
Poe, Burchinal, Roberts (2004)	Durham, NC, Preschool to School Study	ECERS	48 mos. CELF Language; WJ-R incomplete words, broad reading	Gender, maternal IQ, maternal education, HOME total, maternal involvement, maternal book reading	ECERS unstandardized coefficient (standard error): language = 3.24 (1.36),* WJ-R phonemic skills = 1.90 (0.86),* reading = 0.09 (1.47)
Votruba-Drzal et al. (2004)	Welfare, Children, and Families	ECERS/FDCRS and CIS—a composite formed	WJ: Applied Problems, letter-word identification	Child age; race; gender; mother's age, marital status, education, work status; number of minors in HH; income-to-needs ratio; child care hours; center care	Quality composite B(se): WJ Applied Problems = 1.98 (1.95), WJ Letter-word = −0.39 (1.25); Interactions—hours × quality, home × quality, and gender × quality are significant for both outcomes
Loeb et al. (2004)	1998 CA welfare-to-work programs evaluation	CIS	Bracken total score school readiness; FACES story comprehension	Site, child age, child race, mother's PPVT, mother's education, site, months in setting	CIS unstandardized coefficient (standard error): Bracken total score = 1.05 (1.57), school readiness = 1.66 (2.18), story comprehension = 0.52 (0.25)*

(continued)

Table 2.1. (continued)

Author/year	Study	Quality measures	Child outcomes	Covariates	Coefficients with controls
NICHD ECCRN (2006)	NICHD SECCYD	ORCE	Bayley 24 mos., Reynell Language Scale 36 mos., Bracken school readiness 36 mos., WJ-R academic composite (LW & AP), memory 54 mos., language composite (PLS & WJ-R Voc) 54 mos., continuous performance task 54 mos.	Site, child gender, ethnicity, partner status, income-to-need ratio, mother's psychological adjustment, HOME quality, % in center care, hours in child care	High- versus low-quality effect size: 15mos. Bayley = 0.23, 24mos. Bayley = 0.34,***, 36mos. Bracken = 0.38,***, Reynell language receptive = 0.39,***, expressive = 0.34,**, 54mos. language total = 0.26,*, WJ preacademic = 0.32,**, memory = 0.16, CPT omission = −0.10
Howes et al. (2008)	NCEDL Multi-State Study of Pre-Kindergarten	ECERS interaction and activities factors & CLASS Emotional & Instructional Support	Language—PPVT, OWLS, letter naming, WJ-R applied problems	State, gender, age at fall assessment, ethnicity, maternal education, poverty, household size	Quality with gain scores effect size: CLASS Instructional Support & PPVT = 0.06,*, OWLS = 0.07,*, math = 0.01
Gallagher, Lambert (2006)	Head Start Partnership Study, Charlotte, NC	Assessment Profile for Early Childhood Programs	ASBI comply, express, disruption, prosocial; FACES problem behavior; print concepts, story retelling	Maternal education, maternal depression, household income, child gender, violence exposure, child age, special need of child	Profile unstandardized coefficient (standard error) Social skills: comply = 0−0.214 (0.208), express = −0.085 (0.216), prosocial = −0.170 (0.216), problem behaviors disruptive = 0.575 (0.243),*, problem behavior = −0.296 (0.157), print concepts = 0.541 (0.194),**, story retelling = −0.424 (0.190)*
Schliecker, White, & Jacobs (1991)	Montreal area day care centers	ECERS	PPVT	Socioeconomic status, family structure, mother's and father's ages, education, occupation	Standardized coefficients: PPVT β = 0.57***
Kontos & Wilcox-Herzog (1997)	Midwestern Early Childhood Program N = 114	Teacher involvement	Cognitive competence, social competence	Child age, teacher presence, peer presence, activities rating	Teacher involvement—standardized coefficients: cognitive competence = 0.08, social competence = 0.29
NICHD ECCRN (2002)	NICHD SECCYD	Process quality composite (latent variable)	Cognitive competence (latent variable)	Mother's education, family income, child-teacher ratio, caregiver education	Process Quality—standardized coefficients: Cognitive competence = 0.10**

Study	Sample	Quality measures	Outcome measures	Controls	Results
Blau (1999)	NLSY $N = 12652$	Group size, child–teacher ratio, caregiver training	PIAT-Reading, PIAT-Math, PPVT, BPI	Amount of care, number of care arrangements, type of care	Group Size—unstandardized coefficient (standard error): BPI = 0.17 (0.10), PIAT–math = −0.21 (0.10), PIAT–reading = −0.25** (0.11), PPVT = −0.40*** (0.15) Ratio–B(SE): BPI = 7.16 (2.81), PIAT–math = 1.75 (2.45), PIAT–reading −0.56 (3.58), PPVT = −1.06 (3.08) Training—B(SE): BPI = 0.52 (2.36), PIAT–math = 0.83 (2.12), PIAT–reading 3.43 (2.43), PPVT = 4.28 (2.99)
Herrera (2005)	Chilean child care centers $N = 526$	ECERS	Vocabulary, social development, adaptive behavior	None	ECERS—Pearson correlation: vocabulary = 0.20, social development = 0.17, adaptive behavior = 0.09

*p < .01; **p < .05; ***p < .001

Key: Studies: CQO, Cost, Quality, Outcomes Study; FACES, Family and Child Experiences Surveys; NCEDL, National Center for Early Development and Learning; NICHD SECCYD, National Institute of Child Health and Human Development Study of Early Child Care and Youth Development.

Child care quality measures: AIS, Adult Interaction Scale; CELF, Comprehensive Early Language Scale; CIS, Caregiver Involvement Scale; CLASS, Classroom Assessment Scoring System; ECERS, Early Childhood Environment Rating Scale; ECOF, Early Childhood Observation of the Family; FDCRS, Family Day Care Rating Scale; HOME, Home Observation for the Measurement of the Environment; ORCE, Observational Rating of the Caregiving Environment.

Child outcome measures: ALI: Adaptive Language Inventory; ASBI, Adaptive Social Behavior Index; BPI, Behavior Problems Index; CBCL, Child Behavior Checklist; CBI, Classroom Behavior Inventory; CDI, Child Development Inventory; EOWPVT, Expressive One Word Picture Vocabulary Test; MDI, Mental Development Index; OWLS, Oral & Written Language Scale; PIAT, Peabody Individual Achievement Test; PLS, Preschool Language Scale; PPVT, Peabody Picture Vocabulary Test; SSRS, Social Skills Rating System; TBRS, Teacher Behavior Rating Scale; WJ-R, Woodcock Johnson-Revised Achievement Battery.

Table 2.2.   Estimated child care quality effect sizes and confidence intervals by age and type of outcomes

	All ages r_p (CI)	2-year-olds r_p (CI)	3-year-olds r_p (CI)	4-year-olds r_p (CI)
Overall	0.109 (0.098−0.120)	0.111 (0.099−0.122)	0.135 (0.121−0.149)	0.081 (0.072−0.089)
Academic/ cognitive	0.120 (0.101−0.139)	0.119 (0.100−0.138)	0.156 (0.131−0.180)	0.085 (0.072−0.098)
Language	0.144 (0.094−0.194)		0.166 (0.118−0.214)	0.122 (0.087−0.158)
Social	0.085 (0.069−0.101)	0.100 (0.081−0.119)	0.101 (0.084−0.123)	0.051 (0.042−0.061)

Table 2.2 and Figure 2.1. Table 2.2 shows the estimated effect size across the studies in the meta-analysis as the weighted average partial correlation. The analysis indicated that all estimated ECE effects, overall, by age and by type of outcome, were statistically different from zero, as illustrated by the fact that none of the confidence intervals contained zero. Comparisons of the effect sizes for differences related to the age of the child and the type of outcome that was assessed revealed that associations were stronger at 3 years of age than at 4, for overall effects and for academic/cognitive effects. Also, across all ages, effects for language were stronger than for social skills.

In sum, the meta-analysis indicated that widely used measures of ECE quality were statistically related to children's outcomes, but these associations were modest. Partial correlations were in the range from $0.05 < r_p < 0.17$. Stronger associations were observed for younger children than for older children and for academic and language outcomes than for social outcomes.

Secondary Data Analysis: Child Care Quality and Outcomes Among Low-Income Children

Next, we examined the association between child care quality and child outcomes among low-income children. We selected five data sets that included child care quality and child outcome assessments for at least 100 children observed in at least 50 class-rooms. The five studies were the NICHD Study of Early Child Care and Youth Development (NICHD SECCYD; NICHD Early Child Care Research Network, 2003); Cost, Quality, and Outcomes Study (CQO; Peisner-Feinberg & Burchinal, 1997); National Center for Early Development and Learning (NCEDL) 11-State Pre-Kindergarten

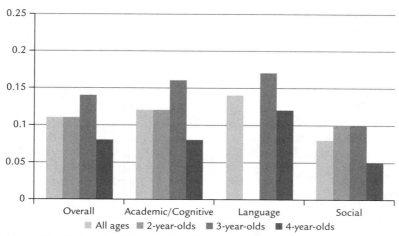

Figure 2.1.   Estimated child care quality effect sizes by age and type of outcomes.

Evaluation (Howes et al., 2008); and the Head Start Family and Child Experiences Surveys (FACES) from 1997 and 2000. The complete data were available for the first three studies, and the public-release data sets were acquired for the FACES data sets.

Methods

Each of the five studies included at least 100 low-income children in at least 50 classrooms but varied in many other ways (see Table 2.3). All included multiple sites and were designed to reflect variation in ECE experiences in the United States. The FACES provided a description of Head Start services in 1997 and 2000, the NCEDL evaluation described mature pre-K programs in 2001–2003, and the NICHD SECCYD described the child care experiences of children randomly selected at birth in 10 sites within the United States. Each study is briefly described next. Table 2.3 provides a descriptive summary of the children from the five data sets included in subsequent analyses.

The NICHD SECCYD was designed to examine the relationship between child care experiences and characteristics, on the one hand, and children's developmental outcomes, on the other. The participating children were a conditional random sample selected shortly after birth during hospital visits at 10 locations across the United States. The locations were associated with the 10 principal investigators, but included sites in the Northeast, Southeast, Midwest, and West. Data were collected in whatever ECE setting the children attended. The current analyses include ECE setting and child assessments over 54 months. (For more information on this study's methodology, see https://secc.rti.org or a report by the NICHD study [NICHD Early Child Care Research Network, 2006].)

The CQO study was conducted in child care centers in four states. The centers were randomly selected from lists of for-profit and not-for-profit centers in the greater Los Angeles area of California, the Frontal Range area of Colorado, the greater Hartford area of Connecticut, and the greater Greensboro area of North Carolina. Quality in a randomly selected infant/toddler and preschool classroom was carefully assessed in 101 centers. Up to 10 children in the preschool classrooms were randomly selected, and their academic, language, and social skills were assessed in the spring of their second-to-last year of child care before they entered elementary school (see Peisner-Feinburg & Burchinal, 1997, for details).

The NCEDL conducted two studies of state-funded pre-K: the Multi-State Study of Pre-Kindergarten and the Study of State-Wide Early Education Programs (SWEEP). The goals and methodologies of the two studies were largely similar, so they have been combined for the current analyses. Both studies sought to describe state-funded pre-K programs in states that had large, well-established programs. In all, 11 states participated. Each state submitted a list of sites providing state-funded pre-K, and sites were randomly selected from this list. Then, at each site, one classroom serving primarily 4-year-olds was selected at random. Within each classroom, children who were old enough to attend kindergarten the following year were selected. The current analyses include the children's assessments from the fall and spring of the pre-K year. (For further details about the methodologies for these studies, see Early et al., 2005.)

The primary purpose of FACES was to describe the quality of Head Start programs in a nationally representative sample, with an eye toward achieving the goals of implementing a system of program performance measures and improving accountability for Head Start programs. The longitudinal data set comprised a sample of 63 randomly selected Head Start programs, stratified by census region; percent minority; and whether the programs were in rural, urban, or suburban areas. The FACES cohorts from

Table 2.3.   Descriptive information for the five studies on low-income children and their classrooms

		NICHD SECCYD $N = 129$	CQO $N = 140$	NCEDL Pre-K eval. $N = 1,465$	FACES 1997 $N = 1,493$	FACES 2000 $N = 1,739$
Background						
Maternal education	M (SD)	12.6 (1.8)	13.0 (1.7)	11.8 (1.9)	11.7 (1.9)	11.9 (1.8)
Child gender (male)		48%	51%	49%	51%	50%
Child age in months	M (SD)	54	51.1 (4.4)	60.6 (2.3)	55.4 (6.3)	54.0 (6.5)
Child ethnicity/race						
African American		36.4%	32.4%	20.7%	21%	38%
Hispanic		9.3%	13.7%	36.0%	36%	29%
White		49.6%	46.0%	28.6%	29%	24%
Other		4.7%	7.9%	14.7%	14%	5%
Quality measures						
ECERS total	M (SD)		4.2 (0.9)	3.8 (0.8)	5.1 (0.6)	4.9 (1.0)
Language and Reasoning	M (SD)		4.38 (1.40)	4.5 (1.1)	5.0 (1.0)	5.0 (1.3)
Interactions	M (SD)		4.62 (1.24)	4.7 (1.5)	5.0 (0.7)	5.6 (1.6)
CIS total	M (SD)		78.0 (10.4)		73.1 (11.1)	72.8 (13.0)
CLASS total	M (SD)			4.5 (0.6)		
Emotional Support	M (SD)			5.5 (0.7)		
Instructional Support	M (SD)			2.1 (0.8)		
ORCE total	M (SD)	2.9 (0.6)				
Child outcomes						
PPVT	M (SD)		83.6 (17.1)	92.0 (13.4)	84.1 (15.1)	84.6 (16.7)
PLS	M (SD)	86.2 (18.5)				
WJ-Letter-Word	M (SD)	91.9 (12.8)	94.7 (10.9)	99.5 (13.0)	90.2 (10.1)	92.5 (10.3)
WJ-Applied Problems	M (SD)	93.4 (15.7)	96.6 (12.8)	96.0 (12.2)	84.9 (17.7)	86.6 (17.5)
CBCL Externalizing	M (SD)	53.3 (10.0)				
CBCL Internalizing	M (SD)	52.8 (10.1)				
CPSCS Social Competence	M (SD)	98.4 (16.6)				
CBI Task Orientation	M (SD)		3.3 (1.0)			
CBI Behavior Problems	M (SD)		2.7 (1.0)			
TCRS Social Competence	M (SD)			3.6 (0.8)		
TCRS Behavior Problems	M (SD)			1.5 (0.6)		
BPI Social Skills	M (SD)				16.4 (4.5)	16.5 (4.6)
BPI Behavior Problems	M (SD)				4.9 (4.5)	5.5 (5.0)

M = Means; SD = Standard Deviation

Key: Studies: CQO, Cost, Quality, Outcomes Study; FACES, Family and Child Experiences Surveys; NCEDL, National Center for Early Development and Learning; NICHD SECCYD, National Institute of Child Health and Human Development Study of Early Child Care and Youth Development.

Child care quality measures: CIS, Caregiver Involvement Scale; CLASS, Classroom Assessment Scoring System; ECERS, Early Childhood Environment Rating Scale; ORCE, Observational Record of the Caregiving Environment.

Child outcome measures: BPI, Behavior Problems Index; CBCL, Child Behavior Checklist; CBI, Classroom Behavior Inventory; CPSCS, California Preschool Social Competency Scale; PLS, Preschool Language Scale; Comprehension Scale; PPVT, Peabody Picture Vocabulary Test; TCRS, Teacher-Child Rating Scale; WJ, Woodcock-Johnson Tests of Achievement.

1997 and 2000 represent four phases of data collection that followed 4-year-old Head Start children from program entry through the spring of kindergarten. The current analyses are restricted to children who were in 4-year-old classrooms in the spring of either 1997 or 2000 and include the children's assessments from the fall and spring of their first year of Head Start. (For more information on this study and its methodology, see Zill and Resnick, 2005, and Zill et al., 2003).

Five measures of ECE quality were collected across the studies (see Table 2.3). The Early Childhood Environment Rating Scale (ECERS; Harms & Clifford, 1980) or the Early Childhood Environment Rating Scale-Revised (ECERS-R; Harms, Clifford, & Cryer, 1998) was collected in all studies except SECCYD. The original was, and now the revised ECERS is, a widely used measure of global classroom quality, specifically designed for use in classrooms serving children between 2 and 5 years of age. Scores on the ECERS-R range from 1–7, with 1 indicating *inadequate* quality, 3 indicating *minimal* quality, 5 indicating *good* quality, and 7 indicating *excellent* quality. The scale's authors reported a total scale internal consistency of 0.92. In addition to the total score, analyses involved the Language and Reasoning Scale and an Interaction factor score. The Language and Reasoning Scale consists of seven items measuring the degree to which the lead caregiver encouraged elaborated language and reasoning. The Interaction factor was identified in a factor analysis of the CQO and NCEDL data and consisted primarily of items describing how the primary caregiver interacted with children, both in general and during specific activities. The Observational Record of the Caregiving Environment (ORCE) was designed specifically for the SECCYD to assess the quality of caregiver–child interaction experienced by individual children. Observations of child care quality used in the present analyses were made during a single half-day visit when the child was 54 months of age. The quality measure used for the current analysis is the positive caregiving rating composite, the mean of 4-point ratings of caregivers' sensitivity/responsiveness, stimulation of cognitive development, intrusiveness (reflected), and detachment (reflected). Scores range from 1 (*unresponsive or harsh caregiving*) to 4 (*frequent responsive and stimulating caregiving*). The Caregiver Involvement Scale (CIS; Arnett, 1989) was collected in the CQO and the FACES studies. It is an observational scale consisting of 26 items—reflecting teacher sensitivity, harshness, and detachment—that are rated on a 1–4 scale indicating how characteristic they are of the teacher, from not at all (1) to very much (4). Psychometric analyses suggest that a single factor most parsimoniously represented these data (Cronbach's α = .93). The Classroom Assessment Scoring System (CLASS™; Pianta, La Paro, & Hamre, 2008) was used by the NCEDL study to rate teacher–child interactions for both emotional support, in terms of sensitivity and responsiveness, and instructional support, in terms of developing concepts and providing productive feedback.

The projects also used a variety of measures to assess child outcomes (see Table 2.3). All of the projects but CQO administered the same battery of assessments in the fall and spring. All studies measured language. The CQO, NCEDL, and FACES studies used the Peabody Picture Vocabulary Test-Revised (PPVT; Dunn & Dunn, 1997). The SECCYD used the Preschool Language Scale-3 (PLS-3; Zimmerman, Steiner, & Pond, 1992). According to the developers, both measure receptive language reliably for 3- to 5-year-olds (PPVT 0.92–0.98; PLS-3 0.89–0.92). All studies administered two subtests from the Woodcock-Johnson Tests of Achievement (WJ), the Letter–Word Identification subtest to measure early reading skills, and the Applied Problems Subtest to measure early math skills. The NCEDL used the Woodcock-Johnson III (Woodcock, McGrew, & Mather, 2001). According to the developer, reliability for 3- to 5-year-old children ranged from

0.92 to 0.99 for Letter–Word and 0.91 to 0.94 for Applied Problems. All of the language and academic achievement measures were individually administered standardized tests with a mean of 100 and a standard deviation of 15 in the norming sample.

The five studies administered a variety of measures of social-emotional development. The SECCYD had teachers complete the Child Behavior Checklist (CBCL; Achenbach, 1991), a widely used measure of internalizing and externalizing behavior problems. The SECCYD measured social skills with the Social Skills Rating System (SSRS; Gresham & Elliott, 1990; test–retest reliability of 0.75 to 0.88). The CBCL has a mean of 50 and a standard deviation of 10 in the norming sample. CQO teachers rated each child on the Classroom Behavior Inventory (CBI; Schaefer, Edgerton, & Aaronson, 1978). Factor analysis of the 10 CBI scale scores from the first year yielded three factors (75% of the variance): a task orientation factor ($\alpha = 0.84$), a social skills factor ($\alpha = .65$), and a problem behaviors factor ($\alpha = 0.77$). CBI scales are computed as the mean of items with a maximum score of 5 and a minimum score of 1. The NCEDL teachers completed the Teacher–Child Rating Scale (TCRS; Hightower et al., 1986), a behavioral rating scale that assesses children's social competence and problem behaviors. The Social Competence scale was computed as the mean of 20 items and had a Cronbach's α of 0.95. The Problem Behavior scale was computed as the mean of 18 items and had a Cronbach's α of 0.91. TCRS scales also are computed as the mean of items that have a maximum score of 5 and a minimum score of 1. The teachers in the two FACES studies completed the 28-item Behavior Problems Index (Zill, 1985) to assess problem behaviors related to emotional status, school behavior, and interpersonal relationships, with items drawn from several other child behavior scales (e.g., CBCL, SSRS). Zill reported a 2-week test–retest reliability of 0.92.

Results

Quality Effect Sizes

The first set of analyses involved computing partial correlations between ECE quality and fall–spring gains in child outcome, measured in the spring for each study. The spring scores were correlated with that project's measure of quality, including site, maternal education, ethnicity, and gender as covariates. The results are shown in Table 2.4.

As you can see, most of the partial correlations are very small. Partial correlations of 0.1 are considered modest; 0.3, moderate; and 0.5, large (Cohen, 1987). The partial correlations should be positive for the measures of language, reading, math, task orientation, and social skills and negative for the measures of externalizing, internalizing, and general behavior problems. They range from $r_p = 0.00$ to $r_p = 0.23$. Most of the correlations are less than $r_p < 0.10$. Some projects and some quality measures appear to have yielded stronger associations, but even those tended to be quite modest. The partial correlations obtained in the FACES studies tended to be smaller, in general, perhaps due to truncation of the range of the quality measures in Head Start. Averaging the correlations across the 12 associations between quality and language measures yielded a mean correlation of 0.06 (SD = 0.06, range = −0.04 to 0.17). Averaging across the 16 correlations between quality and academic outcomes yielded a mean correlation of 0.03 (SD = 0.08, range = −0.06 to 0.23). Similarly, averaging across the 19 associations between quality and social skills or with behavior problems (reversed) yielded a mean correlation of 0.02 (SD = 0.06, range = −0.09 to 0.10).

Follow-up analyses computed other correlations between ECE quality and child outcomes. We computed the simple, or the zero-order, correlations as the most liberal

Table 2.4. Partial correlations between ECE quality measures and child outcomes for low-income children in center-based ECE, controlling for site, maternal education, gender, and ethnicity

	ORCE SECCYD	ECERS/ECER-R				CIS			CLASS NCEDL
		CQO	NCEDL	FACES 97	FACES 00	CQO	FACES 97	FACES 00	
Expressive Language	0.00		0.04						0.04
Receptive Language	0.03	0.13	0.08	0.01	0.07	0.17	−0.04	0.10	0.07
Math-WJ Applied Problems	0.01	−0.04	0.03	0.01	−0.03	0.03	−0.02	0.04	0.08
Reading-WJ Letter-Word	−0.09	0.16	−0.02	−0.02	−0.02	0.24	0.01	−0.03	0.03
Task Orientation		0.08				0.06			
Social Skills			−0.07	−0.07	0.07		0.08	0.05	0.10
Externalizing Problems	0.02								
Internalizing Problems	0.03								
Behavior Problems		−0.06	−0.05	0.09	0.02	−0.03	−0.00	−0.03	−0.08

Key: Studies: CQO, Cost, Quality, Outcomes Study; FACES, Family and Child Experiences Surveys; NCEDL, National Center for Early Development and Learning; NICHD SECCYD National Institute of Child Health and Human Development Study of Early Child Care and Youth Development.

Child care quality measures: CIS, Caregiver Involvement Scale; CLASS, Classroom Assessment Scoring System. ECERS/ECERS-R, Early Childhood Environment Rating Scale/Early Childhood Environment Rating Scale-Revised; ORCE, Observational Record of the Caregiving Environment.

Child outcome measures: WJ, Woodcock-Johnson Tests of Achievement.

estimate of the association because they do not take into account family characteristics that may be confounders. We also computed the correlations between ECE quality and change in child outcomes from fall to spring, considering correlations from this period as the most conservative index. (Data from CQO could not be included because only spring scores were collected.) These correlations are the most conservative because they adjust for the effects of the family and other experiences prior to the experience in the studied ECE setting reflected in the fall score, and they will have more error than correlations with only the spring scores due to the manner in which they were computed. Even so, findings indicated modest associations. The zero-order correlations tended to be about twice as big as the partial correlations reported in Table 2.4, with mean correlations between quality and language of 0.14 (SD = 0.06, range = 0.02–0.26), academic achievement of 0.06 (SD = 0.09, range = −0.06–0.26), and social-emotional development of 0.06 (SD = 0.07, range = −0.08–0.16). The partial correlations excluded data from CQO, the study with the strongest associations. These partial correlations involving the change scores were substantially smaller, averaging 0.01 (SD = 0.04, range = −0.09–0.06) for language, 0.00 (SD = 0.04 range = −0.09–0.05) for academic achievement, and 0.02 (SD = 0.06, range = −0.08–0.15) for social-emotional development.

Aligned Quality–Outcome Associations

Next, we looked at more specific quality measures instead of the global scores. We asked whether associations were stronger in quality indicators that measured specific aspects of the environment thought to promote specific child outcomes. We wanted to know whether child outcomes were strongly predicted from quality measures of

Table 2.5.   Partial correlations between child outcomes and aligned quality measures

	CLASS Instructional Support		ECERS Language and Reasoning		ECERS Interactions		CLASS Emotional Support	
Language	NCEDL	0.08	NCEDL	0.07	NCEDL	0.06		
			CQO	0.19	CQO	0.21		
			FACES97	0.04	FACES97	−0.01		
			FACES00	0.09	FACES00	0.10		
Reading	NCEDL	0.09	NCEDL	0.05	NCEDL	0.04		
			CQO	0.10	CQO	0.11		
			FACES97	0.01	FACES97	0.00		
			FACES00	0.02	FACES00	−0.01		
Math	NCEDL	0.08	NCEDL	0.03	NCEDL	0.06		
			CQO	−0.04	CQO	0.11		
			FACES97	0.03	FACES97	0.02		
			FACES00	0.01	FACES00	0.02		
Social Skills					NCEDL	0.08	NCEDL	0.10
					FACES97	−0.04		
					FACES00	0.09		
Behavior Problems					NCEDL	−0.08	NCEDL	−0.08
					CQO	0.03		
					FACES97	0.07		
					FACES00	−0.02		

Key: Studies: CQO, Cost, Quality, Outcomes Study; FACES, Family and Child Experiences Surveys; NCEDL, National Center for Early Development and Learning.
Child care quality measures: CLASS, Classroom Assessment Scoring System; ECERS, Early Childhood Environment Rating Scale.

specific aspects of the child care experience than from global quality measures. The CLASS Instructional Support Scale, ECERS Language and Reasoning Scale, and ECERS Interactions Scale were thought to measure specific aspects of the child care environment that should promote language and academic skills, whereas the CLASS Emotional Support Scale and ECERS Interactions Scale were thought to measure aspects of the child care environment that should promote social-emotional development. (The items in the ECERS Interactions Scale include indicators about both language and interactions, so that scale was included in both sets of analyses. However, this "specific" ECERS quality measure is not as specific as the CLASS quality measures.)

Results are shown in Table 2.5. Note that associations are somewhat stronger, but still modest. There are clear differences across the projects, likely reflecting differences in the variability of the quality measures. The associations between language and these more specific quality measures ranged from −0.01 to 0.21, with about half of the partial correlations exceeding $r_p > 0.10$. The partial correlations for the other outcomes were more modest, but tended to be above $r_p \geq 0.05$. The CLASS scales appeared to provide slightly stronger associations, even when measures were compared within the single study that collected data on both the CLASS and the ECERS.

Nonlinear Quality–Outcome Associations

Further, we asked whether the reason that the associations between observed quality and child outcomes were so modest might be because the association is nonlinear. We tested this hypothesis with regression analyses that included quality as both linear and quadratic terms (i.e., quality × quality) and site, maternal education, ethnicity, and gender as covariates.

Results are shown in Table 2.6, listing the coefficients and standard errors in parentheses for the models in which the quality-squared term was significant. Figures shown in Appendix A display these associations. The regressions provide a hint that quality may

Table 2.6. Regression coefficients predicting child outcomes from quality as a linear predictor and a quadratic predictor

	ORCE SECCYD	CQO	ECERS/ECER-R NCEDL	ECERS/ECER-R FACES 97	FACES 00	CLASS NCEDL
Receptive Language	NS	NS	NS		NS	NS
Linear quality				−18.62** (6.01)		
Quadratic quality				1.92** (0.60)		
Math-WJ Applied Problems		NS	NS		NS	NS
Linear quality	−52.65* (23)			−20.90* (8.00)		
Quadratic quality	9.32* (4.0)			2.11** (0.80)		
Reading-WJ Letter-Word	NS		NS	NS	NS	−14.0* (6.0)
Linear quality		17.3* (6.6)				1.70* (0.70)
Quadratic quality		−1.8* (0.8)				
Social Skills	NS	—	NS	NS		NS
Linear quality					1.76* (0.88)	
Quadratic quality					NS	
Behavior Problems	—	NS			NS	NS
Linear quality			0.35* (0.15)	−5.70** (2.00)		
Quadratic quality			0.04* (0.02)	0.64** (0.20)		

*p < .01; **p < .05; ***p < .001

Key: Studies: CQO, Cost, Quality & Outcomes Study; FACES, Family and Child Experiences Surveys; NCEDL, National Center for Early Development and Learning; NICHD SECCYD, National Institute of Child Health and Human Development Study of Early Child Care and Youth Development.

Child care quality measures: CLASS, Classroom Assessment Scoring System; ECERS/ECERS-R, Early Childhood Environment Rating Scale/Early Childhood Environment Rating Scale-Revised; ORCE, Observational Record of the Caregiving Environment.

Child outcome measures: WJ, Woodcock-Johnson Tests of Achievement.

be more strongly related to outcomes when quality is in the higher range. The positive quadratic associations indicate that the association between quality and outcomes is stronger at higher levels of quality, whereas a negative quadratic association indicates that the association is stronger at lower levels of quality. In one study, FACES 1997, ECERS scores were positively related to language scores when quality was in the good-to-high range. In three studies, NCELD, SECCYD, and FACES 1997, quality was more strongly related to math skills when quality was in the good-to-high range. In another study, conducted by the NCEDL, the two quality measures were more strongly related to reading skills when they were in the good-to-high range. However, in yet another study, CQO, quality was more strongly related to reading when quality was in the low-to-average range. Finally, in two studies, the NCEDL evaluation and FACES 1997, quality was more strongly negatively related to behavior problems when quality was in the good-to-high range.

Analysis of Individual Items

Finally, we asked whether individual items on either the ECERS or the CLASS may be more or less predictive of child outcomes. This was examined because many professional development programs focus on these scales in self-study programs, using teachers to help improve the quality of their classrooms. Such professional development programs should benefit from the identification of items that are the strongest predictors of child outcomes. First, we looked at the 37 items on the ECERS-R, as measured in the NCEDL 11 state Pre-K Evaluation and CQO study. Although none of the items showed strong correlations ($r > 0.30$), the items with the strongest correlations with language, academic, or social outcomes were all of the items on the Interaction Scale (e.g., staff–child interactions) and the Program Structure Scale (e.g., free play, group time). The items with the weakest correlations were the items in the Activity and Personal Care Scales.

Similarly, we looked at the correlations among the nine items on the CLASS, collected in the NCEDL 11-State Pre-K Evaluation. The items with the strongest correlations with language, academic, or social outcomes were Negative Climate and Positive Climate with all outcomes; Productivity with language and academics outcomes; and Behavior Management with behavioral outcomes. The items with the weakest correlations were Learning Formats with all outcomes and the Instructional items with social-behavioral outcomes.

Conclusions

Both the meta-analysis and the secondary data analysis indicated that higher quality ECE is associated with higher language, academic, and social skills and fewer behavior problems; however, the associations found were quite modest. There are three possible explanations for why such modest associations were obtained.

First, the true association between ECE quality and child outcomes is modest. This conclusion, however, seems to contradict the findings from randomized studies in which low-income children were randomly assigned to high-quality center-based programs such as the Abecedarian Project (Campbell et al., 2001), HighScope Perry Preschool (Nores et al., 2005), and Infant Health and Development Program (McCormick et al., 2006). Those programs produced large effects on language, academic, and social outcomes while the children were enrolled; and the outcomes were maintained, albeit diminished, into early adulthood. Similarly, evaluations of carefully implemented pre-K programs, such as the Tulsa (Gormley et al., 2005) and Miami pre-K programs (Winsler et al., 2008), also have yielded large effects. Therefore, it seems unlikely that the true associations between child care quality and child outcomes are really as small as the findings reported here would suggest.

Second, the estimates of association could be underestimated in our analyses. Our estimates are constrained in several ways. Some of the projects in the secondary data analysis did not have wide variation in quality (e.g., FACES). Almost all of the studies measured the children for the posttest only 6–8 months after they measured them for the pretest, perhaps not enough time for large changes in child outcomes to occur. However, again, it seems unlikely that these explanations account for such small associations obtained in these analyses.

Third, the associations would be underestimated if the quality or outcome measures did not provide adequate measurement. Most preschool child outcomes have good reliability and validity, especially those from standardized tests of language and academic achievement. Therefore, it seems unlikely that poor measurement of child outcomes accounts for the modest associations. In contrast, the ECE quality measures tend to be global and were developed conceptually but not psychometrically. Each has good reliability, requiring extensive training of the data collectors. Each also has some validity. Each has been related to child outcomes, and some recent studies suggest that scale-based quality enhancement may improve quality and child outcomes (Bryant, 2007; Pianta et al., 2008). However, it appears that we may need more specific and more aligned measures, and we may especially need more psychometric development based on a wider set of items and on more advanced psychometric methods. Such a focus on the psychometric development of quality measures could result in the observation of stronger associations thereby providing better measures of improving and monitoring children's experiences in ECE.

References

Achenbach, T.M. (1991). *Manual for the Child Behavior Checklist/4–18 and 1991 profile.* Burlington, VT: University of Vermont Department of Psychiatry.

Arnett, J. (1989). Caregivers in day-care centers: Does training matter? *Journal of Applied Developmental Psychology, 10,* 541–552.

Barnett, W.S., Hustedt, J.T., Hawkinson, L.E., & Robin, K.B. (2006). *The state of preschool 2006: State preschool yearbook.* New Brunswick, NJ: National Institute for Early Education Research, Rutgers University.

Blau, D.M. (1999). The effect of child care characteristics on child development. *The Journal of Human Resources, 34,* 786–822.

Borenstein, M., Hedges, L., Higgins, J., & Rothstein, H. (2005). Comprehensive Meta-analysis Version 2, Englewood, NJ: Biostat.

Bryant, D. (2007, November). *Delivering and evaluating the Partners for Inclusion model of early childhood professional development in a five state collaborative study.* Presentation at the meetings of the National Association for the Education of Young Children, Chicago, IL.

Burchinal, M.R., & Cryer, D. (2003). Diversity, child care quality, and developmental outcomes. *Early Childhood Research Quarterly, 18,* 401–426.

Burchinal, M.R., Roberts, J.E., Riggins, R., Zeisel, S., Neebe, E., & Bryant, D. (2000). Relating quality of center-based child care to early cognitive and language development longitudinally. *Child Development, 71*(2), 339–357.

Campbell, F.A., Pungello, E.P., Miller-Johnson, S., Burchinal, M.R., & Ramey, C. (2001). The development of cognitive and academic abilities: Growth curves from an early intervention educational experiment. *Developmental Psychology, 37*(2), 231–242.

Campbell, F.A., Ramey, C.T., Pungello, E., Sparling, J., & Miller-Johnson, S. (2002). Early childhood education: Young adult outcomes from the Abecedarian project. *Applied Developmental Science, 6*(1), 42–57.

Cohen, E.A. (1987, April). *A critical analysis and reanalysis of the multisection validity meta-analysis.* Paper presented at the annual meeting of the American Educational Research Association, Washington, DC.

Dunn, L. (1993). Proximal and distal features of day care quality and children's development. *Early Childhood Research Quarterly, 8,* 167–92.

Dunn, L.M., & Dunn, L.M. (1997). *Peabody Picture Vocabulary Test–Third Edition (PPVT-III).* Circle Pines, MN: American Guidance Service.

Early, D., Barbarin, O., Bryant, B., Burchinal, M., Chang, F., Clifford, R., et al. (2005). *Pre-Kindergarten in eleven states: NCEDL's Multi-State Study of Pre-Kindergarten and State-Wide Early Education Programs (SWEEP) study.* Retrieved December 1, 2005, from http://www.fpg.unc.edu/~ncedl/pdfs/SWEEP_MS_summary_final.pdf

Gallagher, P.A., & Lambert, R.G. (2006). Classroom quality, concentration of children with special needs, and child outcomes in Head Start. *Exceptional Children, 73,* 31–52.

Gormley, W.T., Gayer, T., Phillips, D., & Dawson, B. (2005). The effects of universal pre-K on cognitive development. *Developmental Psychology, 41*(6), 872–884.

Gresham, F., & Elliott, S. (1990). *Social skills rating system.* Circle Pines, MN: American Guidance Service.

Harms, T., & Clifford, R.M. (1980). *The Early Childhood Environment Rating Scale.* New York: Teachers College Press.

Harms, T., Clifford, R.M., & Cryer, D. (1998). *Early Childhood Environment Rating Scale (ECERS) (Rev. ed).* New York: Teachers College Press.

Herrera, M.O., Mathiesen, M.E., Merino, J.M., & Recart, I. (2005). Learning contexts for young children in Chile: Process quality assessment in preschool centres. *International Journal of Early Years Education, 13,* 13–27.

Hightower, A.D., Work, W.C., Cowen, E.L., Lotyczewski, B.S., Spinell, A.P., Guare, J.C., et al. (1986). The Teacher–Child Rating Scale: A brief objective measure of elementary children's school problem behaviors and competencies. *School Psychology Review, 15,* 393–409.

Howes, C., Burchinal, M., Pianta, R., Bryant, D., Early, D.M., Clifford, R., et al. (2008). Ready to learn? Children's pre-academic achievement in pre-kindergarten programs. *Early Childhood Research Quarterly, 23,* 27–50.

Karoly, L.A., Kilburn, M.R., & Cannon, J.S. (2005). *Early childhood interventions: Proven results, future promise*, MG-341, Santa Monica, CA: The RAND Corporation.

Kontos, S., & Wilcox-Herzog, A. (1997). Influences on children's competence in early childhood classrooms. *Early Childhood Research Quarterly, 12*, 247–262.

Lamb, M. (1998). Nonparental child care: Context, quality, correlates, and consequences. In W. Damon (Series ed.), I. Sigel, & A. Renninger (Vol. eds.), *Handbook of child psychology: Vol. 4. Child psychology in practice*, (5th ed). New York: Wiley.

Lazar, I., Darlington, R., Murray, H., Royce, J., & Snipper, A. (1982). Lasting effects of early education: A report from the consortium for longitudinal studies. *Monographs of the Society for Research in Child Development, 47* (Serial No. 195).

Loeb, S., Fuller, B., Kagan, S.L., Carrol, B. (2004). Child care in poor communities: Early learning effects of type, quality, and stability. *Child Development, 75*, 47–65.

Love, J.M., Kisker, E. E., Ross, C., Raikes, H., Constantine, J., Boller, K., Brooks-Gunn, J., Chazan-Cohen, R., Tarullo, L.B., Brady-Smith, C., Fuligni, A.S., Schochet, P.Z., Paulsell, D., & Voge.l, C. (2005). The effectiveness of Early Head Start for 3-year-old children and their parents: Lessons for policy and programs. *Developmental Psychology, 41*, 885–901.

Martin, A., Brooks-Gunn, J., Klebanov, P., Buka, S.L., & McCormick, M.C. (2008). Long-term maternal effects of early childhood intervention: Findings from the Infant Health and Development Program (IHDP). *Journal of Applied Developmental Psychology, 29*, 101–117.

McCartney, K. (1984). Effect of quality of day care environment on children's language development. *Developmental Psychology, 20*, 244–260.

McCormick, M.C., Brooks-Gunn, J., Buka, S.L., Goldman, J., Yu, J., Salganik, M., et al. (2006). Early intervention in low birth weight premature infants: Results at 18 years of age for the Infant Health and Development Program. *Pediatrics, 117*, 771–780.

Nelson, G., Westhues, A., & MacLeod, J. (2003). A meta-analysis of longitudinal research on preschool prevention programs for children. *Prevention & Treatment, 6*(1). Available from http://journals.apa.org/prevention/

NICHD Early Child Care Research Network. (2000). The relation of child care to cognitive and language development. *Child Development, 71*, 960–980.

NICHD Early Child Care Research Network. (2002). Child-care structure → process → outcome: Direct and indirect effects of child-care quality on young children's development. *Psychological Science, 13*(3), 199–206.

NICHD Early Child Care Research Network. (2003). Does quality of child care affect child outcomes at age 4½? *Developmental Psychology, 39*(3), 451–469.

NICHD Early Child Care Research Network. (2005). Early child care and children's development in the primary grades: Results from the NICHD Study of Early Child Care. *American Educational Research Journal, 42*(3), 537–570.

NICHD Early Child Care Research Network. (2006). Child-care effect sizes for the NICHD Study of Early Child Care and Youth Development. *American Psychologist, 61*(2), 99–116.

NICHD Early Child Care Research Network, & Duncan, G.J. (2003). Modeling the impacts of child care quality on children's preschool cognitive development. *Child Development, 74*, 1454–1475.

Nores, M., Barnett, W.S., Belfield, C.R., & Schweinhart, L.J. (2005). Updating the economic impacts of the High/Scope Perry Preschool program. *Educational Evaluation and Policy Analysis, 27*(3), 245–262.

Peisner-Feinberg, E.S., & Burchinal, M.R. (1997). Relations between preschool children's child-care experiences and concurrent development: The cost, quality, and outcomes study. *Merrill-Palmer Quarterly, 43*, 451–477.

Peisner-Feinberg, E.S., Burchinal, M.R., Clifford, R.M., Culkin, M.L., Howes, C., Kagan, S.L., et al. (2001). The relation of preschool child-care quality to children's cognitive and social development trajectories through second grade. *Child Development, 72*, 1534–1553.

Phillips, D., McCartney, K., & Scarr, S. (1987). Child-care quality and children's social development. *Developmental Psychology, 23*, 537–543.

Pianta, R.C., La Paro, K.M., & Hamre, B.K. (2008). *Classroom Assessment Scoring System™ (CLASS™) Manual, Pre-K*. Baltimore: Paul H. Brookes Publishing Co.

Pianta, R.C., Mashburn, A.J., Downer, J.T., Hamre, B.K., & Justice, L. (2008). Effects of web-mediated professional development resources on teacher–child interactions in pre-kindergarten classrooms. *Early Childhood Research Quarterly, 23,* 431–451.

Poe, M.D., Burchinal, M.R., & Roberts, J.E. (2004). Early language and the development of children's reading skills. *Journal of School Psychology, 42,* 315–332.

Reynolds, A.J., Temple, J.A., Robertson, D.L., & Mann, E.A. (2002). *Age 21 cost–benefit analysis of the Title I Chicago Child–Parent Centers.* Madison, WI: Institute for Research on Poverty.

Schaefer, E.S., Edgerton, M., & Aaronson, M. (1978). *Classroom Behavior Inventory.* Unpublished manuscript, University of North Carolina at Chapel Hill, Chapel Hill, NC.

Schliecker, E., White, D.R., & Jacobs, E. (1991). The role of day care quality in the prediction of children's vocabulary. *Canadian Journal of Behavioral Science, 23,* 12–24.

Vandell, D. (2004). Early child care: The known and the unknown. *Merrill-Palmer Quarterly, 50,* 387–414.

Votruba-Drzal, E., Coley, R.L., & Chase-Lansdale, P.L. (2004). Child care and low-income children's development: Direct and moderated effects. *Child Development, 75,* 296–312.

Winsler, A., Tran, H., Hartman, S.C., Madigan, A.L., Manfra, L., & Bleiker, C. (2008). School readiness gains made by ethnically diverse children in poverty attending center-based childcare and public school pre-kindergarten programs. *Early Childhood Research Quarterly, 23,* 314–329.

Woodcock, R.W., McGrew, K.S., & Mather, N. (2001). *Woodcock-Johnson III: Tests of achievement.* Itasca, IL: Riverside Publishing.

Zill, N. (1985). *Behavior problem scales developed from the 1981 Child Health supplement to the National Health Interview Survey.* Washington, DC: Child Trends.

Zill, N., & Resnick, G. (2005). Emergent literacy of low-income children in Head Start: Relationships with child and family characteristics, program factors and classroom quality. In D. Dickinson & S. Neuman (Eds.), *Handbook of early literacy research* Vol. II, 347–371. New York: Guilford Publications.

Zill, N., Resnick, G., Kim, K., O'Donnell, K., Sorongon, A., McKey, R.H., et al. (2003). *Head Start FACES 2000: A whole-child perspective on program performance. Fourth progress report.* Washington, DC: U.S. Department of Health and Human Services, Administration for Children and Families.

Zimmerman, I.L., Steiner, V.G., & Pond, R.E. (1992). *Preschool Language Scale-3.* San Antonio, TX: Psychological Corp.

Appendix A: Figures Showing Nonlinear Associations

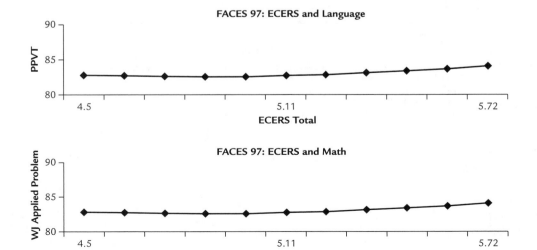

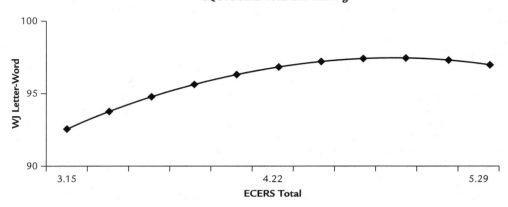

CQO: ECERS Total and Reading

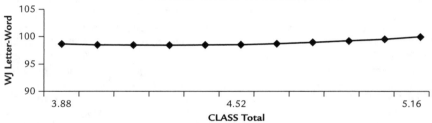

NCEDL: WJ Letter-Word Standard Score

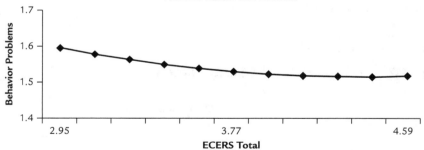

NCEDL: ECERS and Behavior

Key: Studies: CQO, Cost, Quality, and Outcomes Study; FACES, Family and Child Experiences Surveys; NCEDL, National Center for Early Development and Learning.

Child care quality measures: CLASS, Classroom Assessment Scoring System; ECERS, Early Childhood Environment Rating Scales.

Child outcome measures: PPVT, Peabody Picture Vocabulary Test; WJ, Woodcock Johnson Achievement Battery.

Appendix B: Meta-Analysis—Technical Details

The meta-analysis presented in this chapter involved three steps. First, each of the 20 identified studies was coded in terms of sample size, the child care quality instrument, the child outcomes examined, and the magnitude of the association. A separate entry was created for each association so that studies with multiple quality measures and multiple outcomes contributed a separate entry for each observed association between a quality measure and a child outcome. Altogether, there were 97 associations across the 20 studies. Specifically, each entry in this data matrix included the following variables: study, the ages of the children at assessment, the quality measure, the type of outcome (math, literacy, language, or behavior), the partial correlation, and the standard error of the correlation.

Second, we ensured that all 97 of these reported associations were transformed into partial correlations, using software from the company Comprehensive Meta-analysis (Borenstein, Hedges, Higgins, & Rothstein, 2005). We transformed the coefficients from regression analyses by using standard transformation for the regression coefficients for continuous predictors. We transformed group means to partial correlations by using Fisher's transformation for categorical predictors.

Third, a meta-analysis was conducted according to the hierarchical linear model in order to compute the average association between child care quality and child outcomes. The partial correlations were the dependent variable. The study was a repeated measure. A random intercept was computed for each study to adjust for the fact that some studies were represented many times in these data. The analysis was weighted by study sample size so that larger studies contributed more to cross-study averages. We computed the average effect size across all studies, by type of outcome (categorized into language/cognitive, academic, and social-emotional outcomes), by age of child (categorized as 2–3, 3–4, and 4–6 years of age), and by age × type of outcome.

CHAPTER 3

Empirical Approaches to Strengthening the Measurement of Quality

Issues in the Development and Use of Quality Measures in Research and Applied Settings

Donna M. Bryant, Margaret Burchinal, and Martha Zaslow

S trengthening the measurement of quality in early care and education (ECE) will require the consideration of empirical as well as conceptual issues. Multiple chapters in this volume consider the conceptual issues emerging from very recent research on approaches to strengthening children's development in particular domains. (See the chapters on strengthening the measurement of quality as it pertains to young children's well-being and development of skills in the areas of literacy (4), math and science (5), social and emotional development (6), cultural identity (9), health (7), mastery of two languages (11), and development when special needs are present (10).) These chapters indicate that measures development focusing on in-depth assessment of particular facets of quality can benefit from a consideration of the findings from recent descriptive longitudinal studies, as well as evaluation studies examining the linkages between particular aspects of quality and specific child outcome domains.

The next generation of quality measures will need to combine such work with a rigorous psychometric development of scales. Just as the recent substantial expansion in the number of descriptive and intervention evaluation studies of early childhood environments has been providing new input for strengthening the measurement of quality, recent empirical work on measures development, particularly in the assessments of child outcomes, has been providing new tools for strengthening the measurement of environmental quality.

This chapter begins with a discussion of how recent research has raised the possibility that measures of quality could be strengthened through greater attention to measurement issues. It notes important distinctions between empirical approaches that can be applied in the development of scales and the development of indices for the measurement of quality. A final section notes the need for different approaches to measures selection and development, data collection, and data use, according to the purposes of the quality measurement. We emphasize new issues related to the reliability and validity of quality measures that arise with the widespread use of quality measurement in evaluations of quality initiatives and quality rating systems intended to inform parents in their choice of early childhood settings throughout a state or community.

Implications of Analyses on Quality–Outcome Associations for Measures Development

Burchinal, Kainz, and Cai (Chapter 2, this volume) report significant, but relatively modest, associations in both the meta-analysis of published studies and the analysis of data from multiple large-scale data sets focusing on children of low-income families. Furthermore, evidence from some of the analyses reported in Chapter 2, as well as evidence from the long-term follow-up of the National Institute of Child Health and Human Development (NICHD SECCYD) Study of Early Child Care and Youth Development (Vandell et al., 2010), suggest that there may be thresholds in the association between child care quality and child outcomes such that associations between quality and child outcomes are present only when quality is moderate to high. These findings have implications for policy development and the measurement of quality.

At the same time, quality–outcome associations are statistically significant across the analyses reported by Burchinal and colleagues, suggesting that, although modest, the associations between quality and child outcomes are quite consistent. The reported associations may be overestimated because the preexisting differences between children who attend higher quality child care and those who attend lower quality child care cannot all be taken into account. (See Snow & Van Hemel, 2008, for details of experimental and quasi-experimental studies that address issues of selection bias.) Nevertheless, on the basis of the available evidence, we believe that there is a real link between higher quality child care and better cognitive and social skills. The important question concerns the strength of that link.

The findings of modest associations have at least two possible explanations. First, it could be that the true association is modest, although results from experimental studies contradict this conclusion. Experimental studies involving randomly assigning children from low-income families to attend high-quality child care programs over sustained periods have had much larger effect sizes (e.g., $d = 0.75$ for the Abecedarian Project at entry to school, according to Campbell, Pungello, Miller-Johnson, Burchinal, & Ramey, 2001). Similarly, quasi-experimental studies such as the Tulsa Prekindergarten Evaluation also reported moderate-to-large effect sizes ($d = 0.38–0.79$, in Gormley, Gayer, Phillips, & Dawson, 2005) when comparing children of similar age who have and have not experienced prekindergarten.

The discrepancy in the findings between the correlational studies involving observed quality and the experimental studies could be due to a number of other differences. First, the two different types of research use different analytic approaches, one involving experimental or quasi-experimental comparisons of groups that did or did not receive high-quality care for a particular period and the other involving the study of associations between varying quality and child outcomes with no requirement for length of exposure to low- or high-quality care. Further, the experimental and quasi-experimental studies did not necessarily involve direct observations of quality, but rather made the assumption based on program requirements that children in the treatment groups were exposed to high quality. The results of these studies of presumably high-quality programs are consistent with the recent analyses suggesting a threshold effect such that associations between child care quality and child outcomes are larger when quality is moderate to high and possibly nonexistent when quality is low.

The second possible explanation for the modest associations between quality and child outcomes is that any association will be underestimated if the assessment tools are not sufficiently sensitive. The observed association will be smaller than the true association when the assessment tools have limited reliability (Burchinal, 2008). Many different sources of error exist: A measure may not assess all of the important components of a particular skill set involving a caregiver or early educator's interactions with children, a particular aspect of quality may be very difficult to assess within a reasonable amount of time (e.g., it might take a very long time to obtain a representative sample of the caregiver's behavior in the classroom), or the instrument may not score the selected items in the best manner (e.g., it might equally weight items that are of different importance for predicting child outcomes). The different sources of error contribute both to the observed score and to the variability of that score (Lord & Novick, 1968) and thereby reduce the association between that instrument's scores and other measures. Careful psychometric development of instruments should increase the reliability of measurement and, accordingly, associations between the scores from that instrument and other measures. The next section addresses this need.

Need for Psychometric Development of Tools

Ideal psychometric development of instruments entails several steps that are different for scales than for indices (Lambert, Nelson, Brewer, & Burchinal, 2006). Scales consist of multiple items that are supposed to measure a single construct. Indices consist of multiple items reflecting important practices that are not necessarily assumed to be related to each other.

Quality Scales

Most recent quality instruments (e.g., Early Childhood Environment Rating Scale-Revised [ECERS-R], Harms, Clifford, & Cryer, 2005; Classroom Assessment Scoring System [CLASS™], Pianta, La Paro, & Hamre, 2008; Early Language & Literacy Classroom Observation [ELLCO], Smith, Brady, & Anastasopoulos, ELLCO-PreK (2008) comprise multiple scales in which the developers attempted to identify a set of items that would reliably and validly assess selected dimensions of quality. The psychometric development of scales involves several steps. First, the conceptual domains covered by the instrument are defined and refined through expert opinion and feedback. In the case of measuring quality, it is important that the developer define exactly which conceptual domains of quality he or she intends to measure: Will the measure assess caregiver sensitivity and responsiveness, intentional instruction in general, math instruction specifically, behavior management, or some combination of these? A single quality measure is unlikely to assess adequately all of the different conceptual constructs entailed in quality child care.

One approach to achieving construct validity involves the development of a consensus by an expert group as to key constructs that a measure should cover. A recent example in early math is the National Council of Teachers of Mathematics (NCTM) and National Association for the Education of Young Children's (NAEYC) (2002) joint statement on early mathematics skills and instruction. Similarly, in early literacy, *Eager to Learn* (National Research Council, 2000) and the National Institute for Literacy (2008) consensus document provide a firm foundation in terms of the important constructs.

The expert consensus approach has also been used in developing revisions or extensions of measures—for example, in moving from the original ECERS to the ECERS-R (see discussion in Sakai, Whitebook, Wishard, & Howes, 2003). State-developed measures have been created by this approach as well. For example, pilot work for Missouri's quality rating and improvement system included convening a panel of experts to identify key constructs to measure in infant and toddler care (Thornburg et al., Chapter 16, this volume).

However, our field lacks consensus statements in important areas, although we are closer to developing consensus statements in the area of supporting social and emotional development than in the area of teaching children from diverse backgrounds. In the social-emotional development domain, several research syntheses, *What Works* briefs, fact sheets, and practical strategies videos are available from the Center on the Social and Emotional Foundations for Early Learning (2009) and are widely used by practitioners. The National Research Council and Institute of Medicine (2000) published a frequently cited literature review identifying the interactions that characterize supportive and nurturing relationships between early childhood providers and children. Agreement with these documents is quite widespread, and they seem to have become the de facto consensus statements in the domain of social-emotional development.

In terms of coming to agreement on the best teaching strategies for diverse learners, a consensus statement would be useful for guiding caregivers and teachers in ways to convey respect for diversity through their interactions with and instruction of children and through their structuring of the physical environment. A limited number of studies have considered how existing measures of quality function in diverse samples (e.g., Aboud, 2006; Burchinal & Cryer, 2003; see Bryant, 2010, for a discussion of this issue). However, it is only recently that groups have convened to identify the features of quality related to culture in early childhood settings. The Quality Benchmark for Cultural Competence Project at the NAEYC (2009) is an example of a project with this goal. Measures development work providing detailed consideration of cultural sensitivity and respect in early childhood settings is at an early stage (Shivers & Sanders, Chapter 9, this volume).

When they exist, consensus statements are very helpful to measure developers, but the consensus process is not easy. Major stakeholders need to be included in the decision-making process, or validity will be questioned on the grounds of perspectives not taken into account. Further, the procedures required to identify key constructs for measures need to be clearly stated and agreed upon.

The second step in the psychometric development of scales is developing items to measure the important conceptual domains. In the ideal scenario a large pool of items is developed and pilot testing identifies the set of items that most accurately and precisely measures those concepts. Approaches like item-response theory (IRT) are especially useful in determining which items should be included and whether the set of items is adequate to measure the construct (see Lambert et al., 2006, for an overview). IRT is also known as *latent trait theory*. For example, a measure of quality focusing on literacy instruction may tap a teacher's latent trait to structure and equip a classroom for literacy and to interact with children and teach them in a way that promotes literacy. Among other things, IRT provides a framework for evaluating how well this assessment measures the quality of literacy instruction and how well the individual items on the new literacy scale work. IRT approaches offer the added benefit that attention is paid to developing an instrument which provides reliable assessment when scores are high and when they are low, as well as when scores are close to the mean.

Whereas some child outcomes have been measured with instruments developed by the IRT approach (e.g., academic achievement, language, intelligence tests), none of the ECE quality tools have been developed by this approach. The further refinement of quality measures, through developing an adequately large pool of items and testing them by IRT, has the potential to greatly increase the ability of instruments to measure ECE quality competently, especially in classrooms that vary widely in quality.

The third step in the psychometric development of measures involves refining the instrument on the basis of pilot work, continuing the process until the smallest set of items that most precisely measures the construct(s) of interest is identified. Reliability and validity of the measure across classrooms that vary in age group and diversity of backgrounds should be assessed. The structure of the data can be examined to determine whether the measure differs between classrooms of 2- and 3-year-olds versus 4- and 5-year-olds or between a classroom with a heterogeneous mix of children compared with a classroom in which all children are from families with similar demographic backgrounds (e.g., all low-income families).

The fourth psychometric step is to test a measure's performance across a broad range of quality. Does it do a good job of differentiating *very* low quality from low quality, or moderate quality from very good quality? Recent threshold analyses suggest that the selection of items that carefully measure moderate-to-high levels of quality may be more sensitive in detecting associations with child outcomes (Burchinal et al., Chapter 2, this volume; Vandell et al., 2010). If this finding continues to be replicated, then instrument developers may want to ensure that instruments permit differentiation among gradations of higher quality practices. It is also possible, however, that measures that have been developed by empirical approaches will do a better job of differentiating among quality levels across the full quality spectrum. It will be important to replicate analyses of thresholds with newly developed or refined measures of quality.

In sum, our most widely used existing measures of quality were developed theoretically, often with considerable expert and stakeholder input, and have been used enough for the researcher to know a great deal about their reliability, validity, and ability to predict child outcomes (Halle, Vick Whittaker & Anderson, 2010). However, we see the need for more methodological work in which new measures are developed by the IRT approach. Such work could confirm that the IRT criteria used in developing and refining child outcome measures are directly applicable to the measurement of environmental quality.

Quality Indices

A few quality instruments consist of a set of items measuring important practices, but these practices are not necessarily considered related to each other. As discussed in detail by Hegland and colleagues (Chapter 7, this volume), measures of health and safety in early childhood settings may be best thought of as indices rather than scales because they consist of items which assess important health and safety practices that are not conceptually related. Items related to hand washing, the safety of play equipment, posting information about children's food allergies, fire drill procedures, and/or having sufficient space between sleeping cots may not be assumed to be intercorrelated; yet, all of these items may need to be measured for a complete picture of ECE health and safety practices to be obtained.

Just as with the development of a scale, the development of an index requires thoughtful consideration and rigorous empirical approaches. The selected items should reliably measure the most important practices and take into account whether they occur routinely in early childhood settings. One should consider whether comparable numbers of items measuring different types of practices are included or whether the items need to be weighted in order to account for the greater importance of particular practices or to maintain the equivalence in emphasis placed across different practices. With scales, all items are thought to measure the same construct, so weighting items is not a concern. By contrast, in an index, the number of items measuring each type of practice will determine the degree to which the index reflects those practices. For example, scores from a health index with four items about hand washing and two items about nutrition will always be more focused on hand washing than nutrition unless the index score is computed by weighting them differently.

Providing In-Depth Focus on Particular Facets of Quality

There are growing concerns that our quality measures for early childhood settings are too broad and may lack sufficient attention to all-important dimensions of quality. The analyses conducted by Burchinal and colleagues (Chapter 2, this volume) provide evidence that when subscales of measures, rather than total summary scores, are considered and the particular subscales are aligned in content with specific child outcomes, the associations between quality and child outcomes are stronger, though still modest. For example, the CLASS Instructional Support domain summary score is more closely related to child reading and math achievement outcomes than is the CLASS total score. Similarly, the CLASS Emotional Support domain summary is more closely positively related to measures of child social skills and negatively related to measures of child behavior problems than the CLASS total score.

These findings underscore the importance of continued work toward providing in-depth consideration of particular facets of quality. Such work should incorporate the empirical approaches noted previously, with the first key steps being to identify whether the approach needed is the development of a scale or an index, to generate a broad item pool by experts, and to pilot and winnow out the set of items—where possible, by IRT approaches. Empirical work will then be needed to examine the prediction of the measures, focusing in depth on the relation of particular quality features to specific child outcomes, testing the assumption that more closely aligned measures will show stronger prediction.

In this process, it will be useful to distinguish between measures of program implementation and measures of quality. Often, program developers create a measure of "quality" that reflects the extent to which a program or curriculum is being implemented. Such implementation measures are necessary to determine whether the program is being implemented faithfully. Similarly, programs often will develop measures of student progress within the context of what a program is covering. The student progress measure should be expected to relate to the measure of fidelity of program implementation, but should not be used as a general measure of skills in a particular domain of development. Ideally, program evaluation would test the associations between faithfulness of program implementation and student progress and between quality of instruction in a particular content area and demonstrated skills in that area.

Implications for Selecting and Using Quality Measurement Tools

As communities and states invest in initiatives to improve the quality of early care and education, policy decision makers want assurance that the measures being used to assess quality are good ones. They often select, and sometimes adapt, measures that have been developed and used in research (Bryant, 2010). Sometimes the selection process does not focus closely enough on the specific purposes for which a quality measurement is needed and on the alignment of those purposes with the measure chosen. As noted in detail in Zaslow, Tout, and Halle (Chapter 17, this volume; see also Zaslow, Tout, Halle, & Forry, 2009), there are multiple purposes for measuring quality, including 1) guiding improvements in practice for individual practitioners or programs, 2) determining whether program or policy investments have resulted in changes in quality, 3) understanding more clearly the contributors to and outcomes of quality, and 4) rating quality in early childhood settings in a geographical area with the intent of informing parental choice.

   With multiple purposes possible for using a particular quality measure, the selection of the measure, the way data are collected, and the way information about quality is used and communicated ought to be aligned with the underlying purpose. This section summarizes the quality measurement issues that exist when quality tools are used for multiple purposes. We focus especially on issues pertaining to reliability and validity as they differ by purpose.

Guiding Improvements in Practice

Many early childhood programs collect data on quality as a diagnostic tool, both to help individual providers and centers identify the areas in which improvements are needed and to use as a basis for formulating an improvement plan. Often, these data are collected by an outside agent, such as a quality enhancement consultant from the local child care resource and referral agency, but sometimes quality data are collected by someone within the program (e.g., the director), or even by the provider, as a self-assessment (Buysse & Wesley, 2004). The assessment acts as a starting point to identify specific areas in need of strengthening, and it also might act as a monitoring tool at a later time to see whether improvements have indeed been made.

Measuring Selection and Development Issues
Broad-based and well-known quality measures often are used for this purpose because so much information exists about them and because training is widely available. These measures include the ECERS-R (Harms, Clifford, & Cryer, 2005) and Program Quality Assessment (PQA) (HighScope Educational Research Foundation, 2003). A well-collected baseline assessment provides extensive information to guide quality improvement, but decisions typically need to be made regarding priorities, possibly by focusing first on the

weakest subscales or those in which the provider is most interested. For most early childhood educators and/or providers, it would be daunting to try to address all areas at once. If a program is especially keen on improving a particular aspect of quality (e.g., language, literacy), the best selection might be a language-focused measure such as the ELLCO (Smith et al., ELLCO PreK 2008).

Many programs want to focus on improving classroom supports for social-emotional development, but unfortunately, in this area we have few robust and suitable measures. Therefore, providers and those who help them will use subscales or relevant individual items of the existing global quality measures. Similarly, we lack tools for in-depth consideration of health, cultural sensitivity, support for the development of dual language learners, and support for the development of children with special needs. (See chapters 7, 9, 10, and 11 on these issues for an assessment of the most recent status of measures development in each of these areas.)

Data Collection

In order to guide improvements in practice, it is essential for individuals who collect quality observations to have had some level of training in the assessment tool. An accurate baseline provides better guidance for areas that need the most attention. If the data are to be used over time, the reliability of the data collector at multiple time points would make the data more useful.

In a recent evaluation, systematic differences were found between the environmental quality ratings completed by researchers and those providing consultation on improving quality in the same early childhood settings (Bryant, Wesley, & the Quality Initiatives for Early Care and Education [QUINCE] Study Team, 2009). Although the patterns of high and low scores were similar, the ratings of the study's trained research assistants were systematically lower than consultants' ratings. The researchers noted that this could be attributable to differences in the focus and stringency of training or to the existence of a personal relationship between consultant and provider. As noted by Zaslow and colleagues (2009), one solution to the possibility of systematic differences in ratings of the same settings by researchers and consultants might be to use one set of rigorously completed ratings for all purposes, but to require further training of consultants in ways to select aspects of quality for quality improvement and in ways to communicate with providers about ratings.

Sometimes consultants or providers and/or educators might use part of a measure rather than the full measure to guide quality improvement. Researchers may be concerned about the use of selected scales—specifically, whether the evidence on validity for a full instrument pertains to particular scales. It may be important to articulate "best practice" guidelines on the use of selected components of instruments when the aim of assessing the data is quality improvement rather than program evaluation, research, or the provision of information on program quality to parents.

Data Use

If the highest standards of rigor in training and reliability have not been met for quality measurement used for program improvement, high stakes should not be attached to the resultant ratings. As noted earlier, however, some have recently proposed a single collection of quality ratings following the most stringent standards for training and reliability, as well as the subsequent use of the ratings for multiple purposes. This could include conveying the ratings to consultants, who would then use the rigorously collected ratings in their work with providers to develop and communicate quality improvement plans. In addition, self-assessment data should never be part of an accountability system, because those who collect such data are not necessarily trained and reliable. We want to encourage, not discourage, programs to self-assess and participate in quality improvement efforts, so self-assessments should be used only internally. Thus, a careful consideration and communication of the purpose or purposes for data collection is critical.

Determining Whether Quality Investments Have Resulted in Change

A wide variety of technical assistance programs have been conducted all over the United States for the purpose of quality improvement of early childhood education programs. The activities implemented by states and communities generally are based on the research linking certain factors to child care quality. For example, quality initiatives may offer early educators and caregivers college scholarships in order to increase providers' education or may implement supplementary compensation and benefits programs in order to reduce staff turnover. On-site consultation and coaching and mentoring programs are now widely employed to enhance the quality of early childhood care. Quality assessments often are used in evaluations to determine whether these program or policy investments have resulted in a change in quality over time.

Measure Selection and Development Issues

Evaluations of quality improvement initiatives typically utilize broad-based and well-known quality measures. The use of global quality measures seems quite appropriate when the improvement strategy aims to increase a wide variety of teaching and caregiving behaviors via, for example, furthering education or providing on-site coaching or consultation to help address numerous developmental areas. However, we also have seen the development and use of domain-specific measures designed to align more closely with the aim of the quality improvement initiative—for example, in quality improvement initiatives focusing on supporting young children's early mathematics skills (Clements & Sarama, 2008) or early literacy skills (Smith et al., 2008). As with the work of Burchinal and colleagues (Chapter 2, this volume) analyzing data from multiple large-scale data sets that focus on early childhood settings and children's development, the early evidence in this area shows stronger prediction of child outcomes when the quality measure selected is more closely aligned in content with the child outcome domain (Clements & Sarama, 2008). These findings underscore the importance of continuing to develop domain-specific measures of quality.

Data Collection

For assessing quality improvement, data collectors need to be well trained and to demonstrate reliability, not only initially but also as the data collection proceeds. When a quality initiative is implemented throughout a community or state, in some instances training and reliability assessments may be provided and assessed locally rather than by the developer of the measure. An important issue here is the need for confirmation that both training and reliability are in keeping with the intent of the developers of the measure. Otherwise, when a measure is widely used, differences in levels of quality across states or communities may be attributable to different training practices or reliability assessment procedures. Some measures have developed standardized procedures for assessing reliability in relation to master coders through the use of video segments intended specifically for the assessment of reliability. As new measures are developed, it will be important to take into account how to ensure consistency in training and in the measurement of reliability.

Data Use

Quality assessment data—whether aggregated for treatment and control groups or examined over time for those participating in a quality initiative—are usually reported to those funding the quality initiative. These data also may be shared with early childhood programs. A key issue here is the provision of background information sufficient for the summary ratings of quality to be interpreted appropriately. Some attention should be given to "training" the recipients to help them better understand the quality data, not just training for carrying out quality ratings reliably. For example, the Instructional Support domain scores of the CLASS (Pianta et al., 2008) are typically lower than scores on Emotional Support. Providing contextual information about the average score and range of scores found in previous data collection efforts for each of these domains would help programs interpret their own scores. What might seem like a low score on Instructional Support may be very close to the average in previous data collection efforts using the CLASS. Thus, although a particular program might still want to and need to focus on improving Instructional Support, the program staff would not view their scores as unusual or extraordinarily low. They would understand that there is a need in many programs to work to strengthen practices in this domain.

Understanding the Contributors and Outcomes of Quality

We have noted the substantial recent expansion in research seeking to understand better the contributors to, and outcomes of, quality in early childhood settings. (For an overview, see Zaslow, Tout, Halle, Vick, & Lavelle, 2010.) Intervention research considering how to strengthen young children's development overall or in particular aspects of development is identifying whether and to what extent quality is malleable when specific approaches are taken and the extent to which improvements in quality are associated with improvements in child outcomes. In addition to the intervention and evaluation research, longitudinal descriptive analyses are helping to specify the particular facets of quality that support young children's development (Forry, Vick, & Halle, 2009). For example, the amount of preschool teachers' spontaneous talk about mathematics has been found to be related to gain scores in young children's mathematical skills during the year prior to kindergarten (Klibanoff, Levine, Huttenlocher, Vasilyeva, & Hedges, 2006).

Measure Selection and Development Issues

As we have noted, most of the quality measures currently available provide global pictures of quality, with possibly a few strong factors or subscores focused on specific domains. In general, however, they do not allow studies to consider particular domains in depth. However, this body of descriptive and intervention research has been, and likely will continue to be, an important source of new measures of quality.

Data Collection

In any new research efforts to develop additional measures of quality, it would be extremely helpful to the field if researchers collecting observations would simultaneously use existing measures and newly developed measures. This would assist in assessing whether improvements have been made in terms of different subtypes of validity (such as construct validity and predictive validity), as well as in terms of reliability (e.g., internal consistency reliability, test–retest reliability, difficulty in attaining and maintaining reliability by observers).

Data Use

As new quality measures are developed through research, a challenge will be to determine when enough evidence has accumulated to warrant communicating this research to practitioners and policy makers. When does a new measure have sufficient evidence to justify its use in broad initiatives for evaluating quality investments or informing consumers of quality? There is no straightforward answer to this question. In addition to evidence of reliability and validity, evidence also might be needed to confirm sensitivity to interventions of particular kinds and the ability to differentiate quality, especially at higher levels. Here, too, work toward providing best-practice guidance would be valuable.

Measuring Quality Throughout a Geographical Area as Part of a Quality Rating System

Since 2000, when North Carolina incorporated quality ratings based on the environmental rating scales (current versions: Infant/Toddler Environment Rating Scale-Revised ITERS-R, Harms, Cryer, & Clifford, 2003; ECERS-R, Harms, Clifford, & Cryer, 2005; and Family Child Care Environment Rating Scale FCCERS, Harms, Cryer, & Clifford, 2005) in its state child care licensing system, many states have begun to include quality observation measures in their licensing systems and to increase the measurement below a "floor" of quality in order to encompass multiple levels of quality in a rating system. Whereas licensing typically sets only a minimum level of basic health and safety routines and provisions, many states now use quality ratings as a way to encourage programs to attain a higher level of quality, with higher subsidy reimbursement rates given to programs that meet higher quality levels. States also are investing resources and technical assistance for programs to improve quality. Not only do states want to ensure that young children are safe and engaged in learning in their care environments but also they want these rating systems to help inform parent choice.

Measures Selection and Development Issues

The selection or development of a measure of quality for a rating system to be used throughout a geographical area involves multiple issues, including, but going beyond, issues of reliability and validity. In the states that currently have quality rating systems, the ratings often involve direct observations of quality, but also fold in other quality features, most often indicators of educator or caregiver professional development and program policies for communicating with and engaging parents (Tout, Zaslow, Halle, & Forry, 2009). A key issue identified by Tout and colleagues in the development of the quality ratings at different quality levels is the need to confirm the validity of these composite ratings. Whereas they may be based on components with evidence of validity, there is also a need for evidence that the way in which components have been combined and weighted makes valid distinctions in quality and that the composite ratings predict child outcomes. Similarly, there is a need for evidence of reliability not only for the components of a composite quality rating but also for the rating with all of its components incorporated. According to Zellman and Perlman (2008), as well as Tout and colleagues (2009), thus far limited work has been conducted establishing the validity and reliability of composite quality ratings. There appears to be a widespread assumption that the extant evidence for the validity and reliability of the components suffices.

The selection of an observational measure and the selection or creation of composite measures also require affirmation by key stakeholders, including providers, that they perceive the measurement of quality to be a valid representation of their understanding of quality. Without such a "buy-in," there will be limited participation in a quality rating system if it is voluntary.

Data Collection

New issues are emerging regarding data collection for the widespread measurement of quality in quality rating systems (Zaslow, Tout, & Martinez-Beck, 2010). These issues include the frequency with which quality needs to be measured in order to assign a valid rating, as well as the number of classrooms that need to be assessed in order to obtain an overall rating of quality for a center-based program. (See Thornburg et al., Chapter 16, this volume, for evidence pertaining to these issues.) In order to limit the cost of a statewide or communitywide measurement of quality in early childhood settings, self-report data rather than direct observation may be used; however, Thornburg and colleagues (Chapter 16, this volume) note important issues pertaining to the reliability of self-reporting. They propose that reliability checks be carried out for such data, or that the data be collected on an ongoing basis, through early childhood professional development registries that regularly verify such data.

Another key issue regarding reliability is the level at which reliability needs to be ascertained for summary ratings of quality. In some systems, observations of quality are included in the quality rating only if a center or home-based care setting receives a fairly high level on an overall rating of self-report indicators. In such systems, the direct observation of quality may contribute to a distinction only at higher levels of quality—for example, distinguishing between a rating indicating an overall level of quality that is very good versus one that is excellent. If this is the only distinction to which an observational measure is contributing, then it is preferable to ensure that raters can make *that* distinction reliably rather than ensuring that they are reliable overall. Here again, a document providing best-practice guidance for data collection would be extremely valuable.

With consequences for early childhood settings related to ratings, such as differences in reimbursement rates for parents receiving subsidies, eligibility for quality improvement supports for child care settings, and the potential use of quality information by parents in selecting care, it is absolutely essential that data collection be objective (free of any biases associated with familiarity or support for particular programs) and that data collectors demonstrate interrater reliability according to the most stringent standards.

Data Use

Data collected for this purpose are intended for use by parents in the selection of early childhood settings. However, we have limited knowledge, as yet, of whether parents actually understand and/or utilize such quality ratings (Zaslow & Forry, 2009). Witte and Queralt (2004) found a jump in utilization of online information about child care licensing inspections when there was active media outreach that informed parents of the availability of such information. Yet there was no evidence of any change in enrollment in centers with and without licensing violations. Zaslow and Forry (2009) noted that there is some discussion as to whether parents prefer information in the form of composite ratings (e.g., overall number of stars in a quality rating system) or would rather receive the information on the separate components making up a quality rating in order to identify the quality features that they are most concerned about. It will be important to have research that directly examines the issue of parental understanding and the use of quality information.

Conclusion

In sum, we need empirical as well as conceptual approaches to strengthening the measurement of quality. The empirical approaches widely applied in the development of child assessment instruments should be used for strengthening and developing new measures of quality for early childhood settings. As measures are developed and refined, it will be important to keep in mind that issues pertaining to reliability and validity differ by the purpose of data collection on quality. New challenges are emerging, particularly as the measurement of quality is conducted on a broad scale throughout a state or community in order to provide summary ratings of quality so as to inform parental choice in quality rating systems and to measure the outcomes of policy and program investments. When the quality measures become widely used, there will be a clear need for guidance on best practices for the collection and use of data on quality in early childhood settings. High priorities for further work should include an empirical examination of whether there are thresholds of quality that policy makers and program developers should focus on, as well as the development of quality measures providing an in-depth examination of quality features related to particular domains of children's development.

References

Aboud, F.E. (2006). Evaluation of an early childhood preschool program in rural Bangladesh. *Early Childhood Research Quarterly, 21,* 46–60.

Bryant, D. (2010). ACF-OPRE Research-to-Policy Brief. *Observational Measures of Quality in Center-based Early Care and Education Programs.* Office of Planning, Research and Evaluation, Administration for Children and Families, U.S. Department of Health and Human Services. Washington, DC.

Bryant, D., Wesley, P., & the QUINCE Study Team. (2009, September). *The QUINCE-PFI study: An evaluation of a promising model and delivery approaches for child care provider training.* Grant #90YE0056, Final Report Submitted to Child Care Bureau, Administration on Children, Youth, and Families, U.S. Department of Health and Human Services.

Burchinal, M. (2008). How measurement error affects the interpretation and understanding of effect sizes. *Child Development Perspectives, 2,* 178–188.

Burchinal, M.R., & Cryer, D. (2003). Diversity, child care quality, and developmental outcomes. *Early Childhood Research Quarterly, 18,* 401–426.

Buysse, V., & Wesley, P.W. (2004). *Consultation in early childhood settings.* Baltimore: Paul H. Brookes Publishing Co.

Campbell, F.A., Pungello, E.P., Miller-Johnson, S., Burchinal, M.R., & Ramey, C. (2001). The development of cognitive and academic abilities: Growth curves from an early intervention educational experiment. *Developmental Psychology, 37*(2), 231–242.

Center on the Social and Emotional Foundations of Early Learning. (2009). *What Works briefs,* infant/toddler and preschool training modules, and research syntheses. Retrieved August 27, 2009, from http://www.vanderbilt.edu/csefel/index.html

Clements, D.H., & Sarama, J. (2008). Experimental evaluation of the effects of a research-based preschool mathematics curriculum. *American Educational Research Journal, 45,* 443–494.

Forry, N., Vick, J., & Halle, T. (2009). ACF-OPRE Issue Brief. *Evaluating, Developing and Enhancing Domain-specific Measures of Child Care Quality.* Office of Planning, Research and Evaluation, Administration for Children and Families, U.S. Department of Health and Human Services. Washington, DC.

Gormley, W.T., Gayer, T., Phillips, D., & Dawson, B. (2005). The effects of universal pre-k on cognitive development. *Developmental Psychology, 41*(6), 872–884.

Halle, T., Vick Whittaker, J.E., & Anderson, R. (2010). *Quality in Early Childhood Care and Education Settings: A Compendium of Measures* (2nd ed.). Washington, DC: Prepared by Child Trends for the Office of Planning, Research and Evaluation, Administration for Children and Families, U.S. Department of Health and Human Services.

Harms, T., Clifford, R., & Cryer, D. (2005). *Early Childhood Environment Rating Scale— Revised edition.* New York: Teachers College Press.

Harms, T., Cryer, D., & Clifford, R.M. (2005). *Family Child Care Environment Rating Scale.* New York: Teachers College Press.

Harms, T., Cryer, D., & Clifford, R. (2003). *Infant/Toddler Environment Rating Scale-Revised.* New York: Teachers College Press.

HighScope Educational Research Foundation. (2003). *Preschool Program Quality Assessment (PQA) administration manual* (2nd ed.). HighScope Press: Ypsilanti, MI.

Klibanoff, R.S., Levine, S.C., Huttenlocher, J., Vasilyeva, M., & Hedges, L.V. (2006). Preschool children's mathematical knowledge: The effect of teacher "math talk." *Development Psychology, 42,* 59–69.

Lambert, R.G., Nelson, L., Brewer, D., & Burchinal, M. (2006). Measurement issues and psychometric methods in developmental psychology. In K. McCarthy, M. Burchinal, & K.L. Bub (Eds.), Best practices in quantitative psychology for developmentalists. *Monograph*

of the Society for Research in Child Development, 71(3), 24–41.

Lord, F.M., & Novick, M.R. (1968). *Statistical theories of mental test scores.* Reading, MA: Addison-Wesley Publishing Company.

National Association for the Education of Young Children. (2009). *Quality benchmark for cultural competence project.* Retrieved January 12, 2011 from http://www.naeyc.org/files/naeyc/file/policy/state/QBCC_Tool.pdf

National Association for the Education of Young Children/National Council of Teachers of Mathematics. (2002). *Early childhood mathematics: Promoting good beginnings.* Joint position statement of the National Association for the Education of Young Children and the National Council for Teachers of Mathematics. Washington, DC.

National Institute for Literacy. (2008). *Developing early literacy: Report of the National Early Literacy Panel.* A publication of the National Institute for Literacy, retrieved January 12, 2011 from http://www.nifl.gov

National Research Council. (2000). *Eager to learn: Educating our preschoolers.* B.T. Bowman, M.S. Donovan, & M.S. Burns (Eds.). Committee on Early Childhood Pedagogy, Washington, DC: National Academy Press.

National Research Council and Institute of Medicine. (2000). *From neurons to neighborhoods: The science of early childhood development.* In J.P. Shonkoff & D.A. Phillips (Eds.), Board on Children, Youth, and Families, Commission on Behavioral and Social Sciences and Education, Washington, DC: National Academy Press.

Pianta, R.C., La Paro, K.M., & Hamre, B.K. (2008). *Classroom Assessment Scoring System™ (CLASS™).* Baltimore: Paul H. Brookes Publishing Co.

Sakai, L.M., Whitebook, M., Wishard, A., & Howes, C. (2003). Evaluating the Early Childhood Environment Rating Scale (ECERS): Assessing differences between the first and revised edition. *Early Childhood Research Quarterly, 18,* 427–445.

Smith, M.W., Brady, J.P., & Anastasopoulos, L. (2008). *Early Language & Literacy Classroom Observation PreK: Research edition.* Baltimore: Paul H. Brookes Publishing Co.

Snow, C., & Van Hemel, S. (2008). *Early childhood assessment: Why, what and how?* Report of the Committee on Developmental Outcomes and

Assessments for Young Children. Washington DC: National Academies Press.

Tout, K., Zaslow, M., Halle, T., & Forry, N. (2009). ACF-OPRE Issue Brief. *Issues for the Next Decade of Quality Rating and Improvement Systems.* Office of Planning, Research and Evaluation, Administration for Children and Families, U.S. Department of Health and Human Services. Washington, DC.

Vandell, D., Belsky, J., Burchinal, M., Steinberg, L., Vandergrift, N., & the NICHD Early Child Care Research Network. (2010). Do effects of early child care extend to age 15 years? Results from the NICHD Study of Early Child Care and Youth Development. *Child Development, 81,* 737–756.

Witte, A.D., & Queralt, M. (2004). *What happens when child care inspections and complaints are made available on the Internet?* (NBER Working Paper No. 10227). Cambridge, MA: National Bureau of Economic Research.

Zaslow, M., & Forry, N. (March, 2009). *Understanding parent use of child care quality information resources.* Presentation at the symposium on "Parent Choice and How the Market Is Responding" at the Policy Symposium of the National Association of Child Care Resource and Referral Agencies, Washington, DC.

Zaslow, M., Tout, K., Halle, T., & Forry, N. (2009). ACF-OPRE Issue Brief. *Multiple Purposes for Measuring Quality in Early Childhood Settings: Implications for Collecting and Communicating Information on Quality.* Office of Planning, Research and Evaluation, Administration for Children and Families, U.S. Department of Health and Human Services. Washington, DC.

Zaslow, M., Tout, K., Halle, T., Vick Whittaker, J., & Lavelle, B. (2010). *Towards the identification of features of effective professional development for early childhood educators: A review of the literature.* Literature review prepared for the Policy and Program Studies Service, Office of Planning, Evaluation and Policy Development, U.S. Department of Education.

Zaslow, M., Tout, K., & Martinez-Beck, I. (2010). ACF-OPRE Research-to-Policy Brief. *Measuring Quality of Early Care and Education Programs at the Intersection of Research, Policy and Practice.* Office of Planning, Research and Evaluation, Administration for Children and Families, U.S. Department of Health and Human Services. Washington, DC.

Zellman, G.L., & Perlman, M. (2008). *Child-care quality rating and improvement systems in five pioneer states: Implementation issues and lessons learned.* Santa Monica, CA: RAND Corporation.

Potential to Strengthen Measures of Quality in Specific Domains

Advancing the Measurement of Quality for Early Childhood Programs that Support Early Language and Literacy Development

Susan B. Neuman and Judith J. Carta

The last decade has brought a growing consensus on the range of skills that serve as the foundation for reading and writing ability (Dickinson & Neuman, 2006; National Reading Panel Report, 2000; Neuman & Dickinson, 2001; Snow, Burns, & Griffin, 1998). To become skilled readers, children need a rich language and conceptual knowledge base, a broad and deep vocabulary, and verbal reasoning abilities to understand messages that are conveyed through print. Children also must develop code-related skills: an understanding that spoken words are composed of smaller elements of speech (phonological awareness), the idea that letters represent these sounds (the alphabetic principle), the many systematic correspondences between sounds and spellings, and a repertoire of highly familiar words that can be easily and automatically recognized (McCardle & Chhabra, 2004; McCardle, Scarborough, & Catts, 2001).

To attain a high level of skill, however, young children need opportunities to develop these skills, not in isolation, but interactively. Meaning—not sounds or letters—motivates children's earliest experiences with print (Neuman, Copple, & Bredekamp, 2000). Therefore, although state standards and early learning guidelines may identify a typology of skills that serve as important precursors to eventual literacy, it is important to recognize that, in practice, children acquire these skills in coordination, and through interaction, with meaningful experiences. Given the tremendous attention that early literacy has received recently in policy circles (Roskos & Vukelich, 2006) and the increasing diversity of our child population, it is important and timely to take stock of these critical dimensions, as well as of both the strengths and weaknesses in our ability to measure such skills effectively.

In the sections that follow, we first review the important skills that are related to early language and literacy achievement. We then describe a number of assessment measures, designed to examine aspects of quality in center- and home-based settings, that are tied to these critical dimensions.

The Critical Dimensions of Language and Literacy in Early Childhood Language

Verbal abilities are consistently the best predictors of later reading achievement (Scarborough, 2001). Skilled readers typically draw upon multiple levels of the language system (Dickinson, McCabe, Anastasopoulos, Peisner-Feinberg, & Poe, 2003), through abilities encompassing vocabulary, syntax, and discourse. In optimal settings, vocabulary size may increase exponentially in the early years—some estimate about seven words a day (Snow et al., 1998)—and children learn to comprehend words spoken to them before they are able to produce the language on their own. Word knowledge, however, is not developed through exposure just to increasingly complex language, but to knowledge-building language experiences (Neuman, 2001) that involve children in developing and refining networks of categorically related concepts.

With opportunity and practice, children put word knowledge to use in syntactic structures that grow in length and complexity. Children's sentences often start with two words (Bloom, 1970), but quickly lengthen to four or more words as children increasingly communicate their ideas through language. Snow, Baines, Chandler, Goodman, and Hemphill (1991) have shown that conversations that are physically removed from immediate objects or events (i.e., "What if?" discussions) are tied to the development of abstract reasoning and related to literacy skills such as print production and narrative competence.

With word learning occurring so rapidly, children begin to make increasingly fine distinctions of words on the basis not only of their meaning but also of their sound. Children begin to make implicit comparisons between similar-sounding words, a phenomenon described by linguists as *lexical restructuring* (Goswami, 2001; Metsala, 1999). For example, a 2-year-old child probably distinguishes the words "cat" from "cut" and "hot" from "not." Distinguishing between these similar-sounding words both quickly and accurately, children begin to hear sequences of sound that constitute each known word. Children with large vocabularies become attuned to these segments and rapidly acquire new words; children with smaller vocabularies may be limited to more global distinctions. Consequently, vocabulary size and the rate of acquiring vocabulary are important for lexical restructuring (i.e., making sound distinctions between words; Goswami, 2001) and are strongly tied to the emergence of phonological awareness.

Recent analyses (Dickinson et al., 2003) have made it abundantly clear, however, that oral language skills and, more specifically, vocabulary development not only play a role in phonological awareness but also serve as critical skills for the development of reading comprehension later on. Therefore, it is essential for quality indicators in early childhood programs to recognize that oral language and vocabulary development form the foundation for all other skills critical to successful reading.

Phonological Awareness

According to a massive body of research (e.g., Burgess, 2006; Lonigan, 2006), phonological awareness is a critical precursor, correlate, and predictor of children's reading achievement. Discriminating units of language (i.e., words, segments, phonemes) is strongly linked to successful reading (National Reading Panel Report, 2000). It is, however, as described previously, both a cause and a consequence of vocabulary development and of learning to read (Ehri & Roberts, 2006). Typically, developing children begin to discriminate first among units of language (i.e., phonological awareness) and then within these units (i.e., phonemic awareness). *Phonological awareness* refers to the general ability to attend to the sounds of language as distinct from its meaning. *Phonemic awareness* is the understanding of the concept that every spoken word can be conceived as units of sounds represented by the letter of an alphabet (Snow et al., 1998).

Evidence (Lonigan, 2006; Whitehurst & Lonigan, 1998) suggests that children achieve syllabic sensitivity earlier than they achieve sensitivity to phonemes and sensitivity to rhyme before sensitivity to phonemes. Children's entry to these skills typically begins with linguistic activities such as language games and nursery rhymes (Maclean, Bryant, & Bradley, 1987) that implicitly compare and contrast the sounds of words and include alliterative phrases (i.e., "Peter piper picked a peck of pickled peppers" begins with /p/). But implicit comparisons, alone, may be insufficient. Phonological awareness and phonemic awareness are metalinguistic abilities (Adams, 1990). Children not only must be able to recite and play with sound units but also they must develop an understanding that sound units map onto whole or parts of written language.

Phonological awareness should not be confused with phonics. The term *phonics*, or *decoding*, implies an assumption that children understand the phonemic composition of words and the phoneme–grapheme (sound–letter) relationship. Studies that have attempted to accelerate learning through early phonics training have shown no effects (Snow et al., 1998); in fact, evidence suggests that such training, without promoting a firm understanding of phonemic awareness, may deter the development of remembering words and learning to spell.

Recent reviews and analyses (Dickinson et al., 2003; Scarborough, 2001) have identified phonological awareness as a critical part of a complex braid of language abilities that includes strands of phonology, semantics, syntax, pragmatics, and discourse. Its connection to children's ability to decode has been clearly established. At the same time, phonological awareness skills are integrally connected to other important language skills that need to be strongly bolstered in these early education and care programs.

Letter Knowledge

Knowledge of the alphabet letters is a strong predictor of short- and long-term reading success (Bond & Dykstra, 1967; Chall, Jacobs, & Baldwin, 1990). However, its influence on later reading is not about knowing the letter names per se. Rather, the learning of letter names mediates the ability to remember the sounds associated with the letters (Ehri, 1979). Once again, there is a reciprocal relationship between skills: Letter knowledge plays an influential role in the development of phonological awareness, and higher levels of letter knowledge are associated with children's abilities to detect and manipulate phonemes. For example, a child who knows the letter *b* is likely to remember the sound of /b/. Consequently, letter knowledge may reflect a greater underlying knowledge and familiarity with literacy-related skills such as understanding language and print.

Research (Gibson & Levin, 1975) indicates that children differentiate letters according to their visual form—that is, their horizontal, vertical, and diagonal segments. Given the complexities of the visually distinct forms of letters (uppercase, lowercase, printed form), current learning theory (Adams, 1990) suggests that simultaneously teaching two versions of letters, with their confusable sounds and labels, may be overwhelming to the young child. However, there is no substantial evidence to suggest which particular form (uppercase or lowercase) should be taught first.

A growing body of research suggests that a variety of extrinsic and intrinsic factors influence the development of letter knowledge. Exposure to letters is a primary vehicle for alphabet knowledge. Children who participate frequently in adult–child writing activities that include a deliberate focus on print have better alphabet knowledge relative to those who may spend time on other activities, such as shared reading (Aram & Levin, 2004). Further, some letters tend to be learned earlier than others by children. In a recent investigation, Justice, Pence, Bowles, and Wiggins (2006) reported that the single largest advantage in learning letters was the child's recognition of his or her first initials, compared with the lesser advantage of phonological features of the letters themselves. Given the variability among children in the specific letters they know, multiple methods for gaining letter knowledge are recommended.

Background Knowledge

For children to become skilled readers (Neuman & Celano, 2006), they also need to develop a rich conceptual knowledge base and verbal reasoning abilities in order to understand messages conveyed through print. Successful reading ultimately consists of a relatively small toolbox of unconscious procedural skills, accompanied by a massive and slowly built-up store of conscious content knowledge. It is the higher order thinking skills, knowledge, and dispositional capabilities that enable young children to come to understand what they are reading.

Children's earliest experiences become organized and structured into schemas—building blocks of cognition. By classifying incoming bits of information into similar groupings, schemas (Anderson & Pearson, 1984) provide children with the conceptual apparatus for making sense of the world around them. Stein and Glenn (1979), for example, provided a compelling case for schemas and their usefulness for recalling information about stories. Well-read children internalize a form of story grammar—a set of expectations of how stories are told—that enhances their understanding. Knowledge becomes easier to access (Neuman, 2001) and more knowledge networks are produced. Those with a rich knowledge base find it easier to learn and remember.

Quality indicators of a rich content base for instruction in early childhood programs include a content-rich curriculum in which children have opportunities for sustained and in-depth learning (Neuman, Neuman, & Dwyer, 2009), including play; different levels of guidance to meet the needs of individual children; a masterful orchestration of activities that support content learning and social-emotional development; and time, materials, and resources that actively build verbal reasoning skills and conceptual knowledge.

Print Conventions

Recognizing that concepts about print in the English language are not intuitive, Marie Clay (1979), in her pioneering work with Maori children in New Zealand, identified a set of conventions that could be understood by individuals unable to read. These conventions included, among others, the directionality of print in a book (left to right, top to bottom, front to back), differences between pictures and print, uses of punctuation, and definitional characteristics of a letter and of a word. Knowing these conventions, she found, helped in the process of learning to read.

With the exception of a study by Tunmer, Herriman, and Nesdale (1988) demonstrating the relationship of these skills to later reading success, however, there is little evidence to suggest the predictive power of such skills on later achievement. Rather, print conventions act as an immediate indicator of children's familiarity with text but are not integrally related to the other language-based skills associated with reading success. Therefore, whereas such conventions might be helpful to young children in navigating through books, in the long run these skills may not play a powerful role in children's learning to read.

Children who are English language learners (ELLs) experience each of these critical dimensions in the context of learning two languages, which only increases the complexity of the processes of language and literacy development. In order to become proficient in their second language, young children need a familiarity with the phonology of that language, its vocabulary (typical everyday discourse as well as academic vocabulary), its morphology, and its grammar (Geva, 2006). Further, for children to become literate in a second language, it is important that they have an adequate level of oral proficiency in that language (Bialystock, 2007). Research with second language learners has shown that oral language and literacy skills in the first language contribute to the development of those skills in the second language. For example, phonological awareness skills in the first language have been found to predict phonological awareness and word recognition in the second language (Chiappe & Siegel, 1999; Cisero & Royer, 1995; Durgunoglu, 1998). Although much more research is needed about the ways in which ELLs develop literacy skills, the knowledge established so far can help guide the development of further interventions. (See Chapter 11.)

In sum, research supports a particularly strong linkage in the preschool years among oral language, phonological awareness, letter knowledge, background knowledge, and, to a much lesser extent, print conventions. These skills are highly interdependent. Phonological awareness appears to influence the development of vocabulary size and the rate of acquiring vocabulary. Letter knowledge supports phonological awareness. Code-related skills are highly predictive of children's initial early reading success, whereas oral language skills and background knowledge become highly predictive of comprehension abilities and later reading achievement. Each of these skills, when integrated in meaningful activity, has an important role to play in children's literacy development.

Features of the Classroom Environment that Support Literacy Development

The environment can play a major role in promoting these critical skills for literacy development. The organization, structure, and complexity of the early childhood setting influence patterns of activity and engagement. For example, a fairly sizable number of studies (Morrow, 1990; Neuman & Roskos, 1992, 1997; Vukelich, 1994) have revealed the powerful influence of access to literacy tools on young children's involvement in literacy activities. This research indicates that in settings carefully constructed to include a wide variety of literacy tools, books, and play materials, children read more (Neuman & Roskos, 1992) and engage more in literacy-related play themes (Morrow, 1990), with resulting effects on literacy improvement (Neuman & Roskos, 1990).

The use of space in settings influences learning (Roskos & Neuman, 2001). Children use space and its boundaries to regulate and guide their own responses. For example, studies (Morrow, 1988; Neuman & Roskos, 1997) find that smaller, well-defined niches and nooks seem to encourage greater language exchange and collaboration with peers and adults. Children are likely to use these more intimate settings to interact in longer and richer conversation with others.

Related studies (Fernie, 1985) show evidence that the physical environment can have behavioral consequences. Some materials seem to encourage more sustained activity than others and invoke children's attention at different ages. Materials that involve children in constructive activity, for example, tend to generate more language than "pull toys" (Rosenthal, 1973). Some materials, such as building blocks, elicit greater social interaction and cooperation, whereas others, such as puzzles, encourage more solitary and/or parallel play (see review in Roskos & Neuman, 2001).

The physical placement of objects also influences children's engagement in literacy-related activity. Children become more involved in sustained literacy play when objects are clustered together to create a schema, or *meaning network*. For example, in one study (Neuman & Roskos, 1993), placing props associated with mailing letters (e.g., envelopes, writing instruments, stamps, stationery) together in a play setting led to longer play episodes than scattering these props throughout the room. Further, props that were authentic, familiar, and useful in common literacy contexts, such as telephones in the kitchen area or mailboxes in the office area, encouraged more complex language interactions and routines.

The proximity of quality books to children's eye view supports involvement in literacy-like enactments (Morrow & Weinstein, 1986; Neuman, 1999). In one of the first intervention studies of its type, Morrow and Weinstein (1986) examined the influence of creating library corners in early childhood settings. These library corners were specially constructed to include the following elements: 1) a clear location with well-defined borders; 2) comfortable seating and cozy spots for privacy; 3) accessible, organized materials; and 4) related activities that extended whole- and small-group book activities. Morrow and Weinstein found that the frequency of use rose significantly when library corners were made more visibly accessible and attractive. Similarly, in a large-scale study in 500 child care settings (Neuman, 1999), library settings were created to "put books in children's hands" (p. 286). Observations indicated that children spent significantly more time interacting with books when they were placed in close proximity to children's play activities.

Consequently, there is clear and abundant evidence that certain physical design features in environments support young children's literacy engagement and subsequent achievement. Physical design features, uses of space, and resources may help to focus and sustain children's literacy activity, providing greater opportunity for them to engage in language and literacy behaviors. This research indicates, therefore, that a more deliberate approach to the selection and arrangement of materials in accordance with specific design criteria may enhance children's uses of literacy objects and related print resources.

Interactional Supports for Literacy Learning

Optimal environments for literacy learning include not only physical settings but also psychological settings (Tharp & Gallimore, 1988). Children are influenced by the participants present in a setting, their background experiences, and their values; and it is the integration of place, people, and occasion that supports opportunities for learning. These participants act as social and psychological resources providing information and feedback through demonstrations and interactions. From a Vygotskian perspective

(Vygotsky, 1978), the participants in the setting have the potential to help children perform at a higher level than they otherwise would be able to reach by interacting with their physical environment alone. It is the contrast between assisted and unassisted performance that differentiates learning from development.

A great corpus of research (Dickinson & Neuman, 2006; Neuman & Dickinson, 2001) identifies the types of supports that promote children's language and literacy development. Essentially, these supports highlight both instructional and relational components. There is evidence that, because language represents the foundation for literacy learning in the early years, the amount of verbal input in settings enhances children's language development (Hart & Risley, 1995; Hoff-Ginsberg, 1991). Children whose teachers engage them in rich dialogues have higher scores on tests of both verbal and general ability (Whitehurst et al., 1994). This is especially the case when discussions consist of teachers encouraging, questioning, predicting, and guiding children's exploration and problem-solving (Palincsar, Brown, & Campione, 1993). Such verbal interactions contribute to children's vocabulary growth, which in turn is strongly correlated with phonological awareness, comprehension, and subsequent reading achievement.

Teachers also engage in activities that are highly supportive of literacy development. Reading stories to children on a regular basis is regarded as one of the more potent supports for literacy learning (Bus, van IJzendoorn, & Pellegrini, 1995). Studies (Dickinson & Smith, 1994; Whitehurst & Lonigan, 1998) have shown that a teacher's style or approach to reading storybooks to children has both short-term and long-term effects on language and literacy development. Shared book-reading activities, such as dialogic reading (Whitehurst et al., 1994) and repeated readings (Biemiller, 2006), have been widely studied and identified as an important source of knowledge about vocabulary, letters, and the characteristics of written language. Recent studies (Beck & McKeown, 2007; Duke, 2000) also highlight the importance of introducing children to a wide variety of books in different genres, such as information books, poetry, and popular folk tales.

Teachers' attention to and support of emergent writing (Clay, 1991) has also been shown to strongly connect with children's developing phonological awareness, phonemic awareness, and readiness skills. Activities involving "driting" (drawing and writing) and teacher scaffolding help to build the alphabetic principle (Adams, 1990). Further, teachers' interactions in literacy-related play have been shown to relate to children's length of utterances and to sustainability in play themes (Neuman & Roskos, 1992). Taken together, activities that engage children in reading, writing, talking, and playing create occasions for meaningful communicative interactions involving language and print.

This research highlights the central role of the caregiver who evokes children's interest and engagement in literacy learning. According to Bus, Van Ijzendoorn, and Pellegrini (1995), children build a mental representation of their interactions with caregivers, and those interactions influence the children's expectations and responses to activities. When children feel secure, they engage in learning; when insecure in situations, they may use digressive tactics to avoid activity. For example, in a cross-sectional study of interactive reading with 18-, 32-, and 66-month-old children, Bus and van IJzendoorn (1995) found that the atmosphere surrounding book reading was more positive among securely attached caregiver–child dyads than anxiously attached dyads. For securely attached children, book reading was ultimately an enjoyable task, tied to learning improvement; for insecurely attached children, it was negative, with caregivers often using verbal and nonverbal cues to discipline children for their behavior.

Other studies (Blair, 2002; Blair & Razza, 2007; Hamre & Pianta, 2005; Miles & Stipek, 2006; Pianta, La Paro, Payne, Cox, & Bradley, 2002) also support the linkage between children's emotional security and cognitive activity. For example, Howes and Smith (1995) reported that in child care settings rich with creative play activities and staffed by teachers who provide children with emotional security, children thrive not only socially but cognitively as well. Similarly, Peisner-Feinberg and colleagues (2001) found that the influence of close attachments between caregivers and children yielded even stronger positive effects for children from disadvantaged backgrounds than for children from more advantaged backgrounds. Recent studies (Hamre & Pianta, 2005) have shown that these emotional supports may have important moderating effects during the elementary school years as well. A recent study by Powell, Burchinal, File, and Kontos (2008) revealed that these types of supportive teacher–child interactions are more likely to occur in small-group and one-to-one instructional settings than in whole-group instruction.

Addressing the Needs of English Language Learners

All of these environmental supports are especially important for young ELLs. Their numbers have increased dramatically in the past 15 years in the United States. For example, in 1990, 1 in every 20 children was an ELL—that is, a student who speaks English either not at all or with enough limitations that he or she cannot fully participate in mainstream English instruction. Eight years later, the figure was 1 in 9 (Goldenberg, 2008). Although these children come from more than 400 different language backgrounds, by far the largest proportion of students is Spanish speaking (more than 80%; U.S. Department of Education, 2005).

Recent syntheses of research (August & Shanahan, 2006; Rolstad, Mahoney, & Glass, 2005; Slavin & Cheung, 2005) suggest that when feasible, children should be taught in their primary language. Primary language instruction helps to promote bilingualism and, eventually, biliteracy. Further, children will need support in transferring what they know in their first language to learning tasks presented in English. Engaging children actively in meaningful tasks and providing many opportunities for them to participate at their functional levels will enable the children to feel more efficacious and to become contributing members in mainstream classrooms.

Teachers will need to make adjustments and accommodations—sometimes described as *instructional scaffolding*—to support children who are beginning English speakers (Goldenberg, 2008). The teachers may have to speak slowly and somewhat deliberately, with clear vocabulary and diction; they may need to use pictures or other objects to illustrate the content being taught; or they may find it necessary to ask children to respond either nonverbally (e.g., pointing, signaling) or in one- or two-word utterances (Snow et al., 1998).

The language needs of ELLs are complex. These young children are learning not only a new language but also a new set of social rules and behaviors that may be different from those in their home. Given the great variability among ELL children, teachers will need to know the different stages of language learning for each individual ELL in order to be able to implement the most appropriate accommodations. (For additional information on accommodations, see Carlo et al., 2004; Francis, Rivera, Lesaux, Kiefer, & Rivera, 2006; and Vaughn et al., 2006.) These and other factors are especially important to ensure that ELL children have many opportunities to use their second language (i.e., English) and their native language in meaningful and motivating situations. (See Chapter 11.)

To ensure quality instruction, programs need to monitor children's ongoing progress using valid, reliable, and accessible tools. These measures should look at the totality of instructional benefits, including knowledge, skills, and dispositions (Neuman, Copple, & Bredekamp, 2000), as well as self-regulatory skills (Blair, 2002).

From an ecological perspective, therefore, the physical and psychological environments play vital roles in children's learning about literacy. These supports mediate opportunities for literacy engagement and practice and will likely influence children's attitudes toward, and efforts to engage in, literacy activities, despite any difficulties that the children may encounter as they learn to read proficiently.

To summarize, program features that support literacy development include the following:

- A supportive learning environment in which children have access to a wide variety of reading and writing resources

- A developmentally appropriate curriculum that actively engages children's minds and builds language and conceptual development. (A high-quality curriculum serves as an important scaffold for teachers and encourages careful planning and activities that build knowledge, skills, and dispositions.)

- Teacher engagement in children's learning through conversations, discussions, and contingent responses to children's questions and queries

- A daily, interactive book-reading routine that introduces children to multiple genres, including information books, narrative, poetry, and alphabet books

- Activities that support small-group and one-to-one instruction and differing levels of guidance to meet the needs of individual children

- A masterful orchestration of activities that support play, learning, and social-emotional development

- Adjustments and accommodations for ELLs that allow them to successfully engage in learning activities in the classroom

- Ongoing assessment that is designed to monitor children's programs and tailor instruction to children's needs

Existing Strategies for Measuring Language and Literacy

As research begins to clarify the range of skills that serves as the foundation for reading ability and the features needed by early childhood programs to foster those skills, the measurement of these active ingredients becomes critical. Using standardized classroom observation systems to examine classroom quality related to language and literacy can assist programs that seek to measure caregivers' and/or teachers' strengths and weaknesses, form professional development strategies, and plan and evaluate programs and policy initiatives.

Measuring quality in early care and education (ECE) settings related to language and early literacy presents considerable challenges because of the variety of constructs that support these domains. Measures vary tremendously, but most can be categorized in terms of their use of *environmental ratings* of features of the setting, such as the availability of materials or space to foster learning or interaction, *ratings of specific instructional practices* for improving children's literacy and language, or time-sampling approaches for *coding specific caregiver–child interactions*. (See Table 4.1 for a matrix of some existing tools for measuring the quality of language and early literacy in ECE settings.)

In the next section, we highlight sample measures from each of the preceding three categories. Our intention is not to present an exhaustive review; rather, our purpose is to describe how these measures in each of the three categories attempt to capture aspects of quality in ECE settings that support language and early literacy. Following this review of measures, we discuss the state of our practice for addressing issues of age, functional ability, setting, native language, and culture. Finally, we highlight some of the strengths and the weaknesses in our available measures and talk about future research to inform early childhood professional development that may result in improved outcomes in young children's language and literacy.

Environmental Rating Measures

Environmental rating measures have the longest history of use for measuring quality in ECE settings, and they are still the most frequently used measures for examining the quality of environment support for language and literacy and for other, more general, areas of child development. For example, the suite of measures that includes the Early Childhood Environment Rating Scale-Revised Edition (ECERS-R; Harms, Clifford, & Cryer, 2005), the Infant-Toddler Environmental Rating Scale-Revised Edition (ITERS-R; Harms, Cryer, & Clifford, 2003), and the Family Child Care Environmental Rating Scale-Revised (FCCERS-R; Harms, Cryer, & Clifford, 2007) are broadly used for making global ratings of the quality of child care environments. Observers using these tools spend a few hours observing teachers interacting with children in the child care settings, conduct interviews of the teachers or child care providers, and then rate approximately 40 items that capture structural aspects of quality, such as space and furnishings, personal care routines, and program and staff. Structural aspects of the quality of the environment are rated on a 7-point scale, with a score of 5 generally indicating developmentally appropriate practices and adequate support for learning.

Although this suite of measures was not developed specifically to examine quality related to language or literacy, each of the tools includes some items focusing on their quality of support for the critical dimension of fostering oral language. For example, the ECERS-R has items such as "Encouraging Children to Communicate" and "Informal Use of Language." The FCCERs has items such as "Helping Children Understand Language" and "Helping Children Use Language." The measures can be used both for research and for program improvement, program monitoring, or accreditation. Many states include these environmental rating measures as part of their Quality Rating and Improvement Systems.

Other measures that focus on ratings of environmental quality include the Early Language and Literacy Classroom Observation (ELLCO) Toolkit, Research Edition (Smith & Dickinson, 2002); the ELLCO Pre-K Tool (Smith, Brady, & Anastasopoulos, 2008); and the Child/Home Early Language and Literacy Observation (CHELLO) Tool (Neuman, Dwyer, & Koh, 2007). Designed specifically to measure quality related to language and early literacy by examining features of environmental support as well as instructional or interactional practices, these measures employ 5-point rating scales with descriptive indicators for some or all of the anchor points. The ELLCO Pre-K, for example, contains items

Table 4.1. Matrix of tools for measuring quality of support for language and early literacy in early childhood settings

| Purpose of measure | Literacy dimensions targeted | | | | Measurement methodology employed | Reliability data | Validity data |
	Oral language (OL)	Phonological awareness (PA)	Letter knowledge (LK)	Background knowledge (BK)			
Adult Interactional Engagement Scale (Dickinson, 2006)	X	X	X	X	Direct observation: Y/N ratings	−	−
Assessment of Practices in Early Elementary Classrooms (APEEC) (Hemmeter, Maxwell, Ault, & Schuster, 2001)	X				Direct observation: 7-point rating scale and teacher interview	+	+
Child-Caregiver Observation System (C-COS) (Boller & Sprachman, 1998)	X				Direct observation using time-sampling of frequency of caregiver behavior and ratings of interactional quality	+	+
Child/Home Early Language and Literacy Observation (CHELLO) Tool (Neuman, Dwyer, & Koh, 2007)	X		X		Literacy Observation Checklist (Y/N); Group/Family Observation—5-point rating scale, provider interview	+	+
Classroom Assessment Scoring System™ (CLASS™) (Pianta et al., 2008)	X				Ten dimensions of classroom quality organized into 3 dimensions of interactions, coded on a 7-point scale	+	+

(continued)

Table 4.1. (*continued*)

Purpose of measure	Literacy dimensions targeted				Measurement methodology employed	Reliability data	Validity data
	Oral language (OL)	Phonological awareness (PA)	Letter knowledge (LK)	Background knowledge (BK)			
ClassCIRCLE (Code for Interactive Recording of Children's Learning Environments) (Atwater et al., 2007)	X	X	X	X	Momentary time-sampling of classroom activities, teachers' instructional and verbal behavior, child academic engagement, language, and social behavior	+	+
Emergent Academic Snapshot (EAS) (Ritchie, Howes, et al., 2001)	X	X			Naturalistic observation that uses a partial interval time-sampling system to capture adult level of involvement with children and children's exposure and engagement in academic activities	+	+
Early Childhood Classroom Observation Measure (ECCOM) (Stipek & Byler, 2004)				X	Ratings of the extent of the use of social-constructivist and didactic instructional approaches; checklists of instructional and multicultural materials	+	+
Early Childhood Environment Rating Scale-Revised (ECERS-R) (Harms, Clifford, & Cryer, 2005)	X			X	Ratings of the quality of the interpersonal, spatial, and program-matic aspects of the environment	+	+

Measure	Purpose						Description
Early Language and Literacy Classroom Observation (ELLCO) Toolkit (Smith & Dickinson, 2002) (ELLCO Pre-K) (Smith, Brady, & Anastasopoulos, 2008)	To measure the extent of environmental support for language and literacy in early childhood programs for children from pre-K to third grade; for use in research and evaluation or for program improvement	+	+			X	Literacy Environment Checklist; Classroom Observation, for ratings of language and literacy environment and general classroom environment; and Teacher Interview, Literacy Activities Rating Scale, to provide information on the nature and duration of literacy-related activities
Early Literacy Observation Tool (E-LOT) (Grehan & Smith, 2004)	For research or evaluation, or for monitoring or accreditation, to measure research-based instructional practices, student activities, and environmental settings for children in pre-K and kindergarten settings		+	X	X	X	4-point ratings of extent to which key components are observed
Infant and Toddler Environment Rating Scale (ITERS-R) (Harms, Cryer, & Clifford, 2003)	For research or evaluation or for program improvement, to assess the quality of child care environments with regard to protecting children's health and safety, providing appropriate language stimulation, and engaging in supportive interactions	+	+	X	X	X	39 items organized into 7 categories, with each item rated on a 7-point scale with four anchors
Observation Measures of Language and Literacy Instruction (OMLIT) Snapshot (Goodson, Layzer, Smith, & Rimzius, 2006)	To describe the classroom activities and groupings, integration of literacy in other activities, and language in early education settings; designed for research		+	X	X	X	Records the number of children and adults present across a variety of activities and the language interaction occurring; coding in this way occurs once every 10 mins.

(continued)

63

Table 4.1. (continued)

Purpose of measure	Literacy dimensions targeted				Measurement methodology employed	Reliability data	Validity data
	Oral language (OL)	Phonological awareness (PA)	Letter knowledge (LK)	Background knowledge (BK)			
OMLIT—Reading Aloud Profile (RAP) (Goodson, Layzer, Smith, & Rimzius, 2006)	To measure adult behavior when reading to children and to capture 5 indicators of quality of reading to children; designed for research	X	X	X	X	Records the performance of 36 adult book-sharing behaviors and rates 3 quality indicators of book reading	+	
OMLIT—Classroom Literacy Observation Checklist (CLOC) (Goodson, Layzer, Smith, & Rimzius, 2006)	To provide a rating of the literacy-richness of an early education classroom environment; designed for research			X		Inventories 51 aspects of classroom literacy environment rated on a 3-point scale and organized into 10 categories	+	
OMLIT—Classroom Literacy Instruction Profile (CLIP) (Goodson, Layzer, Smith, & Rimzius, 2006)	To describe the formal and informal instructional activities aimed at developing children's oral language skills, phonological processing skills, and increasing print knowledge and print motivation; designed for research	X	X	X	X	Records 7 features of literacy activities and 3 indicators of quality of adult-child interaction when literacy discussion occurs	+	

Measure	Purpose				Description		
OMLIT–Quality Rating of Language and Literacy Instruction (QUILL) (Goodson, Layzer, Smith, & Rimzius, 2006)	To evaluate the instructional practices that build children's print awareness and oral language skills, expose children to a rich vocabulary, and build children's phonological awareness skills; designed for research	X	X	X	Records the frequency and quality of 6 literacy instructional practices and the quality of 4 practices related to instruction of ELL children		+
Observation Record of the Caregiving Environment (ORCE) (Goodson, Layzer, Smith, & Rimzius, 2006)	To describe the experiences of individual children while in nonmaternal care and provide specific information about 1) the behaviors of the caregivers toward the target child and 2) the behavior of the target child; designed for research	X	X		With 5 different versions for children at 6, 15, 24, 36, and 54 mos. old, each version uses a time-sampling approach to record positive and negative caregiving behaviors and children's behavior	+	+
Teacher Behavior Rating Scale (TBRS) (Landry et al., 2002)	For research, program evaluation, and professional development, to measure early literacy and language qualities of preschool classrooms and, more specifically, to examine instructional practices that promote skills important for school readiness	X	X	X	Observation that uses a 3-point scale to evaluate quantity of behavior and a 4-point scale to evaluate quality of observed behavior	+	+

Key: X present; + included; − not included

for rating "Efforts to Build Vocabulary" and "Opportunities for Extended Conversations." The CHELLO, modeled after the ELLCO, contains similar items that rate physical and interactional features of home-based child care associated with children's developing language and literacy skills. Items specific to support for language include those related to adult–child language interaction, quality of vocabulary-building practices, and responsive interaction strategies.

Ratings of Instructional Practices

Whereas measures employing broad environmental ratings have been available and widely used for many years, a more recent trend in quality measurement is to focus more specifically on measuring the educational or interactional strategies that teachers use to promote early literacy. Measures that rate the quality of instructional practices include the Classroom Assessment Scoring System™ (CLASS™) Pre-K (Pianta, La Paro, & Hamre, 2008); the Center for Improving the Readiness of Children for Learning and Education (CIRCLE) Teacher Behavior Rating Scale (TBRS; Landry, Crawford, Gunnewig, & Swank, 2002) and the Adult Interactional Scale (Dickinson, 2006). These measures are based on the premise that quality in early education must be differentiated not just on the presence of materials or the availability of curriculum but on how a teacher uses materials or implements the curriculum in an intentional way to foster children's learning. These measures typically focus on a single teacher or the entire teaching team in a classroom. The CLASS captures teaching practices related to emotional support, classroom organization, and instructional support. The instructional support items—those most related to language and literacy—allow for the measurement of instructional quality related to concept development, quality of feedback, and language modeling. The area of concept development is noteworthy by its absence from most measures of quality in ECE. This CLASS subscale rates the quality with which teachers focus on the process of learning rather than on rote instruction and recall, how frequently they provide students with opportunities to use reasoning and analysis in problem-solving contexts, and how well teachers bring concepts to life through connections to students' everyday world. Each of these constructs on the CLASS is observed and rated on a 7-point scale with descriptive anchors. An additional unique feature of the CLASS is the availability of the CLASS K–3, which captures similar quality constructs as the CLASS Pre-K, thereby allowing for a consistent metric for examining the quality of children's instructional experiences from ages 4 through 8. The CLASS was designed and is in use for research, program improvement, and monitoring and accreditation purposes.

Another tool for examining the quality of instructional practices is the Teacher Behavior Rating Scale (TBRS). This measure was developed by the Center for Improving the Readiness of Children for Learning and Education (CIRCLE) to evaluate literacy and language quality in classrooms (e.g., Landry, Swank, Smith, Assell, & Gunnewig, 2006). The measure has been used in site-specific research, as well as in large, national - studies (e.g., the national evaluation of Early Reading First, Jackson et al., 2007; the Preschool Curriculum Evaluation Research, Preschool Curriculum Evaluation Research Consortium, 2008). It includes subscales related to instructional practices for the promotion of oral language and for book reading. Examples of Oral Language items include "Uses 'scaffolding' language (nouns, descriptors, action words, linking concepts)" and "Relates previously learned words and concepts to activity." Book-reading behaviors include the following rated items: introducing vocabulary words, pacing the reading to allow for children to be involved through questions and comments, and asking open-ended questions. The TBRS also captures features of specific instructional practices related to print and letter knowledge, such as the frequency with which the teacher engages children in activities that promote letter/word knowledge and those which help children learn to associate names of letters with shapes. Other items in this scale rate the quality of the environment for supporting knowledge of print. The TBRS has one of the most extensive sets of items related to measuring phonological awareness activities (e.g., rhyming, syllable segmenting, blending). The measure allows for the recording of the number of classroom activities in which phonological activities are observed (e.g., circle time, mealtime) and the quality or complexity of those activities. (For example, activities with sentence segmentation would be rated more highly than rhyming activities because the former skills are more complex.) Children's level of engagement in each activity is also rated.

Another measure that to date has been used exclusively for research, but has the potential to serve programs, is the Adult Instructional Engagement Scale (Dickinson, 2006). This measure focuses exclusively on instructional quality related to support for language and literacy. Ratings are provided for both the lead teacher and the assistant teacher across the specific activities of center time, mealtime, and book reading. Items generally have some specified amount of engagement, stated in either time or frequency. For example, items in the Center Time Engagement Scale include "Spends 4–5 minutes engaged in talk related to the area in 3 distinct areas" and "Makes 2+ clear efforts to use and teach vocabulary that children may not know." The scale also includes measurement of whether the lead or assistant teacher provides instructional support related to letters (formation, recognition, or naming).

The Quality of Instruction in Literacy and Language (QUILL) is another research-based measure and is one of a suite of measures called the Observational Measures of Language and Literacy (OMLIT; Goodson, Layzer, Smith, & Rimdzius, 2006). This set of measures was developed specifically to assess the quality of instructional practices and environmental supports that have been identified in the literature as predictors of children's reading outcomes (Dickinson & Tabors, 2001; Lonigan, 2006; NICHD Early Child Care Research Network, 2002; Snow et al., 1998). The QUILL includes measures of both frequency and quality of instructional practices, such as the extent to which children are encouraged to use oral language to formulate their ideas and communicate them, the extent to which children are encouraged to use language in higher order thinking, the depth of verbal interactions, and the extent of scaffolding of children's oral language. The QUILL also captures the quality of instructional practice related to phonological awareness on an item that reads "Attention to Sounds in Words through the Day." Classrooms are rated on a 1 (*minimal*) to 5 (*high*) scale on dimensions of the frequency, variety, and level of integration, throughout the day, of various aspects of phonological awareness (e.g., rhyming, alliteration, sentence segmenting). The QUILL also rates the frequency, consistency, and variety of classroom activities that focus on various *functions* of print, such as labeling, naming, and categorizing, as well as the *features* of print (e.g., the directionality of print). The QUILL also records how well adults provide letter/word knowledge—for example, by drawing children's attention to the same or different letters, names, and words or by associating letter names and shapes. Finally, the QUILL measures how consistently teaching staff provide opportunities for children to use oral language to develop higher level cognitive operations such as categorization, prediction, analysis, and exploration.

Another research measure available in the OMLIT suite of tools, the Reading Aloud Profile (RAP), specifically focuses on the quality with which adults read stories to children. The measure zeroes in on behaviors that adults use when interacting with children beyond the actual text reading—how adults prepare children for the reading and how they extend book reading with activities and discussion. Items specific to support for language include scoring whether the adult introduces and teaches new vocabulary in the story and whether the adult asks open-ended questions that require the child's expanded responses or higher order thinking such as prediction or analysis.

One final measure that contains a few categories of items related to phonological awareness is the Early Literacy Observation Tool (E-LOT; Grehan & Smith, 2004), an observation instrument designed specifically to measure research-based instructional practices, student activities, and environmental settings in early education programs. The E-LOT is used to observe literacy-related instruction and scores the degree to which six categories of literacy-related events are present in early education settings. Among the essential components of early reading identified by the National Research Council and the National Reading Panel, the concepts of print, emergent writing, alphabetic and phonological awareness, vocabulary and oral language development, fluency, and development of cognition and text comprehension are rated by the E-LOT.

Measures of Caregiver–Child Interaction

Researchers have developed another set of measures for examining language support that are much more precise and complex in their approach to observation. Some of these measures employ frequency counts or time-sampling systems to quantify the rates of occurrence of specific activities or caregiver behaviors. The Classroom Code for Interactive Recording of Children's Learning Environments (ClassCIRCLE; Atwater, Montagna, Reynolds, & Tapia, 2007), Ecobehavioral System for the Complex Assessment of Preschool Environments (ESCAPE; Carta, Greenwood, & Atwater, 1985), and Classroom Assessment System for Student Participation and Engagement Recording (CASPER) are computerized observation systems developed to provide a fine-grained assessment of certain features of young children's classroom environments, including 1) the context of children's classroom activities, 2) the behavior of teachers and other adults in the classroom, and 3) the child's engagement with people and objects. All of these measures allow for the evaluation of the three aspects of ECE settings and also of the interrelationships among those aspects within these settings; hence, the measures are referred to as *ecobehavioral*. An additional, unique aspect of such measures is that the foci of the observations are individual children; thus, the measure of classroom quality is derived by examining a sample of individual children's experiences within the classroom. In addition, each of these measures employs technology to support the observational data collection.

The ClassCIRCLE, for example, operates using Personal Data Assistant (PDA) devices. Customized software on the PDA prompts an observer to record, at specific intervals, data regarding activities in which a child becomes engaged and the child's level of engagement across activities. The tool also can record the relative frequency of the teacher's support for language in the classroom (e.g., expanding child talk, requesting communication), as well as categories related to children's engagement in language and literacy (e.g., child talk, child literacy engagement) relative to the target child. The unique aspect of this measure is that it captures how individual children experience their environment and the supports that are available. By sampling individual children, an overall picture is obtained about the quality of the classroom and teaching quality. The use of PDAs, laptops, notebook computers, or other technology-based systems has a number of advantages: 1) A greater range of classroom and teacher interaction variables can be tracked along with children's responses to each; 2) observers can be prompted to record specific variables at specific times, thus sharpening the focus of the observers, reducing the complexity of the task of data collection and improving inter-observer agreement; and 3) observational data records can be immediately available for analysis, thus improving the utility of the data for providing feedback to teachers or researchers.

Another research measure designed to capture the quality of adult–child interactions, the Observational Record of the Caregiving Environment (ORCE), was created for the NICHD Study of Early Child Care Phase I Instrument Document, 2004). The ORCE was created both to assess minute-to-minute evidence of caregiving and quality in a relatively objective, quantitative, and qualitative way and to accommodate the demands of the enterprise and the limitations of the human observers (i.e., we tried to get as much detail and "richness" as our coders could reliably record; NICHD Study of Early Child Care Phase I Instrument Document, 2004). Similar to the ClassCIRCLE, the ORCE focuses on the experiences of the individual child while in nonmaternal care and provides information about 1) the behaviors of the caregivers toward the target child and 2) the behavior of the target child. Variations of the measure have been used to rate the caregiving experiences of children from ages 6 to 54 months, and each variation had items related to adult talk to children.

Measures for Instruction of English Language Learners

Few tools have been developed that focus specifically on measuring the program features that support literacy development for ELLs, although the need for such measures is very great. (See Castro, Espinosa, & Paez, Chapter 11, this volume.) One exception in this regard is the OMLIT-QUILL, used to assess the overall quality of ELL practices. The OMLIT-QUILL includes items that capture strategies for promoting literacy skills, such as instructional scaffolding both in the home language and in English. Items include ratings of how well ELL children are integrated into activities with non-ELL children; how teachers encourage and/or support ELL children in joining conversations with English-speaking children; how much teachers encourage ELL children to speak both English and their home language; how often explicit, contextualized, instructional methods are used for teaching English; and how often ELL children's home language is used in language and literacy activities. Other measures included in the OMLIT suite (e.g., the Classroom Literacy Opportunities Checklist, CLOC; the OMLIT-Snapshot) also have capabilities for measuring quality relating to ELL instruction, but these measures have been developed for research purposes only. Such measures that can be used to assist programs in informing continuous improvement and in guiding professional development are sorely needed by the field.

Measuring the Quality of Instruction of Children with Special Needs

As more children with special needs are included in ECE settings, the importance of determining how well those settings address the individual needs of such children becomes more acute. Whereas only one measure (Assessment of Practices in Early Elementary Classrooms, APEEC; Hemmeter, Maxwell, Ault, & Schuster, 2001) was specifically designed to assess settings in which children with disabilities may be included, some measures, such as the ECERS-R and the ITERS-R, have included an item or two that address how well teachers individualize their instructional approaches to consider children's special needs. Measures that designate the individual child as the unit of analysis, such as ClassCIRCLE or ORCE, can capture the way in which children with and without special needs may vary in their classroom experiences. (See Spiker, Hebbeler, & Barton, Chapter 10, this volume.)

How Do Our Measures "Measure Up"?

Certainly, the last 10 years have brought enormous growth in the availability of measures for examining quality related to language and literacy in early childhood settings. Table 4.1 provides an overview of many of the existing measures that tap the literacy dimensions of oral language, phonological awareness, letter knowledge, or background knowledge. Clearly, the emphasis in the available tools over the years has been in measuring support for oral language, but recent developments have focused on the other important dimensions of phonological awareness and letter knowledge. Whereas some measures are beginning to be available that assess environmental support for areas related to background knowledge (e.g., verbal reasoning, vocabulary expansion), a critical need exists for additional measures in this essential area. Moreover, although the existing measures across these areas have demonstrated adequate levels of reliability, few tools that rate support for phonological awareness, letter knowledge, or background knowledge have as yet demonstrated their validity. This is especially true with regard to measures demonstrating predictive relationships between environmental quality and children's outcomes. Finally, measures that have strong reliability and validity are limited almost exclusively to measures focusing on oral language.

Other items missing from our toolbox of available measures include approaches for examining the quality of interaction in settings for infants and toddlers and quality in environments other than classroom centers (i.e., in children's homes or family child care). Very few measures are available that capture the instructional or interactional quality that ELLs experience in any early education settings. More information on tools that are available to examine the responsiveness of teachers and classrooms to children who are dual language learners can be found in Castro, Espinosa, and Paez, Chapter 11, this volume. Measures that capture how well teachers individualize teaching for children with specific instructional needs will be important areas for future research and development.

Finally, although the collection of measures for examining the quality of language and literacy in early education environments is growing, these measures are designed predominantly for use in research. If such tools are to be useful in guiding and promoting professional development and more effective programs, they must be accessible and easy to use by programs. A new generation of tools is needed that not only have strong psychometric properties, but also generate information about quality practices that can be used to inform programs.

Future Directions

There is now substantial evidence of the beneficial effects of high-quality preschool classrooms on children's language and literacy development. Studies have identified specific domains of knowledge that support development, as well as the specific features of preschool classrooms that help to foster them. There is a growing consensus that children need both code-related skills and content knowledge in settings that support teacher–child interaction and other environmental supports related to classroom climate, organization and materials in order to thrive intellectually and to develop early literacy skills necessary for school readiness.

There is less consensus, however, on whether we have the measurement tools to examine these important dimensions. Currently, there is a growing number of measures that tap various aspects of the environment. Additional measures have been developed that more carefully examine the subtle features of classroom interactions and curriculum features that best support learning measures such as the CLASS, the Adult Interactional Engagement Scale, the ClassCIRCLE, and the TBRS. These additional measures have only recently become available and may prove to have value for both researchers and programs that are attempting to evaluate and advance instructional and caregiving quality. Still, more efforts are needed to ensure that measures are well aligned with the behaviors associated with language and literacy improvement. Further, these measures must have demonstrated validity and reliability information that reflects different classroom contexts and the diversity of children in those settings.

Within this broad agenda, the field of language and literacy would benefit from the development of tools that enhance the connection between child outcomes and classroom practices. Specifically, measures are needed to

- Tap the instructional practices that we know are linked strongly to children's language and literacy skills and predict successful outcomes in the elementary grades and beyond

- Have strong psychometric qualities (validity and reliability), but are also easy to use by practitioners to guide program improvement, technical assistance efforts, and professional development

- Describe the classroom experience of individual children, capturing how well instruction is differentiated for children with unique needs (e.g., ELLs, children with special needs)

- Capitalize on new technological capabilities (e.g., PDAs, wireless technology, web-based systems)

In sum, the convergence of research and theoretical energy has led to a growing understanding of the cognitive and affective underpinnings of early literacy development. Also encouraging is the deepening understanding of the environmental factors that shape children's access to literacy-enhancing experiences. We anticipate that our increasingly sophisticated understanding of the complex web of factors that give rise to early literacy will translate into even more sophisticated tools to measure its development. Greater precision in measurement tools is essential if we are to significantly enhance language and literacy opportunities for all children.

References

Adams, M. (1990). *Beginning to read.* Cambridge, MA: M.I.T. Press.

Anderson, R.C., & Pearson, P.D. (1984). A schema-theoretic view of basic processes in reading comprehension. In P.D. Pearson (Ed.), *Handbook of reading research* (pp. 255–291). New York: Longman.

Aram, D., & Levin, I. (2004). The role of maternal mediation of writing to kindergarteners in promoting literacy achievements in school: A longitudinal perspective. *Reading and Writing: An Interdisciplinary Journal, 17*, 387–409.

Atwater, J., Montagna, D., Reynolds, S., & Tapia, Y. (2007). *Classroom Code for Interactive Recording of Children's Learning Environments (ClassCIRCLE).* Unpublished research instrument, Juniper Gardens Children's Project, University of Kansas, Kansas City.

August, D., & Shanahan, T. (Eds.). (2006). *Developing literacy in second-language learners: Report of the National Literacy Panel on language-minority children and youth.* Mahwah, NJ: Lawrence Erlbaum Associates.

Beck, I., & McKeown, M. (2007). Increasing young low-income children's oral vocabulary repertoires through rich and focused instruction. *Elementary School Journal, 107*, 251–271.

Biemiller, A. (2006). Vocabulary development and instruction: A prerequisite for school learning. In D. Dickinson & S.B. Neuman (Eds.), *Handbook of early literacy research (Vol. II,* pp. 41–51). New York: Guilford.

Blair, C. (2002). School readiness: Integrating cognition and emotion in a neurobiological conceptualization of children's functioning at school entry. *American Psychologist, 57(2),* 111–127.

Blair, C., & Razza, R.P. (2007). Relating effortful control, executive function, and false belief understanding to emerging math and literacy ability in kindergarten. *Child Development, 78(2),* 647–663.

Bloom, L. (1970). *Language development: Form and function in emerging grammars.* Cambridge, MA: The M.I.T. Press.

Bond, G., & Dykstra, R. (1967). The cooperative research program in first-grade reading instruction. *Reading Research Quarterly, 2,* 5–142.

Burgess, S. (2006). The development of phonological sensitivity. In D. Dickinson & S.B. Neuman (Eds.), *Handbook of early literacy research: Volume II* (Vol. II, pp. 90–100). New York: Guilford.

Bus, A., & van IJzendoorn, M. (1995). Mothers reading to their 3-year-olds: The role of mother–child attachment security in becoming literate. *Reading Research Quarterly, 30,* 998–1015.

Bus, A., van IJzendoorn, M., & Pellegrini, A. (1995). Joint book reading makes for success in learning to read: A meta-analysis on intergenerational transmission of literacy. *Review of Educational Research, 65,* 1–21.

Carlo, M., August, D., McLaughlin, B., Snow, C., Dressler, C., Lippman, D., et al. (2004). Closing the gap: Addressing the vocabulary needs for English language learners in bilingual and mainstream classrooms. *Reading Research Quarterly, 39,* 188–215.

Carta, J.J., Greenwood, C.R., & Atwater, J.B. (1985). *Ecobehavioral system for complex assessment of preschool environments—(ESCAPE).* Kansas City, KS: Juniper Gardens Children's Project, Bureau of Child Research, University of Kansas.

Chall, J., Jacobs, V., & Baldwin, L. (1990). *The reading crisis: Why poor children fall behind.* Cambridge, MA: Harvard University Press.

Chiappe, P., & Siegel, L. (1999). Phonological awareness and reading acquisition in English and Punjabi-speaking Canadian children. *Journal of Educational Psychology, 91,* 20–28.

Cisero, C., & Royer, J. (1995). The development and cross-language transfer of phonological awareness. *Contemporary Educational Psychology, 20,* 275–303.

Clay, M. (1979). *The early detection of reading difficulties.* Portsmouth, NH: Heinemann.

Clay, M. (1991). *Becoming literate.* Portsmouth, NH: Heinemann.

Dickinson, D. (2006). Toward a toolkit approach to describing classroom quality. *Early Education and Development, 17,* 177–202.

Dickinson, D., McCabe, A., Anastasopoulos, L., Peisner-Feinberg, E.S., & Poe, M.D. (2003). The comprehensive language approach to early literacy: The interrelationships among vocabulary, phonological sensitivity, and print knowledge among preschool-aged children. *Journal of Educational Psychology, 95,* 465–481.

Dickinson, D., & Neuman, S.B. (2006). *Handbook of early literacy research (Vol. II.)* New York: Guilford Press.

Dickinson, D., & Smith, M. (1994). Long-term effects of preschool teachers' book readings on low-income children's vocabulary and story comprehension. *Reading Research Quarterly, 29,* 104–122.

Dickinson, D.K. & Tabors, P.O. (2001). *Beginning literacy with language young children learning at home and school.* Baltimore: Paul H. Brookes Publishing Co.

Duke, N. (2000). For the rich it's richer: Print experiences and environments offered to children in very low- and very-high socioeconomic status first-grade classrooms. *American Educational Research Journal, 37,* 441–478.

Durgunoglu, A. (1998). Acquiring literacy in English and Spanish in the United States. In A.Y. Durgunoglu & L. Verboeven (Eds.), *Literacy development in a multilingual context. Cross-cultural perspectives.* (pp. 135–145). Mahwah, NJ, Lawrence Erlbaum Associates.

Ehri, L.C. (1979). Linguistic insight: Threshold of reading acquisition. In T.G. Waller & G.F. MacKinnon (Eds.), *Reading research: Advances in theory and practice* (Vol. 1 pp. 63–111). New York: Academic Press.

Ehri, L., & Roberts, T. (2006). The roots of learning to read and write: Acquisition of letters and phonemic awareness. In D. Dickinson & S.B. Neuman (Eds.), *Handbook of early literacy research* (pp. 113–134). New York: Guilford.

Fernie, D. (1985). The promotion of play in the indoor play environment. In J. Frost & S. Sunderlin (Eds.), *When children play* (pp. 285–290). Wheaton, MD: Association for Childhood Education International.

Francis, D. Rivera, M., Lesaux, N., Kiefer, M., & Rivera, H. (2006). *Practical guidelines for the education of English language learners: Research-based recommendations for instruction and academic intervention.* Retrieved from http://www.centeroninstruction.org/files/ELL1-Interventions.pdf

Geva, E. (2006). Learning to read in a second language: Research, implications, and recommendations for service. In *Encyclopedia on early childhood development.* Center for Excellence for Early Childhood Development. May 11, 2006. Retrieved from http://www. child-encyclopedia.com/Pages/PDF/ GevaANGxp.pdf

Gibson, E., & Levin, E. (1975). *The psychology of reading.* Cambridge, MA: M.I.T. Press.

Goldenberg, C. (2008). Improving achievement for English language learners: Conclusions from recent reviews and emerging research. In S.B. Neuman (Ed.), *Educating the other America: Top experts tackle poverty, literacy, and achievement in our schools.* (pp. 139–162). Baltimore: Paul H. Brookes Publishing Co.

Goodson, B., Layzer, C.J., Smith, W., & Rimdzius, T. (2006). *Observation Measures of Language and Literacy Instruction in Early Childhood (OMLIT).* Cambridge, MA: Abt Associates.

Goswami, U. (2001). Early phonological development and the acquisition of literacy. In S.B. Neuman & D. Dickinson (Eds.), *Handbook of early literacy research* (pp. 111–125). New York: Guilford.

Grehan, A., & Smith, L. (2004). Early Literacy Observation Tool (E-LOT). Memphis, TN: University of Memphis Center for Research in Educational Policy.

Grehan, A., Smith, L., Boyraz, G., Huang, Y., & Slawson, D. (2006). *Tennessee Reading First formative evaluation.* TN: Center for Research in Educational Policy, University of Memphis.

Hamre, B., & Pianta, R. (2005). Can instructional and emotional support in first grade make a difference for children at risk of school failure? *Child Development, 76,* 949–967.

Harms, T., Clifford, R., & Cryer, D. (2005). *Early childhood environmental rating scale-Revised edition.* New York: Teachers College Press.

Harms, T., Cryer, D., & Clifford, R. (2003). *Infant/Toddler Environmental Rating Scale-Revised edition.* New York: Teachers College Press.

Harms, T., Cryer, D., & Clifford, R. (2007). *Family Day Care Rating Scale-Revised edition.* New York: Teachers College Press.

Hart, B., & Risley, T. R. (1995). *Meaningful differences in the everyday experience of young American children.* Baltimore: Paul H. Brookes Publishing Co.

Hemmeter, M., Maxwell, K., Ault, M., & Schuster, J. (2001). *Assessment of practices in early elementary classrooms (APEEC).* New York: Teachers College Press.

Hoff-Ginsberg, E. (1991). Mother–child conversation in different social classes and communicative settings. *Child Development, 36,* 782–796.

Howes, C., & Smith, E.W. (1995). Relations among child care quality, teacher behavior, children's play activities, emotional security, and cognitive activity in child care. *Early Childhood Research Quarterly, 10,* 381–404.

Jackson, R., McCoy, A., Pistorino, C., Wilkinson, A., Burghardt, J., Clark, M., et al. (2007). *National evaluation of Early Reading First: Final report.* Washington, DC: Institute of Education Sciences.

Justice, L., Pence, K., Bowles, R., & Wiggins, A. (2006). An investigation of four hypotheses concerning the order by which 4-year-old children learn the alphabet letters. *Early Childhood Research Quarterly, 21,* 374–389.

Landry, S., Crawford, A., Gunnewig, S., & Swank, P. (2002). *Teacher Behavior Rating Scale.* Unpublished research instrument. Houston Center for Improving the Readiness of Children for Learning and Education, University of Texas Health Science Center.

Landry, S., Swank, P., Smith, K., Assel, M., & Gunnewig, S. (2006). Enhancing early literacy skills for pre-school children: Bringing a professional development model to scale. *Journal of Learning Disabilities, 39,* 306–324.

Lonigan, C. (2006). Conceptualizing phonological processing skills in pre-readers. In D. Dickinson & S.B. Neuman (Eds.), *Handbook of early literacy research* (Vol. II, pp. 77–89). New York: Guilford.

Maclean, M., Bryant, P., & Bradley, L. (1987). Rhymes, nursery rhymes, and reading in early childhood. *Merrill-Palmer Quarterly, 33,* 255–281.

McCardle, P., & Chhabra, V. (Eds.). (2004). *The voice of evidence in reading research.* Baltimore: Paul H. Brookes Publishing Co.

McCardle, P., Scarborough, H., & Catts, H. (2001). Predicting, explaining, and preventing children's reading difficulties. *Learning Disabilities Research & Practice, 16*(4), 230–239.

Metsala, J. (1999). Young children's phonological awareness and nonword repetition as a function of vocabulary development. *Journal of Educational Psychology, 91,* 3–19.

Miles, S., & Stipek, D. (2006). Contemporaneous and longitudinal associations between social behavior and literacy achievement in a sample of low-income elementary school children. *Child Development, 77,* 103–117.

Morrow, L.M. (1988). Young children's responses to one-to-one readings in school settings. *Reading Research Quarterly, 23,* 89–107.

Morrow, L.M. (1990). Preparing the classroom environment to promote literacy during play. *Early Childhood Research Quarterly, 5,* 537–554.

Morrow, L., & Weinstein, C. (1986). Encouraging voluntary reading: The impact of a literature program on children's use of library centers. *Reading Research Quarterly, 21,* 330–346.

National Reading Panel Report. (2000). *Teaching children to read.* Washington, DC:

National Institute of Child Health and Development.

Neuman, S.B. (1999). Books make a difference: A study of access to literacy. *Reading Research Quarterly, 34,* 286–312.

Neuman, S.B. (2001). The role of knowledge in early literacy. *Reading Research Quarterly, 36,* 468–475.

Neuman, S.B., & Celano, D. (2006). The knowledge gap: Implications of leveling the playing field for low-income and middle-income children. *Reading Research Quarterly, 41,* 176–201.

Neuman, S.B., Copple, C., & Bredekamp, S. (2000). *Learning to read and write: Developmentally appropriate practice.* Washington, DC: NAEYC.

Neuman, S.B., & Dickinson, D. (2001). *Handbook of early literacy research.* New York: Guilford.

Neuman, S.B., Dwyer, J., & Koh, S. (2007). *Child/Home Environmental Language and Literacy Observation (CHELLO).* Baltimore: Paul H. Brookes Publishing Co.

Neuman, S.B., Newman, E. & Dwyer, J. (2009, December). *The impact of vocabulary teaching on low-income preschoolers' word knowledge and conceptual development: Results from a randomized trial.* Paper presented at the National Reading Conference, Albuquerque, NM.

Neuman, S.B., & Roskos, K. (1990). The influence of literacy enriched play settings on preschoolers' engagement with written language. In S. McCormick & J. Zutell (Eds.), *Literacy theory and research: Analyses from multiple paradigms* (pp. 179–187). Chicago: National Reading Conference.

Neuman, S.B., & Roskos, K. (1992). Literacy objects as cultural tools: Effects on children's literacy behaviors in play. *Reading Research Quarterly, 27,* 202–225.

Neuman, S.B., & Roskos, K. (1993). Access to print for children of poverty: Differential effects of adult mediation and literacy-enriched play settings on environmental and functional print tasks. *American Educational Research Journal, 30,* 95–122.

Neuman, S.B., & Roskos, K. (1997). Literacy knowledge in practice: Contexts of participation for young writers and readers. *Reading Research Quarterly, 32,* 10–32.

NICHD Early Child Care Research Network. (2002). Early child care and children's development prior to school entry: Results from the

NICHD study of early child care, *American Educational Research Journal, 39,* 133–164.

NICHD Study of Early Child Care and Youth Development. Phase I Instrument Document. (2004). *Observation Ratings of the Caregiving Environment (ORCE): Behavior Scales, Qualitative Scales, and Observed Structural Variables for 6, 15, 24, & 36 Months.* Retrieved July 30, 2008, from the NICHD Study of Early Child Care and Youth Development website: http://secc.rti.org/instrument.cfm

Palincsar, A.S., Brown, A., & Campione, J. (1993). First-grade dialogues for knowledge acquisition and use. In E. Forman, N. Minick, & C. A. Stone (Eds.), *Contexts for learning* (pp. 43–57). New York: Oxford University Press.

Peisner-Feinberg, E., Burchinal, M., Clifford, R., Culkin, M., Howes, C., Kagan, S., et al. (2001). The relation of preschool child-care quality to children's cognitive and social development trajectories through second grade. *Child Development, 72,* 1534–1553.

Pianta, R.C., La Paro, K.M., & Hamre, B.K., (2008). *Classroom Assessment Scoring System™ (CLASS™).* Baltimore: Paul H. Brookes Publishing Co.

Pianta, R.C., La Paro, K.M., Payne, C., Cox, M., & Bradley, R. (2002). The relation of kindergarten classroom environment to teacher, family, and school characteristics and child outcomes. *The Elementary School Journal, 102,* 225–238.

Powell, D., Burchinal, M., File, N., & Kontos, S. (2008). An eco-behavioral analysis of children's engagement in urban public school preschool settings. *Early Childhood Research Quarterly, 23,* 108–123.

Preschool Curriculum Evaluation Research Consortium (2008). *Effects of preschool curriculum programs on school readiness (NCER 2008-2009).* Washington, DC: National Center for Education Research, Institute of Education Sciences, U.S. Department of Education.

Rolstad, K., Mahoney, K., & Glass, G. (2005). The big picture: A meta-analysis of program effectiveness research on English language learners. *Education Policy, 19,* 572–594.

Rosenthal, B.L. (1973). *An ecological study of free play in the nursery school.* Unpublished doctoral dissertation, Wayne State University, Detroit, Michigan.

Roskos, K., & Neuman, S.B. (2001). Environment and its influences for early literacy teaching and learning. In S.B. Neuman & D. Dickinson (Eds.), *Handbook of early literacy research* (Vol. I, pp. 281–294). New York: Guilford.

Roskos, K., & Vukelich, C. (2006). Early literacy policy and pedagogy. In D. Dickinson & S. B. Neuman (Eds.), *Handbook of early literacy research* (Vol. II, pp. 295–310). New York: Guilford.

Scarborough, H. (2001). Connecting early language and literacy to later reading (dis)abilities: Evidence, theory, and practice. In S.B. Neuman & D. Dickinson (Eds.), *Handbook of early literacy research* (Vol. I, pp. 97–110). New York: Guilford.

Slavin, R., & Cheung, A. (2005). A synthesis of research on language of reading instruction for English language learners. *Review of Educational Research, 75,* 247–281.

Smith, M.W., Brady, J.P., & Anastasopoulos, L. (2008). *Early Language and Literacy Classroom Observation ELLCO Pre-K Tool.* Baltimore: Paul H. Brookes Publishing Co.

Smith, M.W., & Dickinson, D.D., (with Sangeorge, A., & Anastasopoulos, L.). (2002). *Early Language and Literacy Classroom Observation* (ELLCO) Toolkit, (Research ed.) Baltimore: Paul H. Brookes Publishing Co.

Snow, C., Baines, W., Chandler, J., Goodman, I., & Hemphill, L. (1991). *Unfulfilled expectations: Home and school influences on literacy.* Cambridge, MA: Harvard University Press.

Snow, C., Burns, M.S., & Griffin, P. (1998). *Preventing reading difficulties in young children.* Washington, DC: National Academies Press.

Stein, N., & Glenn, C. (1979). An analysis of story comprehension in elementary school children. In R.O. Freedle (Ed.), *Advances in discourse processing* (Vol. 2, pp. 53–120). Norwood, NJ: Ablex.

Tharp, R., & Gallimore, R. (1988). *Rousing minds to life.* New York: Cambridge University Press.

Tunmer, W.E., Herriman, M.L., & Nesdale, A. (1988). Metalinguistic abilities and beginning reading. *Reading Research Quarterly, 23,* 134–158.

U.S. Department of Education. (2005). *Biennial evaluation report to Congress on the implementation of the State Formula Grant Program, 2002-2004: English Language Acquisition, Language Enhancement and*

Academic Achievement Act (ESEA, Title III, Part A). Washington, DC: U.S. Department of Education.

Vaughn, S., Cirino, P., Linan-Thompson, S., Mathes, P., Carlson, C., Hagan, E., et al. (2006). Effects of a Spanish intervention and an English intervention for English language learners at risk for reading failure. *American Education Research Journal, 43,* 449–487.

Vukelich, C. (1994). Effects of play interventions on young children's reading of environmental print. *Early Childhood Research Quarterly, 9,* 153–170.

Vygotsky, L.S. (1978). *Mind in society: The development of higher psychological processes* (M. Cole, V. John-Steiner, S. Scribner, & E. Souberman, Trans.). Cambridge, MA: Harvard University Press.

Whitehurst, G., Arnold, D., Epstein, J., Angell, A., Smith, M., & Fischel, J. (1994). A picture book reading intervention in day care and home for children from low-income families. *Developmental Psychology, 30,* 679–689.

Whitehurst, G.J., Epstein, J., Angell, A., Payne, A., Crone, D., & Fischel, J. (1994). Outcomes of an emergent literacy intervention in Head Start. *Journal of Educational Psychology, 86,* 542–555.

Whitehurst, G., & Lonigan, C. (1998). Child development and emergent literacy. *Child Development, 69,* 848–872.

CHAPTER 5

Measuring the Quality of Early Childhood Math and Science Curricula and Teaching

Kimberly Brenneman, Kimberly Boller, Sally Atkins-Burnett,
Deborah Stipek, Nicole D. Forry, Barbrina B. Ertle, Lucia French,
Herbert P. Ginsburg, Ellen Frede, and Thomas Schultz

We begin this chapter by giving away the ending. Our conclusion, after we have reviewed child care and instructional quality measures[1] in mathematics, science, and general cognition, is that there are few such tools that have been psychometrically validated and are available for wide use. This situation could be seen as a reflection of the field itself, as early mathematics and science learning have only recently become a focus of educators and policy makers as critical, foundational domains for school readiness. Mathematics and science are also viewed as rich content for the development of important general cognitive skills such as memory, problem solving, representation, logical thinking, categorization, reasoning, and so forth. Because *cognition* is so broad a term, both supporting and being supported by learning in specific content areas and by language development, defining it in a way that can be meaningfully addressed by a quality measure is difficult. In fact, our review of measures that exist or are under development found that general cognition has not been a focus; therefore, our discussion addresses mainly classroom observation measures of instructional quality and teacher pedagogical and content knowledge for mathematics and science learning—both in terms of what exists and what we believe should exist.

In this section, we describe why we need to measure quality of instruction for early mathematics and science and what aspects of quality should be assessed. The next section discusses the measures currently available and their characteristics. Finally, we provide recommendations for immediate and longer term follow-up to improve the field's options for measuring various aspects of instructional quality that influence children's learning outcomes in mathematics and science.

Until recently, the predominant philosophy in the field of early childhood mathematics education stressed the "developmentally appropriate practice" of facilitating children's learning by providing rich learning environments and then capitalizing on teachable moments that arise during play. Early childhood educators generally rejected the idea that direct instruction could be appropriate as a key component of either math or science education (Ertle et al., 2008). However, fundamental approaches to instruction in both math and science are now changing, partly as the result of new research.

In recent years, both the American Association for the Advancement of Science (1998) and the National Research Council (NRC, 2005) have convened meetings and issued reports that focus on math and science education in early childhood. The NRC has convened committees to study and report on K–8 science (Duschl, Schweingruber, & Shouse, 2006) and mathematics (Cross, Woods, & Schweingruber, 2009) learning in early childhood. A growing body of research shows that preschool children are capable of learning more mathematics and science than has been previously thought or expected. (Some of this research is reported in a special issue of the *Early Childhood Research Quarterly*: Golbeck & Ginsburg, 2004; see also Bowman, Donovan, & Burns, 2001; Brenneman, Stevenson-Boyd, & Frede, 2009; Ginsburg, Cannon, Eisenband, & Pappas, 2006).

With respect to mathematics, young children have a spontaneous interest in many different mathematical ideas—not just the idea of number. For example, this can be seen in block-area play in which young children spend a good deal of time exploring concepts of measurement, shapes, symmetry creation, and patterns (Seo & Ginsburg, 2004). Also, young children are more competent in key aspects of early mathematics than many researchers formerly believed. From an early age, they seem to understand the basic ideas of addition and subtraction (Brush, 1978), ratios (Hunting, 1999), and spatial relations (Clements, 1999). They can spontaneously develop various methods of calculation (Groen & Resnick, 1977). Furthermore, young children are capable of learning some rather complex mathematics when they are explicitly taught (Greenes, 1999).

With respect to science, preschoolers can participate in discourse involving descriptions, predictions, and explanations (e.g., Cassata-Widera, Kato-Jones, Duckles, Conezio, & French, 2008; Peterson & French, 2008). They are motivated to clarify ambiguous evidence (Schulz & Bonawitz, 2007), and they persist in asking questions until they receive the information they are seeking (Chouinard, 2007). These dispositions support later, more sophisticated scientific reasoning. Such thinking skills are supported, and they grow, when children participate in science experiences in preschool. Preschoolers also possess conceptual competence in areas such as causality, growth, and the animate–inanimate distinction that relates to scientific understandings (Bowman et al., 2001; Duschl et al., 2006; Gelman, Brenneman, Macdonald, & Román, 2009).

Although research has shown that young children have considerable competence in mathematics and science, it has also revealed limitations. For example, although children are able to develop some complex mathematical ideas and strategies (e.g., in addition), they are not always accurate, nor are they always efficient (Baroody & Dowker, 2003). Also, many children lack sufficient language with which to express their mathematical and scientific understandings (Duschl et al., 2006; Jordan, Huttenlocher, & Levine, 1994). Because these limitations can conceal children's competencies in math and science, teachers may underestimate students' abilities and, consequently, might not provide them with challenging instruction. This underestimation could be especially dangerous for low-income children, whose cognitive and mathematics achievement is already lower than that of middle-income children's prior to and at the time of kindergarten entry (Administration for Children and Families, 2006; Cross et al., 2009; Denton & West, 2002; Halle et al., 2009; Tarullo, West, Aikens, & Hulsey, 2008; U.S. Department of Health and Human Services, Administration for Children and Families,

2005). To narrow this gap, it is critical that we accurately assess understandings and involve children in high-quality early mathematics and science experiences.

Duncan et al. (2007) showed that early mathematics achievement is a powerful predictor of later school success in mathematics and even in literacy. Research has also shown that early intervention programs in schools and with parents can be effective in reducing SES-based achievement disparities in mathematics (e.g., Dowker, 2001; Reynolds, 1995; Starkey & Klein, 2000). One feature of effective preschool classrooms seems to be that they provide learning experiences in which mathematics is the main focus, not supplementary to other learning goals (Cross et al., 2009). In general, the consensus is that providing educational supports as early as possible could potentially reduce or prevent later mathematical difficulties and the need for remediation (Cross et al., 2009; Bowman et al., 2001).

Research findings about early competence disparities among children from different backgrounds and about the long-term impacts of early achievement have led professional organizations to recommend mathematics instruction during the early childhood years. The National Association for the Education of Young Children (NAEYC) and the National Council of Teachers of Mathematics (NCTM) have together recommended the use of organized curricula for teaching mathematics to young children (NAEYC and NCTM, 2002), and NCTM has included early childhood standards in its set of mathematics standards (NCTM, 2006). The consensus of NAEYC and NCTM is that young children are ready for mathematics and need more than free play to learn it. There currently is general agreement among early mathematics experts that standards should be research based and should focus on the big ideas of mathematics, including number and operations, geometry and spatial relations, and algebraic thinking and problem solving (Brenneman et al., 2009; Clements, Sarama, & diBiase, 2004; NAEYC and NCTM, 2002; NCTM, 2006). Individual states also publish learning standards for early mathematics. According to a 2005 analysis, most of these lists include number and operations and geometry and spatial relations, but the specific learning goals in these areas vary considerably (Neuman & Roskos, 2005). The recent early math report from the NRC (Cross et al., 2009) recommends that mathematics experiences in early childhood focus on number (whole number, operations, and numerical relations) and geometry, spatial relations, and measurement; and that instruction should be based on research that illuminates learning pathways in these areas of mathematics. Along with NCTM, NAEYC, NRC, and state governments, many public officials and other professional organizations are demanding new efforts to provide early childhood education, including mathematics and science education, to young children, especially those from low SES backgrounds (Ginsburg, Lee, & Stevenson-Boyd, 2008; National Science Board, 2009).

Together, the NAEYC–NCTM position statement and the NCTM preschool standards, based on the research literature, have laid the groundwork for the design of early mathematics curricula, including *Number Worlds* (Griffin, 2000), *Pre-K Mathematics Curriculum* (Klein & Starkey, 2002; Klein, Starkey, & Wakeley, 2004), *Big Math for Little Kids* (Ginsburg, Greenes, & Balfanz, 2003), *Building Blocks* (Clements & Sarama, 2004a), and a Head Start curriculum (Sophian, 2004). The first round of evaluations has indicated that many of these curricula are effective in improving child outcomes, at least as shown by broad and crude measures of achievement (Ginsburg, Lewis, & Clements, in press).

Science standards have been established and published by both the American Association for the Advancement of Science (1993) and the NRC (1996). Congruent with the lesser emphasis on science than on mathematics instruction in the early childhood years, neither of these sets of standards addresses science learning during the preschool years, beginning instead at the level of kindergarten to Grade 2. The Head Start Child Outcomes Framework does include science and math among its eight developmental domains, and the 2007 Head Start reauthorization also states that teachers should include classroom learning experiences that strengthen children's science, mathematics, and approaches to learning because these are critical for school readiness. Most states have established standards or learning expectations for science during the preschool years. Greenfield and colleagues (2009) reviewed the content of state learning standards and 10 preschool curricula, including the few that focused on science. They reported that the topic areas covered by curricula and standards span life sciences, earth/space sciences, and physical/energy sciences, and that eight common process skills emerged: observing, describing, comparing, questioning, predicting, experimenting, reflecting, and cooperating.

In brief, standards and expectations have changed in recent years. Clearly, there is a movement toward implementing early mathematics education and, to a lesser extent, science education. Several mathematics and science curricula have already been developed, and some have been shown to be effective, at least in terms of broad measures of achievement. The next step is to examine these programs in more detail and depth. To increase access to early childhood instruction in mathematics and science, and to be sure that we are making the most of early educational opportunities, we need to define quality in curriculum, teaching, and learning and to develop methods for measuring quality in these three areas. Consistent with the various standards for math and science described earlier, learning goals for early mathematics and science include providing opportunities for engaging deeply with a range of mathematics and science concepts and skills, not just rote counting or learning facts about animals. Considerations of quality should drive our efforts in curriculum development and teaching, and the effectiveness of curricula and practice should be evaluated in terms of student learning. Like measures of instructional quality in math and science, assessments of student learning in these domains are just now being developed. (For a brief review, see the next section and Brenneman et al., 2009.) Appropriate instruments will be required if we are to be certain that the demands being placed on the educational community are met and that young children receive the education they need.

Measuring Quality

What is quality instruction in early mathematics and science? What do we need to measure to effectively meet the demands for better mathematics and science education? Within the domains of math and science, we have not defined quality well as a construct. The field needs to consider what quality is and how to measure it. The next section focuses on factors that influence quality of instruction, such as curriculum and pedagogical content knowledge, and on ways that one could measure various aspects of quality.

High-quality curricula are aligned with developmental trajectories (Clements & Sarama, 2004b; Cross et al., 2009; Duschl et al., 2006). The topics being taught, the order in which they are taught, the ways in which they are presented, and the kinds of teaching recommended should reflect what we know about the development of young children's mathematics and science understandings. Clements and Sarama

(Clements, 2007; Sarama & Clements, 2008) provided a detailed framework that can be used to develop research-based curricula and to evaluate existing curricula with regard to the extent to which they align with children's typical developmental pathways in these two academic domains. Another strategy for judging the quality of a curriculum is to assess how consonant it is with the recommendations outlined by organizations such as the NCTM, the NAEYC, and the NRC. For example, does the curriculum include specific ways for children to engage in reasoning about the big ideas of mathematics, or does it support only counting skills? Alternatively, does the curriculum inappropriately focus on drilling on number facts?

Even good curricula and activities can be taught badly. Efforts to improve math and science understanding in young children, therefore, must consider the quality of instruction. As discussed in the next section, few extant classroom observation instruments examine even the mere presence of mathematics and science teaching, and even fewer assess quality. Many of the instruments currently in use in classrooms evaluate materials, the social environment, and general instructional quality, but most do not include multiple items that assess instruction in mathematics or science (see Table 5.1). A few existing classroom quality measures, however, address these specific domains, as outlined in Table 5.2, and others are under development. In addition, some available classroom quality measures assess instruction in general, without specifying the subject (e.g., CLASS™; Pianto, La Paro, & Hamre, 2008), and measures in other areas, such as literacy, could be used to guide the development of items that assess math or science teaching. Furthermore, it will be useful to measure factors known to influence children's learning in general, such as positive relationships between staff and children, use of language, engagement of children, behavior management, and so forth. These may contribute to the quality of mathematics teaching, just as they do to the quality of teaching in other subject areas. Finally, as we address these content domains, it is important that we also pay attention to children's social and emotional development and dispositions toward learning.

Any instrument that purports to assess specifically the quality of instruction in mathematics or science will have to be aligned with the latest recommendations for teaching in these areas; thus, it will have to measure supports for learning across multiple subareas of mathematics and science (i.e., more than just counting and number) and for instructional strategies that encourage children to problem solve and reason about mathematical and scientific concepts. It should also assess important pedagogical issues, such as teachers' effective use of manipulatives, meaningful introduction of symbols, and clear communication of mathematical and scientific ideas.

Finally, we can hypothesize what constitutes quality and how to measure it, but the real proof is in children's learning outcomes. Quality teaching and quality curricula should yield student learning. Investigating this proposition in a meaningful and useful way requires sound child outcome measures. Few extant measures of students' mathematical skills assess learning beyond numeracy (Cross et al., 2009), and some that include other skills pay only cursory attention to them. For example, the Early Childhood Longitudinal Study—Kindergarten mathematics assessment (ECLS-K) (U.S. Department of Education, National Center for Education Statistics, 2002; West, Denton, & Germino-Hausken, 2000) examines children's understanding of patterns, shapes, and measurement—in addition to their assessment of number—but does so only minimally. There are current efforts, though, to develop measures that examine children's understanding of mathematics more broadly and deeply (e.g., Ginsburg,

Table 5.1. Comprehensive child care environment quality measures with mathematics, science, or general cognition content for use in settings that serve children from 3 to 5 years old

Measure name and source	Math-specific constructs assessed	Science-specific constructs assessed	General cognition constructs assessed	Age range and setting	Observation period	Training requirements
Assessment Profile for Early Childhood Programs (APECP; includes versions for Toddler, Preschool, and School Age Center-Based Care)[a,b,c,d]; Assessment Profile for Family Child Care Homes (APFCCH)	APECP—Math/numeracy materials available (1 item) and accessible (1 item)	APECP—Science materials available (1 item) and accessible (1 item); nutrition/health materials available (1 item) and accessible (1 item)	APECP and APFCCH—Memory of specific information (1 item); APECP—problem solving, reasoning and logical relationships; opportunities to use concrete materials to experience abstract concepts (1 item); teachers integrate learning abstract concepts by allowing children to explore (1 item)	Toddler–2nd grade; center-based classrooms, family child care providers	Center-based programs: 1 day per 2-3 classrooms; Family child care homes: approximately 4-6 hours	2-3 days to achieve preestablished interrater reliability requirement
Caregiver Observation Form and Scale (COFAS)[e]	None	Cooking experiences that reinforce nutritional concepts (1 item)	Show impatience with questions (1 item), use terms above child's reasoning level (1 item), deal in abstract concepts without concrete examples (1 item), show intolerance for mistakes (1 item)	0-12 years; center-based classrooms	1 day per approximately 60 children	1-2 days classroom training; 3-4 days on-site interrater reliability assessment
Child Care Assessment Tool for Relatives (CCAT-R)[f]	None	Encourages experimentation with object (1 item)	Encourages concept learning (1 item)	0-6 years; home-based care by relatives	2-2½ hours with 30-minute interview	2-day training through The Institute for a Child Care Continuum; observers must have training in early childhood, parent education, or family support
Child Observation in Preschool (COP)[g]	Child is working with mathematics materials, or teacher is focused on a mathematics topic (1 item); blocks (1 item); child's activity is math-related (1 item)	Child is working with science materials, or teacher is focused on a science topic (1 item); child's activity is science-related (1 item)	None	3-5 years; center-based classrooms	No information available	No information available

Measure	Mathematics	Science	Ages; settings	Observation length	Training requirements
Classroom Assessment Scoring System™ (CLASS, includes versions for preschool and K-3)[h,i]	None	Analysis and reasoning, creating, integration, and connections to the real world (1 item)	Pre-K through 3rd grade; center-based and school classrooms	Four 20-minute intervals	2-day training; trainings held at the University of Virginia and the University of North Carolina at Greensboro, and on-site training available
Early Childhood Classroom Observation Measure (ECCOM)[j]	Uses mathematical processes to solve problems (1 item), encourages math conversations (1 item), uses authentic math activities (1 item), assesses children's understanding in a range of ways (1 item), uses assessment for individualization (1 item)	Conceptual understanding (1 item), problem solving (1 item), the learner role (1 item), learning facts or procedures (1 item), supports talking about cognitive skills or concepts (1 item)	4–7 years; center-based and school classrooms	3-hour period that includes math and literacy instruction	2-day training followed by successful completion of reliability test (demonstrates 80% reliability)
Early Childhood Environment Rating Scale-Revised Edition (ECERS-R)[k]	Math/number activities (1 item), block activities promoting early math (geometry) reasoning (1 item); each item includes a number of indicators observers look for as part of the rating	Nature/science activities (1 item), sand/water activities promoting scientific exploration (1 item); each item includes a number of indicators observers look for as part of the rating	2–5 years; center-based classrooms	At least 2–3 hours each of 20–30 teacher interviews	Authors offer training sequence that includes video training and 3–4 days of in-field practice and reliability testing
Emergent Academic Snapshot (EAS)[m]	Child engagement in math activities, worksheets, shapes, or measuring (1 item)	Child engagement with science materials, doing exploration (1 item)	10 months to 8 years; home-based, center-based, and school classrooms	1–2 hours	Bachelor's degree and experience working with children; training and certification by authors
Family Child Care Environment Rating Scale-Revised (FCCERS-R)[n]	Math/number activities (1 items), block activities related to early math (geometry) reasoning (1 item); each item includes a number of indicators observers look for as part of the rating	Nature/science activities (1 item), sand and water activities related to scientific exploration (1 item); each item includes a number of indicators observers look for as part of the rating	Birth through elementary school; home-based child care	3 hours of observation followed by 20–30 minutes for provider interview	Authors offer training sequence that includes video training and 3–4 days of in-field practice and reliability testing

(continued)

Table 5.1. *(continued)*

Measure name and source	Math-specific constructs assessed	Science-specific constructs assessed	General cognition constructs assessed	Age range and setting	Observation period	Training requirements
Observational Record of the Caregiving Environment (ORCE)[o]	None	None	6- and 54-month scales: cognitive development stimulation	6, 15, 24, 36, and 54 months; any nonmaternal child care setting	2–4 observation cycles of 44 minutes each	2 days formal ORCE training followed by administration and coding practice; must obtain 90% agreement to be certified, and should be reexamined every 4 months
Preschool Classroom Implementation Rating Scale (PCIRS)[p]	Staff help children compare number and amount in a functional way (1 item); extend children's thinking about classification, seriation, time, and space (1 item)	None	Quality in a cognitive-development or constructionist classroom (52 items)	3–6 years; center-based classrooms using the HighScope curriculum; generic cognitive developmental version is also available	1 day per classroom, multiple times throughout the year	Initial 1-day training with 3 days of reliability observation at 80% agreement
Preschool Classroom Inventory: Enhancing Children's Cognitive Development (abridged version of PCIRS, shown previously)[q]	Same as PCIRS; also, staff help children compare shape, size, and color in a functional way (1 item)	None	Quality in a cognitive-development or constructionist classroom (11 items total)	3–6 years; center-based classrooms	3 hours	Same as PCIRS
Quality of Early Childhood Care Settings: Caregiver Rating Scale (QUEST)[r]	Teaches early math concepts (1 item), encourages children to use math in everyday contexts (1 item), provides opportunities and materials for building (1 item)	Gives children opportunities to explore the natural environment (1 item), encourages children to use math in everyday contexts (1 item)	Helps children plan their own activities (1 item)	0–5 years; variety of care settings ranging from informal home-based care to center-based classrooms	2.5–3.0 hours	2½ day training

Measure					
Ramey & Ramey Observation of Learning Essentials (ROLE)[s]	Math/science/reasoning activities (1 item)	Math/science/reasoning activities (1 item)	Celebrate development-specific new skills/academic advancements in the cognitive/intellectual/academic domain (1 item)	3–4 years; center-based classrooms	2–3 hours	About 1–2 weeks
School-Age Care Environment Rating Scale (SACERS)[t]	Math/reasoning activities (1 item), block activities (1 item); each item includes a number of indicators observers look for as part of the rating	Science/nature activities (1 item); each item includes a number of indicators observers look for as part of the rating	Math/reasoning activities (1 item); each item includes a number of indicators observers look for as part of the rating	5–12 years; center-based classrooms	2.5 hours	Authors offer training sequence that includes video training and 3–4 days of in-field practice and reliability testing

Note: Information on measures has been abstracted from published or online documents/presentations or provided by the author/publisher.

[a]Abbott-Shim, M., & Sibley, A. (1987). *Assessment profile for early childhood programs (APECP).* Atlanta, Georgia: Quality Assist Inc.

[b]Abbott-Shim, M., Lambert, R., & McCarty, F. (2000). Structural model of Head Start classroom quality. *Early Childhood Research Quarterly, 15*(1), 115–134.

[c]Wilkes, D. (1989). *Administration, classroom program, sponsorship: Are these indices of quality care in day care centers?* Doctoral dissertation. Dissertation Abstracts International 50, AAI8922912. Atlanta: Georgia State University.

[d]Abbott-Shim, M. (1991). *Quality care: A global assessment.* Unpublished manuscript. Atlanta: Georgia State University.

[e]Fiene, R. (1984). *Child Development Program Evaluation Scale and COFAS.* Washington, DC: Children's Services Monitoring Consortium.

[f]Porter, T., Rice, R., & Rivera, E. (2006). *Assessing quality in family, friend, and neighbor care: The Child Care Assessment Tool for Relatives (CCAT-R).* New York: Institute for a Child Care Continuum.

[g]Farran, D.C., Kang, S., & Plummer, C. *Child observation in preschool (CCOP).* Culp, A.M., & Farran, D.C. (1989). *Manual for observation of play in preschools.* Unpublished manuscripts. Both are available from D.C. Farran, Peabody College, Vanderbilt University, Nashville, TN 37212.

[h]Hamre, B.K., Mashburn, A.J., Pianta, R.C., Lacasle-Crouch, J., & La Paro, K.M. (2006). *Classroom Assessment Scoring System technical appendix.* Charlottesville, VA: University of Virginia.

[i]Pianta, R.C., La Paro, K.M., & Hamre, B.K. (2008). *Classroom Assessment Scoring System™ (CLASS).* Baltimore: Paul H. Brookes Publishing Co.

[j]Stipek, D., & Byler, P. (2004). The Early Childhood Classroom Observation Measure (ECCOM). *Early Childhood Research Quarterly, 19,* 375–397.

[k]Harms, T., Clifford, R.M., & Cryer, D. (2005). *Early Childhood Environment Rating Scale-Revised Edition (ECERS-R).* New York: Teachers College Press.

[l]Ritchie, S., Howes, C., Kraft-Sayre, M., & Weiser, B. (2001). *Emergent Academic Snapshot Scale (EAS).* Unpublished instrument. Los Angeles: UCLA.

[m]Howes, C., Burchinal, M., Pianta, R.C., Bryant, D., Early, D., Clifford, R., & Barbarin, O. (2008). Ready to learn? Children's pre-academic achievement in pre-kindergarten. *Early Childhood Research Quarterly, 23*(1), 27–50.

[n]Harms, T., Cryer, D., & Clifford, R.M. (2007). *Family Child Care Environment Rating Scale-Revised Edition (FCCERS-R).* New York: Teachers College Press.

[o]NICHD Study of Early Child Care and Youth Development Phase I Instrument Document. Observational Record of the Caregiving Environment (ORCE): Behavior Scales, Qualitative Scales, and Observed Structural Variables for 6, 15, 24, & 36 months. Retrieved from http://secc.rti.org/instdoc.doc

[p]Frede, E.C., & Miller, A. (1998). *The Revised Preschool Classroom Implementation Rating Scale (PCIRS) and Manual.* New Brunswick, NJ: National Institute for Early Education Research (NIEER).

[q]Frede, E. (2000). *The Preschool Classroom Inventory.* New Brunswick, NJ: National Institute for Early Education Research (NIEER).

[r]Goodson, B.D., Layzer, J.I., & Layzer, C.J. (2005). *Quality of Early Childhood Care Settings: Caregiver Rating Scale (QUEST).* Cambridge, MA: Abt Associates Inc.

[s]Ramey, S.L., & Ramey, C.T. (2002). *The Ramey Observation of Learning Essentials (ROLE).* Washington, DC: Georgetown University Center for Health and Education.

[t]Harms, T., Jacobs, E., & Romano White, D. (1996). *School-age Care Environment Rating Scale (SACERS).* New York: Teachers College Press.

Table 5.2. Domain-specific environmental quality measures for mathematics or mathematics and science for use in settings that serve children from 3 to 5 years old

Measure name and source	Mathematics-specific subscales, number of items per subscale, and illustrative items	Science-specific subscales, number of items per subscale, and illustrative items	Setting and age range	Observation period	Reliability information	Validity information	Training requirements
Classroom Observation of Early Mathematics—Environment and Teaching (COEMET)[a][b]	Sections: 1) Classroom Culture (9 items; e.g., teacher used teachable moments to develop math ideas; teacher appeared to be knowledgeable and confident about mathematics); 2) Specific math activities (19 items; e.g., the mathematical content of the activity was appropriate for the developmental levels of the students; teacher encouraged mathematical reflection)	Not applicable	Center-based pre-K classrooms	No less than a half day	Internal consistency = .96 (Rasch model)[a] Interrater = .88[a]	Predictive validity: .50 correlation with children's gain scores on the Early Maths Assessment	Self-study of the manual; practice observations until satisfactory reliability is achieved
Early Childhood Environment Rating Scale-Extension (ECERS-E) *Note:* Includes literacy and diversity subscales as well	Counting and application of counting (1 item); reading and writing sample numbers (1 item); mathematical activities—shape and space *or* sorting, matching, and comparing (observer chooses 1 item to score)	Natural materials (1 item); areas featuring science/science resources (1 item); science activities—nonliving science processes, living processes and the world around us, *or* science processes and food preparation (observer chooses 1 item to score)	Center-based classrooms for children 3–5 years old	Half day with 15 minutes to speak with staff and children and answer any additional questions	Interrater agreement between .88 and .98; Kappas between .83 and .97[c,d,e]	Concurrent validity: correlation with ECERS-R = .78[c] Predictive validity: math subscale reliably associated with nonverbal reasoning measures; average total (includes literacy and diversity subscales) shows positive associations with prereading scores, early number concepts, and nonverbal reasoning[d,e]	Half-day orientation and 2 guided observations

Early Mathematics Classroom Observation (EMCO)[f] and Numeracy Environment Checklist (NEC)[g]	EMCO: Dimensions of support for mathematical development: 1) time spent in math activities, 1 item on child time and 1 on teacher time; 2) type of mathematics activity, 1 item on focal activities and 1 item on embedded; 3) mathematics content, 1 item with 7 possible responses including number, arithmetic, space/geometry. Other items on activity description (full or small group), teacher presence and participation, child participation, number of children	Not applicable	Center-based classrooms for children 3–6 years old	Half-day	Not reported[f]	Minutes spent in focal math activities associated with children's scores on the Child Math Assessment[f]	Not specified[f]
Preschool Classroom Mathematics Inventory (PCMI)[h]	Subscales: 1) Materials (4 items; e.g., materials for classifying and seriating); 2) Numeracy and Other Mathematical Concepts—teacher practices (7 items; e.g., teachers encourage counting for a purpose)	Not applicable	Center-based classrooms for children 3–5 years old	3 hours minimum	Internal consistency = 0.86[i] Interrater = 0.87[i]	Predictive validity demonstrated with Woodcock Johnson, Revised, Applied Problems Subscale[j]	1-day formal training followed by 3 consecutive observations with interrater reliability of 70% exact agreement with an expert observer
Preschool Rating Instrument for Science and Mathematics (PRISM)[k]	Subscales: 1) Materials (4 items; e.g., materials for measuring and comparing amount, materials for exploring geometry and spatial positions/relationships) 2) Staff Interactions (7 items; e.g., supports for thinking about numerical operations and supports for classifying, seriating, patterning)	Subscales: 1) Materials (2 items; e.g., materials for biological and nonbiological science exploration), 2) Staff Interactions (3 items; e.g., modeling and encouraging recording of science information; supports for observing and predicting)	Center-based classrooms for children 3–5 years old	3 hours minimum	Internal consistency = 0.84[l]	Concurrent validity with ECERS-R = 0.55[l]	1-day formal training followed by 3 consecutive observations with interrater reliability of 70% exact agreement with an expert observer

(continued)

Table 5.2. (continued)

Note: Information on measures is abstracted from published or online documents/presentations or is provided by the author/publisher.

[a]Clements, D.H., & Sarama, J. (2008). Experimental evaluation of the effects of a research-based preschool mathematics curriculum. *American Educational Research Journal, 45*(2), 44–94.

[b]Sarama, J., Clements, D., Starkey, P., Klein, A., & Wakeley, A. (2008). Scaling up the implementation of a pre-kindergarten mathematics curriculum: Teaching for understanding with trajectories and technologies. *Journal of Research on Educational Effectiveness, 1,* 89–119.

[c]Sylva, K., Siraj-Blatchford, I., & Taggart, B. (2006). *Assessing quality in the early years: Early Childhood Environment Rating Scale-Extension (ECERS-E).* Stoke-on-Trent, UK: Trentham Books.

[d]Sammons, P., Sylva, K., Melhuish, E., Siraj-Blatchford, I., Taggart, B., & Elliot, K. (2002). Measuring the impact of pre-school on children's cognitive progress over the pre-school period. Technical Paper 8a London: Institute of Education.

[e]Sylva, K., Siraj-Blatchford, I., Melhuish, E., Sammons, P., Taggart, B., Evans, E., Dobson, A., Jeavons, M., Lewis, K., Morahan, M., & Sadler, S. (1999). Characteristics of the centres in the EPPE sample: Observational profiles. Technical Paper 6. London: Institute of Education.

[f]Starkey, P., & Klein, A. (2001). Early Mathematics Classroom Observation (EMCO). Berkeley, CA: University of California.

[g]Starkey, P., & Klein, A. (2001). Numeracy Environment Checklist (NEC). Berkeley, CA: University of California.

[h]Frede, E., Weber, M., Hornbeck, A., Stevenson-Boyd, J., & Colón, A. (2005). *Preschool Classroom Mathematic Inventory (PCMI).* New Brunswick, NJ: National Institute for Early Education Research.

[i]Frede, E., Jung, K., Barnett, W.S., Lamy, C.E., Figueras, A. (2007). *The Abbott Preschool Program Longitudinal Effects Study (APPLES).* Interim report. New Brunswick, NJ: National Institute for Early Education Research.

[j]Frede, E., Lamy, C.E., & Boyd, J.S. (2005). *Not just calendars and counting blocks: Using the NAEYC/NCTM joint position statement "Early Childhood Mathematics: Promoting Good Beginnings" as a basis for measuring classroom teaching practices and their relationship to child outcome.* Paper presented at the annual National Association for the Education of Young Children conference, Washington, DC.

[k]Stevenson-Boyd, J.S., Brenneman, K., Frede, E. & Weber, M. (2009). *Preschool Rating Instrument for Science and Mathematics (PRISM).* New Brunswick, NJ: National Institute for Early Education Research.

[l]Jung, K. (2010). Unpublished analyses. New Brunswick, NJ: National Institute for Early Education Research.

2009; Klein, Starkey, & Wakeley's Child Math Assessment, 2000; Clements, Sarama, & Liu's Research-Based Early Maths Assessment, 2008). Preschool science is the focus of a direct assessment, based on item response theory (IRT), developed by Greenfield, Dominguez, Fuccillo, Maier, and Greenberg (2008).

Strengths and Weaknesses of Existing Classroom Observation Measures

Available measures of the quality of instruction in preschool and the elementary grades examine content, materials, activity setting, teacher and instructional interactions, and teachers' pedagogical content knowledge. Methods of data collection include observations by external raters, logs, teacher reports, teacher tests, and examination of instructional materials. Whereas most early childhood observation tools use rubrics, other observation tools include checklists, ratings, or time samples (measuring frequency or duration of instructional practices or focus on specific content). Most measures use summary scores or mean scores that give every item and/or aspect equal weighting, whereas some newer measures such as the Classroom Observation of Early Mathematics Environment and Teaching (COEMET, Sarama & Clements 2007) and measures of pedagogical content knowledge use IRT to support measures development.

In this section we present information about the existing early childhood program quality measures gleaned from: 1) reviewing measures summaries (Halle & Vick 2007; Kilday & Kinzie, 2009; Kisker et al., 2004) and available measures when possible; 2) identifying new measures presented at the 2008 National Head Start Research Conference and the 2009 Biennial Meeting of the Society for Research in Child Development; and 3) polling colleagues in the field for information about measures that are being developed. Here, we focus on observational measures of classroom quality, but we acknowledge that important and innovative work is being done to assess teacher pedagogical and content knowledge and children's learning opportunities through other types of data collection methods. Our review yielded measures for math and science alone and together and one elementary school measure, expected to be adapted for early childhood settings, which identifies supports for memory strategies (Ornstein, Grammer, & Coffman, 2009). These tools were in various stages of development when this chapter was written. In general, the measures that have been psychometrically evaluated, are widely available, or have been used in published studies are presented in Tables 5.1 and 5.2, and measures that are earlier in the development process are mentioned in the text. Table 5.1 summarizes the characteristics of the many general measures that include at least one item focused on mathematics, science, or general cognition. Table 5.2 presents information about content-specific measures for mathematics or both mathematics and science and provides reliability and validity data.

A number of research teams have made progress in measuring the math or science environment in the context of developing a fidelity-of-implementation rating tool for a given curriculum. On the one hand, these measures are important first steps in the development of the field because they require deep thinking about the logic of an intervention and about what is expected to change in the setting to ultimately affect children's outcomes. On the other hand, the measures are often so closely aligned with the intervention that they cannot be generalized to other curricula and may miss measuring instruction that promotes student learning. We include here only those measures that could be used in any classroom and are not limited to assessing implementation of a specific curriculum.

Comprehensive Measures of Early Childhood Program Quality that Include Items/Scales Addressing Some Aspect of Mathematics, Science, or Cognition

Most of the 15 measures included in Table 5.1 were designed to assess a broad range of environmental or instructional factors that are expected to influence children's learning. To be included in the table, a measure had to have at least one item in one of the three domains (mathematics, science, or cognition). For a given measure, the number of items focused on mathematics, science, or cognition ranges from 0 to 52. Although one measure has 52 items focused on cognition and its short form has 11 items (the Preschool Classroom Implementation Rating Scale, PCIRS), most of the measures have only one or two domain-specific items for math, science, or cognition. Eleven of the measures include at least one item in the domains of mathematics or cognition, and 10 include at least one science item. Four of the measures have at least one item in all three domains.

A few characteristics of these measures limit their utility for documenting quality of instruction for children's development in mathematics, science, and cognition. First, they generally were not designed for documentation purposes, and with only a few items assessing the three domains, coverage of key supports for children's learning in these domains is low. For example, mathematics and science items in the family of measures developed by Harms and colleagues (the Early Childhood Environment Rating Scale-Revised, ECERS-R; the Family Child Care Environment Rating Scale-Revised, FCCERS-R; and the School-Age Child Care Environment Rating Scale, SACERS) are part of a subscale called "activities," which includes a number of other types of activities, such as water play.[2] Second, even for measures that include more than one or two items in one of the domains, a meaningful and psychometrically sound subscale score usually cannot be derived. Third, without further analyses, the relative ease or difficulty in achieving interrater reliability on these items is unknown. Studies that document the interrater reliability of these comprehensive measures depend on certification or passing rules that include thresholds based on only a proportion of the items matching the trainer's or gold standard's ratings (either exact agreement or within a certain number of rating scale points). We are unable to assess how easy or challenging it may be for a rater to become reliable on the smaller, domain-specific set of items. Fourth, most of the measures are for center-based, and not family, child care settings. Finally, a number of the measures are 10 or more years old and have not been updated to reflect the current early learning standards and research about what is important in supporting children's development in these domains.

Although the scope of this chapter focuses on measures suitable for assessing the quality of settings for preschool children (because the bulk of assessments that include math, science, and cognition are geared toward that age group), many comprehensive quality measures cover a range of child ages, from birth (the Caregiver Observation Form and Scale, COFAS; the Child Care Assessment Tool for Relatives, CCAT-R; the Quality of Early Childhood Care Settings [QUEST]: Caregiver Rating Scale; and the FCCERS-R) through 12 years (the COFAS and the SACERS). As discussed in previous chapters, development and innovation in measures of the quality of child care for infants and toddlers lag behind the more robust pace of measure development for settings serving older children. This is becoming an increasingly critical issue as we learn more about what infants and toddlers need as a foundation for later success in mathematics, science, and cognition. Child care quality measures designed to assess such supports for infant and toddler learning and skill development are important for moving the field forward.

The measures listed in Table 5.1 generally require from one-half to a full day of observation time. Some require observation and questioning of teachers about anything that was not observed, including center and classroom policies and practices. Supplementing observations with verbal reports is consistent with most child care quality observations.

Mathematics-specific Measures of Early Childhood Program Quality

Table 5.2 summarizes key characteristics of three mathematics-specific measures (the COEMET; the Early Mathematics Classroom Observation and Numeracy Environment Checklist, EMCO/NEC; and the Preschool Classroom Mathematics Inventory, PCMI) and two broader measures (ECERS-E and PRISM) that include mathematics subscales. All five assess the quality of prekindergarten center-based classrooms. None of the measures assess mathematics-specific environment quality for infants/toddlers. The observation period specified for each measure is generally half of a program day, ranging from 3 to 4 hours. The ECERS-E also specifies the need for 15 minutes to speak with staff members and children. Generally, the measures demonstrate internal consistency reliability and interrater reliability that meet heuristics used by experts in the field (values greater than .70 and .85, respectively). However, some of these measures use exact agreement or agreement to within 1 scale point to compute interrater reliability rather than methods that are becoming more prevalent in the field (such as intraclass correlations or computing kappa coefficients). For four of the five measures included in Table 5.2, researchers have documented significant correlations with direct assessments of child math outcomes at the time of the final classroom assessment or at some point in the future, providing evidence for the validity of the observation measure. (Note that the one without such evidence is the PRISM, which is a new measure.) What is known about the relative contribution of the content, materials used to support learning, and time on explicit instruction is discussed next.

Training requirements for these measures range from self-study of the manual to half-day classroom training/orientation, as well as some time for practice in the field (two to three interrater reliability visits with experienced observers). The PCMI requires exact agreement with the gold standard on 70% of the items.

Science-specific Measures of Early Childhood Program Quality

The science-specific measures described in this section are not yet published or widely available. They are included here as an indication of the current state of the field and to identify research teams that are moving forward with efforts to assess classroom supports for science learning. Given that there is not yet a body of evidence supporting the reliability and validity of these measures, we simply provide a brief overview of the measures and some information about the research teams for interested readers.

As part of an evaluation project, researchers and educators affiliated with the Council of Three Rivers American Indian Center (COTRAIC) Head Start created a tool to assess the integrity with which participating centers implemented a preschool science program (Chase & Buffton, 2008). Administrators and supervisors are interviewed about their level of involvement with teachers around science, supports for professional development, and the extent to which they create partnerships with community science resources. Teachers are interviewed in conjunction with ratings of classroom materials, supplies, activities, and teacher resources.

The Science Teaching and Environment Rating Scale (STERS; Chalufour, Worth, & Clark-Chiarelli, 2009) utilizes classroom observation and a teacher interview to score instructional supports for science learning in early education classrooms. The rated components of science teaching are as follows: 1) creates a physical environment for inquiry and learning, 2) facilitates direct experiences to promote conceptual learning, 3) promotes use of scientific inquiry, 4) creates a collaborative climate that promotes exploration and understanding, 5) provides opportunities for extended conversations, 6) builds children's vocabulary, 7) plans in-depth investigations, and 8) assesses children's learning. Each of these components is rated on a 4-point rubric (1 = deficient through 4 = exemplary) that describes the sorts of materials and interactions one would find in a classroom meeting each numerical level. Psychometric validation of the STERS is currently underway (N. Clark-Chiarelli, personal communication, May 2010).

Other areas of research on science teaching include the quality of teacher–student interactions during science activities, teacher pedagogical content knowledge (e.g., Van Egeren, Watson, & Morris, 2008), and teacher attitudes. Greenfield and colleagues at the University of Miami are developing and testing a teacher attitudes survey about science (personal communication, June 2009) in conjunction with their work interviewing educators about the educators' self-efficacy and attitudes toward teaching science (Greenfield et al., 2009). Similarly, Ginsburg and colleagues (personal communication, May 2009) have tested attitude and self-efficacy measures in early mathematics for preschool teachers.

Mathematics- and Science-specific Measures

In addition to the published and validated ECERS-E (Sylva, et al., 2006), described in Table 5.2, a new tool, the Preschool Rating Instrument for Science and Mathematics (PRISM; Stevenson-Boyd et al., 2009), assesses both math and science. The PRISM is a comprehensive, 16-item instrument designed to measure the presence of classroom materials and teaching interactions that support mathematics and science learning. It is currently undergoing field testing and further validation studies are planned.

Cognition-specific Measures of Early Childhood Program Quality

Cognition is a multifaceted construct that includes many critical functions required to perceive, acquire, retain, and master preacademic knowledge and skills. As is described in Chapter 6, recent research on interventions designed to improve children's executive functioning include a focus on a number of behaviors and skills that historically have been conceived of as *cognition.* Likewise, other types of cognition, such as short- and long-term memory, attention, categorization, sequencing, and estimation are required in all learning. In the mid-1990s, proponents of developmentally appropriate practice viewed the idea of expressly working on these types of cognitive skills as misguided. Today, basic research in early cognitive development is informing a more nuanced understanding of the environmental and instructional supports that may help children enhance their cognitive skills, knowledge, and ability to apply what they learn to new circumstances.

Eleven of the fifteen measures in Table 5.1 include one or more items that assess some aspect of children's cognitive development or skills. Among these assessment items are observational items that capture teacher integration of abstract concept learning, problem solving, and making connections to the real world. In addition to the growing body of research on executive function and attention, and interventions designed to support them, researchers also are beginning to focus on memory strategies as another approach teachers can use to reinforce learning and improve student performance. By applying to the classroom setting advances in the basic science of memory development in young children, Ornstein and colleagues (2009) have studied how teacher instruction on and use of memory strategies, such as rehearsal, organization, and elaboration affects children's learning and skill development (across a range of outcomes). They have developed a classroom coding system to assess teacher use of speech about explicit strategies and teacher prompting of children's metacognitive skills to choose and apply a given memory strategy to the material the class was learning. In Grades 1, 2, and 4, students whose first-grade teachers rated high on using mnemonic strategies as part of instruction performed better on a range of memory and school skill assessments than students whose teachers did not use such strategies. Ornstein and team planned next to implement tests of classroom interventions focused on teachers providing memory strategies to students and to study their effects on children's memory skills. These lines of research on cognitive supports for children's learning and generalization may provide a missing link that brings together the different domains of inquiry about child care quality documented in this volume. If, indeed, development and school readiness in areas such as early literacy, mathematics, science, and interpersonal competence require foundational competence in basic cognitive and attention skills, then focusing on instructional and environmental supports that cut across these domains may be a priority for future research on child care quality.

Quality Measurement Areas in Mathematics and Science Instruction

Four main areas of measurement must be taken into consideration in attempting to characterize early childhood program quality in mathematics, science, and cognition: 1) content of instruction, 2) materials, 3) teacher interactions, and 4) characteristics of teachers. Here we describe each area and provide examples from the measures discussed previously.

Content

Mathematics curricula in the United States have been described as a mile wide and only an inch deep. In response, more emphasis in the early years is being placed on early number concepts, measurement, and geometry and spatial sense (Cross et al., 2009; NCTM, 2006; National Mathematics Advisory Panel, 2008). The mathematics content examined in observation tools emerging for use in early childhood and K–12 classrooms reflects this trend, moving from assessments that are broad but shallow, to measures that examine the classroom supports for deeper, more cognitively complex learning. For example, K–12 classrooms, support for cognitive complexity is examined by observing whether instructional activities require memorization and performance of routine procedures versus demonstration of understanding, metacognitive thinking, conjecture and proof, and/or making connections and solving nonroutine problems (Atkins-Burnett, 2007a; 2007b; Porter, Smithson, Blank, & Zeidner, 2007). In elementary school mathematics research, student learning has been linked to the intensity (time spent per week on mathematics topics) and the difficulty of the mathematics content (Odden, 1994; Raudenbush, Hong, & Rowan, 2002). The content covered by instruments designed for elementary classrooms is also much more comprehensive than that covered by instruments designed for preschool, going beyond number and counting. Among the early childhood measures described in Table 5.2, the ECERS-E includes items for shape and space and for sorting, matching, and comparing. (Note that only one of these items is scored, depending on what is happening in the classroom at the time of observation.) PCMI, COEMET, PRISM, and EMCO focus more specifically on mathematics than does the ECERS-E (which includes literacy and diversity subscales, as well as science) and assess it even more comprehensively.

Few measures of the quality of science instruction exist. Research-based knowledge of the benefits of depth over breadth or of spiraling content (repeating and reinforcing key concepts across years) in science in early childhood is limited, but recent reports recommend focusing on a few key ideas in science domains and exploring how these can be built upon and developed across grade bands (Duschl et al., 2006; Michaels, Shouse, & Schweingruber, 2007). Some developers of preschool science learning materials take this position as well (e.g., Gelman & Brenneman, 2004). It is generally agreed that teaching the processes of science (observing, comparing, wondering, and drawing conclusions) and providing scientific vocabulary repeatedly and in the context of exploration are important.

The ECERS-E, STERS, and PRISM assess materials and teaching methods that support children's learning about the content and processes of science. Emphasis is placed more on providing children with opportunities to engage in scientific inquiry and to explore content deeply (STERS and PRISM) than on *specific* topics covered. A recent approach used by O'Donnell and colleagues to examine the quality of elementary science instruction was guided by the American Association for the Advancement of Science's (AAAS's) Project 2061 instructional strategies.[3] These observation tools measure how the teacher conveys purpose, attends to student thinking and guides reasoning, engages children, introduces and represents ideas, provides practice, and encourages children to explain their ideas (O'Donnell 2007; Lynch, O'Donnell, Lastica, & Merchlinsky, 2007). Many of these strategies focus on supporting important cognitive functions that students use in learning science and math.

Materials

The environment rating scales (ECERS-R, FCCERS-R, SACERS, and ECERS-E) include items that address the availability of math and nature/science materials and activities, and whether adults encourage children's involvement with these materials (the infant/toddler version, the ITERS-R, includes one item on nature/science). Whereas the original ECERS (1980) had items that assessed the availability of block and water play, none of the items specifically addressed mathematics or nature/science. The current version has one item for each of these areas.[4] The ECERS-E assesses specific materials that should be available in a high-quality classroom. For example, a classroom must include a math area that is equipped with number games, countable objects, and counting books. In science, natural materials must be available for observation. Observation tools, print materials depicting living things, food, and reference books are also mentioned. One limitation of this family of environment rating scales is that, to score at the highest levels (a score of 6 or 7 out of 7) on a particular item, all of the conditions required for a lower rating must be met before a higher score can be awarded to the setting. The conditions required for the lower scores tend to focus on the materials and displays for children (posters, calendars) that support learning in a given area, whereas the conditions required to obtain higher scores involve how the teacher interacts with the children around materials and the specific ways in which he or she supports children's learning. In a setting where there are few materials and displays of math/science information, but many rich interactions that embed math and science in routine activities, scores will be lower. (See also Snow & Van Hemel, 2009.) Materials and interactions are scored separately for the COTRAIC science assessment, the PCMI, the PRISM, and the STERS.

Teacher Interactions

Teacher interactions are often examined as part of curriculum-specific measures such as HighScope's Program Quality Assessment (HighScope Educational Research Foundation, 2003) and Klein and Starkey's Pre-K Mathematics Fidelity of Implementation Record (2002; Klein, Starkey, Clements, Sarama, & Iyer, 2008). The kinds of interactions, both planned and unplanned, that staff have with children are directly observed and rated by the ECERS-E, the COEMET, the ECMO, the PCMI, the PRISM, and the STERS. Other global measures draw on the research literature and include instructional activities and teacher actions that are associated with more optimal outcomes for children (La Paro, Pianta, & Stuhlman, 2004; Sarama & Clements, 2007). Teacher interactions are measured in terms of quantity of interaction; types of questions; how much the teacher directs the interaction (demonstrating and telling versus questioning and guiding); how well the interactions scaffold, or match, the child's level of understanding; and the feedback that the teacher provides to the child, usually in terms of type and frequency (Atkins-Burnett, 2007a; 2007b; Moely et al., 1992; Sarama & Clements, 2007). Some measures also assess the ways in which the teacher engages the children with the content (for science, Van Egeren, Watson, & Morris, 2008), as well as whether the children in the classroom become engaged (Pianta, La Paro, & Hamre, 2008; O'Donnell 2007).

Characteristics of Teachers

Although a teacher's level of education often has been used as a proxy for teacher quality, the field is now moving toward more focused questions about teacher preparation. These include examinations of the specific preservice and inservice coursework that teachers have completed in a particular content area, teachers' knowledge or academic proficiency in the content area, their pedagogical knowledge about teaching young children, or their pedagogical content knowledge (PCK)[5] about the best ways to support early mathematics and science learning (Goldhaber & Anthony, 2004; Hill, Ball, & Schilling, 2008). Professional development programs that allow preschool teachers to explore deeply and reflect on their own teaching and children's mathematical and scientific thinking (as recommended by NAEYC and NCTM, 2002) have been linked to positive math learning outcomes for preschool students (Copley & Padrón,

1999). PCK measures have been related to student outcomes in elementary school (Hill, Rowan, & Ball, 2005). Most of this work concerning PCK has been done with elementary school teachers, but with ever-increasing attention on preschool math and science, this situation is changing. New tools to assess teachers' attitudes toward early mathematics and science learning and their knowledge about its development are also being developed and tested (Hartman, 2009; Maier, Greenfield, & Bulotsky-Shearer, 2010; Platas, 2008).

Methods of Data Collection

In early childhood, the most common method for assessing the quality of support for mathematics, science, and cognition is observation guided by checklists or rubrics. Strong rubrics are difficult to create. The anchors need to be clearly described in terms of specific behaviors and materials required so that raters can be consistent in the use of the rubric. The descriptions of each level must build on the previous level and represent an increase in quality. Anchor points at the ends of the rubric and at steps in the scale help to ensure that raters use the scale consistently.

The amount of time spent in the classroom and the number of observations made will influence findings. In content areas such as science and mathematics, the teacher's interactions may vary as a function of the specific content (life science versus space science) and the point in the study of the content (initial exploration or instruction versus practice and review). Further, as we assess quality of supports for math and science in preschool classrooms, we encounter a critical issue: If we wait for a math or science interaction to occur so that we can assess its quality, we are likely to wait for a long time. (For reviews, see Brenneman et al., 2009; Ginsburg et al., 2008.) If we ask the teacher to set up a math or science lesson, we can gauge what he or she believes is a high-quality learning experience, but this is an artificial picture of what usually occurs in the classroom. Rather, a hybrid approach might be required to get a fuller picture of the everyday levels and the potential levels of support for scientific and mathematical thinking in classrooms.

Teacher surveys, teacher logs, and review of lesson plans are other ways that information is collected about what occurs in the classroom. Teachers participating in such research are asked to report on the content that they teach, the types of questions that they use, the activities (including the level of cognitive demand of the activity), and the engagement of the students (Odden, 1994; Rowan, Harrison, & Hayes, 2004). Information from teachers also can be used to augment rating scales and rubrics or to clarify what is seen during a classroom observation period. In assessing the implementation fidelity of their preschool science program, researchers with the COTRAIC (Chase & Buffton, 2008) utilized interviews with teachers, supervisors, and administrators, as well as an observation of the classroom environment. Budget reports, professional development records, and staff meeting notes also were examined to yield a full picture of classroom, instructional, and administrative fidelity to a preschool science program.

Research findings suggest that, on some quality measures, multiple observations may be necessary to fully capture environmental supports for math and science learning. One study showed that teacher logs at the elementary school level called into question the reliability of observations of teaching collected at a single point in time. The majority of the variance in instruction was found between observation occasions in the same classroom rather than between classrooms (Rowan, Camburn, & Correnti, 2004).

Summary and Recommendations

There are few measures available to assess the quality of preschool settings and instruction in the areas of mathematics, science, and cognition. A number of global measures of quality include items on these topics, but overall, the coverage of supports for children's learning in mathematics and science is thin. Most measures have only one or two items. A few content-specific measures of mathematics instruction that address areas deemed important by researchers are available, and assessments of science-specific instruction have been developed and are undergoing field testing. We did not identify any cognition-specific quality measures for preschool settings, but one elementary classroom observation measure is being considered for adaptation in preschool classrooms.

As policy makers and educators focus attention on the mathematics and science learning of young children, new measures to assess classroom quality and learning supports in these domains and other areas of cognition will continue to be developed. To maximize the usefulness of these tools, developers must ensure that measures are reliable by using clear behavioral terms to describe the characteristics and interactions being observed or measured. The predictive validity of these tools will also have to be carefully assessed, and the assessment will depend on the development of valid, reliable, and comprehensive measures of children's learning in these domains. Such measures are being developed and validated. For example, researchers at the University of Miami are using IRT to develop a direct assessment of preschool children's science skills and knowledge (Greenfield et al., 2008; 2009), and Clements and Sarama (2008) used IRT to develop a measure of children's early mathematical knowledge and skills.

IRT is useful for item development because it utilizes empirical information from all of the items in a measure and from all of the subjects to estimate scores. The method provides information about where each item is located on the underlying factor of interest and how strong its relationship to that factor is. This information can then be used to estimate the amount of information provided by a given item. The information function for all of the items can then be combined to estimate the overall test information (Edwards, 2009). Better measurement of instructional quality and learning outcomes will help in examining relationships among aspects of these and will allow benchmarks of quality to be set by empirical approaches. Child care quality measures that employed IRT in development found significant, positive associations with child outcomes (Clements & Sarama, 2008; Hill et al., 2008; O'Donnell, 2007). For the field to progress, it is critical that child care quality measures meet the same high standards set for child outcome measures. This is challenging because measures development, standardization, and validation are costly and there is no natural market driving development of quality measures as there is driving clinical assessments of children. The federal government and foundations have funded some of this work, but more funding will be required to support development and research over the years.

To improve child outcomes is the main reason that we assess instruction and classroom quality. We want to know how to maximize young children's learning by identifying the environmental features that relate to positive child outcomes. We need practical means of assessing quality efficiently. For this reason, more research is needed to clarify the frequency of observations and the types of information required to accurately identify instruction that promotes (or does not promote) student learning. Another design issue researchers face is whether to create a measure that requires observing a whole program day in the hope of being present during a mathematics or science activity (or simply to document whether these activities happen at all or are connected to other activities, such as literacy or music and movement), or to develop a measure focused on observing a specific instructional activity. The latter requires that the researcher request that he or she come at a time when a mathematics or science activity or lesson is taking place. In this case, the researcher likely sees the teacher's best effort in mathematics or science, but perhaps trades off the "representativeness" of the observation as an example of educational activities that typically occur in the classroom. The answer to the question of whether requesting to observe a given activity results in a representative measure of instructional quality requires further study. Both types of observation—what actually occurs on a given day and what occurs if science and math are the focus of a lesson—should be studied with respect to their links to child outcomes and as measures of the state of math and science instructional quality in pre-K classrooms. Mathematics and science instruction researchers face this issue to a greater extent than literacy researchers, because so little time in the classroom is devoted to mathematics and science compared with the time devoted to literacy.

The current trend in the field of developing content-specific measures of child care quality is part of the progression of a science that aims to understand how to improve specific outcomes for children. Clearly, in the areas of preschool mathematics and science, these efforts are just now gaining the attention of the field, and measures of classroom environments, instruction, and teacher knowledge are being developed, validated, and published. Alignment among these measures makes sense, especially in the context of studying the effects of a content-specific intervention. It is possible that the field will proceed with a focus on content-specific measures for the next 5 to 10 years, given the emphasis on alignment with state standards and the current focus on improving outcomes for students in domains beyond literacy. At the same time, policy makers and researchers are asking whether it will be possible to take the best from the newer, most reliable, and most valid measures and develop a comprehensive measure that will assess quality more globally, but still will provide content-specific information about a given classroom or setting. We believe that if, after we identify strong measures of quality in mathematics and science, attention is focused on creating a global measure with good coverage of specific content areas (not just an item or two), this would be an important contribution to the field.

It is likely that multiple methods will be required to capture converging evidence of quality in classrooms and to assess children's learning in mathematics and science. Better measures of environmental and learning constructs will enable more productive explorations of the relations between the two.

References

Administration for Children and Families. (2006). *Preliminary findings from the Early Head Start prekindergarten followup. Early Head Start Research and Evaluation Project report.* Washington, DC: U.S. Department of Health and Human Services.

American Association for the Advancement of Science. (1993). *Benchmarks for science literacy.* New York: Oxford University Press.

American Association for the Advancement of Science. (1998). *Dialogue on early childhood science, mathematics, and technology education.* Washington, DC: Author.

Atkins-Burnett, S. (2007a). *Observation of Math Instruction.* Washington, DC: Mathematica Policy Research, Inc.

Atkins-Burnett, S. (2007b, June). *IES evaluations and tools: Assessing implementation.* Presented at the U.S. Department of Education Mathematics and Science Partnerships Programs Annual State Coordinators Meeting, Washington, DC.

Baroody, A.J., & Dowker, A. (Eds.). (2003). *The development of arithmetic concepts and skills: Recent research and theory.* Mahwah, NJ: Lawrence Erlbaum Associates.

Bowman, B.T., Donovan, M.S., & Burns, M.S. (Eds.). (2001). *Eager to learn: Educating our preschoolers.* Washington, DC: National Academies Press.

Brenneman, K., Stevenson-Boyd, J., & Frede, E. (2009). Early mathematics and science: Preschool policy and practice. *Preschool Policy Brief, 19.* New Brunswick, NJ: National Institute for Early Education Research.

Brush, L.R. (1978). Preschool children's knowledge of addition and subtraction. *Journal of Research in Mathematics Education, 9*(1), 44–54.

Cassata-Widera, A.E., Kato-Jones, Y., Duckles, J.M., Conezio, K., & French, L.A. (2008). Learning the language of science. *The International Journal of Learning, 15*(8), 141–152.

Chalufour, I., Worth, K., & Clark-Chiarelli, N. (2009). *Science Teaching Environment Rating Scale (STERS).* Newton, MA: Education Development Center.

Chase, S., & Buffton, S. (2008). *Model Integrity Checklist: Science outcomes program classroom review and teacher interview, administrator interview, and supervisor interview.* Pittsburgh: Author.

Chouinard, M.M. (2007). Children's questions: A mechanism for cognitive development. *Monographs for the Society for Research in Child Development, 72,* 1–129.

Clements, D.H. (1999). Geometric and spatial thinking in young children. In J.V. Copley (Ed.), *Mathematics in the early years,* (pp. 66–79). Reston, VA: National Council of Teachers of Mathematics.

Clements, D.H. (2007). Curriculum research: Toward a framework for "research-based curricula." *Journal for Research in Mathematics Education, 38,* 35–70.

Clements, D.H., & Sarama, J. (2004a). Building blocks for early mathematics. *Early Childhood Research Quarterly, 19,* 181–189.

Clements, D.H., & Sarama, J. (2004b). Learning trajectories in mathematics education. *Mathematical Thinking and Learning, 6,* 81–89.

Clements, D.H., & Sarama, J. (2008). Experimental evaluation of the effects of a research-based preschool mathematics curriculum. *American Educational Research Journal, 45*(2), 443–494.

Clements, D.H, Sarama, J., & diBiase, A. (Eds.). (2004). *Engaging young children in mathematics: Standards for early childhood mathematics education.* Mahwah, NJ: Lawrence Erlbaum Associates.

Clements, D.H., Sarama, J., & Liu, X. (2008). Development of a measure of early mathematics achievement using the Rasch model: the Research-Based Early Maths Assessment. *Educational Psychology, 28*(4), 457–482.

Copley, J., & Padrón, Y. (1999). Preparing teachers of young learners: Professional development of early childhood teachers in mathematics and science. In *Dialogue on early childhood science, mathematics, and technology education* (pp. 117–129). Washington, DC: Project 2061, American Association for the Advancement of Science.

Cross, C., Woods, T.A., & Schweingruber, H. (Eds.). (2009). *Mathematics learning in early childhood: Paths toward excellence and equity.* Committee on Early Childhood Mathematics, National Research Council. Washington, DC: National Academies Press.

Denton, K., & West, J. (2002). *Children's reading and mathematics achievement in kindergarten and first grade.* Washington, DC: National Center for Educational Statistics.

Dowker, A. (2001). Numeracy recovery: A pilot scheme for early intervention with young children with numeracy difficulties. *Support for Learning, 16*(1), 6–105.

Duncan, G.J., Dowsett, C.J., Claessens, A., Magnuson, K., Huston, A.C., Klebanov, P., et al. (2007). School readiness and later achievement: Supplemental materials. *Developmental Psychology, 43*(6), 1428–1446.

Duschl, R.A., Schweingruber, H.A., & Shouse, A.W. (2006). *Taking science to school: Learning and teaching science in grades K–8.* Board on Science Education, Center for Education, Division of Behavioral and Social Sciences and Education. Washington, DC: The National Academies Press.

Edwards, M.C. (2009). An introduction to Item Response Theory using the need for cognition scale. *Social and Personality Psychology Compass, 3*(4), 507–529.

Ertle, B.B., Ginsburg, H.P., Cordero, M.I., Curran, T.M., Manlapig, L., & Morgenlander, M. (2008). The essence of early childhood mathematics education and the professional development needed to support it. In A. Dowker (Ed.), *Mathematical difficulties: Psychology and intervention* (pp. 59–84). San Diego: Elsevier.

Frede, E., Jung, K., Barnett, W.S., Lamy, C.E., Figueras, A. (2007). *The Abbott Preschool Program longitudinal effects study (APPLES): Interim report.*

Frede, E., Lamy, C.E., & Boyd, J.S. (2005). *Not just calendars and counting blocks: Using the NAEYC/NCTM joint position statement "Early childhood mathematics: Promoting good beginnings" as a basis for measuring classroom teaching practices and their relationship to child outcome.* Paper presented at the annual National Association for the Education of Young Children conference, Washington, DC.

Frede, E., Weber, M., Hornbeck, A., Stevenson-Boyd, J., & Colón, A. (2005). *Prekindergarten Classroom Mathematic Inventory (PCMI).* New Brunswick, NJ: National Institute for Early Education Research.

Gelman, R., & Brenneman, K. (2004). Science learning pathways for young children. *Early Childhood Research Quarterly, 19,* 150–158.

Gelman, R., Brenneman, K., Macdonald, G., & Román, M. (2009). *Preschool pathways to science (PrePS): Facilitating scientific ways of thinking, talking, and understanding.* Baltimore: Paul H. Brookes Publishing Co.

Ginsburg, H.P. (2009). *Early Mathematics Assessment System (EMAS).* New York: Author.

Ginsburg, H.P., Cannon, J., Eisenband, J., & Pappas, S. (2006). Mathematical thinking and learning. In K. McCartney & D. Phillips (Eds.), *Blackwell handbook of early childhood development* (pp. 208–229). Malden, MA: Blackwell.

Ginsburg, H.P., Greenes, C., & Balfanz, R. (2003). *Big math for little kids.* Parsippany, NJ: Dale Seymour Publications.

Ginsburg, H.P., Lee, J.S., & Stevenson-Boyd, J.S. (2008). Mathematics education for young children: What it is and how to promote it. *Society for Research in Child Development Social Policy Report, 22,* 3–22.

Ginsburg, H.P., Lewis, A., & Clements, M. (in press). School readiness and early childhood education: What can we learn from federal investments in research on mathematics programs? Retrieved from http://aspe.hhs.gov/hsp/10/SchoolReadiness/apb3.shtml.

Golbeck, S., & Ginsburg, H.P. (Eds.) (2004). Early learning in mathematics and science [Special Issue]. *Early Childhood Research Quarterly, 19*(1), 1–200.

Goldhaber, D., & Anthony, E. (2004). *Can teacher quality be effectively assessed?* Washington, DC: Urban Institute.

Greenes, C. (1999). Ready to learn: Developing children's mathematical powers. In J.V. Copley (Ed.), *Mathematics in the early years* (pp. 39–47). Reston, VA: National Council of Teachers of Mathematics.

Greenfield, D.B., Dominguez, M.X., Fuccillo, J.M., Maier, M.F., & Greenberg, A.C. (2008, June). *The development of an IRT-based direct assessment of preschool science.* Poster presented at the Ninth National Head Start Research Conference, Washington, DC.

Greenfield, D., Jirout, J., Dominguez., X., Greenberg, A., Maier, M., & Fuccillo, J. (2009). Science in the preschool classroom: A programmatic research agenda to improve science readiness. *Early Education & Development, 20,* 238–264.

Griffin, S. (2000). *Number Worlds: Preschool level.* Durham, NC: Number Worlds Alliance, Inc.

Groen, G., & Resnick, L.B. (1977). Can preschool children invent addition algorithms? *Journal of Educational Psychology, 69*(6), 645–652.

Halle, T., Forry, N., Hair, E., Perper, K., Wandner, L., Wessel, J., & Vick, J. (2009). *Disparities in early learning and development: Lessons from the Early Childhood Longitudinal Study—Birth Cohort (ECLS-B).* Executive Summary. Washington, DC: Child Trends.

Halle, T., & Vick, J.E. (2007). *Quality in early childhood care and education settings: A compendium of measures.* Washington, DC: Office of Planning, Research, and Evaluation. Administration for Children and Families, U.S. Department of Health and Human Services.

Hartman, G. (2009, in preparation). *Teacher Understanding of Student Knowledge (TUSK).* New York: Teachers College.

HighScope Educational Research Foundation. (2003). *PQA preschool program quality assessment: Administration manual.* Ypsilanti, MI: Author.

Hill, H.C., Ball, D.L., & Schilling, S.G. (2008). Unpacking pedagogical content knowledge: Conceptualizing and measuring teachers' topic-specific knowledge of students. *Journal for Research in Mathematics Education, 39*(4), 372–400.

Hill, H.C., Rowan, B., & Ball, D.L. (2005). Effects of teachers' mathematical knowledge for teaching on student achievement. *American Educational Research Journal, 42*(3), 371–406.

Hunting, R.P. (1999). Rational-number learning in the early years: What is possible? In J.V. Copley (Ed.), *Mathematics in the Early Years* (pp. 80–87). Reston, VA: National Council of Teachers of Mathematics.

Jordan, N.C., Huttenlocher, L., & Levine, S.C. (1994). Assessing early arithmetic abilities: Effects of verbal and nonverbal response types on the calculation performance of middle- and low-income children. *Learning and Individual Differences, 6,* 413–432.

Kilday, C.R., & Kinzie, M.B. (2009). An analysis of instruments that measure the quality of mathematics teaching in early childhood. *Early Childhood Education Journal, 36*(4), 365–372.

Kisker, E.E., Boller, K., Nagatoshi, C.T., Sciarrino, C., Jethwani, V., Zavitsky, T., Ford, M., &, Love, J.M. (2004). *Resources for measuring services and outcomes in Head Start programs serving infants and toddlers.* Princeton, NJ: Mathematica Policy Research.

Klein, A., & Starkey, P. (2002). *Pre-K Mathematics Curriculum.* Glenview, IL: Scott Foresman.

Klein, A., Starkey, P., Clements, D., Sarama, J., & Iyer, R. (2008). Effects of a pre-kindergarten mathematics intervention: A randomized experiment. *Journal of Research on Educational Effectiveness, 1*(3), 155–178.

Klein, A., Starkey, P., & Wakeley, A. (2000). *Child Math Assessment (CMA): Preschool Battery.* Berkeley, CA: University of California, Berkeley.

Klein, A., Starkey, P., & Wakeley, A. (2004). Enhancing young children's mathematical knowledge through a pre-kindergarten mathematics intervention. *Early Childhood Research Quarterly, 19,* 99–120.

La Paro, K.M, Pianta, R.C., & Stuhlman, M. (2004). The classroom assessment scoring system: Findings from the prekindergarten year. *The Elementary School Journal, 104*(5), 409–426.

Lynch, S., O'Donnell, C., Lastica, J., & Merchlinsky, S. (2007). *Analyzing the relationship between fidelity of implementation and student outcomes in a quasi-experiment.* Retrieved July 26, 2008, from http://www.gwu.edu/~scale-up

Maier, M.F., Greenfield, D.B., & Bulotsky-Shearer, R. (2010, in preparation). *Development and initial validation of an early childhood teachers' attitudes and beliefs toward science questionnaire.* Miami: University of Miami.

Michaels, S., Shouse, A.W., & Schweingruber, H.A. (2007). *Ready, set, SCIENCE!: Putting research to work in K–8 science classrooms.* Board on Science Education, Center for Education, Division of Behavioral and Social Sciences and Education. Washington, DC: National Academies Press.

Moely, B.E., Hart, S.S., Leal, L., Santulli, K.A., Rao, N., Johnson, T., & Hamilton, L.B. (1992). The teacher's role in facilitating memory and study strategy development in the elementary school classroom. *Child Development, 63,* 653–672.

National Association for the Education of Young Children (NAEYC) and National Council of Teachers of Mathematics (NCTM). (2002). *Early childhood mathematics: Promoting good beginnings.* Washington, DC: National Association for the Education of Young Children.

National Council of Teachers of Mathematics (NCTM). (2006). *Curriculum focal points for prekindergarten through grade 8 mathematics: A quest for coherence.* Reston, VA: Author.

National Mathematics Advisory Panel. (2008). *Foundations for Success: The Final Report of the National Mathematics Advisory Panel,* Washington, DC: U.S. Department of Education.

National Research Council. (1996). *National Science Education Standards.* National Committee on Science Education Standards and Assessment. Center for Science, Mathematics, and Engineering Education. Washington, DC: National Academies Press.

National Research Council. (2005). *Mathematical and scientific development in early childhood.* Summary of a 2005 National Academy of Sciences Workshop, Washington, DC.

National Science Board. (2009). *National Science Board STEM education recommendations for the President-Elect Obama administration.* Retrieved January 20, 2009, from http://www. nsf.gov/ nsb/publications/2009/01_10_stem_rec_ obama.pdf

Neuman, S., & Roskos, K. (2005). The state of state pre-kindergarten standards. *Early Childhood Research Quarterly, 20,* 125–145.

Odden, A. (1994). *Costs of measuring and providing opportunity to learn: Preliminary thoughts. Selected Papers in School Finance 1994.* Washington, DC. Retrieved April 3, 2008, from http://nces.ed.gov/pubs/web/96068cmp.asp

O'Donnell, C.L. (2007). Fidelity of implementation to instructional strategies as a moderator of curriculum unit effectiveness in a large-scale middle school science quasi-experiment. *Dissertation Abstract International, 68*(08). (UMI No. AAT 3276564). Retrieved February 2, 2008, from ProQuest Dissertations and Theses Database. The George Washington University.

Ornstein, P.A., Grammer, J.K., & Coffman, J. (2009). Teachers' "mnemonic style" and the development of skilled memory. In H.S. Waters & W. Schneider (Eds.), *Metacognition, strategy use, and instruction* (pp. 23–53). New York: Guilford.

Peterson, S.M., & French, L.A. (2008). Supporting young children's explanations through inquiry science in preschool. *Early Childhood Research Quarterly, 28,* 395–408.

Pianta, R.C., La Paro, K.M., & Hamre, B. (2008). *Classroom Assessment Scoring System™ (CLASS™).* Baltimore: Paul H. Brookes Publishing Co.

Platas, L.M. (2008, June). *Measuring teachers' knowledge of early mathematical development and their beliefs about mathematics and its teaching and learning in early childhood programs.* Presented at the Ninth National Head Start Research Conference, Washington, DC.

Porter, A.C., Smithson, J., Blank, R., & Zeidner, T. (2007). Alignment as a teacher variable. *Applied Measurement in Education, 20,* 27–51.

Raudenbush, S.W., Hong, G., & Rowan, B. (2002, March) Presentation. *Studying the causal effects of instruction with application to primary school mathematics.* Presented at Research Seminar II: Instructional and Performance Consequences of High-Poverty Schooling. Washington, DC.

Reynolds, A.J. (1995). One year of preschool intervention or two: Does it matter? *Early Childhood Research Quarterly, 10,* 1–31.

Rowan, B., Camburn, E., & Correnti, R. (2004). Using teacher logs to measure the enacted curriculum in large-scale surveys: A study of literacy teaching in third-grade classrooms. *Elementary School Journal, 105,* 75–102.

Rowan, B., Harrison, D., & Hayes, A. (2004). Using instructional logs to study elementary school mathematics: A close look at curriculum and teaching in the early grades. *Elementary School Journal, 105,* 103–127.

Sarama, J., & Clements, D.H. (2007). *Manual for Classroom Observation of Early Mathematics–Environment and Teaching (COEMET)*–Version 3. University at Buffalo, State University of New York: Author.

Sarama, J., & Clements, D.H. (2008). Linking research and software development. In G.W. Blume & M.K. Heid (Eds.), *Research on technology and the teaching and learning of mathematics: Volume 2. Cases and perspectives* (pp. 113–130). New York: Information Age Publishing.

Schulz, L.E., & Bonawitz, E.B. (2007). Serious fun: Preschoolers engage in more exploratory play when evidence is confounded. *Developmental Psychology, 43,* 1045–1050.

Seo, K-H., & Ginsburg, H.P. (2004). What is developmentally appropriate in early mathematics education? Lessons from new research. In D. Clements, J. Sarama, & A. diBiase (Eds.), *Engaging young children in mathematics: Standards for early childhood mathematics education* (pp. 91–104). Mahwah, NJ: Lawrence Erlbaum Associates.

Snow, C.E., & Van Hemel, S.B. (Eds.). (2009). *Early childhood assessment: Why, what, and how.* Board on Children, Youth, and Families, Board on Testing and Assessment, Division of Behavioral and Social Sciences and Education. Washington, DC: National Academies Press.

Sophian, C. (2004). Mathematics for the future: Developing a Head Start curriculum to support mathematics learning. *Early Childhood Research Quarterly, 19,* 59–81.

Starkey, P., & Klein, A. (2000). Fostering parental support for children's mathematical development: An intervention with Head Start families. *Early Education & Development, 11*(5), 659–680.

Stevenson-Boyd, J., Brenneman, K., Frede, E., & Weber, M. (2009). *Preschool Rating Instrument for Science and Mathematics (PRISM).* New Brunswick, NJ: National Institute for Early Education Research.

Sylva, K., Siraj-Blatchford, I., & Taggart, B. (2006). *Early Childhood Environment Rating Scale (Extension).* Staffordshire, England: Trentham Books.

Tarullo, L., West, J., Aikens, N., & Hulsey, L. (2008). *Beginning Head Start: Children, families, and programs in fall 2006.* Washington, DC: Mathematica Policy Research.

U.S. Department of Education, National Center for Education Statistics. (2002). *Early Childhood Longitudinal Study-Kindergarten Class of 1998–99 (ECLS–K), Psychometric Report for Kindergarten Through First Grade,* NCES 2002–05, by D.A. Rock and J.M. Pollack, Educational Testing Service, E. Germino Hausken, project officer. Washington, DC: National Center for Education Statistics.

U.S. Department of Health and Human Services, Administration for Children and Families. (2005, May). *Head Start Impact Study: First Year Findings.* Washington, DC.

Van Egeren, L.A., Watson, D.P., & Morris, B.J. (2008, June). *Head start on science: the impact of an early childhood science curriculum.* Presented at the Ninth National Head Start Research Conference, Washington, DC.

West, J., Denton, K., & Germino-Hausken, E. (2000). *America's Kindergartners.* Publication No. NCES 2000-070. Washington, DC: U.S. Department of Education, National Center for Education Statistics.

Endnotes

[1] As discussed in multiple chapters in this book, child care and instructional quality measures include a range of indicators of the experiences that children have in out-of-home care settings. These include measures of the physical environment (e.g., furnishings, room arrangement, outdoor play space), available materials (e.g., the number of books), and instruction and teacher–provider interactions (e.g., how intentional the adult is in teaching children skills and sharing knowledge, how warm and supportive interactions are with children), as well as the level of training and education of teachers and their pedagogical and content knowledge in areas such as literacy, mathematics, and science.

[2] Water play can be a science exploration experience for children alone and when facilitated by an adult.

[3] AAAS founded Project 2061 in 1985 to help all Americans become literate in science, mathematics, and technology.

[4] Note that in the ECERS-R a single item includes a number of indicators that are assessed in completing the rating.

[5] Item-writing recommendations for mathematics PCK items are available at http://www.sii.soe.umich.edu/documents/Appendix%20C%20Item%20writing%20Hill%20Schill%20Ball.pdf

Measuring the Quality of Environmental Supports for Young Children's Social and Emotional Competence

Marilou Hyson, Jessica E. Vick Whittaker, Martha Zaslow,
Deborah Leong, Elena Bodrova, Bridget K. Hamre, and Sheila Smith[1]

The purpose of this chapter is to summarize the status of measurement of environmental supports for social and emotional competence (ESSEC) in early childhood settings and to indicate the potential for further measures development.

The first section of the chapter begins by defining the domain of social and emotional development. We then describe an emerging consensus about the importance of this domain, both for later social-emotional competence and for other aspects of children's development and learning. We present evidence that recent progress in understanding children's social and emotional development, and in intervention research seeking to strengthen that development, makes this an opportune time to pursue the further development of in-depth measures of this aspect of the early childhood environment. Whether children are in center-based child care, family child care, state prekindergarten (pre-K) programs, Head Start, or other settings, many features of early childhood settings have the potential to either promote or inhibit social and emotional competence. It is therefore critical to assess how well early childhood programs are addressing this aspect of development. Using an ecological framework, we will draw upon what is known about key dimensions of children's social and emotional competence, proposing categories of potential environmental support for that competence.

The second section of the chapter examines the extent to which we now have in-depth, valid, and practical measures to assess those supports. In reviewing existing measures, we will report both good and bad news. On the positive side, a number of widely used measures that provide overall or summary ratings of quality do have components that are directly relevant to supports for social and emotional competence. For example, the Early Childhood Environment Rating Scales (ECERS-R and its variants—e.g., Infant/Toddler Environment Rating Scale, ITERS-R Family Child Care Environment Rating Scale, FCCERS Harms, Clifford, & Cryer, 2005; Harms, Cryer, & Clifford, 2003, 2007) rate environments on items such as the comfort of the physical environment, the supportiveness and warmth of adult–child interactions, and the constructiveness with which teachers and caregivers handle challenging behavior. The Classroom Assessment Scoring System™ (CLASS™; Pianta, La Paro, & Hamre, 2008) is organized into three domains of quality, one of which, termed Emotional Support, includes the dimensions of positive climate, negative climate, teacher sensitivity, and regard for students' perspectives.

The third section builds on this review to propose a comprehensive set of supports that, if adequately measured, would yield a useful picture of the quality of early childhood environments in this domain. The section highlights theoretically and empirically significant supports (or quality features) that are missing from the reviewed measures, as well as those supports measured with insufficient depth or with methods that may not yield informative results.

Finally, the fourth section of the chapter proposes priorities for new measures development and suggests ways to make maximum use of existing measures. In this section we also take up the specific conceptual and empirical challenges to measures development in this area, suggesting ways that these challenges may be addressed in the future.

Defining Social and Emotional Development, Evidence of Importance, and Conceptualization of Environmental Supports

If early childhood environments are to support children's social and emotional competence, and if we are to measure the quality of that support, we need a clear delineation of the social and emotional domain. Yet, perhaps more than in any other domain of development, social and emotional development has been variously and often imprecisely described. Some subsume the social and emotional dimensions into one category: *socioemotional,* or *social-emotional.* Some prefer to keep the emotional domain distinct from the social, in large part because of the rapidly growing body of theory and research on early emotional development (e.g., Saarni, Campos, Camras, & Witherington, 2006; Thompson & Lagatutta, 2006). Many states include in their early learning standards one distinct category combining social and emotional outcomes, whereas other states embed social and emotional items within content domains such as literacy and social studies (Scott-Little, Lesko, Martella, & Milburn, 2007). The school readiness domain of "approaches to learning" (Hyson, 2008; Kagan, Moore, & Bredekamp, 1995), including children's motivation to learn, flexibility, attention, and engagement, sometimes is considered part of the social and emotional arena, sometimes a primarily cognitive dimension, and sometimes a category in its own right.

A related issue is the sheer number of constructs and items that may be found under the social-emotional "tent." Again, state early learning standards are instructive, with some states listing more than 40 separate items in the social-emotional domain (Scott-Little, Kagan, & Frelow, 2003). Some of these items appear well justified in research as predictors of important later outcomes, whereas others appear to be little more than socially desirable behaviors (e.g., "does not call inappropriate attention to self"; "demonstrates respectful and polite vocabulary"). In this chapter we propose to take a parsimonious approach, examining measures of environmental supports for just a few dimensions of social and emotional functioning. Following the framework used by Raver (2008) in a recent synthesis of federally funded research on social-emotional interventions and a similar framework used by the National Research Council's (2008) Committee on Developmental Outcomes and Assessments for Young Children, we focus on three specific dimensions that are important in their own right, that are also known to be important for later social and emotional development as well as other school readiness domains, and that have been shown to be amenable to intervention within early childhood settings. Each has received much attention from developmental and education researchers, whose work influences the following brief descriptions:

1. The *prosocial skills and social cognition* dimension includes and is related to children's understanding of their own and others' feelings; their ability to express emotions appropriately; their interpersonal problem-solving skills; and their ability to engage in close relationships with peers and adults (including their teachers), free of sustained or frequent conflict.

2. The *self-regulation* dimension includes and is related to children's capacity to focus attention upon, engage in, and persist at learning tasks; their ability to modulate and manage both positive and negative emotions in a group setting; and their capacity to plan and follow through on their plans.

3. The *behavior problems* dimension focuses on negative behavior—both externalizing (acting out, aggressive) and internalizing (withdrawn, depressed)—problems that may affect children's ability to function effectively both in the preschool years and beyond.

Although no consensus has arisen about how the social and emotional arena should be subdivided, or about what specific subskills should be assessed (NRC, 2008), a focus on these three broad categories should simplify the task of describing and identifying appropriate measures of features of early childhood environments.

Why Measure Environmental Supports for Social-Emotional Competence?

Recent research makes a compelling case for strengthening our measurement of supports for children's social-emotional competence in early childhood settings. The synthesis paper by Raver (2008), bringing together research on children's early social and emotional development, is drawn upon extensively in the discussion that follows.

Research Indicates that Early Social-Emotional Competence Plays a Critical Role in School Readiness

There is an extensive knowledge base both about the typical course of early social and emotional development and about the effects of that development on other aspects of children's progress and learning, concurrently and in later years (e.g., Duncan et al., 2007; Blair, 2002; Fabes, Gaertner, & Popp, 2006; Hyson, Copple, & Jones, 2006; Raver, 2002; Thompson & Laguttuta, 2006). In particular, social-emotional competence has been shown to foster children's engagement in a range of learning opportunities (McClelland & Morrison, 2003); conversely, children who have difficulties with self-regulation (Bodrova & Leong, 2007) and other aspects of executive functioning are likely to be less engaged with learning opportunities in the classroom and to have less positive relationships with others (Fantuzzo, Bulotsky-Shearer, Fusco, & McWayne, 2005). Preschoolers who were rated as more attentive and persistent in their approaches to learning also have more positive interactions with others (Fantuzzo, Perry, & McDermott, 2004).

Recent research has also underscored the benefits of children's supportive relationships with teachers and caregivers (hereafter referred to together as *early educators*) in the preschool years. A close, supportive relationship with early educators has been shown to enhance the quality of children's future relationships with teachers (Mashburn & Pianta, 2006) and to increase both children's engagement in learning and their academic success (O'Connor & McCartney, 2007; Hamre & Pianta, 2001; Palermo, Hanish, Martin, Fabes, & Reiser, 2007). With respect to behavior problems, much effort has been devoted to identifying and intervening to change the trajectory of early-appearing maladaptive behaviors. Behaviors such as aggression and disruptive behavior often predict later social and emotional difficulties. Further, learning opportunities are lost when both the child with behavioral issues and others in the classroom are affected by the prevalence of these behaviors (Campbell, 2002; Campbell, Shaw, & Gilliom, 2000; Raver et al., 2008; Tremblay, Hartup, & Archer, 2005).

State and National Policy Makers and Early Childhood Practitioners Increasingly Recognize the Importance of Social-Emotional Competence for School Readiness and School Success

Early childhood educators have long understood the importance of social and emotional competence. In surveys, preschool and kindergarten teachers often consider children's interest in learning, their social skills, and their ability to listen and be part of a group as more important aspects of readiness than specific academic skills (Ackerman & Barnett, 2005; Lin, Lawrence, & Gorrell, 2003). In early childhood settings, early educators usually identify children's challenging behaviors as the most pressing issue that they must address (Hemmeter, Corso, & Cheatham, 2006), and higher education faculty find it difficult to adequately prepare their students to work with children who have challenging behaviors (Hemmeter, Santos, & Ostrosky, 2008). When kindergarten teachers estimate how many children are "unready" for school, again they focus on social and emotional indicators, such as being unable to concentrate, follow directions, or cooperate with others (Rimm-Kaufmann, Pianta, & Cox, 2000).

Social and Emotional Development Is Promoted Through Strengthening the Early Childhood Environment

Most researchers consider early social and emotional development to be malleable, subject to a range of environmental influences, albeit with neurobiological and temperamental underpinnings. Correlational research suggests, for example, that children who are in settings with warm, sensitive early educators are more interested and engaged in learning activities (Ridley, McWilliam, & Oates, 2000). This research also indicates that adult modeling and labeling of emotions is associated with children's enhanced understanding of their own and others' feelings and with more empathy for other children (Denham, Zoller, & Couchoud, 1994).

As summarized by Raver (2002; 2008), new randomized evaluation studies provide growing evidence that effective interventions in the social and emotional domains are possible, especially among children whose development may be at risk because of poverty or other factors.

Moving Forward in Measuring Environmental Supports: What Is Needed?

This brief discussion underscores the promise of early childhood programs: Young children's social and emotional competence can be enhanced through high-quality experiences, and the promise is greatest for those children at highest risk of poor developmental outcomes. But to gain a more precise understanding of *why* certain interventions and practices may or may not be effective, and to target areas for improvement in the provision of early childhood services, good measurement of a range of environmental supports is essential.

An Ecological Perspective on Potential Environmental Supports

The work group of researchers and other stakeholders that focused on this measurement domain began its efforts by defining an overall perspective or conceptual framework for measuring potential supports for social and emotional competence. The work group participants believed that, especially in this domain, it is essential to use an ecological or systems perspective that takes into account multiple levels of potential support (e.g., Bronfenbrenner, 1979; Bronfenbrenner & Ceci, 1994; Bronfenbrenner & Morris, 1998). These may include both proximal supports (such as specific interactions between an early educator and an individual child) and distal supports (such as the availability of professional development or other institutional supports for staff).

1. *Responsive and supportive behaviors and interactions with children.* This category encompasses early educator behaviors and interactions that support children's positive social-emotional functioning in the caregiving setting. Evidence points to the salient influence of responsive and supportive early educator behaviors and interactions on young children's emotion regulation, social competence, and behavioral functioning (e.g., Denham & Burton, 1996; Howes, Matheson, & Hamilton, 1994; Stuhlman & Pianta, 2001). Both the quality of relationships and the responsiveness of interactions appear to be important (Walters & Pianta, in press). Studies have consistently shown that children who have more supportive and less conflictual relationships with their early educators are more accepted by their peers (Birch & Ladd, 1997; Hughes, Cavell, & Wilson, 2001; Taylor, 1989). Furthermore, teachers and caregivers who engage in high-quality interactions with children can help them to regulate their emotions and behavior by guiding their attention, assisting them in interpreting emotions, and regulating the emotional demands of the classroom (Thompson, 1994). In sum, research suggests that the following responsive and supportive behaviors and interactions of early educators with children are associated with children's social-emotional development:

   • Supports for children's social understanding and guidance on peer interactions

   • Supports for children's development of conflict resolution skills and positive social behavior

- Supports for emotion expression and emotion regulation

- Supports for children's independence and decision making

- Appropriate responses to children's behavior problems

2. *Routines and activities.* Structuring children's experiences through the use of well-established routines and varied activity settings can promote their social-emotional competence (e.g., Bodrova, Leong, Norford, & Paynter, 2003; Rimm-Kaufman, La Paro, Downer, & Pianta, 2005; Webster-Stratton, Jamila Reid, & Stoolmiller, 2008). Research indicates that expert early educators are adept at creating well-established routines, but are also flexible in responding to children's needs and can make adaptations when necessary (Westerman, 1991). Furthermore, a growing body of research suggests that implementing a social-emotional curriculum can strengthen children's social competence and emotion regulation (Webster-Stratton et al., 2008). Finally, research suggests that not only content of instruction but also early educators' choice of classroom activities, including using a combination of whole- and small-group activities and facilitating positive peer play, is linked to children's social competence (e.g., Bodrova et al., 2003; Kontos & Keyes, 1999; Rimm-Kaufman et al., 2005). Taken together, this research indicates that the following routines, instruction, and activities may foster children's positive social-emotional development:

- Organization of the day, including consistency and predictability

- Use of a curriculum that incorporates social and emotional development as a part of the daily routine

- Activities that are structured to promote children's engagement and that provide opportunities for positive interactions with early educators and peers

- Appropriate balance of time in large groups, small groups, and pairings of children

3. *Physical features of the environment.* Research suggests that physical features of the environment (space, furnishings, materials) can support multiple aspects of development, including physical well-being, academic engagement and achievement, and social and emotional development, which is our focus here. Acknowledging that the physical environment contributes to children's development in multiple domains, researchers have found positive associations between the subscales of the environmental rating scales that focus on space and furnishings and both the emotional climate in the classroom and teacher sensitivity as measured by the CLASS (La Paro, Pianta, & Stuhlman, 2004). Although not demonstrating causal relationships, these associations raise the possibility that a sufficiently spacious, well-supplied, and well-organized physical environment reduces sources of possible conflict in the classroom and frees the early educator to engage in positive interactions. Some research also suggests that there is an inverse relationship between a high-quality physical environment and children's antisocial and/or worried behaviors (Sammons et al., 2003). The following physical features appear to be important components of an environment that fosters children's social-emotional competence:

- Organization of space, including space for children to play and learn with peers or to be alone

- Provision of furnishings that are cozy

- Materials (e.g., books about emotions, art materials, props for pretend play) that support social and emotional competence

Institutional Supports

Institutional supports refer to a range of resources that programs can use to promote social and emotional competence. For example, several recent studies underscore the critical importance of caregivers' access to mental health consultants (Gilliam & Shahar, 2006; Raver et al., 2008). A study of children's expulsions from preschool in the state of Massachusetts by Gilliam and Shahar (summarized in Gilliam, 2005) found that expulsion rates were lower when teachers had access to an expert who could help them in working with children with emotional or behavioral difficulties. Furthermore, increasing evidence suggests that interventions aimed at improving early educators' behavior management skills and pedagogy related to children's social-emotional development have a positive impact on classroom climate (Raver et al., 2008) and on the children's social-emotional skills (e.g., Domitrovich, Cortes, & Greenberg, 2007).

Separately, each of these categories of environmental supports shows linkages to children's social-emotional development. At the same time, we recognize that the benefits of these supports are likely to go beyond the social-emotional domain: "A rising tide lifts all boats." As Stipek (2002), Raver (2008), and others have emphasized, the same instructional practices and interactions that support social and emotional development—including children's motivation and self-regulation—are likely to lead to more effective learning in content domains such as literacy and mathematics. Supporting this hypothesis, Bouffard and Jones (see Chapter 12, this volume) discuss the interrelatedness of development in different domains, pointing to the need for integrative cross-domain measures of quality.

Review of Existing Measures of Environmental Quality

Identifying the needs for further measures development in the area of environmental supports for young children's social and emotional development requires a careful review of existing measures: What categories (broad, overarching groups of supports—e.g., early educators' behaviors and interactions with children) and constructs (more specific features within categories—e.g., supports for emotion expression and emotion regulation) do these existing measures cover, and how do they map onto the conceptualization we have described? Are positive features of the environment assessed, or do the items focus only on problematic features of the environment? Do the measures provide sufficient detail at the item and indicator levels so that they can serve as a basis to guide improvement in practice? Can the measures be used not only by researchers but also by program directors, teachers, and caregivers, as well as by policy makers who accredit and monitor program quality?

In this section we describe how and to what extent existing measures address the environmental supports for young children's social and emotional development. The section serves as a foundation for the next section of this chapter on suggested steps for strengthening measurement in this area. The quality measures that we review for this section are included in the first edition of a compendium of quality measures entitled *Quality in Early Childhood Care and Education Settings: A Compendium of Measures* (Halle & Vick, 2007; see http://www.researchconnections.org/childcare/resources/13403/pdf. The second edition of the compendium by Halle, Vick Whittaker & Anderson (2010) was not yet available when this chapter was being prepared). We recognize that the measures included in the *Compendium* do not encompass all available measures of environmental quality and that new measures are regularly being developed and validated (e.g., Teaching Style Rating Scale (TSRS); Domitrovich et al., 2009; Teaching Pyramid for Preschool Classrooms, TPOT; Hemmeter, Fox, & Snyder, 2008). However, for the purpose of our review, we chose to focus on the subset of measures included in the *Compendium,* as psychometric information was available for all of the measures and we were able to obtain copies of all of the measures from the developers to review individual items. In addition, we believe that the measures in the *Compendium* represent a large proportion of the measures available at the time of review.

In deciding how to categorize various aspects of these measures, we recognize that measures developers often use varying terminology; for example, the CLASS (Pianta, La Paro, et al., 2008) uses the term *domain*, whereas we use *subscale*. However, for this chapter, we decided to use uniform terms to facilitate comparisons.

Overview of Measures

Although the measures reviewed vary in purpose, scope, and format, there are similarities across measures. The measures target a range of settings (e.g., center-based preschools, family child care homes, schools) and age groups (infants through school-aged children). However, the majority assess quality in center-based programs serving children ages 3–5. Furthermore, measures developers most often cite research and evaluation, program improvement, and/or monitoring and accreditation as their primary purpose.

In general, the measures assess environmental quality through direct observation, usually performed by external observers. Some measures also include an interview with the early educator (e.g., Child/Home Early Language and Literacy Observation Tool, CHELLO; Neuman, Dwyer, & Koh, 2007). The interview questions are often related to lesson content and early educator practices rather than to pedagogical beliefs about social-emotional competence or the rationale behind teachers' decisions.

Measure developers suggest varying lengths of time for observation. Very few measures require observers to assess the classroom on multiple days or during different times of the day (e.g., the morning and afternoon). Most assessments are based on a discrete period of time during a single day. Furthermore, many measures do not specify during what time of year classrooms should be assessed or whether multiple assessments are needed. In identifying areas for future measures development, it is important to consider these general measures characteristics as well as taking a more detailed look at the inclusion of specific supports for social-emotional development. The next section presents a more detailed analysis of the categories and constructs that are and are not well represented in existing measures of environmental quality, with particular attention to constructs that could be more fully covered in future measures of quality.

What Constructs Are Included in Existing Quality Measures?

Our goal in this chapter is not to critique individual measures, but rather to summarize areas that are well covered, as well as to identify gaps that could be addressed through further measures development. Our review found that there is great variability in the degree to which existing measures focus on measuring supports for children's social-emotional development as a dimension of quality. In part, this has to do with the Environmental Rating Scales (ERS) varying focus of the measures included in this analysis. For example, at one end of the continuum, the CHELLO (Neuman et al., 2007) was designed to assess the features of home-based care that support children's language and literacy, and was not intended to focus in any depth on supports for social and emotional development. Several other measures were designed to measure global environmental quality. Examples include the ERS scales—ECERS-R (Harms et al., 2005), ITERS-R (Harms et al., 2003), FCCRS-R (Harms et al., 2007), and SACERS (Harms, Vineberg Jacobs, & Romano White, 1996). Within these measures, supports for social-emotional development are one part of a larger whole, with varying degrees of emphasis. At the other end of the continuum, one measure directs its entire focus toward assessing classroom routines, activities, and early educator behaviors that support children's Social-Emotional growth (Supports for Social-Emotional Growth Assessment [SSEGA] Smith, 2004). Our intent in including all of the measures of quality for which we have reliability and validity data (Halle & Vick, 2007), even those that do not include a central focus on supports for social and emotional competence, is to be able to provide a broad overview of the extent to which our full "toolbox" contains supports for this domain of development.

Despite the variation in depth of coverage, almost all of the measures reviewed include items related to at least one category of support for social-emotional competence.

Responsive and Supportive Early Educator Behaviors and Interactions with Children

Overall, the category that is included most often in the set of existing measures reviewed here is *responsive and supportive early educator behaviors and interactions with children*. The majority of measures (31 out of 35) have at least one item that falls within this category. Many scales seem to use *high-quality early educator relationships and responsive interactions* as the primary items reflecting support for children's social-emotional behavior. However, the number of items used to assess this category varies greatly. For example, the Caregiver Interaction Scale (CIS; Arnett, 1989) focuses completely on the emotional tone and responsiveness of early educators' interactions with children. Other measures have entire subscales with multiple items that measure interactions between early educators and children (e.g., FCCERS-R; Harms et al., 2007; Preschool Program Quality Assessment Instrument, PQA; HighScope Educational Research Foundation, 2003). In contrast, a few measures include only one item that assesses children's interactions with early educators, or an item that has indicators referencing the quality of responsiveness toward children. The measures that tend to have only one item related to interactions of early educators with children are those focused on a domain other than social-emotional development (e.g., the Supports for Early Literacy Assessment, SELA; Smith, Davidson, Weisenfeld, & Katsaros, 2001). Although many measures explicitly aim to assess early educators' interactions with children (whether through entire subscales or only one item), most items are focused unidirectionally on educators' actions toward children, not their interactions.

Under the category *responsive and supportive early educator behaviors and interactions with children*, a construct that is commonly assessed in the measures reviewed is *supports for children's positive social behavior and appropriate responses to challenging behaviors*. Although there are a few noteworthy exceptions (including the SSEGA, Smith, 2004, and the CLASS, Pianta, La Paro, et al., 2008), items under this construct focus primarily on behavior management and discipline techniques rather than supports for children's positive behaviors. Many of the measures ask observers to rate appropriate responses to children's challenging behavior with items such as those found in the Assessment Profile for Family Child Care Homes, APFCCH (Abbott-Shim, 1993): "provider intervenes to stop destructive or disruptive behavior"; "limits are clearly stated when there is destructive/disruptive behavior"; and "behavioral consequences are clearly stated without critical tone." Other measures ask observers to rate separate items on early educators' appropriate and inappropriate responses to challenging behavior. Yet another group of measures focuses primarily on early educators' negative reactions to children's disruptive behavior (e.g., all of the items under this construct in the CIS; Arnett, 1989).

The majority of measures include multiple items that assess early educators' responses (appropriate, inappropriate, or both) to challenging behaviors. In fact, this appears to be the most thoroughly measured construct (greatest number of items per measure) in the category *responsive and supportive early educator behaviors and interactions with children*. Many measures define supports for children's social-emotional competence primarily as the reduction or prevention of challenging behaviors. Such measures tend to focus on inappropriate or problematic discipline strategies and do not include as many positive items related to supports for children's prosocial skills, social cognition, and self-regulation. Despite the fact that some measures are very strong on the positive side in this regard, many current measures do not focus explicitly on early educator behaviors that elicit and sustain children's positive social behavior.

Unlike the construct *appropriate responses to challenging behavior*, the construct *supports for emotion expression/regulation* is not assessed in most of the measures reviewed. Less than half of the measures (14 out of 35) included items that assessed supports for children's emotional expression/regulation. Out of the 14 measures that include at least some items related to this construct, most only include one item, which usually assesses whether early educators encourage children to verbalize their feelings or label their emotions (e.g., Child Caregiver Interaction Scale CCIS; Carl, 2007; Classroom Practices Inventory CPI; Hyson, Hirsh-Pasek, & Rescorla, 1990). Perhaps efforts to refine and extend the measurement of emotion expression and regulation (e.g., Diamond, Barnett, Thomas, & Munro, 2007) will spur corresponding efforts to identify and assess the features of the environment that support development in this area.

Routines and Activities

Over half of the measures reviewed (21 out of 35) include items that assess *routines and activities*. Within this category, *organization of the day* is the most widely measured construct. Most of the items assess whether waiting time is kept to a minimum, whether the early educator provides advance warnings about transitions, and whether children are allowed ample time to complete activities. Several scales also include items related to whether there is a daily schedule. Another construct that is included in many measures concerns *activities*. However, there is great variability in what is assessed with regard to activities as a support for social-emotional competence. Some measures include items that assess the developmental appropriateness of activities (e.g., appropriate content and length), others ask observers to rate whether activities are individualized and designed to fit children's interests, and still others assess the degree to which children are able to make choices and engage in activities that are self-directed. Most measures include only one or two items related to this construct. However, the variability in the content of items across measures suggests that there may be several related social-emotional supports and that many measures are assessing only one aspect. The variability also suggests a lack of agreement about how the structure of program activities may contribute to young children's social and emotional development.

A construct that was identified by the working group as important but that was included in only three of the measures reviewed is whether the *curriculum provides a basis for focus on social and emotional development*. The CCIS (Carl, 2007) includes the item, *promotion of prosocial behavior/social emotional learning*. One of the indicators for this item is whether the early educator uses a social-emotional curriculum, and examples of these types of curricula are provided (e.g., Promoting Alternative Thinking Strategies, PATHS; Domitrovich et al., 2007). The Ready School Assessment (RSA; HighScope Educational Research Foundation, 2006) also includes items related to social-emotional curricula. For the subscale Effective Curricula, observers rate, from *never* to *always*, whether "staff are well informed and well trained on all prosocial methods/materials they are to employ." In addition, observers rate whether procedures are in place to monitor the fidelity of implementation of prosocial curricula. Reflecting emphases in recent research (Bodrova & Leong, 2007; Bodrova et al., 2003), some measures include a focus on whether activities include time for play.

Physical Features of the Environment

Sixteen out of 35 measures include the category *physical features of the environment*. Most of these measures assess the organization of space and materials, usually with one item for each construct. Within the measures, the items measuring organization of space focus primarily on whether there is ample space for children and early educators to move freely and whether there are designated spaces available for children to get away from noisy activities or to work through a disagreement with another child. The Assessment of Practices in Early Elementary Classrooms (APEEC; Hemmeter, Maxwell, Ault, & Schuster, 2001) includes, as an example, an indicator for a high rating of adults' encouragement of children's negotiation: *designated space in classrooms for resolving conflicts*. Several of the literacy-specific measures (e.g., Supports for Early Literacy Assessment, SELA; Smith et al., 2001) ask observers to rate whether there is an inviting, cozy place for children to look at books alone or with friends. Although some measures include a focus on resolving conflicts with peers, the emphasis in existing measures is on having a designated space, rather than a process, for resolving conflicts.

It is interesting to note that literacy-focused measures tend to have a substantial emphasis on physical/environmental supports (e.g., charts, signs) for early literacy development. However, there has been very little focus on these quality features as potential supports for social and emotional development. An exception is the APEEC (Hemmeter et al., 2001), which includes two items that assess the presence of problem-solving posters and rule charts posted in the classroom.

Some measures also assess the availability of materials that support young children's social and emotional development. Many of the materials-related items assess whether materials allow for children's self-direction—that is, whether they are easily within reach, do not require an early educator's assistance, and offer a variety from which to choose. Some items focus on adults' encouragement of children's use of materials. Almost half of the measures include items in this category. In sum, there appears to be a frequent focus on children being able to move freely, withdraw to a quiet and/or cozy area, and use materials autonomously. However, measurement has not yet caught up with research suggesting the need for a process—not just a physical space—for children to work through conflict and develop prosocial skills.

Institutional Supports

Unlike the other four categories of supports identified by the work group and supported by research, *institutional supports for children's social-emotional growth* are not included in most measures.

Even in measures that included questions about early educators' education and training, there was very little focus on training specific to social-emotional development or behavior management. Although six measures do include a question related to opportunities for general professional development, the measures do not assess explicitly whether the professional development includes a focus on children's social-emotional skills. In addition, only five measures include items related to screening and assessment; of those, only two are related specifically to identifying children with social-emotional needs. The measures reviewed thus include a minimal focus on institutional supports for children's social and emotional development.

In sum, the measures reviewed for this chapter tend to focus on the input that early educators provide in interactions. They also focus on the avoidance of harsh responses to child misbehavior and frequently include content related to overall emotional climate and a physical environment that permits autonomy and some privacy.

Indicators and Scoring

Many, although not all, measures use Likert-type scales to score or rate items, with indicators at each score point. This is especially the case for scales based on observation. Ratings on the items (derived in part through raters identifying indicator descriptions that best correspond with their observations) then contribute to a summary rating for the subscale or overall scale.

Our review found great variation in number and level of detail of these indicators. Many scales, particularly for the constructs *behavior management* and *responses to children's problematic behaviors,* include many more negative indicators than positive. Furthermore, scales with indicators/examples at each score point do not always have complementary or aligned information at each level. For example, an inadequate rating might include an indicator about inappropriate responses to problematic behavior, while an excellent rating does not include an indicator for an appropriate response to problematic behavior but instead includes one for high-quality interactions between early educators and children. That is, the indicators for a rated item do not include a continuum for a single underlying construct, but instead mix constructs.

Finally, in reviewing the content of the indicators, it became clear that there is variability in the way that measures developers are defining high-quality supports for children's social-emotional functioning. In some instances, early educator behaviors that are indicators of low-quality support on one measure are considered high quality on another. (There are differences, for example, in how praise of children's accomplishments is viewed in different measures, with some rating such praise positively and others negatively.) Similarly, some measures include items on early educators' ability to prevent conflicts before they occur, whereas other measures include items that assess how well early educators assist children in developing their own conflict resolution strategies. In fact, some peer relationship research suggests that learning how to solve disputes amicably is a critical skill that young children must develop (Dunn, 1993); therefore, early educators should *not* always intervene to prevent conflict. This raises the question of whether measure developers are always in agreement about what may or may not support children's social-emotional competence.

Perhaps the critical follow-up step is to seek (or collect new) evidence that a particular behavior is indeed related in a systematic manner to important child outcomes. It is critical that there be an evidence base for the inclusion of specific constructs. In general, the development of strong measures would be assisted if measures developers would provide *both* information on why certain constructs or items were included (based on theory, research, or practice) and evidence of those items' predictive validity.

Guidance for Early Educators

Explicitness in Providing Guidance

A key issue to emerge from this review is whether measures should be accompanied by information to help early educators understand how to use results from the measures to improve their own practices. Our review found a range in the extent to which measures build in guidance for early educators' expectations and practices for young children. A few of the global environmental quality measures include such guidance.

Measures also vary in the degree to which they provide guidance to early educators on how to effectively engage and involve families, particularly with regard to supporting children's social-emotional development. Many measures include no items related to family involvement, and those that do primarily assess whether early educators have yearly conferences with parents about children's progress. Some measures (e.g., ECERS-R, Harms et al., 2005; FCCERS-R, Harms et al., 2007) ask whether parents are referred to professionals when the need arises. However, these items do not specifically ask whether parents are actually connected with professionals who can help support children's mental health and social-emotional well-being. The SACERS (Harms et al., 1996) has a Health and Safety subscale with an item measuring health practices. One of the indicators of an "excellent" score is that the staff provide feedback to parents about children's physical and mental health and assists parents in meeting children's mental health needs. In our review, this indicator was one of the only places in which helping parents to support children's mental health needs was addressed. The SSEGA (Smith, 2004) was the only measure we reviewed that includes a subscale on Parent Involvement, which directly assesses whether early educators help parents to support children's social-emotional development. In general, guidance for early educators on how to effectively and respectfully partner with families to support children's social-emotional development is lacking in our current measures.

If measures are to be used in supporting change in practice within classrooms, a central issue is the degree to which the measures provide explicit and detailed guidance on how the information the measures provide can actually be used. Many measures lack such information or provide insufficient detail to guide practice. What stands out is a *lack* of guidance for early educators on 1) the responsive aspect of interaction with children; 2) the structuring of interactions and activities to proactively support positive social behavior and not only respond to misbehavior; 3) the explicit recognition, expression, and self-regulation of emotions; 4) ongoing assessment of children's social and emotional development; and 5) institutional supports to address children's mental health and behavioral problems.

Explicitness in Linking Specific Practices to Social and Emotional Development

Increasingly, classroom assessment tools are being used in coaching and quality improvement activities (e.g., Pianta, Mashburn, Downer, Hamre, & Justice, 2008). In these contexts, it would be helpful for early educators to understand the rationale for the types of supports described in an assessment's items. Frequently, this rationale is not explicitly stated in the measures.

Meaningful Overlap with Other Domains

Some child behaviors do not neatly fit into one domain of development, and this creates a challenge for measures that are domain-focused. A notable example is the set of behaviors subsumed under "approaches toward learning," such as sustained attention, enthusiastic engagement in learning activities, and developing and following through on plans. Are these behaviors cognitive, social-emotional, or both? Perhaps because of the complexity of the approaches-to-learning construct, neither cognitive nor social-emotional quality measures have addressed these approaches directly.

The measures reviewed for this chapter have little content focusing explicitly on supports for "approaches to learning." Few scales include constructs that assess supports for children's motivation, planning, or sustained attention, and those that do usually contain one or two items rather than a group of items or a separate subscale. Exceptions are the focus in the SSEGA (Smith, 2004) on motivation, engagement, and mastery, and the focus in the CLASS (Pianta, La Paro et al., 2008) on classroom management practices that maximize engagement. For the most part, however, the few approaches-to-learning items get somewhat buried, tending to be included in subscales on routines or program structure. There is rarely an explicit link between specific practices and support for children's approaches to learning, despite the importance of this construct in many states' early learning standards (Scott-Little et al., 2003) and in Head Start's Child Outcomes Framework (Head Start Bureau, 2001).

To reflect recent research on the importance of children's engagement (McWilliam & Casey, 2008), it will be important for future measures to include ratings summarizing whether learning activities provide for active engagement rather than prolonged periods of watching and listening. Similarly, measures should include ratings of whether early educators encourage children's focused attention. In a parallel manner, we need to acknowledge that some aspects of the environment traditionally assessed in measures of supports for cognitive development have a social and emotional component. For example, learning activities such as whole group time or book reading may have an emotional tone or social structure that either facilitates or deters engagement. In the future, measures should more fully address the emotional tone of learning activities, as well as the extent to which the structuring of those activities promotes active engagement.

Summary of Potential Next Steps to Strengthen Existing Measures of Quality

To summarize, our review suggests that potential next steps for strengthening measures of quality with a focus on children's social and emotional development should include the following objectives:

- Ensuring that there is sufficient detail at the indicator level to provide anchor points for ratings, with specification of positive as well as negative indicators

- Confirming that there is alignment between high and low indicators, so that both address the same underlying construct

- Building a consensus across different measures about what practices support children's social and emotional development

- Providing sufficient detail so that concepts that underlie measures (e.g., about appropriate social-emotional practices at different ages) are not left unspecified

- Providing a clear basis in research, theory, and/or practice for the inclusion of a construct and items, and providing evidence of predictive validity for those constructs and items

- Making more explicit the linkages between measures and practices that support children's social and emotional development, articulating the link where possible within measures, and/or making available professional development materials that are clearly aligned with the measures

We conclude this section by noting an important gap in measurement: Despite the construct's importance in the literature and in standards, in our review we found very little focus on environmental supports for approaches to learning. As noted earlier, because the approaches-to-learning construct includes both cognitive and social-emotional competencies, it may have run the risk of falling through the domain-specific measurement cracks. Moving from an analysis of existing measures, we turn now to a discussion of potential extensions of the measurement of environmental supports for children's social and emotional development.

Extending the Measurement of Environmental Supports for Social-Emotional Development

To look more precisely at the areas in which measurement might be extended, we return to our ecological framework. Taking in turn each of the three previously discussed dimensions of children's social-emotional development (*prosocial skills and social cognition, self-regulation,* and *behavior problems*), we outline suggestions for enhanced measurement of supports for these dimensions within early childhood environments. For simplicity, we refer throughout to environmental *supports*; however, we do so with the understanding that when we are focusing on behavior problems, the key environmental features serve as deterrents rather than facilitators. As in other sections of this chapter, we organize the environmental features into four categories: *responsive and supportive early educator behavior and interactions with children, routines and activities, the physical environment,* and *institutional supports*.

Our urging enhanced measurement of these supports does not mean that we ignore measurement advances (e.g., the CLASS and SSEGA, as well as newer measures under development, such as those by Domitrovich et al., 2009, and Hemmeter, Fox et al., 2008). However, here our goal is to paint a broad canvas of what would be desirable in this measurement arena, recognizing that in some cases the desirable is beginning to be achieved.

To illustrate the scope of measurement possibilities, for each social-emotional developmental dimension (prosocial skills and social cognition, self-regulation, and behavior problems), a brief narrative introduction is followed by a table presenting a comprehensive, proposed set of environmental supports organized around our four categories. Each potential support also is accompanied by classroom-based examples and illustrative comments. The goal is to illustrate opportunities to measure a wide range of relevant environmental supports for these critical aspects of social and emotional development, at the same time recognizing the array of technical and methodological challenges posed by those suggestions. Finally, the third section ends by raising several measurement issues that cut across developmental and environmental categories.

Prosocial Skills and Social Cognition

Considering the importance of this developmental dimension, measurement of environmental supports for children's prosocial skill development and social cognition seems to have a number of missing or underemphasized elements. For example, our analysis of existing measures in the second section showed a strong emphasis on measuring early educators' relationships with children as supports for the dimension of social-emotional development. In contrast, with few exceptions (e.g., SSEGA; Smith, 2004), measures could be expanded to give greater attention to supports for children's development of peer relationships, including environmental supports such as materials and activity contexts that promote positive peer interaction.

Besides paying greater attention to supports for peer relations, the measurement of environmental supports for children's development of social cognition needs augmentation (see work in this direction in measures by Bierman et al., 2008; Hemmeter., Fox et al., 2008; Smith, 2004). Measures might also capture the extent to which support for children's prosocial skills and social cognition is embedded within routine classroom activities. One could assess, for example, the extent to which early educators intentionally direct their practices toward children's prosocial skill development. A related focus for measurement could be early educator efforts that go beyond simply *eliciting* peer interactions, to *sustaining* those interactions over time.

To flesh out these ideas, Table 6.1 provides extended descriptions of possible features of environmental supports for children's prosocial behavior and social cognition, each illustrated with examples.

Self-Regulation

The lack of measures focusing on children's self-regulation reflects the fact that only a handful of intervention programs thus far has emphasized self-regulation. Some of these, such as PATHS, focus on social-emotional self-regulation (Domitrovich et al., 2007), whereas a few, such as Tools of the Mind, address social-emotional and cognitive development together (Diamond et al., 2007).

To further add to the complexity, the definition of *self-regulation* has expanded to include such things as inhibitory control of attention, aspects of working memory, and cognitive flexibility, in addition to emotional self-control. This further increases the range of children's behaviors that need to be intentionally supported in the classroom or home-based group (Blair, 2002, Diamond et al., 2007) and, therefore, that need to be considered for inclusion in measures of program quality. In addition, measures that directly assess child outcomes in this area, such as Head-to-Toes (Ponitz, McClelland, Matthews, & Morrison, 2009), Kochanska's Battery for Effortful Control (Kochanska & Knaack, 2003), and Diamond's computerized measures (Diamond et al., 2007), are still

Table 6.1. Potential extensions of measures of quality to include greater focus on environmental supports for young children's prosocial behavior and social cognition

Level of ecological model	Environmental supports that might be incorporated into future measures	Further explanation and examples of these environmental supports
Responsive and supportive early educator behavior and interactions with children	Early educator planning of social groupings to maximize positive interactions between peers	Early educators intentionally plan for social groupings of pairs, small groups, and large groups to provide peer support for children's social skill development. • Older preschool-age children sometimes form cliques that exclude others. This is less likely to happen if children are regularly paired so that they can make friends with all of the other children in the class. • Whereas children have opportunities to play with others who are already friends, they also are paired so that they play with children they do not know as well.
	Early educator planning for social groupings with attention to children's ages and developmental levels	Whereas early educators can intentionally plan for groupings of children even when they are infants and toddlers, the size and composition of groups for the youngest children will need to differ from those of older children. • When there are mixed-age groups—for example, in family child care—the ratio of older to younger children should be considered, and early educators should provide guidance for positive interactions across age ranges.
	Assessment of children's prosocial skills and the use of this information to help children who need support	Early educators help to explain the social overtures of children to each other, if they don't understand them well, and help children learn ways of making overtures to each other. Early educators can encourage children to help each other in ways consistent with their age and developmental level. • In a family child care home that includes a child with a disability, the early educator can help the children who are typically developing know that when Brenda pulls on your arm, she is asking you to play with her. The early educator can also teach Brenda to say, "Come play" or teach her how to gesture to indicate, "Come play." • When a Spanish-speaking child wants to be the doctor, the early educator can explain to the English-speaking peer, "He wants to know whether you want to play doctor. Do you want to? Say 'si' and nod your head. Show him what you want to do to play doctor." • Instead of helping a child find his or her mittens, the early educator can ask another child to help.
	Proactive help with social skills	If there is a potential for social conflict over a toy or a role, the early educator can have children with verbal ability discuss solutions prior to going to a center or playing with a toy. • The early educator might observe that "there is only one ballerina costume, but both of you want to be ballerinas. How are you going to solve that problem?" • If children don't know, then the early educator can suggest, for example, "You could share. One person could go first. You can make a second costume. One person could be the audience," and so forth. • If a child is shy, the early educator can coach that child on strategies for entering the group.
	Early educators model and expand children's use of language to describe their own emotions and their friends' emotions and the reasons for these feelings	There is intentional use of language that goes beyond simple labels such as *mad* or *angry*. • Teaching children about emotions and feelings not only takes place in decontextualized activities, such as discussing books or hypothetical social problems, but also is reflected in the early educator's support for children during ongoing activities.

(continued)

Table 6.1.   (*continued*)

Level of ecological model	Environmental supports that might be incorporated into future measures	Further explanation and examples of these environmental supports
Routines and activities	Weaving opportunities to practice social cognition throughout daily activities	Some activities are designed to help children talk about emotions and feelings with each other, and opportunities to talk about feelings and social interactions are integrated into ongoing activities.
		• During read-aloud time, children talk about the feelings of the characters as well as discuss the story. Some stories are chosen for their emotional content, providing a context for discussing feelings.
		• During make-believe play, early educators use a visit to the doctor's office to model how parents help the baby get a shot, using such words as, "Don't worry. It will hurt for only just a second. It will make you feel better. I'll be there. I'll hold you. Don't be afraid."
	Opportunities for children to work with and help each other, integrated into many activities	Early educators maximize the allocation of time toward activities in which children are encouraged to work together and play together.
		• Children read books with a partner instead of always looking at books alone.
		• Even 1-year-olds can sit together, putting blocks in a container together, with early educator support.
Physical environment	Activities and materials that encourage children to interact with each other	Make-believe play themes for older preschoolers are set up so that they encourage interaction between children.
		• Children are more likely to interact with each other when the play theme is "restaurant" rather than "dinosaurs."
		Toys and props for toddlers and younger preschoolers also are chosen to promote their interactions.
		• A 2-year-old playing with a doctor kit will be looking for someone to play "patient."
		Games that children can play with materials are also set up to encourage interactions.
		• Children are encouraged to work together to build.
	Centers organized so that the size of the group optimizes positive social interactions	There are few centers where children are encouraged to play alone. There are also few centers that have more than 4–6 children, to minimize overcrowding.
	In learning centers, the presence of a system to help children maintain a group size that optimizes positive interactions	Early educators may use a system that lets children know that only four children can play in a center.
		• Four clothespins are placed on a card just outside the center. When children enter the center, they take a clip. Once all four clips are gone, other children know that no other children can join the group.
	Materials that provide opportunities for sharing	Materials available for children reflect a balance between each child having one of everything and having toys that children need to share and work with together.

	Materials that support recognition of emotions	Specific, developmentally appropriate materials are used that are designed to help children recognize each other's emotions.
		• Materials include posters and books with illustrations of facial expressions.
		• Such posters and books should include a focus on young children and should encourage children to think about emotions that they can connect to, such as *happiness* and *sadness,* rather than concepts like *respect* or *discipline* that will be more appropriate for older children.
		Early educators use these materials so that children become familiar with different terms to describe emotions.
Institutional supports	Training for early educators in prosocial development and social cognitive development	The training reflects a consistent theoretical and philosophical approach. The training approach is not a scaled-down version of a program for teachers of older children.

not widely used, though utilization is expanding. Thus, identifying and measuring environmental supports for self-regulation that reach beyond "giving the child choices" continue to be problematic.

The challenge is further compounded because some environmental supports—such as child choice—that may seem invariably to support self-regulation, may actually promote disregulation at certain stages of the development of a child's self-regulation. Children who are already relatively self-regulated are likely to benefit from wide choices of activities as an environmental support for their further self-regulation. Yet, for children who have not yet developed regulatory skills (including children with autism spectrum disorders and other disabilities), a high degree of choice may actually increase their impulsive, unregulated behavior (Bodrova & Leong, 2007), and explicit intervention may be needed to increase their skills in making choices (Barry & Burlew, 2004). To measure the optimal, gradual increases in child choice afforded by a high-quality early childhood environment would require measures that take into consideration the time of year and a particular child's capacities, rather than simply measuring the presence or absence of opportunities for children to make choices. But here, practical considerations again arise: Although it may be important to try to capture these subtleties, measuring the developmental nuances of "giving choices" while aiming to develop a reliable way of measuring this construct is likely to be extremely challenging.

With these challenges in mind, note that Table 6.2 provides a summary of our proposals for ways in which measures of quality could be extended to paint a more varied, nuanced picture of environmental supports for young children's self-regulation.

Behavior Problems

If early educators are able to create environments that support prosocial development, social cognition, and self-regulation, then the need to directly address behavior problems is minimized. However, the question of how to measure these environmental supports is complex: An early educator who is providing strong supports for positive social-emotional functioning may "score low" on his or her use of strategies to address behavior problems—because such problems will occur rarely in his or her classroom or home-based group. On the negative side, however, the absence of environmental features that prevent or address problem behavior could also indicate that an early educator does not know how use such features.

Table 6.2.   Potential extensions of measures of quality to include greater focus on environmental supports for young children's self-regulation

Level of ecological model	Environmental supports that might be incorporated into future measures	Further explanation and examples of these environmental supports
Responsive and supportive early educator behavior and interactions with children	Early educator behaviors that show evidence of insightful and intentional interactions to support child independence and decision-making as supports for self-regulation Early educator behavior and interactions support focused attention	This should take into account the early educator's understanding of the child's current level of self-regulation as a basis for his or her interactions. It is unlikely that this could be assessed without interviewing early educators about the thinking behind their specific interactions. • Early educator behavior includes monitoring children's attention and identifying positive ways of creating joint attention in different group contexts: large group, small group, and one-to-one pair. • Fostering task persistence and motivation are seen both in the way an early educator verbally encourages a child to keep trying and in direct intervention if a child looks as if he or she is going to give up. • Early educator behavior also includes modeling strategies for handling anxiety-provoking and difficult learning situations. Early educators may use direct strategies, such as labeling how a child might know that a task is difficult (for example, "I can see you tried to do that, but it isn't working") or may model speech and behavior that might help (for example, "When I can't put it together this way, I try this").
	Specific scaffolds for individual children who lack focused attention	Early educators would need to show evidence of both differentiating support (allowing children who are more self-regulated to function more independently than children who show less self-regulation) as well as planning to decrease support over time so that children develop self-initiated, focused attention. To be self-regulated, children eventually must be able to focus attention without early educator support. Decreasing support, in particular, would be something that would be difficult to observe and might be measurable only through an interview. • Early educator behavior to support focused attention might include sitting close to a child to support his or her sustained attention. • In this and other areas, measurement would need to be sensitive to children's ages (e.g., promoting focused attention in a toddler program is different than in kindergarten), as well as individual characteristics and disabilities.
	Praising effort and persistence	Early educator praise for accomplishments is seen in many quality measures, but to encourage self-regulation—in particular, motivation and mastery—it is important that early educators praise effort and persistence.
	Interactions with children that include strategies to manage emotions	Examples include the following: • Cuing a child who has difficulty with transitions, far ahead of time, that a transition is approaching • Providing some children more time to think about a choice when choice is difficult for them • Helping children who may not get their first choice to use strategies for handling their emotions (e.g., "Six more people until my turn," "I come after Frank," "I pick last today because I picked first yesterday")

	Changes in supports as children develop more self-regulation	Early educators monitor the development of self-regulation in children by assessing it in different activities and contexts. Measures could gather evidence that early educators modify and change their supports for self-regulation as children develop more self-regulation. • This again may be something that would be measurable only through an interview if observations are limited to relatively small samples of time or do not focus on individual children.
	Modeling of planning	Especially in programs for preschoolers, environmental supports for self-regulation would include early educator interactions that model how to plan and that support children in planning activities in advance. • Early educators discuss how to plan for field trips or how to plan for snacks.
	Mistakes handled as part of learning	Early educators help children handle making mistakes and create an environment in which errors are seen as a part of the learning process.
Routines and activities	Helping children remember and use rules and routines	With the youngest children, early educators support children's ability to remember and follow routines (e.g., through a clean-up song). Older children are observed using the rules to monitor their own behavior and follow routines on their own.
	Turn taking and sharing built into the classroom routines	Children are exposed to routines for sharing and taking turns so that they can internalize strategies. For example, a kindergarten program may have a sign-up list for use of the computer so that children know who is next, and may have a set of rules for using the computer (e.g., each turn is 5 minutes long). Such rules provide a mechanism for dividing up scarce resources so that children learn how to do this on their own.
	Routines that allow early educators to release to children responsibility for doing activities	Even 2-year-olds may be observed to pass out napkins to other children. The early educator may start by handing out materials, but soon gives children increased responsibility for such tasks.
	Monitoring the length of activities and transitions to produce optimal attention and self-regulation	Large-group activities are kept short, or are omitted entirely, for the youngest children so that children do not lose attention and self-regulation. The length of time an individual child is required to wait before his or her turn should be included in the calculation for length of an activity in order to maintain optimal attention and self-regulation.
	Regular inclusion of activities and games that promote self-regulation	Developmentally appropriate activities that promote focused attention and encourage children to self-regulate might include picture books that challenge children to find hidden objects, guessing games, freeze-movement games, and finger plays.
	Use of pretend play as a context to support self-regulation	As children engage in pretend play, they learn to monitor how they and their friends are following the rules they set by themselves for such things as how each of the roles is acted out and how props are used. Early educators provide scaffolding to help children become engrossed in a role and a scenario or to discover new ways to engage in object-oriented play and exploration.
	Transitions that are predictable to children	Early educators use visual aids, like a picture schedule, so that children can anticipate transitions and routines. In a mixed-age group of children, such as in family child care, early educators would make sure that these aids are appropriate for varied levels of understanding.
	Responsive pacing of activities	The pace of classroom or group activities is sensitive to child cues so that children do not feel rushed, but at the same time are not bored. The pace takes into account children's different levels of self-regulation.

(continued)

Table 6.2.   (*continued*)

Level of ecological model	Environmental supports that might be incorporated into future measures	Further explanation and examples of these environmental supports
Physical environment	A physical environment that limits distracting stimuli while also being stimulating	Early educators arrange the room to limit traffic through activities so that children can maintain concentration. The classroom environment is not cluttered (with visual, physical, or auditory clutter).
	Organization of the physical environment to maximize children's ability to take age-appropriate responsibility for choosing and putting away materials and their own possessions	The location of materials is predictable, consistent, and organized. There are visual reminders so that children know where to put things.
	Materials that support sustained engagement	Opportunities to learn to be persistent are supported by materials that are challenging, but that are within the child's capacities. For example, play materials for older preschoolers promote children's ability to engage in play scenarios at increasingly extended and complex levels without the need for early educator intervention to keep them playing.
	Materials that allow children to check their own skill or understanding	For example, • Blocks of graduated sizes allow very young children to self-correct. • Certain counting activities also allow older children to check to see whether they are correct.
	Visual displays of classroom rules	In classrooms for children 3 years old or older, classroom rules are posted which are concrete and represented by icons that the children can understand. These can apply not only to general classroom interactions, but also to specific centers/activities. For example, • Rules for being in the "quiet" center or area, or rules for play with sand in the sand table.
	A physical environment structured so that the early educator can observe and monitor children.	The early educator does not have to enter a section of the room in order to see whether children are self-regulating.
Institutional Supports	Training for early educators on self-regulation	Such training includes the development of self-regulation from birth through age 5, its components, and how to support it in an early childhood program. The training is theoretically and philosophically consistent. The administration has a specific approach to the development of self-regulation, and training is chosen to further early educator development and understanding of this approach.
	Scheduling of "specials" within the day to maximize focused attention during key instructional/activity times	In center-based programs, the scheduling of "specials" (library, music, or gym) takes into account the attention demands of other activities. For example, "specials" may be scheduled later in the day so that children's attention is maximized in the morning during activity or instructional time within the classroom.

A related measurement challenge is that, even in the absence of strong prevention strategies, behavior problems usually occur infrequently, making it difficult to reliably observe the occurrence of related environmental supports for preventing and addressing such problems.

With these caveats, as in the previous sections, we refer to Table 6.3, which presents illustrations of how measures of quality could be extended to provide further focus on environmental features relevant to young children's behavior problems.

Measurement Issues Across Categories

Stepping back from these specific illustrations, we note that several measurement challenges recur across the categories into which the preceding discussion was organized.

Intentions of Early Educators

In making suggestions for measuring environmental supports for children's social and emotional development, a key issue is that the early educator's *intentions* in implementing or purposefully excluding an environmental support, as well as his or her *understanding* of the children's developmental levels, appear to be critical to a greater extent than in considering environmental supports for other domains of development.

Behavior Problems: The Duration of Observations

Behavior problems may not occur every day. Yet, how they are handled when they do occur may be quite important to understanding environmental supports for social and emotional development. This raises the critical issue of duration of observations: When, how long, how often, and at what time of day the classroom or home-based early childhood setting is observed may have an impact on the ratings a classroom or group is given—especially with respect to issues such as how early educators address behavior problems. Therefore, when feasible, it may be useful to broaden the typical observational time frame to ensure that a representative sampling of classroom supports for social-emotional development has been obtained.

Contextual Considerations

Developmental and setting contexts make a difference in the provision of environmental supports. Although the underlying dimensions of support for children's social and emotional development may be the same at different ages, their observable manifestations may be age specific. Supports for the social-emotional development for infants and toddlers would not look the same as those for older children, even if the underlying goal (for example, developing positive relationships) were the same. Because most studies in this area have been conducted with children ages 3–5, our foundation for making these developmental distinctions is still under construction.

Specific early childhood settings also may make a difference in what is measured and in interpretation. For example, observations in family child care homes would have to focus on different routines and different features of the physical environment than observations in a center-based care setting. Furthermore, the features of center-based environments may differ, depending on whether the center is housed within a public school or in a separate child care or preschool setting. The nature of these differences,

Table 6.3.   Potential extensions of measures of quality to include greater focus on environmental supports to address behavior problems in young children

Level of ecological model	Environmental supports that might be incorporated into future measures	Further explanation and examples of these environmental supports
Responsive and supportive early educator behavior and interactions with children	Positive emotional relationships with children who have behavior problems	Early educators do not interact only when children are having difficulties; positive interactions are in evidence at other times. For children who often have problems with behavior, positive interactions with early educators occur at the same rate as the positive interactions with other children.
	Anticipation of situations in which children who have behavior problems will have difficulty, taking a proactive approach	The early educator gives proactive support both to the child who needs help handling angry feelings and the withdrawn child who needs help making social connections.
	Preventing isolation	Early educators foster positive social interactions between children with behavior problems and others in the group, not allowing these children to become isolated or socially outcast.
	Specific coaching for peers on how to help and support children with behavior problems (depending on children's age and developmental level)	Early educators may explain how to interpret the social overtures of a child with behavior problems and how to respond.
	Consistency across early educators	If there is more than one early educator in a classroom or group, there is a consistent strategy for how the team will handle behavior problems.
	Discussions not used to humiliate children	Classroom discussions about social problem-solving are not used to humiliate a child who is having behavior problems, but instead such discussions allow the child to rehearse strategies.
	Charting progress of children with behavior problems	Early educators assess the development of children with behavior problems and their progress in overcoming these problems. Early educators evaluate their strategies to make sure that children with behavior problems are making progress toward self-regulation and prosocial skills. Early educators adjust their strategies as children make progress.
Routines and activities	Handling of behavior problems in a way that does not disrupt routines	Behavior problems are handled in a way that does not disrupt the classroom routine for other children.
		• For example, if a child has a behavior problem during snack, one early educator in a classroom continues with snack while another supports the child who is having difficulties.
	Timely response to behavior problems	Behavior problems are handled as they happen rather than at the end of the day or at another time, so that children remember the behavior and its consequences.
	Supports provided during times in routines that are difficult for some children	Classroom routines are organized to allow early educators to provide extra support for children with behavior problems. If a child has difficulty with changing activities, early educators do not take breaks until the children are settled into the next activity so that special support can be given by a staff member.

Physical environment	Physical supports to diminish problem behavior and increase prosocial behavior and self-regulation	Physical supports for a child may include maintaining close proximity to an early educator during an activity, a carpet square to help a child keep within a defined space, or a social narrative (with a series of pictures that prompts social interactions).
Institutional supports	Access to mental health professionals	Early educators have access to mental health professionals who can provide extra support for children with behavior problems.
	Coordination in responding to behavior problems at institutional level	Consistent plans are created among mental health professionals, parents, and early educators for identifying and supporting the development of children with behavior problems.
	Training	Early educators receive developmentally appropriate training focused on working with behavior problems.
	Written guidelines	Written guidelines describe how early educators are supposed to identify, and procedures for how to respond to, children with behavior problems.

particularly between center-based and home-based care settings, is still unspecified because of the prominence of center-based settings in studies that measure supports for social and emotional development.

Conclusion: Next Steps for Measures Development

In this chapter, we have identified 1) what we see as the range of potential supports for children's social and emotional development, 2) what our existing measures of quality focus on and how they do so, and 3) where we see opportunities to extend the measurement of environmental supports for children's social and emotional development. Among the multiple recommendations we have made for future research toward extending our measures of quality, we see some that could be construed as "low-hanging fruit," or extensions of measures that could be made fairly readily, whereas the harvesting of other fruit will require more strenuous efforts.

One extension of existing measures that could be undertaken fairly readily would involve developing measures of visual reminders to support rules and routines, such as posters summarizing class rules or props to limit the number of children participating in an activity. It would also be within reach to add interview items asking early educators whether staff have participated in professional development focusing specifically on children's social and emotional development, whether there are mental health resources for the program to call upon when a child's behavior or emotional well-being elicits concern, and whether a curriculum with an explicit focus on children's social and emotional development is being used.

In the middle range of difficulty, we have noted the relative emphasis in our current measures on the ways early educators address problematic child behavior (rather than the ways they promote positive social-emotional development) and the relatively rare attempts made to capture supports for children's prosocial behaviors. We have also noted the relative absence of measurement of early educators' efforts to help children understand and express their own emotions. Further, we have noted an imbalance in the focus on relationships between children and early educators, compared with child–child relationships. The multiple suggestions we have given for redressing these imbalances require rating the frequency of specific behaviors. Articulating the specific behaviors to be observed and assuring that ratings can be completed with reliability are challenging tasks. However, observations of supports for positive social behavior, for the appropriate expression of emotion, and for facilitating positive peer interactions are all possible within the span of one typical program observation period lasting one-half to a full day. Other specific behaviors that require attention, yet that do not appear more subtle or complex to capture than those in our current measures of quality, include early educators' actions to support children in anticipating social problems and generating a range of solutions to those problems.

Perhaps the most challenging steps for measures development will involve capturing those supports for children's social and emotional development which require longer spans of time to observe, an awareness of how supports are being adapted for individual children, and an understanding of the early educator's intentions. For example, we have noted the need to consider longer time spans than the usual half-day observation in order to be able to take into account consistency in the handling of behavior problems as children participate in activities with different early educators (such as "specials" in many public school programs) over the course of a week. We also have noted the need to take children's initial level of self-regulation into account in understanding whether an early educator is gradually extending the children's choice of activities over time or gradually extending the amount of time children need to spend waiting for their turn. A grasp of individual children's needs and how early educators are responding to them will be required for measuring whether early educators are providing supports for sustained attention for those children having attentional difficulties, whether early educators are reaching out to establish strong positive relationships with the particular children showing behavior problems, and whether early educators are vigilant in ensuring that no child is becoming isolated and that every child in the group is having opportunities to play or cooperate in an activity with every other child. Understanding the function of a classroom or home-based group's "quiet space" for children to retreat to when they are upset may require more than simply observing the use of such a space during the course of an observation. The intention or rationale for such a space may be ascertained only by interviewing the early educator.

One strategy for the short term might be to add extensions to existing measures of quality—extensions which enable observers to document supports for social and emotional development that can be completed in a half-day or full-day observation. However, in the longer term, we need to develop in-depth measures of supports for social and emotional development incorporating those more challenging or nuanced aspects that require both longer periods of observation and a greater understanding of the early educator's approach and underlying philosophy regarding social and emotional development. Although harder to measure, these kinds of supports may indeed be more strongly related to children's development over time than are other, more superficial supports. To bring all of this together, we must have not only measures development but also empirical work documenting the relative contributions that different environmental supports make to children's social and emotional development.

Finally, we acknowledge that the process of developing environmental quality measures of support for social and emotional development is somewhat dependent on well-validated child outcome measures in this domain. Although there has been some progress in this area (e.g., Diamond et al., 2007; Kochanska & Knaak, 2003; Ponitz et al., 2009), without robust, well-validated direct assessment measures, it will be difficult to validate observation tools measuring the quality of supports for children's social-emotional development.

References

Abbott-Shim, M. (1993). *Assessment Profile for Family Child Care Homes.* Atlanta, GA: Quality Assist.

Ackerman, D., & Barnett, W.S. (2005). *Prepared for kindergarten: What does "readiness" mean?* New Brunswick, NJ: National Institute for Early Education Research, Rutgers University.

Arnett, J. (1989). Caregivers in day-care centers: Does training matter? *Journal of Applied Developmental Psychology, 10,* 541–522.

Barry, L., & Burlew, S.B. (2004). Using social stories to teach choice and play skills to children with autism. *Focus on Autism and Other Developmental Disabilities, 19*(1), 45–51.

Bierman, K., Domitrovich, C., Nix, R., Gest, S., Welsh, J., Greenberg, M., et al. (2008, November). Promoting academic and social-emotional school readiness: The Head Start REDI program. *Child Development, 79*(6), 1802–1817.

Birch, S.H., & Ladd, G.W. (1997). The teacher–child relationship and children's early school adjustment. *Journal of School Psychology, 35,* 61–79.

Blair, C. (2002). School readiness as propensity for engagement: Integrating cognition and emotion in a neurobiological conceptualization of child functioning at school entry. *American Psychologist, 57,* 111–127.

Bodrova, E., & Leong, D.J. (2007). *Tools of the Mind: The Vygotskian approach to early childhood education* (2nd ed.). New York: Prentice Hall.

Bodrova, E. Leong, D.J., Norford, J.S., & Paynter, D.E. (2003). It only looks like child's play. *The Journal of the National Staff Development Council, 24*(2), 47–51.

Bronfenbrenner, U. (1979). *The ecology of human development: Experiments by nature and design.* Cambridge, MA: Harvard University Press.

Bronfenbrenner, U., & Ceci, S.J. (1994). Nature–nurture reconceptualized in developmental perspective: A bioecological model. *Psychological Review, 101,* 568–586.

Bronfenbrenner, U., & Morris, P.A. (1998). The ecology of developmental processes. In W. Damon (Series Ed.) & R.M. Lerner (Volume Ed.), *Handbook of child psychology: Volume 1. Theoretical models of human development* (pp. 993–1028). New York: Wiley.

Carl, B. (2007). *Child Caregiver Interaction Scale.* Unpublished doctoral dissertation, Indiana University of Pennsylvania, Indiana, PA.

Campbell, S. (2002). *Behavior problems in preschool children: Clinical and developmental issues.* (2nd ed.). New York: Guilford Press.

Campbell, S.B., Shaw, D.S., & Gilliom, M. (2000). Early externalizing behavior problems: Toddlers and preschoolers at risk for later maladjustment. *Development and Psychopathology, 12*(3), 467–488.

Denham, S.A., & Burton, R. (1996). A social–emotional intervention for at-risk 4-year-olds. *Journal of School Psychology, 34,* 225–245.

Denham, S.A., Zoller, D., & Couchoud, E.A. (1994). Socialization of preschoolers' emotion understanding. *Developmental Psychology, 30*(6), 928–937.

Diamond, A., Barnett, S., Thomas, J., & Munro, S. (2007). Preschool program improves cognitive control. *Science, 318,* 1387–1388.

Domitrovich, C., Cortes, R., & Greenberg, M. (2007). Improving young children's social and emotional competence: A randomized trial of the preschool "PATHS" curriculum. *Journal of Primary Prevention, 28*(2), 67–91.

Domitrovich, C.E., Gest, S.D., Gill, S., Bierman, K.L., Welsh, J.A., & Jones, D. (2009). Fostering high-quality teaching with an enriched curriculum and professional development support: The Head Start REDI Program. *American Educational Research Journal, 46*(2), 567–597.

Duncan, G.J., Dowsett, C.J., Claessens, A., Magnuson, K., Huston, A.C., Klebanov, P., et al. (2007). School readiness and later achievement. *Developmental Psychology, 43*(6), 1428–1446.

Dunn, J. (1993). *Young children's close relationships: Beyond attachment.* Thousand Oaks, CA: Sage Publications.

Fabes, R.A., Gaertner, B.M., & Popp, T.K. (2006). Getting along with others: Social competence in early childhood. In K. McCartney & D. Phillips (Eds.), *The Blackwell handbook of early childhood development* (pp. 297–316). New York: Wiley-Blackwell.

Fantuzzo, J.W., Bulotsky-Shearer, R., Fusco, R.A., & McWayne, C. (2005). An investigation of preschool classroom behavioral adjustment problems and social-emotional readiness competences. *Early Childhood Research Quarterly, 20*(3), 259–275.

Fantuzzo, J., Perry, M.A., & McDermott, P. (2004). Preschool approaches to learning and their relationship to other relevant classroom competencies for low-income children. *School Psychology Quarterly, 19*(3), 212–230.

Gilliam, W.S. (2005). *Prekindergarteners left behind: Expulsion rates in state prekindergarten systems.* New Haven, CT: Yale University Child Study Center.

Gilliam, W.S., & Shahar, G. (2006). Preschool and child care expulsion and suspension: Rates and predictors in one state. *Infants & Young Children, 3,* 228–245.

Halle, T., & Vick, J.E. (2007). *Quality in Early Childhood Care and Education Settings: A Compendium of Measures.* Washington, DC: Prepared by Child Trends for the Office of Planning, Research and Evaluation, Administration for Children and Families, U.S. Department of Health and Human Services.

Halle, T., Vick Whittaker, J.E., & Anderson, R. (2010). *Quality in Early Childhood Care and Education Settings: A Compendium of Measures* (2nd ed.). Washington, DC: Prepared by Child Trends for the Office of Planning, Research and Evaluation, Administration for Children and Families, U.S. Department of Health and Human Services.

Hamre, B., & Pianta, R.C. (2001). Early teacher–child relationships and trajectory of school outcomes through eighth grade. *Child Development, 72*(2), 625–638.

Harms, T., Clifford, R.M., & Cryer, D. (2005). *Early Childhood Environment Rating Scale-Revised Edition (ECERS-R).* New York: Teachers College Press.

Harms, T., Cryer, D., & Clifford, R.M. (2003). *Infant/Toddler Environment Rating Scale: Revised Edition (ITERS-R).* New York: Teachers College Press.

Harms, T., Cryer, D., & Clifford, R.M. (2007). *Family Child Care Environment Rating Scale-Revised Edition (FCCERS-R).* New York: Teachers College Press.

Harms, T., Vineberg Jacobs, E., & Romano White, D. (1996). *School-Age Care Environment Rating Scale (SACERS).* New York: Teachers College Press.

Head Start Bureau. (2001). Head Start Child Outcomes Framework. *Head Start Bulletin, 70.* Washington, DC: Department of Health and Human Services, Administration for Children and Families. Retrieved from http://www.hsnrc.org/CDI/pdfs/UGCOF.pdf

Hemmeter, M.L., Corso, R., & Cheatham, G. (2006, February). *Addressing social-emotional development and challenging behavior: A national survey of early childhood educators.* Poster presented at the Conference on Research Innovations in Early Intervention, San Diego.

Hemmeter, M.L., Fox, L., & Snyder, P. (2008). *Teaching Pyramid Tool for Preschool Classrooms (TPOT).* Nashville: Vanderbilt University.

Hemmeter, M.L., Maxwell, K.L., Ault, M.J., & Schuster, J.W. (2001). *Assessment of Practices in Early Elementary Classrooms (APEEC).* New York: Teachers College Press.

Hemmeter, M.L., Santos, R.M., & Ostrosky, M. (2008). Preparing early childhood educators to address young children's social-emotional development and challenging behavior. *Journal of Early Intervention, 30*(4), 321–340.

HighScope Educational Research Foundation. (2003). *Preschool Program Quality Assessment, 2nd Edition (PQA) Administration Manual.* Ypsilanti, MI: HighScope Press.

HighScope Educational Research Foundation. (2006). Ready School Assessment: Administration manual. Ypsilanti, MI: HighScope Press.

Howes, C., Matheson, C.C., & Hamilton, C.E. (1994). Maternal, teacher, and child care history correlates of children's relationships with peers. *Child Development, 65,* 265–273.

Hughes, J.N., Cavell, T.A., & Wilson, V. (2001). Further support for the developmental significance of the quality of the teacher–student relationship. *Journal of School Psychology, 39,* 289–301.

Hyson, M. (2008). *Enthusiastic and engaged learners: Approaches to learning in the early childhood classroom.* New York: Teachers College Press and Washington, DC: NAEYC.

Hyson, M., Copple, C., & Jones, J. (2006). Early childhood development and education. In K.A. Renninger & I. Sigel (Eds.), *Handbook of child psychology: Volume 4. Child psychology in practice* (pp. 3–47). New York: Wiley.

Hyson, M.C., Hirsh-Pasek, K., & Rescorla, L. (1990). The Classroom Practices Inventory: An observation instrument based on NAEYC's guidelines for developmentally appropriate practices for 4- and 5-year-old children. *Early Childhood Research Quarterly, 5,* 475–494.

Kagan, S.L., Moore, E., & Bredekamp, S. (Eds.). (1995). *Reconsidering children's early development and learning: Toward common views and vocabulary.* Washington, DC: National Education Goals Panel.

Kochanska, G., & Knaack, A. (2003). Effortful control as a personality characteristic of young children: Antecedents, correlates, and consequences. *Journal of Personality, 71,* 1087–1112.

Kontos, S., & Keyes, L. (1999). An ecobehavioral analysis of early childhood classrooms. *Early Childhood Research Quarterly, 14,* 35–50.

La Paro, K., Pianta, R., & Stuhlman, M. (2004). The Classroom Assessment Scoring System: Findings from the prekindergarten year. *The Elementary School Journal, 104*(5), 409–426.

Lin, H.-L., Lawrence, F.R., & Gorrell, J. (2003). Kindergarten teachers' views of children's readiness for school. *Early Childhood Research Quarterly, 18*(2), 225–237.

Mashburn, A.J., & Pianta, R.C. (2006). Social relationships and school readiness. *Early Education and Development, 17*(1), 151.

McClelland, M.M., & Morrison, F.J. (2003). The emergence of learning-related social skills in preschool children. *Early Childhood Research Quarterly, 18*(2), 206–224.

McWilliam, R.A., & Casey, A.M. (2007). *Engagement of every child in the preschool classroom.* Baltimore: Paul H. Brookes Publishing Co.

National Research Council. (2008). *Early childhood assessment: Why, what, and how.* Committee on Developmental Outcomes and Assessments for Young Children, C.E. Snow & S.B. Van Hemel (Eds.), Board on Children, Youth, and Families, Board on Testing and Assessment, Division of Behavioral and Social Sciences and Education. Washington, DC: The National Academies Press.

Neuman, S., Dwyer, J., & Koh, S. (2007). *Child/Home Early Language & Literacy Observation Tool (CHELLO).* Baltimore: Paul H. Brookes Publishing Co.

O'Connor, E., & McCartney, K. (2007). Examining teacher–child relationships and achievement as part of an ecological model of development. *American Educational Research Journal, 44*(2), 340–369.

Palermo, F., Hanish, L.D., Martin, C.L., Fabes, R.A., & Reiser, M. (2007). Preschoolers' academic readiness: What role does the teacher–child relationship play? *Early Childhood Research Quarterly, 22*(4), 407–422.

Pianta, R.C., La Paro, K.M., & Hamre, B.K. (2008). *Classroom Assessment Scoring System™ (CLASS™) Manual: Pre-K.* Baltimore: Paul H. Brookes Publishing Co.

Pianta, R., Mashburn, A., Downer, J., Hamre, B., & Justice, L. (2008). Effects of web-mediated professional development resources on teacher–child interactions in pre-kindergarten classrooms. *Early Childhood Research Quarterly, 23*(4), 431–451.

Ponitz, C.C., McClelland, M.M., Matthews, J.S., & Morrison, F.J. (2009). A structured observation of behavioral self-regulation and its contributions to kindergarten. *Developmental Psychology, 45*(3), 605–619.

Raver, C. (2002). Emotions matter: Making the case for the role of young children's emotional development for early school readiness. *Social Policy Report of the Society for Research in Child Development, 16*(3), 1–20.

Raver, C.C. (2008, October). Promoting children's socioemotional development in contexts of early intervention and care: A review of the impact of federally-funded research initiatives on young children's school readiness. Working paper prepared for *A Working Meeting on Recent School Readiness Research: Guiding the Synthesis of Early Childhood Research.* Washington, DC.

Raver, C.C., Jones, S.M., Li-Grinning, C.P., Metzger, M., Champion, K.M., & Sardin, L. (2008). Improving preschool classroom processes: Preliminary findings from a randomized trial implemented in Head Start settings. *Early Childhood Research Quarterly, 23,* 10–26.

Ridley, S.M., McWilliam, R.A., & Oates, C.S. (2000). Observed engagement as an indicator of child care program quality. *Early Education and Development, 11*(2), 133–146.

Rimm-Kaufman, S., La Paro, K., Downer, J., & Pianta, R. (2005). The contribution of classroom setting and quality of instruction to children's behavior in kindergarten classrooms. *The Elementary School Journal, 105*(4), 377–394.

Rimm-Kaufman, S.E., Pianta, R.C., & Cox, M.J. (2000). Teachers' judgments of problems in the transition to kindergarten. *Early Childhood Research Quarterly, 15,* 147–66.

Saarni, C., Campos, J.J., Camras, L., & Witherington, D. (2006). Emotional development: Action, communication, and understanding. In W. Damon, R.M. Lerner (Series Eds.), & N. Eisenberg (Vol. Ed.), *Handbook of*

Child Psychology: Vol. 3. Social, emotional, and personality development (6th ed., pp. 226–299). New York: Wiley.

Sammons, P., Sylva, K., Melhuish, E., Siraj-Blatchford, I., Taggart, B., & Elliot, K. (2003). *Measuring the impact of pre-school on children's social/behavioural development over the pre-school period* (No. Technical paper 8b). London: Institute of Education.

Scott-Little, C., Kagan, S.L., & Frelow, V.S. (2003). *Standards for preschool children's learning and development: Who has the standards, how were they developed, and how were they used?* Greensboro: University of North Carolina, SERVE.

Scott-Little, C., Lesko, J., Martella, J., & Milburn, P. (2007). Early learning standards: Results from a national survey to document trends in state-level policies and practices. *Early Childhood Research and Practice, 9*(1). Retrieved from http://ecrp.uiuc.edu/v9n1/little.html

Smith, S. (2004). *Pilot of a new classroom assessment instrument: Supports for social-emotional growth.* (Unpublished manuscript). New York: New York University, Child and Family Policy Center, Steinhardt School of Education, Culture, and Human Development.

Smith, S., Davidson, S., Weisenfeld, G., & Katsaros, S. (2001). *Supports for Early Literacy Assessment (SELA).* (Unpublished manuscript). New York: New York University, Child and Family Policy Center, Steinhardt School of Education, Culture, and Human Development.

Stipek, D.J. (2002). Good instruction is motivating. In A. Wigfield & J.S. Eccles (Eds.), *Development of achievement motivation* (pp. 309–332). San Diego: Academic Press.

Stuhlman, M.W., & Pianta, R.C. (2001). Teachers' narratives about their relationships with children: Associations with behavior in classrooms. *School Psychology Review, 31,* 148–163.

Taylor, A.R. (1989). Predictors of peer rejection in early elementary grades: Roles of problem behavior, academic achievement, and teacher preference. *Journal of Clinical and Child Psychology, 18,* 360–365.

Thompson, R.A. (1994). Emotion regulation: A theme in search of definition. In N.A. Fox (Ed.), *The development of emotion regulation: Biological and behavioral considerations. Monographs for Society of Research in Child Development, 59,* 25–52.

Thompson, R.A., & Lagatutta, K. (2006). Feeling and understanding: Early emotional development. In K. McCartney & D. Phillips (Eds.), *The Blackwell handbook of early childhood development* (pp. 317–337). Oxford, UK: Blackwell.

Tremblay, R.E., Hartup, W., & Archer, J. (Eds.). (2005). *Developmental origins of aggression.* New York: Guilford Press.

Walters, T.J., & Pianta, R.C. (in press). Teacher-child relationships: A review of the past decade of research. *Attachment and Human Development.*

Webster-Stratton, C., Jamila Reid, J., & Stoolmiller, M. (2008). Preventing conduct problems and improving school readiness: Evaluation of the Incredible Years Teacher and Child Training Programs in high-risk schools. *Journal of Child Psychology and Psychiatry, 49,* 469–470.

Westerman, D.A. (1991). Expert and novice teacher decision making. *Journal of Teacher Education, 42*(4), 292–305.

Endnote

[1]The first three authors share authorship equally and are listed alphabetically. The authors thank the members of the Work Group on Measuring Social and Emotional Supports in Early Childhood Settings, from the Roundtable on Quality Measurement. The discussions of the Work Group at the meeting helped to shape the conceptualization in this chapter. The additional members of the work group (in alphabetical order) are Donna Bryant, Lori Connors-Tadros, Kathleen Dwyer, Dale Farran, Grace Funk, Stephanie Jones, Kerry Kriener-Althen, Carolyn Layzer, Lauren Supplee, and Kathy Thornburg. The authors thank Carolyn Layzer and Kathy Thornburg for their extremely helpful feedback on drafts of this chapter.

CHAPTER 7

Measuring Health-Related Aspects of Quality in Early Childhood Settings

Susan M. Hegland, Susan S. Aronson, Patricia Isbell,
Sarah Benjamin Neelon, Beth S. Rous, and Marilyn J. Krajicek

What Is This Facet of Quality and Why Is It Important to Consider?

Physical and psychological development are inextricably interlinked (Friedman, Brooks-Gunn, Vandell, & Weinraub, 1994); however, few studies of group care settings have included assessments of both children's health (e.g., illnesses, injuries, nutritional status) and their psychological (e.g., language, cognition, social-emotional) development. Indeed, Zaslow et al. (2006) pointed out that among 65 studies on the impact of child care quality on children's school readiness, only 3 (5%) included assessments of children's physical well-being or motor development. The gravity of this omission is demonstrated by a recent study by Hair, Halle, Terry-Humen, Lavelle, and Calkins (2006), who found that children assessed as at risk for health outcomes upon kindergarten entrance showed significantly lower performance in academic and social outcomes in first grade. Thus, the importance of health outcomes for the cognitive and social aspects of school readiness cannot be ignored. As noted subsequently in greater detail, features of early childhood settings have been found to be related to such health outcomes in young children as rates of accidents and injuries. In turn, health outcomes have been found to be linked to variation in children's cognitive and behavioral development.

The purposes of this chapter are to identify issues that are important to take into account in measuring facets of quality in early childhood settings that are related to children's health, to summarize the evidence linking children's developmental outcomes to the health features of early childhood settings, to determine why this is a promising time to reexamine the measurement of the health facets of quality in early childhood settings, and to point to possibilities for further progress in measuring health quality in early childhood settings.

Children's health is affected by both structural (e.g., physical environment) and process (e.g., adult–child interaction) components of early childhood settings. (See later discussion of the range of early childhood settings that measures of quality focusing on health should be appropriate for.) The importance of assessing both structures and processes or practices in the early childhood setting was recently demonstrated by Kotch et al. (2007), who found that changes both in the physical environment and in hygienic practices produced the greatest reduction in cases of diarrheal illnesses.

Studies of the impact of early care and education (ECE) on children's development have shown that the majority of variance in child outcomes is accounted for by family characteristics (e.g., NICHD ECCRN, 2004). However, characteristics of the family interact with characteristics of the early childhood setting, especially for children from low-income families (e.g., Peisner-Feinberg, Burchinal, Clifford, Culkin, & Howes, 2001). Children's preparedness and performance in school is affected by intrinsic child characteristics such as predisposing health issues, including prematurity, allergies, or other special health conditions. School readiness also reflects family behaviors in the home (e.g., nutrition and food safety for foods prepared for the child at home), the family's use of preventive health services such as immunization and dental screenings, and the safety of transport to and from the child care program.

Children's school readiness is affected not only by the health and safety structures and practices within the early childhood setting but also by the partnerships among the early childhood program, the home and the child's health care providers which are working to ensure that children's health needs are met in all care settings. These partnerships are essential for children with special health care needs and those from at-risk families. However, ensuring collaboration and communication between the home and the caregiver/educator is important for all children. For example, Moon, Sprague, and Patel (2005) suggested that the relatively high rates of sudden infant death syndrome (SIDS) deaths they found among infants of well-educated parents may reflect not only a lack of implementation of back-to-sleep practices by caregivers but also a lack of coordination between parent and provider: Children who had been placed successfully back to sleep at home are at greater risk of SIDS in the early care and education setting. This may be because they have not developed the muscle strength to adjust their position to breathe better when placed in the prone position in the early care and education setting. Therefore, in addition to measuring the characteristics of the setting, including the physical environment and interpersonal interactions, measures of health quality in early childhood settings need to assess parental involvement, and collaboration with caregivers and with health professionals regarding health practices in the program. Schwebel and Brezausek (2007) used Bronfenbrenner's concept of the mesosystem (i.e., linkages between the family and nonfamily caregiving settings) to explain a correlation between injuries in the home and the experience of the caregiver in the early childhood settings.

Measures of health quality and school readiness in ECE programs build on research from both medicine and education; however, the development of such measures faces challenges stemming from the different goals, values, and research traditions across the two disciplines. One challenge in bridging the two disciplines is the nomenclature, or use of terms. In the health discipline, the term *health* has a global meaning that addresses all aspects of physical and psychological well-being, going beyond the prevention of illness (often referred to as *physical health*) and prevention of injury (often referred to as *safety*), to include also mental health, oral health, physical activity, and nutrition. However, in other disciplines such as education, the term *health* is seen as limited to illness prevention, whereas the term *safety* is seen as focusing on injury prevention.

In this chapter, except where indicated, our use of the term *health* will be as in the medical tradition, encompassing all aspects of both physical and psychological well-being. We see six areas as important to consider in seeking to measure facets of quality that support young children's health: physical activity, physical health/illness prevention, oral health, nutrition, mental health, and safety/accident prevention. Each of these six domains involves structures (physical features of the environment), practices, and parental collaboration with caregivers in the early childhood setting:

1. Physical activity includes the availability and accessibility of space and equipment for large and small motor activities; the extent to which the environment supports physical activity; interactions between adults and children around physical activity; and physical activity education provided to staff, children, and families. Measurement of this area includes assessment of the allocation of both time and encouragement for children to engage in gross motor activities during a significant portion of the day, both indoors and out. This includes how much time children spend in minimal, moderate, and vigorous physical activity during free play, as well as the amount of time they spend in structured (teacher-led) physical activities.

2. Health/illness prevention includes both physical structures (e.g., location of sinks in classrooms) and functions (e.g., hygiene and sanitation procedures, ensuring complete and timely immunization of staff and children). Health also includes a) appropriate use of exclusion and inclusion policies for staff and children for illness, b) health assessments that follow nationally recommended screening procedures for both staff and children, c) the management of sick children, and d) education related to health-promoting behaviors for staff, children, and families.

3. Oral health includes regular dental examinations and preventive treatments provided by oral health professionals, as well as healthful daily oral health practices such as avoiding sugar-containing beverages, using feeding bottles and sippy cups only for interval, not grazing feedings, and daily tooth and gum cleaning procedures.

4. Nutrition includes the nutritional quality of meals and snacks, the extent to which the environment supports healthful eating, interactions between adults and children around eating, and the nutrition education provided to staff, children, and families.

5. Mental health includes structures and practices that reduce stress as well as promote positive interactions between staff and children. This area also includes appropriate interventions to manage challenging behavior and emotional disturbances, as well as to promote positive mental health in both adults and children (see Chapter 6).

6. Safety/accident prevention includes materials and equipment which meet nationally recommended evidence-based guidelines that address the size, age, and developmental abilities of the children. This area also deals with the placement of this equipment. Safety related to gross motor equipment requires appropriate fall zones with cushioning surfacing, as well as the adequacy of maintenance and supervision, including assessments of the use and monitoring of such equipment. Measures of safety also include reduction of other known significant risks, safety education for children and families (e.g., use of bicycle helmets), emergency preparedness, and the identification and prevention of child maltreatment.

To Which Settings Should Measures of Health Quality Apply?

Measures of health quality should incorporate the standards that are adapted as appropriate for all ECE settings serving groups of young children, including schools, centers, preschools, and family child care providers. Measures must reflect the needs of all children, including those with special developmental and/or health needs. Although the standards of quality should be the same across settings, the equipment and approaches used may differ, depending on the group size as well as the ages and the special needs of the children served. For example, measures of health in infant/toddler care settings must include items related to diapering, bottle feeding, cleaning of toys mouthed by infants, and sleeping practices of these youngest children (e.g., putting young infants to sleep on their backs).

What Are the Developmental Outcomes of Interest in Relation to Health Quality?

A comprehensive list of measures of child health outcomes that could be used for longitudinal or cross-sectional studies of health features in young children's environments was recently reviewed and compiled by Brown, Zaslow, and Weitzman (2006). Many of these outcome measures would be appropriate for studies of the impact of health features in ECE. The Appendix lists specific measures of children's health included in 26 national surveys, data sets, and studies. Child health measures include assessment of wellness such as premature birth, nutrition status and diet practices (appropriate weight and diet including breastfeeding from birth to a year of age versus low/very low birth weight or failure to thrive, overweight/obese), iron sufficiency, blood lead level, vision, hearing, immunizations, achievement of developmentally appropriate social-emotional and physical landmarks, incidence of injury, acute and chronic illness (e.g., asthma), disability and medical care according to current guidelines. We underscore that in addition to health outcomes, studies of health quality should consider both the direct linkages of health quality to the cognitive and social aspects of children's school readiness and the indirect linkages to cognitive and social outcomes through the influences of health quality on young children's health outcomes.

The largest number of studies have considered health-related features of quality, and participation in ECE in general, in relation to the health outcomes of illnesses and injuries (Gunn, Pinsky et al., 1991). Thus, for example, the multistate longitudinal study funded by the National Institute of Child Health and Human Development reported that children between the ages of 25 and 36 months and concurrently in large-group care were 2.2 times as likely to have a parent-reported upper respiratory tract illness and 1.4 times as likely to have a parent-reported gastrointestinal illness as children reared only at home or in small-group care. However, ongoing contact was protective over time. Children in large-group care in the third year of life had about a 34% decrease in likelihood of having an upper respiratory tract illness between ages 3 and 54 months and a 24% decrease in likelihood of having a gastrointestinal illness in that period. These findings were related to the size of the group care arrangement, not other factors (National Institute of Child Health and Human Development, Early Child Care Research Network, 2003). In considering health quality and injuries, Kotch, Hussey, and

Carter (2003) found a decrease in the annual rate of medically attended injuries in regulated child care facilities linked to higher playground safety ratings. Similarly, states with higher education requirements for directors of child care centers generally have lower injury rates (Currie & Hotz, 2004). However, Currie et al. (2004) pointed out that states with higher standards also have lower rates of children enrolled in regulated centers; higher standards and costs may have driven some families out of regulated care into less safe, but cheaper, unregulated care.

Recent studies include child outcomes associated with other aspects of wellness. Given recent dramatic increases in the number of overweight and obese children, attention is being paid to strategies that can be used in child care programs to identify young children at risk for obesity as well as to measure practices fostering healthful habits related to physical activity and diet. After reviewing the research, Small, Anderson, and Melnyk (2007) argued that obesity in children from 4 to 7 years of age predicts later obesity better than does obesity in younger children. Therefore, they reviewed studies of interventions designed to either prevent or treat obesity in 4- to 7-year-olds, several of which occurred in preschool, public school settings, and community centers. In addition, as described later, recent efforts have been made to develop reliable and valid assessments of the quality of nutrition and physical activity in child care centers (e.g., Benjamin et al., 2007; Ward, et al., 2008). Tests of measurements of strategies known to be associated with reducing the risk of overweight for infants, toddlers, and young preschool age children are underway (Benjamin Neelon, S., personal communication to S. Aronson, 2010).

Research has considered the relationship between health practices in ECE and oral health in young children. Because dental caries in young children have been identified as one of the most prevalent infectious diseases in the United States, the American Academy of Pediatrics (2003) has called for the prevention, identification, and treatment of dental caries for high-risk children beginning in the first year of life. Southward et al. (2006) used child care centers as a venue to assess children's oral and dental health, as well as to identify practices in both home and child care environments, in order to lower rates of dental caries in preschool children.

Healthy social-emotional development is the beginning of a continuum of child mental health. As described in detail in Chapter 6, appropriate adult-to-child interactions and physical environments are observable features of quality that can be studied in relation to the acquisition of healthy social-emotional skills and prevention of behavior problems (Jelinek, Patel, & Froehle, 2002). Children who have experienced trauma (physical and emotional), those who are depressed, and those who possess intrinsic neurological or psychiatric factors may be found in out-of-home child care. The symptoms of their illness may be intensified or reduced depending on the quality of the care that they receive. Indeed, children with symptoms of mental illness may first be described as having "challenging behaviors" that require a higher level of intervention. For example, quality of care for children with mental illness may involve pharmacological interventions as well as psychiatrically prescribed management routines. These approaches should be reflected in the policies of the facility and the practices of the caregivers (Osofsky, 1998). Therefore, measures of supports for young children's mental health in ECE should include the review of the child care facility's policies and procedures with respect to medication administration and caregiver responses to children who are depressed, violent, self-destructive, or otherwise mentally ill. Care for such children requries structured observations of caregiver actions in response to unacceptable behavior (Keren, Feldman, & Tyano, 1999).

Beyond child health outcomes, strong evidence indicates that children's academic and social outcomes are affected by their health, which, in turn, is affected by both structural and process features of health quality in early childhood settings. Currie (2005) summarized evidence from several studies showing that cognitive and behavior problems in young children are exacerbated by chronic health problems such as dental caries, allergies, ear infections, asthma, and lead poisoning. Illnesses that can be detected, offset, or worsened by conditions in ECE settings include infectious diseases, anemia, sensory problems, and environmental injuries (e.g., lead poisoning, exposure to pesticides), as well as the chronic conditions described previously, such as obesity (Currie, 2005). In a recent study of Head Start children, Hubbs-Tait, Kennedy, Droke, Belanger, and Parker (2007) reported that the children's blood levels of zinc and ferritin together explained 25% of the variance in their verbal scores. Furthermore, they reported that the blood lead levels explained over 20% of the variance in teacher ratings of girls' social skills, whereas blood levels of zinc explained nearly 40% of the variance in teacher ratings of boys' anxiety.

Because such conditions are more likely to be untreated in low-income households, screening and assisting families in obtaining treatment for such conditions have been emphasized in programs that target this population, such as Head Start (Currie, 2005). Currie and Neidel (2005) found evidence of the impact of these efforts in a study of Head Start programs where higher percentages of program expenditures on health and education services were linked to fewer behavior problems and fewer retentions in grade.

Another child outcome that reflects health status and is a contributor to learning is attendance. Associations between attendance and learning have been found both at the level of the school for elementary school children (e.g., Lamdin, 1996) and at the level of the individual child for preschool (i.e., Head Start) children, (Hubbs-Tait et al., 2002). Attendance can be affected by the child's health, as well as by other family circumstances such as substance abuse and transportation challenges. Caregiver as well as child outcomes may be affected by health-related aspects of quality. Provider outcomes such as illness-related absences and diarrheal illnesses can have important implications for children's health and learning outcomes.

Although the major focus of this chapter is on strengthening the measurement of health-related aspects of quality, attention also must be paid to strengthening the measurement of health outcomes in children if we are to be able to assess the strength and consistency of the quality–outcomes relationship in this domain. Zaslow and colleagues (2006) found problems with the degree to which the psychometric properties of child health outcomes were reported in research relating quality and child outcomes, with the use of measures in cultures for which they were not originally developed, and in adapted versions without further assessment of how they were functioning. Further methodological issues relate to the informant (who provides the information on child outcomes) and the severity of health outcomes considered (for example, whether both major and minor injuries are encompassed). Analyses in studies linking ECE participation and child health outcomes are often conducted, of necessity, at an aggregate level. Whereas in educational assessment it is possible to assess an individual child's acquisition of new knowledge or skills in relation to educational practices, this is not possible for such health outcomes as injuries, which are relatively infrequent events in center-based child care. Thus, for example, recent research considers observed caregiver health behaviors or written health and safety policies, documented by child care health consultants (with data collected at the facility level), in relation to facility-level illness or injury rates (Kotch et al., unpublished manuscript).

In summary, research to date has focused especially on injuries and illnesses as child outcomes in relation to participation in ECE and health-related "best practices" recommended to achieve quality in early childhood settings. Other child outcomes considered that are health-related facets of quality include obesity, oral health, and mental health. Emerging evidence links children's learning outcomes and social competence to health quality through effects on child health status. The research on the associations between health quality and child outcomes is impeded not only by limitations in the measurement of health quality but also by methodological issues in the measurement of child health outcomes.

Why Is Now a Fruitful Time to Take Stock of Strengths and Gaps in Measurement Approaches in This Area?

In spite of the large size of the body of research on health issues in early childhood settings, the overall impact of this research on state and national policies and initiatives to improve practices is limited. For example, a recent white paper developed through the Center on the Developing Child at Harvard University (2007) was designed to use evidence to support improved outcomes in learning, behavior, and health for vulnerable children. However, health was omitted both from the principal elements of out-of-home care identified as responsible for positive impacts on children as well as from the list of child outcomes affected by out-of-home care.

A recent analysis of quality rating systems across states reported that only 1 of 14 states considered in the analysis included a category related to health and safety in its statewide quality rating system (Child Care Bureau, 2007). In contrast, 13 of the 14 states included staff professional development qualifications and training, 11 states included parent/family involvement, and 10 states included the learning environment/curriculum (Child Care Bureau, 2007). Although national efforts have been made to increase the role of child care health consultants (Ramler, Nakatsukasa-Ono, Loe, & Harris, 2006), the omission of health standards from quality rating systems (QRS) is likely to limit their visibility and investment among quality improvement interventions.

One possible explanation for the limited impact of the health research on state quality improvement efforts is that the discipline bases from which ECE quality improvement activities are launched are typically psychology or education, but not health. These fields have different research traditions. Although individual studies of health interventions in ECE have reported on interrater reliability and face validity through expert reviews, they do not report on analyses in which summary measures of features of the environment related to health are used to predict child outcomes related to school readiness. Unlike other widely used measures of global quality in early childhood settings, the focus in measuring health has been to compile individual items, each of which is associated with a specific positive or negative health outcome, such as rates of diarrheal illnesses. Summed scores have been used to demonstrate the outcome of an intervention, such as the results of consultation, rather than to predict children's school readiness (e.g., Alkon et al., 2009).

The body of research on health in child care has contributed valuable insights into the specific knowledge and practices required for ECE programs to promote healthful, safe outcomes for children. For example, research on the frequency of serious injuries in children using playground equipment in home and out-of-home settings (e.g., Kotch, Chalmers, Langley, & Marshall, 1993) has influenced guidelines for outdoor home and public playground safety (i.e., U.S. Consumer Products Safety Commission, 2005 and 2008, respectively). Results of health and safety research have also influenced national accreditation standards for center-based and home-based care. For example, both the National Association for the Education of Young Children (NAEYC, 2006) and the National Association for Family Child Care (NAFCC, 2005) have included health among the categories required for accreditation. Research on health issues has become incorporated into both state regulations (e.g., Moon, Aird, & Kotch, 2006) and national standards for child care in nonparental home and center-based settings, as represented in *Caring for Our Children* (National Resource Center for Health and Safety in Child Care, 2nd edition 2002, with 3rd edition in press for publication early in 2011) and in *Stepping Stones to Using Caring for Our Children: Protecting Children from Harm* (National Resource Center for Health and Safety in Child Care, 2003). The latter is a subset of the *Caring for Our Children* standards most closely associated with the highest risk of death, disability, and disease. These standards, in turn, have influenced the development of checklists widely used by child care health consultants to evaluate the quality of health and safety in child care settings (e.g., Alkon, To, Wolff, Mackie, & Bernzweig, 2008).

Glasgow, Lichtenstein, and Marcus (2003) argue that health-related research, in general, has not had an impact on health practices, because the majority of research studies in health interventions have focused on the efficacy, rather than the effectiveness, of interventions. The goal of efficacy studies is to determine whether a given intervention is successful when implemented under controlled conditions. In contrast, the goal of effectiveness studies is to determine whether the intervention *is* usually successful in actual practice. Efficacy is a necessary, but not sufficient, condition for effectiveness, and ideally is established through randomized, controlled, experimental studies (Moher, Schulz, & Altman, 2001). But efficacy studies in the health literature, according to Glasgow et al. (2003), typically lack the description of moderating variables (e.g., characteristics of staff and participants) required for large-scale effectiveness studies. These studies also typically lack cost–benefit analyses that would demonstrate that the cost of the interventions is justified by their outcomes. Glasgow and his colleagues (2003) argued that more effectiveness studies, rather than efficacy studies, of health care interventions are needed in order to impact actual practice. Not mentioned by Glasgow and his colleagues is the need for more transparent operational definitions that would facilitate efficient interrater agreement training in a larger group of assessors involved in large-scale effectiveness studies.

High-stakes funding decisions made through systems using Quality Rating Scales (QRS) in many states make reliable and valid measures of QRS items especially important. Too often in educational settings, what is measured determines what is practiced (Center for Educational Policy, 2007). Unless direct-evidence linkages from health practices to child outcomes are demonstrated, championed, and measured as part of the quality review process, assessing health practices is likely to be acknowledged but then ignored as less important. Administrators are likely to focus on assessing narrow program components that they perceive are directly linked to children's academic and social competence, such as the teaching practices that are the focus of recently developed measures such as the Classroom Assessment Scoring System™ or CLASS™ (Pianta, La Paro, & Hamre, 2008).

Of course, the need for individual children to receive health interventions should not be linked to programwide assessments of health quality. For example, we know that, for individual children with visual impairments and for those with anemia, health interventions will improve their learning (e.g., Sachdev, Gera, & Nestel, 2005; Schoenthaler, Bier, Young, Nichols, & Jansenns, 2000). Systems of assessment, referral, and follow-up that enable these children to obtain the care they need are essential in ECE, particularly in programs serving children at risk. Recent national emphasis on academic achievement (e.g., No Child Left Behind) has been accompanied by state efforts to implement school-based voluntary prekindergarten programs. The health and safety components of quality in early childhood settings that are acknowledged to have linkages to school readiness outcomes are poorly represented in measures of quality and focused interventions that states are using. This is true despite the observation of the developers of the most frequently used observational measure within QRS that low performance on the health and safety items that are included is the norm. (D. Cryer, personal communication to S. Aronson, 2006). The indirect linkages summarized earlier, such as the role of child health in contributing to early learning through fewer absences for illness or injury, may not be considered.

Thus, the development of reliable and valid measures of the health components of quality in ECE settings is essential to safeguard the health of children and staff in these settings. Furthermore, given the evidence that the psychological development and health status of children are inextricably linked (Currie, 2005), such measures play a key role to ensure children's school readiness in all areas. Measures of health quality should be included in the aspects of quality required for financial incentives and awards that are part of many state quality rating systems. Such financial incentives and awards transform the required quality measurements into high-stakes assessments that drive performance. Again, because what is measured in high-stakes assessments too often determines what is practiced, high-stakes assessments in other areas of quality, such as literacy and mathematics, are likely to draw the attention, resources, and efforts of administrators, staff, and parents—away from the equally important, but poorly measured, components of health quality.

Research Identifying the Health and Safety Features of Environment and Interactions that Are Linked to Children's Outcomes

Research incorporating measures of health quality in ECE typically focuses on one of three questions: 1) How do early childhood settings affect children's health? 2) What characteristics in early childhood settings are associated with higher or lower levels of child health? 3) Can targeted interventions alter the level of children's health in early childhood settings?

For the first question about how ECE settings affect children's health, studies report on the epidemiology of illnesses and infections among staff and/or children in early childhood settings. Typical studies either have contrasted rates of injury or illness found in the early childhood setting with those of children who received no nonparental care or have contrasted children in family child care with those in center-based care (e.g., Schwebel et al., 2006). To address the second question about characteristics in ECE settings associated with levels of child health, researchers have assessed the knowledge and implementation of health treatments and/or prevention practices in early childhood settings. In both of these areas of research, children in ECE settings typically have been studied as a unitary population, without analysis of moderating variables (i.e., family characteristics or variations among the facilities studied in which these conditions may occur) or mediating variables (i.e., how these conditions occur, or what are likely causal vectors). To address the third question regarding the impact of interventions, studies typically have employed pre/post, time series, or randomized control trials.

As an example of the first type of study, which focuses on identifying conditions related to health and safety in early childhood settings, Cordell (2001) reviewed a number of studies that found higher rates of infection from several diseases (e.g., shigellosis, hepatitis A, cryptosporidiosis, cytomegalovirus, parvovirus B19) among child care center staff than in the general population. Another study reported that group size is related to incidence of infectious illness in that higher rates of infectious diseases occurred in small child care centers than in family child care settings (Collet et al., 1994). In another study, Tulve et al. (2006) collected data in 168 child care centers across the country both through interview and by direct assessment (i.e., surface wipe and soil samples) from indoor surfaces. They found a particular pesticide, now banned by law, in 89% of the centers and concluded that children were still being exposed to residual levels of a banned pesticide. Therefore, they recommended that efforts to minimize children's exposure to toxic substances include monitoring for pesticides and other toxic compounds that are currently permitted as well as for those that have been banned.

Research conducted over the past 20 years has repeatedly shown higher rates of communicable illnesses (e.g., gastrointestinal tract illnesses, upper respiratory infections, ear infections) among children who participated regularly in ECE settings than among those who exclusively received parental care during their first 2 years of life. As previously mentioned, this finding is related to group size, is most marked among children in the first year of life and disappears by age 3 (National Institute of Child Health and Human Development, Early Child Care Research Network, 2003). Among the specific types of infectious agents that have been reported to affect children in ECE settings more frequently than those exclusively home-reared are cytomegalovirus, hepatitis A, and agents that cause bacterial meningitis (Churchill & Pickering, 1997). This increased rate of infection is reduced by duration of group exposure. Indeed, children who participated in group care during early childhood are less likely to experience both respiratory illness and asthma in their early school years than children who were not exposed to group care during early childhood (Ball, Holberg, Aldous, Martinez, & Wright, 2002).

Researchers in this area have typically reported rates of illness or injuries in ECE settings without assessing potential moderating variables (e.g., family or child care program characteristics) or mediating variables (e.g., staff training or practices) that might affect the rates. Recently, researchers have begun to assess moderators. For example, Moon et al. (2000) found that a larger proportion (20%) of SIDS cases occurred during the time children were in ECE settings than when children were home. This high rate of SIDS occurred most frequently to children of older, more highly educated parents (moderators) in the first few weeks in which they were receiving care in family child care homes. The available data that revealed this finding did not include an assessment of program characteristics, such as caregiver practices, training or education, which could provide additional explanatory evidence related to higher or lower rates of SIDS (mediators). In their discussion of the findings, the investigators suggested that the reason for the higher proportion of SIDS cases that occurred during child care hours might be due to caregivers using the prone (tummy) placement of infants who are accustomed to back sleeping at home.

A second body of research focuses on the knowledge and use of health treatment and/or prevention practices in child care centers (e.g., Clements, Zaref, Bland, Walter, & Coplan, 2001). For example, Clements and his colleagues reported that increased levels of varicella (i.e., chickenpox) vaccine coverage in 11 child care centers were associated with decreases in varicella incidence. This body of research has typically treated early childhood settings as unitary and omitted any description of structural or functional differences in programs that might be linked to variations in the implementation of these practices (Glasgow et al., 2003). Few of these studies examined the linkages of individual differences in the rates of injuries or illnesses to such variables as profit versus nonprofit status, education level of staff, turnover rates of staff, urban versus nonurban location, or socioeconomic status of participating families. One exception is a study by Alkon, Genevro, Tschann, Kaiser, Ragland, and Boyce (1999), which identified child behaviors (i.e., one child pushing another child) that contributed more to higher rates of child injuries than did environmental factors in child care centers.

A third body of research reports the impact of interventions to improve health practices in ECE settings (e.g., Aronson & Aiken, 1980; Kotch et al., 2007; Kotch et al., 1994). For example, in a quasi-experimental time series design study, Ulione (1997) found a significant decrease in children's upper respiratory illnesses and injury rates following staff training in primary care information, infection control, injury prevention, and first aid. Hurwitz et al. (2000), using a randomized control design study, reported that household contacts of preschoolers in child care inoculated with an influenza vaccine had significantly lower rates of febrile respiratory illnesses compared with household contacts of unvaccinated preschoolers in child care. Using self-report measures, Moon and Oden (2003) reported that caregivers increased their awareness, knowledge, and use of the supine position for sleeping infants, and maintained this practice over at least 6 months, following a brief training session. Furthermore, center directors reported an increase in policies related to sleep positions for infants.

Other contributions to this body of work demonstrate that some potentially harmful effects on children's health by children's spending time in ECE settings can be ameliorated or prevented by focused interventions. For example, in randomized controlled trials, two studies by Roberts and her colleagues found that education about hygienic practices reduced episodes of diarrhea in children older than 2 years of age, whereas infection control measures reduced the frequency of respiratory illness in children younger than 2 years of age (Roberts, Jorm, et al., 2000; Roberts, Smith, et al., 2000, respectively). Similarly, Kotch and his colleagues (2007), using a randomized controlled trial design, found that a combination of education and structural modification to foster improved hygienic practices worked better than education alone in reducing illness among both staff and children, as well as in reducing staff absenteeism. Alkon, Sokal-Gutierrez, and Wolff (2002) concluded that child care health consultants made a positive impact on both the knowledge and the implementation of health standards by child care staff.

In many of these studies, the researchers used measures of knowledge, practices, or child outcomes that produced a total score. The researchers reported that the measures met standard psychometric criteria such as content validity and interrater reliability. Such measures contribute to broader and more meaningful assessment of quality health and safety practices that could demonstrate links both to children's general health outcomes and to programwide performance on more general measures of school readiness. The measures used to assess knowledge, practices, and child outcomes in these studies typically have been used by only a single group of researchers and not published for broad-scale use by other researchers. Furthermore, the studies previously described have typically been small-scale demonstrations of the efficacy of a given intervention under tightly controlled conditions, rather than demonstrations of the effectiveness of these interventions implemented across broad populations (Glasgow et al., 2003).

Huskins (2000) reviewed several studies on the impact of interventions designed to reduce the frequency of common respiratory and gastrointestinal infections in child care. He reported inconsistent findings across the studies. For example, some researchers found that certain interventions led to reductions in upper respiratory infections, that others did not. Similarly, some researchers reported that certain interventions led to reductions in gastrointestinal infections; others did not. Although questions have been raised about potential bias due to the sponsorship of some of these studies by manufacturers of the products involved, independent financing is not commonly available for these studies. In attempting to explain such discrepancy in the findings, Huskins (2000) identified several methodological weaknesses among the studies. Although Huskins focused on child health outcomes rather than the health quality of the programs, his criticisms provide helpful reminders for all studies linking health interventions to child outcomes.

First, only a few of the studies incorporated evidence of interrater reliability or any measure of the level of implementation of the intervention strategy (e.g., hand washing) following training. Second, the child health outcomes (e.g., upper respiratory infections, gastrointestinal infections) were based on subjective determinations. For example, assessments of stool consistency and frequency are usually defined by the norm for each individual child. Although these criteria are very appropriate, it is highly likely that some individual staff or parents may not have applied these definitions in the same way either over time or across children. Third, assessment methods varied across the studies, sometimes involving records kept by staff and other times involving parent interviews or questionnaires. Again, inconsistent data across children, classrooms, programs, and studies can result from these different sources. The resulting measurement error from different sources and different definitions reduces the likelihood that the impact of an intervention could be detected in a given study.

Huskins (2000) argued that researchers need to include evidence for the criterion validity of more subjective measures by comparing them with more objective measures, such as records of deaths, emergency room visits or evaluation of symptoms and signs of illness by reliable and valid assessments used by health professionals. Huskins's concerns regarding the consistency of data gathered from staff and parents were echoed by Brown and colleagues (Brown, Zaslow & Weitzman, 2006), who raised concerns about the validity of data collected by parent or staff report in contrast with data collected directly by medical professionals who are kept unaware of potentially biasing information. Because of differences in staff/parent understanding of health conditions, data collection by medical professionals, although more expensive, is more likely to be sensitive to the quality of health practices and environmental factors in the early childhood setting. Another example of potential problems in interpretation can result when staff members or individuals involved in providing interventions, rather than impartial observers, collect data. Findings such as those reported by Alkon et al. (1999; i.e., children's actions, not staff or environmental issues, led to most minor injuries) can be viewed as problematic because the reporting staff member, who completed the report following the child's injury, could have been biased against reporting potential environmental factors, such as the level of supervision or the placement of equipment, for which the staff member could have been blamed.

Huskins also criticized the intervention studies for the use of control groups that are vulnerable to the Hawthorne effect, a common threat to findings in treatment/control studies. In the Hawthorne effect, participants in the treatment group respond positively to any intervention, including the process of assessment itself that might be used to do a pre-intervention, post-intervention comparison, regardless of its actual effectiveness. To minimize the Hawthorne effect, Huskins (2000) recommended that future intervention studies use a comparison of at least two treatment methods, one predicted to have a larger effect than the other, rather than a no-treatment control group.

Huskins (2000) argued that health intervention studies need to include information regarding the time and resource costs for both trainers and staff involved, or regarding savings (e.g., spared costs of substitutes for ill and absent staff, reduced medications, visits to a health care professional) required for a cost–benefit analysis of the intervention. His concerns regarding the need to document the cost–benefit for interventions were echoed by Glasgow et al. (2003), who argued that more cost–benefit analyses in health intervention research would help increase the impact of this research on actual health practices in the field.

As noted earlier, Glasgow et al. (2003) pointed out that much of the extant research on health practices has not included potential moderating variables such as staff education or the children's family backgrounds. These variables have been shown to be extremely important in other research on ECE. For example, Peisner-Feinberg and her colleagues (2001) found that the quality of child care experienced by preschoolers had a differential impact on the academic and social skills of second graders from low-income families. Research on health quality in early childhood settings needs to incorporate family moderators as well. Such studies of moderating variables are expensive because they require large samples.

Thus, three bodies of literature have demonstrated that children's health is affected by what happens in early childhood settings and that specific interventions can reduce the occurrence of both illnesses and accidents in children. However, whereas general studies of early childhood settings have shown modest, but significant, direct effects of program quality on academic and social school readiness (see Chapter 2), studies of health practices in early childhood settings have relied on implied links of health quality to children's learning and social skills related to school readiness.

What Are the Strengths and Problems of Existing Measurement Strategies in This Domain?

In this section, we turn to an overview of existing measures of the health aspects of environmental quality in early childhood settings. Recent years have been an active period for measures development, particularly in the aspects of health related to physical activity and nutrition. We summarize the efforts at measures development in these areas.

Content Covered by Existing Tools

The majority of the tools included in research to assess the ECE health environment and health practices are either specific assessments developed and used in the intervention studies of a given group of researchers or checklists developed to facilitate the consultation efforts of child care health consultants. The latter group includes the California Childcare Health Program Health and Safety Checklist-Revised (the Checklist; 2005), as well as adaptations of the California tool used in other states, such as Indiana. The current edition of this tool involves a three-point Likert scale. Alkon and her colleagues reported reliability and validity data for the group of observers that they trained on the measure (Alkon, To, Wolff, Mackie, & Bernzweig, 2008). The scale has 66 items grouped into 10 subscales: emergency preparedness, medication, facilities, infant/toddler sleep, indoor and outdoor equipment, staff health, hand washing routines, diapering, food preparation and eating, and supervision. In addition to establishing interrater reliability, the authors established face validity and construct validity by linking the items to national standards listed in *Stepping Stones* (National Resource Center for Health and Safety in Child Care, 2003). However, they reported that they were unable to establish criterion-related validity due to the lack of other standardized health and safety checklists based on national standards. Furthermore, they argued that predictive validity is not relevant to this measure, because the Checklist is designed to measure an outcome variable rather than a predictor variable. ECELS-Healthy Child Care Pennsylvania, a program of the PA Chapter of the American Academy of Pediatrics, developed an updated checklist in 2010 adapted from the 2005 California checklist. This checklist is available from their web site, http://www.ecels-healthychildcarepa.org/content/6-15-2010%20%20Health_and_safety_checklist%20for%20pdf.pdf. Testing of the validity and reliability of this updated tool awaits funding for the work.

Although many tools have been used to measure attendance, one widely available measure documents children's attendance over an 8-week period, without revealing their identities. This tool, created by the University of California at San Francisco School of Nursing (n.d.) is available on their website at http://www.ucsfchildcarehealth.org/html/research/researchmain.htm#ail.

Psychometric Properties of Existing Tools

Strengths of Existing Tools

As described earlier, numerous checklists for health care quality exist; some were developed by individual organizations, some by states, and some for particular research studies. These tools are intended for different audiences—for example, parents and child care consultants. The existing checklist items typically are based on the *Caring for Our Children* standards published in 2002 by the American Academy of Pediatrics, the American Public Health Association and the National Resource Center for Health and Safety in Child Care. However, the research base in the standards supports individual items and is not for summed scores across items in a given scale or subscale; furthermore, the research base sometimes is drawn from settings other than early childhood settings. For example, the 3-feet separation rule for cots is based on research on infection rates in army recruits and in nurseries for newborns. Measures of health and safety also have been developed for military early childhood programs; however, published information regarding the reliability and validity of these measures is not available. Military child care standards are consistent with *Caring for Our Children* (American Academy of Pediatrics, American Public Health Association and the National Resource Center for Health and Safety in Child Care, 2002), as are those used by the General Services Administration.

Gaps or Problems with Existing Tools

Several problems limit the use of health quality measures in broadly implemented quality initiatives such as quality rating systems. First, few studies linked the findings using these measures with intervention studies on health practices in early childhood settings, or linked the overall health quality in these settings to children's academic or social-emotional outcomes. Second, most extant measures of health practices and measures of children's health outcomes were developed and validated in efficacy studies conducted by the same research team. Although researchers typically report interrater reliability statistics (e.g., Alkon et al. 2008; Kotch et al., 2007), this reliability was established among the small group of observers used in each study, not among many observers used in larger effectiveness studies. As evidenced by the extensive scoring notes included in the most recent revision of the Early Childhood Environment Rating Scale-Revised (ECERS-R; Harms, Clifford, & Cryer, 2004), compared with earlier versions of this scale, obtaining reliability across multiple observers at multiple sites can require extensive clarification of operational definitions. As recently published measures such as the California Childcare Health Program Checklist (Alkon et al., 2008) and the Observational Scale for Rating Activity in Preschools (OSRAP-C) (Brown, Pfeiffer, et al., 2006) are widely implemented, additional clarification notes may be needed to ensure interrater agreement.

Third, measures of health in early childhood settings lack evidence of criterion and predictive validity. This psychometric problem may reflect differences in disciplines. Alkon and colleagues (2008) argued that predictive validity is unnecessary for their checklist because validity is designed to be an outcome variable, not a predictor variable. The tool was developed for use by child care health consultants, usually nurses, who are expected to assess child care providers' needs for health and safety training (Ramler et al, 2006). Widespread support for the role of child care health consultants is relatively recent. The written standards for child care health consultants described by Ramler and her colleagues (2006) provided no policy recommendation that consultants attain interrater agreement, or reliability, with other consultants on the assessments they use. When the Caring for Our Children standards were written, there were no widely available reliable and valid measures. Although professional training emphasizes consistent interpretations and definitions of standards, it will be important for child care health consultants to achieve acceptable levels of interrater agreement on published, reliable, and valid measures (Alkon et al., 2008).

Recent Measures Development

Measures development in recent years has focused especially on the areas of quality related to nutrition and physical activity. After reviewing existing measures, Brown, Pfeiffer, McIver, Dowda, Almeida, and Pate (2006) developed the Observational System for Recording Physical Activity in Children-Preschool Revision (OSRAC-P). This tool has eight observational categories and codes for recording both the physical activity and the contexts in which they occur. Five levels of activity codes range from stationary, or motionless, behavior to fast movements. A total of 18 activity-type codes include activities such as climbing, dancing, pulling/pushing, rough and tumble, running, swimming, and walking. The scale also includes location codes (i.e., inside, outside, and transition). Each observation interval requires 5 seconds of observing followed by 25 seconds of recording; therefore, recording 60 observations for each child requires a total of 30 minutes of observation. The authors reported evidence of interrater reliability for the observers, as well as descriptive information on typical activity levels in different locations across three preschools. The authors point out that, as a time-sampling measure, the OSRAC-P does not record "real-time" behavior and context. As with other time-sampling measures, therefore, the tool will be more sensitive to high frequency and regularly occurring activities. This measure has been validated by accelerometers. However, further research is needed, documenting the measure's sensitivity to interventions designed to change children's physical activity levels in child care programs. The authors suggested that the tool can be useful in identifying the indoor and outdoor activity contexts predictive of moderate to vigorous physical activity (referred to as MVPA) or sedentary activity. They also recommended the tool for single-case research designs that would test the impact of an intervention on a given child.

The Environment and Policy Assessment and Observation (EPAO) instrument was developed to quantify the physical and social environmental characteristics likely to affect both the dietary and physical activity behaviors of children in early childhood settings (Bower, Hales, Tate, Rubin, Benjamin, & Ward, 2008). This measure requires the observer to observe the child care center for an entire day and to review documentation during nap time. The eight subscales include active opportunities, sedentary opportunities, fixed play environment (e.g., climbing structures), sedentary environment (e.g., TV in room), staff behaviors that may promote or restrict physical activity, physical activity training and education, and physical activity policies. Response formats vary across the items; however, the authors describe a process for deriving a total physical activity environment score.

In order to validate the measure, the authors used a median split to categorize centers as having a high or low EPAO physical activity environment score. Center scores on EPAO were compared with the level of physical activity observed for a randomly selected group of children in each center, using a modified version of the Observational Scale for Rating Activity in Preschools (OSRAP). Validity of the scale was supported by the finding that, in centers with higher total physical activity environment scores on the EPAO, children showed higher levels of physical activity as assessed by the OSRAP (Bower et al., 2008). The authors pointed out the need to investigate variables such as staff training and education that could be related to scores on the EPAO, as well as the need to incorporate information regarding the level of physical activity in the home to any predictions about the child's learning. Benjamin et al. (2007) cautioned that the EPAO, with scores determined by only one day's observations, will capture behaviors and practices that occur more regularly or ones that happen to occur during that day. Sporadically occurring behaviors may require observations repeated over several days. Evidence for predictive validity is needed, relating scores on these two measures to both health and other school readiness outcomes in children.

Recently, a new Nutrition and Physical Activity Self-Assessment in Child Care (NAP SACC) instrument was developed to assess physical activity as well as nutrition policies and practices in early childhood settings (Ammerman, et al., 2007; Benjamin, Ammerman, et al., 2007; Benjamin, Neelon, et al., 2007). The evidence-based measure was developed through a series of focus groups, interviews, and expert reviews, and it includes items relating to nine areas of nutritional practices (e.g., inclusion in meals of fruits and vegetables; meats, fats, and grains; beverages; feeding practices) and six areas of physical activity (e.g., active play, play environment, supporting physical activity). The measure was used as a self-assessment by child care providers, who worked with consultants to develop an action plan and revised policies and practices on the basis of the assessment results. Participants reported increases in physical activity and nutritional meals after 6 months. The authors used scores on the EPAO, completed by independent observers, to validate the NAP SACC self-assessment instruments completed by directors. Using weighted kappas to compare agreement on each item, the researchers concluded that directors and researchers showed moderate levels of agreement on over 50% of the items; however, not surprisingly, scores on the self-report NAP SACC typically were higher than those on the EPAO. Thus, the authors recommend using the NAP SACC self-assessment instrument as an intervention tool because it helps raise awareness and interest in the issues of nutrition and physical activity. However, due to the bias in self-assessments, they concluded that if resources allow, the EPAO may be more appropriate than the NAP SACC self-assessment instrument as an outcome measure. Finally, on the basis of the work of Munoz and Bangdiwala (1997), they recommend less stringent benchmarks for establishing moderate levels of agreement across individual scale items, with the conservative weighted kappa.

Another observational measure was recently developed by Ball, Benjamin, and Ward (2007) to record the dietary intake of children in early childhood settings. Observers were trained to estimate the amount and type of beverages and foods served to children by staff, as well as the amount remaining after the children had finished their meals. Because child care food regulations prevent observers from measuring the quantity of food being served to each child, the accuracy of observers was maintained by requiring each observer to estimate the amount and type of each item on a 20-food certification test. The test included foods such as a sliced banana, mashed potatoes, spaghetti, yogurt, and milk. Observers were trained first to mastery of the test, and then to acceptable levels of interrater agreement in actual classrooms. The scale was used in a subsequent study (Ball, Benjamin, & Ward, 2008) to compare the food consumption of children in 20 centers with the My Pyramid food group standards. Findings reported by Ball and colleagues (2008) showed that the children were not consuming the recommended amounts of whole grains, fruits (with the exception of 100% fruit juice), or vegetables; in addition, they were consuming excessive amounts of saturated fats and added sugars. Future validation studies could relate these dietary patterns to both health outcomes and other school readiness outcomes.

What Is the Potential for Strengthening Measurement Strategies and Developing New Measures in This Domain?

Although some global quality measures, such as the ECERS-R (Harms et al., 2004), include a few items related to health and safety, the common factors (e.g., activities/materials, language/interaction) identified through exploratory or confirmatory factor analyses typically have not included any of the health and safety items (e.g., Cassidy, Hestenes, Hegde, Hestenes, & Mims, 2005). Indeed, following traditional psychometrics standards (e.g., Wilson, 2005), developers of measures of health and safety in early childhood settings typically report low levels of internal consistency, as assessed by the Cronbach's alpha statistic. For example, Alkon et al. (2008) recently reported reliability coefficients for subscales that ranged from 0.27 for emergency preparedness, 0.29 for food preparation and eating, and 0.39 for hand washing to 0.61 for outdoor/indoor equipment and 0.70 for diapering. Such low levels of internal consistency are problematic because they make it more difficult for relationships (e.g., correlations) with other measures to be detected.

Recently, several authors have questioned the appropriateness of these psychometric standards for some scales (e.g., Bradley, Caldwell, & Corwyn, 2003; Diamantopoulos &

Siguaw, 2006; Streiner, 2004). These authors distinguish between measures of causal indicators, such as environmental measures or life events scales, and measures of effects indicators, such as measures of depression or intelligence. In several papers, Bollen and his colleagues (e.g., Bollen, 2002; Bollen, Glanville, & Stecklov, 2007; Bollen & Lennox, 1991) have argued that psychometric standards of internal consistency were developed for measures that comprise multiple indicators of the effects of unobservable psychological traits such as depression. Depression, which cannot be directly measured, is assessed through its presumed effects, such as loss of sleep, sadness, and loss of appetite. An individual who is depressed is assumed to have high levels of each individual indicator; therefore, the items are interchangeable. Bollen and his colleagues contrast such measures of effects indicators with measures of causal indicators for traits such as quality of life, life events, socioeconomic status, and environmental quality. Causal indicators consist of individual events that may be uncorrelated, but have a cumulative impact, producing the given trait. Bollen (2002) argued that measures of internal consistency, such as the Cronbach's alpha, are not appropriate for measures of causal indicators. For example, a measure of life events might include, in its set of causal indicators, items such as the death of a parent, the death of a child, the death of a spouse, and the loss of a job. Although all of these events would be expected to have a cumulative impact on the individual, there would be no reason to expect these events to covary or to correlate.

Similar arguments can be made for measures consisting of the items involved in assessing environmental quality. Following these arguments, Bradley, Caldwell, and Corwyn argued that internal consistency requirements are not appropriate for the Home Observation for Measurement of the Environment (HOME) because the items are not presumed to have any particular covariance structure (Bradley, Caldwell & Corwyn, 2003). Similar arguments can be made for measures of health quality in early childhood settings.

The procedures to validate measures of causal, or formative, indicators described by Diamantopoulos and Siguaw (2006) have implications for measures of health quality. They argued that in the development of measures of effects indicators, the individual indicators need high levels of correlation because the items are seen as interchangeable. However, in measures of causal indicators, each item is seen as contributing separately to the overall assessment. Indeed, high levels of intercorrelations among items, rather than serving as an asset, present potential problems because the resulting multicollinearity may result in weighting one component of the index over others. However, regardless of the statistical relationships, they argued, the construction of the index needs to be guided by theory.

Regarding measures of health quality or other environmental dimensions as causal, rather than as effects indicators, presents some measurement challenges for those used to working with the psychometrics required for scales of effects indicators. In measures of effects indicators, because individual items are seen as items sampled from a population of equivalent items, scales can be shortened to include only those items that correlate most strongly with the total. For the same reason, on scales of effects indicators, missing responses to individual items can be estimated by substituting the average of the remaining items. However, in measures of causal indicators, no omissions and no substitutions can be made. Each item is seen as contributing individually to the total score; no assumption can be made that the response to one missing item would be similar to that of another (Diamantopoulas & Siguaw, 2006). Therefore, once the researchers have developed the logic model with all of the critical indicators included for a measure of health quality that would lead to specific child outcomes, each indicator must be measured for each study participant.

Although a better quality program might excel in providing multiple measures of safety, an item measuring the depth of surfacing under the climbing equipment would be expected to contribute independently to the overall health quality of the program, as would a measure of the level of supervision provided by adults over children using that equipment. Each individual indicator assessing the consistency of hand washing by adults and children across toileting, eating, and nose-blowing, as well as each indicator assessing the sanitizing of surfaces prior to eating, would be an essential and separate contributor to the overall health quality of the program. Because each item contributes separately to the overall health of the facility, these individual items cannot be perceived as interchangeable. Unlike measures of effects indicators, measures of environmental quality cannot be shortened in order to reduce the time and, therefore, the cost required in assessments, as recommended by some authors (e.g., Cassidy et al., 2005).

The arguments regarding the appropriateness of measures of internal consistency for measures of health care quality may raise questions regarding the high levels of internal consistency typically shown for commonly used measures of quality in early childhood settings. Such instruments as the ECERS-R (Harms et al., 2004) typically show measures of internal consistency above .90 across the entire scale, although such high levels commonly are not found for the subscales measuring health and safety (e.g., Cassidy et al., 2005). It is possible that some components of quality, such as language/interactions and provisions for learning, may show common covariance structure as a result of their historical link to widely held views of best practices in early childhood education curriculum theory. Many of the nonhealth/nonsafety items on classic assessment tools, including the ECERS-R (Harms et al., 2004), are based on traditional views of best practices in early childhood education curricula that are now commonly referred to as developmentally appropriate practice (Copple & Bredekamp, 1997). Generations of early childhood teachers have studied these practices, which were explicated in multiple editions of textbooks from the 1940s (e.g., Katherine Read Baker) to the present (e.g., Essa, 2006; Morrison, 2007).

Neither traditional nor current textbooks on developmentally appropriate curriculum practices include recent advances in health-related practices such as the multistep, timed routines required in hand washing (e.g., using a paper towel to turn off the faucet) or the specific surfacing depths required for the height of playground equipment. Thus, items related to learning activities, guidance, communication strategies, and supervision might correlate together because they are the effects of the practitioner's knowledge and attitudes toward developmentally appropriate practice (e.g., Copple & Bredekamp, S., 1997). In contrast, health and safety indicators practices, especially those not included in typical early childhood curriculum textbooks, have not been routinely taught to early childhood education teachers, as evidenced by textbooks available; furthermore, they have not been assessed in the ongoing performance evaluations of ECE teachers.

Measures of internal consistency (Cronbach's alpha) may not be required for measures of program practices and structures related to health. However, evidence of interrater reliability, test–retest reliability, criterion validity, and predictive validity are necessary for measures of health in early childhood settings linked to measures of children's school readiness. The need for criterion validity and predictive validity presents challenges for measures of health quality. First, as Alkon and colleagues (2008) point out, criterion validity is difficult to assess because no standardized measures based on health standards currently exist. Second, as Alkon and colleagues (2008) also point out, measures of predictive validity have not been required for measures of health practice, because these measures have been constructed to be used as outcome variables, not predictor variables. However, even though the relationship of these measures to overall lifelong wellbeing is widely accepted, evidence of predictive validity linking scores on these measures to children's school readiness is needed.

What Are the Implications of Measurement in This Domain for Policy and Practice?

Psychometrics, including measures of interrater agreement (when appropriate) and test–retest stability, as measures of reliability, need to be included for any scales used in high-stakes assessments. Measures of validity need to go beyond face validity, as assessed by expert panels, to include the assessment of predictive validity—for example, predicting child health, learning, and/or behavior problems.

Most measures of health quality have been validated by links to aggregate measures of children's development, including levels of physical activity or rates of illness. Causal vectors from the quality of health practices at the center level to the school readiness of the child, given all of the other factors that influence the child's development, will be difficult to demonstrate.

One issue heavily related both to cost and validity is the method of assessment. The most sensitive measures are likely to come from observation; however, such measures realistically can be made only of high-frequency behaviors (e.g., hand washing, sanitization procedures, toileting procedures). When observation is not possible—for example, because of rare-occurring events (first aid procedures) or events with high desirability, but unpredictable timing for observation (e.g., variety of food served over the course of more than one day, playground safety checks, emergency evacuation practices, review of injuries to identify safety issues)—measure by documentation is the next best alternative. When neither observation nor documentation is possible, interviews can be conducted with the provider, parents, volunteers, or consultants. However, interviews are most likely to be valid for recently occurring behaviors and questions that lack social desirability. For example, one problem with using self-reported practices to assess the impact of an intervention (e.g., Moon & Oden, 2003) is that the intervention may increase the social desirability of certain practices (e.g., the supine sleeping position for young infants), leading to inflated self-reports of implementation. Furthermore, as Huskins (2000) pointed out, self-report measures present methodological challenges in interrater reliability and in consistency of definitions. In such situations, more costly observation may be needed to verify the link between reported and actual levels of implementation. The most convincing evidence for the impact of an intervention is provided by direct observation, such as that used by Kotch et al. (1994), who, following the implementation of hygiene training, observed changes in hand-washing techniques linked to reductions in diarrheal illnesses in treatment centers, but not in control centers.

As in other process–outcome linkages, some child outcomes (e.g., building healthful habits) are hard to measure over brief periods—and even hard to measure over 2 years. Furthermore, some child outcomes such as major injuries occur so rarely (fortunately) that detecting the impact of practices would require studies with very large samples (e.g., Schwebel et al., 2007) and/or very long periods. Furthermore, some recent, but unclear, findings (e.g., lower rates of childhood leukemia and asthma in children who have attended child care) require logic models with causal vectors (i.e., exposure to infectious diseases) that need to be tested.

Research studies are needed to demonstrate the predictive validity of measures such as the Child Care Health Care Checklist (Alkon et al., 2008) and to demonstrate that interrater reliability can be efficiently reached even when the measure is used beyond the circle of a few select members of the originating research team. Studies of interventions should not be required to produce evaluations without funding to support valid data collection. Child care health consultants using these tools need to reach acceptable levels of interrater reliability before the results of their assessments are used in high-stakes assessments such as quality rating systems. Financial incentives (e.g., increased subsidy rates or program incentives) would encourage programs to use reliable and valid measures rather than measures that lack rigorous testing or enough use to permit aggregate data comparisons for specific variables.

Recommendations for Immediate and Longer-Term Follow-up

Health is a cross-cutting issue. Bridges are needed to facilitate collaboration between health professionals and early educators. Quality improvement in early childhood settings requires sustained, respectful relationships between health professionals and early educators working together to develop best practice approaches that draw from both fields. Parents and providers must do more than acknowledge the importance of health in child care settings; they need to act to ensure health and safety to achieve their goals for children's school readiness.

First, as recommended by Zaslow et al. (2006), experts in health, measurement, and school readiness research need to develop logic models identifying specific aspects of health and safety in early childhood as causal indicators for children's outcomes in all areas of school readiness, including health, academic skills, and social-emotional skills. Such models would need to control for family characteristics and potential moderating characteristics in different early childhood settings (e.g., Head Start versus nursery school versus full-day child care; profit versus nonprofit status; family child care versus center-based child care). Items included in the logic models would require operational definitions sufficiently transparent to facilitate efficient interrater reliability training at the item level across large numbers of observers, such as child care health consultants, who might be involved in effectiveness studies. After the interrater reliability and test–retest stability of scores on these measures are verified, and family characteristics and potential differentiating characteristics of the early childhood setting are controlled for, correlation studies are needed to link scores on these measures to the appropriate child outcomes identified in the logic model. Finally, both efficacy and effectiveness studies are needed to demonstrate that increases in the health quality of child care, as assessed by these measures, lead to improved child outcomes and school readiness. During this process, reporting the reliability and validity of measures in a clearinghouse accessible to both health and education professionals will facilitate communication among researchers, policy makers, and practitioners.

A national clearinghouse for health and safety measures in early childhood settings could be established along the lines of the National Quality Measures Clearinghouse, a clearinghouse established for health measures used in medical care (http://www.qualitymeasures.ahrq.gov/about/about.aspx). This clearinghouse would be able to identify reliable and valid measures of early childhood health quality with a demonstrated relationship to positive health outcomes for children. The measures could be required to provide one or more of the forms of evidence, such as

- One or more research studies published in a peer-reviewed journal

- Evidence of reliability and validity, including predictive validity

- A systematic review of the research literature

- A formal consensus procedure (i.e., expert validity) involving experts in relevant clinical, educational, methodological, and developmental sciences

The issue of the health of children in early childhood settings is a core component of school readiness. Being hurt or ill affects children's learning (Currie, 2005). Children who have been ill or hurt need to recoup skills they have lost; preventing illness and injury promotes children's health, learning, and social competence. Reliable and valid scales of health quality linked to children's health and other measures of school readiness skills can be useful tools to highlight the importance of health policies and practices in early childhood care and education and to identify the specific environmental features and practices that need improvement in individual settings.

References

Alkon, A., Benzweig, J., To, K., Wolff, M., & Mackie, J. (2009). Child care health consultation improves health and safety policies and practices. *Academic Pediatrics, 9* (September), 366–370.

Alkon, A., Genevro, J.L., Tschann, J.M., Kaiser, P.J., Ragland, D.R., & Boyce, W.T. (1999). The epidemiology of injuries in 4 child care centers. *Archives of Pediatric and Adolescent Medicine, 153,* 1248–1254.

Alkon, A., Ragland, D.R., Tschann, J.M., Genevro, J.I., Kaiser, P., & Boyce, W.T. (2000). Injuries in child care centers: Gender-environment interactions. *Injury Prevention, 6*(3), 214–218.

Alkon, A., Sokal-Gutierrez, K., & Wolff, M. (2002). Child care health consultation improves health knowledge and compliance. *Pediatric Nursing, 28,* 61–65.

Alkon, A., To, K., Wolff, M., Mackie, J.F., & Bernzweig, J. Assessing health and safety in early care and education programs: Development of the CCHP Health and Safety Checklist. *Journal of Pediatric Health Care.* 2008; 22: 368–377.

American Academy of Pediatrics. (2003). Policy Statement: Oral health risk assessment timing and establishment of the dental home. *Pediatrics, 111*(5), 1113–1116.

Ammerman, A.S., Benjamin, S.E., Sommers, J.K., Ward, D.S. (2007). *The Nutrition and Physical Activity Self-Assessment for Child Care* (NAP SACC) environmental self-assessment instrument (revised). Raleigh: Division of Public Health, NC DHHS, and Chapel Hill, NC: the Center for Health Promotion and Disease Prevention, University of North Carolina at Chapel Hill.

Ammerman, A.S., Ward, D.S., Benjamin, S.E., Ball, S.C., Sommers, J.K., Molloy, M., et al. (2007). An intervention to promote healthy weight: Nutrition and Physical Activity Self-Assessment for Child Care (NAP SACC) theory and design. *Preventing Chronic Disease 4*(3), A67.

Aronson, S.S., & Aiken, L.S. (1980). Compliance of child care programs with health and safety standards: Impact of program evaluation and advocate training. *Pediatrics, 65,* 318–325.

Ball, S.C., Benjamin, S.E., & Ward, D.S. (2007). Development and reliability of an observation method to assess food intake of young children in child care. *Journal of the American Dietetic Association, 107*(4), 656–661.

Ball, S.C., Benjamin, S.E., & Ward, D.S. (2008). Dietary intakes in North Carolina child care centers: Are children meeting current recommendations? *Journal of the American Dietetic Association, 108*(4), 718–721.

Ball, T.M., Holberg, C.J., Aldous, M.B., Martinez, F.D., & Wright, A.L. (2002).

Influence of attendance at day care on the common cold from birth through 13 years of age. *Archives of Pediatric and Adolescent Medicine, 156,* 121–126.

Benjamin, S.E., Ammerman, A., Sommers, J., Dodds, J., Neelon, B., & Ward, D.S. (2007). Nutrition and physical activity self-assessment for child care (NAP SACC): Results from a pilot intervention. *Journal of Nutrition Education and Behavior, 39*(3), 142–149.

Benjamin, S.E., Neelon, B., Ball, S.C., Bangdiwala, S.I., Ammerman, A.S., & Ward, D.S. (2007). Reliability and validity of a nutrition and physical activity environmental self-assessment for child care. *The International Journal of Behavioral Nutrition and Physical Activity, 4,* 29.

Benjamin, S.E., Ward, D.S., Ammerman, A.S., Ball, S.C., Neelon,. H., & Bangdiwala, S.I. (2008). Nutrition and physical activity in child care: Results from an environmental intervention. *American Journal of Preventive Medicine, 34*(4), 352–356.

Bollen, K. (2002). Latent variables in psychology and the social sciences. *Annual Review of Psychology, 53,* 605–634.

Bollen, K., & Lennox, R. (1991). Conventional wisdom on measurement: A structural equation perspective. *Psychological Bulletin, 110*(2), 305–314.

Bollen, K.A., Glanville, J.L., & Stecklov, G. (2007). Socio-economic status, permanent income, and fertility: A latent-variable approach. *Population Studies, 61*(1), 15–34.

Bower, J.K., Hales, D.P., Tate, D.F., Rubin, D.A., Benjamin, S.E., & Ward, D.S. (2008). The child care environment and children's physical activity. *American Journal of Preventive Medicine, 34*(1), 23–29.

Bradley, R.H., Caldwell, B.M., & Corwyn, R.F. (2003). The child care HOME inventories, assessing the quality of family child care homes. *Early Childhood Research Quarterly, 18,* 294–309.

Brown, B., Zaslow, M., & Weitzman, M. (2006). *Studying and tracking early child development from a health perspective: A review of available data sources.* Commonwealth Fund. Retrieved January 23, 2008, from http://www.commonwealthfund.org/publications/publications_show.htm?doc_id=354865

Brown, W.H., Pfeiffer, K.A., McIver, K.L., Dowda, M., Almeida, J.C.A., & Pate, R.R. (2006). Assessing preschool children's physical activity: The Observational System for Recording Physical Activity in Children–Preschool Version. *Research Quarterly for Exercise and Sport, 77*(2), 167–176.

California Childcare Health Program Health and Safety Checklist-Revised. 2005. Retrieved November 1, 2010, from http://ucsfchildcarehealth.org/html/pandr/formsmain.htm#adef

Cassidy, D.J., Hestenes, L.L., Hegde, A., Hestenes, S., & Mims, S. (2005). Measurement of quality in preschool child care classrooms: An exploratory and confirmatory factor analysis of the Early Childhood Environment Rating Scale-Revised. *Early Childhood Research Quarterly, 20,* 345–360.

Center for Educational Policy, Jennifer McMurrer. (December 2007). *Choices, changes, and challenges in curriculum and instruction in the NCLB era (Rev. ed.).* Washington, DC: CEP. Retrieved November 1, 2010, from http://www.cep-dc.org/

Center on the Developing Child at Harvard University. (2007). *A science-based framework for early childhood policy: Using evidence to improve outcomes in learning, behavior, and health for vulnerable children.* Retrieved November 1, 2010, from http://www.developingchild.harvard.edu

Child Care Bureau (2007). Systematic approaches to improving quality of care: QRS gain ground across the nation. *Child Care Bulletin, 32,* 1–19.

Churchill, R.B., & Pickering, L.K. (1997). Infection control challenges in child care centers. *Infectious Disease Clinics of North America, 11,* 347–365.

Clements, D.A., Zaref, J.I., Bland, C.L., Walter, E.B., & Coplan, P.M. (2001). Partial uptake of varicella vaccine and the epidemiological effect on varicella disease in 22 day-care centers in North Carolina. *Archives of Pediatric and Adolescent Medicine, 155,* 455–461.

Collet, J.P., Burtin, P., Gillet, J., Bossard Ducruet, T., Durr, F., et al. (1994). Risk of infectious diseases in children attending different types of day-care setting. *Respiration, 61 (Suppl. I),* 16–19.

Copple, C., & Bredekamp, S. (1997). *Developmentally appropriate practice in early childhood programs (Revised).* Washington, DC: National Association for the Education of Young Children.

Cordell, R.L. (2001). The risk of infectious diseases among child care workers. *Journal of the*

American Medical Women's Association, 56(3), 109–112.

Currie, J. (2005). Health disparities and gaps in school readiness. *Future of Children, 15*(1), 117–138.

Currie, J., & Hotz, V.J. (2004). Accidents will happen: Unintentional injury, maternal employment, and child care policy. *Journal of Health Economics, 23*(1), 25–29.

Currie, J., & Neidel, M. (2005). *Getting inside the "Black Box" of Head Start quality: What matters and what doesn't.* Working Paper 10091. Cambridge, MA: National Bureau of Economic Research, November 2003.

Diamantopoulos, A., & Siguaw, J.A. (2006). Formative versus reflective indicators in organizational measure development: A comparison and empirical illustration. *British Journal of Management, 17*, 263–282.

Essa, E.L. (2006). *Introduction to early childhood education. (5th Ed.).* Florence, KY: Delmar Cengage Learning.

Friedman, S.L., Brooks-Gunn, J., Vandell, D., & Weinraub, M. (1994). Effects of child care on psychological development: Issues and future directions for research. *Pediatrics, 94*, 1069–1070.

Glasgow, R.E., Lichtenstein, E., & Marcus, A.C. (2003). Why don't we see more translation of health promotion research to practice? Rethinking the efficacy-to-effectiveness transition. *American Journal of Public Health, 93*(3), 1261–1267.

Gunn, W.J., Pinsky, P.F., Sacks, J.J., & Schonberger, L.B. (1991). Injuries and poisonings in out-of-home child-care and home care. *Archives of Pediatrics and Adolescent Medicine, 145*, 779–781.

Hair, E., Halle, T., Terry-Humen, E., Lavelle, B., & Calkins, J. (2006). Children's school readiness in the ECLS-K: Predictions to academic, health, and social outcomes in first grade. *Early Childhood Research Quarterly, 21*, 431–454.

Harms, T., Clifford, R.M., & Cryer, D. (2004). *The Early Childhood Environment Rating Scale-Revised (ECERS-R).* NY: Teachers College Press.

Hubbs-Tait, L., Culp, A.M., Huey, E., Culp, R., Starost, H., & Hare, C. (2002). Relation of Head Start attendance to children's cognitive and social outcomes: Moderation by family risk. *Early Childhood Research Quarterly, 17*, 539–558.

Hubbs-Tait, L., Kennedy, T.S., Droke, E., Belanger, D., & Parker, J. (2007). Zinc, iron, and lead: Relations to Head Start children's cognitive scores and teachers' ratings of behavior. *Journal of the American Dietetic Association, 107*, 128–133.

Hurwitz, E.S., Haber, M., Chang, A., Shope, T., Teo, S., Ginsberg, M., Waecker, N., & Cox, N.J. (2000). Effectiveness of influenza vaccination of day care children in reducing influenza-related morbidity among household contacts. *Journal of the American Medical Association, 284*(13), 1677–1682.

Huskins, W.C. (2000). Transmission and control of infections in out-of-home child care. *The Pediatric Infectious Disease Journal, 19 (Supplement)*, S106–S110.

Jelinek, M., Patel, B.P., & Froehle, M.C. (Eds.). (2002). *Bright futures in practice: Mental health-(vol. 1.): Practice guide.* Arlington, VA: National Center for Education in Maternal and Child Health.

Keren, M., Feldman, R., & Tyano, S. (1999) Assessment of caregiver–child interaction in the context of a preschool psychiatric evaluation. *Child and Adolescent Psychiatric Clinics of North America, 8*(2), 281–296.

Kotch, J.B., Chalmers, D.J., Langley, J.D., & Marshall, S.W. (1993). Child day care and home injuries involving playground equipment. *Journal of Pediatrics and Child Health, 29*(3), 222–227.

Kotch, J.B., Hussey, J.M., & Carter, A. (2003). Evaluation of North Carolina child care safety regulations. *Injury Prevention, 9*, 220–225.

Kotch, J.B., Isbell, P., Savage, E., Gunn, E., Vandergrift, N., Lu, L., et al. (Unpublished manuscript). *Child care health consultation improves child care health policies, health practices, and children's access to health care.* University of North Carolina at Chapel Hill.

Kotch, J.B., Isbell, P., Weber, D.J., Nguyen, V., Savage, E., Gunn, E., et al. (2007). Handwashing and diapering equipment reduces disease among children in out-of-home child care centers. *Pediatrics, 120*, e29–e36.

Kotch, J.B., Weigel, K.A., Weber, D.J., Clifford, R.C., Harms, T., Loda, F.A., et al. (1994). Evaluation of a hygienic intervention in child day-care centers. *Pediatrics, 94 (pt2)*, 991–994.

Lamdin, D.J. (1996). Evidence of student attendance as an independent variable in education production functions. *The Journal of Educational Research, 89*, 155–162.

Moher, D., Schulz, K.F., & Altman, D.G. (2001). The CONSORT statement: Revised recommendations for improving the quality of reports of parallel group randomized trials. Retrieved September 4, 2008, from http://www.biomedcentral.com/1471-2288/1/2

Moon, R.Y., Aird, L., & Kotch, L., (2006). State Child Care Regulations Regarding Infant Sleep Environment Since the Healthy Child Care America–Back to Sleep Campaign. *Pediatrics.* 118, 73–83.

Moon, R.Y., & Oden, R.P. (2003). Back to sleep: Can we influence child care providers? *Pediatrics, 112,* 878–882.

Moon, R.Y., Patel, K.M., & Shaefer, S.J. (2000). Sudden infant death syndrome in child care settings. *Pediatrics, 106*(2), 295–300.

Moon, R.Y., Sprague, B.M., & Patel, K.M. (2005). Stable prevalence but changing risk factors for sudden infant death syndrome in child care settings. *Pediatrics, 116*(4), 972–977.

Morrison, G. (2007). *Fundamentals of early childhood education (5th Ed.).* Upper Saddle River, NJ: Prentice Hall.

Munoz, S.R., & Bangdiwala, S.I. (1997). Interpretation of kappa and *B* statistics measures of agreement. *Journal of Applied Statistics, 24*(1), 105–111.

National Association for the Education of Young Children. (2006). *NAEYC Early Childhood Program Standards.* Retrieved August 17, 2008, from http://www.naeyc.org/academy/standards/

National Association for Family Child Care. (2005). *Quality standards for NAFCC accreditation.* Retrieved August 17, 2008, from http://www.nafcc.org/accreditation/accredstandards.asp

National Institute of Child Health and Human Development, Early Child Care Research Network. (2003) Child care and common communicable illnesses in children aged 37 to 54 months. *Archives of Pediatric and Adolescent Medicine, 157,* 196–200.

National Institute of Child Health and Human Development Early Child Care Research Network. (2004). Type of child care and children's development at 54 months. *Early Childhood Research Quarterly, 19,* 203–230.

National Resource Center for Health and Safety in Child Care. (2002). *Caring for Our Children: National health and safety performance standards: Guidelines for out-of-home child care programs* (2nd ed.). Denver, CO: Author.

National Resource Center for Health and Safety in Child Care. (2003). *Stepping stones to using Caring for Our Children: Protecting children from harm* (2nd ed.). Denver, CO: Author.

Osofsky, J.D. (1998). Infant psychiatry viewed from a world perspective. *Psychiatry and Clinical Neurosciences. 52,* S203–S205.

Peisner-Feinberg, E., Burchinal, M.R., Clifford, R.M., Culkin, M.L., & Howes, C. (2001). The relation of preschool child-care quality to children's cognitive and social development trajectories through second grade. *Child Development, 72,* 1534–1553.

Pianta, R.C., La Paro, K.M., & Hamre, B.K. (2008). *Classroom Assessment Scoring System™ (CLASS™) Manual: Pre-K.* Baltimore: Paul H. Brookes Publishing Co.

Ramler, M., Nakatsukasa-Ono, W., Loe, C., & Harris, K. (2006). *The influence of child care health consultants in promoting children's health and well-being: A report on selected resources.* Newton, MA: Education Development Center.

Roberts, L., Jorm, L., Patel, M., Smith, W., Douglas, R.M., & McGilchrist, C. (2000). Effect of infection control measures on the frequency of diarrheal episodes in child care: A randomized, controlled trial. *Pediatrics, 105,* 743–746.

Roberts, L., Smith, W., Jorm, L. Patel, M., Douglas, R.M., & McGilchrist, C. (2000). Effect of infection control measures on the frequency of upper respiratory infection in child care: A randomized, controlled trial. *Pediatrics, 105,* 738–742.

Sachdev, H.P.S., Gera, T., & Nestel, P. (2005). Effect of iron supplementation on mental and motor development in children: Systematic review of randomized trials. *Public Health Nutrition, 8*(2), 117–132.

Schoenthaler, S.J., Bier, I.D., Young, K., Nichols, D., & Jansenns, S. (2000). The effect of vitamin-mineral supplementation on the intelligence of American schoolchildren: A randomized, double-blind, placebo-controlled trial. *The Journal of Alternative and Complementary Medicine, 6*(1), 19–29.

Schwebel, D.C., & Brezausek, C.M. (2007). The role of context in risk for pediatric injury. *Merrill-Palmer Quarterly, 53,* 105–130.

Schwebel, D.C., Brezausek, C.M., & Belsky, J. (2006). Does time spent in child care influence risk for unintentional injury? *Journal of Pediatric Psychology, 3,* 184–193.

Small, L., Anderson, D., & Melnyk, B.M. (2007). Prevention and early treatment of overweight and obesity in young children: A critical review and appraisal of the evidence. *Pediatric Nursing, 33,* 149–161.

Southward, L.H., Robertson, A., Wells-Parker, E., Eklund, N., Silberman, S.L., Crall, J.J., et al. (2006). Oral health status of Mississippi Delta 3- to 5-year-olds in child care: An exploratory study of dental health status and risk factors for dental disease and treatment needs. *Journal of Public Health Dentistry, 66,* 131–137.

Story, M., Kaphingst, K.M., & French, S. (2006). The role of child care settings in obesity prevention. *Future of Children, 16,* 143–168.

Streiner, D.L. (2003). Being inconsistent about consistency: When Coefficient Alpha does and doesn't matter. *Journal of Personality Assessment, 80,* 217–222.

Thacker, S.B., Addiss, D.G., Goodman, R.A., Holloway, B.R., & Spencer, H.C. (1992) Infectious disease and injuries in child day care: Opportunities for healthier children. *Journal of the American Medical Association, 268,* 1720–26.

Tulve, N.S., Jones, P.A., Nishioka, M.G., Fortmann, R.C., Croghan, C.W., Zhou, J.Y., et al. (2006). Pesticide measurements from the first national environmental health survey of child care centers using a multi-residue GC/MS analysis method. *Environmental Science & Technology, 40,* 6269–6274.

Ulione, M.S. (1997). Health promotion and injury prevention in a child development center. *Journal of Pediatric Nursing, 12*(3), 148–154.

United States Consumer Products Safety Commission. (2005a). *Outdoor home playground safety handbook.* Washington, DC: Author. Retrieved August 17, 2008, from http://www.playgroundsafety.org/standards/index.htm

United States Consumer Products Safety Commission. (2005b). *Public playground safety handbook.* Washington, DC: Author. Retrieved August 17, 2008, from http://www.playgroundsafety.org/standards/index.htm

United States Consumer Products Safety Commission. (2008). *Public playground safety handbook.* Washington, DC: Author. Retrieved August 17, 2008, from http://www.playgroundsafety.org/standards/index.htm

University of California San Francisco School of Nursing. (n.d.). *Absence and illness log.* San Francisco: Author. Retrieved August 17, 2008, from http://www.ucsfchildcarehealth.org/html/research/researchmain.htm#ail

Ward, D.S., Hales, D.P., Haverly, K., Marks, J., Benjamin, S., Ball, S., & Trost, S. (2008). An instrument to assess the obesogenic environment of child care centers. *American Journal of Health Behavior, 32*(4), 380–386.

Wilson, M. (2005). *Constructing measures: An item response modeling approach.* Mahweh, NJ: Lawrence Erlbaum.

Zaslow, M., Halle, T., Martin, L., Cabrera, N., Calkins, J., Pitzer, L., & Margie, N.G. (2006). Child outcome measures in the study of child care quality. *Evaluation Review, 30,* 577–610.

CHAPTER 8

Family-Sensitive Caregiving

A Key Component of Quality in Early Care and Education Arrangements

Juliet Bromer, Diane Paulsell, Toni Porter, Julia R. Henly, Dawn Ramsburg, Roberta B. Weber, and Families and Quality Workgroup Members

This chapter presents a model for conceptualizing and measuring quality in early care and education (ECE) settings that focuses on the sensitivity of providers toward the families of children in care. Drawing from research on working families as well as from literature on Head Start, family support, and home visitation programs, we propose an expanded model of ECE quality that includes family-sensitive care as a key component. We define *family-sensitive care* as the attitudes, knowledge, and practices of providers[1] that aim to align services to the needs and preferences of families.

In this chapter we posit that parents will perceive family-sensitive care to be accessible, trustworthy, consistent, and respectful; and, consequently, that over time they will prefer and sustain family-sensitive ECE arrangements to those which focus less directly on family care needs. In turn, we argue that family-sensitive care may moderate the influence of child-centered aspects of ECE (e.g., aspects of care focused on children's needs and development) on child outcomes. Children may reap the benefits of the child-centered aspects of high-quality programming only if the providers offering such care are accessible, affordable, and available during the days and hours for which families need care. Otherwise, children may not even be able to use the ECE arrangement, and the potential for positive child outcomes will be severely compromised by limited and inconsistent dosages of care.

Our emphasis on family-sensitive care is also motivated by research demonstrating that parents' influence on children's developmental outcomes is substantially greater than that attributable to child care (National Institute of Child Health and Human Development Early Child Care Network, 2001, 2002, 2006). Given the size of parent effects on child outcomes, supporting parents is a reasonable route to more positive child outcomes. Thus, we hypothesize that programming which both nurtures children's development and is sensitive to the needs of parents, such as the need to manage both work and family responsibilities, provides the best chance of positively affecting outcomes for children, especially those children from low-income families.

The purpose of this chapter is to lay out an initial rationale and agenda for future research and the development of measurement tools in the area of family-sensitive care. We review existing research to set the stage for future research on the relationship between family-sensitive ECE and child and parent outcomes and on the dimensions of family-sensitive care that are most important. We also review existing measurement approaches and discuss the need to develop measurement strategies for testing whether enhancing family-sensitive care improves parent and child outcomes. We emphasize that a stronger research base and subsequent development of standards for family-sensitive care may be prerequisites to any future quality measurement strategies.

The chapter is organized into six sections. The first section provides a rationale for including family-sensitive indicators in models and measures of child care quality. The second section presents a logic model for family-sensitive caregiving that includes an elaboration of the construct itself and its potential influences on program, parent, and child outcomes. The third section reviews research supporting the different components of the logic model, identifying gaps in knowledge as appropriate. We next turn to an analysis of existing practice standards and quality measures to better understand how family-sensitive models align with existing measurement approaches. The chapter concludes with a discussion of issues regarding measurement strategies for family-sensitive care, policy and professional development implications, and recommendations for next steps.

Rationale for a Family-Sensitive Model of ECE Quality

Parents have a tremendous influence on their children's development. Research demonstrates that parental mental health, the nature of parent–child interactions, and parenting practices affect child outcomes, particularly those related to social-emotional and cognitive well-being (Halle, Zaff, Calkins, & Margie, 2000; Maccoby, 2000; McLoyd, 1998). Maternal depression, for example, is linked to depression in children (Westbrook, 2007), and coercive parent–child interactions are associated with children's behavior problems (Brooks-Gunn & Markman, 2005). Positive parenting practices, in contrast, contribute to the positive growth and development of children (Brooks-Gunn & Markman, 2005; Westbrook, 2007).

Parents are best able to positively influence their children's development in environments that promote economic, social, and psychological health. Family economic constraints, employment demands, and caregiving responsibilities may compromise these environments (Bianchi, Casper, & King, 2005; Brooks-Gunn & Duncan, 1997), contributing to psychological strain (Repetti, 2005), weakened parenting practices (Halle et al., 2000), and complications managing as well as organizing family life (Henly & Lambert, 2005; Roy, Tubbs, & Burton, 2004; Scott, London, & Hurst, 2005). By promoting a family-sensitive model of ECE that recognizes attention to family circumstances and needs as an important dimension of quality practices, this chapter argues that providers can strengthen parents in their parenting roles and contribute to their ability to improve child outcomes.

Moreover, parents' ECE choices are often constrained by a range of factors—for example, resources to pay for care, work and school schedules, and availability of transportation—that may be addressed to varying degrees by family-sensitive arrangements. Although researchers commonly do not identify these factors as components of ECE quality, the literature on parent perceptions of quality makes clear that parents distinguish between components of quality related to the child's experience in care and those which concern the family's needs (Barbarin et al., 2006; Henly & Lyons, 2000; Hofferth, Shauman, & Henke, 1998; Li-Grining & Coley, 2006). Parents across different racial and ethnic groups value child-focused dimensions of quality such as health and safety, warmth of child–caregiver interactions, skill of caregiver, and richness of environment (Shlay, Weinraub, & Harmon, 2007) as well as parent-focused dimensions such as location and accessibility of the arrangement, flexibility around work schedules and finances, comprehensiveness of services (e.g., health and nutrition services), and parent–caregiver interactions (Barbarin et al., 2006; Emlen, Koren, & Schultze, 2000; Henly & Lyons, 2000; Li-Grining & Coley, 2006; Shlay et al., 2007). Parents understand child- and parent-focused care as unique dimensions of the arrangement—for example, rating child-focused dimensions high and the parent-focused dimensions low in the same arrangement (Emlen et al., 2000).

Parents may not have a choice to secure both aspects of quality. Low-income parents and others, whose children may be at greatest risk and thus most in need of high-quality care, may have particular challenges finding care that is both responsive to their economic and work constraints and also safe, nurturing, and developmentally stimulating for their children. For example, some practices, such as inflexible schedules and a refusal to accept public vouchers, act as barriers to access for low-income families and families with nonstandard work schedules.

The notion of family-sensitive programming in ECE is reminiscent of long-standing models such as Head Start and other two-generational programs that combine support services for parents with child care and educational programming for children (Gomby, Culross, & Behrman, 1999; National Research Council and Institute of Medicine, 2003; Seitz, 1990). These programs seek to capitalize on the frequent interactions that providers have with children and parents and the focus on social-emotional development that many ECE programs embrace. ECE settings, according to these programs, are uniquely situated to assist parents in developing the knowledge and social connections, as well as the concrete supports and referrals, that are understood as protective factors against child abuse and neglect (Caspe & Lopez, 2006; Center for the Study of Social Policy, 2004).

Conceptual Framework: A Logic Model for Incorporating Family-Sensitive Constructs into Measures of ECE Quality

This section proposes a conceptual framework for assessing family-sensitive care and programming across *all* ECE settings, whether center based or home based, and whether licensed or license-exempt (family, friend, and neighbor care that is legally exempt from regulation). In presenting this model, we realize that the practicality of adopting the full array of family-sensitive components of care may vary for providers with differing characteristics, resources, and goals. Moreover, the particular ways in which providers operationalize family-sensitive caregiving will likely differ by provider types and characteristics and according to the needs and characteristics of individual families. For example, family, friend, and neighbor providers may share a strong relationship with parents and have a more complex understanding of a parent's circumstances and needs, putting them in a position to offer a range of family supports. By contrast, center teachers may have access to more formal resources and may have more knowledge about how to help parents navigate these services, but they may be less well positioned to develop close relationships with families (Bromer & Henly, 2004). Similarly, we recognize that families with diverse needs present unique opportunities and challenges for providers. One of the challenges for measuring family-sensitive caregiving is assessing the extent to which providers are responsive to all families in care. We submit that the model offers a continuum of family-sensitive aspects of care that may be useful at different levels of intensity to all providers, programs, and families (see Goode, 2004).

Specific components of family-sensitive ECE are described next, followed by a logic model that illustrates possible pathways through which family-sensitive practices may influence parent and child outcomes (see Figure 8.1). Given our purpose of elaborating the *family-sensitive* dimensions of care, we have not included child-centered aspects of programs or family and child characteristics in our discussion. We recognize, of course, that these are critical contributors to child and parent outcomes and are important, independent of the provider-level attitudes, knowledge, and practices we describe in our model.

Constructs of Family-Sensitive Care: Attitudes, Knowledge, and Practices

We propose three family-sensitive constructs of ECE arrangements, demonstrated by the provider, that should be included in measures of quality: attitudes toward families, knowledge of families, and practices with families (see Box A, Figure 8.1). Next, we describe these constructs in more detail and how they may work together to create family-sensitive ECE arrangements that benefit parents and children. (See Figure 8.1 for the full logic model.)

Attitudes Toward Families

The practices characteristic of family-sensitive care will be facilitated if providers hold positive attitudes toward the families in their care. Attitudes are evaluative judgments (Eagly & Chaiken, 1993) that both shape and are shaped by individual beliefs, knowledge, and past behavior (Marsh & Wallace, 2005), as well as by sociocultural norms, traditions, and conventions (Prislin & Wood, 2005). Moreover, attitudes motivate and direct future actions (Allport, 1935; Eagly & Chaiken, 1993). Of course, positive attitudes are not sufficient to determine positive behavioral responses, as many intervening factors—such as institutional rules and practices, resource availability, social norms, and individual perceptions of control and intentionality—complicate the attitude–behavior relationship (Ajzen & Fishbein, 2005; Fishbein & Ajzen, 1975).

In the case of family-sensitive care, we argue that it is important for providers to hold positive attitudes toward families in care. We expect positive attitudes to include an openness, respect, and acceptance of diverse family cultures, traditions, and practices and an appreciation for diverse family circumstances and situations. Providers who hold such attitudes (or programs with missions that are consistent with such positive orientations toward families) may be better positioned to learn about families' strengths and needs and provide sensitive and responsive care to children and families (Kontos, Raikes, & Woods, 1983).

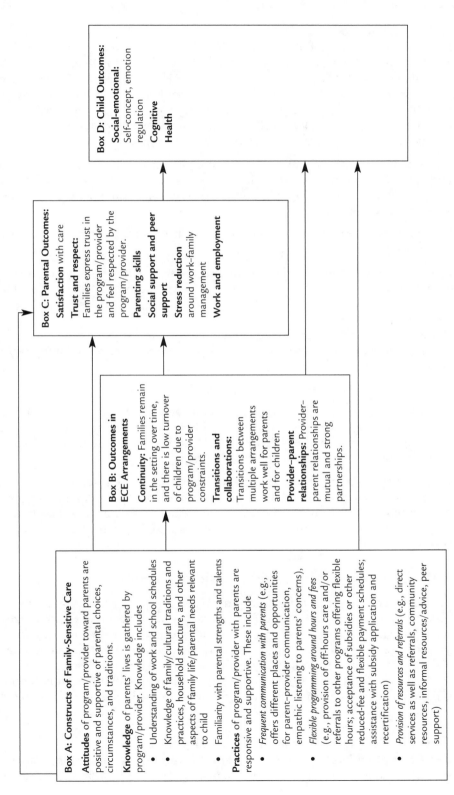

Box A: Constructs of Family-Sensitive Care

Attitudes of program/provider toward parents are positive and supportive of parental choices, circumstances, and traditions.

Knowledge of parents' lives is gathered by program/provider. Knowledge includes

- Understanding of work and school schedules
- Knowledge of family/cultural traditions and practices, household structure, and other aspects of family life/parental needs relevant to child
- Familiarity with parental strengths and talents

Practices of program/provider with parents are responsive and supportive. These include

- *Frequent communication with parents* (e.g., offers different places and opportunities for parent–provider communication, empathic listening to parents' concerns),
- *Flexible programming around hours and fees* (e.g., provision of off-hours care and/or referrals to other programs offering flexible hours; acceptance of subsidies or other reduced-fee and flexible payment schedules; assistance with subsidy application and recertification)
- *Provision of resources and referrals* (e.g., direct services as well as referrals, community resources, informal resources/advice, peer support)

Box B: Outcomes in ECE Arrangements

Continuity: Families remain in the setting over time, and there is low turnover of children due to program/provider constraints.

Transitions and collaborations:
Transitions between multiple arrangements work well for parents and for children.

Provider–parent relationships: Provider–parent relationships are mutual and strong partnerships.

Box C: Parental Outcomes:

Satisfaction with care

Trust and respect:
Families express trust in the program/provider and feel respected by the program/provider.

Parenting skills

Social support and peer support

Stress reduction around work–family management

Work and employment

Box D: Child Outcomes:

Social-emotional:
Self-concept, emotion regulation

Cognitive

Health

Figure 8.1. Conceptual framework underlying a family-sensitive model of ECE quality.

165

Knowledge About Families

Provider knowledge about the lives of families in care is a distinct, yet essential, component of family-sensitive care. Just as high-quality caregiving is based on a sophisticated knowledge of child development and careful observations of children, we posit that knowledge and understanding of individual families is an important contributor to high-quality ECE. We also posit that this knowledge must be used to inform practices and interactions with families. We propose three areas of information that providers should gather that will give them knowledge about families:

- Work-related information about a family's economic and employment circumstances—knowledge about work schedules (including fluctuating and unpredictable work schedules), changing pickup and drop-off schedules, income, ability to pay child care fees from week to week

- Information about family practices—cultural practices, family structure, child-rearing practices, routines

- Information about parents' individual strengths and needs—family resources and supports, health issues, needs of other children in the family, job changes, and job loss

Practices with Families

Positive attitudes toward and knowledge of families can help providers develop responsive and supportive practices with families. We propose three areas of family-sensitive practice with families:

- *frequent and positive communication with parents*

- *flexible scheduling and fees:* flexible hours of care, acceptance of child care subsidies, flexible or sliding-scale fee structures, help navigating the subsidy system; networking assistance to help families find and arrange alternative child care options that provide care during needed hours

- *resources and referrals for parents:* information about community services, events, and activities; information on child development; collaborations with community services and institutions; linkages with programs such as those offering work–family, parenting, and peer services and supports, linking parents to programs that offer economic supports

Potential Outcomes of Family-Sensitive Care

We suggest that provider attitudes, knowledge, and practices will operate together to make the delivery of family-sensitive ECE more likely. In turn, we hypothesize that these family-sensitive arrangements will mediate effects on parents and children. We also acknowledge that family-sensitive care may have different influences on families, depending on familial risk factors and willingness or need for family-sensitive services. For example, family-sensitive care may have larger impacts on children from high-need families if it enables them to access and maintain a high-quality and stable ECE arrangement.

Outcomes in ECE Arrangements (Box B, Figure 8.1)

Family-sensitive providers are expected to affect continuity within arrangements, the success of transitions across ECE arrangements, and strong mutual provider–parent relationships. These arrangement outcomes of family-sensitive providers may be listed as follows:

- *Continuity of care.* Family-sensitive care is hypothesized to result in fewer unantici-pated disruptions in ECE arrangements, longer lasting arrangements for children, and lower turnover rates for providers and/or programs.

- *Transitions and collaborations.* Family-sensitive care is hypothesized to ease transitions and reduce disruptions for children who move between ECE arrangements.

- *Provider–parent relationships.* Family-sensitive provider practices with parents (e.g., frequent communication and interactions) are hypothesized to lead to strong and mutual provider–parent relationships. Parents in arrangements with providers who exercise such practices may feel more comfortable approaching providers for support around the specifics of the ECE arrangement, as well as obtaining referrals for serv-ices, community resources, and advice about child rearing and family management.

Parental Outcomes (Box C, Figure 8.1)

The following are potential parental outcomes that may be affected by family-sensitive ECE arrangements:

- *Satisfaction with care.*

- *Trust and respect.* Parents who use family-sensitive ECE arrangements may be more comfortable with the arrangement and experience greater trust in the caregivers and/or educators. In family-sensitive child care arrangements, parents are expected to feel respected and understood, and they believe that their values are shared and/or recognized as important by the provider.

- *Parenting skills.* Parents whose children are in family-sensitive care may have more information about parenting and child development, as well as more resources and referrals, both of which may enhance their parenting skills and the consistency with which activities in the home and care settings complement each other. In addition, parents' sense of self-efficacy in supporting their children's development may be enhanced as a result of the information about practices, routines, and child develop-ment that they gain from the provider.

- *Social support and peer support.* Parents whose children are in family-sensitive care may experience expanded social support networks as a result of the provider's encouragement of parent-to-parent relationships among families using the arrange-ment. Parents may also experience fewer conflicts in their informal ties to acquain-tances and family members because these personal ties may be called upon less often to help with last-minute child care scheduling problems, to provide child care during off-hours, and to help parents pay for care (see Henly & Lambert, 2005).

- *Parental stress reduction around work–family issues.* Parents whose children are in family-sensitive care may experience reduced psychological stress (or strain-based family-to-work conflict) that can arise from the challenges of meeting the demands of work, child care, and family life (Henly & Lambert, 2005). The reduction in parental stress may result from family-sensitive providers' understanding and knowledge of parental circumstances and needs and from efforts by the provider to accommodate the child care schedule to families' work and education schedules.

- *Parental work and employment outcomes.* Parents whose children are in family-sensitive care may experience improved work outcomes, such as fewer incidents of tardiness at work and more stable employment. Flexible fee arrangements may result in more affordable ECE arrangements, which may, in turn, reduce money-related conflicts between providers and parents. Child care problems—such as those which arise from scheduling conflicts, parents' inability to pay, and interpersonal conflicts between providers and parents—interfere with work productivity and hasten employment exits (Chaudry, 2004; Dodson, 2006; Henly & Lambert, 2005; Press, Fagan, & Laughlin, 2006). Family-sensitive programs may also improve parents' satisfaction with their employment situation and contribute to worker productivity.

Child Outcomes (Box D, Figure 8.1)

We posit that family-sensitive care will enhance child outcomes through two primary pathways. First, family-sensitive care can have an impact on children by moderating the influence of child-focused care on child outcomes. This may happen when arrangements that are considered to be of high quality in their nurturing of children's development are also family sensitive, in that they are accessible and available to those parents who may otherwise not be able to choose such arrangements. For example, children from high-risk families who can benefit most from high-quality ECE settings may show the most improvement in cognitive outcomes in family-sensitive care because this approach to ECE may enable their parents to gain access to such arrangements when they otherwise would not have been able to do so.

Second, family-sensitive care may indirectly have an impact on children through the effects that it has on parents. Given the strong body of research demonstrating the importance of parental mental health and parenting practices on children's outcomes (Halle et al., 2000; Maccoby, 2000; McLoyd, 1998), it is reasonable to hypothesize that if providers who offer family-sensitive care are able to improve the psychological well-being of parents, reduce their isolation, and/or enhance their parenting skills, then children will benefit. Moreover, if family-sensitive care improves the employment productivity of parents by reducing tardiness and turnover, then children may benefit from the increased household earnings that these improved work conditions would bring the family unit.

Drawing from research in child development, we hypothesize that the effects of family-sensitive care on children may be observed in all domains of child development. Yet, we also caution that the effects on child outcomes of child-centered dimensions of quality may be fully realized only when the family-sensitive aspects of care are appropriate to the needs of each particular family. Although an expanded discussion of child outcomes is outside the scope of this chapter, we provide here (also see Box D, Figure 8.1) a brief discussion of key areas in which we would expect family-sensitive care to have the greatest effects:

- *Social-emotional outcomes.* ECE that is sensitive and responsive to families' cultural strengths and needs may improve children's self-concept and identity. Moreover, family-sensitive care may improve the emotion regulation of children through social referencing processes. *Social referencing* is the process by which children gather information about social situations from adults in their lives (Baldwin & Moses, 1996; Sorce, Emde, Campos, & Klinnert, 1985). We hypothesize that if parent–provider interactions and relationships are respectful and responsive, children may pick up positive cues from parents that providers are people to trust and may, as a result, have more positive emotional experiences in the ECE setting. Programs sensitive to families may also buffer children from the detrimental effects of maternal stress, depression, and isolation (Ahluwalia, McGroder, Zaslow, & Hair, 2001) through helping mothers increase their social networks and parenting competence (Burchinal, Follmer, & Bryant, 1996; Crnic, Greenberg, Ragozin, Robinson, & Basham, 1983).

- *Cognitive outcomes.* Family-sensitive care may benefit the cognitive outcomes of children, both directly and through the social-emotional gains made by children in family-sensitive arrangements; however, research is needed in this area. For example, literacy outcomes may be improved for children if the provider is respectful of, knowledgeable about, and sensitive to the literacy and language strengths and needs of families, thereby working with parents to help children develop a foundation for strong literacy learning.

- *Health outcomes.* ECE that is more sensitive to the schedules and budgets of families may reduce the incidence of children left in self-care arrangements or otherwise neglectful situations, in which accidents are most likely to occur. In addition, the reduction of child abuse and neglect may be an outcome of arrangements with providers who are responsive to the needs and strengths of families (Horton, 2003). Finally, providers who offer comprehensive services to families—especially involving health care services—may promote better long-term health outcomes for children (Palfrey et al., 2005).

Research Related to Family-Sensitive Care

In this section we review extant research supporting different components of the logic model, identifying gaps in knowledge as appropriate. Our review has uncovered several studies related to some aspects of our model, but we lack descriptive studies with large representative samples that would allow us to estimate the prevalence of the different aspects of family-sensitive care identified in the model. Research is especially scarce on the relationships between these components of care and parent and child outcomes. Before we can develop measurement strategies for assessing family-sensitive care, we need to understand the constructs of family-sensitive care that are related to improved child and parent outcomes.

Attitudes Toward Families

Scant research has been conducted to examine provider attitudes toward families. Research in this area has focused more on center-based teachers of 3- and 4-year-olds than on providers in other ECE or school-age child care arrangements or in informal family, friend, and neighbor arrangements (Baum & McMurray-Schwartz, 2004; Fiene, 2002; McBride, 1991; Moseman, 2003). Educational research suggests that teacher attitudes are a key element in engaging families in schools and programs (Carlisle, Stanley, & Kemple, 2006; Hoover-Dempsey & Sandler, 1997). Yet, the few studies that do exist in the child care domain provide mixed findings regarding both teacher attitudes and perceptions of families and family involvement. Research conducted by Kontos and colleagues (1983) found that, in general, center-based child care teachers held negative attitudes toward parents, especially those teachers working with single parents and low-income families. Although this study did not look at the relationship between attitudes and practices, the authors suggest that negative attitudes may present a barrier to supportive programs for parents. In contrast, Jones, White, Aeby, and Benson (1997) found more positive overall attitudes toward family strengths in their study of teachers working in elementary school Follow Through programs.

Further research on provider attitudes is needed to examine the influence of demographic factors, such as the race, ethnicity, and social class of providers and families; individual characteristics, such as previous provider experiences and educational background; and program characteristics, such as a program's administrative and organizational climate. Extrapolating from the rather large attitudes and intergroup-relations literature outside of the child care domain (i.e., in the fields of social psychology and sociology), one finds that it is reasonable to expect that factors such as the social structural position of families (e.g., race, ethnicity, class status), provider experience, organizational pressures, and personal/psychological provider characteristics would bear on providers' expectations and attitudes toward their relationships with families in their programs. Future research is also needed to both understand and capture the dynamic nature of provider–parent relationships, including how provider attitudes toward families may influence providers' motivation to seek knowledge about family circumstances, how knowledge may feed back into evaluative judgments about families (i.e., attitudes), and how both attitudes and knowledge might influence practices with families.

Knowledge of Families

Whereas major national studies of Head Start and Early Head Start have examined family involvement, parent engagement, and parent participation in programs, research has not focused on provider knowledge as part of family responsiveness (Administration for Children and Families, 2002a, 2002b, and 2005). The Head Start Program Performance Standards require Head Start and Early Head Start programs to develop individualized family partnership agreements in collaboration with families and to review them regularly. However, methods for developing these agreements and updating them vary across programs. Across arrangements, we lack descriptive data on the kinds of information that providers gather about families, how such information is collected, and how knowledge about families is used by providers. One study that looked at the relationship between parents' perceptions of early childhood program staff knowledge and sensitivity toward families and parent outcomes found that programs rated high on knowledge and sensitivity were positively associated with higher program engagement levels but not with other parenting outcomes, such as parenting competency and quality of the home environment (Green, McAllister, & Tarte, 2004).

Practices with Families

Our review has uncovered significantly more research related to the practice aspect of family-sensitive care, although almost none of this work explores whether these practices are related to other inputs of family-sensitive care, such as provider attitudes or knowledge. Head Start and other two-generation programs have a long history of providing comprehensive services to both parents and children. Family development and health services, separate from early childhood programming, typically are provided by nonteaching staff, such as family service workers. In addition, a growing body of empirical evidence from small qualitative studies has shown that individual providers across arrangements and types report performing informal family support activities in addition to the direct care of children, especially for low-income families (Adams, Rohacek, & Snyder, 2008; Bromer, 2005, 2006; Bromer & Henly, 2009; Hughes, 1985; Joffe, 1977; Uttal, 2002; White, 2002). These qualitative studies describe a range of informal help to families, such as parenting information and advice, marital counseling, legal advice, religious guidance, medical advice, and general emotional support (Bromer, 2005, 2006; Endsley & Minish, 1991; Joffe, 1977; Uttal, 2002; White, 2002).

A few qualitative studies also describe logistical and economic supports that providers reported offering to families (Adams et al, 2008; Henly & Lyons, 2000; Bromer & Henly, 2009). Henly and Lyons (2000) found that low-income parents and their informal (family, friend, and neighbor) providers typically negotiated flexible payment arrangements, inconsistent payments, in-kind exchanges, or no payments at all. Similarly, Bromer and Henly (2009) found that both licensed and informal home-based providers, in particular, offered a range of logistical and economic supports to mothers, including flexible hours and fees, employment advice, help with daily routines, and monetary assistance. Adams and colleagues (2008) similarly found that some family child care providers and centers helped parents to negotiate the subsidy system and maintain continuity of care for their children through the waiver of copayments.[2]

Factors Contributing to Provider Practices with Families

Research on provider practices with families suggests that some home-based providers—especially relatives—may be well positioned to offer family-sensitive care because of familial motivations to help kin and a close familiarity with, and depth of knowledge of family needs and circumstances (Bromer, 2005; Bromer & Henly, 2009; Henly & Lambert, 2005; Porter & Kearns, 2005; Porter & Vuong, 2008). To the extent that family-sensitive practices are related to close parent–provider relationships, center teachers may be less likely than home-based providers to support parents beyond the direct care of children. Studies of parent–staff communication in child care centers have found limited interaction between parents and staff, a mismatch between parent and provider perceptions' of their relationship, and even disagreements around child-rearing issues (Endsley & Minish, 1991; Shpancer, 1998; van IJzendoorn, Tavecchio, Stams, Verhoeven, & Reiling, 1998). In his review of the literature on parent–provider relationships, Shpancer (1998) found that family child care providers consistently had more contact time with parents than did center-based caregivers. Gibbon (2002) reported a similar finding about the co-occurrence of family support roles and close parent–provider relationships in home-based child care settings compared with nonprofit and for-profit centers.

Family-sensitive care in high-quality ECE settings has the potential to draw on the strengths of home-based and center-based settings. We propose that high-quality care and education should include both child- and parent-focused aspects of care. To achieve this, centers may need to increase their focus on providing family-sensitive care and working with parents. Many home- and center-based providers need additional support in other dimensions of quality care, such as supporting language development and providing cognitive stimulation.

Relationship Between Provider
Practices and Parent and Child Outcomes

We also know very little about the effects of provider support roles or of provider–parent relationships on parent and child outcomes. Seitz (1990) suggests that close interactions between teachers and parents in some child care settings may make teachers particularly effective at offering family support. However, this hypothesis requires empirical validation. Many evaluations do not collect data focused on parent satisfaction or experience in child care (Pittard, Zaslow, Lavelle, & Porter, 2006; Porter et al., 2010). In fact, none of the evaluations of home-based child care initiatives reviewed in the literature review undertaken by Porter and colleagues examined parent–caregiver communication or any parent outcomes.

In one study of parent–provider relationships in both child care centers and homes, researchers found that more frequent communication between a parent and provider about the child correlated with providers' more sensitive interactions with the child and higher quality caregiving (Owen, Ware, & Barfoot, 2000). In a study examining child care for working families in four Indiana communities (Elicker et al., 2005), researchers found that positive ratings of the relationship by both the caregiver and the parent were related to higher ratings of children's social-emotional competence. In a field test of the Child Care Assessment Tool for Relatives (CCAT-R) with 92 relative caregivers across the country, researchers found that a parent's interest in the caregiver's life was associated with higher scores for nurturing (Porter, Rice, & Rivera, 2006). These findings provide some preliminary evidence that close, respectful relationships may translate into higher quality child care.

The broader literature on social support suggests that social support from informal network members (some of whom may offer child care supports) is an important contributor to parental and family well-being (Hashima & Amato, 1994), especially for low-income and single mothers (Henly, 2002; Henly, Danziger, & Offer, 2005). Social support from informal networks has been associated with reductions in material hardship in economically disadvantaged families (Henly et al., 2005) and may serve as a buffer against the stresses of poverty, in turn leading to more effective parenting practices (Hashima & Amato, 1994). For example, Burchinal et al. (1996) found that low-income African American mothers with large social support networks employed more sensitive and responsive parenting and may have benefited children's social development, compared with parents with small social networks. Small, Jacobs, and Massengill (2005) found that child care centers in high-poverty communities were important social-capital-generating resources for parents, who benefited from the social ties these centers encouraged.

Finally, although our model of family-sensitive ECE does not assume a separate parent intervention such as home visiting, we examined the literature on family support and home visiting programs because these two-generation programs aim to promote children's development through improving parental capacity (Layzer, Goodson, Bernstein, & Price, 2001) and because these studies purport to demonstrate that parenting and child outcomes can benefit from parent-focused programs.

A meta-analysis of evaluations of 260 family support programs[3] found that this kind of approach offers some promise for improving some of the parent outcomes—*parenting skills, social and peer support, reduction of stress,* and *work and employment*—that we posit in our logic model. The study found that there were small, but statistically significant, effects in all five parent outcome domains across the evaluations.[4] Similarly, evaluations of home visiting programs found that home visiting produces modest benefits for parents, with small effect sizes (Gomby, 2005; Sweet & Appelbaum, 2004).

A large-scale random assignment evaluation of 17 Early Head Start sites (which included center-based programs, home visiting, and/or a combination of both) with 3,001 families found mixed results for parents. This has some implications for the potential for effects from our model (Administration for Children and Families, 2002b). On the one hand, Early Head Start had a positive impact on parents' support for children's emotional and language development. On the other hand, there were no effects on parenting stress or mental health.

These studies suggest that parenting interventions may influence some parent and child outcomes. We hypothesize in this chapter that changing provider attitudes, knowledge, and practices with parents to become more sensitive, understanding, and responsive, even without a specific parenting intervention, may have an impact on some of the parent and child outcomes that have not been affected by targeted interventions. For example, early childhood programs that acknowledge, respect, and reach out to understand and support parents may result in greater parental satisfaction and trust in the arrangement as well as help to reduce parental stress related to work–family management. On the basis of prior research in this area, we suggest that a change in how ECE programs approach and work with parents in their daily routines and interactions may improve both parent and child outcomes by promoting support for parents and by creating continuity for children (Powell, 2005). More research is clearly needed to test these hypotheses and pathways of influence.

Existing Approaches to Defining and Measuring Quality

In this section we review how existing standards for high-quality practice in ECE settings address the constructs of family-sensitive care (see Table 8.1). We also review existing measurement tools of ECE quality (see Table 8.2). We find that although there is considerable acknowledgment in the field of the importance of family-sensitive care, there is only peripheral attention in measurement instruments given to indicators that might tap into the constructs of family-sensitive care.

Quality Standards and Family-Sensitive Care

We next review how four major early childhood organizations have addressed families in their definitions of quality and how the four sets of program quality standards adopted by these organizations align with our proposed constructs for measurement of family-sensitive ECE (see Table 8.1). Our review suggests that there is ample recognition in the field of the importance of families in early childhood programming, but it also points to the need to further elaborate and define how early childhood providers interact with, respond to, and support families. All four sets of standards—the National Association for the Education of Young Children (NAEYC, 2007) Program Accreditation Standards, Head Start Performance Standards (HSPS, 2006), National After-School Association (NAA, 1991) Standards for Quality School-Age Care, and the National Association for Family Child Care Quality Standards (NAFCC, 2005)—include quality standards related to family engagement and involvement and to strong provider–parent relationships.

Table 8.1. Constructs of family-sensitive care included in early care and education/school-age care quality standards

Quality standards	Constructs of family-sensitive care			Training requirements
	Attitudes	Knowledge	Practices	
National Association for the Education of Young Children (NAEYC) Early Childhood Program Accreditation Standards National Association for the Education of Young Children. (2007). *NAEYC Early Childhood Program Standards and Accreditation Criteria: The Mark of Quality in Early Childhood Education.* Washington, DC: Author	None.	Teachers use variety of methods to communicate with parents and consider language of families. Program/teachers gather information about families' race, religion, language, culture, family structure, concerns about child care, socioeconomic background, childrearing practices, interests, and skills. (1.A; 6.A.02; 7A)	Curriculum responsive to family values, experiences, beliefs, and language (2A.04; 2A.08) Staff use knowledge to make program environment, curriculum, and teaching responsive to families. (7A) Family involvement includes family-to-family support, and family schedules are considered in planning events. (7A) Information about resources and services is available, as is help accessing family support services for families that need the services. (7.C.05) Program has linkages with the community and can help families access community resources. (8A; 8B) Administrators have knowledge of family systems and community resources. Responsiveness to parents' work–family schedules and constraints are considered in planning events at the center. (7.A.14)	Teachers have some coursework in "family and community relationships" as part of their formal education and training (phased in over next decade). Teachers are also required to have coursework related to working with children with special needs; coursework is to cover "family-centered practice" and "community supports and resources."
Quality Standards for National Association of Family Child Care (NAFCC) Accreditation The Family Child Care Accreditation Project, Wheelock College (2005). *Quality Standards for NAFCC Accreditation, 4th ed.* Salt Lake City, UT: NAFCC http://www.nafcc.org/documents/QualStd.pdf	Provider respects diverse family styles and strengths. (1.11) An earlier edition of the NAFCC standards stated that providers should accept the decisions of parents to work outside the home.	Provider exchanges information with parents. (5.14) Provider gathers information about parents' values and wishes regarding childrearing. (5.14)	Provider offers reliable child care. Parents can count on child care as described in their "contract." (1.10) Provider offers information about tax credits and subsidies. Provider offers information about community resources and services. (5.12–5.13) Provider individualizes program to respond to parental requests, preferences, values. (1.12) Provider communicates with families effectively. (1.14–1.19)	No training requirements related to family-sensitive care

Source				
The National After-School Association (NAA) Standards for Quality School-Age Care. National After-School Association. *The NAA Standards for Quality School-Age Care: Standards At a Glance.* Washington, DC: NAA http://www.naaweb.org/pdf/StandGlan.pdf	Staff and families interact with each other in positive ways. (7a, b, d) Includes items on making families feel welcome and comfortable, mutual respect, and working together to ensure smooth arrival and departure between home and child care.	Staff share the languages and cultures of the families they serve and the communities they live in. (7c)	Staff support families' involvement in the program (open visitation, new-family orientation, exchange of information). (22a-d) The program builds links to the community (provides information and lists of community resources to meet the needs of families and children). (23a-b) The program makes itself affordable to all families by using all possible community resources and sources of subsidy. (36b) The program's hours of operation are based on families' needs. (36c) Staff receive training on how to work with families. (33a)	Staff receive training in how to work with families.
U.S. Department of Health and Human Services (2003). Head Start Program Performance Standards and Other Regulations. (45 CFR 1304). Revision 8. Washington, DC: Author*	Acceptance and respect for family culture, language, ethnicity, and family composition. (1304.21.a.1.iii; 1304.21.a.3.i.E) Positive attitude toward breast-feeding mothers. (1304.40.c.3)	Exchange of information about families Understanding family customs, beliefs, composition, and service needs Strong relationships as part of knowledge-gathering process	Comprehensive services (e.g., nutrition services. (1304.23.d) Identification and access to community resources and services (1304.40.b) Multiple standards on using family's home language and culture to enhance communication Parent involvement and participation in all aspects of program; standards integrate family involvement into curricular areas. (1304.21.a.2.i) Parents' work and school schedules are considered in arranging parent participation activities. (1304.40d 2) Parent education provided around health, nutrition, child development. (1304.4e & f)	Classroom teachers participate in professional development activities that help them work effectively with parents.

*Note: Some of the items reported here are not standards themselves, but rather are offered in the performance standards as examples to guide programs in meeting the standards. Also, many of the standards regarding family partnerships refer to family support staff and other agency staff who work with families, rather than to classroom teachers.

Table 8.2. ECE quality assessment instruments with constructs of family-sensitive care

Program assessment name, source, and description	Constructs of family-sensitive care			Age range and setting
	Attitudes	Knowledge	Practices	
Child Care Assessment Tool for Relatives (CCAT-R) • Porter, T., Rice, R., and Rivera, E. (2006). *Assessing quality in family, friend, and neighbor care: the Child Care Assessment Tool for Relatives.* New York: Institute for a Child Care Continuum. • In-home observation of caregiver–child dyad, health and safety features of setting, and materials; caregiver interview	Interview includes items on caregivers' motivation for providing care. "He/she values our relationship with each other."	Interview includes items on caregivers' knowledge of parents' schedules, caregivers' knowledge of parents' daily life, and the extent to which caregivers and parents exchange information about the care arrangement and home life	*Flexible programming:* Interview includes items on hours, flexibility in hours, and payment. *Communication:* Interview includes frequency and content of communication between caregiver and parent. *Resources and referrals:* Interview includes other supports caregiver provides to parents, such as errands.	Relatives who provide child care for children under age 6, either in their own home or the child's home
Child Development Program Evaluation Scales (CDPES) • Fiene, R. (1984). *Child Development Program Evaluation Scales and COFAS.* Washington, DC: Children's Services Monitoring Consortium. • 37-item scale with seven domains: administration, environmental safety, child development curriculum, health services, nutritional services, social services, and transportation.	None	Items on staff–parent communication include degree to which staff collects information about child's day, parent conferences, and home visits Item on information exchange about family time, skills, and interests; item that assesses to what degree children's family background (e.g., language spoken, parental attitude toward discipline, and relationships with relatives) is obtained at enrollment Staff are interviewed to see how families share traditional customs with the program.	*Flexible programming:* None *Communication:* Items on culturally appropriate and inclusive practices are included. *Resources and referrals:* Parents are offered parent education; there is some mention of referrals to services to address needs identified in the child health records and for children with special needs.	Child care centers serving infants, toddlers, preschoolers, and school-age children

Program Administration Scale (PAS)	None	One item on open communication with families about their values, beliefs, and culture	*Flexible programming:* Items on family support and involvement include seven types of family supports including work supports (sick child care, extended hours). *Communication:* Items on whether center has multiple modes of communication with families; whether systems exist to ensure daily communication; whether families are involved in evaluating the program; and what mechanisms are used to elicit feedback from the parents on the quality of the program care. *Resources and referrals:* Items refer to information and referral to support services.	Center-based or public school–based early care and education programs
• Talan, T.N., and Bloom, P.J. (2004). *Program Administration Scale: Measuring Leadership and Management in Early Childhood Programs.* New York: Teacher's College Press. • A 25-item scale clustered into 10 subscales.				
Preschool Program Quality Assessment, Second Edition (PQA)	None	One item on whether staff get input from parents regarding the curriculum and its relation to child characteristics and whether staff conduct parent conferences and home visits and have informal conversations with parents about the children's daily experiences; items on whether staff conduct family needs assessments and are familiar with families' needs	*Flexible programming:* None *Communication:* Three items on whether parent participation in children's activities and policy-making committees is emphasized and facilitated. *Resources and referrals:* Items on whether staff provide referrals to families both for children's special educational needs and for the family support services.	Center-based preschool settings
• HighScope Educational Research Foundation. (2003). *Preschool Program Quality Assessment, Second Edition (PQA) Administration Manual.* Ypsilanti, MI: HighScope Press. • A rating instrument comprising seven areas of program quality. Ratings for three areas are based on classroom observations, and the other four are based on teacher and/or director interviews.				

(continued)

177

Table 8.2. (continued)

Program assessment name, source, and description	Constructs of family-sensitive care			Age range and setting
	Attitudes	Knowledge	Practices	
Ready School Assessment (RSA) • HighScope Educational Research Foundation (2006). *Ready School Assessment: Administration Manual.* Ypsilanti, MI: HighScope Press. • Measured eight dimensions of what it means to be a "ready school." Items assessed by a team of teachers, parents, child care and preschool providers, and school principals.	None	Items on school–home communication about program and child's progress, child's life at home, progress and problems; multiple models of school–home communication Item that asks whether kindergarten teachers have access to detailed information (e.g., parent questionnaires, home visits, interviews) about incoming children that help them get to know the child and their family settings	*Flexible programming:* Family participation in school policies is encouraged; barriers related to convenience and transportation are addressed. *Communication:* Multiple items on respecting and embracing cultural and ethnic diversity; parents are encouraged to make recommendations to principal as part of the goal setting and decision making process, and families participate in and have significant influence on school decision-making process and school policies. *Resources and referrals:* Items on parent education and learning opportunities for parents, school–community linkages for services and referrals to families, provision of services to families who cannot receive services in the community, and special attention to families that do not speak and/or read English.	Elementary schools with an emphasis on kindergarten through second-grade classrooms
Emlen Scales • Emlen, A.C., Koren, P., & Schultze, K. (2000). *A packet of scales for measuring quality of child care from a parent's point of view: With summary of methods and findings.* • Parent surveys that assess parental perceptions of child care quality, flexibility, accessibility, and affordability.	A four-item scale that assesses parents' perceptions of caregiver acceptance and supportiveness, including items on the caregiver's acceptance of the way a parent raises his or her child.	A three-item scale that assesses whether the caregiver is open to new information and learning.	Items ask parents to rate the continuity, stability, and reliability of their child care arrangements, as well as support around parenting.	Applies to all ages of children in child care settings

Measure				Setting
Parent-Caregiver Relationship Scale • Elicker, J., Noppe, I.C., Noppe, L.D., and Fortner-Wood, C. (1997). The parent–caregiver relationship scale: Rounding out the relationship system in infant child care. *Early Education and Development, 8*(1), 83-100. • 35-item scale assesses attitudes, perceptions, and feelings about the provider–parent relationship from both parent and caregiver perspectives.	"I truly value this parent's opinions on most matters." "This child's parent is someone I can rely on." "I have a great deal of respect for this parent." "This child's parent and I really seem to value our relationship with each other." "I consider this child's parent to be a true partner in raising this child."	"I am interested in knowing what goes on at home and work." "I trust that this parent will tell me important things about this child."	"If there is a problem, this child's parent and I always talk about it soon." "My communication with this parent is always very open and honest." "If this child's parent had a problem, I would make an extra effort to help him or her out." "I like to work closely with this parent in order to gain a better understanding of her child."	Infant-toddler care; center and family child care
Strengths-Based Practices Inventory • Green, B.L., McAllister, C.L., and Tarte, J.M. (2004). The strengths-based practices inventory: A tool for measuring strengths-based service delivery in early childhood and family support programs. *Families in Society, 85*(3), 326–334. • Face-to-face interviews measure parents' experience working with early childhood and family support staff along four dimensions (16 items) of strengths-based, family-centered programming: empowerment approach, cultural competency, staff sensitivity and knowledge, and relationship supportive practices.	Asks parents whether "program staff help me to see that I am a good parent" Asks parents whether "program staff respect my family's cultural and/or religious beliefs"	Staff knowledge about families is measured through one item that asks parents whether "program staff understand when something is difficult for me."	Several items assess responsive practices with families through asking parents whether they receive information, resources, and support from program staff.	Center-based

179

NAEYC and HSPS offer the most comprehensive and integrated treatment of family-sensitive constructs in their definitions of high-quality care. NAA standards address work–family issues most directly, perhaps because school-age programs are sometimes designed as a work support for families as well as an educational support for children. NAFCC standards have fewer items regarding parents and less integration of family-sensitive constructs.

Family-Sensitive Constructs and Quality Standards

Positive provider *attitudes* toward families are acknowledged in some of the standards through the concept of "respect" for families, although this is not a central focus in any of those standards we reviewed. Each of the standards includes some reference to the importance of provider *knowledge* about families, yet there are few references to knowledge of work–family issues such as work schedules, economic and logistical challenges related to managing work and family demands, and other concerns that may affect families. Moreover, none of the standards explicitly address how providers collect information about families or how this information and knowledge are applied and used in programs.

In our review we found that all four sets of quality standards include several standards related to responsive *practices* of program staff and providers with families, including responsiveness to family diversity, as well as resources and referral to services for families. Finally, with the exception of NAFCC, these standards require providers to participate in some type of training, coursework, or professional development in how to work with parents and families. The content of these activities are not fully articulated, but the inclusion of this professional development requirement indicates the field's awareness that provider–family relationships and interactions are a central aspect of high-quality early childhood programs.

Quality Measurement Instruments and Family-Sensitive Care

Although the quality standards reviewed here include aspects of family-sensitive care as an integral part of programming and quality, most instruments for measuring quality in ECE settings give only peripheral or no attention to families and parents. Some widely used instruments, such as the Classroom Assessment Scoring System (CLASS™; Pianta, & La Paro, & Hamre, 2008), the Observational Record of the Caregiving Environment (ORCE; NICHD, 1996) and the Child Care HOME Inventories (HOME; Bradley, Caldwell, & Corwyn, 2003), for example, do not include assessment items that refer to program responsiveness to parents and families. Other assessment instruments, such as the Early Childhood Environment Rating Scale (ECERS-R) and the corresponding Infant Toddler Environment Rating Scale (ITERS-R), Family Child Care Environment Rating Scale (FCCERS), and School-Age Care Environment Rating Scale (SACERS), have only one item related to parents: "provisions for parents," which includes parental input into programs and referrals to parents as needed (Harms, Clifford, & Cryer, 2005; Harms, Cryer, & Clifford, 2007, 2003; Harms, Vineberg Jacobs, & Romano-White, 1996). Still others include items about programs exchanging information with parents, but these items focus exclusively on the provider sharing information with parents about the program and children. Often, items regarding referrals to services are included only in the context of serving children with special needs. Some instruments that are specific to one domain, such as literacy or emotional development, include one item about parent education in that area (e.g., Neuman, Dwyer, & Koh, 2007).

We identified five instruments for assessing program quality that address some of the components of family-sensitive care as described in this chapter (see Table 8.2): the

Child Care Assessment Tool for Relatives (CCAT-R; Porter et al., 2006), Child Development Program Evaluation Scale (CDPES; Fiene, 1984), Program Administration Scale (PAS; Talan & Bloom, 2004), Preschool Program Quality Assessment (PQA; HighScope, 2003), and Ready School Assessment (RSA; HighScope, 2006).

We also include three instruments that assess aspects of ECE arrangements from parent and caregiver perspectives: Emlen Scales (Emlen et al., 2000), the Parent Caregiver Relationship Scale (Elicker, Noppe, Noppe, & Fortner-Wood, 1997); and the Strengths-Based Practices Inventory (Green et al., 2004). We discuss these parent assessment instruments here because they aim to assess the quality of the parent–provider relationship as well as some of the other ECE and parent outcomes of family-sensitive care described in our logic model in Boxes B and C of Figure 8.1.

As Table 8.2 shows, all three parent assessment tools assess parental *perceptions* of caregiver attitudes as well as of caregiver attitudes toward parents, but only one program assessment (the CCAT-R) includes assessments of provider *attitudes* toward families. All eight assessments address the importance of provider *knowledge* about families' lives and exchange of relevant information. However, the program assessment instruments emphasize knowledge as flowing just one way—providers giving parents information about the program and/or about child development—rather than providers gathering information from parents about family strengths and needs. The CCAT-R offers an exception to this, with items that assess knowledge that both the parent and provider have about each other—"what's happening in the parent's life and what's happening in the caregiver's life." All five program assessment instruments and all three parent assessments include several items that directly assess family-sensitive *practices* with families, including flexibility around hours and payment as well as other work–family logistical supports, such as sick and extended-hours child care.

Although these quality assessments address some of the constructs in our model of family-sensitive care, they do not examine how providers translate attitudes and knowledge into supportive practices with families. None assesses how providers collect information from families and how this information is used to inform planning and programming.

Three of the program assessment instruments we reviewed here (CDPES, PAS, and RSA) use documentation of program communication with parents as evidence of family-sensitive care. Only the PQA and the CCAT-R interview providers about their knowledge of families' lives. The CCAT-R also includes a section on provider–parent communication that specifically assesses the frequency and nature of the communication. All three of the parent assessment instruments rely on parent surveys or in-person interviews to assess the provider–parent relationship and the parents' experience in the ECE arrangement.

Our review suggests that existing measurement instruments do not fully capture the ways that providers are sensitive to the strengths and needs of families. We have very few measures of how to assess provider attitudes toward families and provider knowledge of families. Parental assessment tools that focus on the provider–parent relationship and parental perspectives clearly offer a more fine-tuned measurement of the constructs of family-sensitive care and are able to capture an individual parent's experience of ECE, whereas program assessments may capture only a summative picture of parental experience and engagement. Given the recognition that family-sensitive care may look different for each family in a program and may have different effects on children and parents, depending on family circumstances, risk factors, needs, and strengths, a reliance on measurements that overlook these individual differences may not allow us to accurately capture the effects of quality on outcomes.

Considerations for Future Measurement Strategies of Quality and Family-Sensitive Care

Future efforts to measure family-sensitive ECE should develop both instruments that tap into the three components (attitudes, knowledge, and practices) of family-sensitive care and independent indicators of family-sensitive care itself. In our model, attitudes, knowledge, and practices are proposed to be the ingredients (or inputs) of family-sensitive care (Figure 8.1), whereas continuity within arrangements, successful transitions across arrangements, and strong provider–parent relationships are indicators (or outputs) of these arrangements (Figure 8.1, Box B). An important first test of the conceptual model is whether the components in Figure 8.1, Box A, indeed relate positively to the indicators of Box B. Valid assessments of the relationship between Boxes A and B depend on the development of valid and reliable instruments of each of the underlying constructs in the model.

Future researchers of instruments to assess family-sensitive care can explore the feasibility of using domain-specific instruments (or subscales) as well as integrative measures. Domain-specific instruments have the advantages of focusing the assessment of family-sensitive care on particular dimensions of family-sensitive care (e.g., attitudes, knowledge, practices) and providing the opportunity to empirically examine links between the attitude–knowledge–behavior connection, as well as their potentially unique contributions to family-sensitive care. Our review suggests that it is also important to develop measurement strategies that assess the process by which providers connect the components of family-sensitive care to the delivery of high-quality care to families. On the other hand, our logic model suggests that family-sensitive care is an integral aspect of all areas of care and programming. Thus, future measurement approaches may look toward a more comprehensive approach to measuring family-sensitive care, with indicators across curricular and program areas.

Future measurement strategies also may consider a combination of program and parental assessment of family-sensitive care. This two-pronged approach would allow programs to determine whether there is a good "fit" between provider sensitivity to parents and parental experiences and perceptions of sensitivity. Although parental assessments may be time consuming and burdensome to carry out with every family, they may serve as validity checks for aspects of program assessments.

Another area for consideration in the future development of measures is how to adequately assess different levels of family sensitivity. As described earlier in this chapter, we recognize that some providers may be able to offer higher levels of family-sensitive care. Moreover, some families have a much greater need for family-sensitive care than others with fewer constraints. We need to develop measurement strategies that realistically address these differences in strengths and capacity across settings while at the same time putting forth some universal standards regarding family-sensitive care.

Our review of instruments points to some promising approaches to measurement, including documentation review of family engagement and provider and parent interviews and surveys. In addition to these, other approaches to assessing family-sensitive ECE also may prove useful, such as observational assessment of parent–provider interactions during drop-off and pickup, in-depth interviews with providers about their knowledge and understanding of families, and vignette studies in which providers respond to case studies as a means of assessing attitudes, knowledge, and practices related to families (Finch, 1987). Measurement advances in the study of attitudes (e.g., see Krosnick, Judd, & Wittenbrink, 2005, for review) suggest the benefit of utilizing both explicit measures (i.e., self-reports) and implicit attitude instruments (i.e., unobtrusive measures) in order to account for the complexities with which attitudes may affect actual behavior. All of these approaches raise questions about valid time frames and frequency of measurement, as well as questions about shared assessment and who should be included in assessments of family-sensitive care (e.g., parents, providers, children). Although we do not expect providers to have the resources or time to conduct these kinds of assessments, we propose that a range of alternative approaches be explored in the development of new quality measurement tools that can be used by a wide array of researchers with varied purposes and goals.

Implications and Recommendations

Policy Implications

The model of family-sensitive care that we propose presents both opportunities and challenges. Our review of ECE quality standards indicates that the field recognizes and values family-sensitive care. State efforts to develop quality rating systems (QRS) also suggest a readiness to embrace family engagement as part of quality programming. However, our proposed model for family-sensitive care suggests areas in which these quality-improvement efforts may be strengthened through research, new measurement approaches, and increased and more focused professional-development efforts to promote family-sensitive care.

Promising Strategies for Integrating Family-Sensitive Care into Quality Improvement Initiatives

Two quality improvement efforts—QRSs and professional development systems—offer the most promise for integrating family-sensitive caregiving into definitions and implementation of high-quality ECE programs.[5] A common goal of QRSs is to increase families' understanding of factors related to high-quality care, and most state and local QRSs include parent education and/or family involvement as an indicator of high quality. In a review of state QRSs, the following criteria were used most often as indicators of parent/family involvement: availability of parent advisory boards, parent bulletin boards, parent conferences and meetings, parent resource centers, and/or ways of sharing daily activities with parents (National Child Care Information Center, 2005). Regarding professional development systems, states are beginning to look at the principles of family support and family involvement to design new strategies and approaches, especially as related to defining core knowledge and competencies needed (Connors-Tadros & Ramsburg, 2008).[6]

Challenges to Integrating Family-Sensitive Care into Quality Improvement Initiatives

Despite the recognition that quality ECE should include family engagement, the field is in need of new assessment tools and focused professional development opportunities in this area. As states move forward with their quality improvement efforts, they need cost-effective and feasible strategies to promote and measure family engagement and family-sensitive care. For example, all four states participating in a 2008 Child Care Bureau roundtable looking at QRSs identified "active engagement of parents as a key component of quality in infant/toddler care," yet all felt a lack of adequate measures of the inclusion of these critical indicators in their QRS efforts (National Infant & Toddler Child Care Initiative, 2008, p. 12). Moreover, states are often limited by available resources and tools, and they must weigh program accountability with realistic expectations about both the implementation and the measurement of family engagement.

Efforts to include family-sensitive care in quality improvement initiatives also may need to recognize the strengths and weaknesses of different providers regarding their ability to engage and support families. Providers across settings may need more in-depth and sustained training and education in family systems, family support, and effective work with families. Some providers—especially family, friend, and neighbor caregivers—already may be engaging in family-sensitive care and may need professional development in other aspects of caregiving, whereas center-based teachers may need additional training in working with families. In their work with providers, early childhood degree programs, as well as technical assistance efforts, need to increase and deepen the focus on families. The constructs of family-sensitive care (attitudes, knowledge, and practices) proposed in this chapter may be a useful model for developing and strengthening family-focused coursework.

On the other hand, training and education initiatives also may need to address concerns regarding the providers' burden of support, as well as help providers find realistic ways to meet the needs of families without compromising other aspects of their work with children. Focusing initially on helping providers develop better attitudes toward, and knowledge about, families may be a less threatening and less intensive first step than requiring providers to offer a new range of services to families. For example, most providers conduct some type of intake interview or enrollment procedure with new families, which could be used as an opportunity for gathering the kind of information about families that may help providers understand the work-related, educational, and cultural contexts of the lives of families in their care.

Future Research and Next Steps

This chapter points to several gaps in our knowledge about the ways ECE providers respond and are sensitive to the needs and realities of families. Specifically, future research is needed to develop strategies for measuring family-sensitive care and to test our hypothesis that family-sensitive ECE will lead to better outcomes for children and parents.

There is a great deal more work ahead in understanding how the different family-sensitive constructs identified in this chapter, as well as different levels and intensity of family-sensitive care, relate to child and family outcomes. Further, the factors that promote or inhibit the adoption of family-sensitive care remain empirically untested. A better understanding of the relationship between family-sensitive caregiving and child outcomes may help to explain some of the mixed and modest results from evaluations of ECE programs.

Before we can examine the relationship between family-sensitive care and child or parent outcomes, we clearly need more descriptive research on provider attitudes toward families and the ways in which providers gather and use knowledge about families. Although there is limited evidence that center- and home-based ECE providers can serve as sources of family support, we lack information from representative samples on the prevalence of these practices within or across ECE settings. There also is no research to date that examines the inputs we identify as components of family sensitive care (Figure 8.1, Box A) in relation to the outputs of family-sensitive care (Figure 8.1, Box B). These are critical first steps to understanding the key constructs of family-sensitive care.

In conclusion, given that the effects of parents on child well-being are strong and ongoing, we propose in this chapter that ECE that supports the developmental needs both of children and of parents is essential for giving low-income children access to high-quality child care. Future research on the impacts of family-sensitive caregiving and its constructs and on the subsequent development of assessment tools and professional development opportunities for providers would help guide efforts to improve the quality of ECE for all children and families across all settings.

References

Adams, G., Rohacek, M., & Snyder, K. (2008). *Child care voucher programs: Provider experiences in five counties.* Washington, DC: The Urban Institute.

Administration for Children and Families. (2002a). *Making a difference in the lives of infants and toddlers and their families: The impacts of Early Head Start Volume 1: Final technical report.* Washington, DC: U.S. Department of Health and Human Services.

Administration for Children and Families. (2002b). *Pathways to quality and full implementation in Early Head Start programs.* Washington, DC: U.S. Department of Health and Human Services.

Administration for Children and Families. (2005). *Head Start impact study: First year findings.* Washington, DC: U.S. Department of Health and Human Services.

Ahluwalia, S.K., McGroder, S.M., Zaslow, M.J., & Hair, E.C. (2001). *Symptoms of depression among welfare recipients: A concern for two generations.* Child Trends Research Brief. Washington, DC: Child Trends. Retrieved from http://www.childtrends.org

Ajzen, I., & Fishbein, M. (2005). The influence of attitudes on behavior. In D. Albarracin, B.T. Johnson, & M.P. Zanna (Eds.), *The handbook of attitudes* (pp. 173–222). Mahwah, NJ: Lawrence Erlbaum Associates.

Allport, G.W. (1935). Attitudes. In C. Murchison (Ed.), *Handbook of social psychology* (pp. 798–884). Worcester, MA: Clark University Press.

Baldwin, D.A., & Moses, L.J. (1996). The ontogeny of social information gathering. *Child Development, 67,* 1915–1939.

Barbarin, O.A., McCandies, T., Early, D., Clifford, R.M., Bryant, D., Burchinal, M., et al. (2006). Quality of prekindergarten: What families are looking for in public sponsored programs. *Early Education and Development, 17*(4), 619–642.

Baum, A.C., & McMurray-Schwartz, P. (2004). Preservice teachers' beliefs about family involvement: Implications for teacher education. *Early Childhood Education Journal, 32*(1), 57–61.

Bianchi, S., Casper, L., & King, R. (2005). Complex connections: A multidisciplinary look at work, family, health, and well-being research. In S.M. Bianchi, L.M. Casper, & R.B. King (Eds.), *Work, family, health, and well-being* (pp. 1–17). Mahwah, NJ: Lawrence Erlbaum Associates.

Bradley, R.H., Caldwell, B.M., & Corwyn, R.F. (2003). The Child Care HOME Inventories: Assessing the quality of family child care homes. *Early Childhood Research Quarterly, 18,* 294–309.

Bromer, J. (2005). Ways of caring: How relative providers support children and parents. *Bank Street College of Education occasional paper series. 15, Perspectives on family, friend, and neighbor child care: Research, programs and policy,* 14–21.

Bromer, J. (2006). Beyond child care: The informal family support and community roles of African-American child care providers. (Doctoral dissertation, University of Chicago, 2006). *Dissertation Abstracts International, 68*(01).

Bromer, J., & Henly, J.R. (2004). Child care as family support? Caregiving practices across child care providers. *Children and Youth Services Review, 26,* 941–964.

Bromer & Henly (2009). The work–family support roles of child care providers across settings. *Early Childhood Research Quarterly, 24,* 271–288.

Brooks-Gunn, J., & Duncan, G. (1997). The effects of poverty on children. *The Future of Children, 7*(2), 55–71.

Brooks-Gunn, J., & Markman, L. (2005, March). The contribution of parenting to ethnic and racial gaps in school readiness. *The Future of Children, 15*(1), 139–168.

Burchinal, M.R., Follmer, A., & Bryant, D.M. (1996). The relations of maternal social support and family structure with maternal responsiveness and child outcomes among African-American families. *Development Psychology, 32*(6), 1073–1083.

Carlisle, E., Stanley, L., & Kemple, K.M. (2006). Opening doors: Understanding family and school influences on family involvement. *Early Childhood Education Journal, 33*(3), 155–162.

Caspe, M., & Lopez, E.M. (2006). *Lessons from family strengthening interventions: Learning from evidence-based practice.* Cambridge, MA: Harvard Family Resource Project.

Center for the Study of Social Policy. (2004). *Protecting children by strengthening families: A guidebook for early childhood programs.* Washington, DC: Author.

Chaudry, A. (2004). *Putting children first: How low-wage working mothers manage child care.* New York: Russell Sage.

Connors-Tadros, L., & Ramsburg, D. (2008). Home-based care plays an important role in meeting family needs. In M.M. Cornish (Ed.), *Promising practices for partnering with families in the early years* (pp. 79–102). Charlotte, NC: Information Age Publishing.

Crnic, K.A., Greenberg, M.T., Ragozin, A.S., Robinson, N.M., & Basham, R.B. (1983). Effects of stress and social support on mothers and premature and full-term infants. *Child Development, 54,* 209–217.

Dodson, L. (2006). After welfare reform: You choose your child over the job. *Focus, 24*(3), 25–28.

Eagly, A.H., & Chaiken, S. (1993). *The psychology of attitudes.* Fort Worth, TX: Harcourt Brace Jovanovich.

Elicker, J., Clawson, C., Hong, S-Y., Kim, T-E., Evangelou, D., & Kontos, S. (2005). *Community child care research project final report. Child care for working poor families: Child development and parent employment outcomes.* West Lafayette, IN: Purdue University.

Elicker, J., Noppe, I.C., Noppe, L.D., & Fortner-Wood, C. (1997). The parent–caregiver relationship scale: Rounding out the relationship system in infant child care. *Early Education and Development, 8*(1), 83–100.

Emlen, A.C., Koren, P., & Schultze, K. (2000). *A packet of scales for measuring quality of child care from a parent's point of view: With summary of methods and findings.* Retrieved June 28, 2010, from http://www.hhs.oregonstate.edu/familypolicy/occrp/publications/2000-A-Packet-of-Scales.pdf

Endsley, R.C., & Minish, P.A. (1991). Parent–staff communication in day care centers during morning and afternoon transitions. *Early Childhood Research Quarterly, 6*(2), 119–135.

Fiene, R. (1984). *Child Development Program Evaluation Scales and COFAS.* Washington, DC: Children's Services Monitoring Consortium.

Fiene, R. (2002). Improving child care quality through an infant caregiving mentoring project. *Child & Youth Care Forum, 31*(2), 79–87.

Finch, J. (1987). Research note: The vignette technique in survey research. *Sociology, 21*(1), 105–114.

Fishbein, M., & Ajzen, I. (1975). *Belief, attitude, intention, and behavior: An introduction to theory and research.* Reading, MA: Addison-Wesley.

Gibbon, H.M.F. (2002). Child care across sectors: A comparison of the work of child care in three settings. In F.M. Cancian, D. Kurz, A.S. London, R. Reviere, & M.C. Tuominen (Eds.), *Child care & inequality: rethinking care-work for children and youth* (pp. 145–158). New York: Routledge.

Gomby, D.S. (2005). *Home visitation in 2005: Outcomes for children and parents.* Washington, DC: Committee for Economic Development Invest in Kids Working Group.

Gomby, D.S., Culross, P.L., & Behrman, R.E. (1999). Home visiting: Recent program evaluations—analysis and recommendations. *Future of Children, 9*(1), 4–26.

Goode, T.D. (2004). *Cultural competence continuum.* National Center for Cultural Competence. Washington, DC: Georgetown University Center for Child and Human

Development, University Center for Excellence in Developmental Disabilities.

Green, B.L., McAllister, C.L., & Tarte, J.M. (2004). The strengths-based practices inventory: A tool for measuring strengths-based service delivery in early childhood and family support programs. *Families in Society, 85*(3), 326–334.

Halle, T., Zaff, J., Calkins, J., & Margie, N.G. (2000). Part II: Reviewing the literature on contributing factors to school readiness, in *Background for community-level work on school readiness: A review of definitions, assessments, and investment strategies*. Washington, DC: Child Trends.

Harms, T., Clifford, R.M., & Cryer, D. (1998). *Early Childhood Environment Rating Scale-Revised Edition (ECERS-R)*. New York: Teachers College Press.

Harms, T., Cryer, D., Clifford, R.M. (2003). *Infant/Toddler Environment Rating Scale: Revised Edition (ITERS-R)*. New York: Teachers College Press.

Harms, T., Cryer, D., & Clifford, R.M. (2007). *Family Child Care Environment Rating Scale-Revised Edition (FCCERS-R)*. New York: Teachers College Press.

Harms, T., Vineberg Jacobs, E., & Romano-White, D. (1996). *School-Age Care Environment Rating Scale (SACERS)*. New York: Teachers College Press.

Hashima, P., & Amato, P. (1994, April). Poverty, social support, and parental behavior. *Child Development, 65*(2), 394–403.

Head Start Program Performance Standards. (45 CFR 1304). Retrieved from http://www.access.gpo.gov/nara/cfr/waisidx_06/45cfr1304_06.html

Henly, J.R. (2002). Informal support networks and the maintenance of low-wage jobs. In F. Munger (Ed.), *Laboring below the line: The new ethnography of poverty, low-wage work, and survival in the global economy* (pp. 179–203). New York: Russell Sage Foundation.

Henly, J.R., Danziger, S.K., & Offer, S. (2005). The contribution of social support to the material well-being of low-income families. *Journal of Marriage and Family, 67*, 122–140.

Henly, J.R., & Lambert, S. (2005). Nonstandard work and child-care needs of low-income parents. In S.M. Bianchi, L.M. Casper, & R.B. King (Eds.), *Work, family, health, and well-being* (pp. 469–488). Mahwah, NJ: Lawrence Erlbaum Associates.

Henly, J.R., & Lyons, S. (2000). The negotiation of child care and employment demands among low-income parents. *Journal of Social Issues, 56*(4), 683–706.

HighScope Educational Research Foundation. (2003). *Preschool program quality assessment, 2nd Edition (PQA) administration manual*. Ypsilanti, MI: HighScope Press.

HighScope Educational Research Foundation. (2006). *Ready School Assessment: Administration manual*. Ypsilanti, MI: High/Scope Press.

Hofferth, S.L., Shauman, K.A., & Henke, R.R. (1998). *Characteristics of children's early care and education programs: Data from the 1995 National Household Education Survey*. (NCES 98-128). Washington DC: U.S. Department of Education, Office of Educational Research and Improvement.

Hoover-Dempsey, K.V., & Sandler, H.M. (1997). Why do parents become involved in their children's education? *Review of Educational Research, 67*(1), 3–42.

Horton, C. (2003). *Protective factors literature review: Early care and education programs and the prevention of child abuse and neglect*. Strengthening families through early care and education. Washington, DC: Center for the Study of Social Policy.

Hughes, R. (1985). The informal help-giving of home and center childcare providers. *Family Relations, 34*, 359–366.

Joffe, C.E. (1977). *Friendly intruders: Childcare professionals and family life*. Berkeley, CA: University of California Press.

Jones, I., White, C.S, Aeby, V., & Benson, B. (1997). Attitudes of early childhood teachers toward family and community involvement. *Early Education & Development, 8*(2), 153–168.

Kontos, S., Raikes, H., & Woods, A. (1983). Early childhood staff attitudes toward their parent clientele. *Child Care Quarterly, 12*, 45–58.

Krosnick, J.A., Judd, C.M., & Wittenbrink, B. (2005). The measurement of attitudes. In D. Albarracin, B.T. Johnson, and M.P. Zanna (Eds.), *The handbook of attitudes* (pp. 21–78). Mahwah, NJ: Lawrence Erlbaum.

Layzer, J., Goodson, B., Bernstein, L., & Price, C. (2001). *National evaluation of family support programs: Final report volume a: The meta-analysis*. Cambridge, MA: Abt Associates.

Li-Grining, C.P., & Coley, R.L. (2006). Child care experiences in low-income communities: Developmental quality and maternal views. *Early Childhood Research Quarterly,* 21(2), 125–141.

Maccoby, E. (2000). Parenting and its effects on children: On reading and misreading behavior genetics. *Annual Review of Psychology, 51*(1), 1–27.

Marsh, K.L., & Wallace, H.M. (2005). The influence of attitudes on beliefs: Formation and change. In D. Albarracin, B.T. Johnson, & M.P. Zanna (Eds.), *The handbook of attitudes* (pp. 369–396). Mahwah, NJ: Lawrence Erlbaum Associates.

McBride, B. (1991). Preservice teachers' attitudes towards parental involvement. *Teacher Education Quarterly, 18,* 59–67.

McLoyd, V.C. (1998). Socioeconomic disadvantage and child development. *American Psychologist, 53,* 185–204.

Moseman, C. (2003). Primary teachers' beliefs about family competence to influence classroom practices. *Early Education & Development, 14*(2), 125–153.

National After-School Association (1991). *The NAA standards for quality school-age care: Standards at a glance.* Washington, DC: Author. Retrieved from http://naaweb.site-ym.com/resource/resmgr/Standards_At_A_Glance_Brochu.pdf

National Association for the Education of Young Children. (2007). *NAEYC early childhood program standards and accreditation criteria: The mark of quality in early childhood education.* Washington, DC: Author.

National Association for Family Child Care (2005). *Quality standards for NAFCC accreditation, Fourth Edition.* Salt Lake City, UT: National Association for Family Child Care. Developed by Family Child Care Accreditation Project, Wheelock College. Retrieved from http://www.nafcc.org/documents/QualStd.pdf

National Child Care Information Center. (2005). *Common categories of criteria used in state quality rating systems.* Fairfax, VA: Author.

National Child Care Information Center. (2008). *Quick facts: Quality rating systems.* Fairfax, VA: Author.

National Child Care Information and Technical Assistance Center (2010). *QRIS Definitions and Statewide Systems.* Retrieved January 14, 2011 from http://nccic.acf.hhs.gov/pubs/qrs-defsystems.html

National Infant & Toddler Child Care Initiative. (2008). *Including infants and toddlers in quality rating and improvement systems. QRIS Issues Meeting white paper.* Washington, DC: Author.

National Research Council and Institute of Medicine. (2003). *Working families and growing kids.* Washington, DC: The National Academies Press.

Neuman, S., Dwyer, J., & Koh, S. (2007). *Child/Home Early Language & Literacy Observation Tool (CHELLO).* Baltimore: Paul H. Brookes Publishing Co.

NICHD Early Child Care Research Network. (1996). Characteristics of infant child care: Factors contributing to positive caregiving. *Early Childhood Research Quarterly, 11*(3), 269–306.

NICHD Early Child Care Research Network. (2001). Nonmaternal care and family factors in early development. *Journal of Applied Developmental Psychology, 22*(5), 457–492.

NICHD Early Child Care Research Network. (2002). Parenting and family influences when children are in child care: Results from the NICHD Study of Early Child Care. In J.G. Borkowski, S.L. Ramey, & M. Bristol-Power (Eds.), *Parenting and the child's world: Influences on academic, intellectual, and social-emotional development. Monographs in parenting series* (pp. 99–123). Mahwah, NJ: Lawrence Erlbaum Associates.

NICHD Early Child Care Research Network. (2006). Child-care effect sizes for the NICHD study of early child care and youth development. *American Psychologist, 61*(2), 99–116.

Owen, M., Ware, A., & Barfoot, B. (2000). Caregiver-mother partnership behavior and the quality of caregiver-child and mother-child interactions. *Early Childhood Research Quarterly, 15*(3), 413–428.

Palfrey, J.S., Hauser-Cram, P., Bronson, M.B., Warfield, M.E., Sirin, S., & Chan, E. (2005). The Brookline Early Education Project: A 25-year follow-up study of a family-centered early health and development intervention. *Pediatrics, 116*(1). 144–152.

Pianta, R.C., La Paro, K.M., & Hamre, B.K. (2008). *Classroom Assessment Scoring System™ (CLASS™).* Baltimore: Paul H. Brookes Publishing Co.

Pittard, M., Zaslow, M., Lavelle, B., & Porter, T. (2006). *Investing in quality: A survey of state*

Child Care and Development Fund initiatives. Washington, DC: National Association of State Child Care Administrators and Child Trends.

Porter, T., & Kearns, S. (2005). Family, friend and neighbor care: Crib notes on a complex issue. *Occasional paper series 15. Perspectives on family, friend and neighbor child care: Research, programs and policy* (pp. 5–13). New York: Bank Street College of Education.

Porter, T., Pausell, D., DelGrosso, P., Avellar, S., Hass, R., & Vuong, L. (2010). *A review of the literature on home-based child care: Implications for future directions.* Retrieved from http://www.acf.hhs.gov/programs/opre/cc/supporting_quality

Porter, T., Rice, R., & Rivera, E. (2006). *Assessing quality in family, friend, and neighbor care: The child care assessment tool for relatives.* New York: Bank Street College of Education.

Porter, T., & Vuong, L. (2008). *Tutu and me: The effects of a family interaction program on parents and caregivers.* New York: Bank Street College of Education.

Powell, D. (2005). Searches for what works in parenting interventions. In L. Luster and L. Okagaki (Eds.), *Parenting: An ecological perspective* (2nd ed.) (pp. 343–373). Mahwah, NJ: Lawrence Erlbaum Associates.

Press, J.E., Fagan, J., & Laughlin, L. (2006). Taking pressure off families: Child-care subsidies lessen mothers' work-hour problems. *Journal of Marriage and Family, 68,* 155–171.

Prislin, R., & Wood, W. (2005). Social influence in attitudes and attitude change. In D. Albarracin, B.T. Johnson, & M.P. Zanna (Eds.), *The handbook of attitudes* (pp. 671–706). Mahwah, NJ: Lawrence Erlbaum Associates.

Repetti, R. (2005). A psychological perspective on the health and well-being consequences of parental employment. In S.M. Bianchi, L.M. Casper, & R.B. King (Eds.), *Work, family, health, and well-being* (pp. 241–254). Mahwah, NJ: Lawrence Erlbaum Associates.

Roy, K., Tubbs, C., & Burton, L. (2004). Don't have no time: Daily rhythms and the organization of time for low-income families. *Family Relations, 53*(2), 168–178.

Scott, E., London, A., & Hurst, A. (2005). Instability in patchworks of child care when moving from welfare to work. *Journal of Marriage and Family, 67*(2), 369–385.

Seitz, V. (1990). Intervention programs for impoverished children: A comparison of educational and family support models. In R. Vasta (Ed.), *Annals of child development: A research annual* (Vol. 7, pp. 73–103). London: Jessica Kingsley Publishers.

Shlay, A.B., Weinraub, M., & Harmon, M. (2007). *Racial and ethnic differences in welfare leavers' child care preferences: A factorial survey analysis.* Philadelphia, PA: Temple University, Family and Children's Policy Collaborative. Retrieved from http://astro.temple.edu/%7eashlay/factorialrace.pdf

Shpancer, N. (1998). Caregiver-parent relationships in daycare: A review and re-examination of the data and their implications. *Early Education and Development, 9*(3), 239–259.

Small, M.K., Jacobs, E.M., & Massengill, R.P. (2005). *Childcare centers and inter-organizational ties in high poverty neighborhoods.* Fragile Families Research Brief. Princeton, NJ: Center for Research on Child Wellbeing, Princeton University.

Sorce, J.F, Emde, R.N., Campos, J., & Klinnert, M.D. (1985). Maternal emotional signaling: Its effects on the visual cliff behavior of 1-year-olds. *Developmental Psychology, 21*(1),195–200.

Sweet, M.A., & Appelbaum, M.I. (2004). Is home visiting an effective strategy? A meta-analytic review of home visiting programs for families with young children. *Child Development, 75*(5), 1435–1456.

Talan, T.N., & Bloom, P.J. (2004). *Program Administration Scale: Measuring leadership and management in early childhood programs.* New York: Teacher's College Press.

Uttal, L. (2002). *Making care work: Employed mothers in the new child care market.* New Brunswick, NJ: Rutgers University Press.

van IJzendoorn, M.H., Tavecchio, L.W.C., Stams, G., Verhoeven, M., & Reiling, E. (1998). Attunement between parents and professional caregivers: A comparison of childrearing attitudes in different child-care settings. *Journal of Marriage and the Family, 60*(3), 771–781.

Westbrook, T. (2007). *Mediating influence of parenting styles between exposure to violence, maternal depression and child outcomes: A multigroup analysis.* Dissertation proposal. College Park: University of Maryland.

White, L. (2002). Care at work: In F. Munger (Ed.), *Laboring below the line: The new ethnography of poverty, low-wage work, and survival in the global economy* (pp. 213–244). New York: Russell Sage Foundation.

Endnotes

[1]We use the term *provider* throughout the chapter to refer to individual teachers and caregivers across arrangements, as well as to programs. We recognize that programs (and not individual staff) often are responsible for some of the parental supports described in this chapter.

[2]We do not advocate in this chapter that providers necessarily should offer this range of supports to parents, but we do feel that it is important to understand the kinds of supports some providers informally give parents.

[3]The meta-analysis examined 665 studies that were associated with 260 programs in the United States, Great Britain, and Canada. The studies included evaluations only with experimental or quasi-experimental designs (Layzer et al., 2001).

[4]A smaller study of 13 "family strengthening" programs, including HighScope, an early childhood model, found that approaches such as parent–child workshops and parent–child training can have effects on parents' well-being and parenting, in addition to the family environment and family involvement in learning (Caspe & Lopez, 2006).

[5]As of 2010, 23 states are implementing quality rating systems (QRSs) and many more states are actively discussing, developing, and/or piloting a QRS (National Child Care Information Center, 2010). A QRS is a systematic approach to assess, improve, and communicate the level of quality in early care and education programs (National Child Care Information Center, 2008).

[6]More than 30 states are engaged in efforts to develop comprehensive professional development systems that cover the range of early care and education settings (Connors-Tadros & Ramsburg, 2008).

CHAPTER 9

Measuring Culturally Responsive Early Care and Education

Eva Marie Shivers and Kay Sanders
with T'Pring R. Westbrook

Despite consensus in practice and policy that it is important for early childhood programs to respect and address issues related to cultural diversity, there is little research evidence to help us understand whether, how, and to what extent respecting families' and children's culture and addressing diversity influence the quality of care that children receive and whether these practices also affect children's outcomes. Even a brief review of the literature on multicultural practices in early education reveals very little information on why and how teachers and caregivers should honor and support children's culture in the classroom and home-based care group, and even less information on the impact and effectiveness of such cultural practices (Ramsey, 2006). This dearth of research leaves unanswered many questions related to how early childhood practitioners structure their interactions and activities to be responsive to culture, how structural and organizational factors influence these practices, how culturally responsive pedagogies are aligned with the constructs on widely used measures of observational quality, and how culturally responsive pedagogies relate to children's school readiness.

One of the main reasons that there is scant evidence documenting the impact and relevance of culturally responsive practices in early care settings is that many researchers have misconceptions about the developmental relevance of this work with young children. These misconceptions reflect a lack of knowledge of the most recent scholarship from developmental psychology and the critical, cultural studies of education (Romero, 2008). It is also unclear to many practitioners and researchers exactly how culturally responsive care aligns with various dimensions of quality in early childhood settings. This chapter argues that, to truly understand the impact of culturally responsive care on children's outcomes, definitions must be strengthened and measurement strategies must be improved and expanded. Thus, the broad goals of the chapter are to 1) provide definitions of culturally responsive care, 2) propose a new framework for considering the conceptual links between culturally responsive care and quality, 3) review existing measurement approaches for culturally responsive care, 4) describe new and promising measurement strategies, 5) propose an expansion of school readiness predictors, 6) review and make clear recommendations for continued research on this topic, and 7) review implications for policy.

This review can be contextualized by discussing several key reasons that the measurement of culturally responsive care is critical and timely. First, not only are many in the field aware of the advances and shifts made in our early education systems (e.g., quality rating and improvement systems [QRIS]; universal preschool) and proposals for further initiatives (e.g., proposal for the Early Childhood Challenge Fund; U.S. Department of Education, 2009), but many also are involved in informing these systems through evaluation and research efforts. Understanding how culturally responsive care is embedded in our definitions of, and standards for, measuring quality will help us ensure that we are building a system that is culturally responsive to the families and communities it serves (Bruner, Ray, Stover-Wright, & Copeman, 2009). For example, QRIS now present in many states can serve as powerful drivers of enhancements in current early care and education (ECE) systems. Increasing attention is being paid to whether states' QRIS are developed in ways that ensure cultural responsiveness for all children (Bruner et al., 2009; Tout, Zaslow, Halle & Forry, 2009). Stakeholders, including parents, teachers, directors, community members, policy makers, and researchers, are aware of the influence QRIS are having on shaping provider practices, improvement supports, and definitions of *quality* (Bruner et al., 2009). More and more stakeholders are concerned that if states are not including components related to cultural responsiveness in their QRIS, then formal education to prepare early educators and in-service professional development systems will fail to emphasize cultural responsiveness in their curricula and programs will unwittingly neglect to incorporate attention to cultural issues in their day-to-day practices. In order to address the calls for attention to cultural issues in states' QRIS, we must address the challenge of finding ways to measure dimensions of program quality that are related to cultural responsiveness (Bruner et al., 2009).

Although past research has demonstrated that high-quality ECE provides a buffering effect for numerous children at risk for school failure, many of whom are from ethnic-minority backgrounds (Brunson-Day, 2006a; Burchinal & Cryer, 2003; Shonkoff & Phillips, 2000), recent studies have called into question the low effect sizes present in analyses of the linkages between quality measures and children's outcomes (Burchinal et al., 2009). Separating and studying distinct elements of quality—such as culturally responsive care—and their association with children's outcomes may lead us toward a deeper understanding of whether our current measurement tools are adequate for capturing the experiences of all children.

The next reason for exploring this topic involves the rapidly increasing diversity of the young child population in the United States (see Chapter 1, this volume) and the widening gap separating low-income minority children from their more affluent peers (Klein & Knitzer, 2007). Despite our knowledge about the importance of early development for future developmental outcomes, there seem to be multiple factors that keep low-income children of color from succeeding in school. Many of these factors often are not captured by traditional measures and child care assessments (Brunson-Day, 2006a). There are competing rationales for why children from low-income ethnic-minority backgrounds continue to lag behind their white counterparts in school and in life. One important strategy in addressing this concern is to promote an evolution of models of *risk* and *resiliency*. Examining how culture interacts with children's development in their early childhood settings is one key to understanding risk and resiliency, and therefore the achievement gap, more comprehensively. Finally, recent brain research has provided increasing evidence about the importance of early relationships in the formation of brain architecture (Gunnar & Donzella, 2002). This chapter's approach to decoding culturally responsive care is embedded in the understanding that culturally responsive care is a relational construct. That is, we propose that teachers who are responsively attuned to each child's culture will have a positive impact on children's social and emotional development and, thereby, on their later growth and development.

To briefly anticipate the key conclusions of the chapter, existing measures of quality in early childhood settings tend to address culturally responsive care through the presence of materials (such as books and toys) reflecting a range of cultures. Yet, the conceptual model we present of culturally responsive care underscores the importance also of the characteristics of early educators/caregivers (including their own race/ethnicity and beliefs), the professional preparation they have undertaken, the organizational climate of their ECE settings, and the interactions they engage in with children. Although we are seeing the emergence of measurement approaches addressing these further important components of culturally responsive early childhood care and education, research validating such measurement approaches is extremely limited. For example, studies have focused on early educator race/ethnicity and the match between child and early educator race/ethnicity, and we see work on measurement approaches for capturing early educator/caregiver beliefs about diversity. Yet, these measures of caregiver characteristics have not been examined in relation to overall quality or child outcomes. Although there is descriptive research focusing on the extent to which early educator/caregiver professional preparation includes a focus on diversity and culturally responsive ECE, a critical gap is noted in rigorous evaluation research examining the effects of such professional development. Similarly, there are multiple measurement approaches aimed at describing program goals related to respect for diversity and engagement of families from a range of backgrounds in ECE settings. But these potentially important indicators of organizational quality have not been systematically examined in relation to observational measures of quality or child outcomes. Studies examine the implementation of curricula focusing on cultural diversity, and exploratory studies provide initial descriptions of the effects of curricula, but again, rigorous, longitudinal evaluation studies extending to child outcomes are lacking. Whereas research suffices to articulate the hypothesis that culturally responsive caregiving will be related to the social and emotional domain of school readiness, there is a clear need for further empirical research on this issue. In particular, work is needed that focuses on the quality of teacher–child and child–child relationships, group identification, and self-concept in relation to culturally related features of early childhood settings and how these are affected by intervention approaches to support culturally responsive caregiving.

Key Definitions and Conceptual Framework

A recent call has been issued by researchers to conduct research on ECE that follows a more inclusive agenda for children from ethnic-minority backgrounds (Child Trends, 2009; Graham, 2006; Johnson et al., 2003; Shivers, Sanders, Wishard, & Howes, 2007). One of the recommendations involves developing more culturally relevant definitions to use in conjunction with an evolving definition of quality in ECE. In this section we highlight and define several key terms used throughout the chapter.

Defining Culture

We borrow an inclusive definition of culture:

> Culture is a shared system of meaning, which includes values, beliefs and assumptions expressed through a definite pattern of language, behavior, customs, attitudes and practices, in daily interactions of individuals within a group. The members of a group may or may not be able to articulate the cultural elements that shape their world view and motivate their actions, as much of the cultural knowledge is tacit and gained through participation in activities unique to that group. (Christensen, Emde, & Fleming, 2004, p. 5)

Although we readily acknowledge the breadth of this definition, for purposes of this chapter we discuss culture primarily in the combined context of race, ethnicity, and class. We also present concepts and recommend measurement strategies that employ the use of an insider's perspective to studying cultural phenomena (referred to as *emic* approaches): the perspective from inside the ECE system. Rogoff's (2003) approach to understanding culture can provide us with a basis for examining concrete artifacts of culture in ECE settings. Routines, practices, values, and social interactions provide a way to measure culture in the classroom.

Defining Culturally Responsive Care

Culturally responsive care involves the implementation in early childhood settings of practices, including routines and patterns of social interactions, that represent and support the home cultures and values of the families whose children attend and that thereby support positive outcomes in the children. Our definition of *culturally responsive care* emphasizes the centrality of practices. Program practices may differ, for example, in the degree to which they emphasize individual needs over collective experiences, or child-initiated as opposed to teacher-initiated learning (Howes, 2010; Kessler & Swadener, 1992). By using a practice-focused perspective, we can begin to examine whether and how articulated and observed routines and interactions vary by ethnicity, to identify how culturally relevant practices help to define high quality, and to examine how culturally relevant practices contribute to positive development in children.

Defining Cultural Congruence

Cultural congruence is one aspect of culturally responsive care, and it involves the extent to which various dimensions of continuity and discontinuity exist between the home and early childhood setting. Cultural congruence can be examined as a factor influencing children's development. Traditional standards and markers of quality in early childhood settings fail to take into account the amount of congruence between the values of the home and the early care setting, which, according to Garcia-Coll and colleagues (1996) and Lamb (1999), is a distinctive aspect of the environment. Certainly, compatibility between settings eases transitions for children and enhances communications between parents and child care professionals.

Research has demonstrated that programs serving children from differing cultural communities use different practices in their care of children (Howes, 2010; Sanders, Deihl, & Kyler, 2007; Wishard, Shivers, Howes, & Ritchie, 2003). Furthermore, these practices are rooted in the ethnic and racial identity of the adults who care for children in these early childhood programs. Thus, some programs expect children to bring special objects from home to ease the transition to the early childhood setting, whereas others forbid it, wanting to help children understand that the toys within the early childhood setting belong to the group and not to individuals. When children enter an early childhood setting from a home cultural community that is not the same as the one shared by the adults and children in the program, they may experience discontinuity in practices around basic caregiving.

Conceptual Framework

In order to examine how culture is embedded in the quality of early childhood settings and to investigate the distinct elements of culturally responsive care, this chapter provides a theoretical framework (see Figure 9.1) that places children's development within the context of their care environments, within family systems, and, further, within ethnic and social class contexts. The discussion here of the current status of measurement of culturally responsive care and of next steps for measures development will focus on particular components of this model. We describe measurement of these aspects of the model after highlighting their position within the broader integrative framework.

This integrative framework draws first from ecocultural/ecological theory (Bronfenbrenner, 1979; Gallimore & Goldenberg, 1993; Lerner, 1986, 1991), in which individual development is nested within the broader "sociocultural system," and from more recent work that interprets the development of all children within a cultural context (Garcia-Coll et al., 1996). Garcia-Coll's integrative model helps organize information about how more distal ecological factors, such as social position and culture, impinge on the more proximate contexts of early development (family, ECE settings) for children from ethnic-minority backgrounds. Specifically, in our model we bring variables of social location, such as race and ethnicity, and their derivatives, such as racism, prejudice, oppression, discrimination, and segregation, to center stage and integrate them into a larger, contextually sensitive model that is applied to children's experiences in early childhood settings. We argue that aspects of unique experiences among children from ethnic-minority backgrounds, such as racism, segregation, acculturation, and migration, are normative in their constancy and must be addressed in our exploration of culturally responsive care and quality in early childhood settings (Garcia-Coll et al., 1996; Johnson et al., 2003).

Second, the framework draws on the notion of development as a continuum born in the everyday routines of children, with these routines varying both across and within cultural and linguistic communities (Gallimore & Goldenberg, 1993). In this model, the establishment of daily routines is considered an adaptive issue that all families from all cultures confront. Such routines are organized and maintained to accomplish specific tasks that support the larger cultural values of the community (Weisner, 2002). Daily routines are widely variant, as they are determined and maintained by the specific needs and cultural values of the family unit and are indirectly influenced by the distal features of the environment, such as neighborhood safety and family socioeconomic status, that shape the nature of the activities within the immediate environment (Gallimore & Goldenberg, 1993; Reese, Garnier, Gallimore, & Goldenberg, 2000).

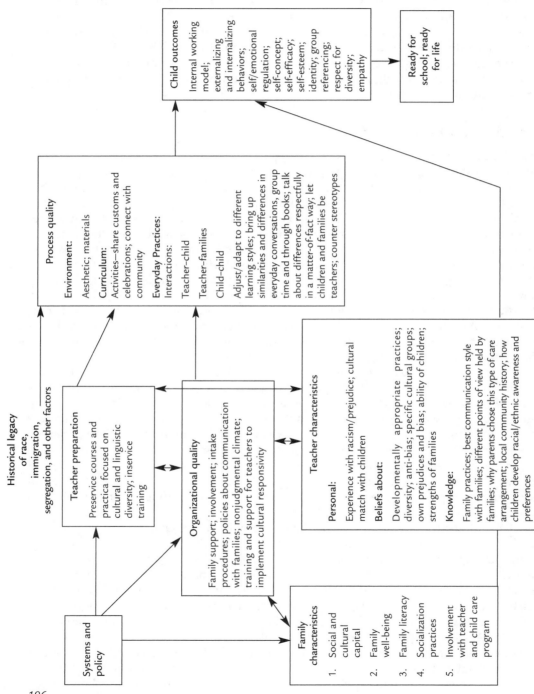

Historical legacy
of race,
immigration,
segregation, and other factors

Process quality

Environment:

Aesthetic; materials

Curriculum:
Activities—share customs and celebrations; connect with community

Everyday Practices:
Interactions:

Teacher-child

Teacher-families

Child-child

Adjust/adapt to different learning styles; bring up similarities and differences in everyday conversations, group time and through books; talk about differences respectfully in a matter-of-fact way; let children and families be teachers; counter stereotypes

Child outcomes

Internal working model;
externalizing and internalizing behaviors;
self/emotional regulation;
self-concept;
self-efficacy;
self-esteem;
identity; group referencing;
respect for diversity;
empathy

Ready for school; ready for life

Teacher preparation

Preservice courses and practica focused on cultural and linguistic diversity; inservice training

Organizational quality

Family support; involvement; intake procedures; policies about communication with families; nonjudgmental climate; training and support for teachers to implement cultural responsivity

Teacher characteristics

Personal:
Experience with racism/prejudice; cultural match with children

Beliefs about:
Developmentally appropriate practices; diversity; anti-bias; specific cultural groups; own prejudices and bias; ability of children; strengths of families

Knowledge:
Family practices; best communication style with families; different points of view held by families; why parents chose this type of care arrangement; local community history; how children develop racial/ethnic awareness and preferences

Family characteristics

1. Social and cultural capital

2. Family well-being

3. Family literacy

4. Socialization practices

5. Involvement with teacher and child care program

Systems and policy

196

Figure 9.1. Conceptual model: Quality and culturally responsive care

Therefore, the model includes routines within the early childhood setting as another expression of culture.

Third, the model uses the construct of *cultural communities* as developed by Rogoff (2003) to mean groupings of people who participate in shared sets of practices and traditions. Practices are particular ways of doing things—for example, how children are greeted as they come to the early childhood program or how caregivers help children sleep during naptime. One kind of cultural community very relevant to the discussion in this chapter is based on shared ethnic or racial identification.

Fourth, the box containing process quality in the model (see Figure 9.1) is informed by a framework developed by Howes (2000) that places children's relationships with their caregiver as one of the most basic features of quality contributing to children's outcomes. In Howes's framework, children's development does not occur outside of relationships; rather, the development of relationships is the cornerstone of children's development. This theme is found also in the emerging application of infant and early childhood mental health theories to policies and practices for early childhood care and education (Hungerford, Brownell, & Campbell, 2000; Zeanah, Stafford, Nagle, & Rice, & 2005). Our approach to decoding culturally responsive care in this chapter is embedded in the understanding that culturally responsive care is a relational construct.

Finally, the model is informed by the most recent work around developmentally appropriate practice and the recent early childhood program standards developed by the National Association for the Education of Young Children (NAEYC) in 2005. That is, we use basic elements of these standards to frame our discussion of quality.

Ultimately, this integrative framework assumes that, in order to understand children's developmental pathways, researchers must examine both the cultural community that forms the context for the interaction of children with others and the nature of routines and interpersonal interactions between children and others.

Current Measurement of Culturally Responsive Care in Early Childhood Settings

In efforts to advance research and conceptualization of culturally responsive caregiving, this section describes the current state of measurement of culturally responsive care in early childhood settings. A review of the current status of measurement of key constructs is organized according to the conceptual framework. We focus specifically on boxes in the conceptual model that pertain to features of ECE settings: the research on teacher characteristics, teacher preparation, and organizational quality as these relate to process quality.

Measurement of Teacher Characteristics Associated with Culturally Responsive Care

Teachers' understanding of, and response to, children's behavior is influenced by the teachers' own personal characteristics. This section explores current measurement strategies related to teacher ethnicity and teacher beliefs.

Teacher ethnicity

There is evidence that teacher race and ethnicity are related to perceptions and expectations of children. Some hold that white teachers perceive children of color as less well adjusted (Gomez, 1994; Payne, 1994), others argue that communication styles account for the differences in perception (Feldman, 1985; Ray, Bowman, & Brownell, 2006), and still others argue that differences in perception are due to limited understanding and socialized stereotypes (Gomez, 1994; Payne, 1994). Some interpretations of the differences imply that the confound between race and class leads to lower expectations of children from low-income families (Pigott & Cowen, 2000).

Usually, child ethnicity and teacher ethnicity are each considered and analyzed in isolation. However, emerging exploratory studies have examined the teacher–child ethnicity match as a single variable (Howes, 2010; Howes & Shivers, 2006; Pigott & Cowen, 2000; Sanders et al., 2007; Shivers, Howes, Ritchie, & Wishard, 2004; Wishard et al., 2003). For example, a study by Wishard and colleagues (2003) found that significantly distinct patterns of cultural practices in early childhood settings emerged only after an analysis using a teacher–child ethnic match was conducted. No significant patterns were found when the analysis used teacher and child ethnicity, each in isolation.

In addition, Johnson and colleagues (2003) argued that ethnicity, race, and culture can be viewed as psychological variables representing a common set of beliefs held about children's socialization. Examining the match between caregiver and child ethnicity as a central variable in this study is another way we can determine whether congruency is present. Researchers recognize that this may be a crude marker for something as nuanced and complicated as cultural congruence. For instance, the task of labeling becomes very complicated when we consider the complexity of interactions among culture, ethnicity, race, and class. Admittedly, broad, simplified labels do not begin to encompass the rich diversity in beliefs and perspectives that exist within ethnic groups.

Teacher Beliefs

Providers form their beliefs about caregiving on the basis of their own experiences of being cared for and their understanding about themselves and others (Howes, 2000; van IJzendoorn, 1992). These beliefs are influenced by the culture of the family and the community of origin, the culture of formal education, and the interplay of culture of origin and experiences with the dominant culture, including formal education (Howes, 2000).

Measurement of teacher beliefs encompasses mainly assessments of child-rearing styles and the level of endorsement a teacher may hold toward developmentally appropriate practices (Rimm-Kaufman, Storm, Sawyer, Pianta, & La Paro, 2006). A less established construct of teacher beliefs pertains to a teacher's understanding, awareness, and endorsement of cultural differences and/or culturally relevant pedagogy. A review of the literature reveals that most studies have relied upon either qualitative methodology (D'Angelo & Dixey, 2001; MacNaughton & Hughes, 2007; Trolley, Magerkorth & Fromme, 1999, van Hook, 2002; Wasson & Jackson, 2002) quantitative survey methods (Buysse, Castro, West, & Skinner, 2005; Huijbregts, Leseman, & Tavecchio, 2008; McDiarmid & Price, 1990; Shechtman, 2002; Tsigilis, Tsioumis, & Gregoriadis, 2007), or a mixed-methods approach (Hsueh & Barton, 2006; Taylor & Sobel, 2002) to measurement of diversity beliefs in teachers. The teaching populations included in these assessments of diversity beliefs have been mostly preservice teachers (Artiles & McClafferty, 1998; van Hook, 2002; Wasson & Jackson, 2002) and established educators within or outside of the United States (D'Angelo & Dixey, 2001; MacNaughton & Hughes, 2007; Trolley, Magerkorth, & Fromme, 1999).

The predominant qualitative methodology has consisted of open-ended question-naires or interviews that were content coded with accompanying frequency counts. However, one study included *concept maps* as part of its assessment of preservice teach-ers that required respondents to represent visually their understandings of effective teaching methods in culturally diverse classrooms (Artiles & McClafferty, 1998). The re-searchers calculated the content of the concept maps according to the density of the teachers' articulations of effective teaching methods. Another study applied a novel approach by presenting to teachers "critical incidents" pertaining to multicultural bias and requiring them to write essays about these incidents (Wasson & Jackson, 2002). The preservice teachers' critical-incident essays were coded thematically for core attitudes and beliefs concerning bias in classrooms. Based on the thematic coding, levels of bias awareness and antibias empowerment categories were established.

None of these studies connected the findings regarding teacher beliefs to children's outcomes. Rather, the main thrust of the qualitative studies was to uncover teachers' perceptions regarding diversity in the classroom and their approaches toward the diverse children they encounter in their classrooms.

In addition to the qualitative assessments, five published scales focus specifically on teachers' beliefs about diversity or cultural relevancy in early education (Buysse et al., 2005; Huijbregts et al., 2008; McDiarmid & Price, 1990; Shechtman, 2002; Tsigilis, Tsioumis, & Gregoriadis, 2007). Like the qualitative assessments, these surveys have not established, nor do they have as a focus, any links to child outcomes. Information about the five published scales is included next. For each scale, we describe the construct measured, the types of studies that have included the scale, and broad findings. After a review of these published scales, we include a summary of a mixed-methods approach to examining and measuring teacher beliefs.

The Pre-Service Teacher Beliefs Survey, produced by the National Center of Research on Teacher Learning (McDiarmid & Price, 1990), includes Likert scale, item-ranking, and multiple-choice questions. It assesses preservice teachers' positions regarding issues asso-ciated with teaching culturally diverse students at all levels of the education spectrum, from preschool to high school, as well as teachers' perspectives on educational adminis-tration. The measure also has been used in other studies on teachers' beliefs about multi-culturalism (Artiles & McClafferty, 1998; Trent, Pernell, & Stevens, 1995).

A frequent approach to the assessment of diversity beliefs has been to assess adults on broad-based cultural belief systems, such as individualistic versus collectivistic orientations or democratic principles. The individual versus collective paradigm is a common theme of research on parental and family cultural belief systems (Trumbull, Rothstein-Fisch, Greenfield, & Quiroz, 2001). The Parental Modernity scale (Schaefer & Edgerton, 1985) is one such scale. The Parental Modernity scale demonstrated high predictive validity for differences in observed parent–child interactions. The Autonomy and Group Questionnaire (Killen & Smetana, 1999) is based on theoretical assumptions similar to those in the Parental Modernity scale and includes three subscales that pur-portedly tap into the balance established between the individualistic and collectivistic beliefs systems of child care teachers. These subscales are Individual Choices, Rules and Order, and Group for the Individual. The Individual Choices subscale assesses the ex-tent to which teachers value individual choice in children and the reasons for valuing it. The Rules and Order subscale measures how much teachers believe a child's adher-ence to the rules of child care is important. The Group for the Individual subscale determines whether teachers believe that group participation is a positive part of a child's individual development.

Huijbregts et al. (2008) adapted the Parental Modernity and Autonomy and Group questionnaires to assess general beliefs and child care–specific beliefs pertaining to the individualistic–collectivistic dichotomy in child care teachers' cultural belief systems. This study revealed that child care teachers' belief systems can be attributed to the cultural community in which an individual resides, the professional experiences in the workplace, and the racial and ethnic diversity of the colleagues who make up the work environment.

Another broad-based approach regarding cultural belief systems of teachers is demonstrated by the Democratic Teacher Beliefs Scale (Shechtman, 2002), a 34-item scale that was validated with a sample population of Israeli teachers, school counselors, and education students. It is unclear, however, whether the sample included individuals who plan to work in early childhood settings. The scale includes items that pertain to the democratic tenets of equality, freedom, and justice. The assumption is that the degree of democratic beliefs held by an individual reveal the degree of openness toward diversity, or a "set of teacher beliefs that are crucial in diverse education" (p. 365). Shechtman found significant criterion validity with the Classroom Coping Scale (Cunningham & Sugawara, 1988).

An additional approach toward assessing belief systems about diversity in classrooms is to focus on the experiences or perception of the needs of a particular cultural group within child care programs. The questionnaire developed by Buysse et al. (2005) assessed administrators' endorsement of six domains of services to Latino families in early childhood programs. The domains of services are related to challenges in serving Latino children and families; strategies for serving Latino children and families; and administrators' beliefs about issues related to language development and early literacy learning, child assessment, approaches to supporting equity and diversity, and parental involvement. This 48-item Likert scale survey was conducted nationally with state administrators of child care and Head Start programs, preschools for children with disabilities, and infant–toddler programs for children with developmental delay. One of the domains (three items) pertains to administrators' endorsement of diversity, access, and equity for Latino children in child care.

Two studies include a mixed methodology for measuring diversity belief systems. Taylor and Sobel (2002) administered a 34-statement Likert scale questionnaire to preservice teachers (which included a small sample of students with a young childhood focus) about teachers' diversity beliefs and perceived skills in teaching children who are different from themselves. In addition, the researchers included open-ended questions that asked the preservice teachers to define key diversity terminology and reflect, in writing, on "the benefits, concerns, and questions that subjects perceived for themselves and their students when teaching in a classroom of learners whose backgrounds and needs differed from their own" (p. 491).

Hsueh and Barton (2006) also incorporated a mixed methodological design to address the cultural differences in early childhood educators' beliefs about the purpose of ECE. Their study is based upon Tobin and colleagues' classic study *Preschool in Three Cultures,* and it included early childhood educators from Head Start programs, non-Head Start child care programs, and students in a university-affiliated early childhood education program (Tobin, Wu, & Davidson, 1989). Tobin and colleagues' study incorporated both an item selection questionnaire with subsequent ranking of those items and teachers' responses to watching a video of a Chinese preschool program.

The Hsueh and Barton questionnaire consisted of three general cultural-belief questions that focused on why society should have preschool, the important learning experiences that should occur there, and the important characteristics of a preschool teacher.

Although the choices for the three questions did not deal with specific stances toward diversity or culture within early childhood programs, the ethnic demographic information of the respondents yielded clear differences in the understandings of these aspects in a preschool context. Like Tobin, the researchers incorporated video viewing of a Chinese preschool to prompt reaction in focus groups that revealed the viewers' "own beliefs and values" (p. 180; Tobin, Wu, & Davidson, 1989). Other studies have incorporated the video methodology to prompt teachers to articulate beliefs and values that may not manifest themselves with more traditional research methods (Cassidy & Lawrence, 2000; Wilcox-Herzog, 2002).

In sum, measures are scant that directly assess diversity or cultural pedagogical beliefs of preschool teachers and how these, in turn, relate to the teachers' practices in early childhood settings. Those which have been developed include a wide assortment of both qualitative and quantitative methodologies. Although these methodologies have been used in widely varying samples, there are no studies, as yet, that include representative or broadly generalizable samples of early educators in the United States. In addition, although the emphasis on qualitative methodology yields interesting findings regarding the diversity attitudes and cultural belief systems of preservice and early childhood professionals, the lack of linkage to child development outcomes and teacher practices makes it unclear whether these diversity beliefs have an impact on teacher practice or childhood experiences.

Measurement of Teacher Preparation and Professional Development

There also is scant research on how early educators and caregivers develop cross-cultural competency. In order for teachers to be effective with diverse students, it is crucial that they first recognize and understand their own worldviews in order to understand the worldviews of their students (Bennett, 1993). Researchers assert that, in order for teachers to interact effectively with their students, they must confront their own racism and biases (Banks, 1992, 1996; McAllister & Irvine, 2000), learn about their students' cultures, and perceive the world through diverse cultural lenses (Banks, 1996; Brunson-Day, 2006b; Middleton, 2002). Although these principles are frequently espoused in preservice teacher education programs, research about the process by which teachers of school-age children develop cross-cultural competency is extremely limited. We know even less about how teacher preparation affects teachers' cultural responsiveness in early childhood classrooms. Likewise, there are very few instruments designed to capture processes and outcomes in this domain (McAllister & Irvine, 2000).

Reviews of research in both early childhood and K–12 teacher-preparation programs have noted that including components of diversity in both coursework and field experiences (or practica) are promising strategies to address the challenges of preparing teachers to work with children and families from diverse backgrounds (Hollins & Guzman, 2005; Lim & Able-Boone, 2005). But there is no real agreement in the field about how much and what type of coursework should be required for effective preparation. Some studies have shown that even a single course may have positive effects on preservice teachers (e.g., Correa, Hudson, & Hayes, 2004; Middleton, 2002). Others have argued that competency in working with diverse children and families cannot be developed unless components of culture and diversity are included throughout the entire preservice program (Banks & Banks, 1995; Stayton, Miller, & Dinnebeil, 2003).

Practica and field experiences are also important in developing teachers' ability to work with children and families who may be linguistically or culturally diverse. Being placed in different internship sites reflecting the range of early childhood services in a community and the diversity of families and children, or in settings in unfamiliar neighborhoods, has been effective in helping student teachers see their own biases and values and attain a more complex understanding of children and families from diverse backgrounds (Hollins & Guzman, 2005; Miller, Fader, & Vincent, 2000). The likelihood that a teacher preparation program will offer courses and/or practica that focus on cultural or linguistic diversity (and the number of courses that will be offered) has been linked to the percentage of ethnically and linguistically diverse faculty (Early & Winton, 2001; Lim, Maxwell, Able-Boone, & Zimmer, 2009), as well as to the geographic location of the college/university (e.g., degree of urbanization, number of nonwhite residents in the state; Lim et al., 2009). In the conceptual model shown in Figure 9.1, the bidirectional arrow indicates that early educator characteristics such as race and ethnicity may affect teacher preparation programs (courses available and race and ethnicity of faculty), which, in turn, may be affected by teacher preparation (i.e., the content and extent of coursework focusing on culturally responsive caregiving).

Measurement strategies used to collect data about cultural and linguistic diversity coursework have included self-report surveys, reviews of course syllabi from university web sites, focus groups, and interviews with faculty and department heads (Early & Winton, 2001; Lim et al., 2009). The quality and reliability of this research is limited by the use of self-reporting and by survey data collection that does not address the depth and quality of multicultural content areas covered in preservice classrooms. Nor do these surveys adequately capture what student teachers actually learn from such courses, how their beliefs and attitudes about diverse children and families have changed, and how those courses have affected teachers' skills and practices with young children (Early & Winton, 2001; Lim et al., 2009; McAllister & Irvine, 2000). In addition, these approaches do not inform us about content areas that are woven throughout the preservice curriculum, as opposed to being addressed in stand-alone courses. This is problematic in that, as noted earlier, some have argued that diversity and multicultural content are optimally infused throughout the curriculum rather than covered in separate courses (Hains, Lynch, & Winton, 2000; Miller, Fader, & Vincent, 2000). We are lacking research that contrasts outcomes when teachers/caregivers are exposed to separate courses on culturally responsive practices and when such content is interwoven across all courses.

We also lack research focused on interventions to strengthen cultural responsiveness. Although other chapters in this book focus extensively on intervention research (see, for example, Chapter 4, by Neuman and colleagues, on the measurement of supports for early language and literacy development; and Chapter 6, by Leong and colleagues, on early social and emotional development), there is a virtual absence of studies on interventions or training on curricula for preschool-age children focusing on culturally responsive caregiving (Ramsey, 2006; Romero, 2008). Whereas some research provides anecdotal evidence, there appears to be no unified approach to evaluation of interventions and training curricula (Ramsey, 2006; Romero, 2008). A key next step is to have rigorous evaluations of diversity training for teachers of preschool-aged children (Banks, 1992, 1996; Delpit, 1995; Eggers-Pierola, 2005; Ladson-Billings, 1994; McLaren, 1995).

Measurement of Organizational Quality

Organizational quality refers to program-level factors such as an early childhood program's articulated mission, goals, and philosophy; programwide use of a curriculum;

policies about involvement with families; reliance on reflective supervision; access to resources; class sizes; teacher–student ratios; and support for ongoing professional development. Some research demonstrates a link among these features of care and children's experiences of culturally responsive care in the classroom (Derman-Sparks & the ABC Task Force, 1989; Sanders et al., 2007; Wishard et al., 2003). This section describes current measurement strategies involving 1) program goals or philosophies about children, families, and communities as these relate to cultural diversity; and 2) the ways in which programs create relationships with families from varying cultural backgrounds and involve them in program and classroom activities.

Program goals embody the intent or mission of the program and can be documented in a systematic way (Howes, 2010; Sanders et al., 2007; Wishard et al., 2003.) Although previous studies have found that program goals significantly influence children's social play behavior (Wintre, 1989; Wishard et al., 2003), this line of research is only just beginning to include the influence of program goals on the more general experiences of children in ECE programs and the extent to which those goals address diversity and cultural responsiveness. Common measurement strategies have included qualitative open-ended interviews with center directors (e.g., Sanders et al., 2007; Wishard et al., 2003) and checklists such as those used in the Head Start Family and Child Experiences Study (West et al., 2007). Further work is needed to understand how program goals translate into practices that are supportive of teachers in their interactions with children and families from varying cultural backgrounds.

A second component of organizational quality that can support culturally responsive caregiving comprises policies and practices that support cultural congruency between home and school. Congruency occurs when there is similarity in child-rearing values, socialization goals, and practices among directors, teachers, and parents. Research agendas that place children from ethnic-minority backgrounds at their core explore questions such as the following: Are parents from ethnic-minority backgrounds more apt to be engaged by early childhood settings that attempt to reflect their culture, or do some parents fear that such a setting will not adequately prepare their child for success in mainstream America? Do higher levels of congruency enhance social competence or ethnic identity? One major hypothesis is that children in early childhood settings that promote higher rates of parent engagement are more likely to experience congruency due to the bidirectional influence between parents and staff. Research on parental engagement finds that teachers who engage families most effectively are those who understand the link between the provision of ECE and parental goals and values. According to Henderson and Mapp (2002), it is the engagement by both teachers and parents that contributes to children's learning, but such engagement requires that teachers incorporate into their practices the cultural knowledge of the families they serve.

The strategies involved with measuring the amount, extent, and quality of family involvement in early childhood settings, and how this promotes cultural congruence, have been mostly exploratory in nature (Shivers et al., 2004; Wishard et al., 2003). Several standardized instruments exist, but these are used primarily to examine the teacher–parent relationship, and they do not focus on program practices intended to support the gathering of knowledge about the families in the early childhood setting. (See Chapter 8, this volume, by Bromer and colleagues, for a discussion of family-sensitive caregiving and a review on attitudes, beliefs, and practices with families).

Measurement of Culturally Responsive Care as an Element of Process Quality

Process quality represents the immediate experience of the children in an early childhood setting—such as the interactions that they have with their providers, activities, and materials—and the everyday practices and routines implemented by their teachers (Phillipsen, Burchinal, Cryer, & Howes, 1997). According to the framework presented in this chapter, process quality is the most proximal to the experience of the child and, therefore, most relevant to children's cultural experiences in ECE. This is the area in which there has been the most effort in terms of measurement development for culturally responsive care.

Researchers, practitioners, and policy makers are questioning the nature and quality of services provided to linguistically and culturally diverse children and their families. Some are concerned because they recognize that multicultural experiences are reduced to a celebration of the artifacts of culture—foods, fashions, and festivals, which, although important, do not penetrate latent value issues associated with culture (Derman-Sparks & the ABC Task Force, 1989). In this approach, culture is regarded as a superficial overlay, a set of activities scheduled for a particular time slot, not a pervasive approach to understanding and nurturing development. Indeed, most of the currently used measures of process quality also measure "culture" or "attention to diversity" in a superficial manner. This section describes current measurement strategies of process quality, with a specific focus on curriculum and environment (see also Table 9.1).

Curriculum and Instructional Practices

Researchers (Ray, 2000; Hale-Benson, 1986; Ladson-Billings, 1994) suggest two critical characteristics of successful schools and teaching practices for culturally, ethnically, and racially diverse students: 1) curricula that embrace, respect, and build on the experiences, abilities, and knowledge that children bring to the classroom; and 2) culturally relevant instruction that is relationship-based and uses students' culture and home language to enhance educational achievement. Multicultural curricula offer tools that teachers may use to help young students understand and appreciate their own and others' rich cultural traditions, behaviors, and beliefs. Culturally relevant strategies also serve as a way for teachers to learn about and respect the diverse backgrounds of students and families (Ladson-Billings, 1994). Culturally relevant pedagogy is intended to convert a relatively monocultural early childhood curriculum into one that embraces the many voices and perspectives of a diverse society (Ray, 2000).

In general, early childhood curricula vary in terms of specificity of goals, with some having specific, stated developmental goals (both social and cognitive), whereas others are based on looser and wider goals. In parallel, early childhood curricula that include a focus on culture differ in terms of the specificity of goals. An example of a curriculum with a focus on culture that has specific goals is the *Anti-Bias Curriculum* for preschoolers (Derman-Sparks & the ABC Task Force, 1989). It shares the same goals as those espoused in the looser curricula of culturally relevant teaching, but it also incorporates a focus on developing children's skills and abilities so that they are able to respond to and resist prejudice and bias in themselves and others. Both approaches aim to change the way that American children think about themselves and others in relation to diversity. They deliberately encourage students to learn about the sources of inequality, the common interests shared by all human beings, and the aspects of culture and heritage that make groups unique.

Table 9.1.   Cultural measures

Name of tool	Author(s)	Domain of quality measured	Methodological approach
Anti-Bias Checklist-3	Howes, 1999	Physical environment	Observed checklist
Anti-Bias Checklist-4	Howes, Ritchie, & Shivers, 2004	Physical environment; interactions; organizational quality; activities	Observed rating scale (1–7) Completed by trained observer
Identification with American Ideals Survey	Phinney, J.S., DuPont, S., Espinosa, C., Revill, J., & Sanders, K., 1994	Beliefs about ideals of American society	Rating scale (1–7) Completed by participant
Diversity Orientation Survey (DOS)	Sanders, 2005	Teachers' beliefs about diversity	Teacher questionnaire
Teaching for Diversity Survey	MacNaughton & Hughes, 2007	Teachers' beliefs about diversity and pedagogy	Teacher questionnaire
Preschool Racial Attitudes Measure (PRAM II)	Hale-Benson, 1990, in ECRQ article	Children's racial bias	Picture test
Child Preference and Identity Test	NICHD	Children's ethnic and social identity	Picture test; self-identification answer test; picture nomination test
Doll Test	Clark & Clark, 1940	Children's racial preference	Doll preference activity
Early Childhood Rating Scale-Revised (ECERS-R) (4 items—Books and Pictures; Music/Movement; Dramatic Play; Promoting Acceptance of Diversity)	Harms, Clifford, & Cryer, 2005	Physical environment; interactions; activities	Observed rating scale (1–7) Completed by trained observer
Early Childhood Rating Scale—Extended (ECERS-E) (3 items: planning for individual learning needs; gender equity and awareness; race equality)	Sylva, Siraj-Blatchford, & Taggart, 2003	Physical environment;	Observed rating scale (1–7) Completed by trained observer
Family Child Care Environmental Rating Scale—(FCCERS-R) (Item #24—Promoting Acceptance of Diversity)	Harms, Cryer, & Clifford, 2007	Physical environment; activities	Observed rating scale (1–7) Completed by trained observer
Program Administration Scale (PAS) (Item # 16—Family Communications; Item #17—Family Support and Involvement)	Talan & Bloom, 2004	Organizational quality	Rating scale (1–7) Completed by trained interviewer; document review
The Early Language & Literacy Classroom Observation (ELLCO) Toolkit, Research Edition (4 items—Recognizing diversity in the classroom; facilitating home support for literacy; presence of books; teacher interview)	Smith, Dickinson, Sangeorge, & Anastasopoulos, 2002	Physical environment; activities; teacher beliefs	Checklist; observation rating scale (1–5); teacher interview
Child Caregiver Interaction Scale (1 item in social domain)	Carl, 2007	Physical environment; activities; interaction	Observed rating scale (1–7)
Supports for Social–Emotional Growth Assessment (1 item on supportive teacher–child relationships)	Smith, 2004	Teacher–child relationships	Observed rating scale (1–5)

(continued)

Table 9.1.   (continued)

Name of tool	Author(s)	Domain of quality measured	Methodological approach
Africentric Home Environment Inventory	Caughy, Randolph, & O'Campo, 2002	Physical environment	Observed rating scale (1–3)
Caregivers' Experience of Racial Socialization	Stevenson, 1999; adapted by Shivers, 2006	Caregiver questionnaire	Teacher/caregiver questionnaire
Perceived Discrimination Scale	Contrada et al., 2001	Teachers' past experiences with discrimination	Teacher questionnaire
Child Rearing Attitudes Scale	Block, 1965; Kontos et al., 1995; Rickel & Biasatti, 1982.	Teacher/caregiver beliefs	Caregiver questionnaire (Likert scale)
Child Development Program Administration Scale	Fiene, 1984	Teacher prep; activities	Observed rating scale (1–5)
Preschool Program Quality Assessment, 2nd Edition (1 item Diversity-Related Materials)	HighScope Educational Research Foundation, 2003	Physical environment; activities	Observed rating scale (1–5)
Ready School Assessment (Respecting Diversity subscale—20 items)	HighScope Educational Research Foundation, 2006	Physical environment; activities; organizational quality	Program self-assessment
Classroom Language and Literacy Environment Observation (Items on teacher interactions with ELLs)	Coviello, 2005	Teacher–child relationships; activities	Observed rating scale (1–5)
Parent's Perception of Caregiver's Cultural Sensitivity	Emlen, 2000	Organizational quality; teacher characteristics	Parent questionnaire

Most practitioners who have implemented some type of multicultural program or curriculum in their classrooms acknowledge the difficulty in evaluating their programs through rigorous designs and in identifying appropriate outcome measures (Romero, 2008). There are very few systematic studies on the effects of multicultural programs in general and even fewer in early childhood settings; moreover, the information that does exist suggests that the implementation of curricular goals is often inconsistent (Ramsey, 2006). In addition, the strategies used in the curricula hardly ever involve more than one approach to multiculturalism (e.g., introducing new material, promoting cross-ethnic friendships; Aboud & Doyle, 1996; Day 1995; Lee & Lee, 2001). However, some of the studies' findings suggest that particular strategies emphasized in some of the curricula showed promising results. Those strategies included focusing on antibias or social reconstructivism, intergroup relationships, and specific accommodations for children from ethnic-minority backgrounds (Ramsey, 2006); they demonstrated the potential to affect outcomes such as children's cognitions, behavior, and academic achievement (Cohen & Lotan, 1995; De Marquez, 2002; Swadener, 1988; Tharp & Gallimore, 1988).

Approaches to the measurement of the effectiveness of these curricula have thus far included qualitative case studies, interviews, observations of cross-ethnic friendships, standardized instruments measuring ethnic group preferences (e.g., Multiresponse Racial Attitude Measure; Racial Relations Survey), and tasks with children involving the recall of stereotyped and counterstereotyped racial images. Ramsey's review of multicultural curricula (2006) reiterates the limitations in this area of the research: No studies have compared outcomes from different curriculum approaches, and no studies have examined the impact of multicultural curricula on longitudinal outcomes for children.

Physical Environment

The structure and content of the environment alert children to what the teacher considers important or not important. Derman-Sparks and the ABC Task Force (p. 5, 1989) state that "children are as vulnerable to omissions as they are to inaccuracies and stereotypes." Classrooms that create a diverse environment can set the stage for children to initiate conversations and for teachers to introduce activities (Derman-Sparks & the ABC Task Force, 1989). Examples of the visual/aesthetic environment related to culture include images and pictures on the classroom walls, as well as materials in the classroom, such as books, dolls, art, and dramatic play materials.

This is the one area of culturally responsive care in which researchers have had the most success at conceptualization and measurement (see Table 9.1). Thus far, we have seen two basic approaches to measurement of the physical environment: inclusion of subscales within global measures of quality, as in the Early Childhood Environment Rating Scale-Revised (ECERS-R) and others (Harms, Clifford, & Cryer, 2005; HighScope Educational Research Foundation, 2003; Smith, Dickinson, Sangeorge, & Anastasopoulos, 2002; Sylva, Siraj-Blatchford, & Taggard, 2003), and the development of separate instruments intentionally designed to capture elements of children's cultural experiences in their care settings. Some researchers argue that, in order to document implementation of culturally focused curricula, it is necessary to go beyond items on a global quality scale and develop separate measures (Chang, 1993).

Thus far, the most widely used strategy for measuring attention to diversity and culture involves the inclusion of subscales on global measures (e.g., ECERS-R, 4 items—*Books and Pictures; Music/Movement; Dramatic Play; Promoting Acceptance of Diversity*; ECERS-E, 3 items: *Planning for individual learning needs; gender equity and awareness; race equality*) (Harms et al. 2005; Sylva et al. 2003). The items contained in these subscales focus on materials in the environment and practices employed by teachers in the classroom, such as inviting parents to share a cultural custom or holiday with the children. The time-sampling approach of these measures may make it difficult to capture instances in which cultural practices actually take place within a classroom when these occur periodically but not daily. It is important to note that, whereas there have been only limited examinations of the relationships of subscales of these global measures to child outcomes, the ECERS-E diversity subscale shows predictive validity with children's nonverbal reasoning and early number concepts (Sammons et al., 2002).

In the early 1990s, three checklist measures were developed to assess classrooms' sensitivity to individual differences with regard to ethnicity, cultural practices, special needs, socioeconomic status, and family lifestyles. Each of the measures (Peisner-Feinberg, Howes, & Jarvis-McMillan, 2004) attempted to assess NAEYC's *Anti-Bias Curriculum (ABC)* guidelines. These measures attempted to capture the degree of implementation of antibias philosophy at the program by recording the presence or absence of images, materials, and general interactions. More specifically, all three measures cover characteristics in the visual environment, books, dramatic play, language, music, art, and manipulatives. For example, the measures document the presence of dolls of different races, ethnic backgrounds, and abilities. The measures also ask observers to note certain teacher–child interactions such as "caregivers respond similarly to boys and girls."

Although these measures indicate progress in terms of documenting more elements of early childhood settings relating to culture, they also show some important limitations. Because they require only one 2-hour observation, they fail to capture interactions that fall outside of the time sampled. As for global measures of quality, it is not clear that one or two observations involving a limited number of hours will capture practices that occur only periodically. Further, by focusing on recording the presence or absence of materials and interactions in the environment, these measures fail to describe the quality of practices. Such measures may tell us whether or not an early childhood setting has dolls of different races, ethnic backgrounds, and abilities, but they do not tell us how the program uses these dolls within the context of the program philosophy (Haines, 1999). In general, there is a clear need for further measures development focusing not only on the presence of materials but also on the quality of practices within early childhood settings related to culture and diversity, and how these practices match with program philosophy and curricular goals.

Promising Strategies for the Measurement of Culturally Responsive Care

Measures of Early Educators' Beliefs and Experiences Not Yet in Wide Use

In this section we highlight two measures that researchers have recently developed to examine how teachers' experiences and beliefs regarding culture can affect children's experiences in early childhood classrooms. These measures build on the broader research conducted on the education of elementary school–age children and adolescents. In each instance, measures developers have taken important steps in documenting the reliability and/or validity of the measure. However, these relatively new measures are not yet in wide use in early childhood studies.

Perceived Discrimination Scale

The Perceived Discrimination Scale contains 16 statements that participants rate on a 7-point scale according to how often the statement pertains to their personal experience of discrimination (with 15 statements rated according to personal experiences in the past 3 months and one statement rated according to lifetime experience). With the exception of the lifetime perception statement, the statements come from the Perceived Ethnic Discrimination Questionnaire (Contrada et al., 2001). Although there are several recently developed discrimination scales, the strength of the Contrada measure is that it can be used for any racial or ethnic group and was tested on diverse samples of nonwhite and white populations. Four subscales provide a mean score of an individual's perceived experiences regarding threat and aggression, verbal rejection, and avoidance and little value in being a member of their racial group. Contrada and colleagues derived the four subscales on the basis of consistent factor loadings ranging from .59 to .88 for the full sample, white samples, and nonwhite samples. Cronbach's alphas point to satisfactory internal-consistency reliability for each subscale in the full sample (.89 for devaluation; .84 for threat/aggression; .78 for verbal rejection; and .74 for avoidance), as well as the white and nonwhite subsamples (ranging from .65 for the avoidance subscale among white respondents to .90 for devaluation for nonwhite respondents).

Identification with American Ideals

The Identification with American Ideals Scale (Phinney, DuPont, Espinosa, Revill, & Sanders, 1994) is a measure of acculturation in terms of identification with mainstream notions of what it means to be American, rather than of the customs or language specific to only one ethnic group or country. Representatives from marginalized communities of color may not be acculturated to mainstream American ideals. Therefore, a measure that accurately assesses acculturation to the mainstream for members of minority ethnic communities is relevant. The American Ideals Scale was developed by soliciting open-ended responses from a diverse sample regarding the members' definition of what it means to be American. Based on these open-ended responses, 12 items, each rated on a 7-point Likert scale, were developed. Participants rank the items as to whether they agree or disagree with the statement (with 1 indicating strongly disagree and 7 indicating strongly agree). The scale has strong internal-consistency reliability (Cronbach's alpha of .85).

Measures in Development

In addition to the measures of teachers' experiences of discrimination and acculturation (seeking to capture Teacher Characteristics in the conceptual framework), several measures are currently being validated for use in early childhood settings that aim to capture culturally relevant classroom practices (seeking to capture Process Quality in the framework). In attempts to combine the strengths of qualitative data and longer observation periods, a fourth measure of the *Anti-Bias Curriculum* is in the process of being piloted and validated (Anti-Bias Curriculum Measure-4, ABCM-4; Ritchie, Howes, & Shivers, 2000). Its format is similar to that of the ECERS-R (Harms et al. 2005) and includes detailed examples of specific ratings. This scale asks the observer to rate a center from 1 (*inadequate*) to 7 (*excellent*) on six different constructs (Race, Home Language and Culture, Gender, Alternative Families, Disability, and Age), using separate scores for five different dimensions (visuals, materials, activities, interactions, and redefining normality) for each construct. Effective use of this measure requires that it be completed by an observer who has spent a considerable amount of time in the program over an extended period (e.g., a child care consultant, a student intern).

A pilot study using this measure with preservice child care teachers at a 4-year university found that child care classrooms housed in programs in which the director was a member of an ethnic minority were more likely to score higher on the following ABCM-4 constructs: race, language and culture, and alternative families (Shivers, 2000). Future plans to validate the use of this measure include examining construct validity and external validity.

Another promising measure currently in development is the Diversity Orientation Survey (DOS; Sanders, 2008). This is a scale that captures an individual's openness and acceptance of a nonmajority orientation in early childhood programs. The DOS assesses beliefs that relate to an individual's acceptance of others, and the scale ranges from a noninclusive to an antibias orientation. The researcher developed the scale while observing diversity education in a large, urban center-based child care program and participating in discussions with individual teachers about the program's practices around diversity education.

A preliminary analysis using multidimensional scaling (MDS) of the responses of approximately 700 early childhood workers revealed two underlying attributes within the scale: similarity and difference dimensions. The similarity dimension ($\alpha = .91$) reflects an individual's orientation to view American culture and European heritage favorably or as superior to other cultures. Individuals who have this orientation tend to believe that the discussion of other cultures or the revealing of differences between people is taboo. The difference dimension ($\alpha = .83$) captures an individual's orientation toward endorsing a broad worldview and the belief that the discussion or focus on differences in others is beneficial.

A pilot study conducted with preservice teachers ($n = 41$) in a 4-year university degree program for early childhood educators used the DOS to capture changes in students' beliefs and attitudes about diversity after a yearlong seminar that included multicultural content integrated into each weekly session (Shivers, 2004). Findings indicated that students of color were more likely to have an increase in the "similarity dimension" score from Time 1 to Time 2. Also, students (both black and white) who worked in child care classrooms where there were more black teachers were more likely to have an increase in the similarity dimension score from Time 1 to Time 2. In other words, contrary to the hypotheses in this study, these two groups of students' attitudes in favor of the superiority of American mainstream culture were more strongly endorsed at the end of the year in comparison with their attitudes at the beginning of the year. Implications of these findings point to research demonstrating that some African American teachers believe that it is important for children of color to "learn" mainstream American culture (Wishard et al., 2003). These findings also could imply a belief among preservice teachers that children who are "bicultural," or adept at functioning well in mainstream cultural contexts as well as in their home cultural context, are more resilient and better prepared for mainstream American schools (Johnson et al., 2003).

Finally, another promising tool still in development is the Quality Benchmark for Cultural Competence Project (QBCCP). The NAEYC has undertaken the QBCCP to determine the key elements of cultural competence for early childhood programs and meaningful ways to integrate these concepts within QRIS criteria. So far, the tool is intended to be used as a guide to spark discussion within programs, and action through implementation of the ideas presented. The tool also includes ways to measure how well the cultural criteria and program goals are being met (J. Daniel & D. McDonald, personal communication, 2009). The QBCCP tool is based on 12 core criteria that focus on themes related to program policies, curricula, materials, partnerships with families, ongoing training for staff, informal and formal instructional strategies, and teachers' awareness of their own beliefs. Alongside each criterion, the tool lists ideas for implementing these different criteria as well as suggested strategies for measuring to what extent the criteria are being met by the program. Although there are plans for the QBCCP tool to be piloted in nine states, it currently is not being validated for specific use as a research tool. The authors and advisory group for this tool are clear in stating that, for now, its intended use is directed toward program discussion and implementation (D. McDonald, personal communication, 2009).

The strengths of the measures reviewed throughout this section are that they evolved from very rich descriptive and exploratory work in early childhood settings, have begun to be validated with diverse groups of teachers, and would be easy to add into an existing research protocol. Work, to date, has not determined whether scores on these measures are significantly associated with other features of care that are known to directly predict children's outcomes. As with most complex phenomena in developmental research, it is likely that there are other measured or unmeasured features of ECE with which these measures may be associated. A full understanding of how early educators' beliefs and practices predict and are manifestations of culturally responsive care will require an examination of the interrelations of these measures with other established measures of ECE, as well as with child outcomes.

Culturally Responsive Practices as Predictors of School Readiness

One unresolved question is whether ECE practices that are culturally responsive significantly affect childhood outcomes. If they do, which outcomes in childhood are linked conceptually to culturally responsive pedagogies? Unfortunately, there is limited conceptual or empirical work connecting culturally responsive practices in early childhood settings to specific childhood outcomes. Although there is acknowledgment by NAEYC and other professional bodies in the early childhood field that quality early childhood care and education must entail an awareness of diversity (NAEYC, 2005), research is needed which demonstrates that the work undertaken to acknowledge diversity in early childhood settings contributes to positive child outcomes.

In this section we focus on the right-hand portion of the conceptual framework (Figure 9.1) linking process quality in ECE to child outcomes. We hypothesize that culturally responsive practice, as a component of process quality, is linked with children's formation of positive relationships with peers and teachers, with children's orientation to their own versus other racial and ethnic groups, and to a positive self-concept, all of which are seen as important components of the social and emotional domain of school readiness. The research focusing on these linkages is very limited. Although it must suffice here to identify the hypothesized linkages, further studies are needed testing the pathways of influence on child outcomes and their relative importance.

Social and Emotional Development as a Key Domain of School Readiness

Although school, community, home, and individual factors contribute to a child's readiness for school (Halle, Zaff, Calkins, & Margie, 2000), *school readiness* commonly refers to the skills and behaviors the child exhibits at the conclusion of participation in early childhood settings or the start of kindergarten that predict positive adaptation to, and achievement in, formal schooling. According to the National Education Goals Panel (NEGP; Kagan, Moore, & Bredekamp, 1995), there are five essential components to a child's school readiness: physical well-being, language and literacy development, cognitive skills (including early mathematical skills and general knowledge), approaches to learning, and social and emotional competencies. School readiness often is mistakenly narrowed to focus exclusively on academic and cognitive skills (Fuller, 2007). However, there is substantial research that documents the importance of the social and emotional domain of school readiness for children's subsequent adjustment to, and achievement in, school.

The *whole child* perspective (Zigler, Gilliam, & Jones, 2006) is one approach toward school readiness that incorporates a wider understanding reflective of the five dimensions identified by the NEGP. A school environment is a dynamic social context, which includes adults, settings, and peers that children successfully must interact with to achieve specific academic goals. This requires the development of a host of emotional and social competencies, rather than only literacy or other cognitive skills. Head Start provides an outcome framework that is reflective of the whole child approach toward school readiness (*Tarullo & McKey, 2001*). In addition to specific academic outcomes, the Head Start child outcomes framework incorporates social and emotional dimensions such as self-concept, self-control, social skills, and social relationships as important features of a child's readiness for school. We hypothesize that culturally responsive ECE is linked especially with the social and emotional domain of school readiness because it supports the formation of positive relationships, a positive orientation towards one's own racial and ethnic group, and a positive self-concept.

Culturally Responsive Caregiving and Relationship Formation

Several recent studies provide evidence that a consideration of culture-related variables, such as racial or ethnic match and diversity of the classroom, helps to predict relationship quality, both of peer relationships and of teacher–child relationships. For example, there is evidence that children who have a peer of the same ethnicity at the start of participation in ECE and are part of an ethnically diverse early childhood classroom increase the complexity of their peer play more over time than those children who do not have a peer of the same ethnicity and attend an ethnically diverse setting (Howes, Sanders, & Lee, 2008). This study extends the person–environment perspective, which posits that social competence with peers can be understood by examining interactions between child characteristics and the environment in which peer competence is developed (Lochman, 2004). The teacher plays a major role in setting up and helping children manage those environments.

A study by Howes and colleagues (Wishard et al., 2003) hypothesized that program- and teacher-articulated practices were deeply rooted in culture and shaped children's daily experiences in ECE settings. This study found that African American teachers who were paired with Latino children were more likely to endorse practices centered on socializing parents and children for "American" schools. This combination of teacher–child ethnic pairing and articulated practices positively predicted children's competent behavior with peers. The authors also pointed out that communities vary significantly in the particular goals that they hold for the children and tailor their ECE practices to nurture these goals (Wishard et al., 2003).

Another study, by Howes and Shivers (2006), examined whether the process of relationship formation or the resulting quality of teacher–child relationships differs on the basis of a match or nonmatch of racial or ethnic heritage. Positive teacher–child relationships are an important aspect of children's emotional development. Studies show that harmonious and positive teacher–child relationships in ECE predict stronger school readiness and better outcomes in kindergarten and first grade (Howes & Ritchie, 2002; Howes & Tonyan, 2000; Peisner-Feinberg et al., 2001). Howes and Shivers found that, on average, children who shared an ethnic or racial heritage with their caregivers were able to form more secure child–caregiver attachment relationships than children who did not share a heritage. They also found that the children who did not share an ethnic or racial heritage with their caregiver and who engaged in more conflicted interactions with her were the least likely to form secure attachment relationships. The authors reasoned that if the child and caregiver lack a common cultural community or understanding of ways of doing things, it is more difficult for the caregiver to disconfirm the child's less-than-optimal behavior (i.e., aggression toward peers) or his or her own less-than-optimal perceptions of the child in order to construct a positive relationship. In contrast, being from the same cultural community seemed to serve as a positive motivator of relationship formation (Howes & Shivers, 2006).

The studies reviewed in this section not only provide evidence of how culturally situated experiences can shape children's social and emotional development but also reiterate the usefulness of considering ethnic pairings (e.g., teacher–child or child–child ethnic matching) in helping to determine whether there are elements of the children's experiences that are common to home and ECE. Using this measurement strategy may help answer the question of whether children can build on familiar ways of interacting socially in developing new social skills. A key issue for future research is whether professional development and curricula focusing on cultural responsiveness can support and enhance the development of positive teacher–child and peer relationships both when there is a racial or ethnic match and when there is no racial or ethnic match.

Social Identity Development

One salient experience for children of color is social identity. Identity is a construct most commonly studied in adolescent populations rather than preschool children because the latter period of childhood is when issues of identity become glaringly relevant. However, social identity, which includes cultural, racial, and ethnic understanding, is a developmental process that children may grapple with as early as infancy (Njoroge, Benton, Lewis, & Njoroge, 2009). Contributions to social identity, such as racial awareness and racial group orientation, have a long-standing research tradition (Quintana et al., 2006; Spencer, 2006; Spencer & Markstrom-Adams, 1990). Features of social identity that are central for young children include four components: race/ethnic/cultural awareness (to be cognizant of one's own ethnic group and the ethnic groups of others), race/ethnic self-identification (labeling of one's group), racial/ethnic attitudes (preference and views toward one's own and other groups), and behaviors (actions and customs related to one's group; Phinney, 1996; Phinney & Rotheram, 1987). Group orientation is determined by one's attitudes toward one's own group (in-group orientation) and other groups (out-group orientation; Spencer, 1990).

One main goal of multicultural education in early childhood settings is to promote children's intergroup tolerance, or *adaptive* ethnic group orientations. Therefore, an appropriate outcome to measure in examining the impact of culturally relevant pedagogy is social identity as it pertains to preferences, attitudes, and awareness of cultural, ethnic, and racial understandings.

Most research associated with group orientation has focused on African American children (Ogbu, 1994; Quintana et al., 2006; Spencer, 2006). Much of this research since the early research of the Clarks (1939, 1940) has found that children of color tend to have an out-group orientation (positive attitudes and preference for the majority racial/ethnic group) during the early childhood years, which will change to an in-group orientation (positive attitudes toward and preference for own racial/ethnic group) during the middle childhood years, usually around age 9 (McAdoo, 2002). Research focusing on Mexican American identity has found that Mexican American children show a similar pattern of transition from out-group to in-group orientation as they became older (Spencer & Markstrom-Adams, 1990).

Out-group preference in minority children may be a logical extension of a young child's lay theory of "familiarity is good" (Cameron, Alvarez, Ruble, & Fuligni, 2001) rather than a negative attitude toward one's group. Since children of color are exposed often to the white majority environment, especially through the media (Graves, 1999), an orientation toward white culture may reflect only a knowledge of what is familiar, not necessarily a rejection of one's own group (Cameron et al., 2001). In fact, the group orientation of children of color may depend on the racial demographics of the environment: Children of color may have an in-group orientation if they are from an environment that is composed primarily of people who are similar (Bagley & Young, 1988) and an out-group orientation if they are from a predominantly white environment (Spencer & Markstrom-Adams, 1990).

The meaning of a child's group orientation, then, may depend on the child's primary care contexts, and it may be that children of color, in certain contexts, such as a multiracial preschool context, reflect neutral orientations (Glover & Smith, 1997). Parents' responses and teachers' reactions to minority groups within a particular context can bend a "familiarity is good" orientation in majority children to that of prejudice (Cameron et al., 2001). Thus, early childhood care and education can play a significant role, not only by exposing children to cultures and ethnicities not experienced in the family unit but also through the multicultural activities and interethnic interactions that are created in the care and education settings.

We have limited understanding of whether having an in- or out-group orientation is beneficial or problematic for young children, in part because of measurement issues (Cameron et al., 2001). Measures often involve forced choice, in which a child must classify a negative attribute such as *ugly* or *mean* to either his or her group or the other group (Aboud, 2003). The option to pick *neither* usually is not present (Cameron et al., 2001). In studies that have tried to address methodological problems, findings are similar to those of previous studies in that minority children show an out-group orientation but switch to an in-group orientation at middle childhood, whereas white children show a consistent in-group orientation (Davey, 1983). Again, however, the contexts in which these preferences are formed (whether children's primary care environments involve mostly same or other-group members) have to be taken into consideration. The forced choice nature of measures and the fact that studies juxtapose a minority with the majority rather than contrasting two minority groups that exist in the same environment must also be taken into account. Therefore, in order for group orientation to be a useful outcome measure in examining the effects of culturally responsive caregiving practices, further development of these measures is necessary and further research into the developmental context of children's orientation needs to be extended. It is too soon to articulate a specific hypothesis, for example, that culturally responsive caregiving practices will accelerate the development of own-group orientation. Rather, we need descriptive studies of group orientation and how it develops in early childhood settings, varying as to diversity and culturally responsive caregiving practices (Njoroge et al., 2009). Building on descriptive research, we also will need to consider group orientation as an outcome of interventions aimed at enhancing culturally responsive practices.

Self-Concept

Self-concept is an aspect of children's self-understanding that refers to the descriptive aspect of the self (Justice, Lindsey, & Morrow, 1999). Although often used interchangeably with self-esteem, self-concept has been found by research to be distinct from self-esteem. Self-esteem appears to tap into the emotional aspect of self-understanding, whereas self-concept reflected a "non-evaluative cognition of a descriptive nature, which delineated characteristics about the self" (Clark & Symons, 2000, p. 92). Work in progress (Sanders, 2005) is beginning to examine the combined influence of overall program quality and racial/ethnic match on children's self-concept. Research in child care programs in Los Angeles is finding that when programs are of low to moderate quality, ethnic match between teacher and children and peer engagement predict lower self-concept.

In sum, this section argues that culturally responsive caregiving practices in ECE will contribute especially to the domain of school readiness in the areas of children's social competencies and emotional development. Promising research findings indicate that peer–peer and teacher–child relationships, group orientation, and self-concept may be key areas of children's social and emotional development that are affected by culturally related features of ECE settings. There is a clear need for further empirical examination of the relationships between social and emotional outcomes and the range of culturally related features of early childhood settings (such as diversity of participating children and ethnic match of children and teacher or children and peers) and interventions to enhance the cultural responsiveness of early childhood settings.

Next Steps for Research

Policy makers are beginning to ask researchers to establish the outcomes in childhood that are linked conceptually to culturally responsive pedagogies. Currently, there is little to no work that directly connects these important issues of culture and race to specific early childhood outcomes. However, before researchers can explore which elements of culturally responsive care predict child outcomes, they first need to develop systematic and valid measures for describing aspects of culturally responsive care that are linked to children's quality day-to-day experiences and for identifying which characteristics of teachers and programs predict those quality, culturally responsive experiences in the classroom.

Further Work on Measures Development and Validation

Current measurement strategies include surveys on teacher beliefs, qualitative descriptions of teacher and program practices, environmental checklists, and diversity-specific items embedded within larger global measures. Researchers do not yet have any validated measures for identifying those aspects of child care that are linked to children's outcomes. There are some recommended immediate and long-term steps that can help move the field toward integrating the current battery of quality measures with systematic measurement of culturally responsive care.

First and foremost, early child care researchers must continue to field-test and validate those measures that are specifically focused on culture and diversity and show promise for use in ECE settings. Systematic data collection on these measures can help us answer questions about pedagogy, teachers' beliefs and knowledge about culture and diversity, and structural and organizational features of culturally responsive care.

Second, moving forward will require more longitudinal studies which examine cultural features of early childhood settings that predict outcomes in kindergarten and beyond. Specifically, research could focus on expanding the list of children's outcomes that are seen as aspects of school readiness, predicting adjustment and achievement in school. Such efforts could determine, for example, what role, if any, young children's positive group identification plays in predicting positive adjustment to, and achievement in, formal schooling.

Last, in order to bolster our understanding of how cultural congruency between home and child care affects children's development, we need to link in-depth data on children's home environment—including parent practices and beliefs—with data on teacher and program practices and beliefs. Addressing these research priorities will move us closer to understanding how we can embed the construct of culturally responsive care within our standardized measurements of quality.

Focus on Operationalizing and Examining the Effects of Cultural Congruence

At present, there is conflicting evidence on cultural congruence between home and early childhood care and education. A strong argument has been made that discontinuity may be particularly disadvantageous for children of color (Garcia-Coll, 1990; Garcia-Coll et al., 1996; Johnson et al., 2003; New, 1994). If practices within early childhood settings reflect those of the dominant culture, children from other cultural communities may feel less valued and have more trouble forming positive relationships with the adults in the program. In addition, as noted previously, researchers argue that a culturally congruent early childhood setting may reinforce family socialization practices.

Alternatively, there is also evidence that sensitive caregiving, rather than specific caregiving practices, may be central to children's optimal developmental outcomes. In other words, children who are cared for in warm and sensitive ways should be able to construct positive child–adult relationships that lead to positive developmental outcomes even when practices in the home and early childhood setting differ. Support for this positive construction of relationships comes from a reanalysis of two very large child care databases: the Cost, Quality and Outcome Study (CQO Study Team, 1995) and the NICHD Study of Early Child Care (Burchinal & Cryer, 2003).

Johnson and colleagues (2003) also presented two competing hypotheses about cultural congruence: 1) On the one hand, greater levels of congruence could promote child competence later; 2) on the other hand, early exposure to settings different from the home could promote adaptability and bicultural coping. An important direction for future research will be to explore cultural congruency in relation to the development of young children of color (Guerra & Jagers, 1998; McLoyd, 1998; Phinney & Landin, 1998). We will need to ask the following questions:

- Is there a cluster of essential practices in early childhood settings which ensure the type of cultural congruency that promotes children's development? In what way do these practices reflect family engagement and authentic knowledge of children and families?

- Is it easier for teachers to engage in these practices when they share the same ethnic background as the children in their class?

- Can cultural practices be rated on a continuum of congruency between home and school?

- Is there a baseline level of congruency that is healthy for all children?

Moving Culture and Ethnicity from Control Variables to a Central Focus

Cultural research in early childhood care and education is a complicated enterprise, and unfortunately, much of the traditional research that addresses minority children is not sufficiently informed by literature that takes a culturally inclusive perspective. For example, many researchers use ethnicity as a control variable. By doing so, researchers are giving the effects of ethnicity a lower conceptual or theoretical priority than other factors simultaneously under investigation. Ethnicity is then seen as a "nuisance" variable, and the researchers attempt to reduce its effects—in essence, to make the "nuisance" go away (McLoyd, 1990; Steinberg & Fletcher, 1998). This common analytical strategy leads to findings that place minority children's developmental outcomes out of context.

There are several other reasons that the development of children of color has been studied out of cultural context. One is the dominance of a Eurocentric middle-class perspective that holds up the social, linguistic, motivational, and cognitive patterns of mainstream white Americans as the goal of all development (Guerra & Jagers, 1998; Ogbu, 1994; Rogoff, 2003). Another reason is that researchers generally believe or assume that mainstream language, socialization, motivation, and cognition are the developmental processes that make children successful in school and make citizens succeed as adults in our institutionalized opportunity structure (Ogbu, 1994). Researchers like Daudi Ajani ya Azibo, whose work focuses on African and African American children, find fault with the paradigm that assumes a white standard reference group, and his work challenges this Eurocentric approach. Azibo (1988) asserted that using an Afrocentric approach—based on conceptual categories and cultural views adopted from African cultures—challenges comparative studies that use theories and methods designed to maintain African American inferiority.

Here are other methodological issues to consider that promote a culturally inclusive research agenda:

1. Use frameworks that match the complexity of the interplay of culture and development.

2. Match ethnicity and language of data collectors with study participants.

3. Ensure cultural validation of existing measures (including translating measures into other languages).

4. Use sampling methodology that includes more within-group samples and a sufficient number of children from ethnic-minority backgrounds to conduct within-group variation analysis and have sufficient representation of various economic groups within cultural groups.

5. Interpret data and findings by using feedback from cultural "insiders."

Conclusion

In order to fully understand developmental processes in young children of diverse cultures, it is important for researchers to examine cultural practices and their relation to human development (Rogoff, 2003). What is evident from the research reviewed in this chapter is that culturally responsive care involves multifaceted relations among many aspects of community, family, program, and teacher functioning.

It is critical and timely that we take further steps to develop and utilize measures of culturally responsive care due to the many state and federal policy initiatives focusing on ECE. One clear policy emphasis is strengthening early childhood professional development. As research becomes more able to measure which features of culturally responsive care are linked to children's outcomes, higher education teacher preparation programs will be able to use this new knowledge to fine-tune their curricula so that more teachers are prepared to work with diverse groups of children and families. Professional development outside of higher education also can emphasize culturally relevant pedagogies and incorporate those elements of culturally responsive care which are linked to quality and achievement outcomes (Bowman, Donovan, & Burns, 2001). Deepening our understanding of culturally congruent care also can lead to professional development strategies that address family involvement by emphasizing awareness of congruities and incongruities between a child's home life and school life (Johnson et al., 2003). Another emerging policy emphasis is the implementation of QRIS. Understanding how culturally responsive care is embedded in our definitions of and standards for "quality" will help us ensure that we are building systems that are culturally responsive to the families and communities they serve (Bruner et al., 2009).

It is of paramount importance that our systems of professional development and quality improvement be informed through evaluation and research efforts that reflect the experiences and challenges of all families.

References

Aboud, F. (2003). The formation of ingroup favoritism and outgroup prejudice in young children. *Developmental Psychology, 39*(1), 48–60.

Aboud, F.E., & Doyle, A.B. (1996). Does talk of race foster prejudice or tolerance in children? *Canadian Journal of Behavioural Science, 28,* 161–170.

Artiles, A.J. & McClafferty, K. (1998). Learning to teach culturally diverse learners: Charting change in preservice teachers' thinking about effective teaching. *The Elementary School Journal, 98*(3), 189–220.

Azibo, D. (1988). Understanding the proper and improper usage of the comparative research framework. *Journal of Black Psychology, 15,* 81–91.

Bagley, C., & Young, L. (1988). Evaluation of color and ethnicity in young children in Jamaica, Ghana, England and Canada. *International Journal of Intercultural Relations, 12,* 45–60.

Banks, J. (1992). African American Scholarship and the Evolution of Multicultural Education. *Journal of Negro Education 61*(3), 273–286.

Banks, J.A. (1996). The African American roots of multicultural education. In J.A. Banks (Ed.), *Multicultural education: Transformative knowledge and action* (pp. 30–45). New York: Teachers College Press.

Banks, J.A., & Banks, C.A.M. (Eds). (1995). *Handbook of research on multicultural education.* New York: Macmillan.

Bennett, M. (1993). Towards ethnocentrism: A developmental model of intercultural sensitivity. In R.M. Paige (Ed.), *Education for the intercultural experience* (2nd ed.). Yarmouth, ME: Intercultural Press.

Block, J. (1965). *The child rearing practices report.* Berkeley: University of California, Institute of Human Development.

Bowman, B., Donovan, S., & Burns, M.S. (Eds). (2001). *Eager to learn: Educating our preschoolers.* National Research Council, Washington, DC: National Academies Press.

Bronfenbrenner, U. (1979). Contexts of child rearing: Problems and prospects. *American Psychologist, 34,* 844–850.

Bruner, C., Ray, A., Stover-Wright, M., & Copeman, A. (2009). Quality rating improvement systems for a multi-ethnic society. Retrieved March 1, 2010, from http://www.buildinitiative.org/files/QRIS-Policy%20Brief.pdf

Brunson-Day, C. (2006a). Leveraging diversity to benefit children's social-emotional development and school readiness. In B. Bowman & E.K. Moore (Eds.), *School readiness and social-emotional development: Perspectives on cultural diversity.* Washington, DC: National Black Child Development Institute.

Brunson-Day, C. (2006b). Teacher-child relationships, social-emotional development, and school achievement. In B. Bowman & E.K. Moore (Eds.), *School readiness and social-emotional development: Perspectives on cultural diversity.* Washington, DC: National Black Child Development Institute.

Burchinal, M., & Cryer, D. (2003). Diversity, child care quality, and developmental outcomes. *Early Childhood Research Quarterly, 18,* 401–426.

Burchinal, P., Kainz, K., Cai, K., Tout, K., Zaslow, M., Martinez-Beck, I., & Rathgeb, C. (2009). OPRE Research-to-Policy Brief. *Early Care and Education Quality and Child Outcomes.* Office of Planning, Research and Evaluation, Administration for Children and Families, U.S. Department of Health and Human Services. Washington, DC.

Buysse, V., Castro, D., West, T., & Skinner, M. (2005). Addressing the needs of Latino children: A national survey of state administrators of early childhood programs. *Early Childhood Research Quarterly, 20*(2), 146–163.

Cameron, J., Alvarez, J., Ruble, D., & Fuligni, A. (2001). Children's lay theories about ingroups and outgroups: Reconceptualizing research on prejudice. *Personality & Social Psychology Review, 5*(2), 118–128.

Carl, B. (2007). Child Caregiver Interaction Scale. (Doctoral dissertation, Indiana University of Pennsylvania, 2007). http://hdl.handle.net/2069/53

Cassidy & Lawrence (2000). Teachers' Beliefs: The "whys" behind the "how tos" in child care classrooms. *Journal of Research in Childhood Education, 14*(2), 193–204.

Caughy, M., O'Campo, P., Randolph, S., & Nickerson, K. (2002). The influence of racial socialization practices on the cognitive and behavioral competence of African American preschoolers. *Child Development, 73,* 1611–1625.

Chang, H. (1993). Racial and cultural diversity in child care centers. In *Affirming children's roots: Cultural and linguistic diversity in early care and education* (pp. 16–43). San Francisco: James G. Irvine Foundation.

Child Trends. (2009). ACF-OPRE Issue Brief. *What We Know and Don't Know about Measuring Quality in Early Childhood and School Age Care and Education Settings.* Office of Planning, Research and Evaluation, Administration for Children and Families, U.S. Department of Health and Human Services. Washington, DC.

Christensen, M., Emde, R.N., & Flemming, C. (2004). Cultural perspectives for assessing infants and young children. In R. Delcarmen-Wiggins & A. Carter (Eds.), *Handbook of infant, toddler, and preschool mental health assessment* (pp. 7–23). New York: Oxford University Press.

Clark, K.B., & Clark, M.P. (1939). Segregation as a factor in the racial identification of Negro preschool children. *Journal of Experimental Education, 11,* 161–163.

Clark, K.B., & Clark, M.P. (1940). Skin color as a factor in the racial identification and preferences in Negro preschool children. *Journal of Negro Education, 19,* 341–350.

Clark, S., & Symons, D. (2000). A longitudinal study of q-sort attachment security and self-processes at age 5. *Infant and Child Development, 9,* 91–104.

Cohen, E.G., & Lotan, R.A. (1995). Producing equal-status interaction in the heterogeneous classroom. *American Educational Research Journal, 32,* 99–120.

Contrada, R., Ashmore, R., Gary, M., Coups, E., Egeth, J., Sewell, A., et al. (2001). Measures of ethnicity-related stress: Psychometric properties, ethnic group differences and associations with well-being. *Journal of Applied Social Psychology, 31*(9), 1775–1820.

Correa, V.I., Hudson, R.F., & Hayes, M.T. (2004). Preparing early childhood special educators to serve culturally and linguistically diverse children and families: Can a multicultural education course make a difference? *Teacher Education and Special Education: The Journal of the Teacher Education Division of the Council for Exceptional Children, 27*(4), 323–341.

Cost, Quality and Outcome Study Team (1995) *Cost, quality and child outcomes in child care centers, public report* (2nd ed.). Denver: Economics Department, University of Colorado at Denver.

Cunningham, B., & Sugawara, A. (1988). Preservice teachers' perceptions of children's problem behaviors. *Journal of Educational Research, 82,* 34–39.

D'Angelo, A., & Dixey, B. (2001). Using multicultural resources for teachers to combat racial prejudice in the classroom. *Early Childhood Education Journal, 29*(2), 83–87.

Davey, A. (1983). *Learning to be prejudiced: Growing up in multi-ethnic Britain.* London: Edward Arnold.

Day, J.A.E. (1995). Multicultural resources in preschool provision: An observational study. *Early Child Development and Care, 110,* 47–68.

Delpit, L. (1995). *Other people's children: Cultural conflict in the classroom.* New York: The New Press.

De Marquez, T.M. (2002). Stories from a multicultural classroom. *Multicultural Education, 9,* 19–20.

Derman-Sparks, L., & the ABC Task Force. (1989). *Anti-bias curriculum: Tools for empowering young children.* Washington, DC: National Association for the Education of Young Children.

Early, D.M., & Winton, P.J. (2001). Preparing the workforce: Early childhood teacher preparation at 2- and 4-year institutions of higher education. *Early Childhood Research Quarterly, 16*(3) 285–306.

Eggers-Pierola, C. (2005). *Connections and commitments: Reflecting Latino values in early childhood programs.* Portsmouth, NH: Heinemann.

Emlen, A.C., Koren, P., & Schultze, K. (2000). *A packet of scales for measuring quality of child care from a parent's point of view: With summary of methods and findings.* Retrieved July 12, 2007 from "http://www.hhs.oregonstate.edu/familypolicy/occrp/publications.html" "parentsperspective" "_parent" http://www.hhs.oregonstate.edu/familypolicy/occrp/publications.html#parentsperspective

Feldman, R.S. (1985). Nonverbal behavior, race, and the classroom teacher. *Theory into Practice, 24,* 45–49.

Fiene, R. (1994). Child development program administration scale. Washington, D.C.: Children's Services Monitoring Transfer Consortium.

Fuller, B. (2007). *Standardized Childhoods: The political and cultural struggle over early education.* Stanford, CA: Stanford University Press.

Gallimore, R., & Goldenberg, C. (1993). Activity settings of early literacy: Home and school factors in children's emergent literacy. In E. Forman, N. Minick, C.A. Stone, et al. (Eds.), *Contexts for learning: Sociocultural dynamics in children's development* (pp. 315–335). New York: Oxford University Press.

Garcia-Coll, C.T. (1990). Developmental outcome of minority infants: A process-oriented look at our beginnings. *Child Development, 61,* 270–289.

Garcia-Coll, C., Lamberty, G., Jenkins, R., McAdoo, H.P., Crnic, K., Wasik, B.H., et al. (1996). An integrative model for the study of developmental competencies in minority children. *Child Development, 67,* 1891–1941.

Glover, R., & Smith, C. (1997). Racial attitudes of preschoolers: Age, race of examiner, and child-care setting. *Psychological Reports, 81*(3), 719–722.

Gomez, M.L. (1994). Teacher education reform and prospective teachers' perspectives on teaching other people's children. *Teaching and Teacher Education, 10*(3), 319–334.

Graham, S.L. (2006). Preface. In D.T. Slaughter-Defoe, A.M. Garret, & A.O. Harrison-Hale (Eds.), *Our children too: A history of the black caucus of the society for research in child development, 1973–1997. Monographs of the Society for Research in Child Development, 283,* 71, 1, xi–xiii.

Graves, S. (1999). Television and prejudice reduction: When does television as a vicarious experience make a difference? *Journal of Social Issues, 55,* 707–728.

Guerra, J.G., & Jagers, R. (1998). The importance of culture in the assessment of children and youth. In V. McLoyd & L. Steinberg (Eds.), *Studying minority adolescents: Conceptual, methodological, and theoretical issues.* (pp. 167–181). Mahwah, NJ: Lawrence Erlbaum Associates.

Gunnar, M.R., & Donzella, B. (2002). Social regulation of the cortisol levels in early human development. *Psychoneuroendocrinology, 27,* 199–220.

Haines, S. (1999). Unpublished master's thesis, An analysis of ant-bias curriculum measures and multicultural educational philosophies in early childhood education. UCLA.

Hains, A.H., Lynch, E.W., & Winton, P. (2000). *Moving towards cross-cultural competence in lifelong personnel development: A review of the literature.* Champaign, IL: CLAS Early Childhood Research Institute.

Hale-Benson, J.E. (1986). *Black children: Their roots, culture, and learning styles.* Baltimore: Johns Hopkins University Press.

Halle, T., Zaff, J., Calkins, J., & Margie, N., (2000, December). *Background for community-level work on school readiness: A review of definitions, assessments, and investment strategies, Part II: Reviewing literature on contributing factors to school readiness.* Final Report to the Knight Foundation, Child Trends, Washington, DC.

Harms, T., Clifford, R.M., & Cryer, D. (2005). *Early Childhood Environment Rating Scale-Revised Edition* (ECERS-R). New York: Teachers College Press.

Harms, T., Cryer, D., & Clifford, R. (2007). *Family Child Care Environment Rating Scale-Revised* (FCCERS-R). New York: Teacher's College Press.

Henderson, A., & Mapp, K. (2002). *A new wave of evidence: The impact of school, family, and community connections on student achievement. (Annual Synthesis).* Austin, TX: National Center for Family & Community Connections with Schools, Southwest Educational Development Laboratory. ERIC Document Reproduction Service #: ED-474 521.

HighScope Educational Research Foundation. (2003). *Preschool Program Quality Assessment, 2nd Edition (PQA) administration manual.* Ypsilanti, MI: HighScope Press.

High/Scope Educational Research Foundation (2006). Ready school assessment. Ypsilanti, MI: High/Scope Press.

Holland-Coviello, R. (2005). Language and literacy environment quality in early childhood classrooms: Exploration of measurement strategies and relations with children's development. Unpublished doctoral dissertation, Pennsylvania State University, University Park.

Hollins, E., & Guzman, M.T. (2005). Research on preparing teachers for diverse populations. In M. Cochran-Smith & K.M. Zeichner (Eds.), *Studying teacher education: The report of the AERA Panel on Research and Teacher Education* (pp. 477–548). Mahwah, NJ: Lawrence Erlbaum Associates.

Howes, C. (2000). Social-emotional classroom climate in child care, child–teacher relationships, and children's second grade peer relations. *Social Development, 9,* 191–204.

Howes, C. (2010). *Culture and child development in early childhood programs.* New York: Teachers College Press.

Howes, C., & Ritchie, S. (2002). *A matter of trust: Connecting teachers and learners in the early childhood classroom.* New York: Teachers College Press.

Howes, C., Ritchie, S., & Shivers, E.M. (2004). Anti-Bias Checklist, Version 4. Unpublished measure, University of California, Los Angeles.

Howes, C., Sanders, K., & Lee, L. (2008). Entering a new peer group in ethnically and linguistically diverse child care classrooms. *Social Development, 17,* 922–940.

Howes, C., & Shivers, E.M. (2006). New child–caregiver attachment relationships: Entering child care when the caregiver is and is not an ethnic match. *Social Development, 15,* 574–590.

Howes, C., & Tonyan, H. (2000). Links between adult and peer relationships across four developmental periods. In K.A. Kerns & A.M. Neal-Barnett (Eds.), *Examining associations between parent–child and peer relationships.* New York: Greenwood/Praeger.

Hsueh, Y., & Barton, B. (2006). A cultural perspective on professional beliefs of childcare teachers. *Early Childhood Education Journal, 33*(3), 179–186.

Huijbregts, S.K., Leseman, P.P.M., & Tavecchio, L.W.C. (2008). Cultural diversity in center-based childcare: Childrearing beliefs of professional caregivers from different cultural communities in the Netherlands. *Early Childhood Research Quarterly, 23*(2), 233–244.

Hungerford, A., Brownell, C., & Campbell, S. (2000). Child care in infancy: A transactional perspective. In C.H. Zeanah (Ed.), *Handbook of infant mental health (2nd ed.).* New York: Guilford Press.

Johnson, D.J., Jaeger, E., Randolph, S.M., Cauce, A.M., Ward, J., & NICHD Early Child Care Network. (2003). Studying the effects of early child care experiences on the development of children of color in the United States: Towards a more inclusive research agenda. *Child Development, 74,* 1227–1244.

Justice, E., Lindsey, L., & Morrow, S. (1999). The relation of self-perceptions to achievement among African American preschoolers. *Journal of Black Psychology, 25*(1), 48–60.

Kagan, S., Moore, E., & Bredekamp, S. (1995). *Reconsidering children's early development and learning: Toward common views and vocabulary.* Washington, DC: National Education Goals Panel, Goal 1 Technical Group.

Kessler, S., & Swadener, B. (Eds). (1992). Introduction: Reconceptualizing curriculum. In S. Kessler & B. Swadener (Eds.), *Reconceptualizing the early childhood curriculum: Beginning the dialogue* (pp. 13–28). New York: Teachers College Press.

Killen, M., & Smetana, J. (1999). Social interactions in preschool classrooms and the development of young children's conceptions of the personal. *Child Development, 70*(2), 486–501.

Klein, L.G., & Knitzer, J. (2007). *Promoting effective early learning: What every policymaker and educator should know.* New York: National Center for Children in Poverty, Columbia University, Mailman School of Public Health.

Kontos, S., Howes, C., Shinn, M., & Galinsky, E. (1995). *Quality in family child care and relative care.* New York: Teachers College Press.

Ladson-Billings, G. (1994). *The dreamkeepers: Successful teachers of African American children.* San Francisco: Jossey-Bass Publishers.

Lamb, M.E. (1999). Nonparental child care. In M. Lamb (Ed.), *Parenting and child development in "nontraditional" families* (pp. 39–55). Mahwah, NJ: Lawrence Erlbaum Associates.

Lee, C.E., & Lee, D. (2001). Kindergarten geography: Teaching diversity to young people. *Journal of Geography, 100,* 152–157.

Lerner, R.M. (1986). *Concepts and theories of human development* (2nd ed.). New York: Random House.

Lerner, R.M. (1991). Changing organism-context relations as the basic process of development: A developmental contextual perspective. *Developmental Psychology, 27,* 27–32.

Lim, C.I., & Able-Boone, H. (2005). Diversity competencies within early childhood teacher preparation: Innovative practices and future directions. *Journal of Early Childhood Teacher Education, 26,* 225–238.

Lim, C.I., Maxwell, K.L., Able-Boone, H., & Zimmer, C.R. (2009). Cultural and linguistic diversity in early childhood teacher preparation: The impact of contextual characteristics on coursework and practica. *Early Childhood Research Quarterly, 24*(1), 64–76.

Lochman, J.E. (2004). Contextual factors in risk and prevention research. *Merrill-Palmer Quarterly, 50,* 311–325.

MacNaughton, G., & Hughes, P. (2007). Teaching respect for cultural diversity in Australian early childhood programs: A challenge for professional learning. *Journal of Early Childhood Research, 5*(2), 189–204.

McAdoo, H.P. (2002). The village talks: Racial socialization of our children. In *Black children: Social, educational, and parental environments* (2nd ed.). (pp. 47–55). Thousand Oaks, CA: Sage Publications.

McAllister, G., & Irvine, J.J. (2000). Cross cultural competency and multicultural teacher education. *Review of Educational Research, 70,* 3–24.

McDiarmid, G., & Price, J. (1990). *Prospective teachers' views of diverse learners: A study of the participants in the ABCD Project.* (Report No. 90-6). East Lansing, MI: Michigan State University, National Center for Research on Teacher Education. ERIC Document Reproduction Service No. ED-324 308.

McLaren, P. (1995). *Critical pedagogy and predatory culture: Oppositional politics in a postmodern era.* New York: Routledge.

McLoyd, V.C. (1990). The impact of economic hardship on Black families and children: Psychological distress parenting and socioemotional development. *Child Development, 61,* 311–346.

McLoyd, V.C. (1998). Changing demographics in the American population: Implications for research on minority children and adolescents. In V.C. McLoyd & L. Steinberg (Eds.), *Studying minority adolescents: Conceptual, methodological, and theoretical issues* (pp. 3–28). Mahwah, NJ: Lawrence Erlbaum Associates.

Middleton, V. (2002). Increasing preservice teachers' diversity beliefs and commitment. *The Urban Review, 34*(4), 343–361.

Miller, P., Fader, L., & Vincent, L. (2000). Preparing early childhood educators to work with children who have exceptional needs. In National Institute on Early Childhood Development and Education, U.S. Department of Education (Eds.), *New teachers for a new century: The future of early childhood profes-*

sional preparation (pp. 91–112). Jessup, MD: U.S. Department of Education, ED Publishing.

National Association for the Education of Young Children (NAEYC). (2005). *NAEYC early childhood program standards and accreditation criteria.* Washington, DC: Author.

New, R. (1994). Culture, child development, and developmentally appropriate practices: Teachers as researchers. In B.L. Mollory & R.S. New (Eds.), *Diversity and developmentally appropriate practices* (pp. 65–83). New York: Teachers College Press.

NICHD Study of Early Child Care and Youth Development, Phase II (1996-1999).

Njoroge, W., Benton, T., Lewis, M., & Njoroge, N. (2009). What are infants learning about race? A look at a sample of infants from multiple racial groups. *Infant Mental Health Journal, 30*(5), 549–567.

Ogbu, J.U. (1994). From cultural difference to differences in cultural frame of reference. In P.M. Greenfield & R.R. Cocking (Eds.), *Cross-cultural roots of minority child development* (pp. 365–392). Mahwah, NJ: Lawrence Erlbaum Associates.

Payne, R.S. (1994). The relationship between teachers' beliefs and sense of efficacy and their significance to urban LSES minority students. *Journal of Negro Education, 63*(2), 181–196.

Peisner-Feinberg, E.S., Burchinal, M.R., Clifford, R.M., Culkin, M.L., Howes, C., Kagan, S.L., et al. (2001). The relation of preschool child care quality to children's cognitive and social developmental trajectories through second grade. *Child Development, 72,* 1534–155.

Peisner-Feinberg, E., Howes, C., & Jarvis-McMillan, V. (2004). *Anti-bias and multicultural classroom observation development study.* Chapel Hill, NC: FPG Child Development Institute.

Phillipsen, L.C., Burchinal, M.R., Howes, C., & Cryer, D. (1997). The prediction of process quality from structural features of child care, *Early Childhood Research Quarterly 12*(3), 281–303.

Phinney, J. (1996). When we talk about American ethnic groups, what do we mean? *American Psychologist, 51,* 918–927.

Phinney, J., DuPont, S., Espinosa, C., Revill, J., & Sanders, K. (1994). Ethnic identity and American identification among ethnic minority youths. In A.M. Bouvy, F. van de Vijver, P. Boski, & P. Schmitz (Eds.), *Journeys into cross-cultural psychology* (pp. 167–183). Lisse, Switzerland.

Phinney, J., & Landin, J. (1998). Research paradigms for studying ethnic minority families within and across groups. In V.C. McLoyd & L. Steinberg (Eds.), *Studying minority adolescents: Conceptual, methodological, and theoretical issues* (pp. 89–109). Mahwah, NJ: Lawrence Erlbaum Associates.

Phinney, J., & Rotheram, M.J. (1987). *Children's ethnic socialization: Pluralism and development (Vol. 81).* Newbury Park, CA: Sage Publications.

Pigott, R.L., & Cowen, E.L. (2000). Teacher race, child race, racial congruence, and teacher ratings of children's school adjustment. *Journal of School Psychology, 38,* 177–196.

Quintana, S., Aboud, F., Chao, R., Contreras-Grau, J., Cross, W., Hudley, C., et al. (2006). Race, ethnicity, and culture in child development: Contemporary research and future directions. *Child Development, 77,* 1129–1141.

Ramsey, P. (2006). Early childhood multicultural education. In B. Spodek & O.N. Saracho (Eds.), *Handbook of research on the education of young children* (pp. 279–301). Mahwah, NJ: Lawrence Erlbaum Associates.

Ray, A. (2000). Understanding multicultural and anti-bias education. In C. Howes (Ed.), *Teaching 4- to 8-year olds: Literacy, math, multiculturalism, and classroom community* (pp. 135–156). Baltimore: Paul H. Brookes Publishing Co.

Ray, A., Bowman, B., & Brownell, J.O. (2006). Teacher–child relationships, social-emotional development, and school achievement. In B. Bowman & E.K. Moore (Eds.), *School readiness and social emotional development: Perspectives on cultural diversity.* Washington, DC: National Black Child Development Institute, Inc.

Reese, L., Garnier, H., Gallimore, R., & Goldenberg, C. (2000). Longitudinal analysis of the antecedents of emergent Spanish literacy and middle-school English reading achievement of Spanish-speaking students. *American Educational Research Journal, 37*(3), 633–662.

Rickel, A., & Biasatti, L. (1982). Modification of the Block child rearing practices report. *Journal of Clinical Psychology, 38,* 129–134.

Rimm-Kaufman, S., Storm, M., Sawyer, B., Pianta, R., & La Paro, K. (2006). The Teacher

Belief Q-Sort: A measure of teachers' priorities in relation to disciplinary practices, teaching practices, and beliefs about children. *Journal of School Psychology, 44*(2), 141–165.

Ritchie, S., Howes, C., & Shivers, E.M. (2000). Anti-Bias Curriculum Measure—Version 4. Unpublished measure, University of California, Los Angeles.

Rogoff, B. (2003). *The cultural nature of human development.* New York: Oxford University Press.

Romero, M. (2008). *Promoting tolerance and respect for diversity in early childhood: Toward a research and practice agenda.* New York: National Center for Children in Poverty Report, Columbia University, Mailman School of Public Health. Retrieved March 1, 2010, from http://seedsoftolerance.org/downloads/DTRD%20%20Toward%20a%20Research%20and%20Practice%20Agenda.pdf

Sammons, P., Sylva, K., Melhuish, E., Siraj-Blatchford, I., Taggart, B., & Elliot, K. (2002). *Measuring the impact of pre-school on children's cognitive progress over the pre-school period.* Technical Paper 8b. London: Institute of Education.

Sanders, K. (2005). *It takes a village: Early race socialization of African American & Latino children in child care.* Unpublished Dissertation, University of California, Los Angeles.

Sanders, K. (2008). *Diversity Orientation Survey.* Unpublished Manuscript.

Sanders, K.E., Deihl, A., & Kyler, A. (2007). DAP in the 'hood': Perceptions of child care practices by African American child care directors caring for children of color. *Early Childhood Research Quarterly, 22*, 394–406.

Schaefer, E., & Edgerton, M. (1985, April). *Parental modernity in childrearing and educational attitudes and beliefs.* Paper presented at the Biennial Meeting of the Society of Research in Child Development, Boston, MA. (ERIC Document Reproduction Service No. ED-202 605).

Shechtman, Z. (2002). Validation of the Democratic Teacher Belief Scale (DTBS). *Assessment in Education: Principles, Policy & Practice, 9*(3), 363–377.

Shivers, E.M., (2006, November). Ways of caring: Examining racial-ethnic socialization practices and emotional availability among African American FFN providers. Paper presented at the National Alliance of Family, Friend and Neighbor Child Care Annual Meeting, Chicago, IL.

Shivers, E.M. (n.d.) *Does using the anti-bias curriculum measure impact pre-service teachers' attitudes about diversity?* Unpublished manuscript.

Shivers, E.M., Howes, C., Wishard, A., & Ritchie, S. (2004). Teacher-articulated perceptions and practices with families: Examining effective teaching in diverse high quality child care settings. *Early Education & Development, 15*(2), 167–186.

Shivers, E.M., Sanders, K., Wishard, A., & Howes, C. (2007). Ways with children: Examining the role of cultural continuity in early educators' practices and beliefs about working with low-income children of color. *Journal of Health and Social Policy, 23*, 110–132.

Shonkoff, J.P., & Phillips, D.A. (Eds.). (2000). *From neurons to neighborhoods: The science of early childhood development.* Washington, DC: National Academies Press.

Smith, M.W., Dickinson, D.K., Sangeorge, A., & Anastasopoulos, L. (2002). *Early Language & Literacy Classroom Observation (ELLCO) Toolkit: Research Edition.* Baltimore: Paul H. Brookes Publishing Co.

Smith, S. (2004). Supports for social-emotional growth assessment. Unpublished measure. New York University.

Spencer, M.B. (1990). Development of minority children: An introduction. *Child Development, 61*, 267–269.

Spencer, M.B. (2006). Revisiting the 1990 special issue on minority children: An editorial perspective 15 years later. *Child Development, 77*, 1149–1154.

Spencer, M.B., & Markstrom-Adams, C. (1990). Identity processes among racial and ethnic minority children in America. *Child Development, 61*, 290–310.

Stayton, V.D., Miller, P.S., & Dinnebeil, L.A. (Eds). (2003). *DEC personnel preparation in early childhood special education: Implementing the DEC recommended practices.* Longmont, CO: Sopris West.

Steinberg, L., & Fletcher, A.C. (1998). Data analytic strategies in research on ethnic minority youth. In V. McLoyd & L. Steinberg (Eds.), *Research on minority adolescents: Conceptual, methodological, and theoretical issues.* Newbury Park, CA: Sage.

Stevenson, H. (1999). Parents' experience of racial socialization. Unpublished measure. University of Pennsylvania.

Swadener, E.B. (1988). Implementation of education that is multicultural in early childhood settings: A case study of two day care programs. *Urban Review, 20*, 8–27.

Sylva, K., Siraj-Blatchford, I., & Taggart, B. (2003). *Assessing quality in the early years: Early childhood environment rating scale extension.* Sterling, VA: Trenthan Books Limited.

Talan, T., & Bloom, P.J. (2004). *Program Administration Scale: Measuring Early Childhood Leadership and Management.* New York: Teachers College Press.

Tarullo, L.B., & Hubbell McKey, R.H. (2001). *Design and implications of the Head Start family and child experiences survey (FACES).* Administration on Children, Youth and Families, U.S. Department of Health and Human Services. Washington, DC: Ellsworth Associates.

Taylor, S., & Sobel, D. (2002). Addressing the discontinuity of students' and teachers' diversity: A preliminary study of preservice teachers' beliefs and perceived skills. *Teaching and Teacher Education, 17*, 487–503.

Tharp, R.G., & Gallimore, R. (1988). *Rousing minds to life: Teaching, learning, and schooling in social context.* Cambridge, U.K.: Cambridge University Press.

Tobin, J., Wu, D., & Davidson, D. (1989). *Preschool in three cultures.* New Haven, CT: Yale Press.

Trent, S.C., Pernell, E., & Stephens, K. (1995, April). *Preservice teachers' beliefs about teaching culturally and linguistically diverse exceptional learners.* Poster session presented at the annual meeting of the Council for Exceptional Children, Indianapolis, IN.

Trolley, B., Magerkorth, R., & Fromme, R. (1999). Preschool teachers' perceptions of and responses to differences: Disability, family, and racial/cultural variation. *Early Child Development and Care, 155*, 17–30.

Trumbull, E., Rothstein-Fisch, C., Greenfield, P., & Quiroz, B. (2001). *Bridging cultures between home and school: A guide for teachers: With a special focus on immigrant Latino families.* Mahwah, NJ: Lawrence Erlbaum Associates.

Tsigilis, N., Tsioumis, K., & Gregoriadis, A. (2007). Applicability of the planned behavior theory to attitudes of students in early childhood education toward teaching culturally diverse classes: The role of self-identity. *Psychological Reports, 100*(3), 1123–1128.

U.S. Department of Education. (2009, July). *Early learning challenge fund.* Retrieved August 7, 2009, from http://www.ed.gov/about/inits/ed/earlylearning/elcf-factsheet.html

van Hook, C. (2002). Preservice teachers' perceived barriers to the implementation of a multicultural curriculum. *Journal of Instructional Psychology, 29*(4), 254–264.

van IJzendoorn. (1992). Intergenerational transmission of parenting: A review of studies in nonclinical populations. *Developmental Review, 12*(1), 76–99.

Wasson, D., & Jackson, M. (2002). Assessing cross-cultural sensitivity awareness: A basis for curriculum change. *Journal of Instructional Psychology, 29*(4), 265–276.

Weisner, T. (2002). Ecological understanding of children's developmental pathways. *Human Development, 45*, 275–281.

West, J., Tarullo, L., Aikens, N., Sprachman, S., Ross, C., & Carlson, B.L. (2007, March). *FACES 2006 study design.* Princeton, NJ: Mathematica Policy Research, Inc.

Wilcox-Herzog, A. (2002). Is there a link between teachers' beliefs and behaviors? *Early Education and Development, 13*(1), 81–106.

Wintre, M.G. (1989). Changes in social play behavior as a function of preschool programs. *The Journal of Educational Research, 82*(5), 294–301.

Wishard, A. G, Shivers, E.M., Howes, C., & Ritchie, S. (2003). Child care program and teacher practices: Associations with quality and children's experiences. *Early Childhood Research Quarterly, 18*, 65–103.

Zeanah, P.D., Stafford, B.S., Nagle, G.A., & Rice, T. (2005). *Addressing social-emotional development and infant mental health in early childhood systems.* (Building State Early Childhood Comprehensive Systems Series No. 12). Los Angeles: University of California, Los Angeles, National Center for Infant and Early Childhood Health Policy.

Zigler, E., Gilliam, W., & Jones, S. (2006). *A vision for universal preschool education.* Cambridge, U.K.: Cambridge University Press.

Cross-Cutting Issues

CHAPTER 10

Measuring Quality of ECE Programs for Children with Disabilities

Donna Spiker, Kathleen M. Hebbeler, and Lauren R. Barton

This chapter addresses the measurement of quality of early care and education (ECE) programs for children with disabilities. The reasons for measuring quality for this population are the same reasons for which we would measure quality for any group of children: 1) to guide program improvement for individual practitioners or programs, 2) to examine changes in program quality over time, 3) to contribute to knowledge about program quality, and 4) to describe quality for parental choice (Zaslow, Tout, Halle, & Forry, 2009). The ultimate goal for undertaking measurement of quality for any of these purposes is the promotion of optimal child development. The fundamental assumption is that children will have more growth-promoting experiences and positive interactions in high-quality, compared with low-quality, environments (Wolery, 2004). The connection between what young children experience and their subsequent development is supported by a substantial body of research on both children who are typically developing and children with delays and disabilities (Guralnick, 2005a; National Research Council and Institute of Medicine, 2000; Shonkoff & Meisels, 2000). Although there are measurement challenges to documenting the precise nature and magnitude of the relationship between program quality and child outcomes, as discussed throughout this book,[1] the evidence linking early experience and child outcomes is overwhelming (NICHD Early Child Care Research Network, 2005). This well-documented relationship is the underlying rationale for measuring and promoting quality in ECE settings. The promotion of high quality is especially important for children with delays and disabilities because these children need specialized services and supports, in addition to the healthy environments considered necessary for all children, if they are to achieve their developmental potential.

To provide a framework for our discussion of the measurement of program quality for children with disabilities, we begin with a description of the ways in which children with disabilities can participate in ECE. There are currently two service systems serving young children with disabilities and their families. Children may participate in either or both of them, and for children participating in both systems, the two systems may or may not be integrated. The first service system is the diverse array of family and center-based child care and prekindergarten programs available in communities across the country. We will refer to this system as *general early care and education* (GECE). The second system is made up of the programs that provide publicly funded, specialized services and supports for young children with disabilities under the auspices of the Individuals with Disabilities Education Improvement Act (IDEA) of 2004 (PL 108-446). For children under age 3, these services, known as *early intervention* (EI), are provided by public or private agencies under the supervision of a state lead agency (Spiker, Hebbeler, Wagner, Cameto, & McKenna, 2000). Children from age 3 to kindergarten age receive early childhood special education (ECSE) provided through the public schools, although the school system may contract with private providers. EI and ECSE encompass a variety of services and supports, such as educational, developmental, and therapeutic activities; along with facilitating families' use of their informal support network and the formal support networks of public services (Sandall, McLean, & Smith, 2000). These services are individualized to a child's and family's needs, so there is considerable variation across children and families as to what, where, and how much service they receive and with what kind of professionals they work. It is also important to note that there is considerable variation in the types and severity of disabilities that children have, and states vary with regard to eligibility requirements and the percentage of the population of young children served.

Figure 10.1 shows the GECE and the IDEA systems and their possible intersection. Children in segment A are children with disabilities who participate in GECE but are not receiving EI or ECSE services through IDEA. These children could be those whose delays or disabilities have not been identified, or children with disabilities whose families are not aware of, are not interested in pursuing, or who have declined IDEA services. Children in segment B are children who are receiving only EI or ECSE; they

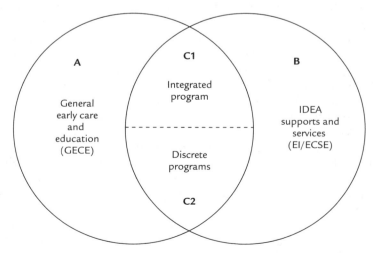

Figure 10.1.   Four types of participation in the Early Care and Education System for young children with disabilities

are not participating in a community preschool or in center-based or family child care. Children in segment C are children with disabilities participating in both service systems. Here we find two options. For the children in C1, the two programs have coordinated to provide an integrated program for the children. Examples of this kind of program would be one with an early interventionist who works with the family child care provider on strategies to facilitate the child's feeding skills, or one with a speech therapist who observes the child in a regular preschool and works with the classroom teacher to plan a program to enhance the child's acquisition of communication skills. The children in the C2 segment of the diagram also participate in both systems, but for these children, the systems operate independently.

The possibility of participation in two systems has significant implications for what constitutes quality and how to measure it. If a child with a disability participates in only a general early childhood program, the "single-system" quality question is this: Is this program a high-quality program for all children, including children with disabilities? This is an important question, but it does not address quality of programs for children who are participating in an IDEA program as an exclusive or supplemental intervention. From the perspective of the IDEA programs, the single-system quality question is this: Is this program high-quality EI or ECSE? This is a meaningful quality question as well, but only for children who are participating solely in IDEA programs and not in GECE. For children who are "dually enrolled" in both systems, the measurement of quality needs to look at the intersection of the two systems in order to understand, monitor, and promote the quality of their experience. For these children, the quality question is: How are these two systems working together to produce a high-quality experience for the child and family? As will be discussed later in the chapter, even if both programs are of high quality as stand-alone programs, the overall experience for the child is likely to be of lower quality if the programs do not intentionally coordinate their service delivery.[2] Any measurement of quality for children with disabilities needs to address the quality of the components of the ECE in which they are participating and, if they are participating in both the GECE and the EI/ECSE, the extent to which these two systems are integrated. In sum, the three critical quality questions for children with disabilities are as follows:

- Does this GECE program provide a high-quality experience for children with disabilities?

- Does this EI/ECSE program provide high-quality services?

- Are the GECE program and the EI/ECSE program coordinating to provide a high-quality experience for children with disabilities?

Population Estimates of Children with Disabilities

The data are incomplete with regard to how many children are in each of the segments shown in Figure 10.1. The most comprehensive data are available for children receiving services through IDEA. These are children in segments B, C1, and C2 in the figure. In 2007, over 1 million children between birth and age 5 in the United States were receiving EI or ECSE (U.S. Department of Education Office of Special Education Programs, 2007). Most of these children—more than 700,000—were between 3 and 5 years of age. This represents 5.7% of the population of children in this age group, or slightly more than 1 out of every 20 preschool-age children. In 2007, 86% of the 322,000 infants and toddlers participating in EI received services in their homes, with 5% receiving services in community-based settings. The percentage of children and families receiving EI services in the home has increased substantially in recent years, from 68% in 1998. EI services in community-based settings also increased, but only from 4% to 5% from 1998 to 2007. Since these data do not tell us about any other settings in which the children who received services in the home might have spent portions of their days, all we can say with certainty from these data is that at least 5% of the 0- to 3-year-old population with disabilities was also participating in the GECE system (C1 or C2). A national study of children receiving EI services suggests that a higher percentage of children in EI also participates in GECE, although the proportion may be somewhat lower than the number using GECE in the general population (Hebbeler, Scarborough, Snyder, Robinson, & Nelson, 2009). At entry to EI services, when children ranged in age from newborn to 31 months, 24% were in child care at least 10 hours a week. This percentage compares with 43% of children less than 3 years of age in child care in the general population. When EI participants were approximately 36 months old, the proportion in child care increased to 41%, which was still less than the general population, with 54% of children 3 years of age in child care (Hebbeler et al., 2009).

In 2007, 65% of the 3-through-5-year-olds who received ECSE spent part of their day in a regular classroom (U.S. Department of Education Office of Special Education Programs, 2007). The fact that at least two-thirds of the 3- through 5-years-olds receiving ECSE were in either category C1 or C2 further emphasizes the importance of examining the extent to which the two systems are working together to produce a high-quality experience for the children.

National data on the percentage of young children with disabilities currently participating in the GECE system (segments A, C1, and C2) are sketchy at best, but it has been estimated that at least 60% of young children with disabilities (5 years old and younger) participate in some kind of ECE program outside of their home (Booth-LaForce & Kelly, 2004). At least 10% of children enrolled in Head Start are required to be children with disabilities. In 2005–06, over 111,000 children with disabilities under 5 years of age were served through Head Start (Administration for Children and Families, 2008). When the same question is examined from the program perspective, it appears that there are many GECE programs that are not serving children with disabilities. Recent research found that only one-third of providers surveyed have children with disabilities in their GECE settings (Thornburg et al., 2004).

Challenges in Serving Children with Disabilities

Participation in the GECE system has been found to present some challenges for families with young children with disabilities (Booth & Kelly, 1998; Brandon, 2000; Warfield & Hauser-Cram, 1996). Issues raised by parents as obstacles include the cost of care, the location of and transportation to access desired care, and locating care that will integrate a child's special service needs into programming (Booth & Kelly, 1998). Access is especially problematic if the child has special health care needs (Kelly & Booth, 1999) or the disability is severe rather than mild in nature (Knoche, Peterson, Pope Edwards, & Jeon, 2006; Warfield & Hauser-Cram, 1996). Finally, there is almost no information available on how many children in the GECE system may have disabilities that are not identified or whose parents have declined services (segment A in Figure 1). A study of children in Early Head Start, a program for children under age 3, found that 87% of the children in the sample had indicators of disabilities but only 5% were receiving IDEA services (Peterson et al., 2004). These data would suggest that there may be a fairly large number of children in segment A who are eligible for IDEA services but who have not been identified, a finding that further supports the importance of measuring and improving coordination across the two systems.

Measuring Program Quality

Much work needs to be done, both in conceptualizing the key elements of quality and the development of tools, to capture these elements. Some tools in current use for measuring quality of GESE programs look at one or more aspects of quality for children with disabilities. A few tools also look at one or more aspects of program quality specifically for children with disabilities. However, in 2010, there is no unified theory that has provided a foundation for instrument development or guidance on what items to include in general program quality measures for children with disabilities. We summarize the related work, acknowledging that this activity is only a small step toward the goal of having valid measures of program quality that can be used in research, in program self-assessment, and in quality rating systems to assess the quality of programs for children with disabilities.

We offer a program model from Carta (2002, as cited in Wolery, 2004) as an organizing structure for thinking about the program elements that need to be considered in measuring program quality for children with disabilities. Carta's model has four levels of quality: 1) *interactions* between the child and teachers and peers, the most proximal aspect of process quality; 2) *classroom features* in which these interactions are embedded—curriculum, instructional practices, scheduling, nature of activities, and materials; 3) *staff characteristics and the classroom structure*, to include staff education, training, experience, beliefs, and goals, as well as child-to-staff ratios, group size, arrangement of physical space, equipment and furnishings, and hours of operation; and 4) *administrative characteristics*—referring to program governance and including philosophy (e.g., program goals; beliefs about children, families, and early education), structures (e.g., policies, compensation), context (e.g., funding adequacy, accreditations, connections to other agencies), and supports (e.g., professional development activities, availability and quality of specialists, supervision of staff).

We propose two modifications to this model to make it more applicable to all programs serving young children with disabilities. First, the language of the model assumes a center- or classroom-based program, which is not the service setting for all young children with disabilities. Substituting the word *program* for *classroom* will allow the model to be applied to a broader range of program and service arrangements. Second, as will be discussed later, the concept of parent partnerships is so critical to quality services for young children with disabilities that we believe that it merits its own category within the framework. The major areas of the framework provide an organizing structure for how to think about the measurement of program quality for children with disabilities; however, it is important to understand that the framework areas are not independent but interrelated. For example, the kinds of interactions a teacher can have with a child with special needs will depend on the staff ratios. Similarly, the types of practices a teacher can implement will be related to both the support within the program for professional development and coordination with other programs that can provide access to specialists.

Organization of the Chapter

The discussion of quality measurement in this chapter is organized around the two systems through which children with disabilities are currently served. The first section discusses the inclusion of children with disabilities in GECE programs and the approaches for measuring quality for children with disabilities in such programs. These are the children in segments A and C in Figure 10.1. The next section discusses the measurement of quality for EI and ECSE, programs providing specialized services. Children in these programs are in segments B and C. Finally, we conclude with a discussion of suggested future directions for the development of measures that will capture quality in programs for children with disabilities and reflect the reality of multiple service systems.

Defining and Measuring the Quality of General Early Childhood Programs for Children with Disabilities

The word *inclusion* is used to describe children with disabilities attending ECE programs together with children who have more typical developmental patterns. As more research has accumulated on this phenomenon, the multiple ways in which different authors use the word *inclusion* have become apparent. Although numerous studies have used the word to refer simply to the physical presence of children in the classroom (see discussion in Bricker, 2000), more recent work recognizes the multiple and critical dimensions of inclusion (see Buysse, Skinner, & Grant, 2001; Guralnick, 2001b; Odom, 2000). Inclusion has legal status in legislation mandating educational services for all children with disabilities from birth on. Inclusion involves "efforts to maximize the participation of children and families in typical home and community activities" (Guralnick, 2005b, p. 59), including "full involvement of the child in family routines and in social activities with relatives and friends, as well as taking advantage of the entire array of educational and recreational opportunities that communities have to offer" (p. 59). For an experience to promote growth in a child with a disability, the experience itself must be inclusive, resulting in the child's full participation in the routines and activities of the setting.

In early 2009, the Division for Early Childhood (DEC) and the National Association for the Education of Young Children (NAEYC) adopted a joint position statement that defines early childhood inclusion:

> Early childhood inclusion embodies the values, policies, and practices that support the right of every infant and young child and his or her family, regardless of ability, to participate in a broad range of activities and contexts as full members of families, communities and society. (DEC/NAEYC, 2009, p. 1)

The position statement asserts that the defining features of inclusion that identify high-quality early childhood programs are 1) *access* (i.e., providing a wide range of activities and environments and offering multiple ways to promote learning and development), 2) *participation* (i.e., using a range of instructional approaches to promote engagement in play and learning activities and a sense of belonging), and 3) *supports* (i.e., infrastructure to support staff, such as appropriate professional development opportunities and opportunities for collaboration and communication). DEC and NAEYC recognized the need for a common definition for influencing policies and practices and improving services for children with disabilities. Viewing inclusion as multidimensional provides a lens through which to examine research on inclusion and to define the key dimensions of quality associated with it.

Bailey, McWilliam, Buysse, and Wesley (1998) argued that there is a strong empirical basis for including children with disabilities in programs serving typically developing children. They cited a review of 22 studies which have found that preschool-age children with disabilities have better outcomes on standard measures of development, social competence, play behavior, and engagement when the children are served in inclusive versus segregated settings (Buysse & Bailey, 1993), findings that are supported by more recent data as well (Guralnick, 2001b). These authors argue that several values that have driven the history of EI and special education programming for young children with disabilities need to be considered when defining the quality of inclusive programs. They proposed that, in implementing inclusive programs for young children with disabilities, the programs need to be "of high quality, consistent with family preferences, and capable of supporting each child's unique learning needs" (Buysse & Bailey, 1993, p. 28).

Parents and professionals sometimes face a dilemma in trying to include children with disabilities in GECE programs when the available program options are not of sufficiently high quality. Achieving the optimal balance between the promotion of developmental outcomes and the principle of normalization can be challenging.

Measuring the Quality of GECE Programs Serving Children with Disabilities

To date, only a few studies have examined the quality of ECE programs that young children with disabilities attend, based on standard global measures of quality. Of these, some studies compare inclusive versus segregated settings for children with disabilities and some compare programs available to typically developing children that include children with disabilities with those who do not. A little over a decade ago, using the Early Childhood Environmental Rating Scale (ECERS), La Paro, Sexton, and Snyder (1998) found similar levels of quality in segregated preschool special education classrooms and early childhood settings serving children with disabilities (e.g., Head Start, child care, prekindergarten programs). A study of 180 community-based child care centers across diverse regions of North Carolina found that 62 (34%) of the programs served at least one child with a disability (birth to age 5) and that the inclusive child care programs had higher ratings on the ECERS than did the noninclusive programs (overall mean of 4.44 versus 4.15; Buysse, Wesley, Bryant, & Gardner, 1999). Additional analyses of predictors of quality across both types of programs revealed that teachers with higher education levels, more experience in early childhood, and higher self-report ratings of knowledge of typical child development had higher ECERS scores. Similarly, a study by Hestenes, Cassidy, Hegde, and Lower (2007) compared quality ratings on the Infant/Toddler Environment Rating Scale–Revised (ITERS-R; Harms, Cryer, & Clifford, 2003) for infant and toddler classrooms in North Carolina that included children with disabilities ($n = 64$) with a group that did not ($n = 400$). The number of children with disabilities in the inclusive classroom ranged from one to seven, with an average of two. Children's disabilities included developmental delays, physical disabilities, Down syndrome, and other diagnosed conditions that put children at risk. The results showed that the inclusive classrooms had higher ITERS-R ratings (5.24 versus 4.89). Higher teacher education levels were predictive of higher global quality in both types of programs, whereas higher teacher–child ratios predicted better quality in inclusive classrooms, but not in noninclusive classrooms.

The Association Between Quality and Outcomes

Findings from the research literature provide insights into defining and measuring quality in GECE programs for young children with disabilities. If we start with the assumption that high-quality GECE programs promote development and learning, then it is critical to look to the empirical research to identify the indicators, environmental characteristics, and practices associated with the best child outcomes. For instance, in summarizing how preschool instructional practices can lead to the successful and meaningful inclusion of young children with disabilities, Hemmetter (2000) described how teacher–child instructional interactions need to 1) target functional and developmentally appropriate goals and objectives; 2) use approaches that are implemented in the context of ongoing classroom activities and routines; and 3) focus on acquiring, generalizing, and maintaining skills. Examples of specific types of research-based instructional approaches or strategies that could be captured in quality measures include the use of naturalistic teaching, response-prompting and embedded instruction.[3]

The wide range of types and severity of disability and functioning among children with disabilities presents a challenge for defining and measuring the quality of inclusive practices. The successful inclusion of a child with a mild disability would likely be qualitatively different from the successful inclusion of a child with multiple and significant disabilities. It is important to note, however, that the empirical research documenting strong relationships among specific features of inclusive programs and positive child outcomes for young children with disabilities is relatively sparse and weak. Most of the research about preschool inclusion to date has focused on demonstrating that it is possible to offer inclusive programs and that children with disabilities can make progress when participating in them (Bricker, 2000; Guralnick, 2001a). Recent work in states on defining quality program standards and measuring and improving the quality of GECE programs provides an important foundation, but more research is needed to identify the specific features of inclusive programs that lead to positive child outcomes, the true indication of high-quality programming.

Considerations Related to Measuring Program Quality for Children with Disabilities

Common Elements of Quality

A central question for measurement of quality in inclusive programs is: What are the elements of GECE program quality for children with disabilities? For many years, researchers have noted the similarities between accepted practices in GECE and ECSE (Buysse & Hollingsworth, 2009; Fox, Hanline, Vail, & Galant, 1994; McLean & Odom, 1993; Odom & Diamond, 1998). In the recently revised volume about developmentally appropriate practices (DAP) in GECE programs, it is quite clear that researchers and practitioners endorse the view that program features of quality for typically developing children constitute the foundation of quality for children with disabilities (Copple & Bredekamp, 2009). The description of DAP clearly asserts that GECE program practices—including instructional practices to promote learning and development, teacher–child interactions, assessment practices, and the use of materials and the physical environment—advocated for children who are developing typically apply as well to children with disabilities, with strong recommendations for individualization for *all* children. Any discussions of the quality of inclusive programs for children with disabilities must acknowledge the commonality of the elements of quality across both groups.

Individualization: Adaptations and Accommodations

Implementing DAP also means tailoring programs and activities to the needs of the individual child. Appropriate adaptations in both the structural and process features of the environment can and should be made so that every child can be successful.[4] Throughout the recommendations about program quality with regard to children with disabilities, Copple and Bredekamp (2009) noted the importance of addressing the unique needs of children with disabilities.

Providing quality programs for children with disabilities, as well as measuring quality, requires a thorough understanding of the heterogeneity of the children who make up this population. The phrase *children with disabilities* encompasses children who are extremely different from one another across all areas of functioning. Some children with mild disabilities may need no accommodations. A child with mobility challenges may need physical accommodations. Another child with intellectual challenges, or attentional or behavioral difficulties, may need an adapted curriculum, specialized instructional techniques, or behavioral supports. A child with a communication problem may need specialized strategies for communication. For some children, structural dimensions of quality may be far more important, whereas for others, process dimensions are critical. Consequently, program quality may differ, depending on the nature of the child's special needs; for example, a program could be of high quality for a child in a wheelchair but of low quality for a child with a severe language delay or behavioral problems. Again, the DAP volume (Copple & Bredekamp, 2009) emphasizes these considerations throughout. For example, referring to teaching children with disabilities, the authors state, "However, teachers may use more systematic instruction to help a child acquire a skill or change an unacceptable behavior" (p. 38); "children with motor problems may need assistive technologies" (p. 119); and "space and equipment may need modifications for some children to fully participate" (p. 263).

The discussion of what constitutes DAP addresses several of the major areas of the adapted Carta framework (as cited in Wolery, 2004) for program quality described earlier. Instructional practices and program features such as equipment and physical space are widely acknowledged as part of program quality. Measuring the extent to which these features are present is insufficient; for children with disabilities, the measurement also must address appropriateness for the individual child, which complicates the process of measurement.

Program Quality versus Individualized Quality

Because of the need for individualization, an important question for children with disabilities is whether the overall quality of the GECE program, as measured in standard quality measures, is experienced by every child in attendance. Global quality measures in widespread use (e.g., ECERS-R) may capture the experiences of most, but not all, of the children in a classroom (Wolery, 2004). An overall quality score can provide a ceiling indicator of quality, but an individual child's experiences may be lower than the overall score, especially if the child has a disability.

A recent study of 60 children ages 4 and 5, 30 with and 30 without disabilities, examined global quality compared with individual children's experiences (Clawson &

Luze, 2008). The researchers used the ECERS-R global ratings to assess global quality, and items from the ECERS-R to record the experiences of individual children across 11 classrooms. An average of three children with diagnosed disabilities and five with suspected delays were in the classrooms. Children's special needs included language and cognitive delays, behavioral and physical disabilities, and vision problems. Global and individualized ECERS-R scores were moderately to highly correlated, regardless of disability status. The global ECERS-R scores across all children (5.10) were higher than the individualized scores (4.07), and the individualized scores were higher for the children with disabilities (4.13) than for those without disabilities (4.00). A series of stepwise regressions found that global quality was the strongest predictor of individual child experience in both groups. It is interesting, however, that children's individualized scores were significantly lower for children with higher levels of behavior problems. The authors noted that children in this study tended to have mild disabilities and that levels of teacher education and training were high—factors limiting any generalization of the results to classrooms with children with more significant disabilities or less-well-trained staff. Nevertheless, this study provides the kind of data that are needed to better understand relationships between global quality measures and the quality of experiences for children with a range of types and severities of disabilities.

This study and the principles of DAP raise questions about how to conceptualize and then measure quality for children with disabilities so that the experiences of the individual children are reflected in the overall measure. Thurman (1997) proposed an ecological congruence model that speaks to the issue of the match between the child's characteristics and needs and the characteristics of the environment. The notion of congruence would appear to be critical to any determination of quality for an individual child. The model has three interrelated dimensions: 1) the degree of deviance (difference) of the child's behavior for a given context or setting, 2) the degree of child competence in doing functional tasks in that context or setting, and 3) the degree of tolerance for difference by the child and by adults—adults' tolerance of the child's difference and the child's tolerance for aspects of the setting, including the adult's behavior. A good quality environment would have an "adaptive fit" between the child and the environment. These dimensions relate to the interactions, program features, and program structures of the Carta model. The concept of "adaptive fit" must be considered in measuring program quality for children with disabilities. *Fit* refers to how well the interactions, the instructional practices, the ratios, the staff's expertise, the physical layout of the room, and numerous other features are compatible with the needs of a particular child; these factors have significant implications for how quality is measured. Adaptive fit implies that quality is not a stand-alone feature of a program, but can be determined only with regard to a particular child in the program.

To promote adaptive fit, one must consider how the many different experiences children have throughout the day and in the environment are compatible with the needs of a particular child. The concept of "activity settings" is particularly relevant to adjusting instructional or intervention practices, one area in which the program must fit the child's needs. Wolery (2004) describes research by Dunst and his colleagues in which environments are characterized as "activity settings," which constitute "a situation-specific experience, the opportunity, or event, that involves a child's interaction with people, the physical environment, or both and provides a context for a child to learn" (Dunst et al., 2001, p. 70). This body of research suggests that an important question for the measurement of program quality for children with disabilities is: How are the adults in the child's program structuring, presenting, and exposing the child to appropriate activity settings? The more they do, the more learning the child will experience and the better will be the child's outcomes—compared with being exposed to inappropriate or low-quality activity settings. The implication of this perspective for a child with a disability is that the adult may need to intentionally structure the activity setting somewhat differently than would need to be done for typically developing children. For instance, in a free-play period, a teacher may need to reduce the number of toys in an area of the classroom and provide more verbal structure for a child with an attention problem, or use a child's picture exchange communication method[5] during small-group activities to support full participation of a child with a communication problem.

Implementing a Child's IFSP or IEP

Children with identified delays and disabilities in GECE programs should be receiving services through IDEA EI (for birth to 3-year-olds) or ECSE (3- through 5-year-olds). Through these services, these children will have an individualized family service plan (IFSP) if they are under 3 or an individualized education program (IEP) if they are 3 through 5. The IFSP and IEP outline the focus of individual supports to promote the child's functioning and how the child's IDEA services should be integrated into his or her GECE context (i.e., these children should be included in segment C1 of Figure 10.1). Another dimension of quality for children with disabilities attending GECE programs is the extent to which the child's IFSP or IEP is being implemented as part of the program. Integration is one of the primary ways in which the GECE program and the EI or ECSE program should be coordinated, and it should be captured in measures of quality (Buysse & Hollingsworth, 2009).

Parent Partnerships

Working closely with families is an essential element of high-quality services for children with disabilities. Positive support and communication with parents is included in several GECE program quality measures and also is central to quality as laid out in DAP recommendations (Copple & Bredekamp, 2009) and in best practices in EI and ECSE (Hemmeter, Joseph, Smith, & Sandall, 2001; Sandall et al., 2000; Trivette & Dunst, 2000). Strong relationships with parents are important for all early childhood programs but especially for children with disabilities. Parents of a child with a disability may have more extensive information about best strategies for supporting the child's full and maximal participation in a GECE program, including ways to adapt the activities and the physical environment, special instructional strategies, and other accommodations that meet the child's individual needs and incorporate the IEP goals into the daily activities and routines. Also, continuity of experiences, strategies, or approaches between classroom and home is especially important to promoting development for many children with disabilities.

Programs should be working with the family to promote family, as well as child, outcomes. Family outcomes identified by stakeholders as the responsibility of EI and ECSE include helping families to 1) know how to help their child develop and learn; 2) understand their child's strengths, abilities, and special needs; 3) know their rights and advocate for their child; 4) have support systems; and 5) have the ability to access desired services, programs, and activities in their community (Bailey et al., 2006).

As noted previously in the discussion of the Carta framework, the concept of a partnership with parents is so central to program quality for children with disabilities that it merits being a major part of any approach to quality measurement. There are several measures of family-centered practice from the EI and ECSE field that attempt to capture the degree and quality of parent support and participation, focusing mainly on how parents perceive their partnership with and support from service providers (see review by Mannan, Summers, Turnbull, & Poston, 2006). Constructs captured in these measures, such as the parent–professional partnership and the extent to which the program provided family-centered services, are important constructs for program quality measures for children with disabilities.

Children with Disabilities and Available Program Quality Tools

Addressing the Needs of Children with Disabilities

Possible elements of program quality for children with disabilities that have been discussed thus far include the nature of the interactions among the child, the adults, and other children; the instructional practices and the extent to which these have been adapted to address the unique needs of the children with disabilities; the availability of appropriate equipment and environmental modifications; the role of parents in the child's program; the extent to which the program is working at the classroom and administrative levels with other providers and systems that are working with the child and family; and the extent to which the program's features are well matched to the individual needs of a given child.

A review of literature and Internet sources revealed no existing tools that measured even this limited subset of quality features of GECE environments for children with disabilities. However, because many of the features of quality care for young children with disabilities are identical to those for children in the broader population, the content of tools outlined in other chapters of this book have considerable applicability for children with disabilities. As the previous discussion indicated, the content in existing measures is necessary, but not sufficient, for measuring the quality of GECE for children with disabilities. Information about quality for children with disabilities obtained from most measures of program quality usually is embedded within other questions in the tool, making it difficult or impossible to distinguish the extent to which quality GECE experiences fully cover children with many different types of disabilities. The interpretation of scores is further complicated in global quality measures because they tend not to provide 1) the extent to which the program serves any children with disabilities, 2) the type and severity of disabilities of children served in the program, and 3) detailed information about whether or not the classroom observation included interactions with one or more children with disabilities.

The ways that existing assessment tools measure quality for children with disabilities are typified by the content and approach of the most widely used GECE quality assessment tool: the ECERS-R. The ECERS-R contains one item that addresses overall how well programs include children with disabilities. A rating of 1 to 7 on one item, "37-provisions for children with disabilities," aims to assess all aspects of successful inclusion. In rating this item, observers are expected to consider the program's assessment and instructional practices, parent participation, staff involvement in intervention planning, and effectiveness in modifying activities to include all children or effectiveness at integrating special activities within the regular classroom routines. A few sample questions are included about activities that were not observed. The ECERS-R item 37 rating also is intended to provide a global sense of program provisions for all children with disabilities, regardless of the severity or types of disability of children in the program. The item is not scored if no children with disabilities are included in the program; no follow-up or scoring relates to the GECE program's history of enrolling children with disabilities or to the reasons that no children with disabilities are enrolled.

In addition to this global item, the ECERS-R makes reference to the need for modifications or accommodations for children with disabilities with regard to scoring on a number of the other quality indicators. For instance, for an item addressing discipline, the manual specifies that "a specialized program may be needed to help a child with a disability." For an item on "informal use of language," the manual mentions that staff should encourage communication among children; if a child uses American Sign Language, the teacher should teach key signs to the other children. Another example is that scoring criteria for the item "furniture for routine care, play, and learning" examine the extent to which "children with disabilities have the adaptive furniture they need" and "adaptive furniture permits inclusion of children with disabilities with peers." Under "fine motor activities," scoring is based in part on whether "materials on different levels of difficulty are accessible (e.g., regular and knobbed puzzles are available for those with varying fine motor skills)." Although some items clearly reference quality considerations for children with disabilities, other items, such as "free play" and "staff–child interactions," do not specifically mention children with disabilities.

Other commonly used quality assessment tools in addition to the ECERS-R also address children with disabilities by including one or more global ratings within the assessment or by mentioning children with disabilities in examples or scoring guidance in sections of the assessment tool and sometimes embedding these examples in training experiences and materials. Table 10.1 shows examples of how selected tools address children with disabilities. Other tools, such as the Classroom Assessment Scoring System™ (CLASS™, Pianta, La Paro, & Hamre, 2008) and the Early Language and Literacy Classroom Observation (ELLCO; Smith, Brady & Anastasopoulos, 2008), provide virtually no instructions in their manuals about how to interpret or modify use of the tools for classrooms that include children with disabilities.

Challenges in Using Existing Quality Assessment Tools

Even those tools that integrate some content about children with disabilities into the tools or include a few global items specific to disability are not adequate as effective measurement tools to understand the quality of GECE environments for children with disabilities. We have identified five challenges that lessen the usefulness and validity of these tools in measuring the quality of GECE environments for children with disabilities.

First, the manuals do not contain enough specific details for most observers to judge adequately whether or not the characteristic being assessed by most items is well implemented for children with disabilities. The items are very broad and therefore require the observers to be familiar with the range of instructional techniques, accommodations, and assistive technology that apply to children with different kinds of disabilities. For

Table 10.1. Strategies for assessing program quality for children with disabilities in selected assessment tools

Program quality assessment tool	Strategy used for inclusion of children with disabilities
Assessment Profile for Early Childhood Programs (APECP; cited in Halle & Vick, 2007)	Contains one section on "Individualizing" activities and practices
Child Caregiver Interaction Scale (CCIS; cited in Halle & Vick, 2007)	Includes "Engaging children with special needs" in the social domain.
Child Development Program Evaluation Scale (CDPES; Fiene, 1984)	Has "special needs of the child" item in the child development curriculum section
Early Childhood Environmental Rating Scale—Extension (ECERS-E; Sylva, Siraj-Blatchford, & Taggart, 2003)	Contains one section focusing on "Planning for Individual Learning Needs"
Early Childhood Environmental Rating Scale—Revised Edition (ECERS-R; Harms, Clifford, & Cryer, 2005)	Has one global item—"Provisions for children with disabilities" specific scoring instructions or examples given for some (e.g., discipline, furniture for routine care and learning, fine motor, informal use of language). Not every item has specific instructions for children with disabilities.
Infant-Toddler Environmental Rating Scale—Revised Edition (ITERS-R; Harms et al., 2003)	Has one global item—Provisions for children with disabilities; like the ECERS-R, specific scoring instructions or examples given for some, but not all, of the other items
Observation Measures of Language and Literacy–Quality Rating of Language and Literacy Instruction (OMLIT–QUILL; Goodson, Layzer, Smith, & Rimdzius, 2006)	Has "integration of special needs children in the classroom" section on the assessment tool for recording a description of children with disabilities who are present.
Preschool Program Quality Assessment, 2nd Edition (PQA; HighScope Educational Research Foundation, 2003)	Contains section on "Respecting Diversity" focused on recognition of and responses to diversity, including in learning materials; has item on diagnostic/special education services in section on parent involvement and family services
Ready Schools Assessment (RSA; HighScope Educational Research Foundation, 2006a, 2006b, 2006c)	Has a section on "Respecting Diversity" and defines one aspect of diversity as special needs
Supports for Social Emotional Growth Assessment (SSEGA; cited in Halle & Vick, 2007)	Has a section on program identification and support of children with special needs that includes two global items
Teaching Strategies Rating Scale (TSRS; McWilliam, Scarborough, Bagby, & Sweeny, 1998; McWilliam, Zulli, & de Kruif, 1998)	Has several global items (i.e., "inclusion in activities," "teaching specific skills," including extent of individualizing teaching for children with disabilities, "developmental appropriateness")

example, without specialized training, most observers will not be able to adequately assess the language and communication items (e.g., "encouraging children to communicate") or even consider the many details necessary to determine whether classroom space is fully accessible for children with a variety of special needs. Although many of the assessment tools identified have an increasingly established research base supporting distinctions among programs, none have strong psychometric validation for assessing quality GECE with sizeable samples of children with disabilities. More work is needed to demonstrate reliability and validity in rating quality GECE for children with disabilities by existing assessment tools.

Second, the tools do not capture the quality of the program for individual children, which could be different from overall program quality, especially for children with disabilities. Specific items could be assessed as being of high quality for children with typical developmental patterns, but of low quality for some or all children with disabilities. There also may be variation in appropriate ratings for children with different types and severities of disabilities. Alternative approaches are needed to measure quality as experienced by individual children with disabilities, in addition to the overall quality. Recently, efforts have been made to capture quality for individual children within a classroom. An example is the piloting of a new measure called the Individualized Classroom Assessment Scoring System (inCLASS; Downer, Booren, Lima, Luckner, & Pianta, 2010). Although this measure is being piloted with a diverse group of 3- to 5-year-olds, it remains to be seen whether such measures are adequate for capturing quality for children with disabilities.

Third, the approach of having one or two items that address the global quality of a program for children with disabilities poses challenges because these items often span multiple dimensions of program quality. For instance, the ECERS-R item for children with disabilities yields an overall assessment, but could be further differentiated into a number of items assessing dimensions of the provisions with regard to assessment, curriculum, environmental modifications, and parent involvement, all of which are encompassed by this one item. Even on any one dimension, there may be considerable variability in the program's effectiveness in serving children with different disabilities. Greater specificity would yield the differentiated information needed to guide program improvement; it would provide a better sense of GECE quality for individual program features, of which some may be good and others may need improvement.

Fourth, quality tools vary in how they handle scoring in cases where no children with disabilities are in the program. Similar programs could receive different ratings on the same tool due in part to whether or not children with disabilities (and with varying disability characteristics) attend the program. One reason children with disabilities or other special needs may not attend a program is because the program was not welcoming to the child or the child's family. Many tools do not assess the program's preparation for serving children with disabilities as a necessary feature of a high-quality program. It can be argued that inclusion is a value that should be promoted in all GECE programs and thus reflected in quality rating scales. Indeed, good early childhood practice would suggest that a program that has not laid the groundwork for serving children with disabilities through policies and professional development should not be considered a high-quality program. This concept of a low score on one indicator overshadowing scores on other indicators already exists in some tools; for example, programs that do not meet certain indicators of health and safety practices on standard GECE quality tools automatically receive low ratings. How programs prepare to serve a child with a disability, even if none is served in the program at a given point in time, is reflected in some innovative work being done in some states in designing their quality rating systems[6] (National Child Care Information and Technical Assistance Center [NCCIC], 2009).

Fifth, some specific considerations may apply only to children with disabilities and their parents or may have special significance for this group (e.g., the measure of how well the child's IFSP or IEP is being implemented in classroom activities and routines[7] or the relevance of many items in the "parents and staff" subscale of the ECERS-R). Some of these are not included, and others currently are rated for everyone. Identifying the key questions and separating them out would considerably aid interpretation and usefulness of the measures.

Specific Tools Designed to Assess Quality of Inclusion

Several tools have been designed to assess how GECE programs support the inclusion of young children with disabilities. The constructs addressed highlight possible key aspects of a quality environment for children with disabilities. Some of these tools are checklists designed primarily for self-assessment or professional development. An example of this kind of checklist is the Preschool and Kindergarten Inclusion Readiness Checklist (PKIRS; Watson & McCathren, 2009). This checklist contains 59 items that are scored as "yes" or "not yet" for a variety of structural and process aspects of the environment as they apply to children with disabilities. One strength of the PKIRS is that it contains sets of items appropriate for children with different types of disabilities. These items are important for examining whether a program may have better quality for some types of children with disabilities than for others. For self-assessment or professional development related to serving children with disabilities, these kinds of checklists are likely to provide richer information than would be available on more standard measures such as the ECERS-R, and they also could be a source of information for more structured quality measures. Because the checklists were not intended for use across programs, they were not designed with the psychometric rigor needed for research purposes or for state quality rating systems, nor have they been examined carefully for their ability to discriminate between programs with different levels of quality. These checklists vary considerably in their comprehensiveness and in the extent to which detailed instructions are available to guide the completion of the assessment. However, the very existence of so many checklists suggests a need to help programs address effective practices related to including children with disabilities.

In addition to checklists around inclusion practices, two assessment tools have been designed to provide more specific measures of program practices around the inclusion of children with disabilities: the SpeciaLink Child Care Inclusion Practices Profile and Principles Scale (Irwin, 2005) and the Quality of Inclusive Experiences Measure (QuIEM; Wolery, Pauca, Brashers, & Grant, 2000). The contents of these tools include more detailed information related to children with disabilities than is found in common quality measures of GECE. Although published research validating and using the tools remains in its infancy, both measures may be useful for research purposes and for program use. The major content areas in each of these measures are presented in Table 10.2.

SpeciaLink Child Care Inclusion Practices Profile and SpeciaLink Child Care Inclusion Principles Scale

The SpeciaLink Child Care Inclusion Principles Scale (Irwin, 2005), developed at the National Centre for Child Care Inclusion in Canada, was designed as a measure of inclusion progress that complements the ECERS-R. The tool uses the same scoring format as the ECERS-R (1 to 7, *inadequate* to *excellent*) and similar terminology in descriptions and explanations. Eleven overarching items on the Practices profile and the six items on the Principles Scale are intended to be administered together. Unlike the items in the ECERS-R, many of the items cannot be scored wholly with observation. Respectful questioning and document review according to protocols are important for completing the tool. The tool provides a detailed description of elements contributing to item scores

Table 10.2.   Content of two assessment tools designed to measure inclusive program practices for children with disabilities

---

SpecialLink Child Care Inclusion Practices Profile and Principles Scale

Practices Profile

- Physical environment and special needs
- Equipment and materials
- Director and inclusion
- Staff support
- Staff training
- Therapies
- Individual program plans
- Parents of children with special needs
- Involvement of children who are typically developing
- Board of directors and other similar units
- Preparing for transition to school

Principles Scale

- Full participation
- Zero rejected
- Natural proportions
- Same hours/days of attendance available to all children
- Maximum feasible parent participation at the parent's comfort level
- Leadership, proactive strategies, and advocacy for high-quality inclusive child care

Quality Measures of Inclusive Experiences Measure (QuIEM)

- Accessibility and adequacy of the physical environment
- Program goals and purpose
- Staff supports and perceptions
- Individualization of goals, planning, and implementation
- Participation and engagement (with activities, routines, and transitions common for all children in the classroom)
- Child–child contacts and relationships
- Adult–child contacts and relationships

(e.g., for "staff support," the program may have a high level of consultative support for teachers but not have reduced staff–child ratios that would support inclusion or may not have expert resource teachers accessible to staff for support). All 250 specific indicators detailed within the 17 items are completed each time the measure is administered.[8]

Quality of Inclusive Experiences Measure (QuIEM)

This measure (Wolery et al., 2000) includes seven scales of child care program practices that are believed to promote positive outcomes for young children with disabilities. Comprehensive and abbreviated versions of the instrument are available and yield scores for each of the seven scales, as well as a profile across all of the scales. Observation, interview, document review, and questionnaires are used to complete the QuIEM tool over a period of several days. Results provide information about global program quality, quality of various classrooms within the program, and quality of the experience for individual children. A portion of the tool is completed separately for each child with a disability in a class. The QuIEM is intended to be used in conjunction with other global measures of classroom quality, such as the ITERS or the ECERS-R. Training and use of the tool are rather labor intensive, but the QuIEM provides a much richer sense of the children with disabilities' GECE environment than does a global program quality measure.

In sum, obtaining a valid measure of GECE program quality for children with disabilities is challenging. Existing tools designed for general programs may include examples or global questions related to these children. The tools may provide valid information with regard to the common constructs of quality relevant to *all* children. The shortcoming is that they do not adequately address the unique and multidimensional nature of the requisite individualized quality for children with disabilities. A few tools (e.g., the SpeciaLink Child Care Inclusion Practices Profile and Principles Scale and the QuIEM) hold promise, but much work is still needed to investigate the validity and reliability of these tools for distinguishing between programs with different levels of quality.

Measurement of Quality in Early Intervention and Early Childhood Special Education

Conceptualizing and measuring quality for EI and ECSE differs in several fundamental ways from conceptualizing quality in GECE settings. One fundamental difference is that the delivery of EI and ECSE is governed by a federal law—IDEA—and its regulations. Furthermore, state laws and regulations also govern the delivery of these services in many places. Consequently, legal requirements establish some of the parameters of quality for the provision of specialized services. These requirements tend to address structural and procedural elements of quality, such as personnel requirements, time lines, and mandating that children have service plans containing certain elements and that these plans be reviewed annually. A new provision in the 2004 amendments to IDEA requires that federal and state monitoring activities focus on "improving educational results and functional outcomes for all children with disabilities" (20 U.S.C. § 1416). This provision expands the focus of oversight activities to include monitoring the achievement of child outcomes and, presumably, practices to achieve those outcomes. This new emphasis brings IDEA monitoring more in line with the connection between program elements and child outcomes that traditionally has been found in discussions of quality measurement for GECE.

A second way in which measuring quality for EI and ECSE differs from measuring quality for GECE is that the measurement of quality of specialized services is far less developed. Acknowledging the measurement issues in GECE as discussed throughout this volume, we nevertheless have a plethora of tools that have been developed for accessing quality in GECE, especially in center-based settings. That is not the case for EI and ECSE, where much work remains to be done in conceptualizing quality as well as measuring it. There is nothing comparable to the states' quality rating systems for EI and ECSE programs. No rating systems exist that parents can use to learn how one program compares with another or that provide parents with a list of elements to consider as they visit programs. A researcher or evaluator seeking to examine the relationship between program quality and child outcomes cannot review the most recent set of studies as background for tool selection; there is no body of research for EI and ECSE parallel to the large-scale and well-known Cost, Quality and Outcomes Study (Peisner-Feinberg et al., 1999) or the NICHD study (NICHD Early Child Care Research Network, 2005). These studies have produced rich information about the relationships between child outcomes and program quality for GECE; such studies are needed for specialized EI and ECSE services.

The paucity of tools may be connected to the many years during which federal and state monitoring emphasized compliance with procedures as quality rather than espousing a broader definition of quality which would encompass services and supports that produce good outcomes. A second possible reason for the lack of tools is that measuring quality for EI and ECSE is considerably more complex than measuring quality in GECE. Aytch, Cryer, Bailey, and Selz (1999) noted the following challenges for measuring quality in EI, which apply to ECSE as well: 1) The programs represent a broad range of services, 2) the services are highly individualized, and 3) the services seek to address multiple child and family goals. The challenges in service provision do not, however, preclude defining and measuring quality in the provision of EI and ECSE. They do mean that measurement of quality is complicated and, consequently, there are no tools for EI or ECSE that have been broadly adopted to measure quality in the way that the ECERS-R or the CLASS are widely used to measure quality for GECE.

The most comprehensive compendium of what constitutes quality for EI and ECSE is a set of 240 recommended practices from the Division of Early Childhood (DEC) (Sandall, Hemmeter, McLean, & Smith, 2004; Sandall et al., 2000). The compilation is intended to "provide guidance on effective practices for attaining our shared goal of improved development and learning outcomes for young children with disabilities and their families" (Sandall et al., 2004, p. 11). The list of practices was developed through an extensive review of the literature, followed by field validation with experts and practitioners. The practices are organized into five strands addressing "Direct Services" and two strands addressing "Indirect Supports," with organizing principles in each strand. The seven strands and an example of an organizing principle within a strand, together with two corresponding practices, are shown in Table 10.3. Of particular interest (and serving as further evidence of the commonality of the major elements of quality) is that many of the recommended practices are descriptors of quality relevant for all children. The recommended practices also address the specialized nature of services required by children with disabilities, as exemplified especially by specific recommendations around specialized instructional techniques, IFSP/IEPs, legal requirements, assistive technology, and settings for services. It is important to note that, even though we are discussing the recommended practices as part of the discussion of specialized services, the practices cut across all environments in which children receive those services and thus apply as well to children with disabilities in GECE settings.

Materials have been developed to enable programs to use the recommended practices as part of a self-assessment, including several checklists. As the authors note, the sheer number of practices means that programs are not likely to be able to address all of the strands at the same time. Programs are encouraged to identify specific strands or practices upon which to focus. Although the recommended practices were not developed to provide a framework for state quality rating systems or for use as a research tool, the concepts in the practices could provide the foundation for such an endeavor because they are a multifaceted articulation of what constitutes quality in EI and ECSE. However, considerable additional work would be required to convert the practices into a measurement tool with adequate validity and reliability.

Another resource for the development of a tool for measuring quality in EI comes from a work group of experts in the field, who identified seven principles for providing services in natural environments (Workgroup on Principles and Practices in Natural Environments, 2008). The principles are further elucidated by key concepts related to each principle and multiple examples of practices that do and do not embody the principle. Two examples of principles are stated as follows: "Infants and toddlers learn best

Table 10.3.   Division for Early Childhood recommended practices: Strands and examples of practices

Strands

Direct services

1. Assessment
2. Child-Focused Practices
3. Family-Based Practices
4. Interdisciplinary Models
5. Technology Applications

Indirect supports

1. Policies, Procedures, and Systems Change
2. Personnel Preparation

Example

Strand: Child-focused practices

Organizing Principle

Adults design environments to promote children's safety, active engagement, learning, participation, and membership.

Practice

C3. Routines and transitions are structured to promote interaction, communication, and learning by being responsive to child behavior and using naturalistic time delay, interrupted chain procedure, transition-based teaching, and visual cue systems.

C8. A variety of appropriate settings and naturally occurring activities are used to facilitate children's learning and development.

through everyday experiences and interactions with familiar people in familiar contexts" and "The families' priorities, needs, and interests are addressed most appropriately by a primary provider who represents and receives team and community support." Like the DEC recommended practices, the principles are not a quality measure, but they do provide a starting point for the development of such a measure.

A search of the literature found only one tool that had been developed specifically to examine the quality of EI and none for preschool special education. Aytch and colleagues (Aytch et al., 1999; Aytch, Castro, & Selz-Campbell, 2004) developed the Early Intervention Services Assessment Scale (EISAS) as a measure that would parallel the ECERS-R and that could be used to assess the quality of EI services. The developers envisioned EISAS as consisting of a program self-assessment and a parent survey. The initial version of the program self-assessment consisted of five subscales (Assessment, Intervention Planning, Service Provision, Transition Planning, and Administration) and 17 items. Scoring involved a 7-point scale. The parent survey examined family experiences and their perceptions of services. Initially, it consisted of five sections addressing the same five content areas as the program self-assessment. Parents respond to a series of items such as "We helped decide when and where an assessment would take place." The self-assessment was intended to be a collaborative process involving both consumers and practitioners. The authors note two limitations with the tool that compromise its usefulness as a program assessment instrument. First, because it was designed for self-assessment, objective use of the tool by outside observers would be difficult and might not be practical given the subjective nature of many of the items. Second, the length of the tool limits its utility. Initial feedback from providers indicated that the initial version of the instrument was cumbersome and redundant, and there was concern about parents' willingness to complete the entire survey (Aytch et al., 2004). No additional research has been published on subsequent versions of the EISAS.

Although few tools are designed to provide a measure of global quality or multiple dimensions of quality for EI or ECSE in a single tool, numerous measures have been developed to assess a single dimension. For example, the Beach Center Family-Professional Partnership Scale (Beach Center on Disability, 2006) assesses parent satisfaction with the partnership between the family and providers, and the Family Support Scale (FSS; Dunst, Jenkins, & Trivette, 1984) measures parent perceptions of the helpfulness of various sources of support. Many of these scales have been used in research and have good psychometric properties, but they assess only one facet of quality. Using several would result in a time-consuming assessment and still leave important facets of quality in EI and ECSE not assessed.

Next Steps in the Measurement of Quality for ECE Programs Serving Children with Disabilities

Much work remains to be done around the development of measures to assess program quality for children with disabilities. Early childhood professionals increasingly have recognized and supported the inclusion of children with disabilities in general early childhood programs, but the measurement of quality of these children's experiences in the programs lags behind the measurement of program quality for typically developing children. The task of relating quality of program experiences to outcomes for young children with disabilities faces the additional challenge in that these children can be served by two service systems: the GECE systems (i.e., preschools, various child care arrangements) and the system that provides EI or ECSE services under IDEA.

As seen in this review, there is widespread consensus that the indicators of program quality for the general population of young children also are indicators of program quality for children with disabilities. In addition, there are unique features of quality that go beyond the common core for all children that programs need to address to be considered high-quality programs for children with disabilities. Identifying the complete set of features is an undertaking beyond the scope of this chapter, but is an essential step toward the development of measures of quality for programs serving children with disabilities.

In this final section, we summarize some of the common themes and elements related to measuring program quality for children with disabilities that appear across the currently available research and resources. In addition to the literature on effective practices, these resources include existing measures of program quality (e.g., the ECERS-R), the DEC/NAEYC joint position statement on inclusion, measures of inclusive practices (Irwin, 2005; Wolery et al., 2000), the DEC recommended practices, the recommendations of the Workgroup on Natural Environments, and the Early Intervention Services Assessment Scale (EISAS).

The conceptualization of what constitutes quality needs to account for individual needs, but it also needs to account for the two service systems in which children with disabilities may be participating. Because many children with disabilities participate in both the GECE system and the specialized systems that provide IDEA EI and ECSE services, the promotion of optimal development for these children will depend on the extent to which they are receiving high-quality services through both systems. Research suggests that the best outcomes will be obtained when the systems work together and deliver EI or ECSE services in the context of GECE. In an ideal world, these two systems work closely together in the community to ensure that each child and each child's family experience a high-quality program. As suggested by the information in Table 10.4, GECE programs need resources and supports such as professional development, access to specialists, assistive technology, and other kinds of administrative supports to provide a quality program for children with disabilities. It is not necessary that each GECE program become a specialized program. Rather, the early childhood system at state and local levels needs to establish the kind of collaborative infrastructure that can assist GECE programs in developing the expertise and making the specific adaptations necessary to serve the entire range of children with disabilities. Coordination at the systems level will be essential to having quality at the classroom level, and any measurement system will need to capture how the administrative structures are or are not working together. Documenting this type of collaboration may prove challenging because much of the process will not be visible to an observer and will require interview data and other kinds of information.

As growing numbers of children with disabilities are served entirely or partially in inclusive settings, GECE programs will need to understand these requirements, and the developers of new quality measures will need to decide how legal requirements are to be incorporated into their measures.

The development of measures for the assessment of program quality for children with disabilities presents the same dilemma that applies to all measures of program quality: The development of these measures should be based on what is known about how specific program features relate to child outcomes, but much more research is needed to establish such relationships. Existing research supports the importance of some components for children with disabilities (e.g., specialized instructional strategies, environmental arrangements), but research has not been done that would establish what constitutes a high-quality ECE program in its entirety for all children with disabilities. Much more research is needed to thoroughly understand what works for which children and under what circumstances (Guralnick, 2005b). The development of a comprehensive set of quality indicators of children with disabilities will require drawing on the existing research as well as professional wisdom, with an understanding that as the knowledge base addressing effective interventions and instructional practices continues to grow, the elements of quality measures will need to be revised.

In closing, we return to the three dimensions of inclusion: access, participation, and supports (DEC/NAEYC, 2009). With particular regard to access, developers of quality measures will need to determine the scoring weight to place on the importance of a program's demonstrated commitment to serve *all* children. A case can be made that a program that has not laid the groundwork for accessibility to children with special needs and their families cannot, by definition, be considered high quality, regardless of ratings on other dimensions. Participation and supports, the other dimensions of inclusion, make clear that a willingness to enroll children without regard to disability or other special needs is a necessary, but not sufficient, marker of quality. In addition, high-quality ECE programs must promote and support the development of all children. As early childhood systems continue to evolve and become better integrated and coordinated, program quality measures also need to evolve to capture how well programs are structured to promote positive outcomes for all children, including children with disabilities.

Table 10.4.   Framework for program quality for children with disabilities: Major areas, related concepts, and examples

Major areas	Related concepts or examples
1. Interactions • Interactions with peers • Interactions with adults	• Presence of typically developing children • Adult facilitation and support of child's interaction with peers • Adult use of appropriate techniques to address challenging behavior • Adult implementation of specialized techniques to facilitate language development
2. Program features • Curriculum • Instructional practices • Scheduling • Nature of activities • Materials	• Curriculum modifications and adaptations • Instructional practices geared to child's needs • Use of everyday routines to promote development and learning • Availability of specialized materials • Full engagement of child in activities • Implementation of IFSP/IEP • Developmentally appropriate and functional goals • Integration of specialized services
3. Staff characteristics/program structure • Staff education • Staff training • Experience • Beliefs • Goals • Child-to-staff ratios • Group size • Arrangement of physical space, equipment, and furnishing	• Professional development for staff related to children with disabilities in general, and to the child's special needs in particular • Staff support for inclusion • Reduced ratios for classes with a child with special needs • Assistive technology, adapted equipment, modified physical space
4. Administrative characteristics • Philosophy (program goals, beliefs about children, families, and early education) • Structures (policies, compensation) • Context (funding adequacy, accreditations, connections to other agencies) • Supports (professional development activities, availability and quality of specialists, supervision of staff)	• Policy voicing support for inclusion • Zero reject policy • Coordination between general and specialized programs/services • Access to specialists • Time provided to support team planning • Transdisciplinary service provision
5. Parent partnerships • Communication • Program support for family outcomes • Family-centered practices	• Services and supports designed to help parents support child's development and learning • Staff use of parents' knowledge of child's strengths, needs, and interests • Ongoing communication to support continuity of experiences for child between home and center • Important decisions related to child's programs or services made jointly by parents and providers

References

Administration for Children and Families. (2008). *Head Start program fact sheet.* Retrieved June 5, 2009, from http://www.acf.hhs.gov/programs/ohs/about/fy2008.html

Aytch, L.S., Cryer, D., Bailey, D.B., Jr., & Selz, L. (1999). Defining and assessing quality in early intervention programs for infants and toddlers with disabilities and their families: Challenges and unresolved issues. *Early Education & Development, 10*(1), 7–23.

Aytch, L.S., Castro, D.C., & Selz-Campbell, L. (2004). Early Intervention Services Assessment Scale (EISAS)—Conceptualization and development of a program quality self-assessment instrument. *Infants and Young Children, 17*(3), 236–246.

Bailey, D.B., Jr., Bruder, M.B., Hebbeler, K., Carta, J., deFosset, M., Greenwood, C., et al. (2006). Recommended outcomes for families of young children with disabilities. *Journal of Early Intervention, 28*(4), 227–251.

Bailey, D.B., Jr., McWilliam, R.A., Buysse, V., & Wesley, P.W. (1998). Inclusion in the context of competing values in early childhood education. *Early Childhood Research Quarterly, 13*(1), 27–47.

Beach Center on Disability. (2006). *Beach Center Family–Professional Partnership Scale.* Retrieved from http://www.beachcenter.org/resource_library/beach_resource_detail_page.aspx?intResourceID=2478&Type=Tool&JScript=1

Booth, C.L., & Kelly, J.F. (1998). Child-care characteristics of infants with and without special needs: Comparisons and concerns. *Early Childhood Research Quarterly, 13*(4), 603–622.

Booth-LaForce, C., & Kelly, J.F. (2004). Child-care patterns and issues for families of preschool children with disabilities. *Infants and Young Children, 17*(1), 5–16.

Brandon, P.D. (2000). Child care utilization among working mothers raising children with disabilities. *Journal of Family and Economic Issues, 21*(4), 343–364.

Bricker, D. (2000). Inclusion: How the scene has changed. *Topics in Early Childhood Special Education, 20*(1), 14–19.

Bricker, D., & Cripe, J.J. (1992). *An activity-based approach to early intervention.* Baltimore: Paul H. Brookes Publishing Co.

Buysse, V., & Bailey, D.B. (1993). Behavioral and developmental outcomes in young children with disabilities in integrated and segregated settings: A review of comparative studies. *Journal of Special Education, 26,* 434–461.

Buysse, V., & Hollingsworth, H.L. (2009). Program quality and early childhood inclusion: Recommendations for professional development. *Topics in Early Childhood Special Education, 29*(2), 119–128.

Buysse, V., Skinner, D., & Grant, S. (2001). Toward a definition of quality inclusion: Perspectives of parents and practitioners. *Journal of Early Intervention, 24*(2), 146–161.

Buysse, V., Wesley, P.W., Bryant, D., & Gardner, D. (1999). Quality of early childhood programs in inclusive and noninclusive settings. *Exceptional Children, 65*(3), 301–314.

Carta, J.J. (2002). *Measuring program quality: Early childhood.* OSEP Research Project Directors' Conference, Washington, DC.

Clawson, C., & Luze, G. (2008). Individual experiences of children with and without disabilities in early childhood settings. *Topics in Early Childhood Special Education, 28*(3), 132–147.

Copple, C., & Bredekamp, S. (Eds.). (2009). *Developmentally appropriate practice in early childhood programs: Serving children from birth through age 8* (3rd ed.). Washington, DC: National Association for the Education of Young Children.

DEC/NAEYC. (2009). *Early childhood inclusion: A summary.* Chapel Hill: The University of North Carolina, FPG Child Development Institute.

Downer, J.T., Booren, L.M., Lima, O.A., Luckner, A.E., & Pianta, R.C. (2010). The Individualized Classroom Assessment Scoring System (inCLASS): Preliminary reliability and validity of a system for observing preschoolers' competence in classroom interactions. *Early Childhood Research Quarterly, 25*(1), 1–16.

Dunst, C.J., Bruder, M.B., Trivette, C.M., & Hamby, D.W. (2006). Everyday activity settings, natural learning environments, and early intervention practices. *Journal of Policy and Practice in Intellectual Disabilities, 3*(1), 3–10.

Dunst, C.J., Bruder, M.B., Trivette, C.M., Hamby, D., Raab, M., & McLean, M.E. (2001).

Characteristics and consequences of everyday natural learning opportunities. *Topics in Early Childhood Special Education, 21,* 68–164.

Dunst, C.J., Jenkins, V., & Trivette, C.M. (1984). Family Support Scale: Reliability and Validity. *Journal of Individual, Family, and Community Wellness, 1,* 45–52.

Fiene, R. (1984). *Child development program evaluation scale and COFAS.* Washington, DC: Children's Services Monitoring Consortium.

Fox, L., Hanline, M., Vail, C., & Galant, K. (1994). Developmentally appropriate practice: Applications for young children with disabilities. *Journal of Early Intervention, 18*(3), 243–257.

Goodson, B.D., Layzer, C.J., Smith, W.C., & Rimdzius, T. (2006). *Observation Measures of Language and Literacy Instruction (OMLIT) in early childhood.* Cambridge, MA: Abt Associates.

Guralnick, M.J. (2001a). Connections between developmental science and intervention science. *Zero To Three: The Science of Early Childhood Development, 21,* 24–29.

Guralnick, M.J. (Ed.). (2001b). *Early childhood inclusion.* Baltimore: Paul H. Brookes Publishing Co.

Guralnick, M.J. (2005a). Early intervention for children with intellectual disabilities: Current knowledge and future prospects. *Journal of Applied Research in Intellectual Disabilities, 18,* 313–324.

Guralnick, M.J. (Ed.). (2005b). *The developmental systems approach to early intervention.* Baltimore: Paul H. Brookes Publishing Co.

Halle, T., & Vick, J.E. (2007). *Quality in Early Childhood Care and Education Settings: A Compendium of Measures.* Washington, DC: Prepared by Child Trends for the Office of Planning, Research and Evaluation, Administration for Children and Families, U.S. Department of Health and Human Services. Retrieved October 10, 2010, from http://www.researchconnections.org/childcare/resources/18804/pdf

Hamre, B.K., Mashburn, A.J., Pianta, R.C., Lacasle-Crouch, J., & La Paro, K.M. (2006). *Classroom Assessment Scoring System™ technical appendix.* Baltimore: Paul H. Brookes Publishing Co.

Harms, T., Clifford, R., & Cryer, D. (2005). *Early Childhood Environmental Rating Scale–Revised Edition.* New York: Teachers College Press.

Harms, T., Cryer, D., & Clifford, R.M. (2003). *Infant/Toddler Environment Rating Scale–Revised Edition.* New York: Teachers College Press.

Hebbeler, K., Scarborough, A., Snyder, E., Robinson, J., & Nelson, L. (2009). Use of early care and education by families receiving Part C early education services. Unpublished manuscript.

Hemmeter, M.L. (2000). Classroom-based interventions: Evaluating the past and looking toward the future. *Topics in Early Childhood Special Education, 20*(1), 56–61.

Hemmeter, M.L., Joseph, G.E., Smith, B.J., & Sandall, S. (2001). *DEC recommended practices program assessment: Improving practices for young children with special needs and their families.* Longmont, CO: Sopris West.

Hestenes, L.L., Cassidy, D.J., Hegde, A.V., & Lower, J.K. (2007). Quality in inclusive and noninclusive infant and toddler classrooms. *Journal of Research in Childhood Education, 22*(1), 69–84.

HighScope Educational Research Foundation. (2003). *Preschool program quality assessment, 2nd edition (PQA) administration manual.* Ypsilanti, MI: HighScope Press.

HighScope Educational Research Foundation. (2006a). *Ready school assessment: Administrative manual.* Ypsilanti, MI: HighScope Press.

HighScope Educational Research Foundation. (2006b). *Ready school assessment: Questionnaire.* Ypsilanti, MI: HighScope Press.

HighScope Educational Research Foundation. (2006c). *Ready school assessment: Team handbook.* Ypsilanti, MI: HighScope Press.

Horn, E., Lieber, J., Li, S., Sandall, S., & Schwartz, I. (2000). Opportunities supporting young children's IEP goals in inclusive settings through embedded learning. *Topics in Early Childhood Special Education, 20,* 208–223.

Individuals with Disabilities Education Improvement Act of 2004, Pub. L. 108–446, 20 U.S.C. § 1400 *et seq.* (2004).

Irwin, S.H. (2005). *SpeciaLink Child Care Inclusion Practices Profile and Principles Scale.* Winnipeg, Manitoba: SpeciaLink, the National Centre for Child Care Inclusion.

Irwin, S.H. (2009). *The SpeciaLink Early Childhood Inclusion Quality Scale.* Sydney, Nova Scotia: Breton Books.

Kelly, J.F., & Booth, C.L. (1999). Child care for infants with special needs: Issues and applications. *Infants and Young Children, 12,* 26–33.

Knoche, L., Peterson, C.A., Pope Edwards, C., & Jeon, H.J. (2006). Child care for children with and without disabilities: The provider, observer, and parent perspectives. *Early Childhood Research Quarterly, 21*(1), 93–109.

La Paro, K.M., Sexton, D., & Snyder, P. (1998). Program quality characteristics in segregated and inclusive early childhood settings. *Early Childhood Research Quarterly, 13*(1), 151–167.

Macy, M.G., & Bricker, D.D. (2006). Practical applications for using curriculum-based assessment to create embedded learning opportunities for young children. *Young Exceptional Children, 9*, 12–21.

Mannan, H., Summers, J.A., Turnbull, A.P., & Poston, D.J. (2006). A review of outcome measures in early childhood programs. *Journal of Policy and Practice in Intellectual Disabilities, 3*(4), 219–228.

McLean, M.E., & Odom, S.L. (1993). Practices for young children with and without disabilities: A comparison of DEC and NAEYC identified practices. *Topics in Early Childhood Special Education, 13*(3), 274–292.

McWilliam, R.A., Scarborough, A.A., Bagby, J.H., & Sweeny, A.L. (1998). *Teaching Styles Rating Scale.* Chapel Hill: University of North Carolina at Chapel Hill.

McWilliam, R.A., Zulli, R.A., & de Kruif, R.E.L. (1998). *Teaching Styles Rating Scale (TSRS) manual.* Chapel Hill: University of North Carolina, FPG Child Development Institute.

National Child Care Information and Technical Assistance Center (2009). *QRIS standards about the inclusion of children with special needs.* Fairfax, VA: Author.

National Research Council and Institute of Medicine. (2000). *From neurons to neighborhoods: The science of early childhood development.* Washington, DC: National Academies Press.

NICHD Early Child Care Research Network. (Ed.). (2005). *Child care and child development: Results from the NICHD study of early child care and youth development.* New York: Guilford Press.

Odom, S.L. (2000). Preschool inclusion: What we know and where we go from here. *Topics in Early Childhood Special Education, 20*(1), 20–27.

Odom, S.L., & Diamond, K.E. (1998). Inclusion of young children with special needs in early childhood education: The research base. *Early Childhood Research Quarterly, 13*(1), 3–25.

Odom, S.L., & Strain, P.S. (2002). Evidence-based practice in early intervention/early childhood special education: Single subject design research. *Journal of Early Intervention, 25*, 151–160.

Odom, S.L., & Wolery, M. (2003). A unified theory of practice in early intervention/early childhood special education: Evidence-based practices. *Journal of Special Education, 37,* 164–173.

Peisner-Feinberg, E.S., Burchinal, M.R., Clifford, R.M., Yazejian, N., Culkin, M.L., Zelazo, J., et al. (1999). *The children of the Cost, Quality, and Outcomes Study go to school* (Technical Report). Chapel Hill: University of North Carolina at Chapel Hill, FPG Child Development Institute.

Peterson, C.A., Wall, S., Raikes, H.A., Kisker, E.E., Swanson, M.E., Jerald, J., et al. (2004). Early Head Start: Identifying and serving children with disabilities. *Topics in Early Childhood Special Education, 24*(2), 76–88.

Pianta, R.C., La Paro, K.M., & Hamre, B.K. (2008) *Classroom Assessment Scoring System™ (CLASS™).* Baltimore: Paul H. Brookes Publishing Co.

Preston, D., & Carter, M. (2009). A review of the Picture Exchange Communication System intervention. *Journal of Autism and Developmental Disorders, 39,* 1471–1486.

Roper, N., & Dunst, C.J. (2003). Communication interventions in natural environments: Guidelines for practice. *Infants and Young Children, 16,* 215–226.

Sandall, S., Hemmeter, M.L., McLean, M., & Smith, B.J. (Eds.). (2004). *DEC recommended practices: A comprehensive guide for practical application in early intervention/early childhood special education.* Longmont, CO: Sopris West.

Sandall, S., McLean, M.E., & Smith, B.J. (2000). *DEC recommended practices in early intervention/early childhood special education.* Missoula, MT: Division for Early Childhood.

Shonkoff, J.P., & Meisels, S.J. (Eds.). (2000). *Handbook of early childhood intervention* (2nd ed.). New York: Cambridge University Press.

Smith, M.W., Brady, J.P., & Anastasopoulos, L. (2008). *Early Language and Literacy Classroom Observation (ELLCO) Toolkit, Research Edition.* Baltimore: Paul H. Brookes Publishing Co.

Spiker, D., Hebbeler, K., Wagner, M., Cameto, R., & McKenna, P. (2000). A framework for describing variations in state early intervention systems. *Topics in Early Childhood Special Education, 20*(4), 195–207.

Sylva, K., Siraj-Blatchford, I., & Taggart, B. (2003). *Assessing quality in the early years. Early Childhood Environment Scales: Extension (ECERS-E). Four curricular subscales.* Stoke on Trent, England: Trentham Books.

Thornburg, K., Raikes, H., Wilcox, B., Torquati, J., Edwards, C.P., Knoche, L., et al. (2004). *Policy brief # 6: Child care quality for children with disabilities.* Lincoln: University of Nebraska-Lincoln Midwest Child Care Research Consortium, Center on Children, Families and the Law.

Thurman, S.K. (1997). Systems, ecologies, and the context of early intervention. In S.K. Thurman, J.R. Cornwell, & S.R. Gottwald (Eds.), *Contexts of early intervention: Systems and settings* (pp. 3–17). Baltimore: Paul H. Brookes Publishing Co.

Tien, K. (2008). Effectiveness of the Picture Exchange Communication System as a functional communication intervention for individuals with autism spectrum disorders: A practice-base research synthesis. *Education and Training in Developmental Disabilities, 43,* 61–76.

Tout, K., Zaslow, M., Halle, T., & Forry, N. (2009). ACF-OPRE Issue Brief. *Issues for the Next Decade of Quality Rating and Improvement Systems.* Office of Planning, Research and Evaluation, Administration for Children and Families, U.S. Department of Health and Human Services. Washington, DC.

Trivette, C.M., & Dunst, C. (2000). Recommended practices in family-based practices. In S. Sandall, M.L. Hemmeter, M. Mclean & B.J. Smith (Eds.) *DEC recommended practices: A comprehensive guide for practical application in early intervention/early childhood special education (pp. 39–46).* Longmont, CO: Sopris West.

U.S. Department of Education Office of Special Education Programs. (2007). *Data Analysis System (DANS).* Retrieved, July 12, 2010, from http://nces.ed.gov/das

Warfield, M.E., & Hauser-Cram, P. (1996). Child care needs, arrangements, and satisfaction of mothers of children with developmental disabilities. *Mental Retardation, 34,* 294–302.

Watson, A., & McCathren, R. (2009). Including children with special needs: Are you and your early childhood program ready? *Young Children, 64*(2), 20–26.

Wolery, M. (2000). Behavioral and educational approaches to early intervention. In J.P. Shonkoff & S.J. Meisels (Eds.), *Handbook of early childhood intervention* (2nd ed., pp. 179–203). New York: Cambridge University Press.

Wolery, M. (2004). Assessing children's environments. In M. McLean, M. Wolery, & D. Bailey (Eds.), *Assessing infants and preschoolers with special needs* (3rd ed., pp. 204–235). Upper Saddle River, NJ: Pearson Merrill Prentice Hall.

Wolery, M., Pauca, T., Brashers, M.S., & Grant, S. (2000). *Quality of Inclusive Experiences Measure (QuIEM):* Unpublished manuscript.

Woods, J., Kashinath, S., & Goldstein, H. (2004). Effects of embedded caregiver-implemented teaching strategies in daily routines on children's communication outcomes. *Journal of Early Intervention, 26,* 175–193.

Workgroup on Principles and Practices in Natural Environments. (2008). *Seven key principles: Look like/doesn't look like.* Retrieved May 24, 2009, from http://www.nectac.org/topics/families/families.asp

Zaslow, M., Tout, K., Halle, T., & Forry, N. (2009). ACF-OPRE Issue Brief. *Multiple Purposes for Measuring Quality in Early Childhood Settings: Implications for Selecting and Communicating Information on Quality.* Office of Planning, Research and Evaluation, Administration for Children and Families, U.S. Department of Health and Human Services. Washington, DC.

Endnotes

[1]See also Tout, Zaslow, Halle, & Forry (2009).

[2]This coordination also includes coordination at key transition points, such as when a child leaves early intervention at age 3 and enters preschool special education, as well as coordination when there are transitions across child care programs.

[3]*Naturalistic teaching* refers to using the naturally occurring learning opportunities of young children in everyday situations and

activities as the main context to teach children new skills and behaviors, rather than setting up artificial didactic situations to teach children (Dunst et al., 2001; Dunst, Bruder, Trivette, & Hamby, 2006; Roper & Dunst, 2003). *Response prompting* refers to a specific behavioral technique in which reinforcement is used differentially to shape successive approximations to a desired behavior (Wolery, 2000). *Embedded instruction* refers to techniques used in naturalistic teaching in which the teacher intentionally structures natural activities in the classroom to allow the child to have opportunities to practice specific learning goals in ways that are interesting and meaningful to the child (Bricker & Cripe, 1992; Horn, Lieber, Li, Sandall, & Schwartz, 2000; Macy & Bricker, 2006). These techniques, which also can be used by parents in daily routines at home (Woods, Kashinath, & Goldstein, 2004), have demonstrated evidence for their effectiveness in teaching skills to young children (Odom & Strain, 2002; Odom & Wolery, 2003).

[4]*Structural quality* refers to conditions and characteristics of an early childhood setting, such as group size, adult–child ratio, staff qualifications, and materials, that are related to a high-quality experience for children. *Process quality* refers to teacher–child and peer interactions, as well as age-appropriate classroom activities, that support children's development.

[5]A common method is the Picture Exchange Communication System (PECS), which is an intervention approach that uses pictures and a variety of well-established behavioral principles to teach communication skills to children with language and communication deficits (see reviews by Preston & Carter, 2009; Tien, 2008).

[6]Quality Rating Systems (QRS) are meant to provide consumers with a uniform metric to judge the quality of ECE programs within a state or locality. QRS are also used as a tool for quality improvement of programs throughout a state or locality. To date, half of all states in the United States have either established QRS or are developing and/or piloting QRS.

[7]Note that a child's disability and whether or not the child has an IEP or IFSP is confidential information, as are the contents of the child's records related to special education. This information cannot be shared with an observer external to the program without parent permission.

[8]Since this chapter was written, a revision to this scale has been released (Irwin, 2009).

CHAPTER 11

Defining and Measuring Quality in Early Childhood Practices that Promote Dual Language Learners' Development and Learning

Dina C. Castro, Linda M. Espinosa, and Mariela M. Páez

The number of young dual language learners (DLLs)[1] enrolling in early childhood programs has increased steadily over the last 15 years, a trend that is expected to continue. A factor contributing to this trend is the rapid growth of the immigrant population. As of 2005, one in four, or 25%, of young children in the United States were children of immigrant families (Hernandez, Denton, & Macartney, 2008). Although a large percentage (62%) of children in immigrant families live in five states (California, Florida, Illinois, New York, and Texas), their percentages have increased in most of the other states, with children of immigrants accounting for at least 10% of children in 26 states (Hernandez et al., 2008). There is enormous diversity in the origin of immigrant families. Among immigrant parents of children under 6 years of age, the largest percentage come from Mexico and other Latin American countries and the Caribbean (64%), and smaller percentages come from countries in Asia (23%), Europe and Canada (7%), and Africa and the Middle East (6%) (Capps et al., 2005).

The majority of children in immigrant families grow up in bilingual environments. Data from the U.S. Census Bureau indicate that 84% of immigrants ages 5 and older speak a language other than English at home (Pew Hispanic Center, 2009). The linguistic diversity among young children is evident in the increase of young DLLs' enrollment in Head Start programs, over 30% nationally; almost 85% of those children are from families who speak Spanish as their primary language (Office of Head Start, 2007). The percentage of DLLs is larger among the youngest children in the public education system. In 2000–2001, the average percentage of DLLs in prekindergarten (pre-K) through grade 12 education was 10%; however, 44% of all DLLs were enrolled in pre-K to third grade (Kindler, 2002).

Although immigrant families account for most of the families who speak a language other than English at home, not all DLLs are children of immigrants. There are U.S. native-born families who speak English and also speak a language other than English at home; for example, among U.S. born Latinos[2] ages 18 and older, 63% speak a language other than English at home (Pew Hispanic Center, 2009). Also, many children in Native American and Pacific Islander families are part of the DLL population.

There are positive characteristics of immigrant families that can support their children's healthy development and learning, such as the fact that a larger percentage (84%) of children in immigrant families live with two parents as compared with children in native-born families (76%; Hernandez et al., 2008) and the high value that these families give to their children's education (e.g., Zarate & Perez, 2006). On the other hand, there are a number of challenges confronted by immigrant families, including that they are more likely to live in poverty than native-born families (National Center for Children in Poverty, 2007) and a larger percentage of immigrant parents have less than a high school education as compared with native-born parents (Capps, Fix, Ost, Reardon-Anderson, & Passel, 2004). However, averages hide a wide range of differences when attempts are made to characterize a group that is diverse across many dimensions. For example, whereas some immigrant parents have come to the United States with college or graduate degrees, others have less than a high school education. Factors such as employment status, occupation, income level, English proficiency, and social status will influence immigrant parents' access to and utilization of early childhood care and education services, as well as their abilities to communicate with educators and to get involved in their children's early care and education (ECE) in the ways traditionally expected by program administrators and educators.

The negative effects of poverty environments on children's development and school achievement have been well documented in the research literature (see Knapp & Woolverton, 2003, for a review), with fewer studies examining this relationship in DLL populations (see Lindholm-Leary & Borsato, 2007, for a review). Similarly, empirical studies report the positive impact of high-quality early education for low-income children, particularly low-income minority young children (Bowman, Donovan, & Burns, 2001). National data show that children of immigrants are less likely to attend an early education program than children in the U.S.-born population (Matthews & Ewen, 2006). The combination of living in poverty and having limited access to early education increases the vulnerability of young DLLs to negative outcomes.

These contextual factors, along with the lack of adequate preparation of early childhood programs and teachers to successfully educate DLLs, create the conditions for the existing school readiness gap. Nationally, the majority of early childhood educators are monolingual English speakers; few have bilingual teacher assistants; and even when there is a bilingual assistant in the classroom, the lead teacher may not know how to incorporate that resource into her teaching practices. A national survey of state administrators of early childhood programs reported that the limited number of bilingual educators and the lack of appropriate preparation and training of early childhood educators were among the most urgent challenges facing ECE programs that serve the growing Spanish-speaking birth-to-age-5 population (Buysse, Castro, West, & Skinner, 2005). Only a small proportion of institutions of higher education offer academic training programs designed to prepare educators to work with DLLs; academic training programs offering this content to early childhood educators are even rarer (Maxwell, Lim, & Early, 2006; Menken & Antunez, 2001).

Given the demographic changes in the country and the role of high-quality educational practices in promoting young children's development and learning, it is urgent to address issues of quality in the early education of DLLs. It is necessary to rethink what quality means for educating young DLLs. New indicators of quality should take into account the specific developmental characteristics of DLLs as well as the challenges they are facing. This is a vulnerable population at risk of school failure, not only because of family risk factors many share such as poverty and low parental education, but also because early education practices have not been designed to address the linguistic and broader developmental needs of DLLs. Thus, instructional practices need to be modified or changed and measures need to capture whether or not those modifications or changes are being implemented. Also, measures of quality need to assess practices that respond to both short-term and long-term learning goals (i.e., practices that promote development of skills needed to succeed in kindergarten and beyond).

The purposes of this chapter are 1) to discuss important considerations for the development of measures of quality practices to promote DLLs' development, including early bilingual development and how it affects children's cognitive, language, literacy, and socioemotional development; 2) to discuss the elements of high-quality early education for DLLs, including program and teacher characteristics, curriculum and instructional practices, and family involvement; and 3) to review available quality measures and measures in development and propose components of new early childhood quality measures that assess the quality of practices to promote development and learning in DLLs.

Considerations for the Design of Measures of Quality Practices to Promote DLLs' Development

The impact of dual language learning on children's cognitive, language, literacy, and socioemotional development has important implications for programs that are trying to create high-quality educational environments for this population. As noted by Chang et al., early childhood programs are faced with the challenge of educating young children "who are simultaneously trying to develop proficiency in their home language and in English, all the while gaining the pre-academic knowledge and social skills they need to be ready for formal schooling" (2007, p. 244). In this section we discuss important considerations for advancing quality measures of early childhood practices that promote DLLs' development. We focus on four areas related to early bilingual development and learning that should be considered when developing measures of quality in early childhood education: 1) the process of second-language acquisition, 2) the importance of oral language skills, 3) the role of first language in learning English, and 4) the particular language contexts that promote development and learning for these children.

Process of Second-Language Acquisition

Dual language learners are faced with the difficult task of transitioning from their home to the school environment and learning English in a short amount of time. Although there are a variety of early childhood program options for young DLLs, the most typical classroom situation for these children is to attend an English-language classroom (Tabors, 2008). In this type of classroom, English is the main language of interaction and instruction for both the children and the educators. If children have no support for their home language, they might find it very difficult to understand or speak English and become active members of the classroom. This is what Tabors has defined as "the double bind of second-language learning: to learn a new language, you have to be socially accepted by those who speak the language; but to be socially accepted, you have to be able to speak the new language" (2008, p. 33). Early childhood educators often are faced with this challenge in trying to understand and integrate DLLs into their classrooms. Fortunately, most children develop strategies for coping with this "double bind" and can adjust and learn a new language in early childhood settings. However, early childhood educators should be aware of the possible "social isolation and linguistic constraints" that children face when placed in settings where their home language is not available to them (Tabors, 2008, p. 34). In addition, early childhood educators can facilitate the process by learning about the developmental sequence of second-language acquisition and implementing effective practices for working with these children.

Research has shown that young children who are exposed to a second language in an English-language early childhood classroom move through a specific four-phase developmental sequence (Tabors, 2008). Initially, children *speak their home language* as they learn to distinguish between their first language and the new language that is being used in the setting. This is followed by a *nonverbal, or observational, period* where children use alternative methods of communication. During this time, children acquire receptive understanding of the new language and they watch, listen, and rehearse in preparation for its use. Children then begin to use *telegraphic and formulaic language,* which involves labeling and employing common phrases, allowing them to get into the flow of the activities in the classroom and begin to sound like members of the group. As they engage in the process of creating new sentences, children build up to the point where they are able to *productively use the new language*. This developmental sequence is cumulative, and there are individual differences in children's rates of acquisition. Tabors and Snow (2002) have identified at least four factors—motivation, exposure, age, and personality—that may affect how quickly young children acquire a second language.

In addition to these factors, second language acquisition research has focused on societal, familial, and individual factors that can have an impact on language and literacy development (August & Hakuta, 1997; August & Shanahan, 2006). As noted by Snow (2006), stronger research evidence is needed in this area to disentangle the complex factors that are relevant to the development of DLLs. However, we can expect that the process of learning a second language is not the same for all children (Bialystok, 2001). For DLLs, the development of language and literacy involves the integration of component skills (e.g., sound-symbol awareness, grammatical knowledge, vocabulary knowledge), as well as more elusive sociocultural variables critical to the development of reading and writing. Thus, DLLs in early childhood programs could display a variety of skills in each language depending on the child's age, when the languages were learned, and how these languages are supported at home, at school, and in the community. Moreover, there are interactions of linguistic knowledge between the languages that children know and are learning so that skills in a first language can facilitate learning a second language. There is also considerable research evidence concerning the role of individual factors in predicting second-language outcomes. Individual differences, including cognitive abilities, previous learning experiences, cultural background, and knowledge, can all play an important role in the dynamic process of learning a second language (August & Shanahan, 2006). Thus, early childhood programs need to collect information about DLLs' background, including culture, language(s) knowledge, and skills, so that they can know and support these children as bilingual/bicultural learners (Brisk & Harrington, 2007).

Importance of Oral Language Skills

Research has shown that language experiences and early exposure to literacy are important precursors for children's language development and reading success (Snow, Burns, & Griffin, 1998; Dickinson & Tabors, 2001). In particular, several language skills have been identified as important during the early childhood years, including a strong vocabulary, phonological awareness, letter knowledge, background knowledge, and understanding of print concepts (Dickinson & Neuman, 2006; National Reading Panel, 2000; see also Neuman & Carta, Chapter 4, this volume). A report from the National Early Literacy Panel (2008) presented a meta-analysis of research and recommendations for early childhood educators on promoting foundational literacy skills. The report identified the skills and abilities of young children (age birth through 5 years or kindergarten) that predict later reading, writing, or spelling outcomes, and the types of early literacy interventions that promote children's early literacy skills. Their findings support the importance of alphabet knowledge, phonological awareness, rapid auto-naming of letters or digits, rapid auto-naming of objects or colors, writing or writing one's name, and phonological memory as predictive skills for literacy development. An additional five early literacy skills were identified as potentially important variables, including concepts of print, print knowledge, reading readiness, oral language skills, and visual processing.

Research with bilingual populations supports the importance of these critical dimensions of language and literacy for DLLs in early childhood. The National Literacy Panel on Language Minority Children and Youth (August & Shanahan, 2006) concluded that instruction in the key components of reading, as identified by the National Reading Panel (2000), including phonological and phonemic awareness, phonics, fluency, vocabulary, and text comprehension, has clear benefits for DLLs. However, the reviewers added that

> Instruction in the key components of reading is necessary—but not sufficient—for teaching language-minority children to read and write proficiently in English. Oral proficiency in English is critical as well—but student performance suggests that it is often overlooked in instruction (August & Shanahan, 2006, p. 4).

In light of these findings, oral language skills, including vocabulary and listening comprehension, have received particular attention from both educators and researchers who are trying to meet the learning needs of DLLs. Research with both monolingual and bilingual populations recognizes that vocabulary is one of the best predictors of reading comprehension, that it is a complex construct that has many components, and that it is learned in multiple contexts both at home and at school (August, Carlo, Dressler, & Snow, 2005). Research with DLLs has also identified vocabulary skills as a domain of particular weakness for this population (Carlo et al., 2004).

Findings from a longitudinal study with young Spanish-speaking children from low socioeconomic backgrounds has found that these children might be at risk for delays in their early literacy development due to their poor oral language abilities, particularly their low levels of vocabulary in both languages—English and Spanish (Páez & Rinaldi, 2006; Páez, Tabors, & López, 2007; Tabors, Páez, & López, 2003). Results from this study showed limited English vocabulary skills when children in the sample were first assessed as 4-year-olds, with the gap between monolingual norms and the sample persisting through first grade. These findings are corroborated by other research with young Spanish-speaking children, such as the studies by Lindsey, Manis, and Bailey (2003) and Manis, Lindsey, and Bailey (2004) and research with young Spanish-speaking children from high socioeconomic backgrounds (Umbel, Pearson, Fernández, & Oller, 1992). Moreover, a more recent research review of vocabulary and second language acquisition found that Spanish–English DLLs lag behind their monolingual English-speaking peers in both depth and breadth of vocabulary knowledge (August et al., 2005). Recent comparative research with various bilingual populations also has found this deficit in vocabulary with Hebrew–English, Spanish–English, and Chinese–English bilingual students in first grade (Bialystok, Luk, & Kwan, 2005).

There are two important points to note regarding these research findings on vocabulary development. First, uneven vocabulary knowledge is common for young DLLs during this stage in their development. Second, there is a lack of data disaggregated by socioeconomic status, as the majority of studies have focused on bilingual children from low socioeconomic backgrounds. The language gap experienced by young DLLs could be explained by multiple factors including demographic factors such as living in poverty (Hart & Risley, 1995). The limited research with DLLs from high socioeconomic backgrounds indicates that children catch up to monolingual norms during the elementary grades and some even exceed their monolingual peers' achievements in English (Espinosa, Laffey, & Whittaker, 2006; Umbel et al., 1992). More research is needed to specifically address these underlying factors, such as socioeconomic status, and how they influence literacy learning for DLLs (Hart & Risley, 1995; National Early Literacy Panel, 2008).

In sum, research with DLLs demonstrates the importance of oral language development and supports instructional approaches that focus on developing these skills by providing rich and engaging language environments, while at the same time focusing on building early literacy skills. Therefore, it is essential for quality indicators in early childhood programs to recognize the critical importance of oral language and vocabulary development for successful instruction and literacy development.

The Role of First Language in Learning English

Past research with bilingual populations has supported the interdependency theory, or the notion that first-language skills transfer and support the learning of a second language (Cummins, 1979, 1991; Royer & Carlo, 1991). Although studies on the transfer of reading-related skills from one language to another have not been numerous, the evidence for transfer or cross-language relationships of skills related to reading (i.e., phonology, vocabulary, grammar, and discourse-level skills) between first and second languages has been growing (August & Shanahan, 2006).

Specifically, recent studies with bilingual Spanish–English children have shown transfer in vocabulary (Ordóñez, Carlo, Snow, & McLaughlin, 2002; Snow, 1990) and phonological awareness (Lindsey et al., 2003; López & Greenfield, 2004). Focusing on the phonological awareness of 123 Spanish–English bilingual preschool children attending Head Start, Dickinson, McCabe, Clark-Chiarelli, and Wolf (2004) found that phonological skills were stable across the preschool year and showed transfer across languages. Cross-language effects also have been useful in predicting English reading and comprehension skills (Manis et al., 2004; Proctor, August, Carlo, & Snow, 2006). In addition, longitudinal research with Spanish-speaking bilingual children has shown that first language skills and growth in Spanish contribute to the development of reading skills in English (Hammer, Lawrence, & Miccio, 2007; Páez & Rinaldi, 2006; Rinaldi & Páez, 2008). More research is needed in this area of second language acquisition to better understand which language and early literacy skills do and do not transfer and under what conditions (Snow, 2006). Also, more research focused on preschool-age and younger DLLs would be an important contribution to the literature. New research is further examining the role of early bilingualism on children's cognitive processing (e.g., Bialystok, 2009; Carlson & Choi, 2009; de Villiers, de Villiers, & Hobbs, 2009; Yoshida, 2008). Findings from those studies will help develop a deeper understanding of issues such as cross-linguistic transfer and other aspects of young children's dual language learning processes.

To date, the majority of research on linguistic transfer has been conducted with Spanish-speakers learning English. However, transfer of language and literacy skills might vary according to similarities and differences among linguistic features of the first and second languages (August & Shanahan, 2006). Bialystok et al. (2005) examined these cross-linguistic relationships among bilingual children from different language groups such as Chinese, Spanish, and Hebrew and found that the extent of transfer of these skills depends on the relation between languages and the relation between the writing systems. Additional research including diverse groups of DLLs is needed to increase our understanding of the dynamics of transfer across different language systems.

It also is important to note that most of the studies which document transfer are correlational studies. It could be that what researchers have called transfer of language skills might be due to other underlying competencies that explain the relationships between languages. As noted by Snow (2006), intervention studies designed around the concept of linguistic transfer would be able to provide "stronger proof" for this phenomenon while testing hypotheses to further develop theory (p. 637).

Although more research is needed, there is already some knowledge that can guide the development of high-quality early education programs for DLLs. On the basis of the increasing evidence of linguistic transfer from research studies on language and literacy development, experts believe that approaches that support and develop children' first language skills may have important advantages (Barnett, Yarosz, Thomas, Jung, & Blanco, 2007; Páez, Tabors, & López, 2007; Tabors et al., 2003). Further, the review of research on the relationship between first and second language acquisition by the National Literacy Panel concluded that access to bilingual programming can assist young DLLs in their language and literacy development (August & Shanahan, 2006).

In addition to facilitating English learning, there are many benefits to knowing two (or more) languages and encouraging children to maintain and develop their home language as they learn English. Children who know more than one language have personal, social, cognitive, and economic advantages throughout their lives. Children who are proficient in their home language (or first language) are able "to establish a strong cultural identity, to develop and sustain strong ties with their immediate and extended families, and thrive in a global multilingual world" (Espinosa, 2006, p. 2).

Another important reason for home language support in programs serving young DLLs is the vulnerability of these children to losing their first language. Children develop and learn in their home contexts with family members who foster a sense of identity and belonging through language and communication. As children grow, it is important for them to continue to develop their home language. Children who do not develop and maintain proficiency in their home language may lose their ability to communicate with parents and family members (Wong Fillmore, 1991). In addition, loss of the home language could have a potentially negative impact on children's thinking and reasoning skills as well as on development of their self-concept (Bialystok, 2001). Thus, home language support provides benefits for learning English while promoting and supporting children's development at home.

In sum, definitions and measures of quality in early childhood programs need to consider the special case of DLLs by considering the process of second-language development and learning, and the particular language contexts that promote development and learning for these children.

Elements of High-Quality ECE for DLLs

As noted at the beginning of this chapter, the demographic composition of early childhood programs is changing with increasing enrollment of children who are linguistically and culturally diverse. Although diversity in children's backgrounds can enhance the learning environment, it also can create new or increased challenges to accommodating the needs of a wide variety of children.

Research on early childhood education programs indicates that high-quality early childhood experiences can have positive effects on children's early development and learning (see Snow & Páez, 2004, for a review). Moreover, research has also shown that young children at risk for school failure, such as children from poor and minority backgrounds, are significantly more likely to succeed in school when they have attended high-quality early childhood programs (Bowman, Donovan, & Burns, 2001). It is important to note, however, that much of the research on the long-term effects of high-quality early education has been conducted with children who are not DLLs. For example, the Abecedarian and Perry Preschool studies were primarily conducted with African American children (e.g., Campbell, Ramey, Pungello, Sparling, & Miller-Johnson, 2002; Schweinhart et al., 2005). Furthermore, these early childhood studies were comprehensive interventions that included strong family support and the provision for and access to health care and social services, in addition to high-quality educational practices. Therefore, their positive effects are attributed to all intervention components, making it impossible to untangle the effect of individual components.

Although there is emerging evidence of the positive impact of high-quality early education on Latino children's school readiness (e.g., Gormley & Gayer, 2005), studies focusing on early education practices and their effects on DLLs' development and learning are few, assess a limited set of children's developmental outcomes, and most important, do not use longitudinal designs.

In this section we review the literature on the elements of early childhood quality that can promote development and learning among DLLs, including curriculum and instruction, program and teacher characteristics, and family engagement. It is necessary to acknowledge that most ECE research with this population has been conducted in center-based settings and with preschool-aged children. There is an urgent need to address the gap in knowledge about the early childhood experiences of infants and toddlers who are DLLs and those attending home-based programs.

Curriculum and Instructional Practices

The National Association for the Education of Young Children (NAEYC) and the National Association of Early Childhood Specialists in State Departments of Education (NAECS/SDE) in a joint position statement about early childhood curriculum, assessment, and program evaluation support the recommendation that high-quality early childhood programs use a curriculum that is "thoughtfully planned, challenging, engaging, developmentally appropriate, culturally and linguistically responsive, comprehensive, and likely to promote positive outcomes for all young children" (NAEYC & NAECS/SDE, 2003, p. 2). What does this mean for the early education of DLLs? Early childhood programs that serve DLLs should use research-based curricula and instructional practices that support first and second language and literacy development, incorporate elements of children's diverse cultures and languages into the curricula (Gay, 2000), implement activities that view children's emergent bilingualism as an asset rather than as a deficit, and build on children's prior knowledge (Moll, 2000; Zentella, 2005).

Regarding specific instructional practices, a major research review conducted by the National Literacy Panel on Language-Minority Children and Youth (August & Shanahan, 2006) found that, even though there are instructional practices that are beneficial to both monolingual and bilingual children, they may not be sufficient to support a comparable level of academic success among bilingual children, suggesting that instructional enhancements are needed, particularly in classrooms where instruction is provided only in English (Goldenberg, 2008). Research on effective instructional and intervention practices to promote development and learning in young DLLs is limited when compared with the research that has been conducted with monolingual English-speaking children; however, although more research is required to expand our knowledge, there is a growing body of knowledge that provides a basis for the development of interventions with this population. Key principles that have been found to be effective in promoting DLLs' cognitive, language, literacy, and social–emotional development and learning are presented next.

Creating a Supportive and Organized Early Childhood Environment

It is widely acknowledged in the field of early education that effective practices are those that build on children's previous knowledge and experiences. As stated by NAEYC,

> For the optimal development and learning of all children, educators must accept the legitimacy of the children's home language, respect (hold in high regard) and value (esteem, appreciate) the home culture, and promote and encourage the active involvement and support of all families, including extended and nontraditional family units. (1995, p. 2)

An environment that is supportive of all children's culture and languages is an environment in which educators carefully maintain the cultural continuity between home and the early childhood setting, where children can share and maintain their home culture and language. Ways to put these recommendations into practice include providing books in multiple languages; bilingual posters and labels; bilingual music and audio stories; stories that reflect the diverse cultures of children in the classroom or family care setting; as well as room decorations, toys, and dramatic play materials that represent diversity and create positive self-images for the children in the classroom or family child care setting.

How the classroom or family care setting is organized and managed will influence children's comfort levels and provide an environment that is supportive of development and conducive to learning. There are certain characteristics of the classroom that will be particularly helpful for young DLLs. For example, providing a space where children can go when they feel the need to be by themselves will help young DLLs, who may at times be tense or tired and might want to be alone. The space may have a table with manipulatives or may be a quiet corner with pillows and books. Also, providing consistency in classroom routines will be useful for children who are DLLs, because it will help them follow what is happening in the classroom, even when they may not be able to understand every word the educator or the other children are saying in English. Also, it will help them to develop a sense of belonging with the group in the classroom or family care setting (Castro, Ayankoya, & Kasprzak, 2010; Tabors, 2008).

Positive Educator–Child Interactions

For early educators who are not bilingual, interacting with DLLs may be challenging, especially when these children are at the beginning of the process of learning English. Using gestures, visual aids, and props along with words will help educators in communicating with young DLLs, as well as in building their vocabulary and increasing their comprehension. It is very important for educators to be observant and follow closely children's phases of second language learning so that they can provide the support that is appropriate. For instance, during the early phases in which the child knows no or very little English, using visual aids and speaking the child's primary language have been shown to be important. As children progress to the telegraphic and formulaic stages of English acquisition, repetition and modeling have been recommended (Castro, Gillanders, Machado-Casas, & Buysse, 2006).

Positive educator–child interactions can promote DLLs' socioemotional development, positively affecting the social status of children who are DLLs and their inclusion in the classroom or family care community (Gillanders, 2007). Educators can create positive relationships with young DLLs when they are consistent and firm, and support children's positive behaviors (Howes & Ritchie, 2002). Being purposeful in creating positive educator–child relationships becomes especially important when monolingual English-speaking educators are working with children who are DLLs, because the language barriers can strain such relationships. An important aspect of the educator–child relationship is the interpretation of challenging behaviors. Some common behaviors of DLLs that are related to the process of second language acquisition often are misinterpreted as challenging behaviors (e.g., not talking, difficulty expressing ideas and feelings, difficulty following directions). To the extent that educators understand the process of second language acquisition and learn effective strategies for dealing with challenging behaviors, they will be better able to establish positive relationships with children who are DLLs (Santos & Ostrosky, 2004).

Increased Opportunities for Peer Interactions

Increasing these opportunities has been proposed as a strategy to promote English language learning among DLLs. However, peer interaction studies suggest that "creating such opportunities and producing positive oral language outcomes involve more than simply pairing [DLLs] with native or fluent English speakers" (Saunders & O'Brien, 2006, p. 28). It involves, in addition, planning, which includes identifying specific tasks and preparing both the native English-speaking child and the DLL to participate (e.g., Peck, 1987). An important consideration when planning peer interactions is the developmental phase of second language acquisition of the DLL, so that activities are prepared in a way that will provide a positive and rewarding experience to both children.

Strategic Use of a Child's First Language

Recent research syntheses (August & Shanahan, 2006; Rolstad, Mahoney, & Glass, 2005; Slavin & Cheung, 2005) have found that, for DLLs, teaching reading skills in the first language is more effective in terms of English reading achievement than immersing children in English. As described in previous paragraphs, the use of the primary language in the classroom or family care setting has been found to be related to educators' negative perceptions of children's behavior and social competence (Chang et al., 2007). Instructing DLLs in their primary language will offer them opportunities to have rich language interactions and close relationships with their educators. Educators need to know when, how, and for which purposes to use the primary language in the classroom or family care setting, and that will require competence development and planning. The amount and frequency of primary language use may vary depending on the language(s) of instruction in the early childhood program, but even in programs in which instruction is provided only in English, some use of the primary language should be incorporated to support DLLs (Castro et al., 2006).

Explicit Vocabulary Instruction

As stated earlier in the chapter, vocabulary is a skill essential to becoming a reader. For most English-speaking children, vocabulary learning in English occurs incidentally. For DLLs, vocabulary development in English requires a combination of direct teaching of words and incidental learning that occurs in multiple exposures to words in a variety of meaningful social contexts (Carlo et al., 2004). Therefore, an important enhancement for DLLs in early childhood programs is to use instruction time to address, in the context of play, the meanings of everyday and content words, phrases, and expressions not yet learned. Furthermore, educators can promote vocabulary knowledge strategically by using the children's primary language in storybook reading activities (Gillanders & Castro, 2007). Even if educators are not fluent in the children's primary language, learning and using specific core words in the primary language can further support children's learning of the same concepts in English (Castro et al., 2006).

Ongoing and Frequent Assessments of Children's First and Second Language Development and Other Developmental Domains

Assessments are used to inform instruction and to improve the outcomes for young DLLs. For example, measures of phonological processing, letter and alphabetic knowledge, and the process of second language acquisition can help educators plan specific instructional enhancements, such as the use of extra support in small-group instruction (Lesaux & Siegel, 2003). One of the most serious challenges for conducting valid and reliable assessments of DLLs' development and learning is the lack of appropriate measures (see Espinosa & López, 2007, for a review). Even though some measures are available in Spanish and English, few are available in other languages. Furthermore, among available translated instruments, most have been normed on monolingual speaking populations of the non-English language so that they are not comparable to the experience of bilingual children. There is a need for an array of instruments that can reliably assess DLLs' development for different purposes, including screening, monitoring, and classroom planning. In addition, assessments should be multidimensional, gathering information about the child from different sources and utilizing various methods (e.g., observational, direct child assessments, family reports).

Small-Group and One-to-One Activities

Small-group and one-to-one activities will help provide individual children who are DLLs support according to their specific needs as determined by the assessment results.

Randomized control trials of reading interventions for struggling DLLs in Grades K–5 have indicated that small-group and peer-assisted interventions allow children multiple opportunities to respond to questions, to practice reading skills, and to receive explicit instruction on vocabulary and phonological awareness (e.g., Vaughn et al., 2006; McMaster, Shu-Hsuan Kung, & Cao, 2008). These practices will have to be adapted to meet the developmental needs of young DLLs.

Program Characteristics

As mentioned earlier, the research reviewed in this chapter corresponds mostly to DLLs' experiences in center-based programs. Quality indicators in early childhood care and education include both process and structural elements. *Process quality* focuses on the experiences that occur in the early childhood setting such as provider/teacher–child and peer interactions, and types of activities that have been described in previous paragraphs. *Structural quality* refers to conditions that need to be in place in a program to support the implementation of high-quality practices such as class size, provider/teacher–child ratios, qualifications of educators and staff, and availability of materials (Espinosa, 2002). Research studies have found a relationship between process and structural quality; for example, in small classes educators are more likely to have positive and supportive interactions with children (NICHD, 2002).

Providing high-quality early education experiences to young DLLs will require a revision of the indicators of quality being used. Regarding structural quality, adult–child ratios may need to be smaller to allow educators time to conduct small-group and one-on-one activities with DLLs. Also, to implement classroom activities in the children's primary language, to conduct valid and reliable assessments in children's primary language and English, and to plan activities that are responsive to young DLLs' individual developmental and learning needs, programs will need to increase the number of bilingual and qualified staff, as well as offer ongoing professional development. The availability of appropriate teaching resources (e.g., written and audio materials in DLLs' primary languages and English; props; pictures) to work with DLLs is also an important condition. Also, the implementation of outreach and communication strategies that take into account families' diverse cultures and languages will be facilitated by the availability of bilingual, bicultural, qualified staff.

Early Educator Knowledge and Skills

National professional organizations are increasingly acknowledging the importance of specific instructional practices to address cultural and linguistic diversity in early childhood care and education, emphasizing diversity as an important element of quality programs (Association for Childhood Education International, 2006; Hyson, 2003; NAEYC, 1995; NCATE, 2008). Professional organizations have concluded that to be effective educators of DLLs, educators need to be knowledgeable in five major content areas: 1) understanding the structural aspects of language development (e.g., syntax, phonology) and the development of both the first and the second language; 2) understanding the role of culture and its linkage to language development; 3) acquiring knowledge and developing skills about effective instructional practices to promote development and learning in DLLs; 4) understanding the role of assessment and how to implement appropriate assessment strategies with DLLs; and 5) understanding the teacher's role as a professional in the education of DLLs (Zepeda, Castro, & Cronin, 2010).

In order to plan and implement instructional activities that are effective in promoting DLLs' development, educators need to know how language and literacy development unfolds in children growing up in bilingual environments and how the process of learning a second language affects young children's social-emotional and cognitive development. Also, in order to meet the needs of DLLs, educators must be effective in making cultural and linguistic enhancements to the curriculum when teaching the various content areas and must have the ability to conduct assessments that provide valid and reliable information about these children's developmental levels and school readiness. In addition, educators must demonstrate a caring attitude and high expectations toward DLLs' academic learning (Castro et al., 2006).

Family Engagement

The importance of developing strong partnerships with families is recognized widely in the field of early education (e.g., Henderson & Berla, 1994; Marcon, 1999; Miedel & Reynolds, 1999). Providing high-quality early education to DLLs implies that there is a strong connection between DLLs' experiences in the early childhood setting and at home. Families' child-rearing beliefs and practices will influence the ways in which children are socialized and supported at home; for children from diverse cultural and linguistic backgrounds, it becomes essential that educators learn about their families' child-rearing beliefs and practices, which may be different from those of children in the mainstream. In high-quality early childhood settings, educators engage in a dialogue with the families, understand families' expectations, and effectively communicate program and educator expectations with regard to children's learning and families' support of their children's early development and education (Delgado-Gaitán, 2004; Reese & Gallimore, 2000). Families are able to participate on their own terms and are willing to incorporate new activities into their daily routines related to what their children learn in the classroom. Some challenges to engaging families of DLLs include the lack of bilingual staff, differences in communication styles, as well as differences in families' expectations about their children's development and learning.

When teaching children who are DLLs in an English-dominant environment, the building of family–school partnerships becomes especially critical, because the family can provide first language support that children may not receive at school. One way of garnering this support is by providing academic learning materials in the primary language that families can use with children at home. Several intervention studies have found that sending literacy materials to families' homes can increase the frequency of literacy events and, in turn, the literacy achievement of young DLLs (e.g., Goldenberg, Reese, & Gallimore, 1992; Hancock, 2002).

Measures that Capture Quality of ECE Practices for Dual Language Learners

As previously described, ECE quality measures which adequately assess practices that promote DLLs' development and learning will need to address specific dimensions of the learning environment that have been shown to be important for this population.

The program characteristics, early childhood program staffing, educator qualifications and characteristics, as well as certain instructional and assessment practices that are best suited for DLLs may vary from those identified as significant for monolingual English-speaking populations. In particular, dimensions of environmental and structural quality (e.g., physical and material environment, child–staff ratios, staff qualifications, collaboration with parents), as well as dimensions of curriculum and teaching (e.g., language of interactions and instruction, support of primary language of child, assessment practices, individualization of instruction) will need to be adapted. Whereas traditional ECE quality measures capture those dimensions that have been linked to language and literacy outcomes for monolingual English speakers (see Neuman & Carta, Chapter 4, this volume) only a handful of measures has been designed or adapted for early childhood settings that include DLLs.

On the basis of the preceding literature review and recent research reports, we conclude that the following features of quality ECE practices are important for young DLLs:

1. Classroom and family care environments that incorporate the cultures and languages of the children enrolled (e.g., print, books, posters, pictures, stories that reflect the languages and cultures of the children)

2. Educators and related staff who are fluent in the children's primary languages and familiar with the family cultural beliefs, practices, and values

3. Educators and related staff who are knowledgeable about first and second language development and instructional practices that promote both maintenance of home language and English acquisition

4. Amount and type of support for primary language development

5. The quantity and quality of language interactions (e.g., language of interaction, educator responsiveness to child language initiation, richness and context of interactions)

6. Amount and nature of explicit instruction in English language acquisition (e.g., targeted vocabulary instruction; storybook reading; use of cues, props, and gestures; scaffolding of existing knowledge for DLLs)

7. Educators' ability to adapt level of English instruction according to knowledge of child's stage of English acquisition

8. Opportunities and support for DLLs to communicate in their home language

9. Positive educator–child interactions that support the social-emotional development of children who are DLLs

10. Arrangements for small-group and individualized instruction

11. Active teacher support for peer social interactions

12. Appropriate and multidimensional assessments (e.g., observational, direct child assessments, family reports) conducted frequently in both the home language and English

13. Educators' knowledge of each child's early language learning background (e.g., first language spoken to child, by whom, extent of English exposure and usage)

14. Linguistically and culturally appropriate outreach to, and engagement of, families

There are few, if any, valid and reliable ECE quality measures that incorporate these dimensions for DLLs. Whereas many measures that have been commonly used in the past 15 years do address some of these quality dimensions in general—for example, opportunities for small-group and individualized instruction, and level of emotional responsiveness (see the description of CLASS that follows)—these measures do not specifically address the quality enhancements that have been shown to be important for DLLs. Several current measures that are in development or are being validated for dual language populations are addressed next.

Early Language and Literacy Classroom Observation Addendum for English Language Learners

This Early Language and Literacy Classroom Observation (ELLCO; Castro, 2005) adaptation was designed to "obtain information about specific classroom practices related to promoting language and literacy development among children who are English Language Learners" (Castro, 2005, p. 2). The ELLCO Addendum focuses specifically on Latino DLLs who speak Spanish as their primary language. It has 10 items in a Literacy Environment Checklist that rates the amount and quality of literacy materials (e.g., books, tapes, word cards, puzzles, labels, posters) available in Spanish and English in the classroom, eight classroom observational items, and eight items on Literacy Activities (e.g., book reading) that rate the appropriateness of the classroom environment and curriculum for DLLs.

This measure was designed as a complement to the ELLCO for classrooms that had children who were DLLs; each item should be completed first for the ELLCO, then for the ELLCO Addendum, with the same scoring procedures. The classroom observational items are based on corresponding items for the ELLCO and are scored on a five-point scale anchored by ratings of 1 (*deficient*), 3 (*basic*), and 5 (*exemplary*). The ELLCO Addendum was used in a randomized, control, intervention study of teacher professional development called the *Nuestros Niños Early Language and Literacy Project*. The ELLCO Addendum was able to detect significant changes in teacher practices related to supporting preschool Spanish-speaking DLLs' language and literacy development (Buysse, Castro, & Peisner-Feinberg, 2010) that could be attributable to the professional development intervention implemented.

The internal reliability of the ELLCO Addendum derived from the initial study appears quite high, ranging from 91.1% (Classroom Observation Scale) to 100% (Literacy Activities Rating scale). Internal consistency is .78 for the Classroom Observation Scale, 0.57 for the Literacy Environment Checklist, and .30 for the Literacy Activities Rating Scale. At this time, we do not know how well this measure predicts short-term or long-term child outcomes for Spanish-speaking DLLs.

The Language Interaction Snapshot

The Language Interaction Snapshot (LISn) (Sprachman, Caspe, & Atkins-Burnett, 2009) is a time-sampling classroom observation tool that captures the extent to which English or other languages are used in conversations between adults and children. The observation items focus on what language educators use with children in the classroom, the types of language interactions across settings, and which adults interact with DLLs. The LISn specifically addresses four aspects of verbal interactions: 1) language use, 2) child initiation of language use and teacher response, 3) types of adult utterances, and 4) language context. The language codes include the extent to which an educator repeats or confirms child talk and responds to child language; the types of language used by the teacher (e.g., requests, gives directions, provides information contextualized or decontextualized); and whether the language context is reading, singing, or other.

Classroom observers code language interactions at the utterance level for a 20-second period over 10 intervals. Interrater reliability of the LISn was strong in the pilot study, ranging from 85% to 96% across the separate components. The pilot study was conducted in two large urban areas and included 117 children in 44 classrooms. The DLLs in the samples came from both Spanish-speaking and Cantonese-speaking homes. Preliminary analyses of the pilot data suggest strong internal consistency of the measure. Further analyses of the pilot data will examine the relationship of teacher language interactions and child outcomes associated with school readiness.

Observation Measures of Language and Literacy: Quality Rating of Language and Literacy Instruction, Classroom Literacy Opportunities Checklist, Snapshot

The Observational Measures of Language and Literacy (OMLIT)-Quality of Instruction in Literacy and Language (QUILL) (Goodson, Layzer, Smith, & Rimdzius, 2006) is one of the six instruments included in the OMLIT; the total group of instruments was designed as a battery of measures that captured the instructional practices and environmental supports for language and literacy in early childhood classrooms. The OMLIT-QUILL, OMLIT-CLOC, and the OMLIT-Snapshot contain items that focus on the classroom quality for DLLs. Specifically, the OMLIT-QUILL has 4 out of 10 items that address DLLs' needs. The 10 items address the following areas (DLL items in bold):

- Opportunities to engage in writing
- Attention to and promotion of letter and word knowledge
- Opportunities for and encouragement of use of oral language to communicate ideas and thoughts
- Attention to the functions and features of print
- Attention to sounds in words throughout the day
- Attention to and promotion of print motivation
- **DLLs intentionally included in activities, conversations**
- **Development of both primary language(s) and English supported for children who are DLLs**
- **Primary language(s) of young DLLs integrated into language and literacy activities**
- **Language and literacy materials and methods appropriate for children who are DLLs**
- Opportunities for dramatic play and play planning
- Integration of children with special needs into the classroom

The OMLIT-CLOC includes a question on whether there is cultural diversity in literacy materials, and the OMLIT-Snapshot includes a question on whether adults and children are speaking in English or another language. In addition, the OMLIT Classroom Description asks the observer to indicate the proportion of time English, Spanish, or another language was used during instruction with the children. The observer also indicates whether there was at least one adult in the classroom who spoke the language of every child. This group of instruments was designed as a research tool and has been used in several large child care, pre-K, and Even Start studies. The interrater reliability of the OMLIT-QUILL for the four items focusing on activities for young DLLs has not been calculated. The validity of the OMLIT is based on experts' opinion; Abt Associates convened a conference on measuring the quality of language and literacy instruction in early childhood programs in 2003, and items on the OMLIT were derived from the research presented at that conference.

Classroom Assessment of Supports for Emergent Bilingual Acquisition

The Classroom Assessment of Supports for Emergent Bilingual Acquisition (CASEBA) (National Institute for Early Education Research, 2005) is a newly developed research tool designed to assess the degree to which preschool teachers and classrooms are providing support for the social, cognitive, and linguistic development of DLLs (or ELLs), with a focus on language and literacy. Based on an earlier instrument, the Support for Early Language Learners Classroom Assessment (SELLCA; National Institute for Early Education Research, 2005), the CASEBA has been revised to better assess teacher and classroom supports for both first and second language acquisition. The instrument consists of 26 rating scale items that cluster around six broad aspects of the early childhood curriculum: 1) collection of child background information, 2) supports for home language development, 3) supports for English acquisition, 4) social-emotional supports and classroom management, 5) curriculum content, and 6) assessment. Each of the 26 items measures one component of a high-quality classroom environment and instruction on the basis of research about effective language and emergent literacy supports for 3- to 5-year-old children who speak a language other than English at home, and who are in the process of acquiring English as a second language. Each item is rated on a 7-point Likert scale, on which 7 indicates that a specific form of support and accompanying practices are present in a nearly ideal form, whereas 1 represents the total absence of any such practices. The CASEBA currently is undergoing research on the psychometric properties of the instrument, including concurrent and predictive validity. Results from this research are expected by the end of 2010.

The CASEBA is designed to be used by researchers trained to reliability by the developers and is not publicly available. The developers are completing the design of a complementary instrument to be used for systematic professional development that involves self-assessment and coaching. The coaching follows a specific protocol that researchers at the National Institute for Early Education Research (NIEER) used in previous professional development research in math, literacy, and other domains, based on the cognitive coaching cycle (Costa & Garmston, 2002). The NIEER version of this cycle begins with teachers' self-assessment of their teaching practices, using the CASEBA Checklist for Professional Development. The Checklist includes criteria for self-assessment that complement the full research instrument, but call for teachers and coaches to provide specific evidence that a particular criterion has been met. The teacher and coach review the results and set specific objectives for improvement. Within each coaching session, a similar cycle is followed with a planning conference to review focus areas, an observation by the coach, and a review of the observation with specific plans for improvement. In some cases, the coach teaches alongside the teacher if understanding a specific technique is an objective of the session. A heavy emphasis of the coaching is to focus on children's activities and what they imply for the child's understanding and for further teaching.

Some measures developed to assess the quality of practices, without particular emphasis on DLLs (e.g., CLASS and ECERS-R), have been commonly used during the last 15 years in early childhood settings serving the DLL population. They provide useful information about overall classroom quality, although they may lack the specificity that we are arguing is necessary in order to fully capture the extent to which early childhood practices address the needs of children who are DLLs. Next, we describe, as an example, one of the measures that is being studied and that should yield results about its appropriateness for DLLs by end of 2010.

Classroom Assessment Scoring System™

The Classroom Assessment Scoring System™ (CLASS) (Pianta, La Paro, & Hamre, 2008) assesses three domains of child–teacher interactions: social-emotional, organization/management, and instructional. The focus of this observational measure is both on what the teachers do with the materials that they have and on child–teacher interactions. The CLASS™ has four scales: 1) emotional support for children (e.g., class climate, teacher sensitivity, regard for student perspectives), 2) organization of the classroom (e.g., learning format used, time use and productivity, behavior management), 3) support for instruction (e.g., level of concept development, quality of feedback to children, modeling of language), and 4) student engagement. Trained observers rate pre-K classrooms on nine dimensions of child–teacher interactions every 30 minutes during a typical morning. The interrater reliability of trained CLASS observers is reported as 87%. The support for instruction scale was the most robust predictor of children's growth over time, whereas the CLASS emotional support scale was associated with growth in children's expressive and receptive language scores. Although the CLASS has been used widely in large national studies of pre-K classroom quality (Early et al., 2005) and has shown relationships to important child outcomes on tests of language and literacy for English speakers, its utility for DLL populations is still under investigation.

An ongoing study (2010) is examining how well the CLASS functions for classrooms heavily populated with Spanish-speaking DLLs and the extent to which the CLASS is associated with DLL school outcomes assessed in both English and Spanish. The study is part of the National Center for Early Development and Learning's (NCEDL) Multi-State Study of Pre-Kindergarten, and the NCEDL–NIEER State-Wide Early Education Programs Study that included 2,966 children, 23% of whom spoke Spanish. A preliminary analysis of the data shows that the CLASS operated similarly in classrooms with 75% or more young DLLs and those with 74% or fewer. The means, standard deviations, and internal consistencies for each of the scales (i.e., emotional support, classroom organization, and instructional support) were not significantly different across classrooms. Additional analyses will examine the extent to which the CLASS is associated with the school readiness of children who are DLLs.

Summary

Our professional knowledge about the features of early childhood programs that are essential to the growth and development of young DLLs has grown rapidly in the last decade—and continues to be the focus of ongoing research. Concurrently, our early childhood programs are experiencing rapid growth in the numbers and proportions of children participating who are not native English speakers. The most recent achievement data continue to reveal the chronic academic vulnerability of children who are challenged with learning a new language while also mastering cognitive and academic content. As our knowledge about high-quality early childhood practices for young DLLs grows, so must our ability to accurately capture the adequacy of ECE settings. Whereas all of the quality measures described herein show promise for capturing the quality of ECE practices for DLLs, none adequately measures all of the dimensions that have been shown to be important for this population and are available for program evaluation.

Future research and development efforts will need to focus on the qualifications and characteristics of early childhood educators that are linked to effective practices for young DLLs, the methods programs employ to involve and engage families who speak a language other than English in the home, specific instructional enhancements important for children who are DLLs (e.g., more individual and small-group instruction, presentation of material in child's home language prior to presenting it in English, teacher scaffolding of concepts and explicit teaching of vocabulary and literacy skills, adapting expectations and scaffolds on the basis of the child's stage of English acquisition, amount of support for home language), and linguistically and culturally appropriate assessment approaches. Some measures appear quite promising, but have yet to be used in large-scale program evaluations. Others, such as the CLASS, may be suitable for DLL populations, but have yet to be rigorously tested with this group of children. In addition, we need to develop and validate quality assessment tools that can work in family and home care settings for children who are DLLs.

From the information and discussion presented in this chapter, it seems appropriate to conclude that the definition of high-quality practices in ECE programs needs to be expanded to incorporate practices that directly address the needs of the growing numbers of young DLLs attending these programs. As emerging research findings suggest (Buysse et al., 2010), improving the quality of practices to support young DLL's language and literacy development will improve the overall quality of practices, thus benefiting *all* children.

References

Association for Childhood Education International (ACEI). (2006). *Global guidelines for early childhood education and care in the 21st century.* Olney, MD: Author. Retrieved September 10, 2008, from http:// www.udel.edu/ bateman/acei/wguides.htm

August, D., Carlo, M., Dressler, C., & Snow, C.E. (2005). The critical role of vocabulary development for English language learners. *Learning Disabilities Research and Practice, 20*(1), 50–57.

August, D., & Hakuta, K. (Eds.). (1997). Improving schooling for language-minority children. A research agenda. Washington, DC: National Academies Press.

August, D., & Shanahan, T. (Eds.). (2006). *Developing literacy in second-language learners: Report of the National Literacy Panel on Language-Minority Children and Youth.* Mahwah, NJ: Lawrence Erlbaum Associates.

Barnett, W.S., Yarosz, D.J., Thomas, J., Jung, K., & Blanco, D. (2007). Two-way and monolingual English immersion in preschool education: An experimental comparison. *Early Childhood Research Quarterly, 22*(3), 277–293.

Bialystok, E. (2001). *Bilingualism in development: Language, literacy & cognition.* Cambridge, England: Cambridge University Press.

Bialystok, E. (2009). Claiming evidence from non-evidence: A reply to Morton and Harper. *Developmental Science, 12*(4), 499–450.

Bialystok, E., Luk, G., & Kwan, E. (2005). Bilingualism, biliteracy, and learning to read: Interactions among languages and writing systems. *Scientific Studies of Reading, 9*(1), 43–61.

Bowman, B.T., Donovan, M.S., & Burns, M.S. (Eds.). (2001). *Eager to learn: Educating our preschoolers.* Washington, DC: National Academies Press.

Brisk, M.E., & Harrington, M.M. (2007). *Literacy and bilingualism: A handbook for all teachers* (2nd Ed.). Mahwah, NJ: Lawrence Erlbaum Associates.

Buysse, V., Castro, D.C., & Peisner-Feinberg, E. (2010). Effects of a professional development program on classroom practices and outcomes for Latino English language learners. *Early Childhood Research Quarterly, 25,* 194–206.

Buysse, V., Castro, D.C., West, T., & Skinner, M. (2005). Addressing the needs of Latino children: A national survey of state administrators of early childhood programs. *Early Childhood Research Quarterly, 20,* 146–163.

Campbell, F.A., Ramey, C.T., Pungello, E.P., Sparling, J., & Miller-Johnson, S. (2002). Early childhood education: Young adult outcomes from the Abecedarian Project. *Applied Developmental Science, 6,* 42–57.

Carlson, S.M., & Choi, H.P. (2009, April). Bilingual and bicultural: Executive function in Korean and American children. Paper presented at the 2009 biennial meeting of the Society for Research in Child Development, Denver, Colorado.

Capps, R., Fix, M., Murray, J., Ost, J., Passel, J.S., & Herwantoro, S. (2005). *The new demography of America's schools: Immigration and the No Child Left Behind Act.* Washington DC: Urban Institute.

Capps, R., Fix, M., Ost, J., Reardon-Anderson, J., & Passel, J.S. (2004). *The health and well-being of young children of immigrants.* Washington DC: Urban Institute.

Carlo, M.S., August, D., McLaughlin, B., Snow, C.E., Dressler, C., Lippman, D., et. al. (2004). Closing the gap: Addressing the vocabulary needs for English language learners in bilingual and mainstream classrooms. *Reading Research Quarterly, 39,* 188–215.

Castro, D.C. (2005). *Early Language and Literacy Classroom Observation: Addendum for English language learners.* Chapel Hill, NC: The University of North Carolina, FPG Child Development Institute.

Castro, D.C., Ayankoya, B., & Kasprzak, C. (2010). *New Voices ~ Nuevas Voces guide to cultural and linguistic diversity in early childhood.* Baltimore: Paul H. Brookes Publishing Co.

Castro, D.C., Gillanders, C., Machado-Casas, M., & Buysse, V. (2006). *Nuestros Niños Early Language and Literacy Program.* Chapel Hill, NC: University of North Carolina, FPG Child Development Institute.

Chang, F., Crawford, G., Early, D., Bryant, D., Howes, C., Burchinal, M., et al. (2007). Spanish-speaking children's social and language development in pre-kindergarten classrooms. *Journal of Early Education and Development, 18*(2), 243–269.

Costa, A., & Garmsten, R. (2002). *Cognitive coaching: A foundation for Renaissance schools.* Norwood, MA: Christopher-Gordon Publishers.

Cummins, J. (1979). Linguistic interdependence and the educational development of bilingual children. *Review of Educational Research, 49*(2), 222–251.

Cummins, J. (1991). The development of bilingual proficiency from home to school: A longitudinal study of Portuguese-speaking children. *Journal of Education, 173,* 85–98.

Delgado-Gaitán, C. (2004). *Involving Latino families in schools: Raising student achievement through home–school partnerships.* Thousand Oaks, CA: Corwin Press.

de Villiers, P., de Villiers, J.G., & Hobbs, K. (2009, April). False belief reasoning in low-income bilingual preschoolers: Is there an effect of bilingualism? Paper presented at the 2009 biennial meeting of the Society for Research in Child Development, Denver, Colorado.

Dickinson, D.K., McCabe, A., Clark-Chiarelli, N., & Wolf, A. (2004). Cross-language transfer of phonological awareness in low-income Spanish and English bilingual preschool children. *Applied Psycholinguistics, 25,* 323–347.

Dickinson, D.K., & Neuman, S.B. (2006). *Handbook of early literacy research: Volume II.* New York: Guilford Press.

Dickinson, D.K., & Tabors, P.O. (Eds.). (2001). *Beginning literacy with language: Young children learning at home and school.* Baltimore: Paul H. Brookes Publishing Co.

Early, D., Barbarin, O., Bryant, B., Burchinal, M., Chang, F., Clifford, R., et al. (2005). Pre-kindergarten in eleven states: NCEDL's multi-state study of pre-kindergarten and state-wide early education programs (SWEEP) study. Retrieved December 1, 2005, from http://www.fpg.unc.edu/~ncedl/pdfs/SWEEP_MS_summary_final.pdf

Espinosa, L.M. (2002). High-quality preschool: Why we need it and what it looks like. Preschool Policy Matters. Policy Brief. Issue 1, November. New Brunswick, NJ: National Institute for Early Education Research.

Espinosa, L.M. (2006, Fall). Young English language learners in the U.S. *Parents as Teacher News, 2.*

Espinosa, L., Laffey, J., & Whittaker, T. (2006). *Language minority children analysis: Focus on technology use.* Final report published by CREST/NCES in 2006.

Espinosa, L.M., & López, M. (2007). Assessment consideration for young English language learners across different levels of accountability. Paper prepared for the National Early Childhood Accountability Task Force and First 5 LA.

Gay, G. (2000). *Culturally responsive teaching: Theory, research, & practice.* New York: Teachers College Press.

Genesee, F., Lindholm-Leary, K., Saunders, W., & Christina, D.(2005). English language learners in U.S. Schools: An Overview of Research. Journal of Education for Students Placed at Risk, *10*(4), 363–385.

Gillanders, C. (2007). An English-speaking prekindergarten teacher for young Latino children: Implications for the teacher–child relationship on second language learning. *Early Childhood Education Journal, 35*(1), 47–54.

Gillanders, C., & Castro. D. (2007, fall). Reading aloud to English language learners. *Children and Families, the Magazine of the National Head Start Association, 21*(3), 12–14.

Goldenberg, C. (2008, Summer). Teaching English language learners. What the research does—and does not—say. *American Educator, 32*(2), 8–44.

Goldenberg, C., Reese, L., & Gallimore, R. (1992). Effects of literacy materials from school on Latino children's home experiences and early reading achievement. *American Journal of Education, 100*(4), 497–536.

Goodson, B.D., Layzer, C.J., Smith, W.C., & Rimdzius, T. (2006). *Observation Measures of Language and Literacy Instruction in Early Childhood (OMLIT).* Cambridge, MA: Abt Associates.

Gormley, W., & Gayer, T. (2005, *Summer*). Promoting school readiness in Oklahoma: An evaluation of Tulsa's pre-K program. *Journal of Human Resources, 40(3),* 533–558.

Hammer, C.S., Lawrence, F.R., & Miccio, A.W. (2007). Bilingual children's language abilities and early reading outcomes in Head Start and kindergarten. *Language, Speech, and Hearing Services in Schools,* 38, 237–248.

Hancock, D.R. (2002). The effects of native language books on the pre-literacy skill development of language minority kindergartners. *Journal of Research in Childhood Education, 17*(1), 62–68.

Hart, B., & Risley, T.R. (1995). *Meaningful differences in the everyday experience of young American children.* Baltimore: Paul H. Brookes Publishing Co.

Henderson, A.T., & Berla, N. (1994). *A new generation of evidence: The family is critical to student achievement.* Washington, DC: National Committee for Citizens in Education.

Hernandez, D.J., Denton, N.A., & Macartney, S.E. (2008). Children in immigrant families: Looking to America's future. *Social Policy Report,* 21, 3–22.

Howes, C., & Ritchie, S. (2002). *A matter of trust.* New York: Teachers College Press.

Hyson, M. (2003). *Preparing early childhood professionals: NAEYC's standards for programs.* Washington, DC: NAEYC.

Kindler, A. (2002). *Survey of the states' limited English proficient students and available educational programs and services, 2000–2001: Summary report.* Washington, DC: National Clearinghouse for English Language Acquisition and Language Instruction Educational Programs.

Knapp, M.S., & Woolverton, S. (2003). Social class and schooling. In J.A. Banks & C.A.M. Banks (Eds.), *Handbook of research on multicultural education* (2nd ed., pp. 656–681). San Francisco: Jossey Bass.

Lesaux, N.K., & Siegel, L.S. (2003). The development of reading in children who speak English as a second language. *Developmental Psychology, 39*(6), 1005–1019.

Lindholm-Leary, K., & Borsato, G. (2007). Academic achievement. In F. Genesee,

K. Lindholm-Leary, W.M. Saunders, & D. Christian (Eds.), *Educating English language learners: A synthesis of research evidence* (pp. 176–222). Cambridge, UK: Cambridge University Press.

Lindsey, K.A., Manis, F. R., & Bailey, C. E. (2003). Prediction of first-grade reading in Spanish-speaking English language learners. *Journal of Educational Psychology, 95*(3), 482–494.

López, L.M., & Greenfield, D.B. (2004). The cross-language transfer of phonological skills of Hispanic Head Start children. *Bilingual Research Journal, 28*(1), 1–18.

Manis, F.R., Lindsey, K.A., & Bailey, C.E. (2004). Development of reading in grades K–2 in Spanish-speaking English language learners. *Learning Disabilities Research and Practice, 19*(4), 214–224.

Marcon, R.A. (1999). Positive relationships between parent school involvement and public school inner-city preschoolers' development and academic performance. *The School Psychology Review, 28*(3), 395–412.

Matthews, H., & Ewen, D. (2006). *Reaching all children? Understanding early care and education participation among immigrant families.* Washington, DC: Center for Law and Social Policy (CLASP).

Maxwell, K.L., Lim, C.-I., & Early, D.M. (2006). *Early childhood teacher preparation programs in the United States: National report.* Chapel Hill, NC: The University of North Carolina, FPG Child Development Institute.

McMaster, K.L., Shu-Hsuan Kung, I.H., & Cao, M. (2008). Peer-assisted learning strategies: A "Tier 1 "approach to promoting English learners' response to intervention. *Exceptional Children, 74*(2), 194–214.

Menken, K., & Antunez, B., with Dilworth, M.E., & Yasin, S. (2001, June). *An overview of the preparation and certification of teachers working with limited English proficient (LEP) students.* National Clearinghouse for Bilingual Education. Retrieved December 14, 2003, from http://www.usc.edu/dept/education/CMMR/FullText/teacherprep.pdf

Miedel, W.T., & Reynolds, A.J. (1999). Parent involvement in early intervention for disadvantaged children: Does it matter? Chicago Longitudinal Study. *Journal of School Psychology, 37*(4), 379–402.

Moll, L.C. (2000). The diversity of schooling: A cultural historical approach. In M. Reyes &

J. Halcón (Eds.), *The best for our children: Latino researchers on literacy.* NY: Teachers College Press.

National Association for the Education of Young Children. (1995). *Responding to linguistic and cultural diversity: Recommendations for effective early childhood education.* Washington, DC: Author.

National Association for the Education of Young Children & National Association of Early Childhood Specialists in State Departments of Education. (2003). *Early childhood curriculum, assessment and program evaluation: Building an effective, accountable system in programs for children birth through age 8.* Joint Position Statement. Washington, DC: National Association for the Education of Young Children.

National Center for Children in Poverty. (2007). *Low-income children in the United States: National and sale trend data, 1996–2006.* New York: Author. Retrieved June 13, 2008, from http://www.nccp.org/publications/pdf/text_761.pdf

National Early Literacy Panel. (2008). *Developing early literacy: Report of the National Early Literacy Panel.* Washington, DC: National Institute for Literacy.

National Institute for Early Education Research. (2005). *Support for English language learners classroom assessment.* New Brunswick, NJ: Author.

National Reading Panel. (2000). *Teaching children to read: An evidence-based assessment of the scientific research literature on reading and its implications for reading instruction.* Washington, DC: National Institute for Literacy.

NCATE. (2008). *Professional standards for the accreditation of teacher preparation instruction.* Washington, DC: Author.

NICHD Early Child Care Research Network. (2002). Early child care and children's development prior to school entry: Results from the NICHD Study of Early Child Care. *American Educational Research Journal, 39*, 133–164.

Office of Head Start. (2007). *Dual language learning: What does it take?* Washington, DC: Administration for Children and Families, U.S. Department of Health and Human Services.

Ordóñez, C.L., Carlo, M.S., Snow, C.E., & McLaughlin, B. (2002). Depth and breadth of vocabulary in two languages: Which vocabulary skills transfer? *Journal of Educational Psychology, 94*(4), 719–728.

Páez, M., & Rinaldi, C. (2006). Predicting English word reading skills for Spanish-speaking students in first grade. *Topics in Language Disorders, 26*(4), 338–350.

Páez, M., Tabors, P.O., & López, L.M. (2007). Dual language and literacy development of Spanish-speaking preschool children. *Journal of Applied Developmental Psychology, 28*(2), 85–102.

Peck, S. (1987). Signs of learning: Child nonnative speakers in tutoring sessions with a child native speaker. *Language Learning, 37*(4), 545–571.

Pew Hispanic Center. (2009). *Statistical portrait of Hispanics in the United States, 2007.* Washington, DC: Author.

Pianta, R.C., La Paro, K.M., & Hamre, B.K. (2008). *Classroom Assessment Scoring System™.* (CLASS™) Baltimore: Paul H. Brookes Publishing Co.

Proctor, C.P., August, D., Carlo, M., & Snow, C.E. (2006). The intriguing role of Spanish language vocabulary knowledge in predicting English reading comprehension. *Journal of Educational Psychology, 98*(1), 159–169.

Reese, L.J., & Gallimore, R. (2000). Immigrant Latinos' cultural model of literacy development: An evolving perspective on home–school discontinuities. *American Journal of Education, 108*(2), 103–134.

Rinaldi, C., & Páez, M. (2008). Preschool matters: Predicting reading difficulties for Spanish-speaking students in first grade. *Learning Disabilities: A Contemporary Journal, 6*(1), 71–84.

Rolstad, K., Mahoney, K., & Glass, G.V. (2005). The big picture: A meta-analysis of program effectiveness research on English language learners. *Educational Policy, 19*(4), 1–23.

Royer, J.M., & Carlo, M.S. (1991). Transfer of comprensión skills from native to second language. *Journal of Reading, 34*(6), 450–455.

Saunders, W.M., & O'Brien, G. (2006). Oral language. In F. Genesee, K. Lindholm-Leary, W.M. Saunders, & D. Christian (Eds.), *Educating English language learners: A synthesis of research evidence* (pp. 14–63). New York: Cambridge University Press.

Schweinhart, L.J., Montie, J., Xiang, Z., Barnett, W.S., Belfield, C.R., & Nores, M. (2005). *Lifetime effects: The HighScope Perry Preschool study through age 40.* (Monographs of the HighScope Educational Research Foundation, Ypsilanti, MI: HighScope Press.

Slavin, R., & Cheung, A. (2005). A synthesis of research of reading instruction for English language learners, *Review of Educational Research 75*(2), 247–284.

Snow, C.E. (1990). The development of definitional skill. *Journal of Child Language, 17*(3), 697–710.

Snow, C.E. (2006). Cross-cutting themes and future research directions. In D. August & T. Shanahan (Eds.), *Developing literacy in second-language learners: Report of the National Literacy Panel on Language-Minority Children and Youth.* Mahwah, NJ: Lawrence Erlbaum Associates.

Snow, C.E., Burns, M.S., & Griffin, P. (Eds.). (1998). *Preventing reading difficulties in young children.* Washington, DC: National Academies Press.

Snow, C.E., & Páez, M. (2004). The Head Start classroom as an oral language environment: What should the performance standards be? In E. Zigler & , S. Styfco (Eds.), *The Head Start Debates* (pp. 113–128). Baltimore: Paul H. Brookes Publishing Co.

Sprachman, S., Caspe, M., & Atkins-Burnett, S. (2009). *Language Interaction Snapshot (LISn) Field Procedures and Coding Guide.* Princeton, NJ: Mathematica Policy Research.

Tabors, P.O. (2008). *One child, two languages: A guide for early childhood educators of children learning English as a second language* (2nd ed.). Baltimore: Paul H. Brookes Publishing Co.

Tabors, P.O., Páez, M., & López, L.M. (2003). Dual language abilities of Spanish–English bilingual four-year olds: Initial finding from the Early Childhood Study of Language and Literacy Development of Spanish-speaking Children. *NABE Journal of Research and Practice, 1,* 70–91.

Tabors, P.O., & Snow, C.E. (2002). Young bilingual children and early literacy development. In S.B. Neuman & D.K. Dickinson (Eds.), *Handbook of Early Literacy Research* (pp. 159–178). New York: The Guilford Press.

Umbel, V.M., Pearson, B.Z., Fernández, M.C., & Oller, D.K. (1992). Measuring bilingual children's receptive vocabularies. *Child Development, 63*(4), 1012–1020.

Vaughn, S., Matches, P.G., Linan-Thompson, S., Cirino, P.T., Carlson, C.D., Pollard-Durodola, S.D., et al. (2006). First-grade English language learners at- risk for reading problems: Effectiveness of an English intervention. *Elementary School Journal, 107,* 153–180.

Wong Fillmore, L. (1991). When learning a second language means losing the first. *Early Childhood Research Quarterly, 6,* 323–347.

Yoshida, H. (2008). The cognitive consequences of early bilingualism. *Zero to Three, 29*(2), 26–30.

Zarate, M.E., & Pérez, P. (2006). Latino Public Opinion Survey of Pre-Kindergarten Programs: Knowledge, references, and public support. Los Angeles: Tomás Rivera Policy Institute.

Zentella, A.C. (2005). *Building on strength: Language and literacy in Latino families and communities.* New York: Teachers College Press.

Zepeda, M., Castro, D., & Cronin, S. (2010). Preparing early childhood teachers to work with young dual language learners. *Child Development Perspectives, 4*(3), 190–194.

Endnotes

[1] The term *dual language learner* refers to children who are learning English and a language other than English either simultaneously or successively, independently of the settings in which they use each language and the language(s) used in the early childhood program. In this chapter we use the term DLL, but when citing research from other authors we use the terms originally used by the authors (i.e., ELL, bilingual).

[2] The terms *Latino* and *Hispanic* are used interchangeably to refer to individuals with heritage in Mexico, countries in Central and South America and the Caribbean, and Spain.

CHAPTER 12

The Whole Child, the Whole Setting

Toward Integrated Measures of Quality

Suzanne M. Bouffard and Stephanie M. Jones

"Educating the whole child" is a frequent refrain in early childhood education policy and practice. This phrase reflects a widespread acknowledgment among educators and researchers that children must develop multiple skills (e.g., cognitive, social, motor) in order to succeed in school (Zigler, Gilliam, & Jones, 2006) and that learning is influenced by all of the settings and interactions in which children develop (Commission on the Whole Child, 2007). However, although approaches to understanding child development that consider important contexts (e.g., Bronfenbrenner & Morris, 1998; Pianta & Walsh, 1996; Sameroff & Chandler, 1975) and settings in schools, such as classrooms and playgrounds (e.g., Jones, Brown, & Aber, 2008; Tseng & Seidman, 2007), have informed how we conceptualize and study early childhood settings, the approaches have yet to be fully incorporated into the process of quality assessment and, therefore, into quality improvement efforts.

Most existing quality assessment processes and measures focus on a set of specific and discrete program elements and do not address interactions among the elements. Although these processes are valuable and necessary for continuing to build knowledge about the multiple facets of quality, they typically do not enable us to capture the true nature of early childhood settings—that is, as social settings characterized by dynamic sets of interactions and processes. This chapter presents a rationale and strategies for moving toward integrated quality assessments that build on the individual dimensions of quality discussed throughout this volume and brings them together into an integrated perspective. It proposes that such integrated assessments view early childhood settings as dynamic systems comprising a set of social relations and processes (e.g., among children and between children and adults), compositional features (e.g., socioeconomic or behavioral composition of the classroom), and structural characteristics (e.g., alignment among programs and settings; between early childhood settings and children's homes; over time; Jones, Brown, & Aber, 2008). Moving toward integrated approaches to quality assessment, we argue, has the potential to lead to quality ratings that are more accurate representations of the environments in which children live and learn, and therefore has the potential to facilitate more effective efforts to improve and sustain quality in early childhood education.

Decades of theory and research have articulated how developmental domains are interactive and embedded in both the individual's proximal settings (such as a child's home or school) and more distal settings (such as the parents' workplaces and the larger cultural context). Supplementing a long and rich history of person–environment interaction theories (which highlight the developmental influence of bidirectional relationships among individuals and social settings; e.g., Bronfenbrenner & Morris, 1998; Cicchetti, 1993; Pianta & Walsh, 2006; Sameroff & Chandler, 1975) are findings that biological systems also interact in bidirectional ways with environmental contexts (Gottlieb, 1996; Kandel, 1998). Within each of these settings and processes, social processes and relationships are particularly salient (Jones et al., 2008).

These advances in theory and research have informed integrated educational approaches that build "horizontal" and "vertical" alignment—that is, connections across developmental domains, and educational contexts within and across time (Bouffard, Malone, & Deschenes, n.d: Bogard & Takanishi, 2005). Such approaches include city- and state-level early childhood systems, P-16 or P-20 councils, the prekindergarten (pre-K)–3rd movement, community schools, and complementary learning initiatives (Adelman & Taylor, 2007; Blank & Berg, 2006; Bogard & Takanishi, 2005; Commission on the Whole Child, 2007; Economic Policy Institute, 2008; Weiss et al., 2009; Zaff, 2008).

However, to date, quality assessment processes and tools have not reflected this movement toward an integrated perspective. In particular, quality assessment—both for individual early childhood settings and for the multifaceted initiatives just described—has tended to focus on distal and sometimes static indicators of quality such as resources and curricula (Pianta, 2003). Although such measures are useful for capturing specific domains of development and characteristics of settings, as described elsewhere in this volume, they do not examine the relationships among these elements and therefore do not capture the dynamic nature of the setting or its developmental influence on the child. Capturing such processes is both necessary for the field moving forward and more feasible than ever before; although developmental science (particularly psychology) has struggled to develop a "language of environments" (Magnusson & Stattin, 1998, p. 691), recent methodological advances have made it possible to quantify and qualify the dynamic nature of developmental settings and their influence on children.

Drawing on theory, research, and practice, we propose that assessing quality in an integrated way requires attention to four theory- and research-derived principles that guide our understanding of healthy child development and that build on the research on individual dimensions of quality described in this volume: 1) Developmental domains and skills (e.g., cognitive, social, emotional, physical) are interdependent; 2) relationships among the multiple settings in which children develop (e.g., home and educational settings such as programs and schools) are as important as the individual settings themselves; 3) dynamic social processes within discrete settings play a role in the influence of structural features on development; and 4) continuity, stability, and predictability of educational environments over time support healthy child development and sustainability of benefits from early childhood education. Next, we address how each of these developmental-contextual principles is linked to quality and children's development, how it has informed practice and policy, and how it could be more fully and meaningfully integrated into quality assessment. We consider the application of these principles to both center-based and home-based settings; however, as is evident from the discussion that follows, most of the research to date has focused on center-based settings. We then present considerations for quality assessment processes and measures moving forward, including decisions about the design and administration of quality assessment measures and opportunities for leveraging existing tools and resources.

Principles of Developmental-Contextual Integration

Building on the theory described in the previous section, here we present research supporting the four principles of developmental-contextual integration and highlight their unique implications for quality assessment. In a subsequent section of this chapter, we propose a set of issues to consider in designing and implementing quality assessments.

Interdependence of Multiple Developmental Domains

From birth through adulthood, the fulfillment of needs and development of skills in one domain influences other domains (e.g., Cicchetti, 1993). For example, children who are healthy (e.g., whose nutritional and medical needs are met and who are physically active) are better able to attend to what they are learning in educational settings (Rothstein, 2004). Another example that we explore in depth here is the reciprocal relationship between the development of social-emotional and cognitive skills. Although much of the education-reform dialogue since the turn of this century has been framed as a debate about the relative importance of these two sets of skills (Zigler, Gilliam, & Jones, 2006), research and practice suggest that this is a false dichotomy. Jack Shonkoff (2004, p. 9) eloquently summed up the debate:

> Developmental scientists have concluded that you can't really separate these two domains [cognitive and social-emotional] of development within a child. And educators know that it doesn't matter how well you are able to read if you are pre-occupied with anxiety or fear or you can't control your behavior. Since a kindergartner who is emotionally healthy but has not mastered any pre-academic skills also is headed for difficulty in school, why are we wasting our time arguing about the relative importance of reading skills versus emotional well-being? Why can't we simply agree that they are both very important?

This comment is supported by growing evidence for links between successful school adjustment and performance and the development of social-emotional competence (Miles & Stipek, 2006; Pianta, Steinberg, & Rollins, 1995; Rogoff, 1990; Wentzel, 1991; Wentzel & Asher, 1995), and findings from economics research that noncognitive skills play a significant role in later employment and earnings (Heckman, 2006; Heckman, 2008; Levy & Murnane, 1996). The mechanisms of these reciprocal processes include a range of emotional, social, and neurobehavioral factors. In the emotional domain, children who express positive affect, modulate negative affect, and regulate their emotions effectively are rated positively by teachers and do better academically (e.g., Raver, 2002). In the social realm, children who get along better with peers and teachers are more likely to enjoy school (Conduct Problems Prevention Research Group, 2002; Dodge, Pettit, & Bates, 1994; Ladd, Birch, & Buhs, 1999), to be rated positively by teachers, and to perform better academically (Ladd et al. 1999). In the neurobehavioral realm, children's executive functioning skills, such as working memory, attention deployment, and ability to inhibit impulses allow them to meet the demands of the setting and perform better academically (Diamond & Taylor, 1996; Greenberg, Riggs, & Blair, 2007). Relationships among these skills are established in early childhood, but their influence appears to persist into elementary school and beyond (Flay, 2002; Hinshaw, 1992).

Some early childhood interventions, such as Head Start Research Based, Developmentally Informed and Tools of the Mind, have utilized this research to design programs that intentionally integrate academic and social-emotional skill development. Studies of these programs suggest that they benefit children, and that activities designed to target one domain have cross-over effects in other domains (Barnett et al., 2008; Bierman et al., 2008). For example, the Head Start REDI intervention found that the hybrid model of cognitive and social-emotional curricula (along with teachers' provision of emotion coaching and support) led to significant moderate- to medium-sized program impacts for children's emotion understanding and interpersonal problem-solving (Bierman et al., 2008). A randomized trial of Tools of the Mind found that treatment-group classrooms were rated higher on measures of program quality than control classrooms and that children in Tools of the Mind classrooms had better self-regulation, executive functioning, and language development than their control-group peers. Findings from the Chicago School Readiness Project, which primarily targets social and emotional processes, suggest that participating children have not only better emotional adjustment but also better cognitive outcomes, including better language, preliteracy, and math skills (Raver et al., 2008; Raver et al., 2009).

Taken together, theory, naturalistic research, and intervention results have built a case that quality assessments should address how well early childhood settings promote a broad range of skills. Because skills develop interdependently, even quality assessment efforts that primarily assess one target skill (e.g., how well the setting promotes cognitive development) should also assess how well the setting promotes other skills that affect or correlate with the target skill. Assessment of supports for skills in multiple domains can be achieved either through incorporating multiple developmental domains within one quality assessment measure or by utilizing multiple assessments that each capture a subset of skills. The latter approach allows researchers to achieve both breadth and depth in quality assessment (that is, to address a broad range of skills while also assessing detailed information about each one). Although this approach could entail more administrative costs (financial, time, and other costs), many of the challenges could be offset by increased efficiencies that come from following the domain-specific recommendations provided by other authors in this volume who have identified the most important elements of specific domains to measure.

Relationships Among Developmental Settings

Just as children develop multiple skills simultaneously, they develop in multiple settings simultaneously. Not only does each of those settings influence child development independently, but the connections among them (or lack thereof) also influence development. In early childhood, one of the most frequently explored connections is the family–educator relationship. (Here, we use the term *educator* to refer to professionals working in a broad range of educational settings, including preschool and early care and education (ECE) settings.) Positive, ongoing, and bidirectional relationships between families and education professionals are related to positive academic outcomes among children, both concurrently and into the future (Henderson & Mapp, 2002; Weiss, Bouffard, Bridglall, & Gordon, 2009; Weiss, Caspe, & Lopez, 2006). Although the mechanisms of these effects have not been definitively established, it is likely that such relationships both provide educators with valuable information about the child's strengths, challenges, and needs and encourage parents to provide educationally rich and supportive home environments. When parents engage in educationally supportive behaviors, beliefs, and attitudes at home (e.g., providing books, reading with children, using complex speech), their children have better educational adjustment and achievement over time (Henderson & Mapp, 2002; Weiss et al., 2009; Weiss, et al., 2006). Research on family–educator connections suggests that outreach from educators is associated with increases in family educational involvement and better educational outcomes (Schulting, Malone, & Dodge, 2005; Sheldon, 2005; Simon, 2004).

These research findings have informed the development of multiple intervention approaches that aim to build parents' capacity to support learning, including home visiting services, family literacy programs, and family participation in center-based settings (e.g., volunteering, accessing resources at a family resource center). The findings also have informed policies (such as the expansion of home visiting programs for expectant mothers and young children through health care reform legislation) and mandates for family involvement in Early Head Start and Head Start. Evidence on the effectiveness of parenting interventions is mixed, but some model programs such as the Chicago Parent Child Centers and the Perry Preschool Project, as well as the national Early Head Start program, have found positive effects. It is notable that parenting programs that combine and connect home- and center-based services are associated with more positive outcomes than either approach alone (Karoly, Kilburn, & Cannon, 2005; Love et al., 2005; Reynolds et al., 2007; Schweinhart et al., 2005), a finding that may be due to the benefits of consistency across settings, to greater intensity of educational activities across the child's day and year, and/or to the importance of the family–school relationship. Results from the Chicago Child–Parent Centers program, which incorporates a variety of family involvement activities at participating centers, suggest that home–center relationships may be an important mechanism: The program increased family involvement in elementary school, which in turn increased children's achievement through high school (Reynolds et al., 2007).

These findings highlight the need for quality assessments that examine whether and how early childhood settings build connections with other settings such as homes and communities. Relationships with families have been incorporated into many national and state early childhood standards (e.g., National Association for the Education of Young Children and National Board for Professional Teaching Standards, Head Start), but they can and should be incorporated into quality assessment measures in more meaningful ways. A wide range of research measures exist for assessing family–educator connections (Westmoreland, Bouffard, O'Carroll, & Rosenberg, 2009), and quality assessment measures can leverage and learn from them. For example, research on the importance of bidirectional and coconstructed family–school relationships (Bouffard & Weiss, 2008) has led to measures that assess both parents' and educators' perceptions of these relationships (e.g., Kohl, Lengua, McMahon, & the Conduct Problems Prevention Research Group, 2000), and research demonstrating the multidimensional nature of family involvement has led to measures that assess multiple types of family involvement behaviors (e.g., helping with homework, volunteering at school), which occur in multiple settings (e.g., in the home and in the school). Incorporating these developments into quality assessment can allow policymakers and practitioners to attain a more detailed and meaningful picture of relationships between families and ECE settings, without employing stand-alone research measures.

In addition to building connections with families, there is anecdotal evidence that educational programs, particularly formal programs and city- and state-level initiatives, are increasingly building relationships with community institutions (e.g., social services, cultural institutions) and partnering with businesses and universities in order to leverage additional resources (Weiss et al., 2009).[1] To date, however, there has been little research on or assessment of these partnerships. Moving forward, it will be valuable to ascertain whether such community connections influence young children's development, how they do so (for example, by serving as a conduit for families to access other needed resources), and whether they constitute important aspects of quality. Quality assessment measures that incorporate items about community connections can provide an opportunity to build this needed research base and ultimately inform program design and improvement. Because research in this area is at an early stage, it will be important to assess the predictive validity of community-focused items before including them in integrated assessments.

Social Processes within Settings

Although research over decades points to the importance of interactions across settings (e.g., between home and school), more recent research finds that interactions in distinct microcontexts within settings (e.g., classrooms, lunchrooms, and play yards can be considered distinct microcontexts within schools that have unique structural and interactional characteristics) also are associated with a broad range of child outcomes. This research, to date, primarily focused on formal early childhood and primary educational settings, has highlighted the role of classroom culture and climate, including the social and demographic composition of the class and the social interactions within the classroom. Embedded in these social dynamics are both components of quality (e.g., the warmth and support in the teacher–child relationship) and factors that influence those components of quality (e.g., the behavioral and interpersonal dynamics among children that influence teachers' warmth and emotional support). Considering the roles of each can lead to interventions that target the educational setting as a whole (Henry, 2008).

We highlight here three social processes that are particularly relevant to early childhood settings and that research has shown are related to child outcomes: relationships (including both peer and child–adult relationships), classroom norms, and "spillover" effects from peers. Each of these is supported by a growing research base as well as by theories and research on the primacy of social processes in understanding classrooms and other social settings (Jones, Brown, & Aber, 2008; Tseng & Seidman, 2007). Although we focus on these three examples of social processes, we acknowledge that many other social processes are at play in early childhood settings and have the potential to affect quality.

Many studies have found that the nature of the teacher–child relationship has strong associations with children's social adjustment and academic competence (see Raver, Garner, & Smith-Donald, 2007, for review). In fact, one study found that the quality of the teacher–child relationship was a more significant predictor of children's academic outcomes than nine features of pre-K quality from national policy standards (Mashburn et al., 2008). Greater teacher–child conflict is associated with children's decreased classroom exploration, lower academic performance, and greater school avoidance (Burchinal, Peisner-Feinberg, Pianta, & Howes, 2002; Hamre & Pianta, 2001; NICHD Early Child Care Research Network, 2003), and teachers' use of harsh and emotionally negative instructional practices has been associated with teachers' reports of feeling overwhelmed by children's challenging behaviors and poorer school adjustment (Raver et al., 2008). In contrast, teachers' warm and responsive behaviors and efforts to create a positive tone in the classroom (e.g. scaffolding, support for autonomy and creativity, personal connections with students) are associated with positive academic outcomes (see Pianta, 2003, for a review).

Classroom norms constitute another set of dynamic social processes that influence the educational experience for children and adults. Norms operate via feedback systems in which individuals convey information to one another about appropriate and inappropriate behaviors (Henry, 2008; Tseng & Seidman, 2007). All actors in the educational setting (e.g., classroom, program, home-based setting), both children and adults, engage in these feedback systems, although teachers are more likely to be agents of change in norms, whereas children are more likely to reinforce existing norms (Henry, 2008). Understanding whether and how these feedback systems are functioning among both children and adults is important for understanding the educational experience and for modifying it accordingly. For example, understanding the extent to which teachers or caregivers in home-based settings establish "injunctive norms" (i.e., norms that discourage certain disruptive or maladaptive behaviors) can help identify the needs of the classroom or home care setting and drive professional development and other program improvement efforts.

In addition to classroom- and school-specific norms and their parallels in home-based ECE settings, the current and past experiences of the class or group as a whole can influence the setting and therefore indirectly influence individuals within the setting. "Spillover" effects can come from one individual or from multiple individuals in the setting. For example, one child's disruptive behavior can change the teacher's behaviors toward and interactions with the whole group of children, as well as affect other factors such as teachers' and peers' ability to concentrate and focus on the activity at hand. At the other end of the spectrum, the collective previous educational experiences of the class or group can influence the pace of instruction and the skills and knowledge that children share with one another. Whether initiated by an individual or by the group's experience as a whole, the effect "spills over" to the group as a whole. Although there has been relatively little research on spillover effects in early childhood compared with other age groups, Neidell and Waldfogel (2008) found that the spillover effect of prior preschool attendance has an impact on children's math and reading skills in kindergarten. As the number of children in the kindergarten classroom who attended preschool increased, children's achievement scores increased, even after accounting for individual children's own preschool attendance and a host of covariates.

Growing research on these and other social processes in the classroom suggest that quality assessments not only should examine static characteristics of settings but also should place particular emphasis on the dynamic interactions within the setting (La Paro, Pianta, & Stuhlman, 2004). It is likely that many social processes contribute to quality and children's outcomes; in this chapter we do not attempt to determine which social processes should be prioritized in quality assessment processes and measures, although we stress the need for future attention to this issue. Here, we focus our attention on key considerations that apply to assessment of a broad range of social processes.

A promising, and increasingly utilized, approach for assessing social processes is observation of the setting or microcontext environment and the interactions within it. For example, Pianta and colleagues have developed an observational assessment, the Classroom Assessment Scoring System™ (CLASS), to measure the nature and quality of teachers' behaviors and to capture the dynamic nature of classrooms (La Paro, Pianta, & Hamre, 2008). The CLASS™ is based on Pianta and colleagues' identification of three dimensions of teacher behavior that are related to social, emotional, and cognitive outcomes: emotional support (positive climate, negative climate, regard for student perspectives, and teacher sensitivity), classroom organization (behavior management, productivity, and instructional learning formats), and instructional support (concept development, quality of feedback, and language modeling). Observations also can be used to record peer interactions and teacher behaviors that guide them. Many quality assessment measures include some focus on relationships and interactions, and many already utilize some observational methods; however, expanding this focus and the observational techniques used to assess aspects of it could enrich these tools and increase their utility for practice and policy.

Although external observations are undoubtedly valuable, actors within the setting can also offer meaningful perspectives. Averaging ratings from multiple respondents within the setting is one way to capture a direct perspective on social processes, especially processes that are coconstructed, such as norms (Henry, 2008; Shinn, 1990). This approach may not be useful with young children, whose responses tend to be unstable and situationally dependent (La Paro & Pianta, 2001). However, it may be useful with early childhood providers, for example, to assess norms about adults' interactions with children and administrators' support for staff.

Quality assessment processes also could draw on a rich tradition of sociometric measures from peer interaction research, in some cases from early childhood (e.g., Prinstein, Cheah, & Guyer, 2005), but primarily from middle childhood, adolescence, and adulthood. In sociometric assessments, individuals provide ratings or nominations of peers on either positive or negative dimensions (e.g., nominating three best friends or rating all of one's classmates in order of popularity). These ratings allow researchers to examine social relationships, for example, by identifying friend pairs or creating social maps of classrooms. Such measures have been used most widely in studies of children's peer relationships and aggression during middle childhood, but some studies also have used them to assess teachers' social networks (Coburn & Russell, 2008; Penuel, Riel, Krause, & Frank, 2009). Although incorporating sociometrics into broader quality assessment measures may be cumbersome, stand-alone sociometric measures could become part of a multifaceted quality assessment process. This strategy would provide a more complete picture of social environments in early childhood settings—one that provides an indication, from the child's perspective, of the density of the social groupings in the classroom, including the degree to which children are socially isolated or are rejected by their peers.

Continuity of Educational Environments over Time

Both within and across settings, development proceeds in an ongoing and cumulative (albeit not always continuous) fashion in which early experience has a significant impact on later development (Cicchetti, 1993). "Skill begets skill" (Cunha & Heckman, 2006), and earlier skills lay the foundation for later skills; for example, children must learn to read before they can read to learn. For this reason, some suggest that interventions are more cost-effective during early childhood than during middle childhood and adolescence (Heckman, 2006). At the same time, however, because development and the influences upon it are ongoing, early interventions must be followed with ongoing investments and supports (Heckman, 2008), and research suggests that there are benefits to building intentional connections among educational settings and initiatives across time. Facilitating educational transitions is one way to build such connections and, therefore, continuity for children as they develop. Because transitions are not a static moment in time, but instead are ongoing processes (Rimm-Kaufman & Pianta, 2000), transition practices should be an integral and ongoing part of the culture of educational settings (Bogard & Takanishi, 2005).

The transition from early childhood to elementary school is a particularly salient one for children and families, and has long-lasting implications (Pianta, Cox, Taylor, et al., 1999). Policies and practices that aim to bridge this transition are associated with better adjustment and academic development (Kreider, 2002; Schutling, Malone, & Dodge, 2005). For example, research from the Early Childhood Longitudinal Study found that when kindergarten teachers engaged in more transition practices, including reaching "backward" to connect with children's preschool teachers and inviting preschoolers to visit kindergarten classrooms, children had higher achievement test scores at the end of kindergarten (Schulting, Malone, & Dodge, 2005). These results suggest that transition practices are a beneficial area for intervention, but other national studies find that such practices are not the norm: Although most surveyed kindergarten teachers implemented some kind of transition practice, connecting "backward" in time was rare, and most transition activities were implemented only after the kindergarten year began (Pianta, Cox, Taylor, & Early, 1999). Further evidence of the need for more attention to transition practices comes from several other research findings, including the following: The effects of high-quality early childhood programs diminish over time if children do not subsequently have access to high-quality educational settings; children who participate in model education programs both during early childhood and elementary school years have better outcomes than those who participate during only one of those time points; and stable and predictable learning environments are associated with better academic adjustment (Bogard & Takanishi, 2005; Reynolds, Magnuson, & Ou, 2006).

Such research has driven a surge of interest in programs and policies that intentionally build connections across developmental stages and settings (Blank & Berg, 1996; Bogard & Takanishi, 2005; Weiss et al., 2009; Zaff, 2008). For example, the pre-K–3rd movement endorses the alignment of educational standards, curricula, and assessments both within and across grade levels—that is, both "horizontally" and "vertically" (Bogard & Takanishi, 2005). pre-K–3rd approaches also prioritize integration across microcontexts (such as home and school) and attention to issues such as quality, professional development, and activities and policies designed to facilitate transitions, especially the transition to kindergarten. The pre-K–3rd approach, which is being adopted at both school and district levels, shares some components and philosophies with P-16 and P-20 councils (which usually operate at the state policy level) and with some horizontally and vertically aligned city-level early childhood systems (e.g., call out in Broward County, Florida, and Thrive in Five in Boston).

Despite the increasing momentum for pre-K–3rd and similar approaches, there have been few efforts to assess the alignment of early childhood and elementary education settings (Bogard & Takanishi, 2005), and alignment with elementary schools is rarely included in early childhood quality assessments. Incorporating indicators of alignment into quality assessment can provide better estimates about the extent to which early childhood settings are facilitating the transition to kindergarten, and using this information to inform practice may help to reduce the fade-out of early childhood program effects by encouraging more consistency in practices between early childhood and the elementary years.

Early childhood–elementary alignment can and should be assessed at multiple levels, including policy (e.g., the organization and policies of schools and districts, the role of administrators) and practice (e.g., teacher practices, school culture; Bogard & Takanishi, 2005). It also should incorporate the roles of multiple actors (e.g., teachers, administrators, parents) in both early childhood and elementary programs. Particular attention should be paid, however, to the role of teachers, who have the most proximal influence on transitions from one educational setting to another and whose skills should include vertical alignment of curricula and content and professional collaboration within and across grade levels (Sadowski, 2006). Quality assessment efforts could leverage methods and measures from research on how teachers facilitate the preschool-to-kindergarten transition; one notable source of such methods is the Transition Practices Survey (NCEDL, 1996; Pianta et al. 1999), which assesses 21 teacher practices that facilitate the transition to kindergarten, along with potential barriers to implementing these practices.

Moving Forward: Key Considerations for Quality Assessment

The four principles of integration that we have described represent a perspective shift and suggest important avenues for quality assessment measures moving forward. The principles can and should build on the domain-specific recommendations detailed elsewhere in this volume. They can be applied to both multifaceted, multidomain measures and to domain-specific measures, as achieving an integrated perspective does not necessarily require one global measure, but rather consistent attention to an integrated perspective across domains and measures.

We propose that achieving a consistent and coherent approach to integration begins with a process of identifying opportunities for coherence across domains and settings. Such a process could begin with a content analysis of best practices in assessment and future recommendations for individual domains and settings in order to identify the "low-hanging fruit"—that is, clearly evident areas of overlap and similarity that can drive improvements across domains and measures. This content analysis process should be informed by a thorough review and understanding of the research literature, such as has been provided throughout this volume. It may then be supplemented by empirical analyses across domains and settings to validate and expand the opportunities for improvement. Together, these processes can allow researchers and others to assemble a more integrated and complete picture of quality across domains, in order to drive coherence and consistency in practice and policy.

Once opportunities for consistency and integration across domains in quality assessment have been identified, several critical issues will need to be addressed. One is the need to look at the broad picture of multiple domain-specific measures and to include within that picture a multifaceted set of data collection approaches, to allow for triangulation. These approaches should include observations, surveys, and sociometric methods. Researchers should carefully consider which types of assessments are most appropriate for each domain and how the assessments will fit together to form a complete picture. It also will be important for these measures to assess the perspectives of multiple stakeholders, including the perceptions of educators, the opinions of parents, and the skills and competencies of children.

Attending to such issues can help to ensure that integrated quality assessment processes are relevant and useful for both practice and policy. One additional issue to consider is the opportunity to build on existing practice and policy resources (including state and national standards and federally funded and state-funded programs such as Head Start and Smart Start). Another is the need for longitudinal data assessment systems that track children and settings over time. Data collection systems should be developed in parallel with quality assessment measures, and should be designed to balance the levels of structure and consistency necessary to capture change over time with the need for the flexibility required to enable assessment of the setting over time, even when the children and the adults in the setting change.

With these considerations in place, integrated approaches to quality assessment can provide important benefits to multiple constituencies. Integrated approaches can provide policy makers with a more meaningful picture of the quality of the setting as a whole, which can lead to the establishment of more meaningful standards and accountability systems, and to more effective allocation of resources. They can provide families with a more holistic concept of the program, which can help them select the programs that are best suited to their children. Furthermore, they can provide program staff and administrators with information for professional development and continuous improvement throughout the year. For example, assessing the social dynamics of the setting could help teachers identify how to redirect negative peer interactions, and examining the transition to kindergarten could encourage early childhood staff to reach out to elementary school teachers and coconstruct aligned curricula. Incorporating such dimensions into teacher rating systems also could help administrators ensure that early childhood educators have the recommended skills and knowledge. Finally, more integrated measures also present opportunities for research; in particular, measures that capture the true nature of the social setting may improve the predictive validity of quality ratings, which has been inconsistent (Burchinal, Kainz, & Cai, Chapter 2, this volume).

Whether in research, policy, or practice, an integrated perspective on assessment can address the fact that, when it comes to quality, the whole is more than the sum of the parts. By building on the domain-specific recommendations provided throughout this volume, the principles and considerations presented here offer promising opportunities for the measurement of quality in diverse early childhood settings, moving forward, and also may provide models of innovation for other fields.

References

Adelman, H., & Taylor, L. (2007). *New directions for student support: Current state of the art.* Los Angeles: Center for Mental Health in Schools, UCLA.

Barnett, W.S., Jung, K., Yarosz, D.J., Thomas, J., Hornbeck, A., Stechuk, R., et al. (2008). Educational effects of the Tools of the Mind curriculum: A randomized trial. *Early Childhood Research Quarterly, 23,* 299–313.

Bierman, K.L., Domitrovich, C.E., Nix, R.L., Gest, S.D., Welsh, J.A., Greenberg, M.T., et al. (2008). Promoting academic and social–emotional school readiness: The Head Start REDI program. *Child Development, 79,* 1802–1817.

Blank, M., & Berg, A. (2006). *All together now: Sharing responsibility for the whole child.* Washington, DC: Institute for Educational Leadership, Coalition for Community Schools.

Bogard, K., & Takanishi, R. (2005). PK–3: An aligned and coordinated approach to education for children 3 to 8 years old. *Social Policy Report, 19*(3), 3–24.

Bouffard, S.M., Malone, H.J., & Deschenes, S. (n.d.). Complementary learning: Recommended and related readings. Retrieved July 13, 2010, from http://www.hfrp.org/publications-resources/browse-our-publications/complementary-learning-recommended-and-related-readings

Bouffard, S.M., & Weiss, H.B. (2008). Thinking big: A new framework for family involvement policy, practice, and research. *Evaluation Exchange, 14*(1 & 2), 2–5.

Bronfenbrenner, U., & Morris, P. (1998). The ecology of developmental process. *Handbook of Child Psychology, 1*, 993–1029.

Burchinal, M.R., Peisner-Feinberg, E., Pianta, R., & Howes, C. (2002). Development of academic skills from preschool through second grade: Family and classroom predictors of developmental trajectories. *Journal of School Psychology, 40*, 415–436.

Cicchetti, D. (1993). Developmental psychopathology: Reactions, reflections, projections. *Developmental Review, 13*, 471–502.

Coburn, C.E., & Russell, J.L. (2008). District policy and teachers' social networks. *Educational Evaluation & Policy Analysis, 30*(3), 203–235.

Commission on the Whole Child. (2007). *The learning compact: A call to action.* Alexandria, VA: The Association for Supervision and Curriculum Development.

Conduct Problems Prevention Research Group. (2002). Using the Fast Track randomized prevention trial to test the early-starter model of the development of serious conduct problems. *Development and Psychopathology, 14*, 925–943.

Cunha, F., & Heckman, J.J. (2006). *Investing in our young people.* Washington, DC: America's Promise Alliance.

Diamond, A., & Taylor, C. (1996). Development of an aspect of executive control: Development of the abilities to remember what I said and to "do as I say, not as I do." *Developmental Psychobiology, 29*, 315–334.

Dodge, K.A., Pettit, G.S., & Bates, J.E. (1994). Socialization mediators of the relation between socioeconomic status and child conduct problems. *Child Development, 65*, 649–665.

Economic Policy Institute. (2008). *A broader, bolder approach to education.* Washington, DC: Author.

Flay, B.R. (2002). Positive youth development requires comprehensive health promotion programs. *American Journal of Health Behavior, 26*(6), 407–424.

Gottlieb, G. (1996). Developmental psychobiological theory. In R.B. Cairns, G.H. Elder, & E.J. Costello (Eds.), *Developmental science* (pp. 63–77). Cambridge, England: Cambridge University Press.

Greenberg, M.T., Riggs, N.R., & Blair, C. (2007). The role of preventive interventions in enhancing neurocognitive functioning and promoting competence in adolescence. In D. Romer & E.F. Walker (Eds.), *Adolescent psychopathology and the developing brain: Integrating brain and prevention science* (pp. 441–462). New York: Oxford University Press.

Hamre, B.K., & Pianta, R.C. (2001). Early teacher–child relationships and the trajectory of children's school outcomes through eighth grade. *Child Development, 72*, 625–638.

Heckman, J. (2006). Skill formation and the economics of investing in disadvantaged children. *Science, 312*, 1900–1902.

Heckman, J.J. (2008). *Schools, skills and synapses.* Working Paper 14064. Cambridge, MA: National Bureau of Economic Research. Retrieved September 10, 2008, from http://www.nber.org/papers/w14064

Henderson, A.T., & Mapp, K. (2002). *A New wave of evidence: The impact of school, family, and community connections on student achievement.* Austin, TX: Southwest Educational Development Laboratory.

Henry, D.B. (2008). Changing classroom social settings through attention to norms. In M. Shinn & H. Yoshikawa (Eds.), *Toward positive youth development: Transforming schools and community programs,* New York: Oxford University Press.

Hinshaw, S.P. (1992). Externalizing behavior problems and academic underachievement in childhood and adolescence: Causal relationships and underlying mechanisms. *Psychological Bulletin, 111*(1), 127–155.

Jones, S.M., Brown, J.L., & Aber, J.L. (2008). Classroom settings as targets of intervention and research. In M. Shinn & H. Yoshikawa (Eds.), *Toward positive youth development: Transforming schools and community programs* (pp. 58–77). New York: Oxford University Press.

Kandel, E.R. (1998). A new intellectual framework for psychiatry. *American Journal of Psychiatry, 55,* 457–469.

Karoly, L.A., Kilburn, M.R., & Cannon, J.S. (2005). *Early Childhood Interventions: Proven Results, Future Promise.* Santa Monica, CA: Report prepared for PNC Financial Services, Inc.

Kohl, G.O., Lengua, L.J., McMahon, R.J., & the Conduct Problems Prevention Research Group. (2000). Parent involvement in school: Conceptualizing multiple dimensions and their relations with family and demographic risk factors. *Journal of School Psychology, 38,* 501–523.

Kreider, H. (2002*). Getting parents ready for kindergarten: The role of early childhood education.* Cambridge, MA: Harvard Family Research Project. Retrieved April 15, 2009, from http://www.hfrp.org/publications-resources/browse-our-publications/getting-parents-ready-for-kindergarten-the-role-of-early-childhood-education

La Paro, K.M., & Pianta, R.C. (2001). Predicting children's competence in the early school years: A meta-analytic review. *Review of Educational Research, 70,* 443–484.

La Paro, K., Pianta, R.C., & Stuhlman, M. (2004). Classroom assessment scoring system (CLASS): Findings from the pre-k year. *The Elementary School Journal, 104,* 409–426.

Ladd, G.W., Birch, S.H., & Buhs, E.S. (1999). Children's social and scholastic lives in kindergarten: Related spheres of influence? *Child Development, 70,* 1373–1400.

Levy, F., & Murnane, R. (1996). *Teaching the new basic skills: Principles for educating children to thrive in a changing economy.* New York: Free Press/Simon & Schuster.

Love, J.M., Kisker, E.E., Ross, C., Raikes, H., Constantine, J., Boller, K., et al. (2005). The effectiveness of Early Head Start for 3-year-old children and their parents: Lessons for policy and programs. *Developmental Psychology, 41*(6), 885–901.

Magnusson, D., & Stattin, H. (1998). Person–context interaction theories. In W. Damon & R.M. Lerner (Eds.), *Handbook of child psychology, Volume 1: Theoretical models of human development* (pp. 685–759). New York: Wiley.

Mashburn, A.J., Pianta, R.C., Hamre, B.K., Downer, J.T., Barbarin, O.A., Bryant, D., et al. (2008). Measures of classroom quality in prekindergarten and children's development of academic, language, and social skills. *Child Development, 79,* 732–749.

Miles, S.B., & Stipek, D. (2006). Contemporaneous and longitudinal associations between social behavior and literacy achievement in a sample of low-income elementary school children. *Child Development, 77*(1), 103–117.

National Center for Early Development and Learning. (1996). *Transition Practices Survey.* Chapel Hill, NC: University of North Carolina at Chapel Hill.

NICHD Early Child Care Research Network. (2003). Social functioning in 1st grade: Associations with earlier home and child care predictors and with current classroom experiences. *Child Development, 74,* 1639–1662.

Neidell, M., & Waldfogel, J. (2008). *Cognitive and non-cognitive peer effects in early education.* NBER Working Paper Number 14277. Cambridge, MA: National Bureau of Economic Research.

Penuel, W., Riel, M., Krause, A., & Frank, K. (2009). Analyzing teachers' professional interactions in a school as social capital: A Social network approach. *Teachers College Record, 111,* 124–163.

Pianta, R.C. (2003). *Standardized classroom observations from Pre-K to third grade: A mechanism for improving quality classroom experiences during the P-3 years.* New York: Foundation for Child Development.

Pianta, R.C., Cox, M.J., Taylor, L., & Early, D. (1999). Kindergarten teachers' practices related to the transition to school: Results of a national survey. *Elementary School Journal, 100,* 71–86.

Pianta, R.C., La Paro, K.M., & Hamre, B.K., (2008). *Classroom Assessment Scoring System™ pre-K.* Baltimore: Paul H. Brookes Publishing Co.

Pianta, R.C., Steinberg, M.S., & Rollins, K.B. (1995). The first two years of school: Teacher–child relationships and deflections in children's classroom adjustment. *Development and Psychopathology, 7,* 295–312.

Pianta, R.C., & Walsh, D.J. (1996). *High-risk children in schools: Constructing sustaining relationships.* New York: Routledge.

Prinstein, M.J., Cheah, C.L., & Guyer, A.E. (2005). Peer victimization, cue interpretation, and internalizing symptoms: Preliminary concurrent and longitudinal findings for children and adolescents. *Journal of Clinical Child and Adolescent Psychology*, 34(1), 11–24.

Raver, C.C. (2002). Emotions matter: Making the case for the role of young children's emotional development for early school readiness. *Social Policy Report*, 16(3), 3–24.

Raver, C.C., Garner, P., & Smith-Donald, R. (2007). The roles of emotion regulation and emotion knowledge for children's academic readiness: Are the links causal? In R.C. Pianta, M.J. Cox, & K.L. Snow. (2007). *School readiness and the transition to kindergarten in the era of accountability*. (pp. 121–148). Baltimore: Paul H. Brookes Publishing Co.

Raver, C.C., Jones, S.M., Li-Grining, C.P., Metzger, M., Champion, K.M., & Sardin, L. (2008). Improving preschool classroom processes: Preliminary findings from a randomized trial implemented in Head Start settings. *Early Childhood Research Quarterly*, 23, 10–26.

Raver, C.C., Jones, S.M., Li-Grining, C.P., Zhai, F., Metzger, M.W., & Solomon, B. (2009). Targeting children's behavior problems in preschool classrooms: A cluster-randomized controlled trial. *Journal of Consulting and Clinical Psychology*, 77, 302–316.

Reynolds, A., Magnuson, K., & Ou, S.-R. (2006). *PK-3 education: Programs and practices that work in children's first decade*. FCD Working Paper: Advancing PK-3 No. 6. New York: Foundation for Child Development.

Reynolds, A., Temple, J.A., Ou, S.-R., Robertson, D.L., Mersky, J.P., Topitzes, J.W., et al. (2007). Effects of a school-based, early childhood intervention on adult health and well-being: A 19-year follow-up of low-income families. *Archives of Pediatric Adolescent Medicine, 161*, 730–739.

Rimm-Kaufman, S.E., & Pianta, R.C. (2000). An ecological perspective on children's transition to kindergarten: A theoretical framework to guide empirical research. *Journal of Applied Developmental Psychology, 21*(5), 491–511.

Rogoff, B. (1990). *Apprenticeship in thinking.* New York: Oxford University Press.

Rothstein, R. (2004). *Class in schools: Using social, economic, and educational reform to close the black–white achievement gap.* New York: Teachers College Press.

Sadowski, M. (2006). *Core knowledge for PK-3 teaching: Ten components of effective instruction.* FCD Working Paper: Advancing PK-3

No. 5. New York: Foundation for Child Development.

Sameroff, A.J., & Chandler, M.J. (1975). Reproductive risk and the continuum of caretaking causality. In F.D. Horowitz, M. Hetherington, S. Scarr-Salapatek, & G. Siegel (Eds.), *Review of child development research: Vol. 4*. Chicago: University of Chicago.

Schulting, A.B., Malone, P.S., & Dodge, K.A. (2005). The effect of school-based kindergarten transition policies and practices on child academic outcomes. *Developmental Psychology 41*(6), 860–871.

Schweinhart, L.J., Martie, J., Xiang, Z., Barnett, W.S., Belfield, C.R., & Nores, M. (2005). *Lifetime effects: The HighScope Perry Preschool study through age 40*. Ypsilanti, MI: HighScope Press, 2005.

Sheldon, S.B. (2005). Testing a structural equation model of partnership program implementation and parent involvement. *The Elementary School Journal, 106*, 171–187.

Shinn, M. (1990). Mixing and matching: Levels of conceptualization, measurement, and statistical analysis in community psychology. In P.H. Tolan, C.B. Keys, F. Chertok, & L. Jason (Eds). *Researching community psychology: Issues of theory and methods* (pp. 111–126). Washington, DC: American Psychological Association.

Shonkoff, J.P. (2004). *Science, policy, and the young developing child: Closing the gap between what we know and what we do*. Chicago: Ounce of Prevention Fund.

Simon, B.S. (2004). High school outreach and family involvement. *Social Psychology of Education, 7*, 18–209.

Tseng, V., & Seidman, E. (2007). A systems framework for understanding social settings. *American Journal of Community Psychology, 39*, 217–228.

Weiss, H.B., Bouffard, S.M., Bridglall, B.L., & Gordon, E.W. (2009). *Reframing family involvement in education: Supporting families to support educational equity* (Equity Matters Paper Series, Research Review No. 5). New York: Columbia University, Teachers College, The Campaign for Educational Equity.

Weiss, H.B., Caspe, M., & Lopez, M.E. (2006). *Family involvement makes a difference: Family involvement in early childhood education*. Cambridge, MA: Harvard Family Research Project.

Weiss, H.B., Little, P.M.D., Bouffard, S.M., Deschenes, S., & Malone, H. (2009). *The federal role in out-of-school learning: After-school, summer learning, and family involvement as critical learning supports.* Cambridge, MA: Harvard Family Research Project.

Wentzel, K.R. (1991). Relations between social competence and academic achievement in early adolescence. *Child Development, 62,* 1066–1078.

Wentzel, K.R., & Asher, S.R. (1995). The academic lives of neglected, rejected, popular, and controversial children. *Child Development, 66,* 754–763.

Westmoreland, H., Bouffard, S., O'Carroll, K., & Rosenberg, H. (2009). *Data collection instruments for evaluating family involvement.* Cambridge, MA: Harvard Family Research Project. Retrieved May 28, 2009, from http://www .hfrp.org/family-involvement/publications-resources/data-collection-instruments-for-evaluating-family-involvement

Zaff, J.F. (2008). *Putting children front and center: Building coherent social policy for America's children.* Washington, DC: First Focus.

Zigler, E., Gilliam, W.S., & Jones, S.M. (2006). A whole child approach: The importance of social and emotional development. In E. Zigler, W.S. Gilliam, & S.M. Jones (Eds.), *A vision for universal preschool education* (pp. 130–148). New York: Cambridge University Press.

Endnote

[1] To our knowledge, research and policy have not focused on these connections in home-based early childhood settings.

CHAPTER 13

Aligning Measures of Quality with Professional Development Goals and Goals for Children's Development

Robert C. Pianta, Bridget K. Hamre, and Jason Downer[1]

By age 5, an unacceptably large number of children are lacking in competencies fundamental to their school success, notably in the areas of spoken language and literacy (Duncan et al., 2007), self-regulation (Raver, 2008; Halle et al., 2008), social and relational competence (Fantuzzo et al., 2007), and early math (Cross, Woods, & Schweingruber, 2009). The long-term effects of early gaps in achievement and social functioning are so pronounced that effective and efficient interventions targeted toward these gaps in the preschool period are essential not only to the developmental success of children but also to the economic and social health of communities (Heckman, 2006; Heckman & Masterov, 2007; Magnuson, Ruhm, & Waldfogel, 2007). Largely in response to the compelling evidence documenting readiness-skills gaps at the start of school, their long-term costs and developmental consequences, and both experimental trials and quasi-experimental studies of large-scale programs showing positive impacts of exposure to preschool (Howes et al., 2008; Gormley & Phillips, 2003; Magnuson et al., 2007; Ramey & Ramey, 2004), there has been a rapid expansion of preschool services for young children, mostly at ages 3 and 4, and mostly targeted toward low socioeconomic groups (Barnett, Hustedt, Friedman, Boyd, & Ainsworth, 2007). It is now estimated that 22% of all 4-year-olds are enrolled in state-funded prekindergarten (pre-K), with 30 states planning to increase enrollment, and with specific efforts to raise the percentage of children from low-income backgrounds enrolled in preschool.

Unfortunately, despite significant investments in expansion and improvement of programs since the turn of the century, the promise of early education in the United

States is not being realized. Too many children, particularly poor children, continue to enter kindergarten far behind their peers (Jacobson-Chernoff, Flanagan, McPhee, & Park, 2007; Johnson, 2002; National Center for Education Statistics, 2000). Jacobson-Chernoff and colleagues (2007) reported results from the first follow-up of the nationally representative Early Childhood Longitudinal Study–Birth Cohort (ECLS-B) showing a gap of roughly one standard deviation on school readiness skills for children below the 20th percentile on family socioeconomic status. Because the wide-ranging and diverse set of experiences in preschools are not, in aggregate, producing the level and rate of skills gains required for children to be ready to enter school (see Howes et al., 2008; Layzer & Price, 2008), simply enrolling more children in more programs will not close the skills gap at school entry. Rather, there is a dire need for investments (current and future) to substantially enhance the positive impacts of existing and expanding educational offerings on the very child outcomes in which skills gaps are so evident (see Moorehouse, Webb, Wolf, & Knitzer, 2008).

It is the contention of the authors of this chapter that for the early childhood (EC) education system to move toward the goal of active and marked advancement of children's skills and competencies, the quality and impacts of programs must be improved through a system of focused professional development through which skill targets for children are aligned with teacher–student interactions that produce gains in these skills, which in turn are aligned with a menu of professional development supports that foster gains in these teacher–child interactions (Howes et al., 2008; Klein & Gomby, 2008; Raver et al., 2008). Thus, we argue that improvement of program impacts in EC rests on aligning, both conceptually and in terms of empirically demonstrated impacts, on 1) a menu of professional development inputs to teachers (preservice or in-service) with 2) processes in classrooms (e.g., teacher–child interactions) that produce 3) skill gains for children in targeted domains (e.g., language, literacy).

In the remainder of the chapter, we describe our efforts to develop such a system of aligned, focused, and effective professional development for the wide-ranging EC workforce, through the auspices of the National Center for Research on Early Childhood Education (NCRECE). This description focuses on skill targets in children's early literacy and language development as a means of illustrating an aligned and focused approach, which is also evident in current work on EC mathematics (see Cross et al., 2009).

Workforce Needs for Professional Development

Standardized observations involving several thousand U.S. early education classrooms clearly demonstrate that, on average, the quality of child–teacher interactions is not high, and effective curriculum implementation is inadequate (NICHD Early Child Care Research Network, 2002; Peisner-Feinberg & Burchinal, 1997; Pianta et al., 2005). Yet, with enrollment of 3- and 4-year-olds in early education programs (including, but going beyond, state-funded pre-K) approaching 70% of the population and growing (Barnett, Hustedt, Robin, & Schulman, 2004; West, Denton, & Germino-Hausken, 2000), expansion of EC programs is placing notable demands on the supply chain for early childhood educators and for evidence-based in-service training. Some surveys estimate that a total of 200,000 teachers would be needed to staff universal enrollment programs, and 50,000 new teachers would be needed by 2020 (Clifford & Maxwell, 2002). The projected demand on education and training systems for more teachers is tremendous. Many states rely on teachers with elementary grade certifications and teachers with 2-year degrees "grandfathered" into certification (Clifford, Early, & Hills, 1999). Many EC educators take courses while already employed and use worksites for student teaching (Howes, James, & Ritchie, 2003). Several states address the staffing and qualification crisis by improving salaries and benefits, whereas others encourage child care and preschool providers to seek additional training as the EC education system becomes more formal and programmatic (see Peters & Bristow, 2005; Pianta, 2006).

Efforts to meet the demand for "trained" teachers are moving rapidly ahead without rigorous controlled evaluation of their impact(s) on the nature and quality of instruction in classrooms and on child outcomes (Clifford et al., 1999; Hart, Stroot, Yinger, & Smith, 2005; Ramey & Ramey, 2004). That is, states and programs are ramping up professional development requirements and offering teachers a wide variety of courses, workshops, credentials, and the like, but at the same time most, if not all of, these efforts do not have an evidence base of support from research that demonstrates their value. To add to the urgency, there is little evidence that accumulating course credits, advancing in terms of degree status (e.g., from A.A. to B.A.), or attending workshops produce teaching that leads to improved child outcomes (e.g., Early et al., 2005, 2007; National Council on Teacher Quality, 2005); thus, the pressure is exacerbated for professional development that is effective for fostering skill gains (for teachers and children). The National Center for Early Development and Learning's (NCEDL) six-state pre-K study demonstrated that even in state-sponsored pre-K programs with *credentialed* teachers with bachelor's degrees, variation in curriculum implementation and quality of teaching was enormous (Pianta et al., 2005) and *unrelated* to teachers' experience or education, whereas teachers' education and experience was also unrelated to the children's progress in academic or social skills (Early et al., 2005). Like nearly every other form of teacher training, including in K–12, there is virtually no evidence linking *garden variety* preservice or in-service training experiences or teacher credentials to child outcomes or to observed classroom quality (National Council on Teacher Quality, 2005; NICHD Early Child Care Research Network, 2002, 2005; Pianta, La Paro, Payne, Cox, & Bradley, 2002). To the extent that there is evidence of a connection between teacher professional development experiences and improvements in teacher behavior or child outcomes, it is present in studies of very specific forms of teacher support focused on a well-defined set of behaviors (often involved in the implementation of a specific curriculum) that are aligned well with target child outcomes (see Bierman, Nix, Greenberg, Blair, & Domitrovich, 2008; Clements & Sarama, 2008; Ginsburg et al., 2006; Lonigan, 2006; Neuman & Cunningham, 2009).

In short, the early child education system is expanding rapidly, creating great demand for effective teachers, but as the professional development system moves to meet these demands, it is critical that investments be targeted toward forms of teacher support that are demonstrably effective. Otherwise, the unguided accumulation of more and more training is a recipe for continued mediocrity and inequity that ultimately will undermine the promise and potential of early education. We argue that if early education programs are going to achieve high quality and effectiveness at scale (Pew Charitable Trusts, 2005) then two notable efforts must be undertaken: 1) development of effective approaches for preparing, supporting, improving, and credentialing teachers that have demonstrable impacts on teaching and student outcomes, and 2) identifying cost-effective mechanisms for delivery of these approaches both in preservice teacher training and in alternate certification and retraining routes used by large school districts or alternative suppliers (Birman, Desimone, Garet, & Porter, 2000; Borko, 2004;

Clifford & Maxwell, 2002; Cochran-Smith & Zeichner, 2005; Hart et al., 2005; Pianta, 2006; Whitebook, Bellm, Lee, & Sakai, 2005). The primary purpose of this chapter is to focus on the former—the importance of a conceptual and empirically demonstrated alignment of professional development inputs to teachers with behavior in the classroom that fosters child outcomes.

In our conceptual framework, teacher–child interactions are viewed as mediating the effects of professional development on children's skill gains (see Hamre, Pianta, Downer, & Mashburn, 2008). The approach taken by the NCRECE in its program of research on professional development rests on evidence from methodologically rigorous studies demonstrating that objectively assessed teacher–child interactions are active agents of developmental change in preschool classrooms (Domitrovich, Gest, Bierman, Welsh, & Jones, in press; Mashburn et al., 2008; Ramey & Ramey, 2008; Raver et al., 2008). In the sections that follow, we describe our approach to designing and testing professional development interventions aligned with interactions that both change teachers' classroom behaviors (Pianta, Mashburn, Downer, Hamre, & Justice, in press; Raver et al., 2008) and—in classrooms where teachers participate in these supports—children's school readiness (Downer, Pianta, & Fan, 2008; Mashburn et al., 2008; Hamre et al., 2008). Again, we emphasize that our approach is not the only one to have aligned professional development inputs with teacher behaviors and child outcomes (e.g., see Clements & Sarama, 2008), and we view the subsequent discussion as illustrative of other work and as signaling the type of change in professional development that is likely to have the most benefits for teachers and children.

Professional Development for Effective Implementation of Instruction in Language and Literacy

Effective teaching in EC education requires skillful combinations of explicit instruction, sensitive and warm interactions, responsive feedback, and verbal engagement and stimulation intentionally directed to ensure children's learning while embedding these interactions in a classroom environment that is not overly structured or regimented (Burchinal et al., 2000; Hyson & Biggar, 2006). This approach to EC teaching is endorsed by those who advocate tougher standards and more instruction and by those who argue for child-centered approaches, and has strong parallels in the types of instruction and teacher–child interactions that have been shown to contribute to student achievement growth in K–12 studies of teachers' effects on student's achievement gains (see Hart et al., 2005; National Council on Teacher Quality, 2005). The challenge is how to produce such teaching in large numbers of highly diverse teachers working in diverse EC settings.

NCRECE research focuses on developing and testing in rigorous studies, professional development models that produce effective high-quality implementation of instruction, and interactional support for literacy and language outcomes in EC. This aim is based on several foundational elements. First, many children are lacking in spoken language and literacy competencies at the start of school, particularly those in poverty or who are English language learners (ELLs), many of whom actually attended preschool (Snow, Hemphill, & Barnes, 1991; U.S. Department of Education, 2000; Vernon-Feagans, 1996). Because early language and literacy skills contribute causally to later reading achievement (e.g., Anthony, Lonigan, Driscoll, Phillips, & Burgess, 2003;

Lonigan, Burgess, Anthony, & Barker, 1998; Storch & Whitehurst, 2002), interventions in EC education can prevent and reduce the prevalence of reading difficulties among at-risk elementary students (e.g., Torgesen, 1998). Experimental research is now available on effective early language and literacy curriculum interventions that can be used in classrooms and integrated into teacher preparation programs (e.g., Byrne & Fielding-Barnsley, 1993, 1995; Girolametto, Pearce, & Weitzman, 1996; Girolametto, Weitzman, & Clements-Baartman, 1998; Justice & Ezell, 2002; Penno, Wilkinson, & Moore, 2002; Wasik & Bond, 2001; Whitehurst, Epstein, Angell, Crone, & Fischel, 1994).

However, even for teachers who have these curricula available to them in their EC classrooms or who have been exposed to them in courses, observational studies show clearly that demonstrably effective literacy and language interventions have *no* effect on child outcomes when the quality and effectiveness of implementation (i.e., instructional interactions) are low (Dickinson & Brady, 2005; Howes et al., 2008). Preschool teachers have little accurate knowledge about language and literacy development, particularly the high-priority skill targets (Lonigan, 2004) that should be the focus of instruction and interactional supports (Cunningham, Perry, Stanovich, & Stanovich, 2004; Justice & Ezell, 1999; Moats, 1994), they appear drastically undertrained in how to *implement* instructional activities in early literacy and engage in interactions and conversations that promote language skills (Justice & Ezell, 1999; Morrison & Connor, 2002; NICHD Early Child Care Research Network, 2002), they are rarely exposed to multiple field-based examples of objectively defined high-quality practice (Pianta, 2006), and they have few if any opportunities to receive feedback about the extent to which their classroom interactions and instruction promote these skill domains (Pianta, 2006).

The Issue of Curriculum and Implementation

Since the turn of the century, there has been extensive attention given to the importance of utilizing proven-effective manualized curricula or instructional approaches as a means of improving program impacts on children's skills (e.g., Preschool Curriculum Evaluation Research Consortium; see http://ies.ed.gov/ncer/pubs/20082009/index.asp). Research on these curricula often utilizes measures of procedural fidelity to ensure that they are implemented as intended (e.g., Justice & Ezell, 2002; Lonigan, Anthony, Bloomfield, Dyer, & Samwel, 1999a; Reid & Lieneman, 2006; Wasik, Bond, & Hindman, 2006); inclusion of procedural fidelity measures are considered an "essential quality" for intervention research (Gersten et al., 2005). Within practice, procedural fidelity measures are increasingly used to determine whether teachers are applying adopted programs as intended, particularly those that are considered to be "scientifically based" and for which procedural fidelity might be a key moderator of pupil outcomes (see Glenn, 2006).

As important as procedural fidelity is to ensuring that curricula are implemented as intended, it must be distinguished from quality of implementation. Quality of implementation is decidedly more difficult to capture (Sylva et al., 2006) than mere adherence to procedures or scripts, and rather reflects the real-time dynamic and interactive nature of classroom processes: the teacher's ability to work flexibly with students, to differentiate instruction and respond sensitively to what they bring to the task—that is, to exhibit skilled performance within dynamic interactions with children in learning activities that unfold over time in a given instructional episode or "teachable moment." It is important to note that, although measurement of procedural aspects of implementation examines whether teachers can "go through the motions" in following step-by-step aspects of a novel curriculum or approach, measurement of quality of instruction looks globally at relational processes between teachers and children across an entire learning episode.

The extent to which measurement of a teacher's procedural fidelity in implementing a structured curriculum may serve as a proxy for her instructional quality is a timely question, as the availability and implementation of preschool language and literacy curricula are flourishing in response to national and local initiatives focused on improving the quality of language and literacy instruction in preschool programs. These include both comprehensive curricula that organize classroom activities and experiences for the entire classroom day (e.g., Schickedanz, Dickinson, & Charlotte-Mecklenburg Schools, 2004) as well as more focal supplements that are embedded into a general curricular framework to provide encapsulated lessons explicitly focused on language and literacy (e.g., Wright Group, 2004). Both types of curricula typically provide a detailed scope and sequence for language and literacy instruction for the entire academic year; weekly lesson plans specifying a set of language and literacy objectives and corresponding activities; example scripts (and for some, companion web sites) illustrating quality implementation of activities, books, and other manipulatives needed to implement the curriculum; informal assessments to monitor children's progress in the curriculum; and implementation checklists to monitor teachers' fidelity to the curriculum.

In a recent study of 180 pre-K teachers' implementation of a scripted set of lessons in language and early literacy, we found that teachers exhibited high levels of procedural fidelity to the prescribed language and literacy curriculum following minimal training (Hamre, Pianta, Burchinal, & Downer, 2010; Justice, Mashburn, Hamre, & Pianta, 2008). Adherence to lesson plans and general guidelines for curriculum implementation exceeded 90% for most aspects of fidelity measured. Although an important sign of teachers' capacity for fidelity, this result must be considered in light of additional findings showing that, in large part, exhibiting fidelity to the curriculum was *not* associated with observed quality of language and literacy instruction when teacher–child interaction during the language or literacy activity was the focus. Fidelity to specific implementation routines (e.g., calling children's attention to the lesson, preparing all needed materials ahead of time) had no predictive value when the quality of instruction was considered, a finding which suggests that procedural fidelity with regard to adherence to a curriculum or activity captures only a portion of teachers' interactions and behaviors while that curriculum or specific activity is implemented. This is a critical distinction that may account for the reason that treatment effects are often small or moderated by features of the classroom or teacher (Preschool Curriculum Evaluation Research Consortium [PCER], 2008).

This contrasting set of findings brings to mind some of the differences discussed early in this chapter about the distinction between high-quality language instruction and high-quality literacy instruction. Language instruction that is of high quality requires adults to provide well-tuned responsive conversational input to children that features the use of open-ended questions, expansions, advanced linguistic models, and recasts (see Girolametto, Weitzman, & Greenberg, 2003). Because a key characteristic of high-quality language instruction is linguistic responsiveness of adults to children within dynamic exchanges, high-quality language instruction is virtually impossible to script procedurally. That is, one cannot possibly script what children will say, and consequently, one likewise cannot script an understanding of how to interact with and respond to children in ways that maximize language-learning opportunities.

By contrast, a component of high-quality literacy instruction can be explicit and direct instruction that systematically teaches children about the code-based characteristics of written language, including both phonological and print structures. These approaches to teaching reading are more amenable to procedural scripting compared with characteristics of high-quality language instruction, and it stands to reason that adherence to a scripted plan might result in relatively high ratings for instruction in the subset of literacy skills that privilege systematic and explicit instruction. To reference the prior discussion, measures of procedural fidelity for a scripted, highly targeted curriculum in literacy may be more closely related to child outcomes than similar assessments of language curricula. However, even for literacy instruction, quality of implementation remains an issue. In fact, ratings of teachers' instructional interactions are low even during specific skill-focused activities drawn from curricula that in other studies have been shown to be effective (e.g., Justice et al., 2008; Justice & Ezell, 2002; Penno et al., 2002; Wasik & Bond, 2001; Whitehurst et al., 1994). Moreover, demonstrably effective literacy interventions have *no* effect on child outcomes when the quality and effectiveness of implementation is low (Dickinson & Brady, 2006; Howes et al., 2008). In short, the availability of a demonstrably effective curriculum and of procedural fidelity with respect to delivery of that curriculum is not sufficient to ensure student learning.

The NCRECE approach to professional development is focused on learning to skillfully use instructional interactions, implement curricula effectively and intentionally through teacher–child interactions, and provide language-stimulation supports in real-time dynamic interactions that operate at the intersection of children's developing skills and the available instructional materials or activities (e.g., Burchinal et al., 2000; Howes et al., 2008; Hyson & Biggar, 2006; NICHD Early Child Care Research Network, 2002). This approach *aligns* (conceptually and empirically) the requisite knowledge of desired skill targets and developmental skill progressions in a particular skill domain (e.g., language development, early literacy) with extensive opportunities for 1) *observation* of high-quality instructional interaction through analysis and viewing of multiple video examples; 2) *skills training* in identifying and providing appropriate instructional, linguistic, and social responses to children's cues, and how teacher responses can contribute to student literacy and language skill growth; and 3) repeated *opportunities for individualized feedback* and support for high quality and effectiveness in one's own instruction, implementation, and interactions with children. Conceptually, there is a system of professional development supports that allows for a direct tracing of the path (and putative effects) of inputs to teachers, to inputs to children, and to children's skill gains. We describe this system briefly next, starting with skill targets for children's development.

Knowledge of Skill Targets and Developmental Progressions

NCRECE professional development approaches are designed for high-priority skill targets in preschool language and literacy and start with defining these targets and ensuring that there is a curriculum in place that reflects these targets. A high-priority target for preschool literacy instruction (Lonigan, 2004) is one that 1) is consistently and at least moderately linked to school-age reading and language achievement, 2) is amenable to change through intervention, and 3) is likely to be underdeveloped among at-risk pupils. From meta-analyses (e.g., Hammill, 2004; National Early Literacy Panel, NELP, 2004) and longitudinal studies of early language and literacy predicting later reading and language skills (e.g., Bryant, MacLean, & Bradley, 1990; Catts, Fey, Zhang, & Tomblin, 2001; Chaney,

1998; Christensen, 1997; Gallagher, Frith, & Snowling, 2000; Schatschneider, Fletcher, Francis, Carlson, & Foorman, 2004; Storch & Whitehurst, 2002), we selected six targets for *MyTeachingPartner-Language Literacy* activities (MTP-LL). The first three targets (phonological awareness, alphabet knowledge, and print awareness) are literacy skills that consistently predict school-age decoding (NELP, 2004), are amenable to change via interventions (e.g., Justice & Ezell, 2002; Ukrainetz, Cooney, Dyer, Kysar, & Harris, 2000; van Kleeck, Gillam, & McFadden, 1998; Whitehurst et al., 1994) and are underdeveloped in at-risk pupils (e.g., Bowey, 1995; Lonigan et al., 1999b; Snowling, Gallagher, & Frith, 2003). The other targets (vocabulary and linguistic concepts, narrative, and social communication and pragmatics) are moderately associated with school-age decoding (NELP, 2004) and reading comprehension (NELP, 2004). Vocabulary achievement is an area of language weakness for children reared in poverty (Justice, Meier, & Walpole, 2005; Whitehurst & Lonigan, 1998) which can be accelerated by the use of structured interventions that feature ongoing exposure to new words, as occurs through adult–child shared storybook reading (e.g., Hargrave & Senechal, 2000; Lonigan et al., 1999a; Penno et al., 2002; Reese & Cox, 1999; Whitehurst et al., 1988).

For each target, MTP-LL includes a 9-month map of between 10 and 20 ordered instructional objectives and activities (e.g., Bunce, 1995; Lonigan et al., 1999a, 1999b; Notari-Syverson, O'Connor, & Vadasy, 1998). Our next goal was to develop an aligned system of supports for teachers not only to demonstrate procedural fidelity with these lessons and activities but also to demonstrate high-quality and effective implementation through the quality of their interactions.

Teacher–Child Interaction Skills Targets

Teacher training that focuses on interactions and quality of implementation of instructional activities in language and literacy must be based on a way of defining and observing interaction and implementation that has shown strong links to growth in child outcomes, in this case, language and literacy development. In the NCRECE professional development (PD) approaches, teachers learn to observe others' effective and ineffective interactions and their own interactions with children, and they receive feedback and suggestions related to improving quality and effectiveness of interactions. These NCRECE PD supports are anchored to a system of observing interactions that has been shown to predict child outcomes in the desired skill targets for children, the Classroom Assessment Scoring System, or CLASS™ (Pianta, La Paro, & Hamre, 2008). The CLASS was used in over 700 pre-K classrooms in the 11-state NCEDL/State-Wide Early Education Programs (SWEEP) pre-K study and is one of the indices of observed quality of interactions that consistently predicts child outcomes in language and literacy, including growth in receptive vocabulary and alphabet knowledge, with effect sizes (r) ranging from .15 to .28 (Howes et al., 2008; Mashburn et al., 2008). The CLASS focuses exclusively on teachers' instructional, language, and social interactions with children (La Paro, Pianta, & Stuhlman, 2004) and in large-scale studies of pre-K through Grade 3 classes, higher ratings on CLASS dimensions predict greater gains on standardized assessments of academic achievement and better social adjustment, even adjusting for teacher, program, and family selection factors (Hamre & Pianta, 2005; Howes et al., 2008; Mashburn et al., 2008; NICHD Early Child Care Research Network, 2002). Because the CLASS validly measures aspects of teachers' instruction and interaction that predict gains in these language and literacy skills during the pre-K years, the NCRECE professional development models rely on the CLASS as one of the central "targets" for teachers' knowledge and skill training.

Aligning Professional Development Modalities with Teacher–Child Interactions

Preschool teachers need support in identifying high-priority skill targets in literacy and language as they are evident in classroom interactions and instructional activities (Lonigan, 2004; Cunningham et al., 2004; Justice & Ezell, 1999; Moats, 1994). These teachers appear to lack training in ways to *implement* early literacy activities and engage in language-promoting interactions (Justice & Ezell, 1999; Morrison & Connor, 2002; NICHD Early Child Care Research Network, 2002), receive limited exposure to field-based samples of effective teaching practice (Pianta, 2006), and rarely receive feedback about the extent to which their classroom interactions promote language and literacy skills (Pianta, 2006).

The NCRECE program of professional development research has focused on testing the effects of the *MyTeachingPartner* (MTP) system of professional development supports for teachers' skillful use of instructional interactions and effective implementation of curricula (e.g., Burchinal et al., 2000; Howes et al., 2008; Hyson & Biggar, 2006; NICHD ECCRN, 2002). The MTP system is designed to offer extensive opportunities for 1) *observation* of high quality instruction, 2) *skills training* in identifying appropriate and inappropriate responses to children's cues, and 3) repeated *opportunities for individualized feedback* on effective interactions. These outcomes are achieved through delivery mechanisms that include didactic and skills-focused coursework, web-based video exemplars of effective practice, and consultation/feedback focused on a teacher's own classroom interactions.

Web-Based Video Exemplars as Professional Development Supports

Teachers in the NCRECE professional development studies receive access to the MTP website, which offers three types of resources available to teachers to promote high-quality interactions. First, teachers are provided detailed descriptions of *10 dimensions of high-quality teacher–child interactions* that are theoretically derived (Hamre & Pianta, 2007), empirically validated (Hamre, Pianta, Mashburn, & Downer, 2007), and directly associated with children's language, literacy and social-emotional development (Mashburn et al., 2008; Howes et al., 2008): Positive Climate, Negative Climate, Teacher Sensitivity, Regard for Students' Perspectives, Behavior Management, Productivity, Instructional Learning Formats, Concept Development, Quality of Feedback, and Language Modeling. In addition to detailed descriptions, the MTP web site also includes a *video library* with numerous video examples of teachers demonstrating each dimension within their classrooms, which helps teachers become critical observers of classroom behavior and more attuned to the effects that teachers' behaviors have on children. There is also a *teaching challenges* section in which teachers observe a common challenge faced by a teacher in her preschool classroom, suggest teaching practices that might be useful in each situation, reflect on the teacher's approaches to resolving these challenging situations, and develop strategies that will help with resolution of similarly challenging situations that teachers experience in their classes. These web-based supports and video exemplars can be used in conjunction with the NCRECE course described previously, or as a stand-alone professional development support accessed by individual teachers or in the context of professional development communities or consultation (described in the next section).

In-Service Consultation

MTP consultancy provides observationally based, nonevaluative practice-focused support and feedback for teachers through web-mediated remote consultation, providing individualized support *wherever teachers work*, without consultants having to visit classrooms—resulting in a potential cost savings. The starting point for an MTP consultancy cycle is the teacher videotaping up to a 60-minute segment of her implementation of a language or literacy instructional activity every 2 weeks. The MTP consultant edits that tape into a 3-minute video of three smaller segments that focus on indicators of quality teaching identified by the CLASS (Pianta et al., 2003), which is posted with written feedback to a secure web site where it is viewed and responded to by the teacher, whose comments are automatically sent to the consultant. The teacher and consultant then participate in a regularly scheduled video conference, using two-way interactive technologies in real time as they discuss teaching practices face-to-face through a web link.

Results from a Controlled Evaluation Study in Pre-K

An experimental study testing the impacts of the MTP instructional activities, video library, and consultancy was conducted within pre-K classrooms during 2004–2005 and 2005–2006. In the study, teachers were randomly assigned to one of three study conditions: One group received the language and literacy activities only; the second group received the language and literacy activities and access to the video exemplars on the web site; and the third group received the language and literacy activities, were given access to the web site, and participated in the consultancy. In a series of studies, we evaluated the effects of the video-exemplars and the MTP consultancy on teachers' interactions with children and on children's gains in language and literacy skills.

Taking full advantage of the RCT study design and 2 years of intervention implementation, we first evaluated preschoolers' language and literacy outcomes across the three study conditions (Downer et al., 2008); these conditions include the consultancy and web-only groups already described, as well as a third that functioned as a comparison group, in which teachers only received curriculum lesson plans (referred to as the Materials group). We hypothesized that across the treatment conditions the Consultancy group would have the greatest effect on children's performance on language and literacy skills at the end of the academic year, while their performance was controlled for at the beginning of the year. Because our child assessment (the Pre-CTOPPP; Lonigan, Wagner, Torgesen, & Rashotte, 2002) has four subtests (Vocabulary, Blending, Elision, and Print), we modeled the potential intervention effect on the latent construct of *language/literacy* with four measured indicators.

For children in classrooms in which the predominant language spoken was English, relative to the Materials condition, the consultancy treatment showed a positive effect on children's literacy outcome measures, after controlling for prior achievement (fall semester measures). The effect (.10) in the form of standardized regression coefficient, $p \leq 0.05$) is statistically significant, after correcting for the cluster sampling effect, and could be characterized as a "small" effect. On the other hand, the effect of the Web

Only condition in contrast to the Materials condition was very small (.04) and statistically nonsignificant.

Also using this experimental intent-to-treat approach, we examined the impacts of MTP on children's development of teacher-rated social skills, task-oriented competence, and problem behaviors during pre-K (Hamre et al., 2008). Multilevel modeling was used to estimate mean differences in teachers' ratings of children's end-of-the-year social skills (controlling for beginning-of-the-year social skills, gender, maternal education, and language spoken in the home), between classrooms with teachers participating in the Materials, Web Only, and Consultancy conditions. Results indicate that there were no differences across study conditions related to children's development of problem behaviors during pre-K. However, there were significant differences related to children's development of task-oriented competence and one aspect of social skills—assertiveness. Specifically, children whose teachers participated in the Web Only and Consultancy conditions demonstrated higher levels of task orientation and assertiveness compared with children whose teachers participated in the Materials condition. We recognize that these results are limited by the fact that the teachers reported on these outcomes and also were the recipients (or not) of the treatments that purportedly produced changes. Thus, in subsequent work we included direct assessments of self-regulation, and observations of self-regulation and social competence in the classroom.

In a series of quasi-experimental treatment-on-the-treated analyses we examined effects on child outcomes exclusively for teachers in the Consultancy and Web Only conditions, in part because the Materials group did not have access to MTP-related resources aimed at improving teacher–child interactions (Mashburn et al., 2008). During the intervention, the Web and Consultancy teachers varied in their use of MTP web-based resources, including the web site that features video-exemplars of high-quality classroom interactions, and consultation. We therefore examined the associations between teachers' exposure to these resources and children's development of language and literacy skills during pre-K. Controlling for relevant covariates (child, teacher, and classroom characteristics), we found that children showed significant gains in directly assessed receptive language skills when their teachers engaged in more hours of Consultancy support. These results complement the intent-to-treat findings reported earlier showing main effects for the Consultation condition on child outcomes (Downer et al., 2008), as well as the findings showing the Consultation condition to be more effective in changing teacher–child interactions presumed to foster school readiness (Pianta et al., in press).

Analyses of results from direct assessments of children's language and early literacy skills show that when teachers receive observationally focused in-service consultation *and* implement MTP-LL activities in literacy and language, the significantly improved changes in teachers' instructional interactions and implementation described earlier were associated with *gains* in direct assessments of children's performance in language and literacy. In terms of individual variation in improved instruction and interaction, when teachers showed greater *increases in positive interactions with children*, gains were greater on alphabet knowledge and rhyme awareness, whereas gains in *effective behavior management* predicted gains in alphabet knowledge. Increases in *concept development* predicted higher scores on word awareness, whereas teachers who provided more *engaging instructional formats* had children who scored higher on rhyme awareness. Finally, higher gains on teachers' use of high-quality *language modeling* were associated with greater gains for children on word awareness. In sum, shifts in teacher behavior as a consequence of exposure to professional development supports focused on those behaviors were associated with gains in children's literacy and language outcomes shown in prior research to be related to teacher behavior.

Coursework

Building on results and lessons learned from the original MTP evaluation study, NCRECE investigators developed a three-credit course offered in partnership with university-based or community-college programs. The course is an intensive, skill-focused didactic experience in which students learn how the development of language and literacy skills targets is linked to features of interactions with adults (using CLASS as the focus) in family and early education settings, and how high-quality implementation of language and literacy curricula and activities leads to skill growth (again using CLASS as the focus). Teachers learn to identify behavioral indicators of high quality and effective teaching on CLASS dimensions and to identify such indicators in their own teaching. The course draws from the MTP-LL resources, including instructional activities in language and literacy, explicit lesson plans, and linked video examples of actual high-quality implementation. The effects of this course are being evaluated in a randomized controlled trial with implementation by several hundred EC teachers in nine sites across the country.

Preliminary results from the initial wave of tests of the NCRECE course indicate that the course produces significant changes in teachers' knowledge of language and literacy skill targets, knowledge of teacher–child interactions linked to gains in these targets, competence in identifying interactive cues and behaviors, and provision of instructionally supportive interactions during literacy activities (Hamre et al., 2010). Changes in other domains include shifts in beliefs about the importance of intentional and explicit instruction in literacy and language development.

Conclusions and Future Directions

With such a varied and loosely organized and regulated workforce, it is widely held that professional development that is practice focused and tied to teachers' experiences in program and classroom settings is a key component for improving teacher and child outcomes in EC education (Bogard & Takanishi, 2005; NAEYC, 2009; Zaslow & Martinez-Beck, 2006). In fact, public investments in professional development often are seen as the key to improving program quality and impacts, and because this is the case, it is imperative that such investments return gains to teachers and children.

In this chapter, we have argued that for the EC education system to contribute more directly to the advancement of children's skills and competencies, both quality and impacts of programs must be improved through a system of focused and aligned professional development. In fact, we have provided evidence from our work and others' work that when skill targets for children are aligned with teacher–student interactions that produce gains in these skills, and in turn are aligned with a menu of professional development supports that foster gains in these teacher–child interactions, then growth is evident in both teacher skills and child outcomes (e.g., Clements & Sarama, 2008; Klein & Gomby, 2008; Neuman & Cunningham, 2009; Pianta et al., 2008; Raver et al., 2008). Our point is that effective professional development must be systematic and produce gains for teacher skills and child outcomes, and for that to occur it is necessary to align, both conceptually and in terms of empirically demonstrated impacts, the following strategies: 1) a menu of professional development inputs to teachers (preservice or in-service) with 2) processes in classrooms (e.g., teacher–child interactions) that produce 3) skill gains for children in targeted domains (e.g., language and literacy, math). The evidence supports this argument.

If conceptual and empirical connections can be demonstrated and replicated across professional development inputs, classroom processes, and child outcomes, in certain skill domains and for certain professional development models, then the potential for scaling and building incentives and policy structures around these models becomes an important feature of systemic improvement and policy. The development and expansion of quality rating and improvement systems (QRIS) are one such example of a set of policy initiatives that integrates measurement of inputs and outcomes with incentives and resources for improvement. These systems could, and perhaps should, be a tool for scaling up and further evaluating the impacts of the type of models of aligned professional development that have been illustrated in this chapter. In fact, to the extent that alignment, as we have argued, is a property of professional development that is critical for both impact and evaluation, it is not unreasonable to suggest that alignment be an explicit property of the professional development models adopted within QRIS and in fact of QRIS themselves.

Finally, one might also envision professional preparation and credentialing models based on what we are learning from aligned professional development and its evaluation. To the extent that these models of support and education for teachers can be demonstrated to produce gains in teacher competencies that produce child outcome gains, then it seems critical to build such opportunities for professional preparation "back" into the "preservice" sector and to find methods for credentialing and certifying teachers on the basis of participation in effective professional development and demonstration of competence. In fact, new policy statements related to professional development and career development being suggested by the NAEYC (2009) explicitly identify teachers' performance in classroom settings—specifically, their interactions with children—as a dimension of career advancement that should be credentialed and tied to professional development. Such statements by professional organizations reflect an openness to innovation that, paired with demonstrably effective supports for teachers, could pave the way for tremendous positive change in outcomes for teachers and children and exemplify one way that EC education leads.

References

Anthony, J.L., Lonigan, C.J., Driscoll, K., Phillips, B.M., & Burgess, S.R. (2003). Phonological sensitivity: A quasi-parallel progression of word structure units and cognitive operations. *Reading Research Quarterly, 38(4),* 470–487.

Barnett, S., Hustedt, J.T., Friedman, A.H., Boyd, J.S., & Ainsworth, P. (2007). *The state of preschool 2007: State preschool yearbook.* New Brunswick, NJ: National Institute for Early Education Research.

Barnett, S., Hustedt, J.T., Robin, K.B., & Schulman, K.L. (2004). *The state of preschool 2004: State preschool yearbook.* New Brunswick,

NJ: National Institute for Early Education Research.

Bierman, K., Nix, R.L., Greenberg, M.T., Blair, C., & Domitrovich, C. (2008). Executive functions and school readiness intervention: Impact, moderation, and mediation in Head Start REDI program. *Development and Psychopathology, 20,* 821–843.

Birman, B., Desimone, L., Garet, M., & Porter, A. (2000). Designing professional development that works. *Educational Leadership, 57(8),* 28–33.

Bogard, K., & Takanishi, R. (2005). *PK–3: An aligned and coordinated approach to education for children 3 to 8 years old.* (Social Policy Report No. 19-3). New York: Society for Research in Child Development.

Borko, H. (2004). Professional development and teacher learning: Mapping the terrain. *Educational Researcher, 33*(8), 3–15.

Bowey, J. (1995). Socioeconomic status differences in preschool phonological sensitivity and first-grade reading achievement. *Journal of Educational Psychology, 87,* 476–487.

Bryant, P., MacLean, M., & Bradley, L. (1990). Rhyme, language, and children's reading. *Applied Psycholinguistics, 11,* 237–252.

Bunce, B.H. (1995). *Building a language-focused curriculum for the preschool classroom.* Baltimore: Paul H. Brookes Publishing Co.

Burchinal, M.R., Roberts, J., Riggins, R., Zeisel, S., Neebe, E., & Bryant, D. (2000). Relating quality of center-based child care to early cognitive and language development longitudinally. *Child Development, 71,* 339–357.

Byrne, B., & Fielding-Barnsley, R. (1993). Evaluation of a program to teach phonemic awareness to young children: A one-year follow-up. *Journal of Educational Psychology, 85,* 104–111.

Byrne, B., & Fielding-Barnsley, R. (1995). Evaluation of a program to teach phonemic awareness to young children: A 2- and 3-year follow-up and a new preschool trial. *Journal of Educational Psychology, 87,* 488–503.

Catts, H.W., Fey, M.E., Zhang, X., & Tomblin, J.B. (2001). Language basis of reading and reading disabilities: Evidence from a longitudinal investigation. *Scientific Studies of Reading, 3,* 331–361.

Chaney, C. (1998). Preschool language and metalinguistic skills are links to reading success. *Applied Psycholinguistics, 19,* 433–446.

Christensen, C.A. (1997). Onset, rhymes, and phonemes in learning to read. *Scientific Studies of Reading, 1,* 341–358.

Clements, D.H., & Sarama, J. (2008). Experimental evaluation of the effects of a research-based preschool mathematics curriculum. *American Educational Research Journal, 45*(2), 443–494.

Clifford, D., & Maxwell, K. (2002, April). *The need for highly qualified prekindergarten teachers.* Paper presented at the Preparing Highly Qualified Prekindergarten Teachers Symposium. University of North Carolina Child Development Institute, Chapel Hill, NC.

Clifford, R., Early, D., & Hills, T. (1999). Almost a million children in school before kindergarten: Who is responsible for early childhood services? *Young Children, 54*(5), 48–51.

Cochran-Smith, M., & Zeichner, K.M. (Eds.). (2005). *Studying teacher education: The report of the AERA Panel on Research and Teacher Education.* Mahwah, NJ: Lawrence Erlbaum Associates.

Cross, C.T., Woods, T.A., & Schweingruber, H. (Eds.). (2009). *Mathematics learning in early childhood: Paths toward excellence and equity.* Washington, DC: Committee on Early Childhood Mathematics, National Research Council and National Academy of Sciences. Retrieved from http://www8.nationalacademies.org/onpinews/newsitem.aspx?RecordID=12519

Cunningham, A.E., Perry, K.E., Stanovich, K.E., & Stanovich, P.I. (2004). Disciplinary knowledge of K–3 teachers and their knowledge calibration in the domain of early literacy. *Annals of Dyslexia, 54,*139–167.

Dickinson, D.K., & Brady, J. (2006). Toward effective support for language and literacy through professional development: A decade of experiences and data. In M. Zaslow & I. Martinez-Beck (Eds.). *Critical issues in early childhood professional development* (pp. 141–170). Baltimore: Paul H. Brookes Publishing Co.

Domitrovich, C., Gest, S., Bierman, K., Welsh, J., & Jones, D. (in press). Fostering high-quality teaching in Head Start classrooms: Experimental evaluation of an integrated curriculum. *American Educational Research Journal.*

Downer, J., Pianta, R., & Fan, X. (2008). Effects of web-mediated teacher professional development on children's language and literacy development. Manuscript submitted for publication.

Duncan, G., Dowsett, C., Claessens, A., Magnuson, K., Huston, A., Klebanov, P., et al. (2007). School readiness and later achievement. *Developmental Psychology, 43,* 1428–1446.

Early, D., Barbarin, O., Bryant, D., Burchinal, M., Chang, F., Clifford, R., et al. (2005). Are teachers' education, major, and credentials related to classroom quality and children's academic gains in pre-kindergarten? *Early Childhood Research Quarterly, 21,* 174–195.

Early, D., Maxwell, K. Burchinal, M., Alva, S., Bender, R., Bryant, D., et al. (2007). Teachers' education, classroom quality, and young children's academic skills: Results from seven studies of preschool programs. *Child Development, 78*(2), 558–580.

Fantuzzo, J., Bulotsky-Shearer, R., McDermott, P.A., McWayne, C., Frye, D., & Perlman, S. (2007). Investigation of dimensions of social-emotional classroom behavior and school readiness for low-income urban preschool children. *School Psychology Review, 36*, 44–62.

Gallagher, A., Frith, U., & Snowling, M.J. (2000). Precursors of literacy-delay among children at genetic risk of dyslexia. *Journal of Child Psychology & Psychiatry, 41*, 203–213.

Gersten, R., Fuchs, L., Compton, D., Coyne, M., Greenwood, C., & Innocenti, M. (2005). Quality indicators for group experimental and quasi-experimental research in special education. *Exceptional Children, 71*(2), 149–164.

Ginsburg, H., Kaplan, R., Cannon, J., Cordero, M., Eisenband, J., & Galanter, M., et al. (2006). Helping early childhood educators to teach mathematics. In M. Zaslow & I. Martinez-Beck (Eds.), *Critical issues in early childhood professional development* (pp. 171–202). Baltimore: Paul H. Brookes Publishing Co.

Girolametto, L., Pearce, P.S., & Weitzman, E. (1996). Interactive focused stimulation for toddlers with expressive vocabulary delays. *Journal of Speech and Hearing Research, 39*, 1274–1283.

Girolametto, L., Weitzman, E., & Clements-Baartman, J. (1998). Vocabulary intervention for children with Down syndrome: Parent training using focused stimulation. *Infant-Toddler Intervention: A Transdisciplinary Journal, 8*, 109–126.

Girolametto, L., Weitzman, E., & Greenberg, J. (2003). Training day care staff to facilitate children's language. *American Journal of Speech–Language Pathology, 12*, 299–311.

Glenn, D. (2006). Weighing the "scale-up" study. *The Chronicle of Higher Education, 52*(45), A12.

Gormley, W.T., & Phillips, D. (2003). *The effects of universal pre-k in Oklahoma: Research highlights and policy implications* (Working Paper #2). Washington, DC: Public Policy Institute, Georgetown University.

Halle, T., Reidy, M., Moorehouse, M., Zaslow, M., Walsh, C., Calkins, C., Margie, N.G., & Dent, A. (2008). Progress in the development of indicators of school readiness. In B. Brown (Ed.), *Key indicators of child and youth well-being* (pp. 65–102). New York: Lawrence Erlbaum Associates.

Hammill, D.D. (2004). What we know about correlates of reading. *Exceptional Children, 70*, 453–468.

Hamre, B.K., Justice, L., Pianta, R.C., Kilday, C. Sweeny, B., Downer, J., et al., (2010). Implementation fidelity of the MyTeachingPartner literacy and language activities: Associations with preschoolers' language and literacy growth. *Early Childhood Research Quarterly, 25*, 329–347.

Hamre, B.K., & Pianta, R.C. (2005). Can instructional and emotional support in the first grade classroom make a difference for children at risk of school failure? *Child Development, 76*(5), 949–967.

Hamre, B.K., & Pianta, R.C. (2007). Learning opportunities in preschool and early elementary classrooms. In R. Pianta, M. Cox, & K. Snow (Eds.), *School readiness & the transition to kindergarten in the era of accountability* (pp. 49–84). Baltimore: Paul H. Brookes Publishing Co.

Hamre, B.K., Pianta, R.C., Burchinal, M., & Downer, J.T. (2010, March). *A course on supporting early language and literacy development through effective teacher–child interactions: Effects on teacher beliefs, knowledge and practice.* Paper presented at the Annual Meeting of the Society for Research on Educational Effectiveness, Washington, DC.

Hamre, B.K., Pianta, R.C., Downer, J.T., & Mashburn, A.J. (2008). *Effects of web-mediated teacher professional development on children's social skills.* Manuscript submitted for publication.

Hamre, B.K., Pianta, R.C., Mashburn, A.J., & Downer, J.T. (2007). *Building a science of classrooms: Application of the CLASS framework in over 4,000 U.S. early childhood and elementary classrooms.* New York: Foundation for Child Development. Retrieved from http://www.fcd-us.org/resources/resources_show.htm?doc_id=507559

Hargrave, A.C., & Sénéchal, M. (2000). A book reading intervention with preschool children who have limited vocabularies: The benefits of regular reading and dialogic reading. *Early Childhood Research Quarterly. Special Issue: Evaluating, interpreting and debating early interventions: The case of the comprehensive development program, 15*, 75–90.

Hart, P., Stroot, S., Yinger, R., & Smith, S. (2005). *Meeting the teacher education accountability challenge: A focus on novice and experienced teacher studies.* Mount Vernon, OH: Teacher Quality Partnership.

Heckman, J. (2006). Skill formation and the economics of investing in disadvantaged children, *Science, 312,* 1900–1902.

Heckman, J., & Masterov, D. (2007). The productivity argument for investing in young children. *Review of Agricultural Economics, 29*(3), 446–493.

Howes, C., Burchinal, M., Pianta, R., Bryant, D., Early, D., Clifford, R., et al. (2008). Ready to learn? Children's pre-academic achievement in pre-kindergarten programs. *Early Childhood Research Quarterly, 23,* 27–50.

Howes, C., James, J., & Ritchie, S. (2003). Pathways to effective teaching. *Early Childhood Research Quarterly, 18*(1), 104–120.

Hyson, M., & Biggar, H. (2006). NAEYC's standards for early childhood professional preparation: Getting from here to there. In M. Zaslow & I. Martinez-Beck (Eds.), *Critical issues in early childhood professional development* (pp. 283–308). Baltimore: Paul H. Brookes Publishing Co.

Jacobson-Chernoff, J., Flanagan, K.D., McPhee, C., & Park, J. (2007). *Preschool: First findings from the third follow-up of the Early Childhood Longitudinal Study, Birth Cohort (ECLS-B).* (NCES 2008-024). Washington, DC: National Center for Education Statistics.

Johnson, R.S. (2002). *Using data to close the achievement gap: How to measure equity in our schools.* Thousand Oaks, CA: Corwin Press, Inc.

Justice, L.M., & Ezell, H.K. (1999). Vygotskian theory and its application to language assessment: An overview for speech–language pathologists. *Contemporary Issues in Communication Science and Disorders, 26,* 111–118.

Justice, L.M., & Ezell, H.K. (2002). Use of storybook reading to increase print awareness in at-risk children. *American Journal of Speech–Language Pathology, 85*(5), 388–396.

Justice, L., Mashburn, A.J., Hamre, B.K., & Pianta, R.C. (2008). Quality of language and literacy instruction in preschool classrooms serving at-risk pupils. *Early Childhood Research Quarterly, 23,* 51–68.

Justice, L.M., Meier, J., & Walpole, S. (2005). Learning new words from storybooks: Findings from an intervention with at-risk kindergarteners. *Language, Speech, and Hearing Services in Schools, 36,* 17–32.

Klein, L., & Gomby, D.S. (2008). *A synthesis of federally funded studies on school readiness: What are we learning about professional development?* Washington, DC: U.S. Department of Health and Human Services.

La Paro, K., Pianta, R., & Stuhlman, M. (2004). The classroom assessment scoring system: Findings from the prekindergarten year. *The Elementary School Journal, 104,* 409–426.

Layzer, J., & Price, C. (2008, October). *Closing the gap in the school readiness of low-income children.* Washington, DC: U.S. Department of Health and Human Services.

Lonigan, C. (2004). Emergent literacy skills and family literacy. In B. Wasik (Ed.), *Handbook of family literacy* (pp. 57–82). Mahwah, NJ: Lawrence Erlbaum Associates.

Lonigan, C.J. (2006). Development, assessment, and promotion of preliteracy skills. *Early Education and Development, 17*(1), 91–114.

Lonigan, C.J., Anthony, J.L., Bloomfield, B.G., Dyer, S.M., & Samwel, C.S. (1999a). Effects of two shared-reading interventions on emergent literacy skills of at-risk preschoolers. *Journal of Early Intervention, 22,* 306–322.

Lonigan, C.J., Bloomfield, B.G., Anthony, J.L., Bacon, K., Phillips, B., & Samwel, C. (1999b). Relations among emergent literacy skills, behavior problems, and social competence in preschool children from low- and middle-income backgrounds. *Topics in Early Childhood Special Education, 19*(1), 40–53.

Lonigan, C.J., Burgess, S.R., Anthony, J.L., & Barker, T.A. (1998). Development of phonological sensitivity in 2- to 5-year-old children. *Journal of Educational Psychology, 90,* 294–311.

Lonigan, C., Wagner, R., Torgesen, J., & Rashotte, C. (2002). *Preschool Comprehensive Test of Phonological and Print Processing.* Austin, TX: Pro-Ed.

Magnuson, K.A., Ruhm, C., & Waldfogel, J. (2007). Does prekindergarden improve school preparation and performance? *Economics of Education Review, 26*(1), 33–51.

Mashburn, A.J., Pianta, R.C., Hamre, B.K., Downer, J.T., Barbarin, O., Bryant, D., et al. (2008). Measures of classroom quality in prekindergarten and children's development of academic, language, and social skills. *Child Development, 79*(3), 732–749.

Moats, L. (1994). The missing foundation of teacher education: Knowledge of the structure of spoken and written language. *Annals of Dyslexia, 44,* 81–102.

Moorehouse, M., Webb, M.B., Wolf, A., & Knitzer, J. (2008). Welcoming and opening remarks. *A working meeting on recent school readiness research: Guiding synthesis of early childhood research.* Washington, DC: ASPE, OPRE, Abt, and NCCP.

Morrison, F.J., & Connor, C.M. (2002). Understanding schooling effects on early literacy: A working research strategy. *Journal of School Psychology, 40*(6), 493–500.

National Association for the Education of Young Children. (2009). *Position statement on standards for professional preparation programs.* Washington, DC: NAEYC.

National Center for Education Statistics. (2000). *America's kindergartners.* Washington, DC: U.S. Department of Education.

National Council on Teacher Quality. (2005). *Increasing the odds: How good policies can yield better teachers.* Washington, DC: Author.

National Early Literacy Panel. (2004, December). *The National Early Literacy Panel: Findings from a synthesis of scientific research on early literacy development.* Presentation to the National Reading Conference, San Antonio, TX.

Neuman, S.B., & Cunningham, L. (2009). The impact of professional development and coaching on early language and literacy instructional practices. *American Educational Research Journal, 46*(2), 532–566.

NICHD Early Child Care Research Network. (2002). The relation of global first grade classroom environment to structural classroom features, teacher, and student behaviors. *The Elementary School Journal, 102*(5), 367–387.

NICHD Early Child Care Research Network. (2005). A day in third grade: A large-scale study of classroom quality and teacher and student behavior. *The Elementary School Journal, 105,* 305–323.

Notari-Syverson, A., O'Connor, R.E., & Vadasy, P.F. (1998; 2006). *Ladders to literacy: A preschool activity book.* Baltimore: Paul H. Brookes Publishing Co.

Peisner-Feinberg, E.S., & Burchinal, M.R. (1997). Relations between preschool children's child-care experiences and concurrent development: The Cost, Quality, and Outcomes Study. *Merrill-Palmer Quarterly, 43*(3), 451–477.

Penno, J.F., Wilkinson, A.G., & Moore, D.W. (2002). Vocabulary acquisition from teacher explanation and repeated listening to stories: Do they overcome the Matthew effect? *Journal of Educational Psychology, 94,* 22–33.

Peters, H.E., & Bristow, B.J. (2006). Early childhood professional development programs: Accounting for spillover effects and market interventions. In M. Zaslow & I. Martinez-Beck (Eds.), *Early childhood professional development* (pp. 339–350). Baltimore: Paul H. Brookes Publishing Co.

Pew Charitable Trusts. (2005). *National Early Childhood Accountability Task Force Briefing.* Philadelphia: Author.

Pianta, R.C. (2006). Standardized observation and professional development: A focus on individualized implementation and practices. In M. Zaslow & I. Martinez-Beck (Eds.), *Critical issues in early childhood professional development* (pp. 231–254). Baltimore: Paul H. Brookes Publishing Co.

Pianta, R.C., Howes, C., Burchinal, M., Bryant, D., Clifford, R., Early, C., & Barbarin, O. (2005). Features of pre-kindergarten programs, classrooms, and teachers: Do they predict observed classroom quality and child–teacher interactions? *Applied Developmental Science, 9*(3), 144–159.

Pianta, R.C., Kinzie, M., Justice, L., Pullen, P., Fan, X., & Lloyd, J. (2003). *Web training: Pre-K teachers, literacy, and relationships. Effectiveness of early childhood program, curricula, and interventions.* Washington, DC: National Institute of Child Health and Human Development.

Pianta, R.C., La Paro, K., & Hamre, B.K. (2008). *Classroom Assessment Scoring System™ (CLASS™).* Baltimore: Paul H. Brookes Publishing Co.

Pianta, R.C., La Paro, K.M., Payne, C., Cox, M., & Bradley, R. (2002). The relation of kindergarten classroom environment to teacher, family, and school characteristics and child outcomes. *Elementary School Journal, 102*(3), 225–238.

Pianta, R., Mashburn, A., Downer, J., Hamre, B., & Justice, L. (in press). Effects of web-mediated professional development resources on teacher–child interactions in pre-kindergarten classrooms. *Early Childhood Research Quarterly.*

Preschool Curriculum Evaluation Research Consortium-PCER. (2008). *Effects of preschool curriculum programs on school readiness (NCER 2008–2009).* Washington, DC: National Center for Education Research, Institute of Education Sciences, U.S. Department of Education.

Ramey, C.T., & Ramey, S.L. (2004). Early learning and school readiness: Can early intervention make a difference? *Merrill-Palmer Quarterly, 50*(4), 471–491.

Ramey, S.L., & Ramey, C.T. (2008). *The effects of curriculum and coaching supports on classrooms and literacy skills of prekindergarten/Head Start students in Montgomery County Public Schools.* Unpublished manuscript. Washington, DC: Georgetown University Center on Health and Education.

Raver, C.C. (2008, October). *Promoting children's socioemotional development in contexts of early educational intervention and care: A review of the impact of federally funded research initiatives on young children's school readiness.* Washington, DC: U.S. Department of Health and Human Services.

Raver, C.C., Jones, A.S., Li-Grining, C.P., Metzger, M., Smallwood, K., & Sardin, L. (2008). Improving preschool classroom processes: Preliminary findings from a randomized trial implemented in Head Start settings. *Early Childhood Research Quarterly, 23*(1), 10–26.

Reese, E., & Cox, A. (1999). Quality of adult book reading affects children's emergent literacy. *Developmental Psychology, 35,* 20–28.

Reid, R., & Lienemann, T. (2006). *Strategy instruction for students with learning disabilities.* New York: Guilford Press.

Schatschneider, C., Fletcher, J.M., Francis, D.J., Carlson, C., & Foorman, B.R. (2004). Kindergarten prediction of reading skills: A longitudinal comparative analysis. *Journal of Educational Psychology, 96,* 265–282.

Schickedanz, J., & Dickinson, D.K., in collaboration with Charlotte–Mecklenburg, NC, Schools. (2004). *OWL (Opening the World of Learning): A comprehensive early literacy program.* New York: Pearson Early Learning.

Snow, C.E., Hamphill, L., & Barnes, W.S. (Eds.). (1991). *Unfulfilled expectations: Home and school influences on literacy.* Cambridge, MA: Harvard University Press.

Snowling, M.J., Gallagher, A., & Frith, U. (2003). Family risk of dyslexic is continuous:

Individual differences in the precursors of reading skill. *Child Development, 74,* 358–373.

Storch, S., & Whitehurst, G. (2002). Oral language and code-related precursors to reading: Evidence from a longitudinal structural model. *Developmental Psychology, 38,* 934–947.

Sylva, K., Siraj-Blatchford, I., Taggart, B., Sammons, P., Melhuish, E., Elliot, K., et al. (2006). Capturing quality in early childhood through environmental rating scales. *Early Childhood Research Quarterly, 21*(1), 76–92.

Torgesen, J.K. (1998, Spring/Summer). Catch them before they fall: Identification and assessment to prevent reading failure in young children. *American Educator, 22,* 1–8.

Ukrainetz, T.A., Cooney, M.H., Dyer, S.K., Kysar, A.J., & Harris, T.J. (2000). An investigation into teaching phonemic awareness through shared reading and writing. *Early Childhood Research Quarterly, 15,* 331–355.

U.S. Department of Education. (2000). *America's kindergartens: Findings from the Early Childhood Longitudinal Study, kindergarten class of 1998–99, Fall 1999.* Washington, DC: National Center for Education Statistics.

van Kleeck, A., Gillam, R.B., & McFadden, T.U. (1998). A study of classroom-based phonological awareness training for preschoolers with speech and/or language disorders. *American Journal of Speech-Language Pathology, 7,* 65–76.

Vernon-Feagans, L. (1996). *Children's talk in communities and classrooms.* Cambridge, MA: Blackwell Publishers.

Wasik, B.A., & Bond, M.A. (2001). Beyond the pages of a book: Interactive reading and language development in preschool classrooms. *Journal of Educational Psychology, 93,* 243–250.

Wasik, B.A., Bond, M.A., & Hindman, A. (2006). The effects of a language and literacy intervention on Head Start children and teachers. *Journal of Educational Psychology, 98,* 63–74.

West, J., Denton, K., & Germino-Hausken, E. (2000). *America's kindergartners.* NCES 2000-070. Washington, DC: National Center for Education Statistics.

Whitebook, M., Bellm, D., Lee, Y., & Sakai, L. (2005). *Time to revamp and expand: Early childhood teacher preparation programs in California's institutions of higher education.* Berkeley, CA: Center for the Study of Child Care Employment, University of California at Berkeley.

Whitehurst, G.J., Epstein, A.L., Angell, A.C., Crone, D.A., & Fischel, J.E. (1994). Outcomes of an emergent literacy intervention in Head Start. *Journal of Educational Psychology, 86,* 542–555.

Whitehurst, G.J., Falco, F.L., Lonigan, C.J., Fischel, J.E., DeBaryshe, B.D., Valdez-Menchaca, M.C., et al. (1988). Accelerating language development through picture book reading. *Developmental Psychology, 24,* 552–559.

Whitehurst, G.J., & Lonigan, C.J. (1998). Child development and emergent literacy. *Child Development, 69,* 848–872.

Wright Group. (2004). *Doors to discovery.* DeSoto, TX: Author.

Zaslow, M., & Martinez-Beck, I. (Eds.). (2006). *Critical issues in early childhood professional development.* Baltimore: Paul H. Brookes Publishing Co.

Endnotes

[1]The research reported here was supported by the Institute of Education Sciences, U.S. Department of Education, through Grant R305A060021 to the University of Virginia. The opinions expressed are those of the authors and do not represent views of the U.S. Department of Education.

CHAPTER 14

Beyond Classroom-Based Measures for Preschoolers

Addressing the Gaps in Measures for Home-Based Care and Care for Infants and Toddlers

Heather Sandstrom, Shannon Moodie, and Tamara Halle

The majority of research on quality in early care and education (ECE) settings has been conducted in center-based care with children ages 3–5. There is considerably less research focused on the quality of home-based child care and care for infants and toddlers. This lack of research could, perhaps, be due to difficulty in accessing these settings for assessments of quality, or to a lack of adequate measurement tools by which to assess quality in these settings or for this age group. Due to the fact that home-based care is the most common care arrangement for infants and toddlers participating regularly in ECE and is widely used across the age range from birth to 5 years, it is imperative that quality in this type of environment and for this age group be appropriately measured.

This chapter addresses the aspects of home-based care and infant–toddler care that are important to capture in assessments of quality. We first consider characteristics of home-based care and infant–toddler care. We then outline the characteristics of quality for care in home-based settings, as identified by the National Association for the Education of Young Children (NAEYC) and the National Association for Family Child Care (NAFCC), and the characteristics of quality for infant and toddler care as informed by NAEYC's guidance on developmentally appropriate practice (DAP) and Head Start Program Performance Standards. Finally, we review existing measures of quality for use in home-based care settings and for programs that serve infants and toddlers, to determine their coverage of the elements of quality identified as important by the afore-mentioned sources, as well as to determine the gaps in coverage of these elements of quality.

Home-Based Care

Home-based care is one of the most commonly used forms of ECE. In general, home-based child care is viewed as any nonparental early childhood care and education arrangement provided in a child's home or the home of an individual who is entrusted with the care of the child. These caregivers include family child care (FCC) providers as well as family members, friends, and neighbors (FFNs). FCC providers usually are small-business owners who operate child care services from their homes in return for payment and are required to meet state regulations, such as registration or licensing. FFN care is provided by caregivers who are relatives, family friends, or babysitters or nannies who are legally exempt from licensing or subject to minimal regulation, depending on the state (Susman-Stillman & Banghart, 2008).

Home-based care, and specifically FFN care, is the most widely used type of ECE for children under age 5 with employed mothers. This is true among families in both rural and urban settings, with varying income levels, and of different races and ethnicities. Working parents of infants and toddlers who use only one nonparental care arrangement are most likely to use FFN care, whereas parents of preschoolers are more likely to use multiple care arrangements that include FFN care (Susman-Stillman & Banghart, 2008). According to 2005 National Household Education Survey (NHES) data, among children in a nonparental ECE arrangement, approximately one half of infants (48%) and 39% of toddlers are in relative care at least once a week, whereas 33% of infants and 30% of toddlers are in nonrelative home-based care. Although preschoolers are more likely to use center-based care than are infants and toddlers, still 29% of preschoolers use relative care weekly, and 15% are in nonrelative home-based care weekly (Iruka & Carver, 2006). The majority of infants in relative care on a weekly basis are cared for by grandparents (81% of children less than 1 year old; 78% of children ages 1–2). Some are cared for by aunts and uncles (14% of children less than 1 year; 18% of children ages 1–2) or other relatives (13% of children less than 1 year; 12% of children ages 1–2). Seventy-two percent of preschoolers (ages 3–5) in relative care are in the care of grandparents, 20% are in the care of an aunt or an uncle, and 14% are in the care of another relative (Iruka & Carver, 2006).

The variation among the types of home-based providers, their relationships with the children for whom they care, and the contexts in which care is provided have presented some difficulties in measuring and comparing the quality of care across these settings. For the sake of measurement, there is a need to move away from previous categories of home-based care and conceptualize home-based care in a broader and more inclusive way. One such approach is to view home-based ECE along a continuum of professionalism and intentionality, not only from unlicensed and unregistered providers to licensed and registered, but also from nonaccredited providers to accredited providers, with strategies to promote registration for those who are nonexempt by state law (Fiene & Isler, 2007).

Characteristics of Home-based Care

Children in home-based care are cared for most often by relatives, primarily grandmothers (Iruka & Carver, 2006; U.S. Census Bureau, 2008). Thus, there is often a match between the race or ethnicity of the child and the provider (Kontos, Howes, Shinn, & Galinsky, 1997). In addition, providers tend to have income levels similar to those of the families they serve, especially in lower income and subsidy-receiving populations.

Although some children are cared for within their own homes, most caregiving takes place in the provider's home (Susman-Stillman & Banghart, 2008). Relatives are likely to charge little or no payment, whereas nonrelatives are more likely to charge payment because they typically provide the service as a business or to supplement their income from another job (Susman-Stillman & Banghart, 2008).

Besides the obvious difference in setting, home-based care is unique in many ways compared with center- or school-based programs for young children. Home-based care usually involves multi-age groups ranging from infants through school-age children; smaller group sizes, but a single caregiver; longer hours of operation and more flexibility in terms of availability; and more continuity of care and fewer transitions with regard to caregivers and groups (Coley, Chase-Lansdale, & LiGrining, 2001; Galinsky, Howes, Kontos, & Abbott-Shim, 1994). Home-based providers typically have lower education requirements, if any, for licensing, in comparison with center-based providers, and many of those who are more educated eventually leave the FCC profession for positions with higher compensation and benefits (Whitebook, Sakai, Gerber, & Howes, 2001). Although many home-based providers follow state regulations and learning standards, they typically are not required to use a curriculum or an assessment tool to measure children's development and progress (Fuller & Kagan, 2000).

A characteristic of home-based care that varies greatly across providers is intentionality. Doherty, Forer, Lero, Goelman, and LaGrange (2006) described *intentionality* as consisting of three components: 1) commitment to the occupation, 2) professional approach to the work, and 3) a child-related motivation for engaging in the work. Some providers view their service as a long-term career, whereas others are motivated to provide services because it allows them the opportunity to stay home with their own young children. Some providers seek registration and licensing (to legitimize their services and to qualify for child care subsidies if registration or licensing is required in order to qualify), liability insurance, and referrals from agencies (Fiene & Isler, 2007). Other providers show higher levels of intentionality by enrolling in professional development; building relationships in the community and with other providers; and obtaining accreditation, in the case of established FCC programs. This level of intentionality and commitment of the provider to a professional career in the field of ECE is argued to be a strong predictor of the quality of care provided (Fiene & Isler, 2007).

Infant and Toddler Care

The years from birth to 3 are critical for the healthy development of young children. Experiences during the infant and toddler years shape children's cognitive, linguistic, social, and emotional capacities and provide a foundation for future growth (National Research Council and Institute of Medicine, 2000). Nearly 5.8 million children under the age of 3 in the United States spend some time in nonparental care, which makes the ECE environment a primary setting for early learning for many young children (Matthews & Schumacher, 2008).

Characteristics of Infant and Toddler Care

Those providing ECE need to understand each child's development within the context of his or her relationships and must be aware of the various developmental needs of children during these formative years. According to the NAEYC's third edition of

Developmentally Appropriate Practice in Early Childhood Programs Serving Children from Birth through Age 8, security, exploration, and identity formation are the fundamental developmental factors in relationships and learning during the first 3 years of life (ZERO TO THREE, 2009).

For the young infant (birth to 9 months), *security* is most important. Babies need access to warm, responsive caregivers and safe, stimulating environments to explore (Matthews & Schumacher, 2008). The young infant's day revolves around the routines of caregiving: diapering, dressing, eating, and sleeping. Caregivers who spend most of the day interacting one-on-one with infants and who learn and watch for an infant's cues are better able to judge when the baby needs to eat, is uncomfortable, or wants to be held (ZERO TO THREE, 2009). Caregivers who frequently talk with, sing to, and read to infants help to stimulate language development. During and between routines, young infants need opportunities for sensory and motor experiences. They need to be carried and cuddled and to spend some time on the floor, where they can move freely. Babies will explore objects and people by kicking, reaching, grasping, pulling, and letting go, and play areas should offer a variety of touch experiences (ZERO TO THREE, 2009). In a group setting, young infants like to watch other babies and older children and enjoy interacting with them, although they can become overwhelmed by too much stimulation and their excitement can lead to distress (ZERO TO THREE, 2009). Group care also provides opportunities for infants and toddlers to learn to form secure attachments to sensitive, affectionate adults. It is important that babies have caregivers who respond quickly to their cues and help build a sense of security that supports their exploration, learning, and identity formation.

Mobile infants (8–18 months) focus on *exploration* of their environment by creeping, crawling, cruising, walking, holding onto furniture or push toys, and climbing (ZERO TO THREE, 2009). The freedom to move about safely in an engaging environment is vital for this age group. A trusted caregiver can become a secure base from which mobile infants can explore, but they often check back with adults for reassurance and encouragement. Mobile infants develop confidence as their caregivers share in their new discoveries and accomplishments. As they play, these infants can become engrossed in opening and shutting, filling and dumping, and picking up and dropping all kinds of objects. They discover that objects can be out of sight and then found and that objects can be all together, separated into pieces, and put back together again. They learn to push buttons, and they begin to group and compare objects. Infants in the 8- to 18-month age group begin to develop language, first using babbles, squeaks, and grunts to communicate, but over time building their vocabularies by naming familiar objects. Even before they begin to say their first words (around the time of their first birthdays), they learn to respond to their name and follow oral commands. Infants of this age also use gestures such as pointing, reaching up, pushing away, bouncing, and shaking their heads to communicate. Mobile infants practice independence and trust caregivers to protect them as they move on their own to explore the world.

Beginning at about 18 months of age, *identity* is extremely important to young children. Toddlers desire independence and control, and use rapidly developing communication skills to express what they do and do not want. Caregivers help toddlers find ways to assert themselves, give them choices when possible, and introduce social guidelines. During this developmental stage, toddlers need opportunities to do things for themselves, both as individuals and as part of a group. Toddlers experiment with language, objects, and social interactions to construct an understanding of the world. Caregivers who give toddlers opportunities to help with tasks increase the child's sense of him- or herself as a capable person. A consistent but flexible routine gives toddlers a sense of security and creates opportunities for group activities while still accommodating individual needs.

Quality of Infant and Toddler Care

Infants and toddlers are more likely to be in home-based care than are preschoolers and school-age children (Halle et al., 2009; Iruka & Carver, 2006; Susman-Stillman & Banghart, 2008). Conversely, preschoolers are more likely than infants to be in center-based care. The 2005 NHES data show that 28% of infants (under 1 year of age), compared with 78% of preschoolers (ages 3–5), are participating weekly in a center-based ECE setting (Iruka & Carver, 2006).

The prevalence of home-based care for infants and toddlers may be due to the fact that high-quality, licensed, center-based care for infants and toddlers is more expensive for providers to offer than is care for older children. Infants and toddlers need care that is different from that of older children. Specifically, they need more holding; physical attention, including feeding and diapering; and special equipment such as cribs and changing tables. Additional standards for quality center-based programs include a small group size, a ratio involving fewer children per provider, adequate teacher education, and training for infant and toddler child care staff. These materials and services raise the cost of programs, making licensed care for infants and toddlers unaffordable for many families. In 38 states, the average annual cost of center-based infant and toddler care is more than 10% of the average median income for two-parent families and is an even larger percentage of income for single parents (National Association of Child Care Resource and Referral Agencies, 2009). Receipt of child care subsidies makes licensed child care more accessible for low-income families; however, in 2007, fewer than one million families received Child Care and Development Block Grant Program (CCDBG) funded child care assistance.[1]

A Framework for Reviewing Existing Measures of Home-Based Care and Care for Infants and Toddlers

A major purpose of this chapter is to review existing measures of quality for home-based and infant–toddler care and to identify ways in which these measures could be strengthened. In order to provide a framework for this review, we took the initial step of identifying categories or components of quality that recur across accreditation standards for home-based as well as center-based care, recommendations for DAP for infants and toddlers, and the Head Start Program Performance Standards, including those for Early Head Start. Our intent here is to articulate the components of quality that occur consistently across these standards and recommendations in order to then identify whether those components are addressed in existing measures of home-based care and care for infants and toddlers.

More specifically, in developing this framework, we referred to the early childhood program quality standards set forth by two national professional organizations: the

NAEYC (2005) and the NAFCC (2005). These standards typically are used to evaluate the quality of programs for accreditation purposes and to guide practitioners seeking accreditation in their quality improvement efforts. Given our focus on measuring the quality of care for infants and toddlers, we also examined the recommendations for DAP with infants and toddlers, as described by NAEYC and ZERO TO THREE: National Center for Infants,Toddlers, and Children (2009), and Head Start Program Performance Standards (2007), with particular attention to standards for infants and toddlers served through Early Head Start.

From these four sets of standards, we identified 10 broad categories, or components, of quality that are relevant across types of care and age groups. Later, we describe each of the following 10 components, identifying those in which the standards included particular provisions for addressing the needs of infants and toddlers: 1) positive relationships and interactions among children and providers; 2) the physical environment; 3) developmentally appropriate learning activities; 4) effective approaches to teaching and cognitive stimulation; 5) health, safety, and nutrition; 6) schedules and routines; 7) providers' qualifications and professional development; 8) relationships and communication with families; 9) community relationships and resources; and 10) professional business practices. Each component is described in more detail in the subsections that follow. We underscore the fact that each of these components was evident in the program accreditation standards for family child care (as identified in NAFCC's standards), as well as for center-based care (as identified in NAEYC's standards), and in standards for high-quality care for infants and toddlers, as well as for older children. However, our review emphasizes the elements of the components that are especially pertinent to home-based settings and to infants and toddlers. Even though many home-based care settings are not established early childhood programs, but rather, are FFN care and oftentimes for a single child, we believe that these 10 components of quality help to identify the essential factors that all children need for healthy development and learning.

Positive Relationships and Interactions Among Children and Providers

The primary feature across all four sets of standards is the importance of relationships. Positive interactions between children and providers lay the foundation for children's early learning and their language, cognitive, and social-emotional development. When providers are accepting, warm, sensitive, and respectful of and responsive to children's individual needs, children develop a trust in their caregivers and the security to explore and learn from their environment. Providers' display of positive affect and use of effective behavioral management techniques also are reflective of their positive relationships with children. *Particular to infants* is the need for *primary caregiving*, or being cared for by the same one or two adults with whom they can form a secure emotional attachment, and *continuity of care*, or a continuous child care arrangement in which the child is in the same setting over time with the same caregiver and peer group. In addition, high-quality care settings have providers who not only demonstrate cultural competence and sensitivity to children with special needs and to children who are English language learners but also have an ability to engage children of varying ages who are in their care.

The Physical Environment

The second component is the environment in which care is provided. The environment includes the structure of the physical facilities—the amount of available space both indoors and outdoors, the organization of space, and the level of comfort and child-friendliness in the physical design—as well as materials and equipment. A high-quality environment contains a sufficient supply of developmentally appropriate materials and equipment for the number of children and age groups served, such as toys, books, dramatic play props, and art materials; cribs and highchairs; tricycles and ride-on toys; and outdoor climbing equipment. The NAFCC standards note that some of these developmentally appropriate materials may be "real tools" such as shovels, rolling pins, and brooms. The environment should be organized in a way that promotes learning across a variety of domains of development (e.g., it should include a quiet book area and writing table for literacy skills; dramatic play for language and social skills; and open floor space for building blocks, puzzles, and games for early numeracy skills). In addition, space should be provided to address the needs of varying age groups (e.g., play spaces for infants to crawl and explore freely, open areas for toddlers to use push–pull toys, tables where preschoolers can use smaller manipulatives and art supplies). A high-quality care provider also will ensure that the environment is arranged to accommodate children with special needs.

Developmentally Appropriate Learning Activities

Within the prepared environment, children in high-quality care are engaged in activities that are appropriate for their age and ability and that promote positive physical, social, emotional, cognitive, and language development. Activities also address learning in different content areas, including early literacy, language, mathematics, science, social studies, music, art, and technology. In high-quality settings, whether center-based or home-based, providers identify early learning goals and activities that can support each child in that setting, as well as the group as a whole. Providers also plan and provide children with activities according to each child's interests and, preferably, build on spontaneous opportunities to support learning goals—for example, by extending children's self-directed play. Through whole-group, small-group, and individual activities, providers support and encourage children's play and learning. For infants and toddlers, this means that the provider has arranged play spaces that offer children a variety of sensory experiences and that offer daily opportunities for exploratory activity at the child's developmental level. Moreover, in high-quality settings, providers ensure that a balance is set between provider-initiated and child-initiated activities, thus allowing children to develop a sense of independence and creativity in their choice of play.

Effective Approaches to Teaching and Cognitive Stimulation

In addition to promoting warm and positive interactions between providers and children, the standards indicate that providers in high-quality settings demonstrate effective teaching strategies and approaches to stimulating early learning. Rather than simply providing appropriate activities for children, providers in high-quality settings are involved in children's activities as active observers and participants. Quality is reflected in providers' instructional style and in their ability to scaffold learning (i.e., provide support that enables the child to do something beyond his or her independent efforts), ask questions, provide positive feedback, and not be intrusive or controlling. In infant and toddler care, providers in high-quality settings play with children in ways that are sensitive to each child's interests in and tolerance for physical movements, loud sounds, or other changes in the child's surroundings. Within the bounds of what is safe, providers also are careful not to intrude on how the child wants to play or to interrupt the child's concentration.

Health, Safety, and Nutrition

Another key component emphasized across standards is composed of three subparts: health, safety, and nutrition. *Health* describes the provider's ability to promote the health of children, other adults, and the provider him- or herself through maintaining a sanitary environment and implementing healthy habits such as regular hand washing and the use of separate personal items (e.g., pacifiers, toothbrushes, pillows, blankets). *Safety* relates to the proper supervision of children, preparation for emergencies, and prevention of fire and injury through appropriate precautionary measures (e.g., installing safety gates on stairs, keeping poisonous materials out of reach). For infants, safety precautions also include putting them to sleep on their backs. In addition, children should be provided nutritious and sufficient meals that are prepared and served in a sanitary manner. In high-quality settings, meals are eaten family style with the caregiver, to provide opportunities for social conversation and language development and to encourage children to eat independently. Younger infants who do not yet possess the motor skills to hold their own bottles are held by caregivers during bottle feeding, which is healthier for babies than propping a bottle and which instills a sense of security in them.

Schedules and Routines

In high-quality settings, providers maintain a consistent schedule of daily events, including planned learning activities, guided free play, and daily caregiving routines such as helping with toileting or changing diapers, washing hands, preparing and assisting with meals, cleaning up, and initiating and monitoring napping. Schedules help to guide the flow of the day and provide stability for children; however, schedules should be flexible with respect to each child's individual needs and should provide time for smooth transitions.

Providers' Qualifications and Professional Development

High-quality early childhood settings employ providers who have knowledge of child development and early childhood education, as well as the skills needed to care for young children and to foster children's learning and development. For infants and toddlers, providing continuity of care—that is, the same providers stay with the child over the early childhood years—by individuals who are knowledgeable and experienced with this age group is considered important. Providers in high-quality settings are committed to their work and are reflective in their practices, meaning that they thoughtfully consider the types of activities that they provide for the children and adapt their practice in order to best meet the needs of the children in their care. These providers also are eager to gain new knowledge and improve their skills, so they pursue continuing education courses, participate in professional development training, maintain membership in professional organizations, and obtain resources and information through support networks or online sources.

Relationships and Communication with Families

Establishing positive relationships with parents and families is essential to the process of caring for young children. Parents trust providers with the care of their children, and in return, providers must respect parents and their values and be sensitive to cultural and language differences. Providers should encourage parental involvement, communicate regularly and effectively, and work together with parents on issues relating to caring for the child, such as discipline strategies, toilet training, and eating habits. In high-quality settings, providers also discuss with parents children's progress and their developmental needs, help to set goals, and recommend strategies or special services in the community to achieve those goals.

Community Relationships and Resources

To better meet the needs of the young children in their care, providers in high-quality settings connect with the community in which they live, develop relationships with community organizations, and utilize community resources. Providers who are aware of the social services and resources available in the community (e.g., child care subsidies and other federal assistance programs; early intervention and special education screening) can provide this information to the families they serve. Moreover, many communities offer a variety of learning opportunities through community-based organizations, and providers can integrate these opportunities into their programs to enrich their activities. In addition, some communities have established networks of home-based care providers, which can also be utilized to promote professional development, validate the profession, and reduce feelings of isolation among providers. High-quality providers also actively participate in the transition process of preschool-age children into kindergarten, or younger children in home-based care into center-based care, by communicating with new teachers and providing them with pertinent information about the children's individual needs. (Note that although this component of quality is part of the standards for both home-based and center-based settings, it is not explicitly mentioned in the standards of quality for infant and toddler care.)

Professional Business Practices

The final quality component deals with providers following and communicating best business practices when caring for young children. This practice includes implementing policies and procedures regarding issues such as hours of operation and availability, payment, the administration of medication, the transportation of children, and emergencies. Providers in high-quality settings keep organized records and create program quality-improvement plans that outline the actions they will take to improve the quality of the services they provide.

Existing Measures of Quality as Considered within this Framework

We conducted a thorough review of existing measures of quality in early childhood settings by using the *Quality of Early Childhood Care and Education Settings: A Compendium of Measures* (Halle & Vick, 2007) as our main resource. Our goal was to identify measures of quality that were 1) intended specifically for home-based care, including both FFN and FCC; 2) appropriate for use in home-based care settings, but designed for use in other types of ECE settings as well; 3) specific to infants and toddlers regardless of setting; 4) appropriate for a mixed-age group that included infants and toddlers; or 5) specific to infants and toddlers in home-based care.

We found 17 measures that met at least one of those five criteria. Six measures were specific to home-based care: the Assessment Profile for Family Child Care Homes (APFCCH; Sibley & Abbott-Shimm, 2005); the Child Care Assessment Tool for Relatives (CCAT-R; Porter, Rice, & Rivera, 2006); the Child Care Home Inventories (CC-HOME; Bradley, Caldwell, & Corwyn, 2003); the Child/Home Early Language and Literacy Observation (CHELLO; Neuman, Dwyer, & Koh, 2007); the Family Child Care Environment Rating Scale–Revised (FCCERS-R; Harms, Cryer, & Clifford, 2007); and the Business Administration Scale for Family Child Care (BAS; Talan & Bloom, 2009). Seven other measures were designed to be used in a variety of settings, including home-based care: the Child Caregiver Interaction Scale (CCIS; Carl, 2007); the Child-Caregiver Observation System (C-COS; Boller, Sprachman, & the Early Head Start Research Consortium, 1998); the Caregiver (Adult) Interaction Scale (CIS; Arnett, 1989); the Emlen Scales: A Packet of Scales for Measuring Quality of Child Care from a Parent's Point of View (Emlen, Koren, & Schultze, 2000); the Observation Measures of Language and Literacy Instruction in Early Childhood (OMLIT)—Snapshot and Read Aloud Profile subscales (Goodson, Layzer, Smith, & Rimdzius, 2006); the Observational Record of the Caregiving Environment (ORCE; National Institute of Child Health and Human Development [NICHD] Early Child Care Research Network, 1996); and the Quality of Early Childhood Care Settings: Caregiver Rating Scale (QUEST; Goodson, Layzer, & Layzer, 2005).

We found three measures that were specific to infants and toddlers or that had an infant–toddler version: the Infant and Toddler Environment Rating Scale–Revised (ITERS-R; Harms, Cryer, & Clifford, 2003); the CC-HOME: Infant/Toddler Version (Bradley, Caldwell, & Corwyn, 2003); and the ORCE, 6 Month, 15 Month, and 24 Month scales (NICHD Early Child Care Research Network, 1996). All of these measures that are specific to, or that include, home-based care are described as being appropriate for mixed-age groups that include infants and toddlers. The one exception is the C-COS, which is intended for children 1–5 years old and not for young infants. In addition, we found three other classroom-based measures that also were described as appropriate for mixed-age groups that include infants and toddlers: the Assessment Profile for Early Childhood Programs (APECP; Abbott-Shim & Sibley, 1987); the Child Development Program Evaluation Scale (CDPES; Fiene, 1984); and the Child Observation Form and Scale (COFAS; Fiene, 1984). The APECP is organized to look at indicators of quality separately for five components of a center-based program: administration, infant (birth to 12 months), toddler (12–36 months), preschool (3–5 years), and school age (5–10 years). Only one measure—the CC-HOME: Infant/Toddler Version—was found to be created specifically for infants and toddlers in home-based settings.[2] Two of the five scales of the CCAT-R—the Materials Checklist and the Health and Safety Checklist—have two versions, one for infants and toddlers and the other for preschoolers.

The home-based measures that were selected can be described as either a comprehensive or global measure of quality, a measure of caregiver–child interactions, a measure of the literacy environment and instruction, or a measure of business practices. The classroom-based infant–toddler measures either measured global quality or focused on the quality of caregiver–child interactions. All but one measure (the Emlen parent questionnaires) used an observational method to assess quality. Eight of the seventeen measures also had a caregiver–teacher interview component, and four of those required a review of program documents.

Once we identified the measurement tools that fit our criteria, we compared the constructs measured by each instrument with our 10 quality components, as shown in Ch 14 Appendix. We found a great deal of overall alignment between the quality components discussed earlier and what these measures assessed; however, there was some variation in the detail with which the measures covered the components. Next, we describe the coverage of each of the 10 quality components in the items and indicators of the 17 selected measures.

Coverage of Positive Relationships and Interactions

According to the results of our review, all but 2 of the 17 instruments address the relationship between the provider and children in some detail. The two measures that do not address positive relationships include a measure appropriate for use in home-based settings focused on literacy (OMLIT) and the home-based measure focused on business administration (BAS). Constructs include the caregiver's responsiveness and acceptance, respect for children and their needs, tone and affect, and discipline strategies.

Coverage of Physical Environment

Twelve of the seventeen instruments also assess the physical or learning environment. The measures that do not address this construct include three of the measures appropriate for home-based settings and focused on caregiver–child interactions (CIS, C-COS, and ORCE), the center-based measure appropriate for infants and toddlers and focused on interactions (COFAS), and the BAS. The constructs include the size of the space, the comfort and appeal of the space, the organization or arrangement of the environment, and the developmental appropriateness and sufficiency of materials and equipment. However, there is some variation in the number of items designated to measure different environmental components.

The infant–toddler version of the CC-HOME, for example, focuses heavily on specific types of learning materials (e.g., simple eye–hand coordination toys), whereas the early childhood version of the same instrument examines the size and organization of the space (e.g., whether it is overcrowded or cluttered), the lighting, and the quality of the neighborhood (e.g., whether it is aesthetically pleasing). The FCCRS-R examines different aspects of the space (e.g., its privacy or lack of privacy, whether children's work can be displayed in it, the arrangement of the space, whether it is comfortable, whether there is room for furniture), as well as the materials and activities for different age groups across different content areas (e.g., art; music and movement). The QUEST also assesses the presence of a specific number of toys for each age group (i.e., six items for children less than 1 year, eight items for children ages 1–3). Although some measures account for the safety of the materials and space in the outdoor play area through specific items (e.g., CDPES and CC-HOME: Early Childhood), we found that other measures (specifically, APFCCH, CCAT-R, and QUEST) have an entire subscale specific to the outdoor environment. The CCAT-R also has two separate versions of its Materials

Checklist—one for children under 3 years and another for children over 3—and assesses the environment, furnishings, and materials separately for these groups, thus allowing for a better understanding of the quality of the physical environment specific to infants and toddlers versus preschoolers.

Coverage of Developmentally Appropriate Learning Activities

Most of the instruments (13 out of 17) assess the provision of developmentally appropriate activities for children. Again, the exceptions are similar to those lacking coverage of the physical environment: the measures appropriate for home-based settings focused on caregiver–child interactions (CIS, C-COS, and ORCE) and the BAS. However, similar to the variation across measures in the degree of focus on the physical environment, there is a range across measures in the number of items representing this construct. For example, the FCCERS-R assesses the quality of the provision of activities across a variety of domains: fine motor, art, music and movement, blocks, dramatic play, math and number, nature and science, and sand and water play. The CCIS, on the other hand, includes indicators of quality constructs that are less domain specific: "Caregiver demonstrates knowledge of child development by engaging children with age appropriate materials/activities" and "Sets up environment/activities to foster development," but does acknowledge the caregiver's use of curriculum in several of its item indicators—something that most measures do not address. The CHELLO also has an open-ended question that assesses how the teacher plans learning activities for children of different ages and developmental needs.

Coverage of Approaches to Teaching and Cognitive Stimulation

We found a variety of ways in which the instruments capture the providers' engagement of children in learning opportunities. Fourteen of the seventeen instruments address this component of quality. A good example is the CCAT-R Summary Behavior Checklist, which includes such observations as "Encourages experimentation with objects," "Explains/demonstrates how to do or use something," and "Uses routines as learning opportunities." Similarly, the QUEST contains a subscale on supporting cognitive development that includes such items as "Caregiver helps children talk about what they are doing and thinking by asking open-ended questions" and "Caregiver takes advantage of and builds upon natural learning experiences and teachable moments as they arise." The CC-HOME: Infant/Toddler has a more general item ("Provider consciously encourages developmental advance"), whereas the CC-HOME: Early Childhood has separate subscales for Cognitive Stimulation (e.g., "Child is encouraged to learn letters") and Language Stimulation (e.g., "Child is encouraged to learn the alphabet").

The three measures that do not address approaches to teaching include two global measures of quality suitable for home-based settings (the Emlen Scales and CIS) and the BAS.

Coverage of Health, Safety, and Nutrition

All nine of the global measures assess safety, health, and nutrition in some way. In addition, one home-based measure focuses on caregiver–child interactions (CCIS) and the BAS also assesses safety, health, and nutrition. The greatest emphasis is on the safety of the environment, emergency plans, and sanitation (e.g., hand washing; cleaning of tables and diapering areas). Whereas the CC-HOME assesses whether the home environment is "safe," other measures, such as the QUEST, contain an extensive checklist of safety and health requirements. The APECP and the CDPES also specifically assess the administration of medications to children to determine whether sufficient health and safety procedures are followed.

Several instruments address nutrition services in some detail. For example, the APFCCH assesses the provision of nutritionally balanced foods that meet children's individual dietary needs, the encouragement of sound nutritional habits, and the development of social skills at mealtimes. The QUEST examines whether meals are nutritious, sufficient in quantity, and eaten while children are seated. The ITERS-R and FCCERS-R also examine whether staff sit with children during meals and use meals or feeding times as opportunities for social conversation and learning, such as naming foods and encouraging toddlers to talk. The APECP has a subscale devoted to food services within the early childhood program, which assesses the food-handling procedures, the cleanliness of the food preparation area, and the administrator's responsibility for providing nutritionally balanced meals that meet children's individual needs. In addition, the CDPES measures whether staff and children eat together, whether conversation occurs in relation to the food being served, whether children are encouraged to try all of their food, and whether nutritional concepts are integrated into the curriculum.

Coverage of Schedules and Routines

Five of the seventeen measures assess to varying degrees the presence of a structured, yet flexible, schedule of daily activities and routines. For example, the CHELLO assesses the daily schedule in terms of whether there is a written schedule posted, lesson plans, and observations of daily routines, with high-quality programs demonstrating both structure and choice (e.g., "Activities and experiences are planned on the basis of children's individual needs and interest," "Sufficient time is available for children's self-directed activities and independent explorations"). The FCCERS-R and ITERS-R also have an item for "Schedules" with similar high-quality indicators: "Schedule is individualized so that the needs of each child are met" and "Most transitions between daily events are smooth." Similarly, the CCIS measures routines and time spent (e.g., "Allows for change in daily schedule based upon children's needs/interests"). The APECP measures scheduling in terms of whether there exists a balance in the types of learning contexts (i.e., individual, small group, large group) in which planned activities occur and in learning opportunities (i.e., child directed and teacher directed, quiet and active, indoor and outdoor), which also demonstrates the provision of developmentally appropriate activities.

Coverage of Providers' Qualifications and Professional Development

Seven of the seventeen measures address, to some extent, the qualifications or training of the care provider. These seven measures include three of the six measures of global quality appropriate for home-based settings (APFCCH, Emlen Scales, and FCCERS-R), all three center-based measures of global quality that include infants and toddlers (APECP, CDPES, and ITERS-R), and the BAS. For example, the BAS specifically documents providers' qualifications and professional development, with indicators of high quality including a baccalaureate degree, coursework in early childhood education or child development, training in business management, and playing an active role in an early childhood professional association. Both the FCCERS-R and ITERS-R address opportunities for professional growth (e.g., "Provider is working towards or has achieved a CDA, AA, or higher," "Support [is] available for staff to attend courses, conferences, or workshops") and provisions for professional needs (e.g., "Well-equipped office space for program administration," "Convenient, well-organized storage space," "Comfortable, private space for parent conferences"). The APECP also assesses the availability of professional development opportunities for staff and the professionalism of the program administrator in center-based care, whereas the APFCCH examines the FCC providers' demonstrated commitment to ongoing personal and professional growth. The CDPES contains several subscales dedicated to staff and administrator qualifications, staff development (including staff orientation requirements), and employee performance evaluation requirements, all of which require physical documentation. In addition, the Emlen scales ask parents about their beliefs regarding the skillfulness of their children's provider and the provider's commitment to advancing his or her knowledge; however, we note that these scales are more subjective and are not based on evidence collected from providers themselves.

Coverage of Relationships and Communication with Families

Although most of the global quality measures emphasize the provider–family relationship, many of the other instruments do not address relationships with parents. The FCCERS-R, for instance, has the item "Greeting/departing" to measure the quality of the provider–parent interaction and whether parents are welcomed into the home, greeted warmly, and provided with information about their child's day. Similarly, the item "Provisions for parents" examines whether parents are allowed to observe, whether the provider holds a yearly conference with parents to review the child's progress and plan for the future, and whether parents are referred to other professionals for services for their children or family. Also, the CHELLO measures "Family Support and Interaction" through evidence of contact information and communication with families (e.g., "Provider regularly provides strategies for promoting family activities that support children's language and literacy development"). In addition, the BAS addresses provider–parent communication by gathering documentation of various modes of communication, including a parent handbook, newsletters, bulletin boards, daily notes, e-mails, a program web site, and parent conferences, as well as evidence of parent–caregiver exchanges such as parental preferences regarding child-rearing practices.

The measures that tend not to address relationships and communication with families include measures focused on caregiver–child interactions (CIS, C-COS, ORCE, and COFAS). However, the CC-HOME and the QUEST—two global measures appropriate for home-based settings and with infants and toddlers—also lack items that assess the relationship and communication between providers and families.

Coverage of Community Relationships and Resources

Only one instrument—the BAS—sufficiently addresses community relationships and the use of community resources. The item "Community Resources" captures whether an FCC provider knows about and recommends to parents resources in the community, such as a child care resource and referral agency, parent resource centers, and developmental screening services available through local intervention organizations. The item "Marketing and Public Relations" on the BAS also measures whether a provider attends events sponsored by community organizations and plays an active role in at least one community organization. In addition, the item "Provider–Parent Communication" assesses whether "the provider gives parents descriptive information regarding tax credits, child care subsidies, or employer child care benefits." Because this construct of quality was not specified within standards for infant–toddler care, it is not surprising that we do not find coverage of community relationships in the measures designed specifically for use with infants and toddlers (CC-HOME, ORCE, and ITERS-R).

Coverage of Professional Business Practices

To evaluate the instruments on their assessment of professional business practices, we looked for the inclusion of several key items, including program policies or procedures that are documented and communicated, the maintenance of child records, and other evidence of organized business practices. Eight of the seventeen instruments had evidence of this component of quality. The BAS fully addresses professional business practices through several items, including "Fiscal Management," "Recordkeeping," "Marketing and Public Relations," and "Provider–Parent Communication."

Additional Elements of Quality

Two additional elements of quality, although not widely endorsed across the four sources of quality standards we have examined, are worth mentioning: 1) addressing diversity and children with special needs and 2) conducting ongoing assessments of child progress. Next, we explore how the set of 17 measures addresses each of these additional elements of quality.

Coverage of Attention to Diversity and to Children with Special Needs
Several instruments also covered sensitivity to children with disabilities and to English language learners (ELLs), as well as the inclusion of diversity, across a range of indicators (e.g., environment, activities, teaching). For example, the QUEST assesses the availability of books written in children's home languages and supporting language development and early literacy for ELLs. The ITERS-R and FCCERS-R each have one item assessing the provisions for children with disabilities and another item measuring the acceptance of diversity in materials and activities. In addition, the CCIS addresses engaging children with special needs, with high-quality providers being involved in such tasks as implementing objectives of individualized education programs (IEPs) and blending adaptive materials into the classroom.

Coverage of Assessment of Child Progress
Although stated as a requirement only for Early Head Start—and not for other nonparental care settings serving infants and toddlers or for home-based settings in general—the assessment of children's progress in identified areas of development can be very valuable. Conducting regular assessments of children's skills allows providers to identify children's individual skill levels, their strengths, and the areas in which they are still developing. Especially during the infant–toddler years, it is important to

determine whether a child has any developmental delays so that early intervention may occur. The information gathered during assessments or evaluations also may be used to plan activities, to individualize instruction, and to communicate with families about children's progress.

Few instruments (6 out of 17) address in their measurement of quality whether programs use assessments to monitor children's progress. These instruments include the two literacy measures suitable for home-based settings (CHELLO and OMLIT); the three center-based global measures of quality suitable for infants and toddlers (APECP, CDPES, and ITERS-R); and one home-based measure of global quality (FCCERS-R). The APECP measures teachers' implementation and use of systematic and comprehensive child assessments in planning and organizing learning experiences that match the skill level of each child, whereas the CDPES measures a program's ability to identify children's needs and to conduct ongoing assessments of children's development. The FCCERS-R and ITERS-R also observe whether staff contributes to the assessment and intervention plans of children with disabilities; however, ongoing assessments for all children are not monitored by these instruments.

Summary of Coverage of the Components of Quality within the Different Measurement Types

Given the range of settings in which infants and toddlers are cared for, and the range of ages of children who experience home-based care, there are a variety of quality measures that pertain to these two special subgroups. As noted previously, we identified four types of measures that are relevant: 1) measures specific to home-based settings serving children of all ages; 2) measures appropriate for a variety of settings, including home-based care, serving children of all ages; 3) measures specific to center-based settings that include infants and toddlers, in addition to children of other ages; and 4) measures specific to infant and toddler care, regardless of setting. There is, of course, some overlap in this way of parsing the types of measures available. Next, we summarize the coverage of the components of quality for each of these four types of measures, focusing first on those measures specific to home-based care and then on those specific to infant-toddler care.

Measures of Home-based Care for Children of All Ages

The measures designed specifically for home-based settings included three global measures of quality (APECCH, CCAT-R, and FCCERS-R), the CHELLO, and the BAS. The global measures of quality, by definition, covered more categories of quality than other types of measures. Two of the three global measures used exclusively in home-based settings addressed 8 out of 10 components of quality (APECCH and FCCERS-R), and the other (CCAT-R) addressed 6 components. The CHELLO, a measure of literacy in home-based settings, covered 7 of the 10 categories of quality. The areas that were not well covered by these measures included community relationships and resources, schedules and routines, and providers' qualifications. In contrast, the BAS, the only home-based measure focused on business administration, covered some of the areas that were not well covered by the other home-based measures. Specifically, the BAS covered 5 of the 10 quality areas: health, safety, and nutrition; providers' qualifications and professional development; relationships and communication with families; community relationships and resources; and business practices. Using a global measure in conjunction with the BAS may yield more complete information about the functioning of home-based settings.

Measures for Infants and Toddlers Regardless of Setting

We identified three measures specific to infants and toddlers or that had a version specific to infants and toddlers: the ITERS-R, the CC-HOME, and the ORCE. The ITERS-R, as a global measure of quality specific to infants and toddlers but appropriate for use only in center-based settings, covered all areas of quality except for community relationships and resources. Both the CC-HOME and the ORCE had versions that are specific to the infant–toddler age range; the CC-HOME is designed for home-based settings, and the ORCE may be used in any nonmaternal care setting. These measures, however, did not cover as many areas of quality as suggested by the standards in the field. Specifically, the CC-HOME, the only measure that addressed the quality of care for infants and toddlers in home-based settings, lacked coverage of schedules and routines, providers' qualifications and professional development, relationships and communication with families, community relationships and resources, and business practices. Perhaps because the ORCE was concerned with the proximal experience of the child, this measure covered only two quality areas sufficiently: positive relationships between caregiver and child, and approaches to teaching and cognitive stimulation.

Measures of Center-Based Care for Children of All Ages

The two global measures of quality used in center-based settings that were not specific to infants and toddlers, but still included them (APECP and CDPES), covered all but one component of quality: community relationships and resources. The center-based measure that focused on the quality of caregiving behaviors for children between birth and 12 years (COFAS) covered only three quality areas adequately: positive relationships and interactions between children and providers, developmentally appropriate learning activities, and approaches to teaching and cognitive stimulation.

Measures for Multiple Care Settings and Ages

We identified six measures that could be used in a variety of settings, including home-based care, and for a variety of age groups, including infants and toddlers. These included global measures such as the Emlen Scales and the QUEST, and measures focused on caregiver–child interactions, including the CIS, the CCIS, and the C-COS. There was one measure specific to the literacy environment—the OMLIT—which is appropriate for use with children of all ages in all types of early childhood settings, with two specific subscales appropriate for home-based care. Of these six measures, the CCIS stood out as covering the most quality components (8 of the 10). The only two components not covered by the CCIS were providers' qualifications and community relationships and resources. The Emlen Scales covered 6 of the 10 quality components; the quality components that were missing included approaches to teaching, schedules and routines, community relationships and resources, and business practices. The remaining measures that could be used in multiple care sites for multiple age groups tended to focus on specific features of the environment, such as caregiver–child interactions (CCIS and C-COS) or the literacy environment (OMLIT) and therefore covered elements of the physical environment, developmentally appropriate activities, and approaches to teaching, but lacked coverage of other areas of quality, such as health, safety, and nutrition; schedules and routines; providers' qualifications and professional development; relationships with families and communities; and business practices. The QUEST, a measure noted earlier for excellent coverage of several components of quality, still did not have adequate coverage of schedules and routines, providers' qualifications and professional development, relationships with families, community relationships and resources, and business practices.

Summary

Many infants and toddlers are in nonparental care with some regularity, and many of these young children are cared for in home-based settings. Yet, as a field, we know relatively little about the quality of care for infants and toddlers (compared with what we know about care for older children) and the quality of care in home-based settings (compared with what we know about care in center-based settings). This chapter focuses attention on the features of quality that are essential for the youngest children in ECE settings in the United States, as well as for children of all ages in home-based settings. Results of our review of existing measures indicate that there is wide variability in the coverage of the components of quality thought to be important for infants and toddlers, and for care in home-based settings. Further work is needed to develop new measures with strong psychometric properties that can deepen our understanding of the quality of care infants and toddlers are experiencing, especially those cared for in home-based settings.

References

Abbott-Shim, M., & Sibley, A. (1987). *Assessment Profile for Early Childhood Programs: Preschool, Toddler, Infant, School Age and Administration.* Atlanta, GA: Quality Assist.

Arnett, J. (1989). Caregivers in day-care centers: Does training matter? *Journal of Applied Developmental Psychology, 10,* 541–552.

ASPE Office of Human Services Policy. (2005). *Child care eligibility and enrollment estimates for fiscal year 2003.* Washington, DC: Assistant Secretary for Planning and Evaluation, U.S. Department of Health and Human Services.

Boller, K., Sprachman, S., & the Early Head Start Research Consortium (1998). *The Child–Caregiver Observation System Instructor's Manual.* Princeton, NJ: Mathematica Policy Research.

Bradley, R.H., Caldwell, B.M., & Corwyn, R.F. (2003). The Child Care HOME Inventories: Assessing the quality of family child care homes. *Early Childhood Research Quarterly, 18,* 294–309.

Burstein, N., & Layzer, J.I. (2004). *National Study of Child Care for Low-Income Families: Patterns of child care use among low-income families: Final report.* Washington, DC: Abt Associates.

Carl, B. (2007). *The Child Caregiver Interaction Scale.* Unpublished doctoral dissertation, Indiana University of Pennsylvania, Indiana, PA.

Coley, R.L., Chase-Lansdale, L.P., & Li-Grining, C.P. (2001). *Child care in the era of welfare reform: Quality, choices, and preferences.* Policy Brief 01–04. Baltimore: Johns Hopkins University.

Collins, A., Kreader, L., & Layzer, J. (2004). *National Study of Child Care for Low-Income Families: The supply of regulated child care in twenty-five study communities.* Washington, DC: U.S. Department of Health and Human Services, Administration for Children and Families.

Doherty, G., Forer, B., Lero, D.S., Goelman, H., & LaGrange, A. (2006). Predictors of quality in family child care. *Early Childhood Research Quarterly, 21,* 296–312.

Emlen, A.C., Koren, P.E., & Schultze, K.H. (2000). *A packet of scales for measuring quality of child care from a parent's point of view.* Portland, OR: Regional Research Institute for Human Services, Portland State University.

Fiene, R. (1984). *Child Development Program Evaluation Scale and COFAS*. Washington, DC: Children's Services Monitoring Consortium.

Fiene, R., & Isler, M.W. (2007). Home based and family child care: Characteristics and quality issues. In C.J. Groark, K.E. Mehaffie, R.B. McCall, & M.T. Greenberg (Eds.), *Evidence-based programs, practices, and policies for early childhood care and education* (pp. 102–113). Thousand Oaks, CA: Corwin Press.

Fuller, B., & Kagan, S.L. (2000). *Remember the children: Mothers balance work under welfare reform. Growing Up in Poverty Project, Wave 1 findings—California, Connecticut, Florida.* Berkeley: University of California.

Galinsky, E., Howes, C., Kontos, S, & Abbot-Shim, M. (1994). *The study of children in family child care and relative care: Highlights of findings.* New York: Families and Work Institute.

Goodson, B.D., Layzer, C.J., Smith, W.C., & Rimdzius, T. (2006). *Observation Measures of Language and Literacy Instruction in Early Childhood* (OMLIT). Cambridge, MA: Abt Associates, Inc.

Goodson, B.D., Layzer, J.I., & Layzer, C.J. (2005). *Quality of Early Childhood Care Settings: Caregiver Rating Scale (QUEST).* Cambridge, MA: Abt Associates, Inc.

Halle, T., Hair, E.C., Nuenning, M., Weinstein, D., Vick, J., Forry, N. et al. (2009). ACF-OPRE Research Brief. ACF-OPRE Research Brief. *Primary Child Care Arrangements of U.S. Infants: Patterns of Utilization by Family Income, Family Structure, Maternal Work Status, Maternal Work Schedule, and Child Care Assistance.* Office of Planning, Research and Evaluation, Administration for Children and Families, U.S. Department of Health and Human Services. Washington, DC.

Halle, T., & Vick, J.E. (2007). *Quality in Early Childhood Care and Education: A Compendium of Measures.* Washington, DC: Prepared by Child Trends for the Office of Planning, Research and Evaluation, Administration for Children and Families, U.S. Department of Health and Human Services. Retrieved January 22, 2009, from http://www.researchconnections.org/childcare/resources/13403/pdf

Halle, T., Vick Whittaker, J.E., & Anderson, R. (2010). *Quality in Early Childhood Care and Education: A Compendium of Measures* (2nd ed.). Washington, DC: Child Trends. Prepared by Child Trends for the Office of Planning,

Research and Evaluation, Administration for Children and Families, U.S. Department of Health and Human Services. Retrieved October 10, 2010, from http://www.researchconnections.org/childcare/resources/18804/pdf

Harms, T., Cryer, D., & Clifford, R.M. (2003). *Infant/Toddler Environment Rating Scale–Revised Edition.* New York: Teachers College Press.

Harms, T., Cryer, D., & Clifford, R.M. (2007). *Family Child Care Environment Rating Scale–Revised Edition.* New York: Teachers College Press.

Head Start Program Performance Standards, 45 C.F.R. §§ 1304 (2007).

Iruka, I.U., & Carver, P.R. (2006). *Initial results from the 2005 NHES Early Childhood Program Participation Survey* (NCES 2006–075). Washington, DC: National Center for Education Statistics, U.S. Department of Education.

Kontos, S., Howes, C., Shinn, M., & Galinsky, E. (1995). *Quality in family child care and relative care.* New York: Teachers College.

Kontos, S., Howes, C., Shinn, M., & Galinsky, E. (1997). Children's experiences in family child care and relative care as a function of family income and ethnicity. *Merrill Palmer Quarterly, 43*(3), 386–403.

Matthews, H., & Schumacher, R. (2008). Ensuring quality care for low-income babies: Contracting directly with providers to expand and improve infant and toddler care. (Child Care and Early Education Series Paper No. 3). Washington, DC: Center for Law and Social Policy.

National Association of Child Care Resource & Referral Agencies. (2009). *Parents and the high price of child care—2009 update.* Arlington, VA: NACCRRA.

National Association for the Education of Young Children. (2005). *NAEYC early childhood program standards and accreditation criteria: The mark of quality in early childhood education.* Washington, DC: NAEYC.

National Association for Family Child Care and the National Family Child Care Accreditation Project. (2005). *Quality standards for NAFCC accreditation* (4th ed.). Boston: Wheelock College. Retrieved January 22, 2009, from http://www.nafcc.org/documents/QualStd.pdf

National Institute of Child Health and Human Development (NICHD) Early Child Care

Research Network (1996). Characteristics of infant child care: Factors contributing to positive caregiving. *Early Childhood Research Quarterly, 11,* 269–306.

National Research Council and Institute of Medicine. (2000). *From neurons to neighborhoods: The science of early childhood development.* Washington, DC: National Academies Press.

Neuman, S.B., Dwyer, J., & Koh, S. (2007). *Child/Home Early Language and Literacy Observation (CHELLO) Tool.* Baltimore: Paul H. Brookes Publishing Co.

Porter, T., Rice, R., & Rivera, E. (2006). *Assessing quality in family, friend and neighbor care: The child care assessment tool for relatives.* New York: Institute for a Child Care Continuum.

Sibley, A., & Abbott-Shimm, M. (2005). *Assessment Profile for Family Child Care Homes.* Atlanta, GA: Quality Assist, Inc.

Susman-Stillman, A.R., & Banghart, P. (2008). *Demographics of family, friend, and neighbor child care in the United States.* New York: Child Care and Early Education Research Connections.

Talan, T.N., & Bloom, P.J. (2009). *Business Administration Scale for Family Child Care.* New York: Teachers College Press.

U.S. Census Bureau. (2008). *Who's minding the kids? Child care arrangements: Spring 2005, Detailed tables, PPL Table 1A: Child care arrangements of preschoolers under 5 years old living with mother, by employment status of mother and selected characteristics: Spring 2005 (numbers).* Retrieved January 22, 2009, from http://www.census.gov/population/www/socdemo/child/ppl-2005.html

Whitebook, M., Sakai, L., Gerber, E., & Howes, C. (2001). *Then and now: Changes in child care staffing, 1994–2000.* Washington, DC: Center for the Child Care Workforce.

ZERO TO THREE: National Center for Children, Toddlers, and Families (2009). Developmentally appropriate practice in the infant and toddler years—ages 0–3: Examples to consider. In C. Copple & S. Bredekamp (Eds.), *Developmentally appropriate practice in early childhood programs serving children birth through age 8* (3rd ed.; pp. 75–107). Washington, DC: NAEYC.

Endnotes

[1]Estimates of the percentage of potentially eligible families utilizing subsidies vary substantially, with a range from 12% to 39% (ASPE Office of Human Services Policy, 2005; Burstein & Layzer, 2004). Some of this variation depends on which families are included in the denominator of the estimate (e.g., families who are eligible according to federal versus state eligibility guidelines; families leaving welfare versus all income-eligible families). Estimates also do not take into account other forms of early childhood care and education supports that families receive, such as Head Start and prekindergarten. When these other supports are taken into account, estimates of the proportion of families actually receiving some form of assistance are substantially higher (Collins, Kreader, & Layzer, 2004).

[2]The second edition of the *Quality of Early Childhood Care and Education Settings: A Compendium of Measures* (Halle, Vick Whittaker, & Anderson, 2010) includes a profile of the Classroom Assessment Scoring System developed for use with 15- to 36-month-old children in center-based classrooms (CLASS Toddler), which is currently being piloted in 30 classrooms. A separate infant version of the CLASS is also under development. Because limited information on these new measures is available as of the date of publication of this book, they are not included in this chapter's evaluation of measures.

Appendix Matrix of tools for measuring quality for infants and toddlers and in home-based settings

Measurement tool	Setting	Age range	Focus	Constructs/components measured	Measures of home-based care: Global quality — Components of Quality									
					Positive relationships and interactions among children and providers	Physical environment (facilities, equipment, materials, organization)	Developmentally appropriate learning activities	Approaches to teaching and cognitive stimulation	Health, safety, and nutrition	Schedules and routines	Providers' qualifications and professional development	Relationships and communication with families	Community relationships and resources	Business practices (policies, procedures, schedules, records)
Assessment Profile for Family Child Care Homes (APFCCH)	Family child care homes	Mixed-age groups	Overall program quality, including both physical features and interactions	Safety Health and nutrition Learning environment Interacting Outdoor environment Professionalism	✓	✓	✓	✓	✓	✓	✓	✓		✓
The Child Care Assessment Tool for Relatives (CCAT-R)	Relative care	Children under 6 years	Overall quality of care, with emphasis on specific domains of development	Support for physical development, health, and safety Support for cognitive development Support for language development Support for social-emotional development Behavior management Relationship with parents	✓	✓	✓	✓	✓			✓		
The Child Care HOME Inventories (CC-HOME)	Relative and neighbor care outside of child's home; licensed and unlicensed family child care homes	Infant-Toddler (IT) version for children under 3 years; Early Childhood (EC) version for children 3–6 years	Overall quality of care, with emphasis on stimulation and support	Caregiver responsivity (IT; EC) Acceptance of child (IT; EC) Learning materials (IT; EC) Variety of stimulation (IT)/Variety of experience (EC) Organization (IT) Caregiver involvement (IT) Physical environment (EC) Language stimulation (EC) Academic stimulation (EC) Modeling of social maturity (EC)	✓	✓	✓	✓	✓					
Emlen Scales	Any type of child care arrangement	Children of all ages	Quality of child care from parent's point of view	Warmth and interest in my child Rich activities and environment Skilled caregiver Talk and share information Caregiver accepting and supportive Child feels safe and secure Child getting along well socially High-risk care	✓	✓	✓		✓		✓			

(continued)

Measurement tool	Setting	Age range	Focus	Constructs/components measured	Components of Quality									
					Positive relationships and interactions among children and providers	Physical environment (facilities, equipment, materials, organization)	Developmentally appropriate learning activities	Approaches to teaching and cognitive stimulation	Health, safety, and nutrition	Schedules and routines	Providers' qualifications and professional development	Relationships and communication with families	Community relationships and resources	Business practices (policies, procedures, schedules, records)
Family Child Care Environment Rating Scale–Revised Edition (FCCERS-R)	Family child care homes	Birth through 12 years	Overall quality of child care environment, including appropriate stimulation through language and activities, and warm, supportive interactions	Space and furnishings Personal care routines Listening and talking Activities Interaction Program structure Parents and provider	✓	✓	✓	✓	✓	✓	✓	✓		✓
Quality of Early Childhood Care Settings: Caregiver Rating Scale (QUEST)	Variety of settings, from informal and home-based care to formal center-based care	Birth to 5 years	Quality of caregiver warmth, responsiveness, and support for child's development in cognitive, emotional, social, and physical development	*Environmental Checklist* Space and comfort Equipment and materials to support developmentally appropriate play Equipment and materials to support language and literacy development Indoor safety and health Daily routines *Caregiver Rating Scale* The caregiver with children (caring and responding, using positive guidance and supporting social–emotional development) Supporting play Supporting cognitive development (instructional style and learning activities) Supporting language development and early literacy Television and computers	✓	✓	✓	✓	✓					

Measures of home-based care: Caregiver–child interactions

Measurement tool	Setting	Age range	Focus	Constructs/components measured	Positive relationships and interactions among children and providers									
Arnett Caregiver Interaction Scale (CIS)	Classroom or family child care home	Children of all ages in early childhood settings	Quality of emotional tone and responsiveness of caregiver's interactions with children	Sensitivity Harshness Detachment Permissiveness	✓									

Child and Caregiver Interaction Scale (CCIS)	Home-based and center-based child care settings	Infancy through school age	Quality of child-caregiver interactions, with attention to specific domains of development	*Emotional Domain* Tone of voice Acceptance and respect for children Greetings Enjoys and appreciates children Expectations for children, health, and safety Health and safety *Cognitive/Physical Domain* Routines/time spent Physical attention Discipline Language development Learning opportunities Involvement with children's activities Symbolic and literacy materials *Social Domain* Promotion of prosocial behavior/social emotional learning Engaging children with special needs Relationships with families Cultural competence	✓	✓	✓	✓	✓	✓	✓	✓
The Child-Caregiver Observation Scale (C-COS)	All types of child care settings	1–5 years	Quality of interactions that an individual child experiences within a caregiving environment	Type of caregiver talk Focus-child talk Focus-child interactions Focus-child smiling Caregiver interactions Caregiver behavior toward focus child Focus-child behavior toward caregiver Focus-child behavior toward other children	✓							
Observational Record of the Caregiving Environment (ORCE)	All nonmaternal child care settings	6–54 months, with separate versions for 6 months, 15 months, 24 months, 36 months, and 54 months	Quality of the proximal experiences of the child while in nonmaternal care, including behaviors of caregivers toward target child and behaviors of the target child	*Behavior Scales* Positive and negative affect (6, 15, 24, 36, 54) Language focused interaction (6) Stimulation (6, 15, 24, 36, 54) Behavior management (6, 15, 24, 36, 54) Child's activity (6, 15, 24, 36, 54) Child's interaction with other children (6, 15, 24, 36, 54) Adult language (15, 24, 36, 54) Activity setting (15, 24, 36, 54) Child's behavior (15, 24, 36, 54) Physical control (24, 36, 54)	✓							

(continued)

(continued)

Measurement tool	Setting	Age range	Focus	Constructs/components measured	Components of Quality									
					Positive relationships and interactions among children and providers	Physical environment (facilities, equipment, materials, organization)	Developmentally appropriate learning activities	Approaches to teaching and cognitive stimulation	Health, safety, and nutrition	Schedules and routines	Providers' qualifications and professional development	Relationships and communication with families	Community relationships and resources	Business practices (policies, procedures, schedules, records)
CIS				Positive/neutral peer activities (54) Negative peer activities (54) Child alone (54) *Qualitative Ratings* Sensitivity/responsivity to distress (6, 15, 24, 36) Sensitivity/responsivity to nondistress (6, 15, 24, 36) Intrusiveness (6, 15, 24, 36) Detachment/disengagement (6, 15, 24, 36) Stimulation of development (6, 15, 24, 36) Positive regard for the child (6, 15, 24, 36) Negative regard for the child (6, 15, 24, 36) Flatness of affect (6, 15, 24, 36) Child positive mood (6, 15, 24, 36) Child negative mood (6, 15, 24, 36) Child activity level (6, 15, 24, 36) Child sociability (6, 15, 24, 36) Child sustained attention (6, 15, 24, 36) Child positive engagement with caregiver (15, 24, 36) Chaos (54) Overcontrol (54) Positive emotional climate (54) Negative emotional climate (54)										
Measures of home-based care: Literacy based														
Child/Home Early Language & Literacy Observation (CHELLO)	Home-based child care, including friend, family, and neighbor care	Birth through 5 years	Quality of physical and psychological environmental features associated with children's developing language and literacy skills	*Literacy Environmental Checklist* Book area Book use Writing materials Toys Technology *Physical Environment* Organization of the environment Materials in the environment Daily schedule	✓	✓	✓	✓		✓				✓

Observation Measures of Language and Literacy (OMLIT)

Early childhood classrooms; "Read-Aloud Profile" and "Snapshot of Classroom Activities" subscales used in family child care homes

Children of all ages in early childhood settings

Quality of the instructional practices and environmental supports for langauge and literacy

Support for Learning
Adult affect
Adult–child language interaction
Adult control behaviors
Adult Teaching Strategies
Vocabulary building
Responsive strategies
Use of print
Storybook/storytelling activities
Writing activities
Monitoring children's progress
Family support and interaction

Snapshot of Classroom Activities
Environment (including number of children and adults)
Learning activities
Read-Aloud Profile
Support of comprehension
Support of print motivation
Support of phonological awareness/print knowledge
Classroom Literacy Opportunities Checklist
Physical layout of classroom
Print environment
Literacy toys and materials
Books and reading area
Listening area
Writing supports
Literacy materials outside of reading and writing areas
Diversity in literacy materials
Instructional technology
Richness of curriculum theme and integration of theme in classroom activities, materials, and displays
Literacy resources outside of the classroom
Classroom Literacy Instruction Profile
Type of literacy activities (including assessment)
Literacy knowledge afforded
Teacher's instructional style
Text support/context for literacy instruction
Number of children involved in activity with teacher
Languages spoken by staff and children
Teacher's involvement with children
Cognitive challenge in the discussion
Quality of Language and Literacy Instruction

(continued)

Measurement tool	Setting	Age range	Focus	Constructs/components measured	Positive relationships and interactions among children and providers	Physical environment (facilities, equipment, materials, organization)	Developmentally appropriate learning activities	Approaches to teaching and cognitive stimulation	Health, safety, and nutrition	Schedules and routines	Providers' qualifications and professional development	Relationships and communication with families	Community relationships and resources	Business practices (policies, procedures, schedules, records)
										Components of Quality				
Measures of home-based care: Business administration														
Business Administration Scale for Family Child Care (BAS)	Family child care	Birth through 12 years	Overall quality of business practices in family child care settings	Qualifications and professional development Income and benefits Work environment Fiscal management Record keeping Risk management Provider–parent communication Community resources Marketing and public relations Provider as employer							✓	✓	✓	✓
Measures of center-based care for infants and toddlers: Global quality														
Assessment Profile for Early Childhood Programs (APECP)	Early childhood programs	Infant, toddler, preschool, and school-age children	Global quality of learning environment and teaching practices in classrooms for young children	*Classroom* Safety and health Learning environment Scheduling Curriculum methods Interacting Individualizing practices within the classroom *Administration* Physical facilities Food services Personnel Program management Program development	✓	✓	✓	✓	✓	✓	✓	✓		
Child Development Program Evaluation Scale (CDPES)	Classroom settings	Infant, toddler, preschool, and school-age children	Quality of child development program and compliance with basic minimal requirements that ensure child health and safety	Administration Environmental safety Child development curriculum Health services Nutritional services Social services Transportation	✓	✓	✓	✓	✓	✓	✓	✓		✓

| Infant and Toddler Environment Rating Scale-Revised (ITERS-R) | Classroom settings | Birth to 30 months | Overall quality of care, including protection of child health and safety, appropriate stimulation through language and activities, and warm, supportive interactions | Space and furnishings
Personal care routines
Listening and talking
Activities
Interaction
Program structure
Parents and staff | ✓ | ✓ | ✓ | ✓ | ✓ | ✓ | ✓ |

Measures of center-based care for infants and toddlers: Caregiver-child interactions

| Child Observation Form and Scale (COFAS) | Classroom settings | Infant to 12 years | Quality of caregiving behaviors during interaction with children | Language
Socio-emotional
Motor
Cognitive
Caregiving | ✓ | ✓ | ✓ |

Applications in Policy and Practice

CHAPTER 15

Measuring and Rating Quality

A State Perspective on the Demands for Quality Measurement in a Policy Context

Deborah Swenson-Klatt and Kathryn Tout

The measurement of quality in early care and education (ECE) programs entered the realm of policy relatively recently. Before the late 1990's, quality measurement was an activity conducted primarily in research projects and in professional development initiatives aimed at improving program quality. Since then, however, with the advent of states implementing quality rating and improvement systems (QRIS) for care and education programs, quality measurement has become a topic considered by state policy makers including legislators, state agency staff, and community organizations working closely with ECE and school-age care providers (Zaslow, Tout, & Martinez-Beck, 2010).

A QRIS is a strategy for assessing and rating the quality of ECE programs (as well as school-age care programs in some states) and disseminating the ratings to parents and policy makers. The information also may be used to support quality improvement among participating programs. With more than half of the states currently operating statewide, county-level, or pilot QRIS, or considering QRIS development, quality measurement is now relevant to a broad group of stakeholders who are raising new questions and posing challenges to existing measurement strategies.

The purpose of this chapter is to examine the new demands on quality measurement by drawing on the experiences of one state, Minnesota, as it developed an approach to quality measurement and implemented a pilot QRIS. Although some contextual issues and pressures may be unique, the experiences of Minnesota highlight a number of universal questions and challenges shaping work on quality measurement at the state level. The chapter is organized into three sections. The first section addresses key contextual factors at the state level (as well as at the local and federal levels) that shape the way in which a quality measurement strategy and QRIS develop. The second section describes challenges that implementation of quality improvement initiatives at the state level may face and the implications of these challenges for quality measurement strategies. The third section provides a synthesis of issues from the first two sections and an overall summary of potential next steps in measures development and research supporting quality measurement. Thornburg et al. (Chapter 16, this volume) complements the present chapter, illustrating how data can be used to inform key decisions in both the development and implementation of a state QRIS, using Missouri's experience as illustrative of broader issues.

Contextual Factors Shaping Quality Measurement at the State Level

The context for quality measurement in states plays an important role in shaping decisions that are made at all stages of QRIS development (as well as in the development of other quality improvement initiatives). Contextual factors such as the constituencies and leadership that are involved in the initiative, existing regulations and standards, and previous experience with quality measurement are particularly salient in the early stages of goal setting and planning (as the example from Minnesota in this chapter will demonstrate). These factors continue to be influential, however, once a QRIS is fully implemented and operating. This section provides an overview of the interrelated contextual factors and their impact on key design and implementation decisions related to quality measurement. This section also describes the ways in which the targets in a QRIS (e.g., the types of programs that will be included and the characteristics of families that are the focus of the initiative) shape measurement strategies (though these are determined by decisions in the QRIS and are not contextual factors per se). It is useful to note that a number of other critical QRIS design elements (e.g., the provision of financial incentives and the selection of quality-improvement strategies) are influenced by contextual factors, but this chapter focuses specifically on how strategies for the measurement of quality are shaped by context.

Constituencies and Leadership

In a comprehensive guide for developing QRIS, Mitchell (2005) described the importance of engaging a wide range of stakeholders in the QRIS design phase to promote development of a functional system with clear roles and responsibilities. Stakeholders may include representatives from state agencies, professional associations serving care and education providers, advocacy organizations, parents, higher education, business leaders, and legislative representatives. These stakeholders typically engage in a participatory planning process to establish goals, structure, and other features of a QRIS. In a case study of five early QRIS adopters, Zellman and Perlman (2008) found that states indeed involved multiple stakeholders to establish buy-in to the development process; however, these researchers acknowledged the potential for reduced momentum and slow progress when many participants are brought to the table during the development phase. One reason for this tension in the process is that there may be competing priorities for the initiatives among the stakeholders that are involved. The resolution of these tensions will have implications for the final design decisions.

In Minnesota, QRIS stakeholders, led by early childhood and school-age advocates, participated in a development process and the production of a QRIS implementation plan for a pilot program. However, the legislation establishing the pilot program was vetoed by the governor in the 2006 legislative session. In a statement about the veto, the governor stated that "an input-driven rating system is not the best way to provide parents with meaningful results regarding the quality of the child care facility" (Pawlenty, 2006, June 2). The governor then directed the Minnesota Department of Human Services (DHS) and the Minnesota Department of Education (MDE) to collaborate on the development of a QRIS pilot that would better align children's kindergarten readiness to the rating system.

Simultaneously, the Minnesota Early Learning Foundation (MELF) was launched with contributions from the philanthropic and business communities. MELF is a partnership of foundation, corporate, and civic leaders and was established to address growing concerns in Minnesota about school readiness among at-risk children. As part of this mission, MELF was preparing to pilot a QRIS as a cornerstone of an innovative scholarship initiative (the Saint Paul Early Childhood Scholarship program) to promote access to high-quality ECE for low-income children.[1] As the overlap in MELF and state agency efforts became clear, the two were combined. With the financial support of MELF and in-kind contributions from state agency partners, Parent Aware—Minnesota's pilot QRIS—began in July, 2007. (See Box 15.1.)

The leaders of MELF established guiding principles for Parent Aware that have defined and shaped the measurement approach used in the pilot. First, they specified that the goal of Parent Aware and the related Saint Paul Early Childhood Scholarship Program must be the promotion and support of school readiness for at-risk children (a goal aligned clearly with the direction provided to state agencies by the governor). The identification of improved child outcomes as an explicit goal has influenced the choice of tools and rating processes included in the pilot and has differentiated the

---

Box 15.1.   Parent Aware: Minnesota's Quality Rating and Improvement System Pilot

What Is Parent Aware?

Parent Aware is a voluntary quality rating and improvement system (QRIS) for early care and education (ECE) programs, including licensed family child care programs, child care centers, Head Start, and school-based prekindergarten (pre-K) programs. It is being piloted from July 2007 through June 2011 in four Minnesota communities: the city of Minneapolis, the city of Saint Paul, the Wayzata school district, and Blue Earth and Nicollet Counties. More than 300 ECE programs serving more than 20,000 children were participating in Parent Aware as of January, 2010.

The primary purpose of Parent Aware is to support parents by providing information about the quality of ECE programs. Parent Aware uses ratings to recognize quality and promotes quality improvement through a variety of resources. Together, these strategies aimed at parents and ECE programs target an ultimate goal of improving children's school readiness.

How Are Ratings Assigned to ECE Programs?

Programs submit documentation and receive visits from trained observers using the Environment Rating Scales and the Classroom Assessment Scoring System™ (CLASS™; Pianta, La Paro, & Hamre, 2008) that measure their environment, practices, and interactions with children. Programs are awarded one to four stars depending upon the number of points earned in four categories:

- Family partnerships
- Teaching materials and strategies
- Tracking learning
- Teacher training and education

Accredited child care centers, accredited family child care programs, school-based pre-K, and Head Start programs are awarded a four-star rating automatically if they demonstrate current accreditation status and compliance with licensing, or compliance with applicable state or federal program performance standards.

How Do Parents Learn About the Ratings?

Ratings are posted on the Parent Aware web site. Parents can search for programs by pilot area and in a variety of languages including English, Hmong, Spanish, and Somali. They can also call their local child care resource and referral agency for assistance.

Minnesota pilot from earlier QRIS initiatives in other states focused primarily on quality improvement as an explicit goal (Tout, Zaslow, Halle, & Forry, 2009; Zellman & Perlman, 2008). The explicit emphasis on supporting child outcomes for at-risk children as the goal of QRIS in Minnesota and other states has contributed to the focus on recent findings from research showing only modest prediction of child outcomes from existing quality measures (Burchinal et al., 2009; see also Burchinal, Kainz, & Cai, Chapter 2, this volume), and helped to foster consideration of how measures of quality might be strengthened.

Second, MELF emphasized the centrality of parents and their role in supporting school readiness through the choices they make about ECE. This emphasis has been the basis for a directive for the implementation team to consider not only the measures used in the rating process but also how the information is disseminated to parents. However, although parents have been a specific target of state QRIS from the beginning, there is little research evidence documenting whether and how parents process and use QRIS information and the effectiveness of specific dissemination strategies (Tout & Maxwell, 2010; Zaslow & Forry, 2009). Thus, considerable effort by MELF and the implementation team has gone into conducting focus groups to understand what parents would like to see in a QRIS and into developing communication and marketing strategies aimed at parents (DHS & MDE, 2007; Ray, 2010). Stakeholders in the initiative were surprised by the dearth of empirical findings on this topic, given the purported emphasis on parents in QRIS across the nation.

Third, MELF called for an evaluation of the initiative so that the effectiveness of the tools and strategies developed for the Minnesota QRIS pilot could be analyzed and so that key lessons learned could inform a possible statewide scaling up of the QRIS. MELF also requested that the evaluation examine the linkages between the quality ratings and children's school readiness gains. The evaluation is coordinated with other evaluations of MELF initiatives, and MELF leadership has emphasized from the beginning the role that evidence-based decisions should play in the ECE system (MELF, 2009). As the measurement tools were being developed for the QRIS pilot, MELF and the implementation team reminded stakeholders that the evaluation would provide data on whether the processes were working as anticipated, setting clear expectations that feedback loops were in place to allow initial decisions to be revised as more information became available. The presence of business leaders on the MELF board of directors has reinforced this focus on accountability and data-driven decision making.

As the QRIS pilot has progressed in Minnesota, the influence of other constituencies, including professional organizations and providers associations, also has been prominent in shaping aspects of the pilot related to the quality measures. For example, the inclusion of indicators related to the use of a research-based curriculum and assessment tools has led to the provision of free training and resources for providers who need assistance in meeting these indicators. These additions to the pilot were made as it became clear that certain quality indicators would be particularly challenging for the providers in the pilot areas.

Existing Regulations and Standards

Licensing regulations are a foundational element of QRIS (Mitchell, 2005; Tout, Starr, Soli, Moodie, Kirby & Boller, 2010b; Zellman & Perlman, 2008). Indeed, QRIS are intended to provide incentives for scaling "manageable increments" between licensing and accreditation (Mitchell, 2005, p. 5). Thus, existing licensing regulations are another key contextual factor to consider in the development of QRIS measurement strategies. Some states incorporate licensing into the QRIS by using a rated license in which compliance with a mandatory initial licensing assessment results in attainment of the first level of a QRIS; programs can then decide whether they want to participate in the voluntary portion of the system in which they may attain further stars that are posted on their license. Other states may incorporate licensing as an eligibility criteria for the QRIS. Depending on concerns about the adequacy of certain licensing regulations, QRIS may incorporate quality standards related to elements such as ratio and group size to build on perceived deficiencies in the regulations. Other elements such as staff qualifications may be addressed in both licensing and the QRIS, with the QRIS offering standards that build upon those in licensing.

In Minnesota, compliance with licensing is an eligibility criterion for the QRIS. Standards related to ratio and group size were not included, because the perception among the developers was that existing licensing regulations were sufficient.

Standards such as early learning guidelines, core competencies for practitioners, and career lattices (outlining "steps" of professional credentials and qualifications) also may be incorporated into QRIS and can provide a critical connection to align QRIS with other ongoing initiatives. States that prioritize inclusion of these standards will shape their measurement strategy accordingly.

For example, Minnesota included the state early learning guidelines in the pilot QRIS by creating an indicator on curriculum that specifies that a curriculum must be research-based and aligned with the Minnesota Early Childhood Indicators of Progress (the state's early learning guidelines). If a program is not using a curriculum that has been preapproved by Parent Aware, the curriculum can be submitted to an expert review committee that will assess the degree to which it is aligned with the early learning guidelines (as well as assess the degree to which it is in compliance with other criteria).

Previous Experience with Quality Measurement

The state's previous experience with quality measurement and quality improvement initiatives is another important contextual factor to consider. States that have engaged in efforts to collect baseline data on quality prior to implementation of a QRIS may have greater "buy-in" among providers and programs to the concept of measuring and rating quality. States may be inclined to include existing quality measures with which they have gained experience through research or quality improvement activities, rather than starting from scratch and developing new measures.

For example, through the Minnesota Child Care Policy Research Partnership,[2] observational data on child care center quality had been collected in Minnesota with the use of the Early Childhood Environment Rating Scale-Revised Edition (ECERS-R; Harms, Clifford, & Cryer, 2005; Tout & Sherman, 2005). Similarly, Minnesota was involved in the five-state Quality Initiatives for Early Care and Education (QUINCE) Partnerships for Inclusion (PFI) evaluation that involved use of the ECERS-R, the Family Day Care Rating Scale (FDCRS; Harms & Clifford, 1989), and the Early Childhood Environment Rating Scale Extension (ECERS-E; Sylva, Siraj-Blatchford, & Taggart, 2006) in an assessment-based individualized consultation model aimed at improving quality (Bryant et al., 2009). As part of participation in the QUINCE study, consultants in Minnesota resource and referral agencies and a provider association group were trained in the Environment Rating Scales (ERS), and interest grew among decision-makers and the provider community in using assessment tools in ECE settings as a basis for goal-setting and quality improvement. Existing state capacity with the ERS, in addition to the use of ERS in numerous other state QRIS, was a significant influence on the decision to include the ERS in the pilot QRIS. It is likely that experience with these tools (including the ECERS-E) lay the groundwork for inclusion of a measure with an emphasis on instructional quality—the Classroom Assessment Scoring System™ (CLASS™; Pianta, La Paro, & Hamre, 2008)—that also was clearly linked to the MELF and state focus on promoting school readiness.

Targets of QRIS

A final issue to consider with respect to measurement strategy includes the targets of the QRIS, though this is not a contextual factor per se. Decisions about the targets of the initiative—the programs and parents that the QRIS is focused on influencing—become a driving force in shaping the measurement strategy that is used. Three interrelated factors are helpful to review: the types of ECE settings included in the initiative, the characteristics of the workforce affected by the QRIS, and the characteristics of families served. Each of these factors has implications for the measures selected and the quality improvement strategies used.

Types of ECE Settings Included in the Initiative

Nationwide, the majority of QRIS include a full range of ECE programs, including licensed child care centers and family child care programs, Head Start/Early Head Start, and state pre-K programs (Tout et al., 2010b; legally license-exempt home-based providers typically are not included in QRIS). The decision to include a range of programs can be an important signal that acknowledges or promotes system integration. In practice, however, inclusion of different program types with different program standards and requirements (e.g., Head Start Performance Standards and pre-K standards in state statutes) may present implementation challenges, such as, for example, whether to permit programs meeting specific program standards an option to receive an automatic rating instead of going through the "full" QRIS rating process. During QRIS development, efforts may be made to document how well different sets of standards are aligned conceptually (e.g., whether they include goals or requirements for the same program elements). Yet, little empirical evidence exists to help states know whether conceptually aligned standards relate to practices that are actually observed in ECE programs. This is an important research issue for states to consider as they engage in efforts to validate their measurement strategies.

In Minnesota, for example, a policy decision was made midway through the pilot to award school-based pre-K programs an automatic four-star rating (the highest available) in a process similar to that used for Head Start programs and accredited programs (both center-based and family child care programs), which are also automatically awarded a four-star rating in the pilot. This was a change from the beginning of the pilot, when school-based programs were awarded a three-star "provisional" rating indicating that they had not been through the full rating process. Stakeholders have expressed concern about the automatic rating process in general and are awaiting the results of findings from the evaluation that can address further decisions about this process through direct observation of quality in programs receiving automatic ratings (Tout, Starr, Knerr, Cleveland, Soli, & Quinn, 2010a).

Characteristics of the Workforce Included in the Initiative

In addition to program type, it is also critical to consider the characteristics of the workforce employed in the programs targeted by QRIS. Key characteristics to note include the qualifications and credentials of the workforce, the geographic location of programs and providers, cultural background and languages spoken, as well as other demographic characteristics. Measurement strategies will be affected by each of these characteristics, as will strategies for outreach and recruitment and provision of quality-improvement supports.

In the Minnesota pilot, MELF invested in a baseline survey of programs and providers in the pilot areas to identify the context for the Parent Aware pilot, including structural characteristics of programs (staff or provider qualifications, weekly rates) and other important features such as languages spoken and use of a curriculum (Chase & Moore, 2008). Data from the Minnesota Child Care Resource and Referral Network also were used in this effort. These data provided the Parent Aware implementation team with critical information at the outset of the pilot that helped them to make decisions about measurement, recruitment, and quality-improvement supports. The evaluation of Parent Aware provided further documentation after the first year of the pilot on topics related to the characteristics of the workforce such as resistance to Parent Aware by providers in rural areas (particularly family child care programs) and concerns about whether the model or definition of quality promoted in Parent Aware is more appropriate for center-based programs than for family child care programs (Tout, Starr, & Cleveland, 2009). These data informed the development of measurement strategies by, for example, highlighting the need for measurement strategies that could be used in programs in which English was not spoken and the need to develop indicators that could tap training on curriculum and assessment tools (rather than simply including checkboxes for programs to indicate that a specific tool is being used).

Characteristics of the Families Served

As noted, families are key stakeholders in QRIS, and information about the characteristics of families targeted by QRIS can shape its development. In addition to the baseline study of programs and providers conducted by MELF in the Minnesota QRIS pilot, a baseline study of families in the pilot areas was also conducted (Chase & Moore, 2008). The study revealed critical information about the level of disadvantage of families in the pilot areas (with lower incomes noted for families in the urban areas than in the rural pilot areas), the cultural and linguistic diversity of families in the pilot areas (again, with greater diversity found in the urban areas than in the rural areas), the use of ECE arrangements (with greater use of family, friend, and neighbor care among families in the urban pilot areas), and access to the Internet—the primary mechanism for accessing QRIS information (with less use of the Internet found in the urban pilot areas). The findings shaped the way that information about quality is described and disseminated in Parent Aware. The implementation team also developed strategies for collecting information that could be useful to parents, though not necessarily information included in the rating. For example, the administrators of each program in the QRIS pilot submit a philosophy statement that describes in their own words the mission and goals of their program. Using feedback from parents in the focus groups indicating that the health and safety of the children is a primary concern, they also developed a health and safety checklist to be completed by all programs upon enrollment in the rating process.

Summary of Contextual Factors

When quality measurement becomes a central component of a policy initiative, multiple factors will shape the ultimate decisions that are made about design and implementation of the measurement strategy, including the priorities of leaders and stakeholders in the initiative, characteristics of the target participants of the initiative (including both programs–providers and families), the perception and prioritization of existing regulations and standards by QRIS developers, and previous experience and "buy-in" to the use of quality measures among QRIS developers. In the absence of a consensus set of QRIS standards that has been validated across program types, states initiating QRIS have enormous flexibility in the parameters they develop for their measurement strategies. Yet, as will be described in the next section, challenges may emerge in implementation of QRIS strategies or may be raised in evaluation findings that may require reexamination of initial decisions and revision of QRIS features.

Quality Measurement at the State Level: Implementation Challenges

The development of goals, priorities, and a logic model for a QRIS is a necessary first step preceding development of actual procedures and protocols for, and eventual launching of, the initiative. In preparation for implementation of a state QRIS, a number of challenges may arise, highlighting the demands on quality measures that emerge in a policy context. In many ways, these challenges are similar to the contextual influences described earlier and reflect the need to adapt and make decisions based on the realities encountered in the field. Yet, these decisions have profound implications for the integrity of a QRIS, the validity of the approach, and the effectiveness in achieving desired outcomes. In this section, four challenges are illustrated: building consensus around measures, balancing cost with stakeholders' and participants' needs, translating measures for parents, and situating QRIS in a high-profile political environment.

Building Consensus

As noted, the goals of a QRIS initiative are a key driver of design decisions. In the Minnesota pilot, a goal of improved school readiness was established early in the development phase and was used as a guidepost for decisions about quality domains to include in the actual rating tool. Identifying the broad categories of indicators to include in the QRIS was fairly straightforward because many of the other state QRIS could be reviewed and the research base could be turned to for basic confirmation of the positive linkages between certain domains (e.g., the learning environment) and children's outcomes (albeit with modest effect sizes; Burchinal et al., 2009). Yet, decisions about which specific indicators to include were much more difficult, and the research base on QRIS is not advanced enough to provide guidance on these critical decisions. (See Thornburg et al., Chapter 16, this volume, for a description of how data from a QRIS pilot were used to inform critical program decisions.) Building consensus on the quality indicators was time consuming and required careful consideration at multiple levels.

At one level, indicators needed to be developed consistently *within* program type. For example, in addition to the considerations about the inclusion of state early learning guidelines and career lattices, developers wondered, How will the indicators in each domain be structured? What documentation will be required for each indicator? How will the indicators be weighted or scored in the QRIS? In each case, the questions raised in the measures development process outstrip the existing research base (Zaslow, Tout, & Martinez-Beck, 2010). Decisions must be made, extrapolating from the existing evidence and making estimates of face validity. Without a sufficiently detailed research base on how to structure ratings, and especially where to place cut-points, building consensus on indicators is challenging.

A second level requires building consensus on measures across the programs included in the QRIS and determining equivalence of measurement strategies across program types. For example, are the indicators and measurement structure developed for center-based programs appropriate for family child care programs? If not, how will they be adapted? How will decisions be made about "automatic" rating processes that equate a level of the QRIS with the standards set by a different body (e.g., an accrediting body or the statutory requirements for school-based prekindergarten programs)? Very little or no empirical evidence exists that can provide guidance to states asking these questions, though evaluations of the pilot in Minnesota as well as of those in other states are beginning to provide this crucial information.

A third level requires consensus on measures among diverse stakeholders within the communities involved in a QRIS initiative. As noted, the implementation team in Minnesota used baseline survey data to identify characteristics of the communities involved in the Parent Aware pilot. These data revealed the need to consider a variety of cultural groups and languages (including Spanish, Somali, Hmong, and Karen, among others), and in follow-up discussions, stakeholders raised the possibility of including indicators related to the cultural sensitivity of programs. (See Bromer et al., Chapter 8, and Shivers & Sanders, with Westbrook & Najafi, Chapter 9, this volume, for in-depth discussions of practices that are indicative of family-sensitive caregiving and culturally responsive pedagogy, respectively.) However, limited information was available to the implementation team regarding the inclusion of indicators related to cultural or linguistic competence or sensitivity, as noted by Bruner and colleagues in their review of QRIS (Bruner, Ray, Wright, & Copeman, 2009). Work is underway to begin building the research base on this issue (NAEYC, 2009), but QRIS have few resources to draw upon in their systems. In Minnesota, this gap has caused tension between the implementation team and community stakeholders who view the QRIS as unresponsive to their concerns about gaps in the current measurement strategy. Further research linking measures of family sensitivity and cultural responsiveness to family and child outcomes, therefore, not only will strengthen measurement within QRIS but also will provide a basis for greater responsiveness to the priorities of key stakeholders.

Balancing Cost with Needs

A second set of challenges related to implementation concerns the trade-off that states must make across the different activities needed to fully operate a QRIS. As seen in Thornburg and colleagues, Chapter 16, this volume, a pilot phase of a QRIS initiative can facilitate data-based decision making on issues such as the number of classrooms to assess in order to arrive at a rating for a center and the frequency with which measures should be collected. Yet, in the absence of solid evidence gathered across state contexts, states likely feel that these and other measurement decisions must be made within their own policy and economic contexts.

For example, in the Minnesota pilot, the implementation team chose to conduct annual on-site observations by using the ERS (ECERS-R; the Infant and Toddler Environment Rating Scale-Revised Edition, ITERS-R; Harms, Cryer, & Clifford, 2003; the Family Child Care Environment Rating Scale Revised Edition, FCCERS-R; Harms, Cryer, & Clifford, 2007) as well as the (CLASS; Pianta et al., 2008) in classrooms serving preschool-age children in center-based settings. The use of multiple observational assessment tools greatly increased the cost of the pilot because of the training and infrastructure needed to support appropriate use of the tools in the field (including proper training prior to data collection and frequent monitoring of reliability throughout the pilot). It is expected that data from the evaluation will be used to assess this decision and make recommendations about the number and frequency of on-site observations to include if the QRIS is scaled statewide.

A number of other cost questions that relate peripherally to measurement decisions also must be answered in a QRIS initiative, including provision of quality improvement supports to programs (e.g., What criteria should be used to allocate resources to programs and providers), provision of incentives to programs for improving quality, provision of culturally responsive services for both programs and parents (e.g., Into how many languages should materials be translated?), and the level and types of supports for parents (e.g., What kinds of outreach to parents should be planned to help parents understand QRIS ratings?; Into how many languages should information about the ratings be translated?). In Minnesota, for example, the implementation team prioritized outreach and supports to providers from diverse cultural groups and has devoted resources to translation and the development of culturally specific recruitment efforts. In addition, the availability of scholarships and allowances for low-income families was intended to infuse resources into the system that could provide both access to high-quality settings for families and additional resources to programs to improve and maintain quality. Evaluation results from the allowances initiatives indicate that the funds were indeed used for both of these purposes (Gaylor, Spiker, Ferguson, Williamson, & Georges, 2009).

It is also important to note that costs of the program are not incurred only at the level of service provision. Depending on whether and to what extent states offer financial resources to programs undertaking quality improvement, participating programs also may incur costs as they make improvements to meet the quality standards in the QRIS. Further research on these costs and the supports that are most useful in helping programs meet and maintain quality standards is needed.

Translating Measures for Parents

Another challenge encountered in the Minnesota pilot that highlights the new demands placed on current quality measurement strategies relates to parents, their understanding of quality measures, and their potential interactions with a QRIS. As previously noted, MELF identified low-income families as a primary target of MELF initiatives because children in these families are more likely than other children to begin kindergarten not fully prepared. Through focus groups and a survey of parents, the implementation team had learned about parents' perceptions of quality and their hypothetical interest in using a rating system. However, further analysis by a marketing research team revealed that, even though parents are interested in the concept of quality ECE, there is a need first to build a very basic understanding among parents about the importance of children's early learning. Without this knowledge, parents are unlikely to act on information that they learn about quality. The implementation team also took note of the survey data indicating that a significant proportion of low-income families and recent immigrant families, particularly in the urban pilot area, were using care provided by family, friends, and neighbors. The interpretation of these findings was that families may need information not only about early learning and the importance of quality but also about the ECE system in general. Parents may need answers to such questions as, What are the types of care available? What do the different terms used in ECE, such as *licensing* and *accreditation,* mean? Research conducted by the National Association of Resource and Referral Agencies (NACCRRA) confirms this need. NACCRRA research has shown that parents are confused by terms used in QRIS and ECE. This research indicates that parents have misperceptions about the requirements for licensing and the regularity of inspections in child care settings (i.e., they assume that inspections occur on an annual basis, and in many states, this is not the case; NACCRRA, 2009; Smith & Sarkar, 2008).

In addition to the challenges posed by parents' understanding, or lack thereof, of key terms and concepts in the QRIS, additional challenges related to the timing of information provided to parents were identified. From the perspective of a QRIS logic model (see Zellman, Perlman, Le, & Setodji, 2008), parents are expected to drive participation by programs in QRIS and in quality-improvement activities because parents begin to demand information about quality. However, at the beginning of a QRIS initiative, recruiting programs and building an adequate supply of rated programs are critical activities. There is a tension in promoting a QRIS before there is an adequate supply of rated programs because parents may become frustrated if there are few rated programs to choose from. In Minnesota, a radio campaign was launched at the end of the second year of the pilot once it was determined that a supply of rated programs was available to families.

Another timing challenge concerns promoting a consumer demand model without ensuring that parents have adequate resources to purchase high-quality care. Resources may provide target parents with information to help them value, assess, and select higher quality care and education, but there may be unintended, negative consequences if parents are unable to afford access to highly rated programs. Ideally, rollout of a QRIS would occur with information about how to access financial support and with adequate resources to fully fund financial support for parents who need it. In Minnesota, parent mentors were included in the first year of the Saint Paul Early Childhood Scholarship Program to assist parents who received scholarships upon selection of a program with a three- or four-star rating.

Situating QRIS in a Political Environment

The promise of QRIS to produce positive impacts that range from improved quality of ECE programs, to better parental decision-making, to enhanced school readiness has increased the visibility of QRIS among policy makers at the state and federal levels. There is an expectation that outcomes will be achieved quickly, but less attention is paid to the incremental benchmarks that would need to be in place before a QRIS has the full potential to achieve the desired outcomes (Tout & Maxwell, 2010). This pressure on QRIS (particularly those that are new or in a pilot phase) to ramp up quickly and produce rapid improvements creates implementation challenges. For example, in the Minnesota pilot there was pressure to enroll programs quickly because of the colaunching of the Saint Paul Early Childhood Scholarship Program, as well as another financial incentive program for parents called the Pre-Kindergarten Allowances Program (in which income-eligible families could receive $4,000 to use at a program with a three- or four-star Parent Aware rating). Procedures for enrolling programs to be rated automatically at the four-star level were developed, as was a process called a provisional rating (equivalent to a three-star) that would bypass much of the documentation and the observational visits conducted for a full Parent Aware rating. The provisional rating was open to licensed child care centers and family homes that were not accredited. Although many programs took advantage of the automatic rating process for accredited programs, very few applied for the provisional rating (Tout et al., 2010a). Thus, the provisional rating process as originally designed has been modified for use in only limited circumstances. In addition, the rapid speed of the launch of Parent Aware caused some communication gaps, and some stakeholders perceived that "shifting ground" has prevailed, as rules and requirements have been modified along the way. The flexibility to adjust procedures is useful to the implementation team, but clearly can create confusion among staff and program participants.

A QRIS implementation team also is challenged to manage expectations about the timeline on which changes will occur. For example, what density of programs should be enrolled in a QRIS before market-level outcomes can be expected? What level of investment in quality improvement is needed to produce lasting change in quality? What criteria can be put in place to determine with certainty that the measurement tool produces meaningfully different valid quality levels across the rated programs? As QRIS are emphasized in state legislation and in state-level committees such as the Early Childhood Advisory Councils, these questions will need to be addressed.

Summary of Implementation Challenges

On the ground, a number of challenges emerge when quality measures are implemented in a policy context. Forming consensus on specific definitions and quality indicators across diverse stakeholders is difficult, and there is limited research for states to turn to when making these decisions. Trade-offs also must be made to balance the costs of measuring, rating, improving, and disseminating information about quality. Again, the evidence base that can assist states as they wrestle with these trade-offs is limited. Challenges are also encountered when measures and the results of the rating process are translated to parents. The needs go beyond an understanding of whether parents would like to see ratings, to a core issue of whether parents (or all key subgroups of parents) value the concept of early learning and the role that quality plays in early learning. Finally, states implementing QRIS initiatives also must develop strategies for dealing with high expectations for producing change in rapid fashion. The welcome focus on measuring quality and using ratings as part of an overall strategy to improve quality needs to be balanced against unrealistic expectations that change will occur rapidly or translate immediately into improvements in child outcomes.

Next Steps for Research and Development of Quality Measures and Measurement Strategies that Are Responsive to a Policy Context

QRIS are multifaceted initiatives with broad goals, diverse stakeholders, and a limited, though growing, evidence base to guide design and implementation decisions. As the example in this chapter has illustrated, QRIS are influenced by a variety of contextual factors and face numerous challenges in launching sound, quality measurement approaches that are appropriate across settings and the populations served.

Research is needed to address questions in several areas about quality measurement within QRIS.[4] In particular, work in three key research areas could generate findings to strengthen the use of quality measures in policy contexts.

First, what specific quality indicators should be included in a QRIS and how should these be defined? As noted earlier, stakeholders can come to consensus relatively easily on the broad domains of quality to include in a QRIS, but it is much more challenging to agree upon specific quality indicators and the distinctions that they make between different quality levels. For example, even when existing measures are used in a QRIS, decisions still need to be made about which scores (a total score or subscale scores) should be incorporated into a rating scale. If measures (e.g., indicators of family partnerships) for the QRIS are developed by the implementation team, decisions need to be made about which constructs should be emphasized in the indicators and what documentation requirements should be used to establish that an indicator has been met. Research findings could and should play a much stronger role in this aspect of QRIS design and development.

Second, how should quality indicators be combined, and how should thresholds or cutoffs be determined to produce a measurement strategy that accurately identifies meaningful differences in quality? To address this question, QRIS stakeholders and researchers need to agree upon the criterion for these analyses. What is a "meaningful" difference in quality? In the Minnesota pilot, stakeholders specified that a quality differential should be predictive of children's outcomes. However, there may be a need to consider multiple criteria—for example, quality that produces greater stability of children in the program (in terms of attendance) or quality that is linked to better family outcomes. Research that can clarify these concepts and predictive relationships would be very useful.

Third, what logistical parameters and infrastructure requirements should be recommended for quality measures? Measurement of quality in a QRIS is different from measurement of quality in a research project in some ways, but not in others. (See Zaslow, Tout, & Halle, Chapter 17, this volume, for a discussion of different purposes of quality measurement.) Attention to psychometric properties of measures, such as reliability and validity, is paramount in measures used for both purposes. (See Bryant, Burchinal, & Zaslow, Chapter 3, this volume.) However, the field is at a point at which recommendations could be made on standards for reliability, for frequency of measurement, and for documentation when measures are used in policy contexts such as QRIS. There may be important issues to consider when measurement is conducted in an environment with financial and other "high-stakes" consequences at play.

As new research on these critical questions emerges and is added to the existing research base, guidelines for QRIS quality standards measurement strategies and validation studies can be continually refined. An underlying goal for this work could be acceptance by QRIS stakeholders, at multiple levels, of the principle that QRIS, to the extent possible, should use research-based indicators and a measurement approach that has been validated by research.

In conclusion, it is important to highlight that state policy makers are clear about their interest in new research and recommendations from the field: They are eager for information from the research community about how to structure QRIS in a way that brings them closer to achieving the goals they have for programs, families, and children (Child Trends, 2009). The realities of tight budgets and other implementation pressures may continue to influence decisions made in a policy context, but states are looking to improve QRIS and to use their resources wisely and with the greatest impact. New collaborative initiatives—such as the Quality Initiatives Research and Evaluation Consortium (INQUIRE) funded by the Office of Planning, Research and Evaluation in the U.S. Department of Health and Human Services, as well at the QRIS National Learning Network coordinated by the BUILD Initiative and Smart Start's National Technical Assistance Center—are bringing together researchers and policy makers to work toward refinement and improvement of QRIS.

References

Bruner, C., Ray, A., Wright, M.S., & Copeman, A. (2009). *Quality rating improvement systems for a multi-ethnic society.* BUILD Initiative. Retrieved July 21, 2010, from http://www.buildinitiative.org/files/QRIS-Policy%20Brief.pdf

Bryant, D., Wesley, P., Burchinal, P., Sideris, J., Taylor, K., Fenson, C., et al. (2009, September). *The QUINCE-PFI Study: An evaluation of a promising model for child care provider training. Final Report.* Chapel Hill, NC: FPG Child Development Institute.

Burchinal, P., Kainz, K., Cai, K., Tout, K., Zaslow, M., Martinez-Beck, I., & Rathgeb, C. (2009). ACF-OPRE Research-to-Policy Brief. *Early Care and Education Quality and Child Outcomes.* Office of Planning, Research and Evaluation, Administration for Children and Families, U.S. Department of Health and Human Services. Washington, DC.

Chase, R., & Moore, C. (2008, February). *Early learning conditions among low-income families in Minneapolis, Saint Paul, and Blue Earth and Nicollet counties: Baseline study prepared for the Minnesota Early Learning Foundation.* St. Paul, MN: Wilder Research.

Child Trends. (2009). *Meeting on evaluation of state quality rating systems.* Washington, DC: Meeting notes prepared for the U.S. Department of Health and Human Services, Administration for Children and Families, Office of Planning, Research, and Evaluation.

Gaylor, E., Spiker, D., Ferguson, K., Williamson, C., & Georges, A. (2009). *Pre-Kindergarten Allowances Project: Final Evaluation Report.* Menlo Park, CA: SRI International.

Gaylor, E., Spiker, D., Williamson, C., & Ferguson, K. (2010, March). *Saint Paul Early Childhood Scholarship Program Evaluation,* *Annual Report, Year 2.* Menlo Park, CA: SRI International.

Harms, T., & Clifford, R.M. (1989). *Family Day Care Rating Scale.* New York: Teachers College Press.

Harms, T., Clifford, R.M., & Cryer, D. (2005). *Early Childhood Environment Rating Scale–Revised Edition.* New York: Teachers College Press.

Harms, T., Cryer, D., & Clifford, R.M. (2003). *Infant Toddler Environment Rating Scale–Revised.* New York: Teachers College Press.

Harms, T., Cryer, D., & Clifford, R.M. (2007). *Family Child Care Environment Rating Scale–Revised.* New York: Teachers College Press.

Minnesota Department of Education and Minnesota Department of Human Services. (2007, January). *Child Care Information and Rating System—parent focus group results.* DHS-4965-ENG 1-07. St. Paul, MN: Author.

Minnesota Early Learning Foundation. (2009, April). *Annual report: Fiscal year 2008.* St. Paul, MN: Author.

Mitchell, A.W. (2005). *Stair steps to quality: A guide for states and communities developing quality rating systems for early care and education.* Alexandria, VA: United Way of America, Success by 6.

National Association for the Education of Young Children. (2009). *Quality benchmark for cultural competence.* Retrieved March 3, 2010, from http://www.naeyc.org/files/naeyc/file/policy/state/QBCC_Tool.pdf

National Association of Child Care Resource and Referral Agencies. (2009, January). *Parent perceptions of child care in the United States: NACCRRA's national poll, November 2008.* Washington, DC: Author.

Pawlenty, T. (2006, June 2). Letter to Representative Steve Sviggum, Speaker of the House, Minnesota House of Representatives. Retrieved July 21, 2010, from http://www.leg.state.mn.us/archive/vetoes/2006veto_ch282.pdf

Pianta, R.C., La Paro, K.M., & Hamre, B.K. (2008). *Classroom Assessment Scoring System*TM. Baltimore: Paul H. Brookes Publishing Co.

Ray, A. (2010). *Parent priorities in selecting early care and education programs: Implications for Minnesota's pilot quality rating and improvement system.* St. Paul, MN: Minnesota Early Learning Foundation.

Smith, L., & Sarkar, M. (2008). *Making quality child care possible: Lessons from NACCRRA's military partnerships.* Washington, DC: National Association of Child Care Resource and Referral Agencies.

Sylva, K., Siraj-Blatchford, I., & Taggart, B. (2006). *Early Childhood Environment Rating Scale (Extension).* Staffordshire, England: Trentham Books.

Tout, K., & Maxwell, K.M. (2010). Quality rating and improvement systems: Achieving the promise for programs, parents, children and early childhood systems. In V. Buysse & P.W., Wesley (Eds.), *The quest for quality: Promising innovations for early childhood programs.* Baltimore: Paul H. Brookes Publishing Co.

Tout, K., & Sherman, J. (2005). *Inside the preschool classroom: A snapshot of quality in Minnesota's child care centers.* Child Trends and the Minnesota Child Care Policy Research Partnership. St. Paul, MN: Minnesota Department of Human Services.

Tout, K., Starr, R., & Cleveland, J. (2009). *Evaluation of Parent Aware: Minnesota's Quality Rating System pilot: Year 1 evaluation report.* Minneapolis, MN: Child Trends.

Tout, K., Starr, R., Knerr, T., Cleveland, J., Soli, M., & Quinn, K. (2010a). *Evaluation of Parent Aware: Minnesota's Quality Rating System pilot: Year 2 evaluation report.* Minneapolis, MN: Child Trends.

Tout, K., Starr, R., Soli, M., Moodie, S., Kirby, G., & Boller, K. (2010b). ACF-OPRE Report. *A Compendium of Quality Rating Systems and Evaluations.* Office of Planning, Research and Evaluation, Administration for Children and Families, U.S. Department of Health and Human Services. Washington, DC.

Tout, K., Zaslow, M., Halle, T., & Forry, N. (2009). ACF-OPRE Issue Brief. *Issues for the Next Decade of Quality Rating and Improvement Systems.* Office of Planning, Research and Evaluation, Administration for Children and Families, U.S. Department of Health and Human Services. Washington, DC.

Zaslow, M., & Forry, N. (2009, March). *Understanding parent use of child care quality information.* Presentation at the National Association of Child Care Resource and Referral Agencies 2009 National Policy Symposium, Washington, DC.

Zaslow, M., Tout, K., & Martinez-Beck, I. ACF-OPRE Research-to-Policy Brief. *Measuring the Quality of Early Care and Education at the Intersection of Research, Policy and Practice.* Office of Planning, Research and Evaluation, Administration for Children and Families, U.S. Department of Health and Human Services. Washington, DC.

Zellman, G.L., & Perlman, M. (2008). *Child-care quality rating and improvement systems in five pioneer states.* Santa Monica, CA: RAND Corporation.

Zellman, G.L., Perlman, M., Le, V.-N., & Setodji, C.M. (2008). *Assessing the validity of the Qualistar Early Learning Quality Rating and Improvement System as a tool for improving child-care quality.* Santa Monica, CA: RAND Corporation.

Endnotes

[1]The Saint Paul Early Childhood Scholarship Program, developed by Art Rolnick and Rob Grunewald of the Federal Reserve Bank of Minneapolis, promotes a combination of parent empowerment (through provision of information about ECE), increased accountability of ECE programs (through a quality rating system), and financial incentives to parents to purchase high-quality care (see Gaylor, Spiker, Williamson, & Ferguson, 2010, for a detailed description of the model).

[2]The Minnesota Child Care Policy Research Partnership was established with funding

from the Child Care Bureau and the Minnesota Department of Human Services. The purpose was to support research collaborations and projects that could provide data to inform state decision-making.

[3]These decisions were prompted by legislation authorizing the Pre-Kindergarten Allowances, a state-funded program providing up to $4,000 for low-income families in the MELF pilot areas to use in programs with a three- or four-star rating, or a provisional rating.

[4]Research is needed on a variety of other QRIS components, but the focus here is exclusively on quality measurement.

CHAPTER 16

Data-Driven Decision Making in Preparation for Large-Scale Quality Rating System Implementation

Kathy R. Thornburg, Denise Mauzy, Wayne A. Mayfield, Jacqueline S. Hawks, Amber Sparks, Judy A. Mumford, Teresa Foulkes, and Kathryn L. Fuger

The purpose of this chapter is to describe the use of research in both developing the internal structure of a state quality rating system and in developing procedures for implementing it. Research often has served as the starting point in identifying the need to improve quality in early childhood and school-age programs. By describing the process used in Missouri for developing, testing, and implementing a quality rating system (QRS), the chapter illustrates ways in which data can be used beyond the basic rationale for a quality improvement strategy to inform its design and implementation.

Background: History of Missouri's QRS and Initial Decisions

Surveys of early childhood programs in Missouri conducted in 2001 highlighted the need for a systematic, statewide process to evaluate the quality of programs that serve young children (Thornburg, Scott, & Mayfield, 2002). The findings from this research of home- and center-based programs portrayed an early childhood field in need of improvement. Using observation-based measures of learning environment quality, researchers found that more than half of the classrooms and family child care homes scored below "good" quality. In addition, survey data evidenced a work force lacking appropriate child-related formal education.

Despite these statistics pointing to problems in the quality of early childhood programs, there was no statewide, reliable, and valid method for assessing the many dimensions of program quality or for targeting training and technical assistance resources for early childhood and school-age programs. In order to improve the outcomes for young children and youth, Missouri stakeholders agreed to develop a Missouri quality rating system (MO QRS) to coordinate across the early childhood and school-age communities and to combine local and statewide efforts to develop practical tools to measure the overall quality of programs.

In 2003, the QRS State Committee was convened to establish goals for the MO QRS. The goals are as follows:

- Raise public understanding about high-quality programs

- Improve the quality of early childhood programs, and school-age and after-school programs, for Missouri's young children and youth

- Allow subsidy-receiving children access to higher quality programs by linking state child care subsidies to the various QRS levels (pending state approval)

- Target limited resources and monitor the outcomes of early childhood and after-school program investments

To support the QRS development, two Missouri agencies—the Center for Family Policy & Research at the University of Missouri and the Metropolitan Council on Early Learning at the Mid-America Regional Council in Kansas City—secured federal grants to conduct extensive pilot studies on program quality. Findings from these pilots informed the committee's work, and subsequently, the development of the MO QRS models and implementation protocols. Although our main focus was on how data could be used in the design and implementation of a statewide QRS, we first turned to a common set of underlying assumptions that provided a foundation for the MO QRS.

Shared Expectations in MO QRS Development

The QRS State Committee negotiated shared expectations to guide the process. The MO QRS will

- Utilize Missouri's existing early childhood and school-age and after-school infrastructure (e.g., the state registry system)

- Be cost effective to allow the majority of early childhood and school-age and after-school funds to be used in the QRS and other supports in the system

- Be voluntary and include incentives for programs to participate (e.g., increased subsidy payments for higher quality programs)

- Apply to all licensed early childhood and school-age and after-school programs, regardless of size or geographic location

- Provide a number of tiers that build on each other, starting with licensing and progressing to the top tier that includes program accreditation by a state-approved accrediting entity

- Assess all aspects of program quality, using verified data and on-site observations by reliable assessors

- Offer programs constructive feedback based on the assessment process

- Recognize the extent to which program quality varies, thus providing opportunities for all programs to increase program ratings prior to publicizing

- Allow programs a window of opportunity to appeal their QRS rating

We focused on the development of a rating system for licensed programs. The process for development of the MO QRS rating structure included reviewing the literature and other QRS models, analyzing state registry data on the work force and program quality indicators, and identifying areas that needed further investigation. Models were developed and piloted to determine the most effective measures and appropriate thresholds for criteria. This process included collecting data on 122 programs (75 centers and 47 homes) from across the state of Missouri; conducting 16 focus groups with 57 directors, teachers, and parents; and surveying both center and home directors and staff. The qualitative respondents raised questions, offered suggestions, and helped inform decisions throughout the pilot process. The quotes included in this chapter were collected during the pilot project via director surveys and focus groups.

Collectively, these data informed the revisions to the MO QRS. In the sections that follow, we will use the MO QRS pilot experience to illustrate how data can be used in formulating a state QRS. Subsequent sections will focus on using data to inform the implementation of a state QRS.

The revisions to the MO QRS, informed by pilot data, resulted in three models for licensed programs: the center and group home model, the home-based model, and the school-age and after-school model. Although all three models comprise the same progressive components, the requirements within each of the components are designed to recognize the unique aspects of different program types. The shared components of the models and the point values are as follows:

Program Personnel
1. Director Education and Training (10 points)

2. Staff Education (10 points)

3. Education Specialization (5 points)

4. Annual Training (5 points)

Program Content
1. Learning Environment (10 points)

2. Intentional Teaching (5 points)

Program Management
1. Family Involvement (5 points)

2. Business and Administrative Practices (5 points)

The requirements in each component are organized hierarchically, beginning with Tier 1 (licensing) and progressing to Tier 5, which includes accreditation. The tiers within each component are assigned a point value. To obtain the Tier 4 point value in a component, for example, the program must meet all of the criteria in Tiers 1, 2, 3, and 4. Programs add their points from each component according to the tier level they achieve, and then the total number of points from all eight components results in an overall star rating of 1–5. Only accredited programs have the potential to earn enough points to meet the five-star rating, as they are the only programs eligible to earn points at the 5th tier in each component. All of the components are verified. The Program Personnel criteria are verified through the state registry. The Program Content and Program Management criteria are observed and verified on-site by QRS Assessors.

Initial Decisions

In developing MO QRS, the QRS State Committee identified the six structural issues to be addressed before criteria could be set: whether to require programs to be licensed; whether to include specifications for adult–child ratios beyond those in licensing; which accreditation standards to recognize as part of the QRS; how to incorporate Missouri's infrastructure to support the MO QRS; how to assess the quality of school-age programs as part of the QRS; and rating frequency. These decisions sometimes called upon previous or recent state-specific data (as in the case of deciding whether to include observations of ratio in the QRS), but more often were matters of judgment about what was important to include in the QRS.

Licensing Status

A first key decision concerned whether to include only licensed programs in the state QRS or whether to also include license-exempt programs. Missouri regulations include minimal education and training requirements, adult–child ratios, health rules, staff background screenings, injury prevention guidelines, health and safety issues, and space and equipment requirements (Department of Health and Senior Services, 1991). Missouri's licensing regulations reflect legislative compromise, rule interpretation, and public debate. A pivotal distinction is made for license-exempt programs—faith-based programs and programs operated by school districts—allowing them to operate legally while receiving only health and safety inspections, which include annual fire safety and sanitation inspections and an annual health and safety inspection from the Section for Child Care Regulation.

Adult–Child Ratios

The second factor on which the QRS State Committee focused was adult–child ratios. In Missouri, licensing requires adult–child ratios of 1:4 for infants and toddlers; 1:8 for 2-year-olds; 1:10 for preschoolers; and 1:16 for school-agers. Thus, programs meeting licensing standards are presumed to meet these ratios, and verification is the responsibility of child care licensing. However, the general support by research literature for ratio as an important structural quality indicator (Burchinal et al., 1996; Elicker, Fortner-Wood, & Nopp, 1999; NICHD Early Child Care Research Network, 2000; Phillips, Mekos, Scarr, McCartney, & Abbott-Shim, 2001) and the fact that many states include ratio requirements in their rating systems led us to use Missouri-specific pilot data to determine whether ratio differentiated quality levels. Ratio data were collected during two rating cycles from center-based and home-based programs located in rural and urban counties. More than 1,200 ratio checks occurred at different times of the day and on different days of the week. Almost all programs in the pilot exceeded state requirements for ratio. The approximately 350 ratio checks for homes showed programs to be in ratio 96% of the time. In fact, the vast majority of the time, programs had three or four fewer children than licensing would permit. For centers, the approximately 875 ratio checks showed that programs were in ratio 95% of the time. Again, as with homes, the staff–child ratios in centers, on average, exceeded licensing requirements (e.g., programs averaged about seven preschool children per check). Although it would be possible to build into the state QRS ratio requirements that go beyond licensing, the ratio checks suggest that programs often actually exceed requirements. So, providing more stringent requirements at higher levels may not actually differentiate effectively across programs. In addition, Missouri data from the Midwest Child Care Research Consortium (Raikes et al., 2003) showed that ratio was not correlated with other quality indicators, such as director education, teacher education, environment rating scale (ERS) scores, and accreditation status. From these two findings and the fact that it would be costly to collect ratio data, the QRS State Committee decided that adult–child ratios would not be included as one of the components of the QRS criteria. As collection of ratio data is included in the ERS protocol, we have ratio data and can monitor compliance issues to determine whether additional support is needed within licensing. In sum, pilot work and previous research in Missouri indicated that there would not be substantial, further information gleaned from including ratio as part of the state QRS.

Source of Accreditation

The third factor concerned the effects on MO QRS of the variations in accreditation requirements by accrediting entities. Missouri's Department of Social Services currently recognizes six accrediting organizations: National Association for the Education of Young Children (NAEYC), Missouri Accreditation (MO-A), National Association for Family Child Care (NAFCC), National Early Childhood Program Accreditation (NECPA), Council on Accreditation (COA), and the Commission on Accreditation of Rehabilitation Facilities (CARF). The six state-approved accrediting bodies vary significantly in the level of rigor, types of standards, frequency of visits, and cost. As a whole, the small number of accredited programs in the pilot did not score enough points to result in a five-star rating. Thus, we did not feel comfortable automatically assigning a five-star rating for accredited programs at this time. We also were unwilling to develop standards that differ depending on the accrediting entity chosen by a program. In the end, the most logical course of action seemed to be to use the most stringent accreditation criteria among the six approved accrediting entities for each program type (e.g., NAEYC accreditation standards for early childhood centers; NAFCC for family child care programs; National Afterschool Association [NAA] for school-age programs—the NAA accreditation process has since been taken over by COA) as the Tier 5 standard and to step down the requirements from accreditation at the Tier 5 level to licensing at the Tier 1 level. Although programs do not automatically receive a five-star rating by being accredited, they are the only ones eligible to earn points at the Tier 5 level in each component as long as the requirements in previous tiers are met. By earning points at Tier 5, programs have the potential to earn enough points to be awarded an overall five-star rating. Data were informative here in indicating that accreditation did ensure fulfillment of the Tier 5 requirements and helped shape the decision that accreditation would be necessary, but not sufficient, for this level.

Using Missouri's Early Childhood and
School-age Infrastructure to Support the MO QRS

The fourth factor reviewed pertained to which pieces of the early childhood and school-age and afterschool systems would be useful in developing and implementing the MO QRS. We decided to use the state registry, the Professional Achievement and Recognition

System (PARS), to track all staff requirements, as PARS already tracks program staff members' completion of education and annual training hours and assigns professionals an education level based on the education matrix (Missouri Education Matrix; OPEN Initiative, 2005). As PARS offers a standard method for communicating about levels of educational attainment based on the Education Matrix, we decided to use the Matrix to designate the MO QRS education requirements for program staff. Missouri's Education Matrix recognizes the formal education level and vocational credentials of professionals in the early childhood and school-age and afterschool fields. Next, we reviewed the different state standards, resources, and quality improvement initiatives that should be incorporated into the criteria, as many programs are already using these resources in their quality improvement efforts. The state standards included the following:

- Core Competencies for Early Care and Education Professionals (OPEN Initiative, 2011) and Core Competencies for Youth Development Professionals (OPEN Initiative 2006; Missouri AfterSchool Network, 2007)

- Missouri Early Learning Standards (Missouri Department Education, 2002–2005) Literacy, Math, Physical Development, Health and Safety, Science, and Social and Emotional Standards

- Missouri Afterschool Program Standards (Missouri AfterSchool Network, 2007)

Other states developing QRS and their research teams may wish to consider alignment with QRS criteria with other state standards, as well as with other existing data systems, to provide a foundation for key data elements or to work toward aligning data systems in developing the state QRS.

Quality for School-age Children

The fifth factor considered was how to measure quality for school-age children in the MO QRS, regardless of whether we are assessing school-age classrooms that are part of early childhood centers or rating before- and-after-school programs. Missouri is recognized as a national leader for its school-age career development work. This work supported the development of a separate model for school-age-only programs because before- and after-school programs have unique characteristics, including staffing patterns and group configurations, as well as a youth development emphasis in curriculum. Two key system level supports were already in place:

1. The PARS was already assigning Education Matrix designations for staff on the basis of the age of the children with whom they work. For example, the transcript of a group leader in a before-and-after-school program is reviewed for school-age-related coursework and the person is given a School-Age Matrix designation.

2. The Missouri Afterschool Program Standards served as the foundation for the MO QRS School-Age Intentional Teaching Checklist (described later in the chapter).

Although Missouri approaches early childhood and school-age work as a continuum of services and strives to create a seamless system, not all pieces of the larger career development system are seamless. This was the case when developers were considering how to set criteria related to accreditation status for early childhood programs with school-age classrooms, because only one of the six approved accrediting entities accredits all age groups (infant–toddler, preschool, and school-age). Initially, we thought that only programs that had all age groups accredited should be eligible to earn points at Tier 5, because we wanted to ensure that the level of quality would be consistent for all age groups. However, given the negative impact on programs due to being accredited by an agency that accredits only ages birth through age 5, the QRS State Committee decided to wait to implement the policy for all classrooms being accredited to receive points at Tier 5 until more than one state-approved entity accredits all age groups within a program. This decision was made in the anticipation that accrediting bodies would either expand their age groups to include school-age children or partner with other accrediting entities to provide reduced rates for accrediting programs with both early childhood and school-age children. Data here were informative in terms of the number of programs with accreditation for multiple age ranges. This key finding was critical to the decision not to create disincentives for programs that currently have accreditation that does not apply to all groups that are served. This could result in programs being discouraged from participating in QRS as well.

Frequency of Ratings

The sixth factor addressed how frequently programs would be rated. Qualitative data were helpful in determining the frequency of ratings. In addition, considerations included the cost to rate programs, as well as the length of time a rating would be valid. Annual ratings are very costly and do not give programs a chance to fully address the recommended program improvements. Two-year to five-year ratings presented an increased probability that ratings would no longer be valid, given the high staff turnover in the early childhood and school-age fields. The committee decided on an 18-month rating cycle, which allows programs time to make improvements, ensures that QRS assessors will conduct on-site observation visits at different times of the year (rather than just every spring or fall), and produces significant cost savings. Table 16.1 presents an example of a possible implementation plan based on the 18-month cycle over a 5-year period. In this example, by year 5, MO QRS will rate 1,911 programs (50% of licensed programs), but a total of 2,674 (70%) will have an active rating. Therefore, Missouri will save the funds that would have been required to rate the 763 programs that did not have to be rerated in that year.

Data can be used by states and research teams to project the proportions of programs and costs that would have active ratings, given different assessment cycles.

Table 16.1.   Draft implementation plan for MO QRS (18-month cycle)

	Year 1	Year 2	Year 3	Year 4	Year 5
Number of programs rated/rerated	382	764	1146	1529	1911
Percentage of licensed programs rated/rerated	10%	20%	30%	40%	50%
Number of programs with current rating (do not need to be rerated yet)	0	255	509	636	763
Percentage of programs with current rating	0%	7%	13%	17%	20%
Overall number of licensed programs with QRS rating	382	1019	1655	2165	2674
Percentage of overall licensed programs with QRS rating	10%	27%	43%	57%	70%

Establishing the Components and Criteria for MO QRS

In developing and revising the components and criteria for the MO QRS, we tapped four sources of information. First, we examined the research literature for each broad category (Program Personnel, Program Content, and Program Management) to assist us in initially choosing what variables to use and how to measure the separate components. In the Program Personnel and Program Content categories, there is abundant evidence linking these factors to overall quality. In Program Management, however, there is scant literature addressing measurement of family involvement and business practices and their impact on quality. Second, we used the literature on best practices as a guide to measuring quality. Third, we examined other states' QRS models to collect ideas about tier structure and methods of measurement. Finally, we used data from our pilot studies and Missouri's state registry to provide concrete information about how well our initial ideas about meauring various components matched with the realities of Missouri's early childhood and school-age settings. This section of the chapter will provide multiple examples of how data were used to finalize decisions regarding how to distinguish among levels, and what it was realistic to expect, given descriptive data about quality and the workforce.

Program Personnel

The Program Personnel category includes components that measure staff education and training across many areas. The QRS State Committee attempted to find a balance between the need to raise the bar for quality and the reality of the education and training of the work force in Missouri. The director education and training component includes the licensed capacity structure and director approval criteria. Missouri licensing requires different director qualifications depending on the capacity of the program (i.e., 1–20; 21–60; 61–99; and 100 or more). This component assesses the formal education and professional requirements (e.g., number of business-related college credits, membership in a professional association, number of training hours specific to core competencies that relate to a director's role). The staff education component assesses lead staff members' vocational credential and formal education and assistant staff members' vocational credentials and formal education, *or* annual training (workshops without college credit). The education specialization component measures child- and youth-specific coursework or approved curriculum training completed by the director and lead staff. The annual training component assesses the number of clock hours completed by staff members in the previous calendar year.

Establishing Subcomponents for the Staff Education Component

Due to differing responsibilities of lead and assistant staff in the classrooms and considering that pilot data show that the educational attainment of Missouri's assistant staff is much lower than that of lead staff (only 15% of assistant teachers have at least an associate's degree, compared with 30% of lead staff), we decided to differentiate the requirements according to position by dividing the staff education component into two subcomponents: lead staff and assistant staff.

Setting Tier Thresholds for the Education Specialization Component

Due to the low number of child- and youth-related college credits earned by directors and lead staff, we determined that points could be earned in two ways: 1) completion of a specified number of related college credits; or 2) completion of a minimum of 14 clock hours of state-approved curriculum training. We decided to allow two different ways of meeting

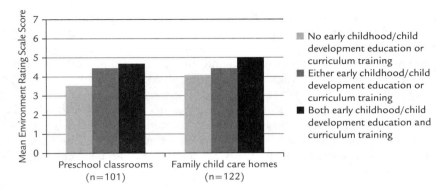

Figure 16.1.   Midwest Child Care Research Consortium data: Mean environment rating scale scores by education and curriculum training and program type. (Data from Raikes et al. [2003]. Child care quality and workforce characteristics in four midwestern states. Lincoln, NE: The Gallup Organization and the University of Nebraska; adapted by permission.)

the requirements for this component because of the results from the Midwest Child Care Research Consortium (Raikes et al., 2003). Figure 16.1 shows that teachers who had either formal curriculum training or child-related education credits scored better than those with neither on the ERS, whereas having both resulted in the highest ERS scores.

Setting Tier Thresholds for the Annual Training Component
In the pilot models, requirements for the Annual Training component were determined on the basis of the percentage of staff that documented at least 12 clock hours of training in the previous year. (Twelve hours is the annual requirement for staff working in licensed programs.) Specifically, 50% of staff had to document 12 clock hours of training for Tier 2; 75% for Tier 3; and 100% for Tier 4.

Other state organizations and research teams working to specify standards for professional development could benefit from the Missouri experience by examining current education and training levels in their respective states. Where possible, state-specific data may be used to examine the relationship between education and training and criterion measures of quality such as observed early childhood environment, to inform the development of alternative criteria to education.

Data-Driven Modifications to the Components in the Program Personnel Category

Many issues had to be addressed in order to achieve the balance between high-quality standards and current circumstances. Descriptive data from the QRS pilot studies suggested the need for alternative ways of progressing across tiers. The following paragraphs describe the modifications made in light of the pilot study data previously discussed:

1. Director Education and Training:
Balancing Formal Education and Professional Requirements
During the pilot, this component consisted of both formal education and professional requirements. As a result, it required that directors meet both the formal education requirements and professional requirements in order to earn points at each tier. Pilot

data showed that directors often met the formal education requirements *or* the professional requirements, negatively affecting the number of points earned by the program in this component. Given that this component was double weighted and worth 10 points, we decided to divide the director education and training component into two equal subcomponents (5 points each) to highlight directors' strengths and to accommodate the wide variety of backgrounds present in the field. The education matrix designation subcomponent assesses the formal education and number of child- and youth-related college credits for the director, and the professional requirements subcomponent assesses the number of training hours completed that relate to the director's role, membership in an approved professional association, and the number of business-related college credits the director has completed.

2. Staff Education: Consideration of Program Size

After receiving feedback from several directors in rural communities, we recognized that staff education criteria were sometimes unfair to smaller programs with only one or two lead teachers. For example, a program with one lead staff member could not earn points at Tier 3 (50% of lead teachers with an associate's degree) because the program either has 0% with the degree (Tier 2) or 100% with the degree (Tier 4). Thus, the QRS State Committee decided to adjust the criteria on the basis of the number of staff.

3. Staff Education: Balancing Formal
Education and Training Requirements for Lead and Assistant Staff

During the pilot, lead and assistant staff requirements were combined and established that both lead and assistant staff meet all criteria within a tier in order to earn points at that tier. As a result, programs earned fewer points. Given that this component was double weighted and worth 10 points, we decided to divide staff education into two equal subcomponents—lead staff and assistant staff. For the lead staff education subcomponent, we maintained the formal education requirements. However, due to the lower levels of education for assistant staff compared with lead staff found in the pilot study, we determined that points for the assistant staff education subcomponent could be earned in two ways: 1) by formal education according to Missouri's Education Matrix, or 2) by earning up to 18 annual clock hours of training. The following quote shows a center director's concern, expressed during a focus group meeting, that lead and assistant staff requirements were not separate in the pilot: "My lead teachers are really at high levels of education but our aides are not. A lot of our aides are moms who have been active in school and came in and have been helping for several years."

4. Education Specialization and
Intentional Teaching: Separating Specialized Training and
Education and Implementation of a Curriculum in a Group Setting

The pilot models included one component called education specialization and program curriculum. The intent of this component was to measure the extent to which program staff members had taken college coursework or state-approved curriculum training that addressed the needs of the age group they educate, and whether the program follows a curriculum. In hindsight, it is obvious that these two ideas are distinct: education specialization is a matter of the education and training of program personnel, whereas the presence of a curriculum (not to mention the quality of its implementation) clearly fits better in the Program Content category. The two concepts were divided in the final model—education specialization is in the Program Personnel category, and program curriculum was renamed intentional teaching and was included in the Program Content category.

5. Annual Training: Compliance with Licensing Requirements versus Raising the Bar for Number of Training Hours

In the pilot models' Annual Training component, if all staff met the 12-clock-hour training requirement, points were awarded at Tier 4. From anecdotal reports, we were aware that many staff did not meet the annual training requirements. However, our pilot data showed that the training-hour compliance was a greater problem than we first had realized. In our pilot study, 26% of center-based administrators ($n = 70$) and 27% of home-based directors ($n = 44$) did not satisfy the 12-hour annual requirement. Even fewer teachers met the annual training requirements: For these, 50% of lead teachers ($n = 292$) and 49% of assistant teachers ($n = 150$) were not in compliance. Overall, only 13% of centers had 100% of staff meet the annual training requirement. Noncompliance rates were found to be even higher when we examined training-hour data from Missouri's registry for the last 2 years. For center-based programs, 59% of administrators ($n = 485$), 68% of lead teachers ($n = 1,080$), and 73% of assistant teachers ($n = 744$) failed to meet the annual training requirements. For home-based programs, 75% of owners were not in compliance. It should be noted that the registry figures likely overestimate noncompliance due to the fact that the registry verifies all training hours, and many participants do not provide complete documentation for their annual training. In addition, it should be noted that the calculation of compliance was based on a calendar year. Missouri licensing allows professionals to count clock hours in the current year that were earned in the last quarter of the previous year if 12 clock hours were earned by the end of the third quarter.

For the approved models, we decided for two reasons to require documentation of compliance at Tier 2 and additional annual clock-hour requirements for higher tier levels for administrative and lead staff. During the pilot, we awarded points at Tier 4 for programs that were meeting the clock hour requirement. Upon reflection, we realized that we were actually supporting programs that were not in compliance by awarding points at the earlier tiers. Second, given that staff training and professional development are facets of our definition of program quality, we determined that it was necessary to "raise the bar" and to provide reasons for programs to exceed the required number of annual training hours.

Setting the specific requirements for quality tiers needs to be informed both by what is realistic within a state and by what research on quality indicates. State data on education and training can help to establish tiers that are reasonable according to existing distribution within the state. These can then be related to and calibrated against the broader body of evidence on what matters in terms of children's early experiences.

Program Content

The Program Content category includes components that measure the daily experiences of children enrolled. The learning environment component addresses the health and safety, room arrangement, activities, and interactions of children and teachers and is a component typically included in most states' QRS. The intentional teaching component focuses on the purposeful implementation of activities and interactions between children and teachers. Both components in this category are scored by QRS Assessors who complete on-site observations. The Learning Environment measure is based on the appropriate ERS instrument.

Setting Tier Thresholds for the Learning Environment Component

The findings of Raikes and colleagues (2003)—which examined observed quality in randomly selected providers from a larger random telephone survey sample of full-day child care providers drawn from state department files of licensed and subsidy-receiving providers in Iowa, Kansas, Missouri, and Nebraska—provided an excellent source of baseline data for learning environment thresholds in Missouri. This study found that the average ECERS-R and ITERS-R scores for Missouri were 4.59 and 4.56, respectively. From these figures, we determined that Tier 3, the middle tier, would encompass an average of 4.00–4.99 on the ERS. We then built the thresholds for the other tiers around Tier 3.

However, because the Raikes et al. (2003) study also indicated that there was substantial variability in classroom quality within a program, we wanted the MO QRS learning environment component to differentiate between programs in which most assessed classrooms were of higher quality. Accordingly, we set basal limits (i.e., "no score below" rules) for each tier threshold in order to safeguard against programs with some low-scoring classrooms being rated higher on this component than merited. See Table 16.2 for the learning environment component criteria.

Data-driven Modifications to the Components in the Program Content Category

No modifications were made to the learning environment component on the basis of pilot data. However, major changes were made to this category by incorporating the new component of intentional teaching.

Adding an Intentional Teaching Component

In the pilot models, there was no intentional teaching component. Instead, we started with a single component called education specialization and program curriculum. For the program curriculum part, we relied on self-report by simply asking the director whether the program used a specific written curriculum. We asked directors and family child care owners, "Do you have a curriculum?" and "Is it written down?" Upon reflection, we realized that this approach documented only the presence of curriculum resources and not how well the identified resources were being used. In our pilot, 93% of centers and 70% of home programs reported that they follow a curriculum. Because this item was not very discriminating (in that the vast majority of programs indicated that they followed a curriculum), and because this approach did not document the quality of curricular activities,

Table 16.2. Missouri QRS learning environment tier thresholds

Tier 1	Tier 2	Tier 3	Tier 4	Tier 5
ERS average: less than 3.50	ERS average: 3.50–3.99	ERS average: 4.00–4.99	ERS average: 5.00–5.49	ERS average: 5.50 or above
or				
Lowest ERS score < 3.00	(no score below 3.00)	(no score below 3.50)	(no score below 4.50)	

we determined that we needed solid assessments of the intentional teaching activities that were taking place. Thus, we decided to split program curriculum from education specialization and rename the new component Intentional Teaching.

It was important that we identify appropriate measures for this new component, Intentional Teaching. We began to investigate our options and reviewed other data collected in the pilot related to this component. For example, although the ECERS-R assesses the necessary component of learning environment quality, it was not intended to be a strong measure of intentional teaching and curriculum, which provide the crucial link between preschool quality and positive child outcomes (Epstein, 2007). We argue that a high-quality learning environment provides the necessary, but not sufficient, conditions for fostering children's development of cognitive and social–emotional skills; teachers also must employ intentional, individualized teaching and assessment strategies to maximize children's development.

Although we did not have the Early Childhood Environment Rating Scale-Extension (ECERS-E; Sylva, Siraj-Blatchford, & Taggart, 2003, 2006) built into the pilot model, we did build it into our data collection protocol for preschool classrooms and home-based programs that had primarily preschool-age children, in order to inform the development process. Our hope was to obtain data that possibly could help us to establish a reliable way to look at teaching practices. The ECERS-E was designed to be used in classrooms with children ages 3–5, focusing on curricular provision of literacy, mathematics, science and nature, and diversity.

The data from one Missouri community that instituted a quality-improvement initiative with 22 programs help to clarify the importance of the intentional teaching component. These programs received targeted technical assistance—including on-site coaching, scholarships, and curriculum training—that was specifically designed to increase pilot QRS scores. After one year, programs significantly increased their mean star rating (from 2.18 to 3.14) and their mean ERS scores (from 3.72 to 4.66). However, the scores on the ECERS-E, the measure of intentional teaching (described subsequently), showed no change (3.05 to 3.04). These results showed us that the learning environment quality and the quality of intentional teaching are not necessarily related.

Our experiences during the pilot helped us to determine how to and how not to measure the quality of teaching practices. We were convinced that we needed three instruments to address the three different age groups in the MO QRS models: infant–toddler, preschool, and school-age. For preschool-age classrooms, we chose to use the ECERS-E (Sylva et. al., 2003, 2006). To address teaching practices in the other groups, we developed checklists for infants–toddlers and school-age children. (See pages 370–371 for descriptions of these instruments.)

For classrooms consisting entirely of 2-year-olds and for home-based programs with mixed-age groups, accommodations were made in the Missouri Additional Notes for Clarification (OPEN Initiative, 2008). Similar to many states' additional notes for the ERS, Missouri's notes applied to the ECERS-E as well. These notes covered space issues in home-based programs and developmentally appropriate expectations for 2-year-old children. The following statements from a home-based provider sensitized us to curricular issues faced by family child care providers:

A lot of the questions were based for centers. I don't know if there would need to be a set for centers and then a set for home-based. Because there was a lot of things I know I questioned. I thought that doesn't even make any sense to me because I am not a center.

For measuring curricular provision in infant–toddler and school-age populations, no instruments existed comparable to the ECERS-E that addressed the age-appropriate intentional teaching aspects we hoped to capture. Therefore, two work groups were formed to create checklists specific to each age group. For the Missouri Infant/Toddler Intentional Teaching Checklist (MITITC), feedback was gathered from state and national experts, including professionals from University of Missouri campuses (Columbia, Kansas City, and St. Louis), Region VII Head Start T/TA Network, Ohio Bureau of Child Care and Development, Parents as Teachers National Center, and National Child Care Information Center. The Missouri School-Age Intentional Teaching Checklist (MSAITC) was cross-walked with the Missouri AfterSchool Standards and included input from the Missouri Afterschool Community Coalition and the Missouri Afterschool Network. The checklists were piloted in QRS demonstration projects, and the MITIC has since been revised according to findings from the most recent data. In addition, the MITIC has been renamed the Missouri Infant/Toddler Responsive Caregiving Checklist (MITRCC).

To maximize cost-effectiveness, the intentional teaching instruments were paired with the corresponding learning environment scales for the observations. The observations for the infant–toddler and preschool-age groups were at least 3.5 hours, and the school-age observations were at least 2.5 hours. Assessors reported that this was sufficient time to complete both the learning environment and intentional teaching instruments.

The packaging of instruments for home-based programs, group homes, and 2-year-old classrooms had special considerations. For home-based programs and group homes with children configured in one group, the FCCERS-R was assigned for the Learning Environment component. The choice of the Intentional Teaching instrument was determined by the majority of children present within each age group during the day of the observation. Therefore, if the majority of children present were 2 years of age or under, the MITITC was selected. If the majority of children were preschool-age, the ECERS-E was used. Likewise, if the majority of children were school-age during the observation, the MSAITC was used. For home-based programs with an equal number of children present in each age group, multiple instruments were completed. Home-based providers had special concerns that the range of ages they serve may interfere with the rating process. One home-based provider gave the following input:

> I feel that we do . . . get compared [to] a center. You know, they do want things out all the time. But we also have infants and little toddlers. And some things you just can't have out all the time. Like . . . they want to have the arts stuff out all the time so kids can just go paint and do whatever they want. And you just can't have that available to them when you've got little kids on the floor that . . . are going to put that stuff in their mouth.

The determination of the instrument package for group homes was based on the configuration of the individual program. If the children were divided into separate groups according to age, the selection would mirror a center-based program. If the children were together in one group, the instrument assignment would follow the same procedures as home-based programs.

For centers or group homes, assignment of instruments to classrooms with children ages 24–36 months proved challenging. The ITERS-R is designed for settings with children from birth to 30 months, whereas the ECERS-R is to be used with children ages 2½ through 5 years. In the pilot, we assigned the instrument according to the ages of the majority of children enrolled. Birthdays, fluctuating enrollment, and the developmental level of each child proved to be problematic in genuinely capturing whether classroom operation more closely resembled that of a toddler room or a preschool room. Directors choose, through a series of questions during the application process, whether the 2-year-old classroom should be assigned an ITERS-R or an ECERS-R.

Preliminary Reliability and Validity Evidence for the Intentional Teaching Measures

Preliminary psychometric data were obtained for the MITITC and MSAITC through samples from the pilot study. Both measures showed good internal consistency reliability as measured by coefficient alpha. For the 20-item MITITC ($n = 76$), alpha was .81; for the 48-item MSAITC ($n = 27$), alpha was .94. For concurrent validity evidence, we correlated the intentional teaching measures with the relevant ERS instrument. The correlation between the ITERS-R total score and the MITITC was .75; the correlation was .87 between the SACERS and the MSAITC.

Setting Thresholds for the Intentional Teaching Component

Similar to the development efforts we put forth for the Learning Environment component, we examined means and distributions of the scores for each Intentional Teaching tool, and, on the basis of these data, we determined the tier thresholds for this component.

Do We Need to Observe All Classrooms?

In some QRS models, all classrooms are observed with ERS instruments to assess the quality of learning environments. Because observations are one of the most expensive aspects of QRS models, we decided to test whether sampling only a portion of the classrooms would provide a sufficiently accurate measure of a program's learning environment level. Specifically, we wondered whether random sampling of one half or one third of the classrooms would provide an accurate snapshot of the learning environment.

To test this hypothesis, we examined data from an earlier Kansas City pilot study (Fuger, 2004), augmented with data from rural sites, in which all classrooms were observed. Only centers with a minimum of two classrooms and a maximum of six classrooms per age group were included, resulting in a sample of 24 programs with 122 classrooms. From this empirical study, we examined the results of the sampling of at least one half and at least one-third of the classrooms from each age group. All possible sampling combinations with the scores of the environment rating scales (ECERS-R and ITERS-R) were calculated. For example, in a center with four preschool classrooms (observed with the ECERS-R) and three infant–toddler classrooms (observed with the ITERS-R), two preschool and two infant-toddler classrooms would be randomly selected for the one-half sampling method. Looking at all possible combinations across the two types of classrooms yielded nine different combinations, three for the preschool classrooms multiplied by the three for the infant–toddler classrooms. (In this case, the number of possible combinations is the same for the one-third sampling method.)

The MO QRS guidelines for rating a program on the Learning Environment component (Tier 1–Tier 5; see Table 16.2 for the guidelines) were then applied to the combinations to determine how frequently the mean of the sampling combinations matched the true component score based on the mean with all classroom data. It is important to note that the MO QRS uses a "no score below" rule for Tiers 1–4, which was applied, when appropriate, to the sampling combinations.

It was found that sampling one half of the classes resulted in an 86% match; that is, 86% of Learning Environment tier levels based on all possible one half sampling combinations matched the component Tier levels calculated from observations of all classrooms. When a sampling of one-third of the classes was calculated, the match rate dropped to 75%.

To verify our results for sampling one half of the classrooms, scores from the second wave of the Kansas City QRS pilot study (41 programs with 199 classrooms) were examined (Fuger, 2004) by the same procedure. (In this second study, the examination included all combinations for sampling one-half of the classrooms.) In this sampling, 81% of the learning environment tier levels matched the tier level, based on all classroom observations.

In both studies, because of the basal limits established in which no classroom scored below a certain threshold for each tier, the tier level based on sampling either overestimated the true tier level rating or was accurate. In other words, with these data, the tier level based on one-half sampling was never lower than the tier level based on all classroom data.

The results from both empirical studies align closely with those reported by Illinois researchers in which they found that one-half sampling yielded a 72% match rate and one-third sampling yielded a 67% match rate, using the Illinois Quality Counts QRS Learning Environment Component thresholds (McCormick Tribune Center for Early Childhood Leadership, 2008). It should be noted that the research in Illinois examined only preschool classrooms and that the Illinois QRS has different thresholds and lacks basal limits. Given the findings from these two studies, we decided to adopt the one-half sampling criteria. Based on our pilot data, the cost savings for observing at least one half of classrooms at each age group will be approximately 33%.

Data were used in multiple ways to revise the program content requirements for the MO QRS. Other states might consider using data on the distribution of environmental ratings within the state, if such data are available, to establish appropriate ranges on observational measures for different tiers. Pilot data can also be used to identify issues with distribution that indicate a necessity to go beyond self-report data, as Missouri did on the use of curricula. Pilot data can also be extremely valuable in determining the number of classrooms that need to be observed in a program or center, and ways to ensure that a rating is not assigned to a program with specific classrooms below a certain threshold of observed quality.

Program Management

The Program Management category includes the family involvement and business and administrative practices components. The Program Management category assesses quality at the level of the organization, which supports and sustains quality at the level of the classroom and the staff. These components reflect both programs' efforts to include family members and programs' attention to implementation of administrative processes needed to sustain a business, which ensures that taxpayers' dollars invested in quality improvements are not wasted on programs that subsequently will close. Upon review of the literature and other state QRS models related to these components, we decided that frequently used measures and criteria did not meet our needs. We believed that it was important to distinguish between measuring families' perceptions about quality and programs' family engagement efforts. Furthermore, QRS models that use parent surveys to inform the rating risk poor measurement if the response rate is low and the sample is biased. There were few examples to guide the development of the criteria and measures for the administrative aspect of quality. We considered the Program Administration Scale (Talan & Bloom, 2004) as one possible measure for this category, but decided against using it due to cost restraints and the duplicative nature of some aspects of the instrument with our Program Personnel category.

In the development of the pilot models, we used the following questions to guide our choice of criteria: What are the most important things that programs and staff should do to engage families? What are the most important things that directors do to retain high-quality staff and run an efficient and viable organization? The criteria for family involvement included frequency and type of communication with families, parent handbooks, advisory boards, workshops, and family–teacher conferences. The criteria for business and administrative practices included job descriptions, staff evaluations, orientations, and paid leave.

Data-driven Modifications to the Components in the Program Management Category

During the pilot, we assessed these components by surveying directors and completing an on-site verification process. In addition, parents completed surveys about the program's family involvement practices. This was done to include the "voice" of the families and also to verify that such practices occurred. The data indicated that parents agreed with the director 96.3% of the time on the activities and practices used in the program, so we chose to eliminate the family surveys. However, we felt the individual items indicating a range of opportunities for family involvement (e.g., social and educational events; parent advisory council; parent–teacher conferences; family resource center) were significant and therefore needed to be included in the program quality rating. To enhance the criteria in these two components, we incorporated the philosophy and strategies presented in *Strengthening Families through Early Care and Education* (Center for the Study of Social Policy, 2004). Advancing the view that programs help build a foundation of protective factors and support family resilience, *Strengthening Families* provides strategies for fostering administrative capacity, engaging families, supporting staff members, and partnering with community agencies.

During the pilot study, it became evident that this category may require a conceptual shift among directors who view their work as caring for children rather than running a business to educate children in partnership with families. In the family involvement component, centers' scores were distributed evenly among the five tiers; homes tended to score in the bottom two tiers. Centers tended to score either very low or very high on the business and administrative practices component, whereas homes scored very low. Table 16.3 illustrates this lack of focus on the administrative aspects of the program. For example, although we were not surprised that no home-based programs operated with an annual budget, we were shocked to learn that 39% of the center-based programs operated without one.

Because of these disappointing results, we felt it necessary to add criteria from *Strengthening Families* to ensure that these components are measured with the same rigor as the other six MO QRS components and that state-specific resources are incorporated (e.g., core competencies and after-school program standards). The reality of programs' striving to meet these requirements is that many of the program management criteria (e.g., budget, orientations) can be met quickly with relatively little cost to the program.

Table 16.3.   Percent of programs that met selected business and administrative practices criteria

Criteria	% Centers ($n = 31$)	% Homes ($n = 37$)
Written professional development plans	48	3
Volunteer orientation	58	22
Policy and procedure manuals	68	54
Budget	61	0
Paid sick leave	68	3

From the perspective of system development, these pilot data can inform how states provide quality improvement resources and what issues the states address. In this case the data indicate that the majority of programs need training in how to develop and implement a program budget. Thus, if developing an annual budget is something that programs can learn to do fairly easily, it appears important for states to allocate resources for technical assistance in this area.

Challenges for Statewide Implementation

With the pilot complete and the three MO QRS models approved by the directors of the state Departments of Social Services, Elementary and Secondary Education, Health and Senior Services, Mental Health, and Higher Education, and the Missouri Head Start-State Collaboration Office, we continue to learn from other states' efforts and our own demonstration projects as we prepare to implement the MO QRS statewide. Challenges we are working to address include

- How to keep our rating and improvement processes separate, but complementary

- Whether license-exempt programs should be eligible to participate in MO QRS

- How to ensure that the MO QRS is updated when state infrastructure or accreditation requirements change

- How to market MO QRS

Separation of Rating and Improvement Processes

We are aware that some states combine rating and improvement processes within the same organization; however, we intentionally maintained a separation to avoid conflicts of interest. The assessment and coaching roles vary greatly. Staff members involved in the rating process must adhere to standardized policies and procedures, showing impartiality in their decision making. Coaches build rapport with program staff as they establish long-term relationships that enable them to provide optimal guidance for improving quality. Although some coaches maintain that it is better for them to rate the programs they serve because they have more details about the day-to-day classroom operations, we believe that maintaining objectivity sufficient to complete reliable and valid classroom assessments would be challenging for coaches. In addition, a coach could find his or her relationship with program staff compromised if staff members were upset about the rating. (See the discussion of this issue in Zaslow, Tout, & Halle, Chapter 17, this volume, on differing purposes for the assessment of quality.)

Eligibility of License-Exempt Programs

Missouri, like many states, considers licensing to be Tier 1 of the QRS. This decision prevents a number of programs (faith-based and school-operated) from participating in MO QRS, because they are exempt from licensing and choose not to become licensed. Some exempt programs would like to participate in MO QRS, but for a variety of reasons choose not to become licensed. There are, however, some exempt programs which are adamant that they do not wish to participate in the system and do not think any exempt programs should be a part of MO QRS. Some licensed providers think that exempt programs should not be able to participate in QRS and access program improvement funds without meeting the same base criteria for licensing. This issue is in part due to the belief that license-exempt providers already have an economic advantage, because they do not have to meet licensing requirements (e.g., ratio) to operate and can afford to charge less.

Although we want all programs to have the opportunity and resources to pursue quality, we must ensure that health and safety standards are met. One possible solution is to create an alternate path for meeting Tier 1 requirements outside of licensing. Given our limited resources, we do not want to duplicate any licensing functions. We continue to engage the exempt and licensed providers in discussions to explore all aspects of this issue in an attempt to find a solution that is satisfactory to all parties involved.

Modifying MO QRS

Because licensing and accreditation anchor MO QRS, it is necessary to build mechanisms in MO QRS for adjusting to revisions made to these systems. In addition, it is important to incorporate new quality initiatives and standards (e.g., infant–toddler early learning guidelines) when appropriate. There is a delicate balance between updating the criteria to reflect current standards of best practice and changing requirements too frequently, thereby frustrating participants. On the one hand, if the system is not updated, it may discontinue to be a valid assessment of quality. On the other hand, program staff members would become overwhelmed if we were to make major changes in the requirements every 2 to 3 years. We plan to continually gather stakeholder input and publish revisions every 5 years. Some of the changes that will be considered for the first major revision are discussed next.

Accreditation as an Automatic Five-Star Rating

Some directors believe that their programs should automatically receive a five-star rating based on their program accreditation. Unfortunately, there were not sufficient numbers of accredited programs in the pilot study to evaluate whether the level of quality according to MO QRS ratings is commensurate with the level of quality documented through accreditation. In addition, most accredited programs in the pilot did not reach the five-star rating. We will continue to collect data through the demonstration and statewide implementation, and then review whether accredited programs should receive a five-star rating when we make revisions to the QRS. For example, if a high percentage of accredited programs earn five stars, then the QRS State Committee will likely recommend this change.

> I think [going] through national accreditation . . . gave us a huge heads up on what to do and how to formulate it. . . . 'Cause a lot of it seems actually redundant—what [QRS] is asking for and national accreditation. *(School-age site facilitator)*

Frequency of Ratings

Program staff provided recommendations about the frequency of ratings ranging from 1 to 5 years. As noted previously, the protocol is to rate programs every 18 months. If a program is willing to pay for the rating, the director may request another rating before the end of the 18-month cycle. As more data are available about the stability of ratings over time, the MO QRS State Committee will revisit this decision to determine whether the 18-month cycle is still appropriate for all programs or if some programs may be eligible for an extended rating cycle.

> If you got this certain rating, how long would you have that before you had the opportunity to change it? *(Home-based provider)*

> If I was at a center and the rating wasn't very good . . . I think . . . it's important as long as there is a recertification or whatever, again, in another year or however long . . . so that people . . . can see the improvement [and] you can get a higher rating. *(Teacher)*

Instruments

We recognize that the School-Age Care Environment Rating Scale (SACERS; Harms, Jacobs, & White, 1996) is the only ERS instrument that has not been revised. During our MO QRS revision cycle, we may need to consider a different observation tool for our school-age groups. In addition, we will continue to gather psychometric data on our intentional teaching checklists to further guide their development.

Marketing

> I moved here from another state and I knew absolutely nobody except for my husband and mother-in-law, and so . . . I was at a grocery store or somewhere, and I saw people with little children, I just asked them, "Where does your kid go to school at?" . . . "Where do you take them?" because I knew nothing about the area. *(Mother of a preschooler)*

As this parent's dilemma illustrates, the MO QRS will be an important tool for families searching for a high-quality program. In a study of 225 parents from over 30 communities across Missouri, the majority of parents (87.5%) reported that they would use a QRS when looking for programs. The three most important factors cited by parents in choosing a program, regardless of income, were reputation, curriculum, and personnel. Not surprisingly, rural respondents reported distance from school or work as a factor more important to them than to urban parents. The vast majority of parents said that they would want their children in at least a three-star program. However, no state has studied how marketing a QRS affects parents' choice of programs.

Communicating About Program Quality

We continue to discuss how much information about the rating should be shared with parents. On the one hand, giving families an overall star rating is easy to understand and market. However, programs may wish to communicate more specific information about the component scores. For example, Tennessee issues a report card that provides information about the director's qualifications, professional development, compliance history, family involvement, ratio and group size, staff compensation, program assessment, and business management.

A key point here is that there is a need for ongoing monitoring as QRS initiatives are implemented. New issues may arise from initial data collection or qualitative data from QRS participants that need to be addressed through implementation of the systems. Caution is needed about whether and how often modifications to a system are made for it to be fully adopted within a state.

QRS as a Source of Data to Inform Decisions About Quality Measurement at the Systems Level

Reframing QRS as an Accountability Measure

During the planning and piloting stages, we viewed the MO QRS as a means to ensure that programs are accountable to the families they serve and the organizations that provide financial support to them. We now realize, however, that MO QRS provides checks and balances for the entire early childhood and school-age system (programs, communities, state departments, and legislators). Up until this point in the chapter, we have shown how pilot data can be used to inform modifications in finalizing a statewide QRS. The focus in this section is to show how the QRS ratings can be used as a source of data in future decision making at the state level about quality measurement. Although the illustrations provided are specific to Missouri, the process of using state QRS data to inform broader decisions is applicable to all states.

Communities

As communities secure local funds (public and private) to support programs in their efforts to improve program quality, MO QRS is a measure for local funders and taxpayers to determine whether the community investments are resulting in higher star ratings and, ultimately, in better outcomes for children and youth. The director of the Greater Kansas City Metropolitan Council on Early Learning noted, "Accountability is critically important. Parents, funders, and the community must know that our work to improve the quality of early learning is happening. The Quality Rating System provides accountability" (J. Caccamo, personal communication, February 13, 2009).

State Departments

Missouri state department personnel oversee contracts for approximately $12.5 million annually for quality-improvement activities. Department personnel will be able to use the MO QRS to better target the allocation of limited resources. In addition, the MO QRS will allow state department personnel to monitor the outcome of the investment and determine whether a service improves the area targeted for quality improvement.

The MO QRS is built on the state infrastructure, with each of the state departments playing a key role (e.g., the Department of Health and Senior Services oversees training approvals, the Department of Education approves curriculum training, and the Department of Social Services provides tiered subsidy). MO QRS has highlighted a need for standardization and centralization of the training approval system. MO QRS pursues consistent decisions regarding counting clock hours toward the annual training requirement. As programs encounter roadblocks or inconsistencies, MO QRS helps state departments to identify the need and make plans to address the issues, thus making them accountable to the providers.

Legislators

MO QRS provides to legislators and community leaders a measure to determine the value of the state's investment in quality improvements and to inform their funding decisions (e.g., higher rates of reimbursement for higher levels of quality). The MO QRS offers education advocates a means of holding legislators accountable for their decisions related to early childhood and school-age funding.

Steps to Help Ensure Data Quality in a QRS

We offer the following six suggestions for maintaining data quality once a QRS initiative is fully implemented:

1. State Registries Can Provide an
Important Resource for High Data Quality

State registries are likely already to collect most of the data to inform the staff education and training material, or can be modified to do so. When QRS and state registries support one another, these benefits are likely to be seen:

a.   Teachers submit their training and education data to one organization to meet the requirements for various quality initiatives (e.g., QRS and accreditation).

b.   Directors have an easy method of tracking staff training and education for multiple purposes, allowing them to focus on the day-to-day operations rather than on paperwork.

c.   State registries experience increased enrollment.

d.   QRS does not require additional program staff data collection and verification (i.e., transcript review) for those programs already participating in quality initiatives—it uses existing state infrastructure.

e.   Use of verified data increases the validity of the QRS rating process.

2. Data Quality Is Best Maintained When
QRS Components Are Verified or Are Directly Observed

In addition to verifying education and training data, as discussed earlier, most QRS initiatives include additional criteria that can and should be verified. For example, in Missouri, information about criteria in the Program Management category is collected through a survey and verified on-site by the QRS Assessor.

3. Transparency

Data quality is best maintained when the data collection processes support program staff members' understanding of the criteria and the scoring process and when directors have sufficient information about the scoring to monitor the progress of the program and to review and approve data used in the calculation of the score.

4. Use of Technology

Web-based technology allows program staff to "manage their QRS account"—by completing program and staff information, tracking data submitted for verification purposes, requesting an observation window, and monitoring the number of points earned.

5. Need to Maintain Breadth

Because QRS models typically provide a global view of quality, they cannot assess all specialized areas. Requests for focused examination of specialized areas (such as provision of mental health services) can overburden QRS and threaten data quality. Adherence to breadth in a QRS need not be seen as undermining the value of addressing more specialized issues, however. These can be addressed through state standards, such as the Core Competencies and the development of best practices technical assistance tools.

6. Schedule for Revisions

A QRS should be updated as state and national standards are updated. Establishing a revision schedule early and communicating the schedule and plan to stakeholders help to ensure that the QRS maintains broad support and remains valid, reliable, and relevant.

Summary: Implications of the MO QRS Experience for the Use of Data to Inform the Development and Refinement of Statewide Quality Measurement in Other States

This summary is divided into two sections: 1) a general discussion on how data can be used to inform the development of a state QRS, and 2) specific findings from the MO QRS pilot that may help inform the development or revision of other state quality rating systems.

Using Data to Develop a QRS

- *Data collected when piloting a QRS can make clear where there is variation in responses and where not.* This can be very important in determining the kind of data that can discriminate across levels of a QRS. For example, there was limited variation in self-report regarding use of a curriculum in the MO QRS pilot, whereas there was substantial variation in observational measures of intentional instruction. The latter appear to be more valuable for creating quality rating levels.

- *Data collected when piloting a QRS can indicate where the funds needed to collect direct observations appear warranted and where this is not the case.* Direct observations of ratio compliance in Missouri revealed that programs nearly always met licensing requirements. Because ratio compliance in licensed programs was not related to quality indicators across several Missouri studies, we deemed it unnecessary and costly to include multiple random ratio checks in MO QRS.

- *Pilot data can indicate where two sets of informants show a high degree of agreement on report data, eliminating the need to collect data from both.* In the MO QRS pilot, program directors and parents agreed closely in their report of administrative practices. Moving forward, it was not considered necessary to collect data on this topic from both sources.

- *Data collected when piloting a QRS can reveal gaps in available instrumentation and provide sufficient data from established measures to assist in the development of new instruments.* The MO QRS pilot data demonstrated that measuring curriculum implementation requires specific observational measures that capture teaching practices in a variety of areas. Our research for appropriate measures across the age ranges led us to realize that the field lacks appropriate instruments for measuring intentional instruction for infants and toddlers and for school-age children. We were also lacking guidelines for observing intentional instruction when home-based care involved mixed-age groups. The MO QRS provided an opportunity to start the development of measures for infant–toddler and school-age groups and for procedures for mixed age groups. Internal consistency reliability was assessed for the new measures, and established measures provided criteria for concurrent validity.

- *Means and distributions can provide important information regarding how to set criteria for differing levels.* In the MO QRS pilot, it became clear that mean scores were not enough data to consider in assigning a tier value for observed quality, because averages could obscure the results from some classrooms with scores that were extremely low. Examination of the distributions suggested the importance of providing a range within which a center's average score across classrooms needed to fall, but simultaneously to require that no scores for individual classrooms fell below a certain level.

- *Pilot data can be informative as to where state resources for quality improvement efforts should be allocated.* In the MO QRS pilot, there clearly were limitations in programs' ability to meet some of the administrative requirements (e.g., development of an annual budget). These findings can be used to help shape quality improvement efforts for programs.

- *Pilot data can be used by state departments that approve accrediting bodies.* The variation of criteria in the approved accrediting entities by program type is significant, so these data could be used to revise the state-approved list.

- *Pilot data can be used to assess whether accreditation is equivalent to the highest quality rating attained through other criteria.* In Missouri, there were insufficient numbers of accredited programs to make this assessment of equivalence. This is a potentially important issue for other states to address through the collection of pilot data.

- *Pilot data can be used to ensure that tiers of a QRS differ on specified criteria.* That is, pilot data can be used to validate the different levels or ratings.

Learning from the Missouri Experience

- The MO QRS pilot data suggest that professional development requirements involving education credits *or* training may both be associated with certain levels of observed quality, leaving open the possibility of creating alternative paths to fulfilling the requirements through education or training. The general issue of providing alternative paths when data indicate that both are related to an external criterion is important to consider, given the background and professional development of the work force.

- Pilot data from the MO QRS helped to identify barriers to increase ratings for small programs. For example, educational requirements indicating that half of the staff needs a certain education level may be inappropriate to very small centers. It is important to consider quality tiers that small programs can progress across.

- The MO QRS pilot data suggest caution in relying on self-report data about use of a curriculum. A very high proportion of programs report such use, yet direct observations of intentional instruction show substantial variation not captured by the self-reports.

- Measures of intentional instruction are lacking for infant–toddler and school-age programs. Experts were consulted to contribute input on how to observe intentional instruction appropriately and reliably in these age groups. The results of the pilot work in Missouri may provide feedback for other states seeking measures of intentional instruction for these age ranges. The Missouri pilot work also provides guidelines for observing intentional instruction in mixed-age home-based care that may be valuable for other states to consider.

- In order to conserve resources for quality improvement, it is important to carefully allocate funds for direct observation of quality. The results of the MO QRS pilot study suggest that when half of the classrooms for each age group in a center-based program are observed, the quality tier is assigned with a high degree of accuracy (over 85%), compared with when all of the classrooms are observed. The rate of accuracy drops substantially when a third of the classrooms are observed. These findings, taken together with those from a similar study in Illinois, suggest that accurate assignment to a quality tier for a center may be made based on findings from half of the classrooms. Further studies will be needed to test the generalizability across quality rating systems with different requirements.

- A high proportion of parents in a sample from across the state indicated that they would use data from the QRS in selecting programs for their children. Although no state has yet studied how QRS data actually affect selection of care, this finding is important in indicating that parents would be receptive to using QRS ratings.

References

Burchinal, M.R., Roberts, J.E., Nabors, L.A., & Bryant, D.M. (1996). Quality of center child care and infant cognitive and language development. *Child Development, 67,* 606–620.

Center for the Study of Social Policy. (2004, April). *Protecting children by strengthening families: A guidebook for early childhood programs.* Washington, DC: Author.

Cost, Quality, & Child Outcomes Study Team. (1995). *Cost, quality, and child outcomes in child care centers, technical report.* Denver, CO: Department of Economics, Center for Research in Economics and Social Policy, University of Colorado.

Elicker, J., Fortner-Wood, C., & Noppe, I.C. (1999). The context of infant attachment in family child care. *Journal of Applied Developmental Psychology, 20,* 319–336.

Epstein, A.S. (2007). *The intentional teacher: Choosing the best strategies for young children's learning.* Washington, DC: National Association for the Education of Young Children.

Fuger, K.L. (2004). Early Childhood Quality Rating System Initiative of Greater Kansas City program data. (Unpublished raw data.)

Harms, T., Jacobs, E.V., & White, D.R. (1996). *School-age Care Environment Rating Scale.* NY: Teachers College Press.

McCormick Tribune Center for Early Childhood Leadership, National Louis University. (2008, Spring). *When quality counts and money matters.* (Research Notes). Chicago: Author.

Missouri AfterSchool Network. (2007). Missouri Afterschool Program Standards. Columbia, MO: Author.

Missouri Department of Education. (2002–2005). Missouri Early Learning Standards. Retrieved 1-14-11 from http://dese.mo.gov/divimprove/fedprog/earlychild/PreK_Standards/Index.html

Missouri Department of Health and Senior Services. (1991). Child care licensing rules. Jefferson City, MO: Author.

NICDH Early Child Care Research Network. (2000). The relation of child care to cognitive and language development. *Child Development, 71,* 960–980.

OPEN Initiative. (2005). Missouri Education Matrix. Columbia, MO: Author. Retrieved 1-14-11 from https://www.OPENInitiative.org (click on "Resources" to find the document).

OPEN Initiative. (2006). Core competencies for youth development professionals. Columbia, MO: Author. Retrieved 1-14-11 from https://www.OPENInitiative.org (click on "Resources" to find the document).

OPEN Initiative. (2010). Missouri's additional notes for clarification. Columbia, MO: Author. Retrieved 1-14-11 from https://www.OPENInitiative.org (click on "Resources" to find the document).

OPEN Initiative. (2011). Core competencies for early care and education professionals. Columbia, MO: Author. Retrieved 1-14-11 from https://www.OPENInitiative.org (click on "Resources" to find the document).

Phillips, D., Mekos, D., Scarr, S., McCartney, K., & Abbott-Shim, M. (2001). Within and beyond the classroom door: Assessing quality in child care centers. *Early Childhood Research Quarterly, 15,* 475–496.

Raikes, H.H., Wilcox, B., Peterson, C., Hegland, S., Atwater, J., Summers, J., et al. (2003). *Child care quality and workforce characteristics in four midwestern states.* Lincoln, NE: The Gallup Organization and the University of Nebraska.

Sylva, K., Siraj-Blatchford, I., & Taggart, B. (2003). *Assessing quality in the early years: Early Childhood Environment Rating Scale, Extension (ECERS-E).* Sterling, VA: Trentham.

Sylva, K., Siraj-Blatchford, I., & Taggart, B. (2006). *Assessing quality in the early years: Early Childhood Environment Rating Scale, Extension (ECERS-E) (Rev. Ed.).* Sterling, VA: Trentham.

Talan, T.N., & Bloom, P.J. (2004). *Program Administration Scale.* New York: Teachers College Press.

Thornburg, K., Scott, J., & Mayfield, W. (2002). *Quality child care among licensed and licensed-exempt centers: Findings from the Midwest Child Care Consortium.* Policy brief. Columbia, MO: Center for Family Policy and Research.

CHAPTER 17

Differing Purposes for Measuring Quality in Early Childhood Settings

Aligning Purpose with Procedures

Martha Zaslow, Kathryn Tout, and Tamara Halle

A s states and communities invest in initiatives to improve the quality of early care and education (ECE), the measurement of quality is becoming more widespread and the importance of measuring quality *well* is gaining increasing attention (Zaslow, Tout, & Martinez-Beck, 2010). Within the broad context of interest in improving quality, this chapter seeks to differentiate among a number of more specific purposes for measuring quality in early childhood settings and to identify the implications of these differing purposes for the careful and appropriate measurement of quality.

In the related, but distinct, area of the assessment of developmental outcomes in young children, distinguishing carefully among different purposes has provided a critical starting point for thinking through the identification of what assessments should be used, how they should be carried out, and to whom information about assessment results should be communicated (Shepard, Kagan, & Wurtz, 1998; Snow & Van Hemel, 2008). By way of background, we begin with an overview of key points in the discussion by Shepard and colleagues (1998) and by Snow and Van Hemel (2008) regarding the importance of having a clearly articulated purpose in carrying out assessments of young children's development. Building on that discussion, we distinguish among different purposes for conducting assessments of quality in early childhood settings. We then identify the implications of the different purposes for assessing quality in terms of the selection of measurement tools, decisions about who collects the information on quality, strategies for how the information is collected, and the determination of in what form and to whom results are communicated.

Having differentiated among four different purposes for measuring quality, we note the need for caution when such assessments seek to address multiple purposes at once. In order to conserve resources, especially so that they can be allocated toward the *improvement* of quality and not only its *assessment*, it is efficient to seek to use the measurement of quality for multiple purposes, particularly when the measurement of quality is carried out in many sites throughout a geographical area. Just as in the work on child assessments, however, we underscore the need for safeguards when the assessment of quality is carried out for multiple purposes. We conclude by providing specific examples of the use of quality measures for multiple purposes, and the kinds of safeguards that may be important to implement in these circumstances.

Purposes for Assessing Young Children's Development as a Starting Point

In *Principles and Recommendations for Early Childhood Assessments,* Shepard et al. (1998) identified four intended uses, or purposes, for carrying out assessments of young children: 1) assessments to support learning, 2) assessments for identification of special needs, 3) assessments for program evaluation and monitoring of trends, and 4) assessments for high-stakes accountability. These differing purposes and the need to distinguish among them is supported and extended by the recent report of the National Research Council's Committee on Developmental Outcomes and Assessments for Young Children (Snow & Van Hemel, 2008).

To illustrate the centrality of starting with a clear sense of underlying purpose, Shepard and colleagues contrasted circumstances involving assessment for the purpose of guiding instruction for individual children and those involving assessments carried out for accountability. Assessments to guide instruction are carried out in the familiar context where care and learning take place (the classroom or home-based care setting) and are conducted by the familiar caregiver or educator. The assessments are intended to help caregivers and early educators understand what new knowledge and skills the child has mastered and where he or she may need help in proceeding to the next step. Because the aim, in part, is to determine what the child is ready to progress to, the assessment may actually involve the caregiver–educator trying to help the child move on to a new skill to see whether he or she is ready to progress when specific information or supports are provided. In addition, because assessments occur on an ongoing basis as new skills are learned, there is no need to restrict assessments to certain times during the year. It takes expertise and discipline to observe and probe a child's level of understanding and skills, but the background required to observe and probe is different from the training required to administer and score a standardized assessment (which may involve, for example, training on how to ask assessment questions in a uniform manner; how to identify the appropriate starting and ending point for an assessment, given the child's age and responses; and how to score responses).

Assessments for the purpose of guiding instruction must meet less stringent standards for reliability than assessments for other purposes. Because the assessments for this purpose are ongoing, if a caregiver or educator reaches a conclusion based on an assessment one week, but a further assessment a couple of weeks later yields different information, the caregiver–educator can quickly change course in terms of targeting activities and instruction for the child. In addition to the assessment information being used to shape instruction for the particular child, the information from ongoing assessments to guide instruction is also intended to be communicated to parents—for example, during parent conferences. Children may also benefit from seeing collections of their own work that may be assembled as part of the ongoing assessment to guide instruction, finding in it evidence of the progress they are making.

As an example of assessments carried out for the purpose of accountability, Shepard and colleagues point to assessments conducted to determine whether a targeted proportion of children in each school in a school district has reached a certain level identified as indicating proficiency. Shepard and colleagues note that when assessments are carried out for the purpose of school accountability, it is important to collect the assessments in a standardized way so that scores are comparable across schools. Because comparability is critical, it is important for the assessments to be carried out at about the same time in the school year. It is also important for teachers not to help or probe when administering an assessment, but for the assessments to be conducted in the same way across classrooms and schools. To guard against errors in decisions about whether individual schools have reached the targeted proportion of children whose scores indicate proficiency, the technical standards for reliability and validity of the chosen assessment need to be stringent. Results at the school level are communicated to policy makers and to the public.

In these contrasting examples, it can be seen that the purpose of an early childhood assessment is central in determining the content that the assessment focuses on, the method of data collection (e.g., whether administration should be strictly standardized), the technical requirements for the assessment, and the way in which the information is communicated and used. Shepard and colleagues caution that

> Serious misuses of testing with young children occur when assessments intended for one purpose are used inappropriately for other purposes. For example, the content of IQ measures intended to identify children for special education is not appropriate content to use in planning instruction. At the same time, assessments designed for instructional planning may not have sufficient validity and technical accuracy to support high-stakes decisions such as placing children in a special kindergarten designated for at-risk children. (1998, p. 7)

Shepard and colleagues noted that "there is a natural tendency for policymakers and educators to want to use assessment data for more than one purpose" (1998, p. 32). However, they urge caution in combining purposes, noting that the appropriate content, technical requirements, and the way in which the assessments need to be collected may differ too much. For example, assessment to guide instruction must be closely tied to the content of ongoing instruction, whereas assessment for purposes of screening involve making "inferences about *ability* to learn and/or the existence of a possible disability" and so should be designed to be "as 'curriculum free' as possible" (p. 32).

When the same content can be addressed in assessments carried out for different purposes, careful planning is nevertheless required regarding technical requirements and practices of collecting data. Shepard and colleagues note that for school-age children, some states have attempted to record children's progress in a portfolio system to guide individual instructional decisions, as well as to report on state-level trends in achievement and for accountability of schools. However, this has necessitated a uniform curriculum for each grade level across the state so that progress of individual students is tracked in light of common curricular goals. Great care has been required to assure that portfolio entries are made in a uniform manner so that state-level trends reflect uniform data collection across schools. "Use for accountability purposes also requires standardization of scoring across schools and rigorous external checks to make sure that the data being aggregated from classrooms are comparable" (1998, p. 33). Thus, although there may be benefits to simultaneously addressing multiple purposes in assessing children, it should not be assumed that this can be done without additional planning and resources.

The Committee on Developmental Outcomes and Assessments for Young Children of the National Research Council recently completed a comprehensive review of the research on early childhood assessments (Snow & Van Hemel, 2008). There are two key principles stressed throughout the committee's report: The selection of assessments and the way in which they are carried out need to be guided by the underlying purpose; and early childhood assessments should not be carried out in isolation, but should be part of a system with other key components, such as the appropriate preparation of those who administer the assessments and those who interpret and use the information from them, procedures to ensure that child assessment results are interpreted in the context of knowledge about program quality and opportunities to learn, and advance planning for the ways that the needs for improvement will be addressed when they are identified.

Similar to the earlier work by Shepard and colleagues, this review underscores the central importance of the purpose of measurement for determining what assessments are carried out and how they are conducted:

> Different purposes require different types of assessments, and the evidentiary base that supports the use of an assessment for one purpose may not be suitable for another. As the consequences of assessment findings become weightier, the accuracy and quality of the instruments used to provide findings must be more certain. Decisions based on an assessment that is used to monitor the progress of one child can be important to that child and her family and thus must be taken with caution, but they can also be challenged and revisited more easily than assessments used to determine the fate or funding for groups of children, such as those attending a local child care center, an early education program, or a nationwide program like Head Start. (Snow & Van Hemel, 2008, pp. 2–3)

The report anticipates a tendency to use early childhood assessment for more than one purpose, and just as the report by Shepard and colleagues does, cautions against this. For example, the report expresses concern about the use of measures designed for program accountability instead for guiding individual children's instruction. Assessment for the purpose of accountability often involves the use of abbreviated versions of standardized measures to make it more feasible to carry out such measures within a limited period in large samples of children. The report cautions that such abbreviated measures may not provide information that is detailed enough to guide the instruction of individual children.

The NRC report builds on and goes beyond the work of Shepard and colleagues by articulating specific protections and guidelines that must be in place when a single assessment is used for multiple purposes. For example, the report anticipates a tendency to use teachers' ongoing observations regarding children's progress in response to instruction (using specific ongoing instructional measures) not only for the purpose of guiding children's progress, but also for purposes of accountability:

> Performance (classroom-based) assessments of children can be used for accountability if objectivity is ensured by checking a sample of the assessments for reliability and consistency, if the results are appropriately contextualized in information about the program, and if careful safeguards are in place to prevent misuse of the information. (Snow & Van Hemel, 2008, p. 11)

This additional step of articulating specific guidelines and protections which should be in place when a measure is used for more than one purpose is a precedent that we can follow for the measurement of quality in early childhood settings. In particular, at the conclusion of this chapter, we will note examples of measures of quality (rather than child assessments) being used for more than one purpose. We propose an initial set of guidelines to be put in place to protect against difficulties that can emerge when data collection on quality addresses multiple purposes.

Distinguishing Among Purposes for Assessing Quality in Early Childhood Settings

Just as the identification of underlying purpose plays a central role in selecting, implementing, and communicating results from early childhood assessments, we propose that the assessment of quality in early childhood environments could be strengthened by articulation of distinct purposes. Lambert (2003) commented on the need to differentiate among measures of quality in an article titled "Considering Purpose and Intended Use When Making Evaluations of Assessments." In this article, Lambert noted that measures of quality can be differentiated both in terms of intended recipient and breadth. Lambert added that different recipients include programs themselves, researchers, or those determining whether a classroom or program has attained an externally determined standard of quality such as accreditation. These different recipients may need information at different levels of detail. For example, programs seeking information to guide program improvement may need detailed information at the level of specific items, whereas summary information may be more relevant for hypothesis generation for researchers or for policy makers. Lambert noted that some quality measures actually have different versions for different audiences, building in these differences in the level of detail. (See, e.g., Abbott-Shim & Sibley, 1997, 1998.) In terms of breadth, Lambert notes that some measures of quality focus on supports for specific domains of development, such as language and literacy development, whereas others provide a broad portrayal of overall quality. The purpose for measuring quality is critical to selecting specific measures. If the goal is for overall quality improvement, a broad measure may be most appropriate, whereas if the goal is to improve practice in a specific domain, a measure focusing in depth on a particular aspect of the environment may be more appropriate. In some instances, underlying purpose may call for a combination of broad and domain-specific measures to be used.

Snow and Van Hemel (2008) also cautioned that there are multiple purposes for measuring quality and a need to align the measure, the way data are collected, and the way information about quality is communicated, with the underlying purpose. We use the discussions of Snow and Van Hemel (2008) and Lambert (2003) as starting points for a more detailed discussion of different purposes for measuring quality in early childhood settings and the implications of these different purposes.

In particular, we see the following as four key purposes for measuring the quality of early childhood settings:

1. To inform and guide improvement in practice for individual practitioners or programs by identifying specific areas in need of strengthening

2. To determine whether program or policy investments have resulted in a change in quality over time, both at the level of the individual program and in a geographical area (such as community or state) where investments in quality have been made

3. To contribute to understanding about the contributors to and outcomes of quality

4. To describe or rate the quality of individual programs in a community or geographical area, with the aim of helping to inform parental choice

Following the precedent set by Shepard and colleagues, as well as Snow and Van Hemel, we next discuss the implications of each of these four purposes for a) who collects the information on quality, b) who receives or uses the information, c) selecting a specific quality measure, d) the training needed for data collection, and e) issues in the implementation process for collecting the data. We also note issues that are emerging in the field as data on quality are collected for each purpose.

For this chapter, we use the term *quality* to refer to the broad range of environmental features and interactions in nonparental care and education settings that have been positively linked to children's development (Zaslow et al., 2010). These include structural characteristics such as child–adult ratio and the education of the teacher or caregiver, as well as process characteristics such as the frequency and tone of activities to promote early literacy. The measures used to capture these dimensions of quality typically go beyond a focus on structural features to include a global assessment of process features as well as an evaluation of the daily routines and environment. This concept of quality differs from the standards used in child care licensing. Although some states utilize well-known quality measures in their licensing system as a way to establish a higher threshold of quality for programs, licensing typically provides only a minimum level of basic health and safety routines and provisions. In this chapter, our focus is on the measurement of quality above the floor established by typical licensing standards.

Cross-cutting Issues

Before turning to the four suggested purposes for assessing early childhood environments, we note two consistent cross-cutting issues: selecting measures with evidence of reliability and validity, and selecting measures appropriate for the populations participating in the early childhood settings.

Irrespective of purpose, a starting point for the selection of a measure of quality will consistently be the demonstrated reliability and validity of the measure. The previous work on child assessments stressed that requirements for reliability and validity, although important to any purpose, needed to be most stringent where there are consequences for individuals or programs, such as when assessments are used for placement of individual children or when funding decisions are made for teachers (e.g., teacher salaries) or programs (Shepard et al., 1998; Snow & Van Hemel, 2008).

Evidence that a measure is reliable (i.e., when a measure results in consistent information across different administrations and different trained administrators) and valid (i.e., when a measure appropriately reflects key underlying dimensions of quality according to experts in the field, or shows evidence of relationships to other established measures of quality and to important child outcomes) is a starting point for the selection of measures of quality for each of the four purposes noted (Bryant, 2010). A key resource that summarizes the evidence on the reliability and validity of measures of quality is the compendium of quality measures for early childhood settings recently completed by Halle, Vick Whittaker, and Anderson (2010).

Although all measures selected for the assessment of quality need to have evidence of reliability and validity, the requirements for reliability in the particular circumstances of implementation can vary. A central question, as is noted shortly, is not just whether a measure has been shown to have reliability under conditions of rigorous administration and as demonstrated by the measure's developers, but how demanding the training and standards of interrater reliability need to be when measures are administered for such purposes as guiding improvement in practice as opposed to gauging whether programs have improved over time. Thus, we distinguish here between a measure's potential for reliability and validity, as documented in the technical manual for the measure, and the reliability and validity of the measure as actually implemented in a particular context. As we will discuss in the conclusion to the chapter, key issues that are emerging in the field are whether it is appropriate for the standard of reliability to be less stringent when the purpose for measuring quality is to guide program improvement, and the precautions that need to be put into place when quality is measured both for informing program improvement and for another purpose, such as creating summary ratings to provide to parents.

An additional cross-cutting issue is the appropriateness of measures for the populations participating in the ECE settings for which quality is being measured. The section of this volume on cross-cutting topics highlights several important considerations. For example, children whose home language is not English may need additional supports, such as instructional scaffolding (Goldenberg, 2008), in order to achieve optimal outcomes for learning. Characteristics of the caregiver—for example, the extent to which caregivers are knowledgeable about the development of dual language learners (DLLs) and their own ability to communicate effectively with the child and parents in their primary language—are also important. (See Castro, Espinosa, & Páez, Chapter 11, this volume.) Instruction in a child's primary language promotes bilingualism and biliteracy, and will influence the degree to which the child and parents feel emotionally and culturally comfortable in the care setting. (See Neuman & Carta, Chapter 4, and Castro et al., Chapter 11, this volume.) These examples of specific elements of quality for DLLs suggest that quality measures should be able to capture specific instructional practices and caregiver–child interactions in order to determine the quality of the environment for DLLs. Another example is when care environments include children with special needs. Here, specific accommodations in the classroom, both for the physical environment and for instructional practices, may be important. (See Spiker, Hebbeler, & Barton, Chapter 10, this volume.) Measures that rate the overall classroom environment and specific instructional practices would need to be sensitive to accommodations for children with special needs. Finally, early care settings which include infants and toddlers have different characteristics that constitute quality, compared with care settings including only preschool-age children. Specifically, measures of quality must be able to distinguish settings in which materials and activities are appropriate for the age of the children. (See Sandstrom, Moodie & Halle, Chapter 14, this volume.)

Purpose #1: To Inform and Guide Improvement in Practice for Individual Practitioners or Programs by Identifying Specific Areas in Need of Strengthening

The first purpose that we have identified for the collection of data on quality in early childhood settings is to serve as a diagnostic tool. Data collected for this purpose can help individual providers and programs identify the areas in which improvements are needed and can be used as a basis for formulating an improvement plan.

Who Collects the Information on Quality?

In most instances, the information on quality collected for this purpose is gathered by an individual providing technical assistance to the early childhood caregiver–educator or program. The measure usually is an observational measure of quality used as a source of feedback about strengths and areas in need of improvement and for planning goals and developing an approach to quality improvement.

Some quality improvement approaches involve providing training to the caregivers– educators so that they can master the observational measure and conduct their own assessment of quality. In the Partnerships for Inclusion (PFI) model, as assessed in the Quality Interventions for Early Care and Education (QUINCE) Evaluation, caregivers–educators learned the assessment tool and then worked jointly with a consultant to implement an action plan for quality improvement (Bryant et al., 2009). For caregivers–educators to learn how to assess their own quality and monitor it over time is considered a central factor in maintaining a higher level of quality after the person providing on-site technical assistance (hereinafter called the *consultant*) has completed the work with the caregivers–educators.

Who Receives the Information on Quality?

When quality is assessed to guide improvement in practice, the recipient of the findings is the caregiver or early educator whose classroom or group was observed, sometimes with feedback also provided to a program director. In all instances, however, the intent is to develop a plan for quality improvement in that particular classroom or home setting and to document whether improvement has occurred and is sustained in that particular setting.

Selecting Measures

As noted previously, the reliability and validity of measures as documented by measures developers is a selection criterion that must be taken into account when measures are chosen, irrespective of purpose. (However, see the subsequent discussion on standards for interrater reliability when the purpose is goal-setting for on-site technical assistance versus other purposes.) Further considerations, however, are specific to purpose. For example, when quality is assessed to guide improvement in practice, it is important that a measure is selected in which the focus aligns with the aspects of quality that the provider or program is seeking to improve. Thus, for example, if the goal is to improve overall program quality, a broad measure of quality may be most appropriate. However, if the focus of program improvement is on a particular facet of quality, such as strengthening the supports in the early childhood setting for early language and literacy development or for young children's social and emotional development, a more in-depth measure focusing on this facet of quality would be more appropriate. The compendium of measures of quality for early childhood settings (Halle et al., 2010) provides multiple examples of both broad measures of quality (of which two illustrations include the Early Childhood Environment Rating Scale-Revised [ECERS-R]; Harms, Clifford, & Cryer, 2005; and the Family Child Care Environment Rating Scale-Revised [FCCERS-R]; Harms, Cryer, & Clifford, 2007) and measures of quality with a more detailed focus on specific facets of quality (of which illustrations include the Early Language and Literacy Classroom Observation [ELLCO]; Smith, Brady, & Anastasopoulos, 2008; Smith & Dickinson, 2002; the Classroom Assessment Scoring System™ [CLASS™]; Pianta, La Paro, & Hamre, 2007; and the Supports for Social-Emotional Growth Assessment, [SSEGA]; Smith, unpublished). Further work toward the development of in-depth measures of quality focusing on specific facets of quality is underway (Child Trends, 2008a).

Training

Training needs to be multifaceted for those who collect information on quality in order to guide improvement in practice. In addition to training to collect the quality data with reliability, showing acceptable levels of agreement with master coders or reliability tapes, training for this purpose also involves understanding how to translate the quality ratings into setting specific and attainable goals toward quality improvement. In order to work with a caregiver–early educator on quality improvement, the consultants need to have skills in building positive working relationships. Training in this area may involve, for example, learning how to emphasize strengths when communicating with a provider before identifying and agreeing upon areas in need of improvement, and helping providers recognize when positive changes are occurring. We note that there are varying approaches to working directly on quality improvement with caregivers or early educators. For example, some approaches involve the caregiver–educator identifying the aspects of quality that she would like to work on, whereas others involve the consultant identifying the areas for improvement and developing the quality improvement plan. Some on-site approaches focus on the implementation of a specific curriculum, whereas others have a broad focus on overall quality. Some involve working with all staff members in a classroom or home setting, whereas others involve working only with the most senior staff member. We are beginning to see efforts to share information on the training for consultants.

Implementation

With the expansion of approaches that involve working with caregivers or early educators to improve quality, one important implementation issue is providing for adequate numbers of qualified consultants. Large caseloads are indeed a reality for many agencies offering on-site technical assistance. For example, in the QUINCE evaluation, consultants in the partner agencies (not necessarily only those who delivered the PFI model) served, on average, 44 clients at a time (Bryant, 2008; Bryant et al., 2009). In addition to the need for substantial numbers of consultants, implementation also requires the availability of staff to provide supervision. Such supervision is needed to help address challenging issues that come up in the field and to help someone who is traveling from site to site to stay well connected to the initiative's goals, as well as to colleagues. A further implementation issue is the need to track quality improvement efforts as they move forward. Tools for describing the focus of joint quality improvement efforts and for tracking progress toward goals are needed.

Emerging Issues

As more is learned about the use of quality data to guide program improvement, one challenge that is emerging is the issue of standards for reliability in such data collection. In some research and evaluation projects, information on quality is collected both by the consultant, who uses the information on quality to help guide quality improvement, and by a research team, whose members are unaware of whether the early childhood site was participating in an intervention or not. In the QUINCE-PFI Evaluation, the quality ratings collected by the consultants were correlated with, though systematically more favorable than, the data collected by the researchers (Bryant, 2008; Bryant et al., 2009). The fact that ratings collected by consultants and researchers were correlated indicates that areas of strength and areas of weakness were perceived similarly, though the extent of the problem in areas of weakness tended to be understated by the consultants. Those who will be working directly with caregivers–educators may tend to emphasize the positive.

A key issue for the field to address is the extent to which consultants should be held to the standards of reliability required for data collectors on a research project. Some states are responding to this issue by increasing the rigor of training in completing observational measures of quality for the consultants (e.g., North Carolina). Another possible approach would be for one team to collect the data as a resource for the technical assistance team as well as for research purposes. The consultant would then utilize the quality data, but not be the source of such data. As the field discusses the costs and benefits of various approaches, another important issue will be the role of the individual caregiver or educator in his or her own assessment and improvement efforts.

Purpose #2: To Determine Whether Program or Policy Investments Have Resulted in Improvements in Quality at the Program Level or for Sets of Programs in a Geographical Area

The second purpose for measuring quality moves from the individual caregiver or educator to a group of caregivers or early educators participating in a program or policy initiative. The goal here is to determine through evaluation whether an investment in improving quality is resulting in the intended changes at the program level or for multiple programs that are part of a quality initiative, and thus whether the investment is warranted. The most rigorous approach to measuring whether a program or policy investment is yielding intended changes involves experimental evaluation, in which some sites are randomly assigned to participate in the initiative, whereas others are randomly assigned to be in a control group. Another rigorous design involves contrasting different program approaches (rather than having a program and a control group) to which sites are randomly assigned to see whether one is more effective than others. Less definitive answers to the underlying question of whether an investment to improve quality is effective come from comparative research designs that do not involve random assignment, such as designating all of the ECE sites in one community to receive the resources of a quality initiative and then comparing quality initially and over time in the facilities in that community with those of a nearby and demographically similar community that did not participate in the quality initiative. Reviews of the growing number of rigorous evaluations of approaches to strengthening quality in early childhood settings have pointed to the centrality of measures of quality for confirming that changes in practice have occurred in response to specific interventions. (For one review of this evidence, see Zaslow, Tout, Halle, Vick Whittaker, & Lavelle, 2010.)

Who Collects the Information on Quality?

Observations of quality for the purpose of assessing whether a quality improvement initiative is effective are generally conducted by specially trained independent observers. Although a working relationship between the observer and the caregiver–early educator was assumed for Purpose #1, this cannot be the case in Purpose #2. Indeed, in a random assignment evaluation, it is a goal for observers to be unaware of whether the settings they are observing have been assigned to participate in the intervention to improve quality or to the control group. Independence of the observer protects against possible bias and helps to ensure that the data that are collected will provide a fair assessment of the investment in improving quality.

Who Receives the Information on Quality?

In contrast with Purpose #1, for which the recipient of the information on quality is the individual caregiver or early educator and, possibly, the program director, for Purpose #2, the main recipients of the information are the funding agency and policy makers who were responsible for the initiative. Results also may be shared with the general public, and a technical report of the results or a journal article may also be made available that is useful to researchers.

Selecting Measures

The issues regarding selection of the measures for Purpose #2 are very much the same as for Purpose #1: In addition to selecting measures with demonstrated reliability and validity, it is important to align the content of the quality measures selected as closely as possible with the focus of the quality initiative. Just as for Purpose #1, we note that further measures development that is in progress may provide in-depth measures of aspects of quality in areas for which few or none now exist. Some evaluations of quality initiatives include multiple measures of quality to ensure that changes are detected both on broad or global measures and on more specific facets.

Although our discussion of measures has focused very heavily on observational assessments, it is important to note that evaluations of quality initiatives also may involve interviews with staff or reviews of program documents for such information as the educational attainment and training of caregivers–early educators, group size, ratio, and staff turnover.

Training

The training required for data collection to evaluate whether an initiative to improve quality is effective or not does not involve preparing to work directly with caregivers–early educators in order to translate quality measures into plans for improving quality. Rather, training needs to focus on reaching and maintaining stringent standards for reliability in data collection. When data on quality are collected for Purpose #2, there are possible consequences in terms of further implementation and expansion, versus discontinuation, of an existing approach to improving quality. Thus, it is absolutely essential to protect, to the extent possible, against wrong conclusions being drawn about a program because of measurement error. Training needs not only to require observers to demonstrate interrater reliability immediately after training and before they begin to collect data but also to require observers to demonstrate that reliability has been maintained across the period of data collection. It is important for the developers of measures of quality to articulate clearly the standards for acceptable interrater reliability on the measure.

Implementation

Implementation issues for Purpose #2 emerge especially when the quality initiative being evaluated is implemented at a broad scale—for example, throughout a community or state. In such instances, it is necessary to put into place an infrastructure for measuring quality that will permit observations in a large number of sites (Zaslow et al., 2010). We have noted in our discussion of measures selection that measures for this purpose may go beyond direct observation of quality and include also information gleaned from interviews or review of program documents regarding such issues as staff education and training, group size and ratio, and staff turnover. Although we have discussed interrater reliability for observational measures of quality, another key issue in terms of guarding against measurement error for Purpose #2 is the verification of data provided through interview or document review. In a meeting on the measurement of quality for statewide quality initiatives (Child Trends, 2008b), some participants noted the need for such information to be obtained from a source that regularly verifies the information (such as ECE registries; see the National Registry Alliance web site[1]), or through request for further documentation to verify program records for a subsample of the data collected.

Emerging Issues
Further work is needed on the best design for an infrastructure for the reliable collection of data and for the verification of reported data in evaluations of widely implemented quality initiatives.[2] As states and communities address the set of implementation issues previously noted, they would be well served to bring together those carrying out evaluations of broadly implemented quality initiatives to help develop best-practice statements regarding these issues.

Purpose #3: To Build Knowledge About What Factors Contribute to Quality and What Aspects of the Environment Strengthen Specific Child Outcomes

Efforts to improve quality are built on a foundation of both cross-sectional and longitudinal studies examining the factors that contribute to quality in ECE and the facets of quality that are most important to children's development in different areas. Thus, for example, if research shows that staff turnover is a strong predictor of observed quality in early childhood settings, then efforts to increase the retention of staff can be prioritized for quality improvement efforts. Similarly, if the amount and quality of caregiver–child verbal interaction emerges as the strongest predictor of how well children build vocabulary over the course of a year in an ECE program, then strengthening this aspect of quality would become a priority. Purpose #3 focuses on the collection of data on quality in the context of research to provide a better understanding of predictors of quality in early childhood environments, and of the facets of quality most closely linked with children's development. Such examinations of quality usually take place in longitudinal research in which children's scores on measures of development are examined in light of the quality of their experiences in an ECE setting. Such research also collects a range of contextual information about the program or home setting in order to learn about the factors that contribute to quality.

Who Collects the Information on Quality?
Although the information that is collected for this purpose is intended to inform practice and policy, the context for data collection for Purpose #3 is generally a longitudinal research study. As such, observations are collected by a research team. Some longitudinal studies, such as the NICHD Study of Early Child Care and Youth Development (NICHD Early Child Care Research Network 2003, 2005) and the Early Childhood Longitudinal Study-Birth Cohort (Flanagan & West, 2004; Flanagan & McPhee, 2009), have involved large national samples. In these instances, data may be collected by multiple collaborating university research teams or by a survey research organization with the capacity to carry out direct observations of quality.

Who Receives the Information on Quality?

Information on quality collected for Purpose #3 is shared with researchers with the goal of building the knowledge base to strengthen quality and child outcomes. However, in order to eventually contribute to the strengthening of practice and policy, the descriptive research also needs to be communicated to the practice and policy communities. There are a number of important mechanisms for the dissemination of research findings. For example, the Child Care and Early Education Research Connections web site serves to improve access to research for decision makers in policy and practice, as well as researchers.[3] In addition, the National Child Care Information Center[4] seeks to build on research in providing technical assistance to state child care administrators and others involved in child care policy and practice within states.

Selecting Measures

As for Purposes #1 and #2, the underlying issue for selection of measures for Purpose #3, in addition to the selection of measures with clearly demonstrated reliability and validity, is the need to align the content and focus of the quality measures with the particular questions under study. This becomes even more critical for Purpose #3 for situations in which the issue under study might be the particular facets of care and education environments and interactions that contribute most to a specific aspect of children's development. For example, if the question under study is, What aspects of quality most strongly predict children's language and literacy development?, it is especially important to select a measure that provides detail on aspects of quality that are hypothesized to be related to language and literacy development. Except for the domain of language and literacy development, there are limited measures available to examine specific facets of quality and their links to children's outcomes, such as a measure looking specifically at aspects of quality that contribute to children's physical health outcomes. This gap needs to be addressed through new research and development of measures.

Training

Training for the collection of data on quality for this research purpose should follow stringent rules for attaining and also maintaining interrater reliability. Bryant (2010) notes some fairly consistent decision rules about the levels of interrater agreement that are appropriate to use as evidence of good interrater reliability and the frequency of reliability checks during data collection considered to be good practice. However, some measures developers provide videotapes coded by groups of master coders and hold to their own specific criteria for attaining and then maintaining reliability with the master coders. (See Halle et al., 2010.)

Implementation

Sometimes a descriptive, longitudinal study is carried out in multiple sites that may be geographically dispersed. As one example, the NICHD Study of Early Child Care and Youth Development (NICHD Early Child Care Research Network 2003, 2005), which provided information both on the predictors of quality and on ways by which quality contributes to children's development, involved multiple research sites around the United States. When research is carried out in multiple sites, procedures need to be developed to confirm that there is consistency across sites in the ways observational ratings are completed, and in the ways the data for other measures of quality are collected.

Emerging Issues

Research by Burchinal and colleagues (2009; Chapter 2, this volume) indicates that statistically significant relationships between widely used measures of quality and child outcomes are found consistently, but are modest in strength. These findings are challenging researchers to work on the development of measures by focusing in greater depth on specific aspects of the environment that are hypothesized to be related to children's development in specific domains (Child Trends, 2008a). Gaps in available measures involve not only in-depth measures focused on particular aspects of quality but also age groups and types of ECE settings. We have few measures specifically focused on the quality of care for infants and toddlers, and we also have limited options for the measurement of home-based care, especially family, friend, and neighbor care (Halle et al., 2010). As noted in Sandstrom, Moodie, and Halle (Chapter 14, this volume), a review of existing instruments designed to capture the quality of nonparental care reveals six measures designed specifically for home-based settings; an additional seven that could be used in a variety of settings, including home-based care; and only three measures designed specifically for infants and toddlers.

Purpose #4: To Describe or Rate the Quality of Individual Programs in a Geographical Area in Order to Inform Parental Choice

Purpose #4 for collecting information about quality is to provide information to parents to help them make informed decisions about care for their children. Quality Rating and Improvement Systems (QRIS) involve the measurement of quality throughout a state or in those settings that elect to participate in the system (Mitchell, 2005; Tout et al., 2010; Zaslow et al., 2010).

Who Collects the Information on Quality?

The collection of data on quality throughout a geographical area, particularly if this is done on a periodic basis as part of a system that requires the rating of quality in a large number of settings, requires the identification or creation of an entity that will be responsible for the data collection. Although some states have partnered with a university or community organization taking the primary responsibility for ongoing collection of quality data in statewide or pilot QRIS, others have created a unit within their licensing agency or human services department to collect the data.

Who Receives the Information on Quality?

QRIS intentionally provide the information on quality to parents as consumers of ECE for their children. The aim is to provide the information in summary formats that can be readily understood. The information on quality from QRIS also is summarized for policy makers so that they can identify specific types of ECE settings and specific aspects of quality in need of improvement.

Selecting Measures

States collecting information on quality for QRIS have generally started by collecting global observational measures, focusing on overall quality. However, as attention has increasingly focused on early childhood care and education as laying the groundwork for the cognitive aspects of school readiness, there has been an emerging tendency to add or substitute measures of quality, with a more explicit focus on aspects of quality that support early learning. The compendium profiling measures of quality in early childhood settings by Halle et al. (2010) includes examples of both global measures (e.g., Harms, Clifford, & Cryer, 2005; Harms, Cryer, & Clifford, 1990) and more content-specific measures of quality (e.g., Pianta et al., 2007; Smith et al., 2002, 2008). Questions about which measure or set of measures would be most appropriate to include in community or statewide measurement of quality have also been fostered by recent findings indicating that, although widely used measures of quality such as the ERS show statistically significant prediction to child outcomes, the associations are modest in strength (Burchinal et al., 2009, Chapter 2, this volume).

Although most states with QRIS collect observational measures of quality, they also collect documentation of structural aspects of quality, such as teacher education and training, and reported group size and ratio. In some cases, data collection includes extensive written documentation of practices related to curriculum and child assessments. Other states collect documentation regarding structural aspects of quality and do not collect observational data. Some states collect observational measures only for settings that have met all of the requirements for higher levels of quality, whereas others collect observational data at all quality levels. Looking across the existing QRIS, it is clear that there are a variety of data collection strategies being used and different processes for combining observational and self-report data (Child Trends, 2008b; Tout et al., 2010).

Training

As with Purposes #2 and #3, for Purpose #4 it is essential for training to be sufficient so that data collection meets stringent standards for reliability. Although for Purposes #2 and #3 the issue was meeting standards generally required for research, for Purpose #4 there is the additional issue that the ratings completed for QRIS have consequences for participating early childhood settings in terms of public perception and in terms of possible enrollment, if parents use the quality ratings in choosing care. States may also recognize higher quality through incentives (e.g., tiered reimbursement: higher subsidy payments for settings that are accredited or that receive higher quality ratings) and may provide resources for improving quality depending upon ratings. It is essential that observational measures of quality are collected to high standards of reliability when such "high stakes" are involved. It also is important for training on data collection to be sufficient for data involving document review so that this also is completed with high reliability.

Implementation

Some states are taking interesting steps to address challenges faced in implementation when the measurement of quality is done on such a large scale. One challenge is the possibility that an ECE facility may feel that the rating it has received is inaccurate or unfair. Most QRIS have put in place explicit appeal procedures for a review of ratings when such issues arise. In addition, some QRIS use application and documentation processes that clearly outline the basis for every component of the quality rating so that participating programs can know what their rating will be and will be unlikely to question it.

A second set of implementation issues concerns the frequency with which ratings need to be completed within QRIS in order for the ratings to be sufficiently current to appropriately reflect quality for consumers. A third implementation issue concerns the number of classrooms in a program that need to be observed in order to reach an overall rating of quality for the program, and the way these classrooms should be selected (Thornburg, 2008; Thornburg et al., Chapter 16, this volume).

Emerging Issues

In order to include all types of care in QRIS, measures of quality need to be available for home-based care that are appropriate for family, friend, and neighbor care, as well as for licensed family child care. At present, we have few options for the measurement of quality in family, friend, and neighbor care (however, see Porter, Rice, & Rivera, 2006). The same issue pertains to the measurement of quality in care for infants and toddlers. As for other purposes, it is easy to focus on issues of reliability of measurement only for observational measures, but it is clear from discussions across states that the reliability of data derived from record review is also an issue.

We are just beginning to understand the extents to which and manners in which parents gain access to and actually utilize quality rating information in selecting care for their children. Additional emerging issues include whether parents prefer summary ratings or instead find component ratings regarding particular facets of care more useful; whether quality ratings are being communicated effectively to parents from differing cultural and economic groups; and whether there are constraints (such as the cost of higher quality care) that limit the capacity of parents to utilize quality information. It will be a high priority for researchers to document parental utilization of quality rating information.

The Use of Measures of Quality for Multiple Purposes: Suggested Guidelines

We have identified four distinct purposes for the use of quality measures, and noted recommendations from experts in the field against the collection of data on quality for multiple purposes without first putting in place provisions to safeguard against specific problems in the collection and use of data. In practice, initiatives at the state and local levels are experiencing pressure toward using one data collection effort for multiple purposes regarding quality. This is especially the case given the expense of carefully and rigorously collecting data on quality in many early childhood settings. It is far more efficient to collect such data with multiple goals in mind. Further, there may actually be pitfalls associated with collecting quality data multiple times in the same settings if there are different purposes. These pitfalls include such unintended outcomes as overburdening ECE settings or providing slightly different quality information from data collected through different measures or different data collection strategies (e.g., sampling a different number of classrooms; using differing standards for reliability).

Given that the need for efficiency pushes states or communities toward using one set of data collection procedures to provide information on quality for multiple purposes, it is important to consider the precautions that should be in place when using data collection on quality for multiple purposes. We are at an early stage of identifying such precautions. Next, we note four possible situations that communities or states collecting data on quality on a broad scale might encounter as they launch data collection. We use examples from emerging practices at the local and state levels that involve putting precautions in place to guard against unintended consequences of collecting quality data in one process of data collection for multiple purposes. In particular, we are beginning to see precautions being put into place to guard against the following:

1. *Problems can result from the use of differing standards for reliability when data are collected for purposes of technical assistance and guiding improvement, as well as for such further purposes as informing consumers or for research.* Many quality rating and improvement systems implement both a rating process and a quality improvement process for the providers who participate in the system. When this is the case, information on quality may be used to inform consumers (Purpose #4). However, it also may be used as a source of information to guide improvement in individual programs (Purpose #1) and summarized to inform policymakers as to whether investments in quality are resulting in progress (Purpose #2). Although, as we have noted, reliability assessments have tended to be less stringent when quality information is collected to guide improvements in individual programs, we are seeing states take precautions to use the most stringent standards for reliability when a single round of data collection is to be used to inform individual programs, consumers, and policymakers. For example, some states allow only data collectors who have demonstrated initial and sustained adherence to strict reliability standards to collect data to contribute to the quality rating in a Quality Rating and Improvement System *and* the technical assistance process being used to help providers improve their quality. The trained data collector shares the results of the quality measure with the technical assistance specialist who has training not only in interpretation of the quality measure but also in relationship-based strategies for helping guide goal-setting and improvement strategies on the basis of the results of the measure. This eliminates the possibility that the data collector and the technical assistance specialist would score the measure differently. It also honors the separate and critical expertise of technical assistance providers who have the skills to help providers in the quality improvement process. (See Thornburg et al., Chapter 16, this volume.)

    In addition, the use of the highest standards for reliability in a measurement syst used for accountability purposes is advisable because of the confidence that the public and decision makers place in the results. The system is responsible for ensuring that the same standards for quality are applied to all participants in the system, and high standards for reliability help make this practice possible.

2. *Safeguards must be in place against using information on quality for research and generalizable knowledge when the initial intent was to collect ratings to inform consumers.* As states or local areas with measurement systems accumulate data across programs and over time, it may be useful to look to the data for information about, for example, the predictors of quality or the characteristics of those who make improvements over time compared with those who do not. This information would be useful to the individual system, but also could inform the field at a national level. Yet, states are confronting the fact that collection of data for generalizable knowledge (Purpose #3) requires specific planning steps that need to occur before, rather than after, data collection. These include the need to confirm that a specific measure of quality has been validated for the purpose of research; the need to follow human research subjects protection procedures, such as having a research protocol reviewed by an institutional review board; and the need to collect informed consent from participants in the data collection process. Lambert (2003) noted that different measures of quality may have been validated only for the purpose of improving program quality, or only for research purposes, with different versions of measures sometimes existing (and having validity confirmed) for only one purpose or the other. Further, even if precautions are in place to protect the privacy of data on quality

(e.g., using only identification numbers rather than names and reporting only aggregate results, not results for individuals), this does not suffice as a protection for participants if the information is going to be used in a generalizable way (e.g., in a journal article, in a research brief available on a web site). States or local areas may want to consider following informed consent procedures with all quality data that are collected if they anticipate using data for these broader purposes.

3. *Problems can occur when information on quality is used to indicate whether quality investments have resulted in intended changes when this was not the initial purpose and contextual information has not been gathered that is needed for appropriate interpretation and decisions on possible consequences.* In the volume on early childhood assessment, the Committee on Developmental Outcomes and Assessment of Young Children (Snow & Van Hemel, 2008) recommends that data collected for accountability purposes be complemented by data collection on corresponding contextual factors, such as demographic risk of children and families, and resources available to follow up on children identified as at risk for developmental problems. Such information can help researchers understand findings and stakeholders target investments. This guideline can be extrapolated to data on the quality of programs. For example, understanding that lower quality ratings are correlated with a lack of access to professional development opportunities can provide information to shape future investments and prevent high-stakes decisions (such as de-funding) from being implemented unfairly. A second recommendation by the Committee on Developmental Outcomes and Assessment of Young Children (Snow & Van Hemel, 2008) is to use data on children's progress over time rather than just a point-in-time assessment. In a similar manner, it may be more helpful in a measurement system focusing on quality to identify where improvements are and are not occurring and to seek to understand what is contributing to different patterns of change over time. Supplementing the quality data with information on program resources, demographic characteristics of the target population, and other contextual information will make it possible to identify contributing factors to changes in quality.

4. *When information on quality is provided to multiple audiences (e.g., parents, programs, and policy makers) when only a research audience was anticipated, resources may not be allocated to providing background on the measures used so that all audiences can fully understand the information being provided.* Our final scenario to describe is one in which data collected for one purpose and one audience are shared more broadly with other stakeholders in the system. The Committee on Developmental Outcomes and Assessment for Young Children (Snow & Van Hemel, 2008) cautioned that part of implementing a system of child assessments involves providing key stakeholders with information about the measures and how to interpret scores so that findings are understood appropriately and misinterpretations are avoided. In a parallel manner, states are finding that it is important to plan for and provide information to all key stakeholder groups about the appropriate interpretation of quality measures. When findings are distributed more broadly than initially intended, some stakeholder groups may not receive important background information. Some states and local areas that have begun using quality measures in their systems offer a range of training on the quality measures, anticipating differing levels of background information and also variation as to whether the aim is to have informed consumers of the information or more active and in-depth users of the information.

For example, some states and local areas with quality measurement systems now provide abbreviated training in order to facilitate familiarity and increased understanding of the measures by those who will need to use the information to guide improvement efforts. Training targeted to different stakeholder groups may contribute to a higher comfort level with the measures and greater buy-in to the measures among stakeholders, and protect against interpretations that are not supported by the measures.

These four scenarios are offered as examples of the kinds of situations that states and communities are beginning to encounter when using information on quality for multiple purposes. It is encouraging to see the emergence of precautionary steps for each of these scenarios. It will be important to continue a discussion about additional scenarios that are emerging and the precautions that are needed when measurement of quality is carried out for multiple purposes.

In addition, as further scenarios are identified in which specific measures of quality that are collected initially for one purpose are serving a second and third purpose, it will be useful for the field to turn to measures developers to ask for clarity on the intended uses of the measures. Measures developers could provide specific guidance on both the appropriate use of the measure, with precautions in place as needed, as well as the purposes for which their measures should *not* be used, even with precautions put it place. This guidance will be useful as increasing weight is put on certain measures to serve multiple roles in a measurement system.

Summary and Implications

The measurement of quality in ECE settings is expanding as states and communities launch initiatives to strengthen quality. Although there may be a common, underlying concern with strengthening quality, there are, nevertheless, important distinctions in the more specific purposes for the collection of data about quality. This chapter has identified four different purposes for measuring quality in ECE settings: to guide improvement in practice by individual caregivers–educators; to determine whether program or policy investments have resulted in improvements in quality at the level of individual programs or multiple programs in a geographical area; to build knowledge about what factors contribute to quality and what aspects of the environment contribute to specific child outcomes; and to describe or rate the quality of individual programs in order to inform parental choice.

Following the precedent of work in the area of the assessment of development in young children, we note that, whereas reliability and validity, as well as the appropriateness of measures for populations served, are cross-cutting issues irrespective of purpose, the purpose underlying assessment of quality in early childhood settings has important implications for what and how data are collected and communicated. These differences in data collection and use underscore the importance of planning a data collection effort with clarity as to underlying purpose.

Just as when assessing young children's development, caution is suggested when data collection involves the assessment of quality in early childhood settings for multiple purposes. We provide examples of measures of quality being used for multiple purposes, and suggest guidelines for the multipurpose utilization of individual measures. There is a need for further discussion about the challenges that can arise when data on quality are collected for multiple purposes, and how best to address these challenges.

We have noted throughout the chapter the importance of selecting the particular measure of quality in a data collection effort so that it aligns with the underlying purpose of data collection. Yet, we have also acknowledged the limited number of quality measures currently available to address specific facets of quality in detail. In addition to a more differentiated sense of the purposes for measuring quality in early childhood settings, there is a need for the development of more differentiated measures of quality that align with these differing purposes.

References

Abbott-Shim, M., & Sibley, A. (1997). *Assessment Profile for Early Childhood Programs: Preschool.* Atlanta, GA: Quality Assist.

Abbott-Shim, M., & Sibley, A. (1998). *Assessment Profile for Early Childhood Programs: Research Edition II.* Atlanta GA: Quality Counts, Inc.

Bryant, D. (2010). ACF-OPRE Research-to-Policy Brief. *Observational Measures of Quality in Center-based Early Care and Education Programs.* Office of Planning, Research and Evaluation, Administration for Children and Families, U.S. Department of Health and Human Services. Washington, DC.

Bryant, D., on behalf of the Partnerships for Inclusion (PFI) Quality Interventions for Early Care and Education (QUINCE) Partnerships for Inclusion (PF1) research team. (2008, July). *Effectiveness of on-site consultation for quality enhancement and children's development.* Presentation at breakout session on Professional Development Strategies: Findings and Implications, at the meeting of the Child Care Policy Research Consortium, Washington, DC.

Bryant, D., Wesley, P., Burchinal, M., Sideris, J., Taylor, K., Fenson, C., et al. (2009). *The QUINCE-PFI Study: An evaluation of a promising model for child care provider training.* Final Report. Chapel Hill, NC: FPG Child Development Institute.

Burchinal, P., Kainz, K., Cai, K., Tout, K., Zaslow, M., Martinez-Beck, I., et al. (2009). ACF-OPRE Research-to-Practice Research-to-Policy Brief. *Early Care and Education Quality and Child Outcomes.* Office of Planning, Research and Evaluation, Administration for Children and Families, U.S. Department of Health and Human Services. Washington, DC.

Child Trends. (2008a). *Roundtable on developing the next wave of quality measures for early childhood and school-age programs.* Meeting notes pre- pared for the U.S. Department of Health and Human Services, Administration for Children and Families, Office of Planning, Research and Evaluation, Washington, DC.

Child Trends. (2008b). *Meeting on evaluation of state quality rating systems.* Meeting notes prepared for the U.S. Department of Health and Human Services, Administration for Children and Families, Office of Planning, Research and Evaluation, Washington, DC.

Flanagan, K.D., & McPhee, C. (2009). *The Children Born in 2001 at Kindergarten Entry: First Findings From the Kindergarten Data Collections of the Early Childhood Longitudinal Study, Birth Cohort (ECLS-B).* (NCES 2010–005). Washington, DC: National Center for Education Statistics.

Flanagan, K.D., & West, J. (2004). *Children Born in 2001: First Results From the Base Year of the Early Childhood Longitudinal Study, Birth Cohort (ECLS-B).* (NCES 2005–036). Washington, DC: National Center for Education Statistics.

Goldenberg, C. (2008). Improving achievement for English language learners. In S.B. Neuman, *Educating the other America* (pp. 139–162). Baltimore: Paul H. Brookes Publishing Co.

Halle, T., Vick Whittaker, J.E., & Anderson, R. (2010). *Quality in Early Childhood Care and Education Settings: A Compendium of Measures* (2nd ed.). Washington, DC: Prepared by Child Trends for the Office of Planning, Research and Evaluation, Administration for Children and Families, U.S. Department of Health and Human Services. Retrieved October 10, 2010, from http://www.researchconnections.org/childcare/resources/18804/pdf

Harms, T., Clifford, R., & Cryer, D. (2005). *Early Childhood Environment Rating Scale-Revised Edition.* New York: Teachers College Press.

Harms, T., Cryer, D., & Clifford, R. (1990). *Infant/Toddler Environment Rating Scale.* New York: Teachers College Press.

Harms, T., Cryer, D., & Clifford, R.M. (2007). *Family Child Care Environment Rating Scale-Revised.* New York: Teachers College Press.

Lambert, R.G. (2003). Considering purpose and intended use when making evaluations of assessments: A response to Dickinson. *Educational Researcher, 32*(4), 23–26.

Mitchell, A.W. (2005). *Stair steps to quality: A guide for states and communities developing quality rating systems for early care and education.* Retrieved May 30, 2008, from http://www.unitedway.org/sb6/upload/StairStepsto QualityGuidebook_FINALforWEB.pdf

NICHD Early Child Care Research Network. (2003). Does quality of child care affect child outcomes at age 4½? *Developmental Psychology, 39* (3), 451–469.

NICHD Early Child Care Research Network. (2005). Early child care and children's development in the primary grades: Results from the NICHD Study of Early Child Care. *American Educational Research Journal, 42*(3), 537–570.

Pianta, R.C., La Paro, K.M., & Hamre, B.K. (2007). *Classroom Assessment Scoring System™.* Baltimore: Paul H. Brookes Publishing Co.

Porter, T., Rice, R., & Rivera, E. (2006). *Assessing quality in family, friend, and neighbor care: The Child Care Assessment Tool for Relatives.* New York: Bank Street College of Education, Institute for Child Care Continuum.

Shepard, L., Kagan, S., & Wurtz, E. (1998). *Principles and recommendations for early childhood assessments.* Washington, DC: National Education Goals Panel.

Smith, M.W., Brady, J.P., & Anastasopoulos, L. (2008). *Early Language and Literacy Classroom Observation, Pre-K Tool.* Baltimore: Paul H. Brookes Publishing Co.

Smith, M.W., & Dickinson, D.K. (2002). *Early Language and Literacy Classroom Observation.* Baltimore: Paul H. Brookes Publishing Co.

Smith, S. (unpublished). *Supports for Social-Emotional Growth Assessment (SSEGA) for early childhood programs serving preschool-age children.* New York: New York University.

Snow, C., & Van Hemel, S. (2008). *Early childhood assessment: Why, what and how?* Report of the Committee on Developmental Outcomes and Assessments for Young Children. Washington DC: National Academies Press.

Thornburg, K. (2008, April). *Evaluation strategies focusing on implementation and outputs.* Presentation at the Meeting on Evaluation of State Quality Rating Systems, Washington, DC.

Tout, K., Starr, R., Soli, M., Moodie, S., Kirby, G. & Boller, K. (2010). ACF-OPRE Report. *Compendium of Quality Rating Systems and Evaluations.* Office of Planning, Research and Evaluation, Administration for Children and Families, U.S. Department of Health and Human Services. Washington, DC.

Zaslow, M., Tout, K., Halle, T., Vick Whittaker, J., & Lavelle, B. (2010). *Towards the identification of features of effective professional development for early childhood educators: A review of the literature.* Washington, DC: U.S. Department of Education.

Zaslow, M., Tout, K., & Martinez-Beck, I. (2010). ACF-OPRE Research-to-Policy Brief. *Measuring Quality of Early Care and Education Programs at the Intersection of Research, Policy and Practice.* Office of Planning, Research and Evaluation, Administration for Children and Families, U.S. Department of Health and Human Services. Washington, DC.

Endnotes

Prepared by Child Trends under Contract #GS10F0030R with the Office of Planning, Research and Evaluation, Administration for Children and Families, U.S. Department of Health and Human Services, with support from the Office of the Assistant Secretary for Planning and Evaluation, U.S. Department of Health and Human Services.

[1] See http://www.registryalliance.org

[2] The evaluations of QRIS may involve research designs that differ depending upon the underlying question. Here we have focused on comparative research designs that permit conclusions about the effectiveness of quality initiatives. In the evaluation of QRIS, for example, such a research design might focus on the question of whether one approach versus another is more effective for providing quality improvement resources

and supports. However, we note that other important questions in the evaluation of QRIS involve looking at changes in quality overall across a state or community. The underlying question here may be, Is the overall availability, throughout the state, of care rated at higher levels of quality becoming greater over time? This question and measurement issues related to it are addressed in the discussion on Purpose #4, which involves the ongoing description of quality, and tracking of changes in quality, for a geographical region with the intent of providing information to consumers.

[3]See http//www.childcareresearch.org
[4]See http//www.nccic.org

Conclusion

Ending with a Beginning: Key Themes and Next Steps

Martha Zaslow, Tamara Halle, and Kathryn Tout

T his book is intended *both* to take stock of the current status of quality measurement for early childhood settings *and* to chart a course for moving forward to strengthen measurement. Accordingly, the concluding chapter should be not only an ending, drawing out key themes about the current status of quality measurement, but also a beginning, identifying next steps for strengthening the measurement of quality in early childhood settings. In keeping with this dual focus, an initial section in this concluding chapter will summarize the rationale for strengthening the measurement of quality at this particular time. A second section will summarize key points raised across the chapters of this book for ways in which we can move forward in strengthening the measurement of quality.

Why Focus on Strengthening the Measurement of Quality, and Why Now?

The introduction to this book identified multiple reasons for working to strengthen the measurement of quality. In this section we return to these key issues, summarizing the more specific and nuanced discussion of the issues from the chapters of this book.

Over time, an increasingly salient goal of quality measurement has become providing a strong basis for predicting child outcomes. It is currently an explicit goal of many local, state, and federal quality initiatives to lay a strong foundation for early learning and a transition to school. New accountability structures and incentives are in place to encourage quality improvement, particularly among programs serving children who are at risk for poor academic outcomes.

Yet, as noted by Burchinal, Kainz, and Cai in Chapter 2, the measures of quality that are in widest use at present predict child outcomes consistently, but do so only modestly in terms of the strength of association. We have hints in the available evidence of why this might be the case. The relationship is somewhat stronger when the aspect of quality examined is aligned well with a particular child outcome (e.g., when it is a measure of the quality of language stimulation rather than a broad and global measure of quality that is related to language outcomes). In Chapter 13, Pianta, Hamre, and Downer discuss the need for intentional planning for alignment: The particular measure of quality selected for use should be in keeping both with the child outcomes that are of the highest priority to strengthen in a particular quality improvement initiative and with the features of professional development put in place to strengthen quality. We also have some indication in the data that the relationship between quality and child outcomes may occur only or especially in some ranges of quality; it may be particularly at higher quality ranges that an increase in quality is associated with an improvement in child outcomes.

Chapter 2 suggests that, when considering our most widely used measures, we focus our attention on a further key reason that the relationship between quality and child outcomes may not be strong: Current measures of quality may be completely lacking, or lacking in sufficient detail, in capturing certain aspects of quality that are important in predicting specific child outcomes. For example, one may be seeking to strengthen young children's capacity to regulate their own behavior, and put in place a professional development approach aimed at helping teachers support behavioral self-regulation in children. Yet, as Hyson and colleagues discuss in Chapter 6, existing measures of quality have a limited focus on supporting young children's self-regulation. Many currently available measures do not always reflect contemporary conceptualizations of how best to support young children's development in specific domains.

There has been enormous growth in both descriptive and evaluation research focusing on early childhood. Much of the recent work assumes that laying a foundation for early learning is essential, and addresses a different set of research questions than earlier research did. For example, the more recent research asks, Is there naturally occurring variation in the vocabulary that early childhood teachers and caregivers use with children and does this matter to the children's vocabulary development? What about spontaneous discussions about numbers and measurement during the course of a day in early childhood settings? Do children in different early childhood settings get differing amounts of vigorous physical activity? What kinds of supports are children receiving to learn how to control their attention and behavior? Do these spontaneously occurring variations in supports for self-regulation matter to children's development in this area? Moreover, are these very specific practices in early childhood settings malleable?

Evaluation research in these very different domains of development is helping to specify what practices in early childhood settings can be strengthened, how they can be strengthened, and whether strengthening particular practices within classrooms and home caregiving settings supports better developmental outcomes. This growth spurt in research on early development provides a challenge for a parallel growth spurt in how we approach the measurement of quality.

In Chapter 3, Bryant and colleagues raise a further caution about our toolbox of quality measures, arguing that available measures are strongly rooted in conceptual frameworks, but often have given minimal attention to the empirical bases for measures development. In contrast, empirical approaches have been used more widely in the development of child assessment tools. Standardized assessments are often developed with a large item pool, and empirical procedures are used for selecting the final set of items and for forming subscales and scales. Empirical procedures are also used to sequence the items by difficulty, using specific statistical approaches.

Strengthening measures of quality will require attention to the empirical as well as the conceptual bases of measures development. For example, an empirical focus to the work will help to clarify instances in which summary scores in measures of quality should be based on scales versus on indices. (See Hegland et al., Chapter 7, for a discussion of this issue in the area of measures of quality focusing on supports for young children's health.)

Although it is an extremely hopeful and positive development that communities, states, and the federal government are devoting resources to the measurement of quality in broadly based quality improvement initiatives, these very initiatives are posing new challenges to measurement. For example, when stakeholders in a state gather to begin to plan for the development of Quality Rating and Improvement Systems (as described by Swenson-Klatt and Tout in Chapter 15 and Thornburg et al. in Chapter 16), the stakeholders are expecting the quality measures to capture aspects of quality that researchers have not anticipated and for which measurement resources are not available. Two particularly important examples are the expectation by stakeholders that measures of quality will capture the capacity of early childhood settings to respond sensitively to the wide range of cultural backgrounds of participating families, and to the needs of children learning English as well as a different home language. Yet, we have seen very limited measures development for assessing the strength of early childhood settings in supporting families from varying cultural backgrounds and facilitating the development of children who are dual language learners. As noted by Shivers and colleagues in Chapter 9 and Castro, Espinosa, and Páez in Chapter 11, work on measures development in both of these areas is at an early stage.

Extensive use of quality measures throughout a geographical region also challenges those using measures of quality to develop best practices for systemwide implementation of quality measurement. If a quality rating pertains not to a classroom, but to a whole center or program, how many classrooms need to be observed and how often? If assigning four as opposed to three stars within a rating system will have consequences in terms of parent perception of quality and also, perhaps, financial incentives within the system, what is a sufficient empirical basis for components of quality to qualify for such a rating difference? As noted in Chapters 15 and 16, measurement challenges are emerging with the widespread use of quality measures in policy initiatives, and there is much to consider in terms of the ways in which data can be used to address these challenges.

Measures of quality may be used for such differing purposes as to guide improvement in individual classrooms or groups, for research identifying the features of quality most important to particular child outcomes, to evaluate the effects of quality improvement initiatives, or to assign a rating of quality that can be used by parents in selecting early childhood settings for their children. Yet, as noted by Zaslow, Tout, and Halle in Chapter 17, we have rarely considered whether and how either the content of quality measures or the way in which we collect data and communicate results should be tailored for these differing purposes. For example, reliability of raters may be needed at the level of summary scores when the purpose is to assign a summary rating of quality to each setting in a community, but raters may need to agree at the level of subscales or items when the goal is to guide improvement on very specific practices in a classroom. Training to conduct quality ratings for research purposes and for guiding professional development may entail high standards for interrater reliability, but for the latter purpose, also may require training in how to communicate results in a way that can be well understood by a practitioner and can motivate change. The independence and stringent objectivity of the observer of quality may be much more critical when the purpose is to track changes in quality over time for policy purposes, in which case there may be financial incentives or consequences involved, than when an individual provider is being guided to improve quality. In some instances, separate measures of quality have been developed for use in research and for guiding program improvement by the same research group. But the design of measures of quality according to underlying purpose has been the exception rather than the rule. This book suggests that greater awareness of underlying purpose should be a starting point for measures development and implementation.

Further, there is a mismatch between available measures of quality and the settings in which most young children are cared for. As summarized by Halle, Martinez-Beck, Forry, and McSwiggan in Chapter 1, approximately 4 in 10 infants under the age of 1 are in regular nonparental care arrangements. Among those participating in a regular nonparental care arrangement, home-based early care and education is the most common type of care for infants and toddlers and for children from impoverished households. Yet, as Sandstrom, Moodie, and Halle discuss in detail in Chapter 14, few measures have been developed specifically to describe quality in home-based care or care for infants and toddlers.

Chapter 1 notes that 64% of mothers with children under the age of 6 were in the labor force in 2008. Early care and education plays a dual role, supporting parents in their work roles and supporting the development of children. Yet, we gauge the strength of our measures of quality only according to the latter role: the strength of prediction to child outcomes. Without in any way dismissing the importance of prediction to child outcomes, in Chapter 8 Bromer and colleagues raise the central question of whether our measures of quality should also predict ways in which early care and education is supporting family life, including the work roles of parents. This chapter suggests that a more complex model of prediction would view family and child outcomes as linked and would test this assumption empirically by examining the relationship between quality and child outcomes, asking whether children's development is more optimal when family needs are well supported through early childhood settings. Thus, a further reason to review our existing measures of quality is to ask whether they fully reflect early care and education's dual role of supporting families as well as caring for and educating children.

Moving Forward in Strengthening the Measurement of Quality

With these issues in mind, what steps will be needed to move forward with strengthening existing measures of quality and developing new measures? We see the next steps as varying by the particular aspect of quality being considered. There is a continuum of measures development needs. At one end of the continuum are facets of quality for which we already have multiple domain-specific measures. The need here is to fill in gaps and add aspects of quality to measurement tools that have only very recently been identified as important. At the other extreme are facets of quality at the earliest stage of measures development, for which there is a lack even of a conceptual framework for identifying the key constructs that measures should address. Next, we describe these different stages of measures development in greater detail and provide examples for each stage on the continuum.

Addressing Gaps Where Measures Exist

An example of a domain in which measures development is fairly well progressed is supports for young children's language and literacy development. Although the research in this area still is progressing, there is a strong starting point for describing the key environmental supports for young children's early language and literacy development. Reliability and validity data exist for existing measures and for the key child outcomes that are used in assessing predictive validity of the measures in this domain. Recent experimental evaluations help to identify features of the environment that can be strengthened and the implications for children's development.

As described by Neuman and Carta in Chapter 4, at present we have in-depth measures of quality focusing specifically on environmental supports for young children's language and literacy development. However, it is only in recent years that these measures have encompassed home-based as well as center-based early childhood settings. Furthermore, there are few measures of the quality of the language and literacy environment that capture supports for the earliest forms of communication among infants and toddlers, or supports for English language learners. In addition, a review of existing measures finds that they still show gaps in terms of key constructs covered. For example, additional measures are needed of environmental supports for the development of background knowledge (e.g., verbal reasoning, vocabulary expansion). As such measures are developed, work will be needed assessing reliability and validity—especially of measures of environmental supports for the development of phonological awareness, letter knowledge, and background knowledge. Finally, work is needed in the development of measurement tools for improving practice as well as for research.

Building on a Strong Research Base to Develop New Measures

To date, we have few in-depth measures focusing specifically on environmental supports in the areas of young children's early mathematics and science learning, social and emotional development, or health. Yet, strong recent developments in research in these areas provide a sufficient basis for the articulation—by Brenneman and colleagues in Chapter 5 regarding math, science, and cognition; Chapter 6 regarding social and emotional development; and Chapter 7 regarding health—of the key constructs that in-depth measures of these facets of quality should cover.

For example, research demonstrates that children have interest and competence in learning math and science earlier than previously thought, and professional organizations now recommend intentional instruction in mathematics as early as possible in order to ameliorate later mathematical difficulties, articulating the key constructs that should be addressed in such instruction. New measures in early mathematical and science learning should focus on the mere presence of math and science instruction and assess the quality of instruction, ensuring that it is aligned with new expectations for teaching in these domains. In the area of social and emotional development, the recent research provides a much clearer picture of how young children develop the capacity to recognize and respond to their own emotions and the emotions of others. The emerging research suggests a need, in measures of quality, to balance the very strong current focus on the relationship of children with their educators and caregivers with greater focus on ways to support the development of positive peer relationships and interactions.

Substantial work is needed to marry an understanding of the key constructs that quality measures should cover in these domains to the empirical approaches to measures development described previously (such as development of a large item pool, and procedures for the selection of the most appropriate items for scales). As noted, such measures development also should be governed by a clear articulation of the underlying purpose for the measure (e.g., whether to guide improvement in practice, provide a broad population-based picture of quality to inform parental choice, or to use in evaluation research).

Although we have emphasized the potential to develop and extend measures of quality in specific *domains* by building on substantial existing research, this potential also exists for measures of quality pertaining to *populations* of particular importance for which we have very limited measurement options as well as for *settings* for which measures are quite limited. For example, the definition of high-quality practices in early care and education programs needs to be expanded to incorporate practices that directly address the unique needs of children with disabilities (see Spiker, Hebbeler, & Barton, Chapter 10) and the growing numbers of young DLLs (Chapter 11). For children with disabilities, this might mean inclusion of measures of specialized instructional strategies and accommodations in environmental arrangements. For children who are DLLs, it might mean including measures of teacher qualifications specifically linked to effective practices for young children learning two languages, measures of engagement with families that do not speak English, and measurement of whether linguistically and culturally appropriate assessment approaches are used.

Many would argue that the research on home-based early childhood settings is much more limited than the research on center-based settings, but there is a growing body of research on care and education in these settings. Although not extensive, the research on home-based early care and education now suffices to provide guidance toward identifying the further features that are important to measure in these early childhood settings. For example, recent research suggests that measures of quality in home-based care might seek to capture "intentionality," or the extent to which caregivers approach their work as a profession.

Where There Is a Limited Research Base on Which to Build

The chapters in this book also identify facets of quality for which we are at an early point in the development of measures. It is not only that we have few or no measures of quality focusing on these facets of the environment, population groups, or settings, but also that the research base itself is limited, with few demonstrations of linkages between facets of quality and child outcomes, and a very limited base on which to build a conceptual framework. Yet, a compelling need has been identified for the development of measures of quality in these areas.

An example falling in this category is cultural responsiveness as a facet of quality, as described in Chapter 9. A recurring theme in states working to develop their own Quality Rating and improvement Systems is that stakeholders call for the inclusion of quality indicators focused on cultural sensitivity. Yet, resources in this area are scarce, and the existing literature does not provide a strong basis for the initial step of providing a conceptual framework pointing to the key constructs that a measure of quality should seek to describe. Chapter 9 takes an important step in providing such a framework.

Similarly, if we accept the assumption that quality measurement should encompass facets of quality that are important to family well-being as well as directly supportive of children's development, then the measurement of family-sensitive caregiving also can be pointed to as an example of measures development at a very early stage. Chapter 8 takes the important step of providing a conceptual framework for measures development in this newly emerging area.

Cross-Cutting Issues

We have distinguished three stages of measures development primarily according to whether quality measures with a specific focus on the facet of quality already exist and whether research is available to help guide the identification of key constructs that should be covered by measures. However, at all three levels, strengthening measurement will require 1) combining clarity as to constructs that should be addressed with utilization of psychometric approaches to measures development; 2) being explicit about the underlying purpose of the measure and following through to match the underlying purpose with how the measure is developed and how it is implemented; and 3) being thoughtful about alignment: thinking through how the newly developed or extended measure is hypothesized to contribute to specific child (and family) outcomes, and what environmental supports and professional development approaches would be needed to foster quality as captured in the measure.

Finally, this book has focused extensively on providing in-depth examinations of particular facets of quality and the development of measures of quality appropriate for particular settings and groups of children that have received limited focus and, yet, for which quality of early childhood settings is critical. We contend that it is a necessary first step to develop in-depth and detailed measures in order to then coordinate across these in order to develop composite or summary measures of quality.

An extensive focus on particular facets of quality and particular population subgroups and settings, however essential, runs the risk of failing to return and reintegrate the in-depth knowledge from these more specific efforts into overall measures of quality. As noted in several chapters in this book, environmental features and aspects of teacher–child or caregiver–child interactions often simultaneously affect multiple domains of development. For example, a verbal interaction between a caregiver or teacher and a child about a book has the potential both to build vocabulary and to clarify for the child how one interprets and discusses emotion (e.g., in discussing a book character's delight about a snowy day). When considering the needs of children who are DLLs or children with disabilities, we are oriented to facets of the environment that actually may be of importance to all children, such as the need to create an inclusive environment and ensure that no children are isolated.

Although it may seem like a long sequence to build from measures appropriate for in-depth consideration of particular domains, population subgroups, or settings, to measures of the whole environment and whole child, Bouffard and Jones argue in Chapter 12 that there is efficiency in such an effort. We can build into integrated measures those items and scales identified to be of particular importance in the in-depth work on particular domains, subgroups, and settings. Empirical work can help identify where and how items and scales predict outcomes across multiple domains of development. Thus, integrated measures can capitalize on the in-depth work in multiple ways.

The underlying theme of alignment underscores the critical importance of careful thinking about the outcomes one is aiming for in seeking to measure and strengthen quality. Clearly, there will be some instances in which the goal is to strengthen specific domains of development (such as early math skills), and therefore, it will be important to select measures of quality and of child outcomes aligned with this effort. Yet, in other instances, the principle of alignment will require that the outcomes of interest include multiple domains of development and a focus on the overall well-being of the child or the family. Accordingly, future research with the goal of strengthening the measurement of quality in early childhood settings will need to encompass both work aimed at strengthening measures of quality that capture domain-specific, setting-specific, and population-specific features of quality; and integrative work examining how facets of quality are interrelated, how they can be measured efficiently and reliably, and how they jointly predict multiple aspects of child and family well-being.

Index

Tables and figures are indicated by *t* and *f*, respectively.

7